# Automobiles and Pollution

Front cover

*ADEME Document*
*(Agence de l'Environnement et de la Maîtrise de l'Énergie)*

**Paul Degobert**

Engineering PhD degree from the University of Paris
Graduate Engineer from ENSPM and ENSCL
Research Engineer at Institut Français du Pétrole

# Automobiles and Pollution

Translated from the French by Nissim Marshall
and reviewed by Frank Carr

SOCIETY OF AUTOMOTIVE ENGINEERS, INC.
400 COMMONWEALTH DRIVE, WARRENDALE, PA 15096-0001

1995

ÉDITIONS TECHNIP
27 RUE GINOUX, 75737 PARIS Cedex 15

Translation (reviewed and enlarged Edition) of
«Automobile et pollution», P. Degobert
© 1992, Éditions Technip, Paris. ISBN 2-7108-0628-2

*Published with the Financial Aid of
the French Ministry of Culture.*

Edition published 1995
by Society of Automotive Engineers, Inc.
Warrendale, PA, USA

ISBN 1-56091-563-3
SAE Order No. R-150
Library of Congress Catalog Card No. 95-69809



ISBN 2-7108-0676-2

Printed in France
by Imprimerie Nouvelle, 45800 Saint-Jean-de-Braye

# Foreword

This book was drafted after two important announcements were made. First came the establishment of the single market in the European Community and then the tightening of pollution control standards. The net result was that catalytic converters would be virtually generalized on all new vehicles running in the *European Union*.

After situating automobile pollution in a general context, I then sought to update and anticipate the evolution in regulations and the solutions developed to comply with them. I dealt with these issues in the area of both engines and exhaust systems. An extensive list of references at the end of each chapter provides further information sources for readers to go more thoroughly into the subjects covered.

I would like to address my thanks first of all to André Douaud, head of the Energy Division at *Institut Français du Pétrole*, who relied on me to write the book. I would also like to thank Philippe Pinchon, head of the Energy Application Techniques Department, who enabled me to carry the project through.

In addition, I am obliged to my colleagues in the Energy Application Techniques Department at *IFP* who were most helpful and gave me the benefit of their experience, each in his own specific field and were good enough to reread the manuscript with a critical eye.

I was able to review health issues thanks to the collaboration of Professor Bernard Festy, head of the city of Paris Health Laboratory, and would also like to acknowledge his contribution.

My special gratitude is extended to Hélène Jaray, documentalist, whose readiness to help, efficiency and kindness allowed me to gather and consult the references mentioned.

Finally, my thoughts turn to my family, who often suffered when I was engrossed in the slow gestation of the book, and to my wife, Nicole, who is now happy to see it publised.

# Table of contents

# Introduction 1

*"Every animal is naturally made for the use of pure, natural and free air";* this declaration appeared in the book 'Tests of the Effects of Air on the Human Body' [2] by John Arbuthnot, a Scottish doctor. This book was translated into French and published in Paris in 1742.

In the fifth and sixth centuries BC, Hippocrates and his disciples were already aware of the influence of different airs and places on health. Pliny the Elder died in 79 BC from breathing air polluted by the eruption of Mount Vesuvius. About the same time, Seneca complained of the stench of smoking urban chimneys [10]. In 1661, the English doctor John Evelyn wrote a treatise on the negative effects of London's smoke and polluted air, which were caused by the burning of coal. This happened centuries before the 1952 London catastrophe that resulted in more than 4000 deaths due to dense smog [13].

Hence, long before Priestley and Lavoisier tried to analyze air, men had already claimed their natural right to breathe air that was unpolluted by 'mephitic' vapors[1]. The term pollution, as it is used today, was unknown in the seventeenth century when doctors wore filtering funnels lined with 'balsamic' substances on their noses to avoid breathing 'miasmas'[2], which they blamed for the spread of the plague. Furthermore, infectious diseases such as malaria were blamed, for a long time, on bad air *(mala aria).*

In thirteenth-century England, the Crown took measures to restrict the burning of coal in homes, due to the smoke and odor it released [3]. These measures were encouraged by taxation, long before the tax on sulfur dioxide emissions was instituted in France by the Agence pour la Qualité de l'Air (Air Quality Agency). Furthermore, in previous centuries, most rural and urban populations breathed smoke-laden air containing emissions from open fires burning wood, peat, or coal. They also breathed air fouled by the sulfur and ammonia that escaped from the stables and sheep pens that were used as 'central heating' in one-room cottages during the winter [7]. This situation still exists in the developing countries where biomass is the basic source of energy [6]; high concentrations of sulfuric and nitric acids are found in dwellings, as well as carbon monoxide and volatile hydrocarbons.

1. Toxic and stinking exhalations.
2. Emanations to which infectious diseases and epidemics were ascribed before Pasteur's discoveries.

The life expectancy of the highlanders of New Guinea, who are still living in smoky huts, is little more than forty years due to respiratory infections [1].

In fact, the so-called 'natural' fuels, championed by the proponents of the return to nature, emit pollutants that are very difficult to control. An example is the burning of wood for heat using traditional techniques [12]. According to the United States Environmental Protection Agency (*EPA*), the yearly emissions of wood-burning appliances are 7 Mt of particles, 19 Mt of carbon monoxide, 0.16 Mt of unburned hydrocarbons, and 52,000 t of polycyclic organic matter [5, 8]. In some areas wood smoke is a major contributor of organic compounds, which are adsorbed onto atmospheric particles, contributing to their mutagenic effect [9].

The nineteenth century brought the first transport vehicles powered by mechanical energy. These vehicles aroused the apprehensions of the very highest medical authorities of the time, who greeted the advent of the railway with concerns about the poisoning of passengers by the smoke from the locomotives, especially in tunnels.

Concerns were raised about the risk potential of automobile exhausts around 1915, before vehicles in California were acknowledged, around 1945, as contributors to the 'smog' problem in the Los Angeles area.

On September 14, 1967, the Council of Europe provided the following definition of air pollution [4]:

*"Air pollution occurs when the presence of a foreign substance or a large variation in the proportion of its components is liable to cause a harmful effect, according to the scientific knowledge of the time, or to create a discomfort."*

The expression 'according to the knowledge of the time' shows that the notion of pollutant can evolve with expanded knowledge of the risks. Also, the expression 'creating a discomfort' means that pollution concerns not only harmful chemical compounds, but also includes nuisances to the human senses, such as bad odors, reduced visibility caused by smoke or fog, and other similar problems.

This book is intended as an overall review of the very pressing problem of automotive pollution. The automotive pollution control measures enacted in the world's nations spring from very different considerations:

- in the United States—California smog
- in Germany—pressure from the 'Greens' to fight the 'death of the forests'
- in the United Kingdom—lead-poisoning of the blood, which was observed in a part of the population (This led to a gradual switch to unleaded gasoline—to reduce lead pollution, not to facilitate the introduction of catalytic converters.)

This book identifies some of the causes and effects of air pollution and provides an estimate of the air pollution attributable to automotive traffic. An initial evaluation of air pollution considers the changes in the Earth's atmosphere as a whole, including the effects of air pollution on the thermodynamic equilibrium of the atmosphere and the potential climatic consequences of these effects. Going to the other extreme on the space scale, a subsequent evaluation considers the problem of indoor pollution in the premises where people in the developed countries spend most of their time. This second evaluation examines the internal pollution of vehicle passenger compartments—a problem more closely linked to automotive air pollution. The various air pollutants are individually reviewed; an attempt is made to evaluate the mass emissions of each one and to assign a percentage of those emissions to automotive sources. The health repercussions of the presence in air of compounds that are 'normally' absent are assessed in the short term (acute toxicity), and in the medium and long terms, by considering genetic modifications and the problem of carcinogenesis.

The consequences on the general environment are examined by considering the potential effects on plant and animal species ('acid rain' and the acidification of lakes and waterways; the degeneration of plants and the 'death of the forests') and on building materials (corrosion, erosion, and soiling of monuments). The present and foreseeable regulatory measures applicable to automotive emissions are reviewed for each of the countries concerned. This presentation covers both the limits imposed by the regulations and the standard procedures used for taking the corresponding measurements (test cycles, etc.).

A subsequent chapter of the book deals with analytical methods applicable to the various automotive exhaust pollutants, which are either regulated or detected but not systematically measured. After a description of indispensable sampling precautions, measurement principles are discussed and then applied to the various compounds of concern. The mechanisms causing the formation of polluting emissions are described by distinguishing between the combustion cycles of the spark-ignition gasoline engine and the compression-ignition diesel engine. The influence of fuel on emissions is considered in the next chapter; this includes consideration of the properties of gasoline and diesel fuels, as well as the influence of lubricants and additives. These considerations indicate what measures are to be applied to engines to minimize pollutant emissions, and to strike the best possible compromise between performance, fuel consumption, and pollutant emissions. To meet the strictest purification levels, chemical reactors must be added to engine exhaust systems. These reactors are designed to finish the incomplete combustion achieved in the engine; 'catalytic converters' and particulate filters are described and discussed.

The final chapter describes the economic factors related to automotive pollution control, details the costs of the systems involved, and describes the positive repercussions anticipated.

This book should enable lay readers to develop an objective opinion of the contribution of automotive traffic to air pollution and should familiarize them with the means and methods employed to control it. The many bibliographic references will enable interested readers to study the corresponding problems in greater detail.

The subject matter of this book deals primarily with air pollution. Although this book does not deal with the problem of noise emitted by automotive engines and traffic, noise should always be kept in mind when discussing solutions for reducing automotive emissions. This book is concerned exclusively with vehicle traffic and vehicle operation; air pollution caused by the manufacture of vehicles or the destruction of derelict vehicles is not addressed herein.

## REFERENCES

[1] Anon., (1978), "Can air pollutants cause chronic lung diseases?" *E.S.&T.*, **12**, 1356-1359.

[2] A. Corbin, (1982), *Le miasme et la jonquille*, Aubier, Paris, 334 p.

[3] L.A. Chambers, (1968), "Classification and extent of air pollution problems", in: *Air Pollution*, A. C. Stern, Academic Press, New York, pp. 1-21.

[4] P. Chovin, (1979), *La pollution atmosphérique*, Que Sais-je No. 1330, PUF, Paris, 128 p.

[5] J.A. Cooper, (1980), "Environmental impact of residential wood combustion emissions and its implications", *J. APCA*, **30,** 855-861.

[6] C.I. Davidson et al., (1986), "Indoor and outdoor air pollution in the Himalayas", *E.S.&T.*, **20**, 561-567.

[7] P. Goubert, (1982), *La vie quotidienne des paysans français au XVII^e^ siècle*, Hachette, Paris, 319 p.

[8] J. Keough, (1986), "Sins of emission", *Energy Rev.*, **13,** 59.

[9] C.W. Lewis et al., (1988), "Contribution of woodsmoke and motor vehicle emissions to ambient aerosol mutagenicity", *E.S.&T.*, **22,** 968-971.

[10] R. Leygonie, (1988), "Les progrès accomplis dans la maîtrise de la pollution atmosphérique urbaine", *Pollution Atmosphérique* (120), 366-374.

[11] F. Lipari et al., (1984), "Aldehyde emissions from wood burning fireplaces", *E.S.&T.*, **18,** 326-330.

[12] T. A. Quaraishi, (1985), "Residential wood burning and air pollution", *Int. J. Environ. Stud.*, **24,** 19-33.

[13] M.J. Suess et al., (1985), *Ambient air pollutants from industrial sources, A Reference Handbook*, Elsevier Sci. Pub., Amsterdam, 843 p.

# Characterization of air pollution 2

*Before describing the relationship between air pollution and automotive exhaust emissions, it is necessary to describe the nature of the atmosphere, its evolutionary changes, and the effects of large scale changes, especially on climate.*

## 2.1 General

The Earth is an enormous thermodynamic machine. Its energy states govern the meteorology in the short term and climatic variations in the long term.

The chemical composition of the atmosphere plays an important role in the kinetics of atmospheric exchanges and the absorption of solar energy or the release of energy into space.

### 2.1.1 Components of the atmosphere

The principal gaseous components now present in the atmosphere, as well as their historical trends, are listed in Table 2.1: column A lists the concentrations in the pre-industrial atmosphere; column B lists the concentrations in the present atmosphere; and column C indicates the annual rate of increase for each component [29]. The average concentration of each of the gases is appropriate for sustaining life on earth:

- Nitrogen, the majority component, is non-toxic. However, excessively high concentrations would be detrimental to respiration. Nitrogen's retention by soil bacteria enables it to participate in life sustaining processes.
- Oxygen, necessary for aerobic life, would be toxic in much higher concentrations.
- Carbon dioxide, in atmospheric concentrations, is also non-toxic. A concentration one hundred times higher would be necessary to cause suffocation, as occurred in the volcanic accident at Nyos Lake. However, carbon dioxide, through its participation in chlorophyll synthesis and its transformation into plant tissue, is indispensable to life.
- Water vapor, also a necessary constituent for life, is naturally limited in its concentration by its saturation vapor pressure—which, when exceeded, causes it to condense into droplets to form clouds.

- Ozone, an essential presence in the stratosphere, is produced by the reaction of an oxygen molecule (created at ground level by photosynthesis) with an oxygen atom (obtained by the dissociation of an oxygen molecule due to solar radiation). Ozone is also created at low altitude in the form of a secondary pollutant from other emissions (see below). In the concentrations shown in Table 2.1, ozone and the other trace gases are far below toxicity limits.

**Table 2.1** Chemical composition of the atmosphere [20, 29, and 34]

| Constituant | % | A | B | C |
|---|---|---|---|---|
| **Troposphere** | | | | |
| nitrogen | 78.084 | | | |
| oxygen | 20.984 | | | |
| argon | 0.934 | | | |
| carbon dioxide | 0.033 | 270 | 340 | 0.4 |
| neon | $18\ 10^{-4}$ | | | |
| helium | $5.30\ 10^{-4}$ | | | |
| methane | $1.70\ 10^{-4}$ | 1.0 | 1.7 | 2 |
| krypton | $1.14\ 10^{-4}$ | | | |
| hydrogen | $0.50\ 10^{-4}$ | | | |
| nitrous oxide | $0.30\ 10^{-4}$ | 0.28 | 0.30 | 0.25 |
| xenon | $0.09\ 10^{-4}$ | | | |
| ozone | $0.02\text{-}0.1\ 10^{-4}$ | | | |
| CO | | 0.05-0.2 | 0.13 | 3 |
| $SO_2$ | | 0.001 | 0.002 | 2 |
| $NH_3$ | | 0.004 | 0.006 | 2 |
| $C_2H_4$ | | 0.0 | 0.0002 | 2 |
| $H_2S$ | | 0.00005 | | |
| CFCs | | 0.0 | 0.00015 | 8 |
| **Stratosphere** | | | | |
| ozone | $0.1\text{-}10\ 10^{-4}$ | | | |
| water vapor | $3\text{-}5\ 10^{-4}$ | | | |

A: ppmV (pre-industrial age). B: ppmV (current). C: %/year.

In addition to these gases, suspended dust also plays a role. Dust acts as a support for adsorbed chemical compounds, as condensation seeds for water vapor, and as absorbers of incident solar radiation. Polycyclic aromatic hydrocarbons (PAH), despite their low concentrations, also play an important role in air chemistry [32].

### 2.1.2 Contribution of atmospheric constituents to the Earth's energy balance

Figure 2.1 illustrates the spectral distribution of solar radiation as it originates from the sun and upon its arrival at sea level. Fortunately for life on earth, solar radiation (in the short wavelengths: $< 4\ \mu$) is neither fully absorbed nor completely reflected.

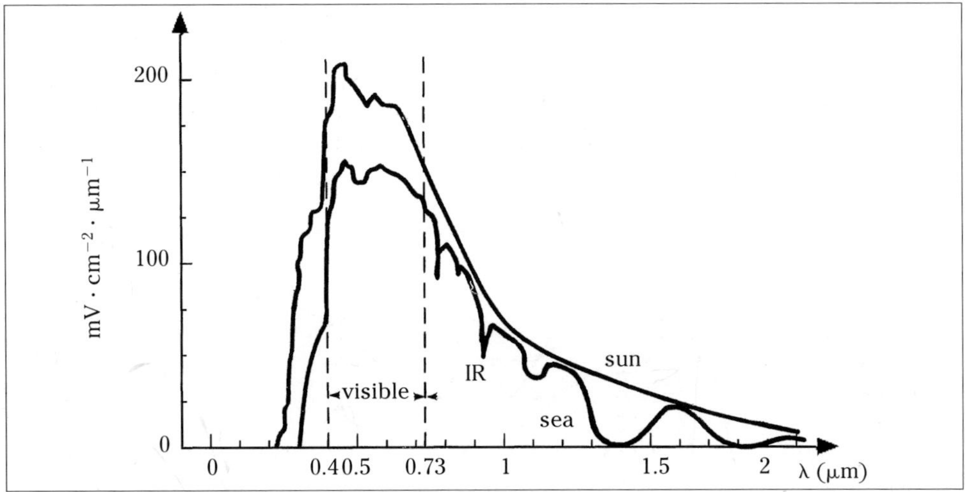


**Fig. 2.1** Solar emission spectrum and spectral distribution of radiation on arrival at sea-level [31]

Atmospheric gases participate in filtering the wavelengths of sunlight [34]:

- Ozone absorbs ultraviolet radiation and filters the solar ultraviolet radiation at high altitude.
- Water vapor absorbs near-infrared radiation (0.8 to 4.0 µm). Due to its abundance and its wide absorption band, water vapor plays the leading role in the re-absorption of terrestrial infrared radiation.
- Carbon dioxide absorbs wavelengths around 15 µm, which are close to the wavelengths at which the maximum energy is radiated by the Earth—in a window left free by water absorption.
- The other trace gases absorb infrared radiation in the wavelengths at which carbon dioxide and water are transparent.

By absorbing a part of the infrared radiation re-emitted by the Earth and by re-emitting it towards the ground (Fig. 2.2), these gases contribute to the warming of the earth's surface—this is known as the 'greenhouse effect' [33].

This effect, similar to the effect observed with the glass roofs of greenhouses, derives from the fact that these gases act as one-way filters [6]:

- they allow 48 percent of the incident solar radiation, which warms the oceans and continents, to pass through
- they absorb 80 percent of the infrared radiation re-emitted by the Earth's surface, preventing it from returning into Space (Fig. 2.3)

This 'greenhouse effect' raises the Earth's surface temperature to an average equilibrium value of +15°C, instead of the value of –18°C that would result from the balance between energy received and energy re-emitted by infrared radiation from the globe [18].

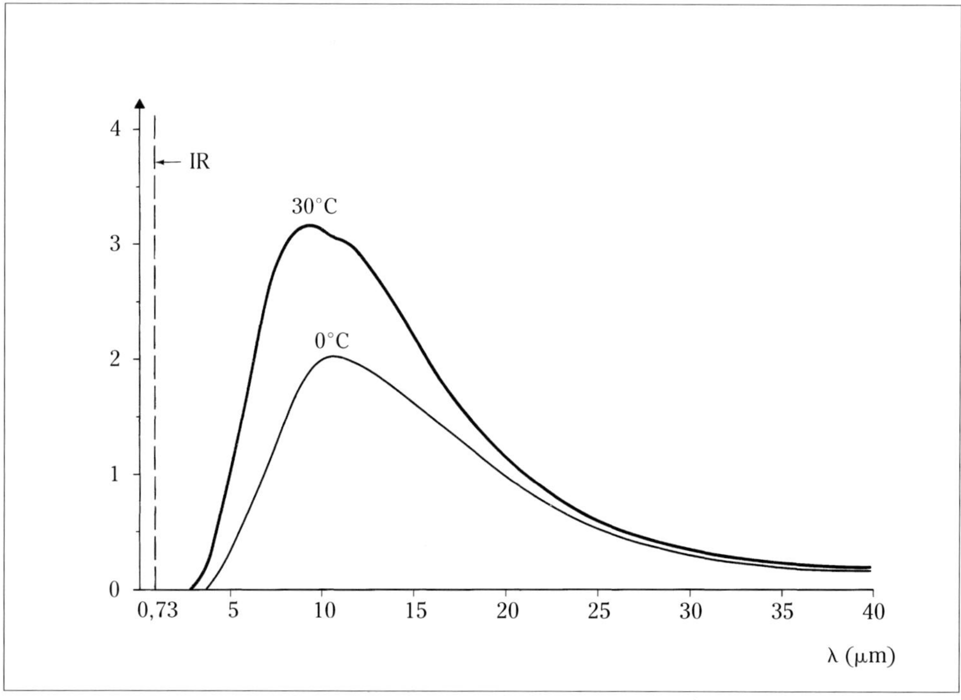


**Fig 2.2** Spectrum of re-emission by the Earth's surface

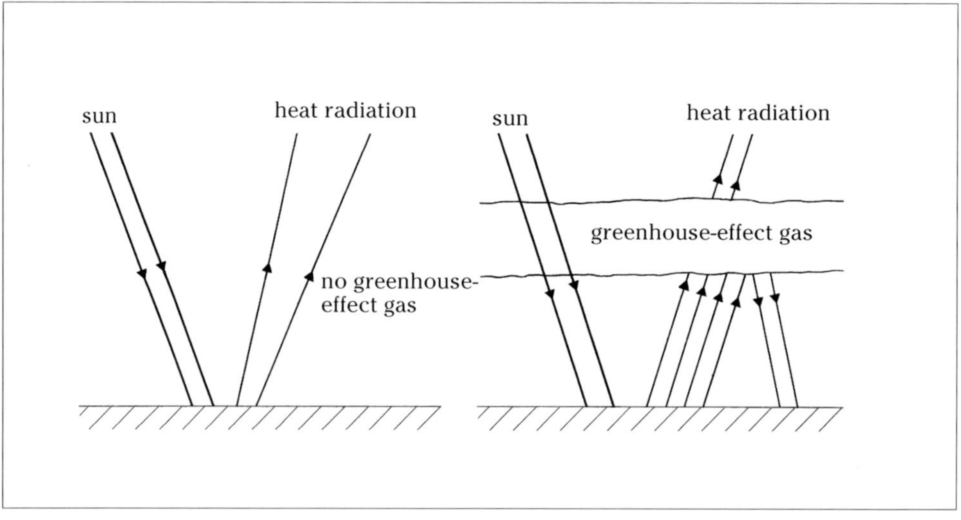


**Fig 2.3** Diagram of the "greenhouse-effect" [17]

### 2.1.3 Interactions of air constituents

While carbon dioxide remains approximately inert within the atmospheric reservoir, the other components participate in many chemical reactions assisted by other factors such as solar radiation.

Thus, the atmosphere contains a large number of minority components that are referred to as secondary components, because they are generated from primary components. These secondary components are of natural origin (biomass, volcanism, storms, etc.) or of anthropogenic origin (industrial, agricultural, or domestic).

The reactions that produce these components take place in a homogeneous gas phase by free radical mechanisms, or in a heterogeneous gas phase on particles of atmospheric aerosols [12].

Photochemical reactions cause the formation of tropospheric ozone [42]. In addition to the nitrogen oxide (NO) molecule, the photolysis of nitrogen dioxide ($NO_2$) produces an oxygen atom, which combines with the oxygen molecule to form ozone:

$$NO_2 + h\upsilon \Rightarrow NO + O^\bullet$$
$$O_2 + O^\bullet \Rightarrow O_3$$

Water vapor reacts with the excited oxygen atom to yield hydroxyl radicals:

$$HO_2 + O^\bullet \Rightarrow 2OH^\bullet$$

These radicals are capable of reacting with hydrocarbons to form aldehydes, which are also primary pollutants formed directly in combustion processes.

Carbon monoxide (CO) is involved in the main mechanisms leading to the removal of hydroxyl ($OH^\bullet$) radicals from the troposphere, thus preventing them from reacting with the other trace gases, such as methane ($CH_4$), and tending to increase their concentration [25].

The hydroxyl radicals thus formed yield peroxide radicals, of the peroxyacetyl type, which combine with $NO_2$ to give peroxyacetyl nitrate. This compound is one example of a family of mutagenic molecules and a contributor to the acid pollution responsible for damaging forests (Chapter 5)[27]. The acetaldehyde and acetone detected in the atmosphere [4] are precursors of peracetylnitrate (PAN):

$$CH_3{-}CHO + OH^\bullet \Rightarrow CH_3{-}CO^\bullet + H_2O$$
$$CH_3{-}CO^\bullet + O_2 \Rightarrow CH_3{-}CO_3^\bullet$$
$$CH_3{-}CO_3^\bullet + NO_2 \Rightarrow CH_3{-}CO_3{-}NO_2$$

Under similar conditions, sulfur and nitrogen compounds form sulfuric and nitric acids. For example:

$$NO_2 + O_3 \Rightarrow NO_3^\bullet + O_2$$
$$NO_2 + NO_3^\bullet \Rightarrow N_2O_5$$

The nitrogen pentoxide ($N_2O_5$) formed in this reaction reacts with water droplets to yield nitric acid, just as the sulfur trioxide produced by the following reactions yields sulfuric acid under the same conditions:

$$
\begin{aligned}
SO_2 + OH^\bullet &\Rightarrow SO_3H^\bullet \\
SO_3H^\bullet + O_2 &\Rightarrow SO_3 + HO_2^\bullet \\
HO_2^\bullet + NO &\Rightarrow OH^\bullet + NO_2 \\
SO_3 + H_2O &\Rightarrow H_2SO_4
\end{aligned}
$$

Olefins also tend to react with atmospheric ozone to produce aldehydes and hydroxyl radicals capable of propagating the formation of tropospheric ozone [7]. Polycyclic aromatic hydrocarbons also undergo atmospheric nitration and oxidation reactions, the products of which may exert an amplified genotoxic effect (Chapter 4) or produce phytotoxins that participate in the destruction of forests [32].

The interactions involved are highly complex and still poorly understood, therefore, only a brief overview can be presented herein.

Ozone formation in the air is related to $NO_x$ and reactive organic gases. Each type of organic gas has a different influence on ozone formation. Recently, W.P.L. Carter of the California Air Resources Board (CARB) [44] examined air modeling based on the ozone-forming reactivities of different types of gases and, following his particular model[1] , proposed the Maximum Incremental Reactivities (MIR) as an index for ozone formation. This index (Table 2.2) shows the maximum increase in ozone formation following the calculation of the specific reactivity (contribution of emission composition to ozone formation) of a mixture, such as automotive exhaust:

$$\text{specific reactivity} = \Sigma(\text{NMOG} \cdot \text{MIR})/\text{NMOG}$$

NMOG (non-methane organic gases) is the sum of non-methane hydrocarbons (NMHC) and oxygenates, including aldehydes.

## 2.2 Evolution of the atmosphere

The chemical composition of the atmosphere is changeable, and has changed considerably through geological time.

Thus, the Earth occupies a special position among the solar planets. Mars, which has neither an atmosphere to retain solar energy nor any ozone layer, has a very low surface temperature, and a soil bombarded by UV radiation. While Venus, with its $CO_2$-rich atmosphere, reaches surface temperatures of 400°C due to the very intense greenhouse effect.

1. In fact, specially fitted to Californian conditions, and at present not widely accepted.

**Table 2.2** Maximum incremental reactivity values (MIR) for ozone formation (expressed in g $O_3$/g NMOG (non-methane organic gases)

| Compound | MIR | Compound | MIR | Compound | MIR |
|---|---|---|---|---|---|
| ethane | 0.25 | ethene | 7.29 | benzene | 0.42 |
| propane | 0.48 | ethyne | 0.50 | toluene | 2.73 |
| 2-methylpropane | 1.21 | propene | 9.40 | ethylbenzene | 2.70 |
| n-butane | 1.02 | propadiene | 7.29 | m-xylene | 8.16 |
| 2,2-dimethylpropane | 0.37 | propyne | 4.10 | p-xylene | 6.60 |
| 2-methylbutane | 1.38 | 2-methylpropene | 5.31 | styrene | 2.22 |
| n-pentane | 1.04 | 1-butene | 8.91 | o-xylene | 6.46 |
| 2,2-dimethylbutane | 0.82 | 1,3-butadiene | 10.89 | isopropylbenzene | 2.24 |
| cyclopentane | 2.38 | 1,2-butene | 9.94 | n-propylbenzene | 2.12 |
| 2,3-dimethylbutane | 1.07 | 1-butyne | 9.24 | 1,3-methylethylbenzene | 7.20 |
| 2-methylpentane | 1.53 | c-2-butene | 9.94 | 1,4-methylethylbenzene | 7.20 |
| 3-methylpentane | 1.52 | 3-methyl-1-butene | 6.22 | 1,3,5-trimethylbenzene | 10.12 |
| n-hexane | 0.98 | 2-butyne | 9.24 | 1,2-methylethylbenzene | 7.20 |
| 2,2-dimethylpentane | 1.40 | 1-pentene | 6.22 | 1,2,4-trimethylbenzene | 8.83 |
| methylcyclopentane | 2.82 | 2-methyl-1-butene | 4.90 | Iso-butylbenzene | 1.89 |
| 2,4-dimethylpentane | 1.78 | 2-methyl-1,3-butadiene | 9.08 | 1,2,3-trimethylbenzene | 8.85 |
| 2,2,3-trimethylbutane | 1.32 | t-2-pentene | 8.80 | indane | 1.06 |
| cyclohexane | 1.28 | c-2-pentene | 8.80 | 1,3-dimethylbenzene | 6.45 |
| 2-methylhexane | 1.08 | 2-methyl-2-butene | 6.41 | 1,4-dimethylbenzene | 6.45 |
| 2,3-dimethylpentane | 1.51 | cyclopentadiene | 7.66 | 1,2-dimethylbenzene | 6.45 |
| 3-methylhexane | 1.40 | cyclopentene | 7.66 | 1-methyl-2-propylbenzene | 6.45 |
| c-1,3-dimethylcyclopentane | 1.85 | 4-methyl-1-pentene | 4.42 | 1,4-dimethylethylbenzene | 9.07 |
| t-1,3-dimethylcyclopentane | 1.85 | 3-methyl-1-pentene | 4.42 | 1,2-dimethyl-2-ethylbenzene | 9.07 |
| 2,2,4-trimethylpentane | 0.93 | t-3-hexene | 6.69 | 1,3-dimethyl-2-ethylbenzene | 9.07 |
| n-heptane | 0.81 | t-2-hexene | 6.69 | 1,2,4,5-tetramethylbenzene | 9.07 |
| methylcyclohexane | 1.85 | 3-methyl-t-2-pentene | 6.69 | 1,2,3,5-teramethylbenzene | 9.07 |
| 2,5-dimethylhexane | 1.63 | 2-methyl-2-pentene | 6.69 | methylindane | 1.06 |
| ethylcyclopentane | 2.31 | c-3-hexene | 6.69 | 1,2,3,4-tetramethylbenzene | 9.07 |
| 3,3-dimethylhexane | 1.20 | c-2-hexene | 6.69 | | |
| 2,3,4-trimethylpentane | 1.60 | 3-methyl-c-2pentene | 6.69 | methyl-t-butylether | 0.62 |
| 2,3-dimethylhexane | 1.32 | 3-methylcyclopentene | 5.69 | ethyl-t-butylether | 1.98 |
| 2-methylheptane | 0.96 | 3-methyl-1-hexene | 3.48 | | |
| 4-methylheptane | 1.20 | t-2-t-3-heptene | 5.53 | methanol | 0.56 |
| 3-methylheptane | 0.99 | 2-methylhexene | 5.53 | ethanol | |
| di-trimethylcyclic C5/C6 | 1.94 | c-2-heptene | 5.53 | | |
| 2,2,5-trimethylhexane | 0.97 | 1-methylcyclohexene | 5.52 | formaldehyde | 7.15 |
| octane | 0.61 | t-4-octene | 5.29 | acetaldehyde | 5.52 |
| t-1,3-dimethylcyclohexane | 1.85 | 1-nonene | 2.22 | acrolein | 6.77 |
| 2,4-dimethylheptane | 1.34 | | | propionaldehyde | 6.53 |
| c-1,2-dimethylcyclohexane | 1.94 | | | n-butyraldehyde | 5.26 |
| 3,5-dimethylheptane | 1.14 | | | crotonaldehyde | 5.41 |
| 2-methyloctane | 1.14 | | | pentanaldehyde | 4.40 |
| 2-methyloctane | 1.14 | | | hexanaldehyde | 3.79 |
| n-nonane | 0.54 | | | benzaldehyde | –0.56 |
| 2,2-dimethyloctane | 1.01 | | | p-tolualdehyde | –0.56 |
| 2,4-dimethyloctane | 1.01 | | | acetone | 0.56 |
| branched $C_{10}$'s | 1.01 | | | butanone | 1.18 |
| 3-methylnonane | 1.01 | | | | |
| n-decane | 0.47 | | | | |
| n-undecane | 0.42 | | | | |
| n-dodecane | 0.38 | | | | |

### 2.2.1 Evolution through time

Carbon dioxide and water, at first condensed, evaporated during the progressive warming of the Earth to reach very high concentrations about three billion years ago. On subsequent cooling, water vapor condensed and atmospheric carbon dioxide dissolved in the ocean to bring its concentration to about 0.3 percent some five hundred million years ago, and then to 0.03 percent at the onset of the industrial era (around 1860).

Figure 2.4 shows the evolutionary trends of the different gases up to historical times. In the last few decades, however, man has directly influenced the intensity of the sources, and for certain gases, the anthropogenic component of the variations has reached approximately the same level as the natural component [9].

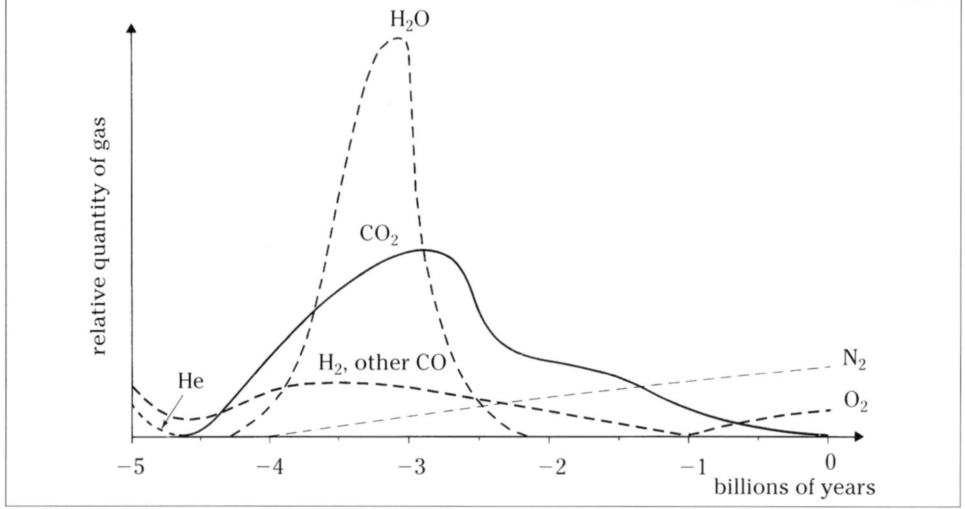


**Fig 2.4** Trends in atmospheric gases during geologic eras [11]

For example, the $CO_2$ content is rising steadily, going from 280 ppm at the dawn of the industrial age to about 340 ppm, at an annual rate of 1.5 ppm.

The increased extraction of energy from fossil fuels (coal and oil), increased biomass combustion to expand arable areas (slash and burn, deforestation, etc.), and the elimination of forests, which absorb $CO_2$ by the chlorophyll function, are the main factors responsible for the increase in $CO_2$. It is estimated that one hectare of new forest can capture 6.24 t of carbon annually in the form of $CO_2$. That means 465 million hectares, or 75% of the area of the USA not covered by forests, would have to be planted to absorb the $CO_2$ released into the atmosphere [41].

Other trace gas concentrations are also increasing:

- Methane ($CH_4$): With an annual increase estimated at 1.5%, methane had an estimated pre-1700 concentration of 0.7 ppmv [11]. Its concentration remained stable during the previous millennium [24], then increased to 1.5 ppmv in 1980 and 1.7 ppmv in 1990 (an annual rise of 0.0165 ppmv per year, estimated in 1990 [26]). Methane has a stratospheric lifetime of about ten years.

The most widely mentioned sources of $CH_4$ are:

- anaerobic fermentation: emissions of ruminants (manure gas), and marshes and rice paddies (marsh gas)
- combustion of fossil fuels and biomass
- leaks from coal mines, and natural gas fields and pipelines

The $CH_4$ concentration is growing at the same rate as the world population.

- Carbon monoxide (CO): With an annual increase of 0.8 to 1.4%, CO has an average concentration estimated at 0.08 ppmv [25], about half of it due to human activities (automotive traffic, burning of fossil fuels, and biomass).
- Nitrous oxide ($N_2O$): While increasing at a lower rate than $CH_4$ (0.4%/year), $N_2O$ has reached an average concentration of 0.3 ppmv today. Its stratospheric lifetime is about 125 years.

  The main processes responsible for the formation of $N_2O$ are microbial nitrification and denitrification. The action of these processes is amplified by the increasingly widespread use of nitrogen and ammonia fertilizers. Added to this main source are combustion processes: the combustion of coal, especially in fluidized beds, and to a lesser degree, the combustion of fuels in internal combustion engines (the production of $N_2O$ by turbojet engines operating at high altitude is a hotly debated subject).
- Chlorofluorocarbon compounds (freons): Though their presence was detected in the atmosphere only in the early 1970s, freon concentrations are increasing rapidly. For the various molecules involved, freon concentrations are increasing at an annual average of 5%, with current concentrations about 0.25 ppmv. Freon's lifetime is 70 to 100 years.

  Freon compounds are essentially synthetic products, used as aerosol propellant gases and heat transfer fluids in refrigerators and air-conditioners. Freons are discharged into the atmosphere during purging and drainage of these appliances.
- Ozone: Mainly produced from $NO_2$, ozone is increasing in the troposphere. Its basic pre-industrial age concentration is estimated at 0.01 ppm in Paris [43], whereas its stratospheric concentration is decreasing.

## 2.3 Potential effects on climate and environment

### 2.3.1 Consequence of the greenhouse effect

The increase in gases reflecting the Earth's infra-red (IR) radiation can upset the thermal equilibrium of the globe [8].

Various forecasting models exist to estimate the effects of such changes on the conditions of life on earth. A doubling of the $CO_2$ content, a hypothesis considered for the next century, would incur the following consequences [34]:

- warming of the air by an average of 2 to 3°C

- melting of the Arctic and Antarctic ice and a rise in sea level of 5 to 7 m, the rise due in part to the thermal expansion of the ocean
- changing of the landscape, since the anticipated warming will not be uniformly distributed over the Earth's surface: the appearance of deserts in areas of current vegetation and the emergence of vegetation in areas that are arid today, warming of some areas and cooling of others, and accompanying changes in wind and rainfall patterns [35],
- evaporation (and hence precipitation) due to the warming of the air.

However, these effects will not be simultaneous due to different inertias and retroaction processes (the $CO_2$ content affects the climate and the change in the climate reacts on the $CO_2$ content).

Moreover, other hypotheses assume that the temperature rise, by directly causing additional evaporation, would cause an increase in cloudiness. This cloud screen could thus reduce the incident solar energy reaching the ground and oppose the warming process.

### 2.3.2 The problem of ozone

The maintenance of the stratospheric ozone layer, created by the photochemical dissociation of oxygen, depends on the equilibrium between the formation and destruction reactions catalyzed by the trace gases containing nitrogen, chlorine, or hydrogen.

The ozone layer filters the UV/B radiation (280 to 320 μm). Otherwise, this radiation would cause the proliferation of skin cancer and biological mutations. The action of radiation on DNA molecules can cause viral mutations and the emergence of new diseases resistant to current therapeutic remedies. Radiation can also cause changes in the bacterial population of the soil, with predictable consequences on vegetation and therefore on climate [14]. This would ultimately prevent any life on earth, in a manner analogous to the conditions prevailing on Mars.

Lately, a decline has been observed in this stratospheric ozone layer [1 and 2]. The decline is attributed to a predominance of destructive catalytic reactions by nitrogen oxides and halogenated compounds. This has lead the industrial nations to restrict and ultimately prohibit the manufacture and use of chlorofluorinated hydrocarbons, and to be concerned about combustion sources generating high nitrous oxide emissions [28].

## 2.4 Indoor pollution

The majority of individuals in most modern societies spend the bulk of their time indoors, inside various premises, residences, and workplaces. It is estimated that working men in Europe and the USA spend 80 to 90% of their time indoors—their wives spend even longer [39]. Hence, indoor air quality appears to be just as important as outdoor air quality, from the standpoint of health and comfort [13].

Although many of the pollutants found indoors are connected with the very human activities that generate them—such as smoking, cooking, the use of coating materials, and professional activities—some of them still come from outside. For various indoor pollutants, one can estimate the contribution of outdoor pollution and, associated with it, a share attributable to automotive emissions. This share obviously depends on parameters such as the season (windows open or closed), the air renewal rate, the possible use of air-conditioners with filters, etc.

The following penetration rates are obtained for various pollutants:

- $SO_2$: 15 to 50%
- $NO_x$ : 33 to 60%; in cities, the outdoor portion derives primarily from heavy automobile traffic
- particulates: about 30%; where windows are left open, up to 70% for submicron fractions
- lead: 50 to 70%; essentially of automotive origin
- CO: 33 to 100%; also caused by automotive emissions
- other pollutants ($O_3$, PAH, aldehydes, etc.), of which the penetration rates have not been estimated, but which are partly due to outdoor pollution

### 2.4.1 Pollution inside vehicle passenger compartments

A specific case of indoor pollution occurs in automotive vehicles, especially due to the small interior volume (0.3 $m^3$ for a private car). For most people, this situation accounts for only a small fraction of their time spent indoors, but for certain professions (taxi, bus, coach, truck, and utility vehicle drivers), the cab of the vehicle is a preponderant place of residence. In heavy traffic, drivers are the victims of emissions from vehicles in front of them. This situation is aggravated in winter by heaters that draw ambient air into the vehicle through 'fresh' air intakes, which are often placed at the level of the exhaust pipe of the car in front.

To date, the few studies [3] that have dealt with this specific problem show that the concentrations measured inside the vehicle reflect outdoor concentrations [36]. Concentrations are higher in heavy traffic than on expressways [10], mainly to the detriment of CO. They are generally higher than those found on sidewalks, but can reach up to 75% of the concentrations found near the vehicle [15]. A more detailed study has shown that the concentrations of CO, benzene, toluene, xylenes, lead, and ethyl halogenides could be three to four times higher than ambient concentrations. These concentrations are even higher if the vehicle is old, the traffic is slow, and the vehicle is running with windows closed and the heater on [31]. The presence of these pollutants may also arise from the level of pollutants present in garages when the vehicles depart [16].

Thus, 230 to 700 μg/m$^3$ of NO, 70 to 110 mμ/m$^3$ of $NO_2$, and up to 250 ppm of CO can be found inside passenger compartments. Table 2.3 gives the concentrations of benzene measured in passenger compartments. This situation obviously reaches a peak in traffic jams in tunnels [21]. On the road, the vehicle itself may be a source of its own internal pollution, due to a defective exhaust system, open windows, or a badly-closed hatchback [20]. Since the passenger compartment is under negative pressure, the vehicle's own exhaust emissions are drawn inside.

**Table 2.3** Benzine levels measured in vehicle passenger compartment

| Location | Date | Type of trip | Average value (μg/m$^3$) |
|---|---|---|---|
| Deft | 1981 | Commuter 4184 trips | 66 max. 2500 |
| Deft | 1981 | Freeway 86 trips | 27 max. 300 |
| Frankfurt | 1981 | Commuter 4 (itinerary ≠) | 305 max. 840 |
| Hamburg | 1979 | City | 55 |
| Sarrebruck | 1974 | City 1 trip | 560 |
| Munich | 1981 | City 1 trip | 69 |
| Munich | 1981 | Freeway 2 trips | 9.6 |
| Munich | 1983 | City 2 trips | 112 |

Even when parked, internal hydrocarbon concentrations, especially aromatics [36 and 38], are higher than outdoor concentrations. This is probably due to evaporation from the fuel tank, due to an imperfect seal. Therefore, internal concentrations of 2700 μg/m$^3$ can be reached after parking in open sunlight with the windows closed. The maximum permissible value for benzene is 3000 μg/m$^3$.

For riders who may be inconvenienced by the odor of the exhaust gases from a preceding diesel vehicle, an activated-carbon filter has been evaluated for installation in vehicle ventilation systems [3 and 40].

## 2.5 Conclusion

In this chapter, we have tried to assess the overall importance of air pollution and its potential repercussions on the evolution of the Earth's environment, from the standpoint of major biogeochemical cycles.

The highly complex investigations that are under way are not yet sufficiently advanced to draw irrefutable conclusions. Despite the sharp increase in pollutant concentrations, exaggerated alarmism would be inappropriate. Natural phenomena (volcanic eruptions, for example) often generate tonnages of pollutants greater than those contributed by human activities, and the globe has retroactive capabilities that have often come into effect through the centuries.

The following chapters discuss the quantities of various pollutants and describe their effects on human health and plant life.

# REFERENCES


[1] P. Aimedieu, (1986), "Inquiétante disparition de l'ozone dans l'Antarctique?", *La Recherche*, **17** (181), 1249-1252.

[2] P. Aimedieu, (1988), "La querelle de l'ozone", *La Recherche*, **19** (196), 270-282.

[3] G. Arendt and H.J. Decker, (1986), "Luftqualität in Fahrgastraümen", *Forschungsvereinigung Automobiltechnik e.V. (FAT) Schriftenreihe* No. 59, 94 p.

[4] F. Arnold et al., (1986), "Acetone measurements in the upper troposphere and lower stratosphere, Implications for hydroxyl radical abundances", *Nature*, **321**, 505-507.

[5] R. Atkinson, (1990), "Gas phase tropospheric chemistry of organic compounds, A review", *Atmosph. Environm.*, **24A,** 1-41.

[6] A. Bertrand, (1987), "L'effet de serre par le $CO_2$ et les gaz traces", *Rev. Inst. Franç. du Pétrole*, **42,** 655-669.

[7] P.M. Berglund and G. Petersson, (1990), "Hazardous petrol hydrocarbons from refuelling with and without vapour recovery", *The Sci. Tot. Environm.*, **91,** 49-57.

[8] B. Bolin et al., (1986), *The greenhouse effect, climatic changes and ecosystems*, John Wiley and Sons, New York, 541 p.

[9] C. Boutron et al., (1980), "L'homme a-t-il pollué l'atmosphère à une échelle globale?", *La Recherche*, **109,** 340-343.

[10] R.M. Brice and J.F. Roesler, (1966), "The exposure to carbon monoxide of occupants of vehicles moving in heavy traffic", *J. APCA*, **16,** 597-600.

[11] J. Carbonnelle et al., (1987), "Le gaz carbonique et l'effet de serre", *CEA/FAR SPIN Report*, 10.2.1.3(140), 144 p.

[12] P. Carlier and G. Mouvier, (1988), "Initiation à la physico-chimie de la basse troposphère", *Poll. Atmosph.* (January/March), 12-24.

[13] J. Carmes, (1987), "État des connaissances en matière de pollution atmosphérique à l'intérieur des locaux en France", *Ministry of Health Report*, 37 p.

[14] S. Cieslik, (1976), "L'ozone stratosphérique", *La Recherche*, **7** (68), 510-519.

[15] D.M. Colwill and A.J. Hickman, (1980), "Exposure of drivers to carbon monoxide", *J. APCA*, **30,** 1316-1319.

[16] P.G. Flachsbart et al., (1987), "Carbon monoxide exposures of Washington commuters", *J. APCA*, **37,** 135-142.

[17] H. Grassl, (1987), "Klimaveränderung durch Spurengase, Stand der Forschung", *Energiewirtschaftliche Tagesfragen*, **37,** 127-133.

[18] J. Hansen et al., (1981), "Climate impact of increasing atmospheric carbon dioxide", *Science*, **213,** 957-966.

[19] B. Henderson-Sellers, (1984), *Pollution of our Atmosphere,* Bristol, Adam Hilger Limited, 210 p.

[20] F. Henry and M. Sanchez, (1983), "Mesure des taux de CO émis par un véhicule dans son habitacle, Analyse du phénomène", *IRT/CERNE Report*, 88 p.

[21] R. Joumard et al., (1984a), "Risques dus à la pollution de l'air pour les usagers et les professionnels du tunnel de Fourvière à Lyon", *IRT/CERNE Report*, 33 p.

[22] R. Joumard, (1989), "Quels polluants?", Contribution des transports, *Poll. Atmosph.*(121), 5-8.

[23] R. Joumard, (1991), "Pollution de l'air dans les transports", *Poll. Atmosph.* (January/March), 20-24.

[24] M.A.K. Khalil and R.A. Rasmussen, (1987), "Atmospheric methane, Trends over the last 10,000 years", *Atmosph. Environ.*, **21,** 2445-2452.

[25] M.A.K. Khalil and R.A. Rasmussen, (1988), "Carbon monoxide in the earth's atmosphere, Indications of a global increase", *Nature*, **332,** 242-245.

[26] M.A.K. Khalil and R.A. Rasmussen, (1990), "Atmospheric methane, Recent global trends", *E.S.&T.*, **24,** 549-553.

[27] S.L. Kopczynski, (1974), "Photochemical reactivities of aldehyde nitrogen oxide systems", *E.S.&T.*, **8,** 909-918.

[28] J.C. Kramlich et al., (1988), *EPA/NOAA/NASA/USDA $N_2O$ Workshop, EPA Report* 600/8-88-079, Boulder, Colorado, 67 p.

[29] M. Lal et al., (1986), "Potential climatic consequences of increasing anthropogenic constituents in the atmosphere", *Atmosph. Environ.*, **20,** 639-642.

[30] G. Lambert, (1987), "Le gaz carbonique dans l'atmosphère", *La Recherche*, **18** (189), 778-787.

[31] C.S. Liu et al., (1989), "In-vehicle air toxics characterization study in the Los Angeles region of California", in: *Man and His Ecosystem*, Vo. 1, L. J. Brasser, Elsevier Science Publications, Amsterdam, pp. 247-252.

[32] P. Masclet and G. Mouvier, (1988), "La chimie atmosphérique des hydrocarbures aromatiques polycycliques", *Poll. Atmosph.* (January/March), 25-31.

[33] G. Megie, (1988), "Les modifications chimiques de l'atmosphère et leurs effets sur l'environnement", *Poll. Atmosph.* (January/March), 5-11.

[34] S. Midot, (1987), "Les effets du $CO_2$ sur le climat, un bilan des connaissances actuelles", *Poll. Atmosph.* (July/September), 199-225.

[35] I. Mintzer, (1989), *The $CO_2$ problem, Energy World Yearbook 1989*, pp. 89-91.

[36] W. Mücke et al., (1984), "Luftverunreinigungen in Kraftfahrzeugen", *Staub*, **44,** 374-377.

[37] C. Parfait and D. Dallest, (1991), "Étude comparative de l'exposition bioclimatique des voyageurs suivant différents types de transport", *Poll. Atmosph.* (January/March), 25-33.

[38] M. Pasquereau and P. Degobert, (1987), *unpublished results.*

[39] M.L. Perrin et al., (1988), "Pollution de l'air à l'intérieur des locaux. Études effectuées à l'étranger", *SPIN Report* No. 88/1, 270 p.

[40] H. Rohlfing and A. König, (1985), *Zuluftfilter als technische Maßnahme zur Verringerung der Geruchsimmission in Kraftfahrzeuginnenräumen, VDI Symposium 'Geruchstoffe'*, Baden-Baden, 2/4 October, pp. 34-36.

[41] R.A. Sedjo, (1989), "Forests, A tool to moderate global warming?", *Environment*, **31,** 14-20.

[42] G. Toupance, (1988), “L’ozone dans la basse troposphère, Théorie et pratique”, *Poll. Atmosph.* (January/March), 32-42.

[43] A. Volz and D. Kley, (1988), “Evaluation of the Montsouris series of ozone measurements made in the nineteenth century”, *Nature*, **332,** 240-242.

[44] W.P.L. Carter, (1970), “A method for evaluating the atmospheric ozone impact of actual vehicle emissions”, *SAE Paper* No. 900710.

# An inventory of air pollutants 3

*This chapter introduces the various pollutants allegedly responsible for air pollution, with particular emphasis on automotive pollutants, and further attempts to determine the respective share of automotive pollutants as a part of the whole.*

## 3.1 Definition of pollutants

The term pollutant is normally applied to any substance added to the environment in a sufficient concentration to have a measurable effect on humans, animals, vegetation, or building materials [31].

Hence, air pollutants include all natural and artificial airborne substances, including gases, solid particles, liquid droplets, and mixtures of these different items.

Two main classes of pollutants are considered:

- primary pollutants emitted directly by identifiable sources
- secondary pollutants produced in the atmosphere by the interaction between the various primary pollutants (or reactions between the pollutants and the normal constituents of the atmosphere, with or without photochemical activation)

The problem of secondary pollutants has already been touched on briefly (Section 2.2.1). Therefore, the following discussion will focus essentially on primary pollutants.

### 3.1.1 Primary pollutants

The following substances can be considered air pollutants:

- carbon compounds
- nitrogen compounds
- organic compounds—volatile, irritating, or odoriferous
- sulfur compounds
- halogen compounds
- metallic compounds
- fine particles ($\Phi<100$ μm)
- coarse particles ($\Phi>100$ μm)

Water vapor, the final combustion product of most fuels, is not considered a pollutant since it is a major constituent of the Earth's crust.

The following sections discuss the various pollutants, with particular emphasis on those of mainly automotive origin, especially engine exhausts. Special mention is made of the evaporative emissions of volatile hydrocarbons.

The following chapters examine the effects of different categories of pollutants on human health, on plants, and on materials.

## 3.2 Carbon compounds

These compounds are carbon-based gases, essentially carbon dioxide ($CO_2$) and carbon monoxide (CO).

### 3.2.1 Carbon dioxide

Carbon dioxide is a normal final-combustion product of every fuel containing carbon (biomass, wood, coal and its variants, oil and petroleum derivatives) and a product of aerobic metabolism (respiration). On the other hand, it is reconverted to carbonaceous solids by the chlorophyll function in plants. We have already discussed the problems caused by increased carbon dioxide concentration in the air (Section 2.3.1), which risks altering the carbon cycle and modifying the climate by the greenhouse effect.

In 1983, carbon emissions from fossil fuels were estimated at approximately 5 Gt per year, with an equivalent amount being contributed by other human activities [26]. Other studies have set the share of carbon emissions retained by the Earth's atmosphere at 2.9 Gt of the 5.8 Gt emitted annually from different sources [142]. Emissions have since been re-assessed for 1990 [72] at 26 Gt of $CO_2$, with 15% being attributable to road traffic.

The emission factors listed in Table 3.1 are established by CITEPA [6] and indicate the emissions attributable to various fuels. Corresponding $CO_2$ emissions from the consumption of petroleum products, which are based on 1986 petroleum consumption [36], are listed in Table 3.2 and highlight transport-related emissions.

**Table 3.1** Fuel emission factors CITEPA [6]

| Fuel | kg $CO_2$/t |
|---|---|
| solid fuels | 2984 |
| heavy fuel oil | 3113 |
| home heating oil | 3142 |
| light fuel oil | 3142 |
| diesel | 3149 |
| regular- and premium-grade gasolines | 3137 |
| natural gas | 2290 |
| propane | 2700 |

Of the total industrial $CO_2$ emissions in France in 1986, estimated by CITEPA at 326 Mt, the portion attributable to transportation (determined by adding only the contributions of regular- and premium-grade gasolines and diesel fuel, since the contribution of LPG is still negligible in France) amounted to about 95.3 Mt, or 29% of the total. A similar calculation for the whole world (excluding China, the ex-USSR, and Eastern Europe) attributes 4416 Mt to transportation, out of a total emitted tonnage of about 18 Gt of $CO_2$ (5 Gt of carbon) [114], or about 25% of the total.

**Table 3.2** Distribution of $CO_2$ emissions in 1986

| Fuel | Consumption | | kt $CO_2$ | |
|---|---|---|---|---|
| | France (kt) | World (Mt) | France | World |
| heavy fuel oil | 6834 | 437.5 | 21,274 | 1,361937 |
| home heating oil | 21,097 | | 6629 | |
| diesel | 11,850 | 757.5 | 37,316 | 2,385367 |
| regular- and premium-grade gasoline | 18,484 | 647.5 | 57,984 | 2,031207 |
| LPG | 2917 | | 7876 | |
| motor LPG | 0.059 | | 0.159 | |

## 3.2.2 Carbon monoxide

CO is a colorless, odorless, and highly toxic gas, with a density close to that of air, (Section 4.5.1) It is produced under excessively rich combustion conditions (Section 10.3).

CO is primarily generated by combustion processes. Anaerobic microbial metabolisms, similar to those that generate methane, produce only negligible amounts of CO: Emissions from these sources amounted to 200,000 t/year of the estimated total of 1600 to 5000 Mt/year that is discharged into the atmosphere [35] In 1990, approximately 200 Mt was of anthropogenic origin [72]. The output of emissions corresponding to different sources has been published [37].

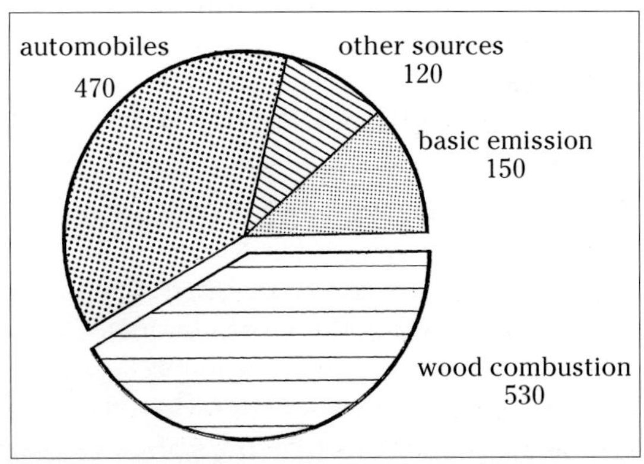


**Fig 3.1** Sources of CO in winter in Oregon [84]. (Values in ppbV)

Stationary sources, operating with fixed air/fuel ratios that are easy to regulate, emit considerably less CO than spark ignition engines running on relatively rich and variable mixtures. In certain parts of the USA, however, the spread of wood-burning appliances, supposedly 'ecological' and conserving of fossil fuels, generate winter CO concentrations similar to those blamed on automotive traffic [84] (Fig. 3.1).

The atmospheric reactivity of CO fortunately prevents its accumulation with time. The $OH^\bullet$ (Section 2.1.3) radicals oxidize it to $CO_2$ by a mechanism involving NO [28]:

$$\begin{aligned} CO + OH^\bullet &\longrightarrow CO_2 + H^\bullet \\ H^\bullet + O_2 &\longrightarrow HO_2^\bullet \\ HO_2^\bullet + NO &\longrightarrow OH^\bullet + NO_2 \end{aligned}$$

Automotive CO emissions in France rose from 4.1 Mt in 1970 to 5.5 Mt in 1984 [92], of which 80% was from private vehicles and 20% from utility vehicles. For 1988 [4], emissions from light vehicles were estimated at 8.67 Mt (including 1.5% for light diesel vehicles).

Other evaluations estimated 1988 automotive emissions at about 8.9 Mt, accounting for 80% of all French emissions that totaled 10.8 Mt [4].

In Germany during 1982 and 1989 [89, 131, 133, and 134], the shares attributable to transportation represented 63% and 73% respectively of all CO emissions, which were estimated at a total of 8.38 and 8.44 Mt respectively. Of this proportion, truck emissions amounted to 78,000 t/year, with an emission factor of 10 g of CO per kg of fuel [7]. In the Netherlands during 1980, CO emissions were estimated at 1.35 Mt, including 0.971 Mt (72%) due to automotive traffic [159]. In the USA, the share of CO emissions attributable to transportation is estimated at 66% [54]; around 1983, the average concentration was about 7 ppm. World emissions were estimated in 1961 at 200 Mt/year [149].

CO occurs primarily in urban traffic, when gasoline engines are often idling, and concentrations can rise to over 100 $mg/m^3$. In the Ludwigshafen area, with its very heavy traffic, up to 550 t/year · $km^2$ of CO has been recorded [134].

## 3.3 Nitrogen compounds

### 3.3.1 Nitric oxide and nitrogen peroxide

NO and $NO_2$ are usually analyzed simultaneously and expressed in the form of $NO_x$ with $1 < x < 2$. NO is the most abundant of all nitrogen derivatives present in the atmosphere and it represents about 95% of $NO_1 + NO_2$ emissions. NO is a natural emission of soil bacterial activity. The amounts estimated vary with latitude as follows:

- in Australia, 0.005 to 0.01 $g/m^2$ per year expressed as nitrogen
- in Germany, 0.009 to 0.09 $g/m^2$ per year expressed as nitrogen
- in France, about 0.004 $g/m^2$ per year expressed as nitrogen
- in the rain forests of Côte d'Ivoire, about 0.08 $g/m^2$ per year expressed as nitrogen

Expressed as $NO_2$, total worldwide emissions of $NO_x$ amount to 177 Mt/year (76 to 315 Mt/year according to the source, and even 66 Mt [72]), including ≈68% of natural origin and ≈32% of human origin (combustion of fossil fuels). Of this total mass, ≈22% results from the combustion of biomass, ≈15% from soil bacterial activity,

≈15% from lightning, ≈4% from nitrogen fertilizers, ≈10% from ammonia oxidation, ≈1% from the oceans, and ≈1% from the stratosphere (oxidation of $N_2O$) [89].

The rather wide range reported for all worldwide nitrogen emissions stems from the uncertainties concerning the scale of natural and biogenic emissions. Some of these can be attributed to secondary pollution caused by the oxidation of ammonia in the atmosphere. Another portion results from $N_2O$ emissions (see below).

The worldwide contribution of artificial nitrogen oxide emissions to the atmosphere is estimated at about 66 Mt/year of $NO_2$. Most of these emissions are generated by the use of fossil fuels by the steel industry, by glassworks, by the chemical industry in the production of nitric acid, and by automotive traffic (generating 70 to 80% of the emissions).

In France, $NO_2$ emissions were estimated in 1989 at ≈1.76 Mt (a declining total: 1980 ≈5.5% is generated by industry and agriculture, and ≈75% by road traffic. The latter figure rose from 56% in 1980 to 76.3% in 1989 due to increased traffic and to the drop in emissions from power plants (switching to nuclear) and industry. In West Germany, anthropogenic sources emitted ≈3.0 Mt of $NO_2$ in 1980 (2.68 Mt in 1989 [131 and 133]), of which ≈54% is attributed to mobile sources [127]: 15% of this 54% is generated by trucks [134]. Truck $NO_x$ emissions in Germany reached 460,000 t in 1985 [7], with an emission factor of 60 g of $NO_x$ per kg of diesel fuel. Total traffic emissions are estimated at 1.6 Mt/year of $NO_x$. In automotive emissions, $NO_2$ can account for as much as 35% of the total $NO_x$ for diesel vehicles, and 38% for gasoline vehicles equipped with exhaust air injection [95]. Table 3.3 gives the emission factors.

**Table 3.3** Emission factors for $NO_x$ expressed as g $NO_2$ per kg of fuel [129]

| | **Vehicles** | | | | |
|---|---|---|---|---|---|
| **Type of traffic Average speed (km/h)** | **Urban 10 to 50** | **Rural 50 to 80** | **Expressway 80** | **100** | **120** |
| **private cars:** | | | | | |
| • gasoline: | | | | | |
| - four-stroke | 23 | 41 | 44 | 55 | 62 |
| - two-stroke | | 7 (average) | | | |
| • diesel | | 15 (average) | | | |
| **vans (< 3.5 t)** | | | | | |
| • gasoline | | 42 (average) | | | |
| • diesel | | 15 (average) | | | |
| **trucks (> 3.5 t)** | | | | | |
| • diesel trucks | 50 | 55 | 60 (average) | | |
| • buses | 50 | 60 | 70 (average) | | |
| • gasoline trucks | | 20 (average) | | | |
| **motorcycles and mopeds** | | | | | |
| • (gasoline) | | 5.5 (average) | | | |
| **locomotives** | | 20 (average) | | | |
| **interior navigation craft** | | 70 (average) | | | |
| **farm tractors** | | 50 (average) | | | |

For all the European countries of the OECD in 1980, anthropogenic emissions were estimated at ≈12 Mt with the same proportion (≈54%) for mobile sources. These figures agree with Dutch estimates [8 and 43]. European refineries account for 1.5 to 3.5% of total $NO_x$ emissions of anthropogenic origin. For 1980, Table 3.4 gives the share of $NO_2$ emissions attributed to traffic [104] in a number of European countries. Another artificial cause of nitrogen oxide emissions is biomass combustion (forest and brush fires, etc.), where it is estimated that the $NO_x$ results from nitrogen present in the plant matter. The estimate is about 1 to 2 g of $NO_2$ per kg of plant matter burned [49]. This production is estimated at 5 to 40 Mt of nitrogen on a worldwide scale.

**Table 3.4** Relative share in 1980 of different pollutants emitted by road traffic in Europe [104] Countries indicated by country registration code

| **Pollutant** | **Country** | | | | | | | | | | | |
|---|---|---|---|---|---|---|---|---|---|---|---|---|
| (% total emitted) | **A** | **DK** | **SF** | **F** | **D** | **I** | **NL** | **N** | **P** | **S** | **CH** | **GB** |
| $SO_2$ | 3 | 2 | 1 | 3 | 2 | 2 | 3 | 3 | 3 | 2 | 4 | 1 |
| $NO_x$ | 64 | 33 | 43 | 37 | 47 | 55 | 51 | 32 | 45 | 48 | 66 | 34 |
| VOC (traffic) | 25 | 35 | 11 | 37 | 33 | 29 | 42 | 14 | 10 | 18 | 24 | 33 |
| VOC (natural) | 36 | 21 | 71 | 34 | 11 | 26 | 5 | 57 | 63 | 64 | 13 | 4 |

The sharpest increases in nitrogen oxide emissions due to human activities are observed mainly in the northern hemisphere. In the USA, for example, it is estimated that $NO_x$ emissions rose from 3 Mt in 1900 to 22 Mt in 1980 [56].

### 3.3.2 Nitric acid

Measurements of diesel exhaust show that direct emissions of $HNO_3$ are negligible in comparison to those produced in the atmosphere by the oxidation of $NO_x$ [128].

### 3.3.3 Nitrous oxide

$N_2O$ is a gas considered apart from $NO_x$, because it displays much greater stability (125 year lifetime) and is measured by different analytical techniques, which are still subject to debate (Section 8.5).

It also appears in the biochemical processes of the soil by nitrification of nitrogen-bearing compounds: the average release in the Netherlands is about 0.5 g/ha per hour of $N_2O$ from well-worked soils. In Germany, it is estimated that this figure may be as high as 1.35 g in the days immediately following the spreading of fertilizer. Tropical savannas are also sources of $N_2O$ [61]. Worldwide biochemical emissions vary between 0.5 and 10 Mt/year expressed as nitrogen.

$N_2O$ is also generated during combustion from nitrogen included in the fuel. It is also generated in processes that operate in the temperature range in which $N_2O$ is formed and then rapidly 'quenched', subsequently leaving the zone of the reaction. This occurs, for example, with combustion in a circulating fluidized bed.

Problems of analysis make it difficult to estimate the proportion of 'industrial' $N_2O$ emissions in worldwide emissions, but anthropogenic emissions were estimated at 5000 to 7000 Gg/year of $N_2O$ in 1992 [72 and 173]. However, it appears that the share of automotive emissions is low, about 3.3% of the worldwide total, which is estimated at 200 Gg/year of $N_2O$ [93 and 173]. This also applies to high-altitude turbojet engine emissions.

Nitrous oxide is a relatively inactive pollutant in the troposphere due to its low reactivity. However, it is an active factor in the attack on the stratospheric ozone layer (Section 2.3.2).

### 3.3.4 Ammonia

Atmospheric ammonia is a major indirect source of nitrogen oxides. Apart from the direct volatilization of ammonia compounds in fertilizers, it is essentially formed by the bacterial transformation of urea in animal manure—primarily from livestock.

Traffic and the combustion of coal account for only a few per cent—negligible compared with agricultural emissions. The automobile normally only emits ammonia if the catalytic $NO_x$ reduction systems fail to work efficiently (Section 12.11.5).

The average value quoted in the Netherlands for $NH_3$ emissions is about 0.5g/ha per hour, from the spreading of synthetic fertilizers and manure. Livestock produce 3 to 18 kg/year of $NH_3$ per animal.

In France, the production and use of fertilizer accounts for 140,000t/year of $NH_3$, with livestock being responsible for about 2.5 Mt of $NO_2$ through $NH_3$.

In Europe, $NH_3$ emissions due to livestock were estimated in 1980 at about 3.45 Mt, with record production in the Netherlands of 3.1 t/km$^2$ [11]. On the world scale, the production of $NO_x$ attributed to $NH_3$ is estimated at between 1 and 10 Mt/year of nitrogen.

Despite its alkaline character, $NH_3$ does not display a tendency to neutralize 'acid rain'—on the contrary, the nitrogen oxides it gives rise to are essential contributors to acidic precipitation in certain countries.

### 3.3.5 Hydrocyanic acid and cyanogen

Hydrocyanic acid HCN and cyanogen $(CN)_2$ are, respectively, a liquid and a gas—non-flammable, colorless, and toxic. Cyanogen has been detected in the upper atmosphere, where it is formed by electron bombardment of $CO_2$ and $N_2$.

Hydrocyanic acid is a normal product of plant metabolism, present in particular in peach leaves and flowers [130].

These are exceptional pollutants in the automotive context and are emitted only when purification systems fail to work efficiently (Section 12.11.4). Turbojet engines are also very low contributors (9 to 42 ppb) [138].

### 3.3.6 Nitrosamines

This class of compounds, particularly N-nitrosodimethylamine (NDMA) and N-nitrosodiethylamine (NDEA), is obtained by the reaction between nitrogen oxides and amines. They have been detected in tobacco smoke and in air near certain roads [144]. NDEA could be generated by a reaction between diethylamine and nitrous acid (formed from water and NO and $NO_2$) [60]:

$$(C_2H_5)_2NH + NOOH \longrightarrow (C_2H_5)_2N{-}NO + H_2O$$

However, amine emissions from vehicles equipped with catalytic converters are too low to implicate the automobile (<2.2 mg/mile) [24].

Apart from the production of nitrogen oxides that are precursors of these pollutants, the responsibility of the automobile in the production of nitrosamine emissions has not yet been clearly established [53 and 146].

These products are recognized as carcinogenic to animals and a potential source of other carcinogens such as benzo(a)pyrene [99].

## 3.4 Organic compounds

The compounds implicated in air pollution are mostly volatile organic compounds, since aerosols of solids or heavier liquid compounds are rarely found in the atmosphere.

### 3.4.1 Volatile organic compounds and evaporation losses

This category includes a wide variety of different products. The definition provided by the EPA in the USA [20] states:

*"A volatile organic compound (VOC) is any organic compound which, once released into the atmosphere, can remain there for a sufficiently long time to participate in photochemical reactions. Although there is no clear demarcation between volatile and non-volatile compounds, compounds that evaporate rapidly at ambient temperatures account for the main share of VOC. Virtually all organic compounds which can be considered as VOC have a vapor pressure >0.1 mmHg in standard conditions (20°C and 1 atm)."*

The definition of 'hydrocarbons' differs slightly from that of VOC. These are generally organic compounds, such as those measured by the FID method (Section 7.2.2). The emission parameters of the different compounds are still poorly understood and the composition of the mixtures concerned depends on the type of industry involved [46 and 160]:

- oil industry (refining and distribution)
- mobile sources (automobile, aviation, railroad)
- industries employing solvents (rubber, plastics, paints, printing, adhesives, organic chemicals, alcoholic fermentation)

Table 3.5 gives the figures currently assumed for these emissions.

**Table 3.5** VOC emission factors [46]

| Emitting activity | Emission factor |
|---|---|
| diesel-powered vehicles | 5 kg/t diesel |
| petroleum industry | 0.04% of crude oil treated |
| solvents | 85% of tonnage consumed |
| natural gas production | 3.1 $g/m^3$ |
| heating fuel oil | 0.15 kg/t |
| heating gas | 0.05 $g/m^3$ |
| coal (power plant) | 0.15 kg/t |
| coal (industry) | 0.7 kg/t |
| coal (domestic use) | 2.0 kg/t |
| forest | 30 $\mu g/m^2$ per min of terpenes |
| grasslands | 2.7 $\mu g/m^2$ per min in summer |

In 1990 [72], worldwide anthropogenic emissions were estimated at 20 Mt. For 1980 [127], the emissions of the European countries of the OECD were estimated at ≈11 Mt, which included 44% attributable to mobile sources. France accounts for ≈2 Mt, which includes 57% due to road traffic, and West Germany for 2.5 Mt (45% from mobile sources). In these European countries, natural sources account for ≈5 Mt.

For motor fuel consumption, the determination of an emission factor is difficult due to the constant improvements made in engines and the progressive installation of catalytic converters. Table 3.6 shows the distribution of European emissions by the different industry branches.

This list includes gasoline lost by evaporation from the vehicle, estimated at 0.8 g/km travelled [46] or at about 7.4 g/day per vehicle [112], which is included with gasoline-powered vehicle emissions. Of the 3390 kt indicated, 2428 kt correspond to exhaust emissions and 962 kt to evaporation losses at the carburetor and the fuel tank. Service station refuelling losses are included in 'distribution'. In the Netherlands, traffic represents 211 kt of VOC out of a total of 465 kt emitted in 1985: 138 kt due to gasoline vehicle exhaust emissions, 18 kt due to evaporation from these vehicles, 41 kt for trucks, and 14 kt for two-wheeled vehicles [8].

On the basis of a large number of vehicles in an underground carpark, evaporation losses have been estimated at about 10 g/vehicle per day [123].

According to surveys in California, refuelling losses amount to a total of 9.6 g/gallon (2.54 kg/$m^3$) [12], 44% of which is due to the filling of storage tanks, 47% to the refuelling of vehicles, 5% to respiration losses, and 5% to spillage. For France, in 1987, this factor would give a total of 57,785 t of hydrocarbons emitted in the distribution of motor fuels (22.75 million $m^3$).

Light hydrocarbons (butanes and isopentanes) account for about 30% of evaporated compounds in the USA [145]. In Europe, due to the increasing use of cat-cracked gasolines, gasoline vapors contain a higher proportion of olefins, up to 10% butenes and pentenes [18].

Table 3.4 gives the percentages of VOC emitted attributable to road traffic in the different European countries [104].

As shown in Table 3.6, the contribution of natural phenomena is practically equal

**Table 3.6** VOC emissions in Europe in 1983 not including methane [46 and 160]

| Source | OECD | | EEC-10 | |
|---|---|---|---|---|
| | kt | % | kt | % |
| **mobile sources:** | | | | |
| • gasoline-powered vehicles | 3390 | 34.4 | 2725 | 36.0 |
| • diesel-powered vehicles | 300 | 3.0 | 225 | 3.0 |
| • aviation | 40 | 0.4 | 30 | 0.4 |
| • railroads | 40 | 0.4 | 30 | 0.4 |
| • coastal and barges | 10 | 0.1 | 10 | 0.1 |
| **total** | 3780 | 38.3 | 3020 | 39.9 |
| **petroleum industry:** | | | | |
| • production | 20 | 0.2 | 15 | 0.2 |
| • transport and terminals | 50 | 0.5 | 15 | 0.5 |
| • refineries | 220 | 2.2 | 180 | 2.4 |
| • distribution | 510 | 5.2 | 415 | 5.5 |
| **total** | 800 | 8.1 | 650 | 8.6 |
| **solvents** (all types) | 4020 | 40.8 | 2850 | 37.7 |
| **industry** (except solvents) | 405 | 4.2 | 300 | 4.0 |
| **natural gas** | | | | |
| • production | 75 | 0.8 | 300 | 4.0 |
| • distribution | 570 | 5.8 | 550 | 7.1 |
| **total** | 645 | 6.6 | 605 | 7.9 |
| **refuse dumps** | 110 | 1.1 | 65 | 0.9 |
| **combustion of fixed sources** | 85 | 0.9 | 58 | 0.8 |
| **anthropogenic total** | 9845 | 100 | 7565 | 100 |
| **natural total** | 10,000 | | 7500 | |

to that of industrial sources: methane (not in the table) is formed in the anaerobic fermentation of organic matter (swamps), trees emit terpenes, and grasslands emit esters, ketones and other oxygenated compounds. This is shown clearly by Table 3.4. In densely-wooded Finland, VOC of natural origin account for 71% of the total and traffic for 11%. These figures are practically the reverse in the Netherlands, at 5% and 42% [104].

### 3.4.2 Hydrocarbons

Typical exhaust compositions of gasoline engines, diesel engines, and the compositions of vapors escaping from gasoline tank farms are given in Tables 3.7, 3.8, and 3.9 respectively. In France in 1983, VOC emitted by automotive vehicles (traffic evaporation and distribution) was estimated at 1.22 Mt of a total of 3.11 Mt of VOC, or 39% [21]. Other estimates indicate less than 1 Mt/year [94]. Refuelling losses amount to about 2.54 g/liter of gasoline, of which 47% is due to evaporation and 5% to spillage: 81.9% of traffic emissions come from exhaust gases, 13.6% from onboard evaporation, and 3.3% from tank filling.

For Europe in 1983, automotive VOC emissions under the same conditions represent 4.2 Mt of the total anthropogenic emissions of 9.84 Mt, or 43% [46].

**Table 3.7** Typical composition of an exhaust gas of a gasoline-fuelled engine [46]

| Chemical compound | % Weight |
|---|---|
| $C_2$ alkanes | 1.2 |
| $C_5$ alkanes | 7.5 |
| $C_6$ alkanes | 4.6 |
| **total alkanes** | 13.3 |
| $C_2$ alkenes | 10.0 |
| $C_3$ alkenes | 6.0 |
| $C_4$ alkenes | 1.5 |
| **total alkenes** | 17.5 |
| $C_6$ aromatics | 8.8 |
| $C_7$ aromatics | 16.5 |
| $C_8$ aromatics | 19.3 |
| $C_9$ aromatics | 10.8 |
| **total aromatics** | 55.2 |
| **other** | 14.0 |
| **total** | 100.0 |

**Table 3.8** Composition of VOC from a diesel exhaust [46]

| Compound | Total hydrocarbons (mol %) | |
|---|---|---|
| | Idling | Full load |
| $C_2$ to $C_5$ | 32 | 44 |
| $C_6$ to $C_{11}$ | 14 | 2 |
| $C_{12}$ to $C_{18}$ | 35 | 38 |
| $C_{18}$ to $C_{24}$ | 10 | 15 |
| other | 9 | 1 |
| **total** | 100 | 100 |

**Table 3.9** Hydrocarbon composition of gasoline storage effluents [46]

| Hydrocarbon | % By weight |
|---|---|
| $C_{4+}$ alkanes | 89.2 |
| $C_{3+}$ alkenes | 6.9 |
| aromatics: | |
| • benzene | 1.1 |
| • toluene | 2.0 |
| • xylenes | 0.8 |
| **total** | 100.0 |

In Germany, VOC emitted by automotive traffic (not including fuel distribution) account for 38% of total emissions: 0.6 Mt/year in 1982, out of a total of 1.6 Mt attributed to corresponding human activities [134]. Emissions in 1989 were estimated at 2.42 Mt including 52% from traffic [133]. The emission factor reported by the UBA for trucks is 11 g HC per kg of fuel, and their emissions amounted to 83 000 t in 1985 [7].

**Benzene**

Benzene represents a special case due to its toxicity and its carcinogenic effect (Section 4.5.4.1). Although it is also emitted in other industrial activities, it is estimated that 80 to 85% of the benzene in the atmosphere comes from the automobile [153 and 159]. Worldwide emissions were estimated in 1988 to be 21 Mt of benzene. In 1991, emissions were estimated at 5.6 Mt just for the EEC countries. In Germany in 1989, traffic was responsible for 90% of an estimated total of 43,000 t emitted [133]. In heavy traffic, up to 20 to 30 $\mu g/m^3$ of benzene can be found in the air. Despite the limitation of its maximum content to 5% by volume, and an average value of around 2 to 3% by weight [57], this measure only partly reduces the quantities emitted. All the aromatics act to form benzene at the exhaust, whereas the other hydrocarbons, alcohols, and lead have no effect [55].

Three processes are involved in these emissions:

- Refuelling losses, which depend on the ambient temperature at the time, are determined by the following equation:

$$Bz_e = 0.23\ Bz_d + 0.21\ Bz_r$$

  where:
  - $Bz_e$ = mass fraction in the HC vapor emitted
  - $Bz_d$ = mass fraction in the gasoline distributed
  - $Bz_r$ = mass fraction in the gasoline in the tank
- Evaporation losses from the carburetor and the fuel tank, which result from the dissipation of heat when the engine is turned off and from variations in temperature between day and night (respiration). The following equations have been established:
  - engine stopped: % weight of $Bz$ in vapor = 0.45% of the weight of $Bz$ in the gasoline
  - respiration: % weight of $Bz$ in vapor = 0.89% of the weight of $Bz$ in gasoline
- Benzene in the exhaust, with an equation of the following type:

$$Bz_{exh} = 0.50 + 0.44\ Bz_{gas} + 0.04\ Ar$$

  where:
  - $Bz_{exh}$ = % weight of $Bz$ in the exhaust
  - $Bz_{gas}$ = % weight of $Bz$ in the gasoline
  - $Ar$ = % weight of other aromatics in the gasoline

On a European vehicle fueled with gasoline containing 3.1% by weight of benzene and 30% by weight of other aromatics, it has been found that 44% of the benzene emitted has survived combustion, and that 56% was created during combustion, from other aromatics, olefins, and cycloparaffins [153].

Exhaust catalysts (Section 12.11.7) significantly reduce benzene emissions [135]. Average benzene emissions of 20 mg/mile (FTP-75 cycle) (Section 6.2.1.2) have been measured on American automobiles equipped with catalytic converters [122], this amount from an average total of 0.7 g/mile of all HC. European automobiles without catalytic converters emit about 270 mg/km of benzene [64] in the ECE cycle (Section 6.2.2.1).

### 3.4.3 Polynuclear aromatic hydrocarbons

PAH are aromatic hydrocarbons with two or more benzene or cyclopentane rings (2 to 6) joined in various more or less clustered forms from indane to coronene [57].

The special attention paid to them stems from their recognized carcinogenic effect on animals and their suspected effect on humans, which depends on the steric structure of the specific PAH concerned (Table 4.1 in Section 4.5.4.2).

Most PAH are formed in high-temperature reactions, involving pyrolysis and incomplete combustion of organic matter and carbon compounds in a partly-reducing atmosphere. The presence of aromatic compounds in fuel favors the formation of PAH, but the pyrolysis of pure methane in a nitrogen atmosphere already produces a complete range of the different PAH [90].

PAH have been found in cigarette smoke [51], in the effluents from the combustion of dead leaves, in the smoke from wood [120], peat, and coal combustion, and in grilled foods (meats, etc.) particularly from barbecues [108]. Most of the PAH are found adsorbed on the carbon particles produced by the combustion of the different carbon-containing fuels (coal, fuel oil, diesel engines). However, they are also detected in the gas phase, particularly in gasoline engine exhaust gases [47], with the lowest molecular weight PAH (3 and 4 rings) being found in this case. In diesel emissions, a large part of these light PAH are adsorbed on particulates accompanied by much higher molecular weight PAH (5 rings or more) [165]. Benzo(a)pyrene is emitted at practically the same rate by a gasoline and a diesel vehicle [169]. The differences in profile of the different PAH as a function of the emission sources help to distinguish their respective share in the ambient air [110].

It is difficult to provide an idea of the annual masses of PAH emitted by the different pollutant industries. Some estimates indicate average quarterly concentrations in urban locations of 0.4 ng/m$^3$ for benzo(a)pyrene and 4.4 ng/m$^3$ for benzo(ghi)perylene [38]. Depending on the urban location, it is also estimated that 35 to 100% of the PAH measured is generated by automotive traffic [73]. In the automobile industry, PAH are mainly emitted by diesel engines, with a factor of 5 as the differential between two vehicles of the same type, one spark ignition, one diesel, tested under the same conditions. Unlike diesel engines, gasoline and turbojet engines emit lighter PAH with 3 to 4 condensed rings [139].

Still found in the environment are PAH derivatives considered to be even more harmful, although present in lower concentrations: the nitro-PAH. It is uncertain whether they are generated in combustion chambers or whether they are created during sampling by reaction of the PAH with $NO_2$ [96], or if they are formed in the atmosphere by the reaction with $NO_2$, $HNO_3$, and $O_3$ [52]. Nitro-PAH may be mutagenic, contrary to the initial PAH (Section 4.5.4.2) [121], and have been discovered in effluents of many industrial activities [137]. Their presence in the atmosphere may also be due to the reaction of atmospheric $NO_2$ with existing PAH [125]. The derivative 1-nitropyrene has also been detected in spent engine oils [76]. Other PAH derivatives also suspected to be mutagenic, particularly ketones and quinones, have been detected in the environment [136]. However, like the nitro-PAH, it is not known whether they are actually formed during combustion or during analytic trapping by PAH oxidation. Alkyl-9-fluorenones, quinones [32] and hydroxylated nitropyrenes [126] have been detected in diesel [50] and gasoline [2] particulates, but not in significant concentrations. Halogen derivatives of PAH have also been identified (1-chloropyrene) or suspected (by GC/MS) in gasoline engine exhausts [58].

### 3.4.4 Carboxyl compounds

By definition, these are compounds containing the carboxyl group —CO— in their molecule, namely aldehydes and ketones.

Ketones are compounds that are practically absent from combustion effluents, especially in exhaust gases. Their presence in the atmosphere is essentially due to their use as solvents.

By contrast, aldehydes are products of the incomplete combustion of carbon compounds, either wood, coal, gas, gasoline, diesel, etc. Hence they are found in automotive exhausts, effluents from electric power plants and boilerhouse installations, incineration plants, and in cigarette smoke.

The main aldehyde—most frequently found in air—is formaldehyde HCHO, which is also formed in the atmosphere by a reaction between the hydroxyl radical and methane. It is also found in the effluents of specialized chemical plants that use it as a synthesis intermediate and in many widely-consumed products (urea/formol resins employed as particle board adhesives and in coatings) [148].

The lightest aldehydes have an irritant sensory effect, which is reinforced by the presence of double bonds (acrolein, crotonaldehyde). As the molecular weight rises, the odorant effect becomes preponderant. Moreover, toxic light aldehydes are in themselves suspected of being co-factors of carcinogenesis (Section 4.5.5).

Table 3.10 offers an idea of the formaldehyde concentrations found in different locations [87]. It shows that automotive traffic accounts for a large share of the figures found in urban areas, but that photochemical processes are a predominant factor in Los Angeles. Formaldehyde is also found in combustion gases of natural gas, coals and fuel oils, and also in effluents of refuse incinerators and various industries [148]. In the USA, it is estimated that wood-burning heaters emit 54 Mt/year of aldehydes, comparable to those emitted from power plants and automobiles combined [101].

Formaldehyde is also a major factor in indoor pollution.

It is difficult to estimate the total quantities of aldehydes or HCHO emitted in a given area.

In the Netherlands in 1980, formaldehyde emissions were estimated at 5 kt, including 1.75 kt (34%) due to automotive traffic. The corresponding figures for acrolein are 0.213 kt and 0.182 kt (85%) [159].

**Table 3.10** HCHO concentrations of air at different locations [87]

| Location | [HCHO] ppb |
|---|---|
| above the ocean | up to 5 |
| rural areas | up to 12 |
| urban areas: | |
| • normal traffic | up to 16 |
| • dense traffic | up to 56 |
| • Los Angeles | up to 165 |
| pure air zone | 0.4 to 3.8 |
| in residential rooms and offices | 8.3 to 833 |

In Germany, automotive emissions of formaldehyde are estimated at an average of 30 mg/km, giving annually-emitted quantities of 9000 t. This emission factor falls to about 2 mg/km in the United States with the use of catalytic converters [102]. In the standard FTP cycle (Section 6.2.1.2), total aldehyde emissions are about 63 mg/mile for a gasoline-fueled vehicle, dropping to 8 mg/mile with a catalytic converter, whereas a corresponding diesel vehicle emits 44 mg/mile [97]. Other measurements [47] indicate about 28 mg/km, dropping to 13 mg/km with a three-way catalyst, and 30 mg/km for a diesel-powered vehicle.

On gasoline-fueled vehicles in service in the USA [145], it has been found that aldehydes account for 2.5% by weight of the hydrocarbons emitted, made up of 51% formaldehyde, 25% acetaldehyde, and 6% acrolein [172].

The contents of carbonyl products at the exhaust increase if oxygenated alternative fuels are employed (Section 10.3).

### 3.4.5 Organic acids

It is mainly the lighter components, formic and acetic acids, that can be detected in the air. They are generally not emitted in automobile exhausts, but result from the corresponding aldehydes. Formic acid is monitored mainly because of its recognized toxicity.

### 3.4.6 Halogenated organic compounds

The presence of scavengers[1], added to leaded premium-grade gasolines [57] to facilitate the volatilization of lead in anti-knock additives in the form of lead halogenides, causes the formation of halogenated hydrocarbons. These lead scavengers, which consist essentially of dibromoethane or dichloroethane, give rise to emissions of bromophenols and brominated alkylbenzenes [119] whose exhaust concentrations are nevertheless quite low (23 $\mu g/m^3$ of brominated compounds).

1. Used to prevent lead deposits on valves and spark-plugs (see section 11.1.5).

Although 70% of the bromine produced by industry goes into motor fuels, only 2 to 4% of the quantities added are released into the air [63]. They could yield chlorinated PAH (chloropyrenes, -fluoroanthenes and -benzopyrenes) and brominated PAH (bromopyrenes and -fluoroanthenes), which are detected in exhausts and in the atmosphere in very low concentrations (~10 pg/m$^3$ of 1-chloropyrene) [58].

Ortho-substituted bromophenols are the potential precursors of polyhalogenated dibenzo-p-dioxins. Among these compounds, which are the ones most closely monitored by health specialists, are chlorodioxins and particularly 2378-TCDD (2,3,7,8-tetrachlorodibenzo-p-dioxin) that caused the Seveso disaster. They are products emitted mainly in industrial chemical processes (production of pesticides). The uniform dispersion of these products implies that more widespread sources exist, other than refuse incinerators, and automotive traffic has been mentioned in this regard [15]. The compound 2378-TCDD has also been detected in the incineration of spent engine oils contaminated with polychlorinated biphenyls [23 and 154].

According to the EPA, these products have been detected in diesel particles and in exhaust pipe corrosion slag [27]. However, they are emitted in traces at the detection limit (<ng/mile) (3.3 to 7.7 pg/km). The low chlorine content of motor fuels (about 0.14 g/l), contributed by scavengers [57], makes the emission of these types of products by engines negligible. However, they are totally eliminated by catalytic converters, whereas they are detected in amounts of 30 to 550 pg/km of 2378-TCDD equivalent and up to 1700 pg/km of 2378-TCDF (dibenzofuranes) on exhausts of vehicles unequipped with converters and running on leaded fuel [109 and 154]. This risk will be eliminated with the transition to unleaded gasoline.

## 3.5 Sulfur compounds

### 3.5.1 Sulfur dioxide

$SO_2$ is the main sulfur compound emitted into the atmosphere. It is the major factor responsible for acid rain (Section 5.3.3.4). All combustion processes of products containing sulfur yield $SO_2$ emissions, hence, fossil fuels are mainly blamed for atmospheric $SO_2$.

Among these fuels, coal, whose use is tending to increase in most industrial and industrializing countries due to the oil crises, generally contains a high portion of sulfur (in France, Gardanne coal contains 5% S) (Table 3.11).

**Table 3.11** S content of different fuels [57, 6 and 115]

| Fuel | S (% by weight) |
|---|---|
| coals | 1 (average) to 4 (maximum) |
| lignites | 1 |
| petroleum coke | 4 |
| wood and charcoal | 0 |
| household refuse | 0.17 |
| residual fuel oil | 3 |
| diesel | 0.3 |
| gasolines | 0.08 |

The $SO_2$ emission factors corresponding to these different fuels are declining with the gradual installation of smoke desulfurization systems.

Apart from the activities using fossil fuels, $SO_2$ is also produced by non-ferrous metallurgy (Pb, Zn, Cu, etc.) and pyrite roasting. Table 3.12 provides a rough worldwide estimate of emissions in the 1980 to 1985 period [89 and 115]: ≈208 Mt compared with 186 Mt from natural sources (volcanoes, oxidation of sulfides in the oceans, swamps, rice paddies, etc.).

**Table 3.12** Worldwide $SO_2$ emissions 1980 to 1985 [89 and 115]

| Fuel | Millions of tons of $SO_2$ |
|---|---|
| coal and lignite | 128 |
| oil | 52 |
| ore processing | 22 |
| miscellaneous | 6 |
| **total** | 208 |

In the case of oil, about 10% of the S present in crude oil is found in distilled products [44]. The same proportion is emitted into the atmosphere in the form of $SO_2$ with the major portion (41%) being contributed by heavy fuel oils. Constant advances in crude oil desulfurization processes have increased the proportion of S recovered from 10% in 1979 to 23% in 1985.

In France, $SO_2$ emissions were estimated to be 1580 kt/year in 1986 [30] and 1227 kt/year in 1988. Table 3.13 gives the breakdown of these emissions.

The transportation share is essentially contributed by diesel engines running on diesel or home-heating oil containing 0.3% S (upper limit of French specifications), whereas gasolines generally contain a maximum of 0.08% S, although the corresponding specifications allow for 0.15% (premium) to 0.20% (regular) S [57].

A calculation made from French consumption figures for 1987 indicate emissions of 30,000 t of $SO_2$ for automotive fuels and 72,000 t for diesel fuels, an amount close to the figure already mentioned in Table 3.13 [94].

**Table 3.13** $SO_2$ emissions in France in 1988 (Source: *CITEPA*)

| Activity | kt/year | % |
|---|---|---|
| thermal power plants | 233 | 19.0 |
| industry and agriculture | 344 | 28.1 |
| residential and tertiary | 230 | 18.8 |
| oil (refining and natural gas) | 9 | 5.6 |
| processes | 107 | 15.4 |
| transport | 123 | 10.0 |
| **total** | 1227 | 100.0 |

In Germany in 1982, annual $SO_2$ emissions due to transportation were estimated to be 100 kt/year, accounting for 3.4% of total emissions [134], a lower proportion than in France, where the spread of nuclear power plants is reflected by a relatively higher share attributed to transportation. In 1985, truck emissions were estimated at 42,000 t/year [131], with an emission factor of 0.54 g $SO_2$/kg of diesel. In the Netherlands, transport accounted for 16 kt of a total 275 kt emitted in 1985, or 5.8% of the total [8]. Table 3.4 shows an approximately identical share in the various European countries [104].

In the United States in 1976, $SO_2$ emissions due to transport (including 50% on freeways) were estimated at 800,000 t (2.9%) of an annual total of 27 Mt [83].

$SO_2$ is formed by the combustion of the residual sulfur compounds in the fuels, specifically thiophene, mercaptans and sulfides in gasolines [164], and substituted benzothiophenes and dibenzothiophenes in diesel fuels [57].

### 3.5.2 Sulfur trioxide and sulfuric acid

Apart from its actual toxicity, $SO_2$ is harmful mainly as a precursor of $SO_3$ and $H_2SO_4$ in atmospheric interactions (Section 2.1.3).

As such, very little sulfur trioxide and sulfuric acid are emitted, since their high solubility in water limits their atmospheric diffusion. They are found in chemical industry effluents (sulfuric acid and fertilizers, plaster plants, etc.) but no statistics are available on the corresponding amounts emitted.

In transportation, catalytic converters—particularly oxidation reactors with certain catalysts and excess air—favor the conversion of $SO_2$ to $SO_3$ before its release into the atmosphere.

Fortunately this reaction exhibits relatively slow kinetics, which limits the conversion rate. This is favored by a lower temperature and higher oxygen concentration [83].

Three-way catalysts do not generally increase sulfate emissions, which retain the same level as that found on vehicles without catalytic converters [147], and Pt/Rh catalysts form fewer sulfates than Pt/Pd catalysts [83].

Diesel engines emit relatively few sulfates, which account for only 1 to 3% of the corresponding $SO_2$ emissions [22]. However, the addition of catalytic filters containing precious metals is liable to favor sulfate and sulfuric acid emissions, due to the higher S content of diesel fuel. Sulfuric acid predominates, representing over 90% of the sulfates emitted [156], with the remainder consisting of ammonium sulfates and other metallic sulfates [69].

### 3.5.3 Hydrogen sulfide, sulfides, and mercaptans

Atmospheric emissions of reduced sulfur compounds ($H_2S$, mercaptans, or R—SH thiols and R—S—R disulfides) are incomparably lower than those due to the combustion of sulfur. In 1970, $H_2S$ emissions were estimated at 3 Mt/year of S, compared with 60 Mt of $SO_2$ at the same time [116].

These emissions are generated by specific industries: oil refineries, natural gas production, paper plants, viscose plants, etc. Added to these industrial sources are agricultural emissions and those of the marine and land biosphere, whose estimates vary widely, according to the different authors, from 3 to 100 Mt, of which more than half is $H_2S$ [116].

These products are chiefly identified by their nauseating odors and are precursors of air acidity.

The transportation sector rarely emits these compounds. Motor fuels are sufficiently desulfurized to avoid releasing sulfur products, and only certain very brief operating conditions of catalytic converters can generate sulfurous odors [42] by the reduction of the sulfur compounds stored in the catalysts (Section 12.11.3) [157].

## 3.6 Halogenated compounds

Besides halogenated organic compounds, halogenated compounds are essentially hydrochloric, hydrobromic, and hydrofluoric acids.

Apart from the emissions of the chemical industry itself, HCl is emitted in incineration plants that pyrolyse chlorinated plastics (polyvinyl chloride, etc.). These plants are being progressively equipped with scrubbers to recover this acid instead of discharging it into the atmosphere.

Automotive traffic emits mainly halogenides, lead bromides, and chlorides, which are volatile at the exhaust gas temperature. HBr and HCl is then generated in the atmosphere by the hydrolysis of these salts. On the basis of the lead consumption figures for motor fuels in France, estimated at about 7672 t of Pb metal in 1990, and the amount of scavengers required for its volatilization, it can be estimated that 2100 t of HCl and 2400 t of HBr are emitted in exhausts. This assumes that the average anti-knock additive contains one 'theory' of dichloroethane for each 0.5 'theory' of dibromomethane [57], and that 80% of the lead is emitted into the air, with the rest remaining in the engine or in the lubricating oil. These acids, HCl and HBr, do not generally remain in gaseous form, but are adsorbed on atmospheric dust. Assuming that practically all the bromine found in the atmosphere is generated by automotive traffic, the measured Br/Cl ratio serves to determine the automotive contribution to atmospheric chlorine, and to estimate, in Paris for example, that 14% of particulate chlorine results from automotive emissions [48].

The rest of the atmospheric chlorine is generated by industrial sources, particularly the incineration of household refuse, which contains many polyvinyl chloride objects. In Germany, 15% of the PVC (800,000 t in 1984) is used for packaging and produces about 50% of its chlorine weight by incineration [103]. Another survey indicates annual chlorine emissions of 640,000 t of HCl for Western Europe [98].

## 3.7 Metallic compounds

Heavy metals are the main metallic compounds implicated in air pollution due to their greater harmfulness (Section 4.5.9.1).

As an example, Table 3.14 gives the average contents recorded in Paris in the 1976 to 1982 period [81]. The fourth column corresponds to the analyses of the same elements in a Paris highway tunnel (with lead as the baseline).

**Table 3.14** Average particulate contents in Paris [81]

| Element | Urban average (ng/m³) | General relative importance | Relative importance in highway tunnel |
|---|---|---|---|
| iron | 830 | 1.08 | 0.68 |
| lead | 770 | 1.00 | 1.00 |
| aluminum | 265 | 0.34 | 0.03 |
| zinc | 250 | 0.32 | 0.06 |
| magnesium | 220 | 0.29 | 0.07 |
| barium | 57 | 0.07 | – |
| vanadium | 42 | 0.05 | – |
| copper | 38 | 0.05 | 0.06 |
| manganese | 38 | 0.05 | 0.007 |
| nickel | 22 | 0.03 | 0.0012 |
| cadmium | 14 | 0.02 | – |
| arsenic | 6 | 0.008 | – |
| chromium | 4 | 0.005 | 0.0012 |
| mercury | 3 | 0.004 | – |

In the urban environment, the main sources responsible for the metals are:

- soil erosion and corrosion
- combustion of coal, fuel oil and urban refuse
- vehicle emissions

Besides lead, which is very specific to automotive traffic, vehicles emit relatively more copper than all the other pollutants combined. However, no other element appears to be specifically emitted during the passage of dense traffic.

### 3.7.1 Lead

Together with arsenic, lead is one of the most active toxic elements (Section 4.5.9.1). This toxicity results from the ingestion of lead in foods, drinks, and drinking water. Lead compounds also enter the body with air as a result of breathing dust containing lead (attrition of white lead paints, rust inhibiting primer, adsorption of lead salts from exhausts on suspended particles in air, etc.).

A survey of the amount of lead ingested daily by English children [16] provides an estimate that 30 to 40 μg came from food and 2 to 3 μg, or less than 10%, came from the atmosphere. This air-borne intake stems chiefly from the exhaust gases of gasoline-fueled vehicles burning fuels containing lead alkyls as an anti-knock agent. It is estimated that in the cities, 90% of atmospheric lead comes from gasolines [25] and lead accounts for about 25% of the composition of particulates emitted by vehicles running on gasoline containing 0.4 g Pb/liter [167]. In 1979, of the 450,000 t of lead emitted into the atmosphere, half was generated by automotive emissions; the remainder came from industrial activities (batteries, electric insulation, piping, paints, additives, welding, munitions, etc.) and refuse incineration. Measurements of household refuse incinerators help to estimate by plant the releases by these installations at about 11 t/year of lead adsorbed on solid particles [161].

On the basis of 1990 French automotive fuel consumption figures, about 15.6 Mt (19.18 million $m^3$) of fuels were burned and contained 0.25 g Pb/litre. This corresponds to 7672 t of lead. Therefore, the quantity of metal released into the air can be estimated at 5700 t if 75% of the lead is found in the exhaust gases. The figure from the French Environmental Ministry is 8000 t/year of Pb emitted in 1988 [94]. AQA forecasts for 1990 estimate 5300 t of lead emissions, 85% of automotive origin [5].

While certain countries still use high lead content fuels (0.84 g/litre in Saudi Arabia) [1], lead emissions are declining sharply, as the concentrations of lead additives are being steadily reduced in the various developed countries, with the future goal being no-lead motor fuels.

### 3.7.2 Precious metals

The development of catalytic converters and the resulting progressive deterioration of catalyst-impregnated ceramic elements causes the emission of fine particulates impregnated with platinum and palladium, which are deposited in the neighborhood of major traffic arteries or are transported by surface runoff.

In the United States, it is estimated that cars emit about 1.3 to 5 μg/km [10] of Pt, and dust containing Pt and Pd is beginning to be found near highways, in the proportions used in the catalysts. The concentrations of these fines already approach those of the 'rich' ores of South Africa [68].

### 3.7.3 Cadmium and zinc

Cadmium is also considered to be one of the most toxic of metals. Tobacco combustion, beverages, and food are the major sources of cadmium ingestion [132]. Cadmium is emitted into the atmosphere by specific industries and household refuse incinerators, which pyrolyse plastics containing cadmium derivatives used as stabilizers or dyes [103]. A typical incinerator can release about 500 kg/year of cadmium [161].

On the other hand, the combustion of motor fuels is not a source of cadmium. Yet cadmium can be emitted from zinc-based additives in lubricants, where cadmium is an impurity combined with the zinc. Cadmium is also emitted by the wearing of tires containing cadmium naphthenate and octoate additives, which are used as rubber stabilizers.

Zinc is a much less harmful pollutant than cadmium (Section 4.5.9.2). Like cadmium, it results primarily from waste incineration. Automotive emissions of zinc correspond to the zinc dithiophosphate-based additives employed in lubricants. An oil consumption of 0.12 liters/1000 km would cause zinc emission of 0.15 mg/km, a rate that has been observed on vehicles without catalytic converters [17].

### 3.7.4 Manganese

Manganese is not in itself considered toxic in ambient concentrations [100 and 170]. The concentrations found in ambient air are mostly due to soil erosion. It was emitted in automotive exhausts between 1975 and 1978, when it was used as an anti-knock additive to replace lead, in the form of methylcyclopentadienyl manganese tricarbonyl (MMT) [57], which was incorporated in gasolines at the rate of 0.03 g/liter. Economics (cost/benefit ratio) and the risk of clogging catalytic converters, rather than the danger to health, have led to its abandonment as an additive. A 1977 amendment to the *Clean Air Act* banned its use in the USA [77]. Canada continues to use it in a concentration of 16.5 mg/liter [70] and the advent of unleaded fuels in Europe may lead to its use there as an anti-knock additive.

### 3.7.5 Other metals

The other metals found in the atmospheric environment of urban centers result from the wear of rocks and soils (Mg, Al, Fe, Cr), the combustion of coal (Al, Cr, Fe, As) and fuel oils (V, Ni), or from various poorly-defined sources (Cu, Co, Ba) [81].

Catalyst attrition can release small amounts of metals such as nickel, copper, and chromium from the catalysts containing them [17].

## 3.8 Particles

The term 'particle' generally applies to aerosols created by the dispersion in air of atomized solids and liquids, powders or droplets, and hence includes the terms "fines, dust, soot, mist, fog, and smog."

Particles in suspension in the atmosphere are generated by a wide variety of physical processes (e.g. condensation of saturated vapors, mechanical erosion of materials including rocks, etc.) and chemical processes. They are emitted into the atmosphere by numerous sources, including combustion, industrial processes (steel mills, collieries, cement plants, etc.), and natural phenomena.

These natural phenomena include volcanic eruptions (Krakatoa, Mount Saint Helens, Pinaatubo, etc.), forest fires and wind erosion. It can be estimated [40] that half of the 5 to 8 Mt of dust deposited in the northern hemisphere comes from the Sahara.

Annual worldwide particulate emissions are estimated at 2.6 Gt, of which 89% are of natural origin and 11% are of anthropogenic origin [40].

The term 'particles in suspension' refers to dust smaller than 10 μm with a low sedimentation rate. Larger particles tend to fall back rapidly near the emission source [150].

These particles in suspension are important because they affect the following:

- health, by penetrating deeply into the pulmonary system (Section 4.5.8)
- the environment, by contributing to the soiling of buildings and monuments (Section 5.4)
- atmospheric visibility and climate, by increasing the diffusion of incident sunlight (a cooling tendency) and by absorbing this radiation as black particles (a warming tendency)

It is estimated that 10 to 90 Mt/year of particles smaller than 20 μm are emitted worldwide by direct emission [150].

In Germany [131], it was estimated in 1978 that 720,000 t of dust was emitted per year, 64% from industry, 24% from thermal power plants, 8% from households, and 4% (30,000 t) from transportation. The tonnages corresponding to industry and power plants have declined sharply due to newly installed purification systems.

In 1988 in France, according to CITEPA, particulate emissions due to transportation were estimated at 26.6% of the total industrial particle emissions [30] of about 280,000 t/year (Table 3.15)—a substantial drop from the 1980 figure of 427,000 t.

**Table 3.15** Anthropogenic emissions of dusts in France in 1988 (Source: *CITEPA*)

| Activity | kt/year | % |
|---|---|---|
| thermal power plants | 25 | 9.0 |
| industry and agriculture | 23 | 8.3 |
| residential and tertiary | 18 | 6.6 |
| oil (refining and natural gas) | 6 | 2.3 |
| processes | 132 | 47.2 |
| transport | 74 | 26.6 |
| **total** | 280 | 100.0 |

## 3.8.1 Mineral particles

In addition to dust of natural origin (windborne erosion of rocks, for example), most mineral particles are generated by industry and agriculture: cement plants, fertilizer industry, steel mills, coal upgrading, fly ash from boilers and electric power plants, soil tilling, harvesting, etc.

Automotive traffic generates mineral dust by travelling on soils and roadways (quartz particles placed in suspension) and by wearing down tires . However, this wear tends to generate relatively large particles (>7 μm) [78] and the particles placed in suspension are negligible in comparison with exhaust emissions. A specific case arises in winter with the use of studded tires [71].

Another source of automotive mineral particles is the wearing of brake and clutch linings that contain a certain amount of asbestos fibers. Although part of the asbestos in the linings is thermally converted to non-fibrous fines [106] (chrysotyl converted to forsterite [140]), annual emissions of 80 t of asbestos have been estimated in the USA, which includes 85% falling to the ground and 3.2% passing into the atmospheric air [74 and 75]. This would correspond to emissions ranging between 18 and 55 μg/km per passenger car or truck respectively. Replacement fibers help to eliminate these asbestos emissions. These replacements include Kevlar, attapulgite[2] [162], and cellulose [86].

Metallic oxides can also be emitted by vehicle exhausts. These include calcium oxides from lubricant additives and aluminum oxide resulting from the attrition of catalyst converters [17]. However, the level of these emissions is very low, less than 0.45 mg/km aluminum and about 0.1 mg/km calcium.

### 3.8.2 Organic particles

These particles result from the incomplete combustion of motor and other fuels due to excessively rich mixtures. The oxygen deficiency appears clearly in the combustion of wood with a bright flame; the soot and tars are rich in PAH, with emissions of about 8 to 9 g of particles per kg of wood (including 5 to 7 g of extractable organic compounds) [34], and represent a major contribution to pollution (Table 3.16).

In transportation, these emissions are generated mainly by diesel engines (Section 10.5.2), which accounted for 30% of black smoke emissions in the United Kingdom in 1984 and 80% of the carbon emissions in Europe in 1978 [14]. Combustion malfunctions in engines can contribute strongly to elemental carbon emissions.

**Table 3.16** Black smoke emissions in the United Kingdom in 1984 [14]

| Fuel | Emission factor (g C/kg fuel) | Annual emissions (kt) |
|---|---|---|
| domestic coal | 35.00 | 190 |
| industrial coal | 25.00 | – |
| smokeless fuel | 5.60 | 17 |
| heavy fuel oil | 1.00 | 34 |
| home-heating oil | 0.25 | 7 |
| gasoline | 1.50 | 30 |
| diesel | 6.00 | 122 |
| **total** | | 400 |

2. Hydrated silicate of magnesium and aluminium.

Emissions are about 4 mg/g of fuel consumed [80], with the highest values resulting from only a very small number of vehicles [59].

In Germany, 70,000 t per year are emitted by diesel engines, with 20% from cars, 60% from trucks, and the remaining amount from off-road machines, army vehicles, etc.

These organic particles generally consist of a carbon skeleton impregnated with different unburned or incompletely burnt materials, which are extractable by suitable solvents and are accordingly referred to in US terminology (Section 9.20.5) as SOF[3].

Particle emissions depend on the wide variety of diesel engines (direct injection or pre-combustion chamber, and power range) and on the operating conditions. It is therefore difficult to indicate general emissions.

For trucks, however, emissions can be estimated at at least 6 g/kg of fuel, including 1 to 2 g/kg of 'dry' carbon [7], with a generally higher proportion of organic compounds in truck emissions [168].

In the USA, truck emissions range between 1 and 10 g/kg of fuel depending on the engine, its settings, and the fuel employed [13]. Of an annual total of 180,000 t of dust emitted in 1986 (35%), and based on French diesel fuel consumption in 1986 (Table 3.2), annual emissions can be estimated at about 70,000 t/year of diesel particles (including 15,000 t due to passenger vehicles) [94].

Particles emitted by diesel engines are very opaque [152] and of small grain size, around 0.3 μm on average, enabling them to penetrate deeply into the pulmonary system (Section 4.5.8). Their harmful effect is largely due to the compounds adsorbed onto carbon particles: PAH and nitro-PAH, which are responsible for mutagenic effects.

## 3.9 Odors

Foul odors conveyed into the surrounding air also cause air pollution. Malodorous materials do not generally raise a health problem, because they are normally detected by the sense of smell in concentrations that are often far below those considered hazardous (in contrast, other dangerous products such as CO are totally odorless).

They nonetheless cause an annoyance that is as unpleasant as that caused by noise, and may have harmful effects on the behavior of individuals forced to put up with them (aggressiveness, loss of attention, etc.) (Section 4.3.2).

Despite current attempts to quantify the nuisance (Section 9.2.1), it is obviously not yet possible to draw up a classification of the intensity of the nuisance caused by

3. Soluble organic fraction.

the various sources of bad odors. Among these sources are the following:

- agricultural processes: animal husbandry, pigsties
- food industries, e.g. coffee-roasting plants, chocolate plants, breweries, sugar refineries, etc.
- industrial processes, e.g. oil refineries, petrochemicals, chemical industry, etc.
- waste disposal facilities: rendering plants, water purification stations, household refuse incinerators, etc.
- combustion processes: coke ovens, combustion in diesel engines

In fact, due to visible smoke, diesel exhaust gases represent an essential factor in sensory pollution [79 and 85] as 'felt' by the population, which is obviously not directly alerted by an increase in the CO or PAH content.

The concept of bad odor covers not only the purely olfactory sensation, but mainly the irritation of the eyes, the nose, and the throat caused by the presence in these exhaust gases of irritating compounds such as aldehydes, formaldehyde, and acrolein [29 and 41].

Moreover, the odors result from the simultaneous action of different chemical compounds that form complex blends, in which the olfactory action of each of the components is relatively unrelated to their respective concentrations in these mixtures.

## 3.10 Parameters influencing automotive emissions

Automotive emissions are not only dependent on the type of engine system and its power, but also on other factors that are discussed in greater detail in Chapter 10: road profile, altitude, ambient temperature, speed limits, vehicle wear, type of driving, etc.

An expression of the following form has been suggested, combining parameters that are a function of the vehicle and others that are a function of the travel concerned [134]:

$$B_e = \frac{b_e}{\eta_u}\left(m(gf + g\sin\alpha + b) + \frac{1}{2}C_w A \rho_L V^2\right)$$

where:

- $B_e$ = factor characterizing consumption and emissions, and (specific vehicle factors):
- $\frac{b_e}{\eta_u}$ = engine efficiency,
- $m$ = vehicle weight,
- $g$ = condition of transmission and tires,
- $\frac{1}{2}C_w A$ = a body shape

and (parameters depending on traffic conditions):

- $f$ = state of driving surface,
- $g \sin \alpha$ = path profile,
- $b$ = circulation flow (which affects acceleration),
- $V$ = traffic speed,
- $\rho L$ = air specific gravity.

All these variables affect pollutant emissions.

These conditions mean that actual emissions in traffic, related to the distance travelled by the vehicle, do not always correspond to the regulatory measurements taken in clearly-defined driving conditions (Chapter 6). As an example, Table 3.17 gives the values recorded in the Netherlands for various vehicles in urban traffic. The same measurements taken in Athens, with vehicles that are generally much more poorly maintained, yield far higher values [105].

**Table 3.17** Emission factors in 1986 indicated by the TNO for vehicles travelling in the Netherlands in urban traffic [105] (Emissions expressed in g/km)

| Vehicle | | CO | VOC | $NO_x$ | Particulates |
|---|---|---|---|---|---|
| private cars | gasoline | 17.0 | 3.2 | 1.58 | 0.06 |
| private cars | diesel | 3.5 | 1.1 | 1.20 | 1.00 |
| vans | gasoline | 28.0 | 4.5 | 2.80 | 0.11 |
| buses and coaches | diesel | 14.0 | 10.0 | 15.00 | 5.00 |
| trucks (3.5 to 5.5 t) | diesel | 4.0 | 2.0 | 6.00 | 1.50 |
| trucks (5.5 to 12 t) | diesel | 10.0 | 7.0 | 10.00 | 3.50 |
| trucks (>12 t) | diesel | 13 to 16 | 9 to 12 | 13 to 20 | 5 to 7 |
| mopeds | 2 stroke (<55 $cm^3$) | 5.0 | 4.0 | 0.05 | 0.06 |
| motorcycles | 4 stroke (>55 $cm^3$) | 20.0 | 2.0 | 0.20 | 0.05 |

## 3.11 Emissions from other mobile sources

The considerations presented so far in this chapter on mobile sources have essentially concerned automotive vehicles, the primary subject of this work.

Other mobile sources contribute to air pollution. These include railroads, maritime and river transportation, air transportation, agricultural machinery, and motor-driven leisure equipment, which ranges from outboard motor boats to lawnmowers.

Their pollution is obviously very low compared with the other means of transportation and industrial activities, but may nevertheless cause annoyance in certain areas where their concentrations are high. In 1987 in California, it was estimated that the 'off-the-road' share of total emissions represented respectively

9.3% of HC emissions, 8.1% of CO emissions, and 25.4% of $NO_x$ emissions [10]. From the VOC emissions standpoint, one hour's use of a lawnmower, a chainsaw, or an outboard motor is respectively equivalent to a travel distance of 80, 320, or 1300 km in an emission controlled vehicle. In terms of $NO_x$ emissions, one hour of caterpillar tractor operation corresponds to 1500 km by car [9].

### 3.11.1 Emissions from 'two-wheeled' vehicles

Many motorcycles, and nearly all pedal motorcycles, are equipped with two-stroke engines.

These engines often run on a mixture of gasoline and a lubricant, causing emissions of unburned oil. Even with separate lubrication, HC emissions remain high due to the direct passage of a part of the fresh carburetted mixture into the exhaust.

Compared with a similar four-stroke engine, a corresponding two-stroke engine generally emits up to twice as much CO, about eight times more HC, but two to four times less $NO_x$ [45 and 91]. Aldehyde emissions are also higher in two-stroke engines.

### 3.11.2 Aircraft emissions

The gas-turbine engines used on most airplanes and helicopters today are characterized by very low emission levels of CO, HC, and $NO_x$, whose concentrations remain lower than 200 ppm [45]. However, since the discharge gas flow rates are very high, the hourly emissions may exceed a few dozen kg per jet engine, depending on the operating conditions (Table 3.18). Fortunately, the emissions are rapidly dispersed by the gas jet emitted by the engines [143]. Emissions per passenger/km are nevertheless lower than in cars, even those equipped with catalytic converters [67]. The high $NO_2$ concentrations in the neighborhood of crowded airports may accordingly raise a number of problems [151]: 3000 t/year of $NO_x$ is attributed to aircraft movements at Charles de Gaulle Airport [66].

Advances have since been made in the design of gas-turbines, which simultaneously reduce consumption and emissions, but the quest for maximum efficiency tends to mean higher combustion temperatures and hence $NO_x$ (Section 9.2) emissions [67 and 141]. Gains in fuel consumption nevertheless reduce the tonnages emitted, provided this is not countered by an increase in air traffic [82].

A new-concept gas-turbine with 'pilot combustion' may yield a 40% reduction in $NO_x$ emissions during the approach phase.

Turbojet engines also emit smoke and particles, in the extracts of which nitropyrenes have been detected, leading to an estimate of the daily emissions at a typical American airport of 7 kg of nitropyrene and 20 g of dinitropyrene [107].

**Table 3.18** Emissions from a Boeing 747 with four JT 9D engines [45]

| Operating conditions | CO (kg/h) | HC (kg/h) | $NO_x$ (kg/h) |
|---|---|---|---|
| idling on ground | 168.0 | 36.0 | 12.4 |
| take-off | 12.8 | 4.0 | 1340.0 |
| climb | 21.6 | 4.0 | 840.0 |
| approach | 72.0 | 6.4 | 104.0 |
| landing | 72.0 | 6.4 | 104.0 |

**Table 3.19** Emissions from large diesel engines

| Pollutant | ($mg/m^3$)(1) | (g/kWh)(2) | (g/kWh)(3) |
|---|---|---|---|
| $NO_x$ | 2500 to 5000 | 5 to 15 | 8 to 15 |
| CO | 300 to 1500 | 1 to 2.7 | 0.5 to 3.0 |
| HC | 150 to 700 | 0.3 to 1.3 | 0.2 to 1.3 |
| soot | 20 to 15 | | |

(1) Fixed engines at an average speed of 1500 r.p.m.
(2) Cooled supercharged engines with bore <170 mm for bmep. between 0.8 and 1.4 MPa (at lower loads, $NO_x$ may exceed 25 g/kWh, and HC and CO can exceed 4 g/kWh).
(3) Cooled supercharged engines with bore >1700 mm for bmep. between 1.2 and 2 MPa.

## 3.11.3 Other sources

It is not our intention here to dwell on atmospheric emissions of motor-driven systems lying beyond the automotive world. However, California also plans to regulate emissions from small internal combustion engines (less than 25 kW) employed in garden appliances and small industrial appliances [166]. These systems generally emit a lot of CO (up to 600 g/kWh) because they are often set to a rich mixture to guarantee ease of operation. They emit a great deal of aldehydes (up to 2.5 g/kWh) and HC (up to 250 g/kWh: approximately the consumption of the engine), especially the two-stroke engines that also form aerosols (up to 9 g/kWh of 'particulates') from the lubricant mixed with the gasoline. However, $NO_x$ emissions are relatively low, especially for two-stroke engines, due to the rich mixtures employed [166]. Table 3.20 offers American examples of typical quantities of pollutants emitted, without guaranteeing any possibility of extrapolation to European conditions [163 and 171]. Little is known about emissions from ships [39].

Large direct injection diesel engines used on ships, locomotives, shipboard generators, heavy vehicles (construction machinery), etc. produce emissions that appear in the ranges listed in Table 3.19 [88].

Maritime navigation, which burns cheap sulfur-rich fuels, is responsible for more than 4% of worldwide $SO_2$ emissions and about 7% of $NO_x$ emissions [111]. Since cold starting and warm-up times are relatively long, marine diesel engines and locomotive engines spend a large part of their time idling in a relatively high pollution mode, to be ready to respond when required [163].

Outboard engines represent a special case, because the passage of the exhaust into the water leaves part of its components there [62]: 37% for HC, 5% for CO, 40% for $CO_2$, 15% for $NO_x$, and 5% for $SO_x$. Aldehydes are also retained in the water.

**Table 3.20** Emissions from off-road systems [33, 117, 118 and 171]

| Equipment | Pollutant (g/kWh) | | | |
|---|---|---|---|---|
| | HC | CO | $NO_x$ | $SO_x$ |
| passenger locomotive 2 stroke | 9.00 | 4.00 | 11.00 | 2.6 |
| passenger locomotive 4 stroke | 5.00 | 13.00 | 17.00 | 1.9 |
| goods locomotive 2 stroke | 4.00 | 1.80 | 9.40 | 1.5 |
| goods locomotive 4 stroke | 0.70 | 4.00 | 8.20 | 1.4 |
| turbo goods locomotive 4 stroke | 2.20 | 4.00 | 10.00 | 1.3 |
| tugboat | 15.00 | 14.00 | 27.00 | 5.8 |
| motor ship | 12.00 | 13.00 | 22.00 | 4.8 |
| steam ship | 0.04 | 0.25 | 1.30 | 4.7 |
| helicopter (piston) | 500.00 | 30,000.00 | 200.00 | – |
| helicopter (turbine) | 680.00 | 2,600.00 | 680.00 | – |
| tractor (gasoline) | 3.90 | 160.00 | 7.30 | 0.3 |
| tractor (diesel) | 1.90 | 3.10 | 10.00 | 0.9 |
| combine (gasoline) | 7.60 | 230.00 | 5.70 | 0.3 |
| combine (diesel) | 1.80 | 3.60 | 9.10 | 0.9 |
| windrower (gasoline) | 7.60 | 230.00 | 5.70 | 0.3 |
| windrower (diesel) | 1.80 | 3.60 | 9.10 | 0.9 |
| lawnmower two-stroke | 210.00 | 490.00 | 1.60 | – |
| lawnmower four-stroke | 20.00 | 290.00 | 4.30 | – |
| motor tiller | 20.00 | 290.00 | 4.30 | – |
| snowmobile | 640.00 | 1,000.00 | 10.00 | – |
| outboard engine | 27.00 | 69.00 | 0.13 | – |

## 3.12 Conclusion

This chapter has shown the different chemical compounds involved in air pollution, with an attempt, whenever possible, to identify and quantify the different human activities responsible for the corresponding emissions.

Automotive traffic appears to be an important factor, especially for CO emissions, concentrated in urban zones, and for $NO_x$ emissions, where it accounts for half and is equivalent to industrial sources.

For hydrocarbons and volatile compounds, in which automobile emissions account for less than 40%, gasoline-fuelled engines are mainly concerned, whereas diesel engines are major emitters of particles, which, although representing less than 20% of industrial emissions, worry the health authorities due to the associated organic fraction.

The next chapter will discuss this specific subject.

Figure 3.2 shows the concentrations of the main gaseous and particulate pollutants found in rural areas, in cities, and in indoor spaces.

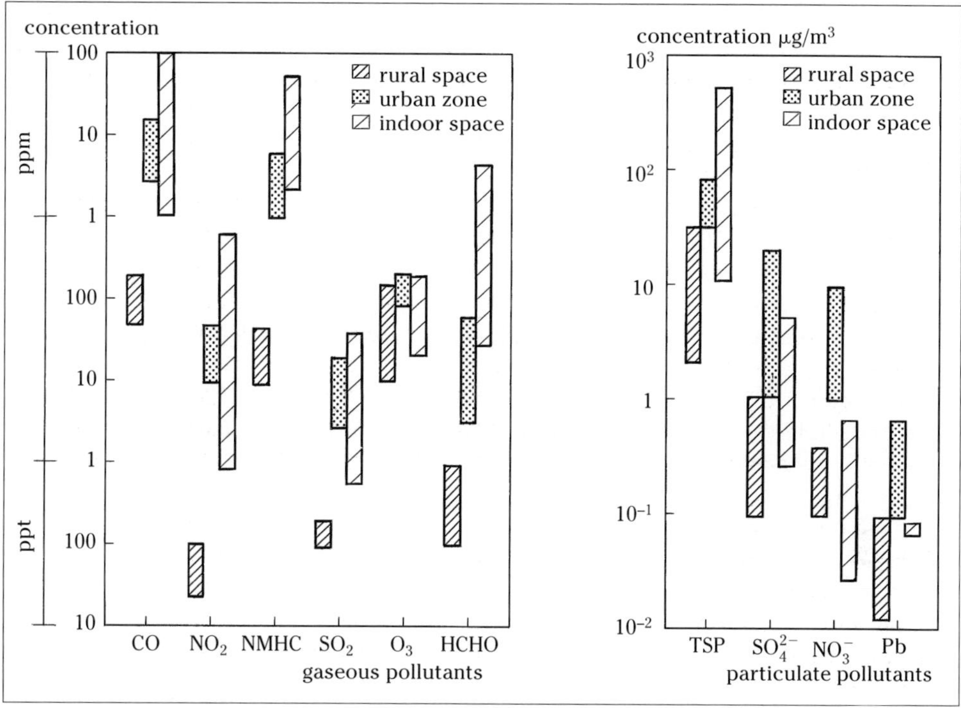


**Fig 3.2** Concentration ranges of different pollutants [54]

# REFERENCES


[1] I.S. Al-Mutaz, (1987), "Automotive emission in Saudi Arabia", *Environm. Int.*, **13,** 335-338.

[2] T. Alsberg et al., (1985), "Chemical and biological characterization of organic material from gasoline exhaust particles", *E.S.&T.*, **19,** 43-50.

[3] Anon., (1990), "Poursuite de la hausse des émissions de $NO_x$ en 1989", *Air Environnement*, No. 9, June.

CITEPA, (1990), *Études Documentaires*, No. 96, March.

[4] Anon., (1990), "L'automobile, une source de pollution majeure", *Air Environnement*, No. 10, September.

[5] Anon., (1990), *Pollution automobile, La mobilisation!*, AQA Document, 13 p.

[6] Anon., (1984), "Combustion et émissions de polluants, calculs des facteurs de conversion et expressions des émissions", CITEPA, *Études Documentaires*, No. 77, 34 p, October.

[7] Anon., (1985), "Reduzierung der Schadstoffemissionen bei Nutzfahrzeugen", *Umweltbundesamt*, 18 January, 12 p.

[8] Anon., (1987), *Interim evaluation of acidification policy in the Netherlands, Ministerie van Volkshuisvesting, Ruimtelijke Ordening en Milieubeheer*, Leidschendam, 117 p.

[9] Anon., (1991), "Non-road engine and vehicle emission study", *NTIS Report* 92-126960.

[10] Anon., (1990), "Proposed California utility engine regulations", *SAE Off-Highway Conf.*, Milwaukee, 11 September.

[11] H.P. Apsimon et al., (1987), "Ammonia emissions and their role in acid deposition", *Atmosph.Environm.*, **21**, 1939-1946.

[12] T.C. Austin and G.S. Rubinstein, (1985), "A comparison of refueling emissions control with onboard and stage II systems", *SAE Paper* No. 851204, 30 p.

[13] T.M. Baines et al., (1979), "Heavy duty diesel particulate emission factors", *J. APCA*, **29,** 616-621.

[14] D.J. Ball, (1987), "Particulate carbon emissions and diesel vehicles", *Paper* C337/87, *IMechE Conf., "Vehicle emissions and their impact on European Air Quality"*, London, 3/5 November, pp. 83-88.

[15] K. Ballschmitter et al., (1986), "Automobile exhaust versus municipal waste incineration as sources of the polychloro dibenzo dioxins (PCDD) and furans (PCDF)", *Chemosphere*, **15,** 901-915.

[16] D. Barltrop, (1983), *Medical issues, seminar on the health, economic and energy issues related to lead in petrol*, Bruxelles, 30 November, 1 p.

[17] M. Beltzer, (1976), "Non-sulfate particulate emissions from catalyst cars", *SAE Paper* No. 760038, 11 p.

[18] P.M. Berglund and G. Petersson, (1990), "Hazardous petrol hydrocarbons from refuelling with and without vapour recovery", *Sci. Tot. Environm.*, **91,** 49-57.

[19] R. Bouscaren, (1985a), "Évolution des émissions de polluants en France", *CITEPA Report*, 9 p.

[20] R. Bouscaren, (1985b), "Que sont les composés organiques volatils?", *CITEPA Report*, 4 p.

[21] R. Bouscaren, (1986), *Inventaire des émissions de composés organiques en France, ENCLAIR '86 Proceedings*, Taormina, Italy, 28/31 October, pp. 267-270.

[22] J.N. Braddock and P.A. Gabele, (1977), "Emission patterns of Diesel powered passenger cars", Part II, *SAE Paper* No. 770168, 11 p.

[23] G. Bröker and H. Gliwa, (1986), "Dioxin- und Furanemissionnen bei der Verbrennung von Altöl", *Staub*, **46,** 435-438.

[24] S.H. Cadle and P.A. Malawa, (1980), "Low molecular weight aliphatic amines in exhaust from catalyst-equipped cars", *E.S.&T.*, **14,** 718-723.

[25] E. Caplun et al., (1984), "Le plomb dans l'essence", *La Recherche*, **15,** 270-280.

[26] J. Carbonelle et al., (1987), "Le gaz carbonique et l'effet de serre", *CEA/FAR SPIN Report* 10.2.1.3(140), 144 p.

[27] A.W. Carey, (1967), "Smoke reduction in diesel engines", *SAE Paper* No. 670224, 4 p.

[28] P. Carlier and G. Mouvier, (1988), "Initiation à la physico-chimie de la basse troposphère", *Poll. Atmosph.* (January/March),12-24.

[29] N.P. Cernansky0, (1983), "Diesel exhaust odor and irritants", A review, *J. APCA*, **33,** 97-104 [30] L. Chabasson et al., *État de l'Environnement, Ministry of the Environment*, Édition 1987, Paris, 262 p.

[30] L. Chabasson et al., *État de l'Environnement, Ministry of the Environment*, Édition 1987, Paris, 262 p.

[31] L.A. Chambers, (1968), "Classification and extent of air pollution problems", in: *Air Pollution*, A.C. Stern, Academic Press, New York, pp. 1-21.

[32] D.R. Choudhury, (1982), "Characterization of polycyclic ketone and quinone particulates by gas chromatography/mass spectrometry", *E.S.&T.*, **16,** 102-110.

[33] S.W. Coates and G.G. Lassanske, (1990), "Measurement and analysis of gaseous exhaust emissions from recreational and small commercial marine craft", *SAE Paper* No. 901597 (SP-835), pp. 25-39.

[34] J.A. Cooper, (1980), "Environmental impact of residential wood combustion emissions and its implications", *J. APCA*, **30,** 855-861.

[35] R. Conrad et al., (1988), "Emission of carbon monoxide from submerged rice fields into the atmosphere", *Atmosph. Environm.*, **22,** 821-823.

[36] CPDP, (1987), "Pétrole 86", *Comité interprofessionnel du pétrole*, Éléments statistiques, May, 367 p.

[37] C.F. Cullis and M.M. Hirschler, (1989), "Man's emissions of carbon monoxide and hydrocarbons into the atmosphere", *Atmosph. Environm.*, **23,** 1195-1203.

[38] A.B. Dash and P.H. Guldberg, (1983), "A generalized model for estimating the concentration of PAH in urban air", in: *Polynuclear aromatic hydrocarbons, formation, metabolism and measurement*, M. Cooke et al., 7th Int. Symp., pp. 379-392

[39] S.L. Dattner et al., (1980), "A method for rapid calculation of merchant vessel combustion emissions", *J. APCA*, **30,** 305-308.

[40] C.N. Davies, (1974), "Particles in the atmosphere, natural and man made", *Atmosph. Environm.*, **8,** 1069-1079.

[41] P. Degobert, (1980), "Diesel exhaust offensive effect, True odor or irritancy?", *SAE Paper* No. 800423, 18 p.

[42] P. Degobert, (1987), "Pollution secondaire des pots catalytiques, Action sur les polluants non réglementés", *Poll. Atmosph.*, Special Issue (November),25-36.

[43] F.A.A.M. De Leeuw, (1989), "Contribution of traffic emissions to mesoscale $NO_x$ and $O_3$ concentrations", *Atmosph. Environm.*, **23,** 49-53

[44] A. de Meulemeester et al., "Sulphur dioxide emissions from oil refineries and combustion of oil products in Western Europe", *CONCAWE Report* No. 10/86, 10. pp. (1986)

[45] J. Delsey, (1979), "La pollution due aux moyens de transports", *INRETS Memorandum* No. 13, 56 p.

[46] A.H. Edwards et al., (1986), "Volatile organic compound emissions, an inventory for Western Europe", *CONCAWE Report* No. 2/86, 18 p.

[47] K.E. Egebäck and B.M. Bertillson, (1983), "Chemical and biological characterization of exhaust emissions from vehicles fuelled with gasoline, alcohol, LPG and Diesel", *snv pm Report* 1635, National Swedish Environment Board.

[48] C. Elichegaray, (1982), "Le rapport Br/Cl dans l'aérosol atmosphérique comme traceur de la pollution automobile", *Poll. Atmosph.* (January/March), 37-41.

[49] C. Elichegaray, (1987), "La part des transports dans le cycle des oxydes d'azote", *Poll. Atmosph.*, Special Issue (November), 214-224.

[50] M.D. Erickson et al., (1979), "Identification of alkyl-9-fluoronones in Diesel exhaust particulate", *J. Chromat. Sci.*, **17,** 449-454.

[51] W. Funke et al., (1984), "Determination of polycyclic aromatic hydrocarbons in mainstream cigarette smoke with respect to particle size", in: *Polynuclear aromatic hydrocarbons, chemistry, characterization and carcinogenesis*, M. Cooke et al., 9th Int. Symp., Columbus, Ohio, 30 October/1 November, pp. 333-341.

[52] T.L. Gibson et al., (1986), "Evidence for the transformation of polycyclic organic matter in the atmosphere", *Atmosph. Environm.*, **20,** 1575-1578.

[53] E.U. Goff et al., (1980), "Nitrosamine emissions from Diesel engine crankcases", *SAE Paper* No. 801374, 8 p.

[54] T.E. Graedel, (1988), "Ambient levels of anthropogenic emissions and their atmospheric transformation products", in: *Air pollution, the automobile and public health*, A.Y. Watson, *National Academic Press*, Washington, pp. 133-160.

[55] D. Gruden, (1988), *Aromaten in Abgas von Ottomotoren*, Verlag TÜV Rheinland, Köln, 126 p.

[56] G. Gschwandtner et al., (1986), "Historic emissions of sulfur and nitrogen oxides in the United States from 1900 to 1980", *J. APCA*, **36,** 139-149.

[57] J-C. Guibet and B. Martin, (1987), *Carburants et Moteurs*, Technip, Paris, 903 p.

[58] P. Haglund et al., (1987), "Analysis of halogenated polycyclic aromatic hydrocarbons in urban air, snow, and automobile exhaust", *Chemosphere*, **16,** 2441-2450.

[59] A.D.A. Hansen and H. Rosen, (1990), "Individual measurements of the emission factor of aerosol black carbon in automobile plumes", *J. Air Waste Managem. Assoc.*, **40,** 1654-1657.

[60] P.L. Hanst et al., (1977), "Atmospheric chemistry of N-nitroso dimethylamine", *E.S.&T.*, **11,** 403-405.

[61] W.M. Hao et al., (1988), "Production of $N_2O$, $CH_4$ and $CO_2$ from soils in the tropical savanna during the dry season", *J. Atmosph. Chem.*, **7,** 93-105.

[62] C.T. Hare et al., (1974), "Exhaust emissions from 2-stroke outboard motors and their impact", *SAE Paper* No. 740737, 27 p.

[63] E. Häsänen et al., (1979), "On the occurrence of aliphatic chlorine and bromine compounds in automobile exhaust", *Atmosph. Environm.*, **13,** 1217-1219.

[64] E. Häsänen et al., (1981), "Benzene, toluene and xylene concentrations in car exhaust and in city air", *Atmosph. Environm.*, **15,** 1755-1757.

[65] P. Henensal and O. Benoît, (1987), "Contribution des véhicules à moteur à la pollution atmosphérique acide", *LCPC Report EG3*, December, 111 p.

[66] O. Herz, (1991), "Transport aérien et pollution atmosphérique", Proc. Int. Symp. *Transport et Pollution de l'Air*, Avignon, 10/13 September, pp. 319-325.

[67] O. Herz, (1991), "Transport aérien et pollution de l'air", *Air Environnement*, October, No. 14, 3 p.

[68] V.F. Hodge and M.O. Stallard, (1986), "Platinum and palladium in roadside dust", *E.S.&T.*, **20,** 1058-1060.

[69] G. Hunter et al., (1981), "The effect of an oxidation catalyst on the physical, chemical and biological character of Diesel particulate emissions", *SAE Paper* No. 810263, 29 p.

[70] R.G. Hurley et al., (1989), "Characterization of automotive catalysts exposed to the fuel additive MMT", *SAE Paper* No. 890582, 11 p.

[71] M. Ikeda et al., (1986), "Upper respiratory symptoms presumably due to studded tire generated dust", *Environm. Int.*, **12,** 505-511.

[72] *International panel for climate changes*, (1990).

[73] G. Israël et al., (1986), "Der Verkehrsanteil an der Immission von Gesamtstaub und polycyclischen aromatischen Kohlenwasserstoffen in deutschen Großstädten", in: *Luftverunreinigungen durch Kraftfahrzeugen*, B. Seifert, G. Fischer, Stuttgart, pp. 59-80.

[74] M.G. Jacko et al., (1973a), "Brake and clutch emissions generated during vehicle operation", *SAE Paper* No. 730548, 18 p.

[75] M.G. Jacko et al., (1973b), "How much asbestos do vehicles emit?", *Automotive Eng.*, **81,** 38-40.

[76] T.E. Jensen et al., (1986), "1-nitropyrene in used Diesel engine oil", *J. APCA*, **36,** 1255.

[77] J.H. Johnson, (1988), "Automotive emissions", in: *Air pollution, the automobile and public health*, A.Y. Watson, National Academic Press, Washington, pp. 39-75.

[78] R. Joumard, (1981), "Les particules émises par les transports terrestres", Étude bibliographique introductive, *INRETS Report*, 56 p.

[79] R. Joumard et al., (1984), "Odeurs et fumées parmi les autres nuisances, une enquête à Marseille", *Poll. Atmosph.*,73-81.

[80] R. Joumard et al., (1990), "Émissions unitaires de polluants des véhicules légers", *INRETS Report* No. 116, 120 p.

[81] B. Juguet et al., (1984), "Étude de la fraction minérale de l'aérosol urbain à Paris, bilan d'une surveillance prolongée", *Poll. Atmosph.*, 3-12.

[82] M. Kawanaugh, (1988), "New estimates of $NO_x$ from aircraft, 1975 to 2025", *APCA Meeting*, Dallas, 19/24 June, 63 p.

[83] J.M. Kawecki, (1978), "Emission of sulfur-bearing compounds from motor vehicle and aircraft engines, A report to Congress", *EPA Report* 600/9-78-028, 436 p.

[84] M.A.K. Khalil and R.A. Rasmussen, (1988), "Carbon monoxide in an urban environment, application of a receptor model for source apportionment", *J. APCA*, **38,** 901-906.

[85] A. König and H. Rohlfing, (1984), "Geruchsbelästigung durch Kfz-Abgase", *Staub*, **44,** 396-398.

[86] J.A. Kovach and R.E. Grambo, (1980), "Performance characteristics of a non-asbestos cellulose fiber composite friction material", *SAE Paper* No. 800979, 14 p.

[87] J. Kraft and M. Kuhler, (1985), "Aldehydes from motor vehicles, toxicity and air quality", *SAE Paper* No. 851661, 11 p.

[88] O. Kruggel, (1985), "Untersuchungen zur Stickoxidminderung an Großdieselmotoren, Emissionsminderung Automobilabgase-Dieselmotoren", *VDI Berichte*, (559), 459-478.

[89] M. Kuhler et al., (1985), "Natürliche und anthropogene Emissionen", *Automobil-Industrie*, **(2),** 165-176.

[90] J. Lahaye, (1987), *Unpublished results.*

[91] F.J. Laimböck, (1991), "The potential of small loop scavenged spark ignition single cylinder engines", *SAE SP* 847, 74 p.

[92] J. Lambert, (1986), "Prévisions globales des émissions de polluants automobiles à l'horizon 2000", *INRETS Report* No. 2, (May), 69 p.

[93] W.S. Lanier and S.B. Robinson, (1986), "EPA Workshop on $N_2O$ emission from combustion, Durham, North Carolina", *EPA Report* 600/8-86-035, 104 p.

[94] H. Legrand, (1988), "La pollution due aux transports", *SIA Conference, Le Moteur à allumage commandé de la prochaine décennie*, Strasbourg, 18/19 May, 7 p.

[95] M. Lenner et al., (1983), "The $NO_2/NO_x$ ratio in emissions from gasoline powered cars, high percentage in idle engine measurements", *Atmosph. Environm.*, **17,** 1395-1398.

[96] K. Levsen et al., (1988), "Artifacts during the sampling of nitro PAHs of Diesel exhaust", *Fresnius' Z. Anal.Chem.*, **330,** 527-528.

[97] K.H. Lies et al., (1986), "Aldehyde emissions from passenger cars", *Staub*, **46,** 136-139.

[98] P.J. Lightowlers and J.N. Cape, (1988), "Sources and fate of atmospheric HCl in the UK and Western Europe", *Atmosph. Environm.*, **22,** 7-15.

[99] W. Lijinsky, (1979), "N-nitrosamines as environmental carcinogens", in: *N-nitrosamines, ACS Symposium Series* 101, J.P. Anselme, pp. 165-173.

[100] P.J. Lioy et al., (1987), *Toxic air pollution*, Lewis Publishers, Chelsea, Michigan, 294 p.

[101] F. Lipari et al., (1984), "Aldehyde emissions from wood burning fireplaces", *E.S.&T.*, **18,** 326-330.

[102] W. Lohrer et al., (1985), "Formaldehyd in der Umwelt", *Staub*, **45,** 239-247.

[103] W. Lohrer and W. Plehn, (1987), "Umweltbelastung durch PVC", *Staub*, **47,** 190-197.

[104] B. Lübkert and S. De Tilly, (1989), "The OECD map emission inventory for $SO_2$, $NO_x$ and VOC in Western Europe", *Atmosph. Environm.*, **23,** 1-15.

[105] B. Lübkert and K.H. Zierock, (1989), "European emission inventory, A proposal of international worksharing", *Atmosph. Environm.*, **23,** 37-48.

[106] J.R. Lynch, (1968), "Brake lining decomposition products", *J. APCA*, **18,** 824-826.

[107] M.A. McCartney et al., (1986), "Airplane emissions, A source of mutagenic nitrated polycyclic aromatic hydrocarbons", *Mut. Res.*, **171,** 99-104.

[108] A.S. McGill et al., (1982), "The polynuclear aromatic hydrocarbon content of smoked food in the United Kingdom", in: *Polynuclear aromatic hydrocarbons, formation, metabolism and measurements*, M. Cooke et al., 6th Int. Symp., pp. 491-499.

[109] S. Marklund et al., "Emissions of PCDDs and PCDFs in gasoline and Diesel fueled cars", *Chemosphere*, **20,** 553-561. (109)

[110] P. Masclet et al., (1986), "Évaluation des contributions respectives des principales sources de HAP dans l'atmosphère", *Poll. Atmosph.* (July/September),197-201.

[111] J-M. Massin and O. Herz, (1991), *La pollution atmosphérique induite par la navigation maritime, Int. Symp. "Transport et Pollution de l'Air"*, Avignon, France, 10/13 September, pp. 327-334.

[112] H. May et al., (1984), *Einfluß von Zündung und Kraftstoffzusammensetzung auf die Schadstoff-Emission, VDI Berichte No. 531, "Emissionsminderung Automobilabgase-Ottomotoren"*, pp. 307-323.

[113] N. Metz, (1990), "Entwicklung der Abgasemissionnen des Personenwagen Verkehrs in der BRD von 1970 bis 2010", *ATZ*, **92,** 176-183.

[114] S. Midot, (1987), "Les effets du $CO_2$ sur le climat, Un bilan des connaissances actuelles", *Poll. Atmosph.* (July/September),199-225.

[115] D. Möller, (1984a), "Estimation of the global man-made sulphur emissions", *Atmosph. Environm.*, **18,** 19-27.

[116] D. Möller, (1984b), "On the global natural sulphur emission", *Atmosph. Environm.*, **18,** 29-39.

[117] G. Monnier and P. Duret, (1991), "IAPAC compressed air assisted fuel injection for high efficiency low emission marine outboard two-stroke engines", *SAE Paper* No. 911849 (SP-883), 123-135.

[118] G. Monnier et al., (1991), "IAPAC compressed air assisted fuel injection for high efficiency low emission marine outboard two-stroke engines", *Japan SAE Paper* No. 911251 (STEC), 16 p.

[119] M.D. Müller and H.R. Buser, (1986), "Halogenated aromatic compounds in automotive emissions from leaded gasoline additives", *E.S.&T.*, **20,** 1151-1157.

[120] D.J. Murphy, (1983), "Ambient particulate and benzo(a)pyrene concentrations from residential wood combustion in a mountain community", in: *Polynuclear aromatic hydrocarbons, formation, metabolism and measurement*, M. Cooke et al., 7th Int. Symp., pp. 567-574.

[121] R. Nakagawa et al., (1983), "Identification of dinitropyrenes in Diesel exhaust particles, their probable presence as the major mutagens", *Mut. Res.*, **124,** 201-211.

[122] G.J. Nebel, (1979), "Benzene in auto exhaust", *J. APCA*, **29,** 391-392.

[123] P.F. Nelson, (1981), "Evaporative hydrocarbon emissions from a large vehicle population", *J. APCA*, **31,** 1191-1193.

[124] B.C. Nguyen and J. Servant, (1984), "Sources Naturelles et sources anthropogéniques des polluants à l'origine de l'acidification des pluies", *Livre Blanc sur les pluies acides*, Ministry of the Environment, 20 June, pp. 37-56.

[125] T. Nielsen and T. Ramdah, (1986), "Determination of 2-nitrofluoroanthene and 2-nitropyrene in ambient particulate matter, Evidence for atmospheric reactions", *Atmosph. Environm.*, **20,** 1507.

[126] M.G. Nishioka et al., (1988), "Detection of hydroxylated nitro aromatic and hydroxylated nitro polycyclic aromatic compounds in an ambient air particulate extract using bioassay directed fractionation", *E.S.&T.*, **22,** 908-915.

[127] OECD, (1990), "Monographie sur l'Environnement No. 21", *Inventaire d'Émissions des Principaux Polluants Atmosphériques dans les Pays Européens de l'OCDE*, 98 p.

[128] W.K. Okamoto et al., (1983), "Nitric acid in Diesel exhaust", *J. APCA*, **33,** 1098-1100.

[129] J. Pacyna et al., (1991), "European survey for $NO_x$ emissions with emphasis on Eastern Europe", *Atmosph. Environm.*, **25A,** 425-439.

[130] P. Pascal, *Nouveau Traité de Chimie Minérale*, Masson, Paris.

[131] R. Petersen, (1984), *Abgasbestimmungen für Dieselkraftfahrzeuge, Heutiger Stand und mögliche zukünftige Entwicklungen*, Umweltbundesamt.

[132] M. Piscator, (1978), "Exposure to cadmium", in: *Trace metals, Exposure and health effects*, E. Di Ferrante, Pergamon Press, Oxford, pp. 35-41.

[133] H.U. Pfeffer, (1991), "Immissionen im Einflußbereich des Kraftfahrzeugverkehrs", *Staub*, **51,** 63-69.

[134] E. Plaßmann, (1986), "Abgas-Emissionen des Kraftfahrzeugverkehrs, Stand und Entwicklung", in: *Luftverunreinigungen durch Kraftfahrzeuge*, B. Seifert, G. Fischer, Stuttgart, pp. 1-28.

[135] D.L. Raley et al., (1987), "Analysis of benzene refueling emissions from vehicles and vehicle refueling", *SAE Paper* No. 841397, 10 p.

[136] T. Ramdahl, (1983), "Polycyclic aromatic ketones in environmental samples", *E.S.&T.*, **17,** 666-670.

[137] T. Ramdahl et al., (1986), "Ubiquitous occurrence of 2-nitrofluorenthene and 2-nitropyrene in air", *Nature*, **321,** 425-427.

[138] D.J. Robertson et al., (1979), "HCN content of turbine engine exhaust", *J. APCA*, **29,** 50-51.

[139] D.J. Robertson et al., (1980), "Organic content of particulate matter in turbine engine exhaust", *J. APCA*, **30,** 261-266.

[140] A. Roussel et al., (1983), "Impact médical des pollutions d'origine automobile", *Poll. Atmosph.*, Supplement 99, (July/September),1-30.

[141] R.F. Sawyer and E.S. Starkman, (1968), "Gas turbine exhaust emissions", *SAE Paper* No. 680462, 7 p.

[142] R.A. Sedjo, (1989), "Forests, A tool to moderate global warming?", *Environment*, **31,** 14-20.

[143] H. Segal and R. Yamartino, (1981), "The influence of aircraft operations on air quality at airports", *J. APCA*, **31,** 846-850.

[144] D. Shapley, (1976), "Nitrosamines, Scientists on the trail of prime suspect in urban cancer", *Science*, **191,** 268-270.

[145] J.E. Sigsby et al., (1987), "Volatile organic compound emissions from 46 in-use passenger cars", *E.S.&T.*, **21,** 466-475.

[146] R.L. Slone et al., (1980), "Nitrosamine emissions from Diesels", *SAE Paper* No. 801375, 8 p.

[147] J.H. Somers et al., (1977), "Automotive sulfate emissions, A baseline study", *SAE Paper* No. 770166, 16 p.

[148] Q.R. Stahl, (1969), "Air pollution aspects of formaldehyde", *PB Report* No. 188081-NTIS, p. 139.

[149] A.C. Stern, (1968), *Air Pollution*, Vol. 3, Academic Press, New York, 2244 p.

[150] M.J. Suess et al., (1985), *Ambient air pollutants from industrial sources, A Reference Handbook*, Elsevier Science Publications, Amsterdam, 843 p.

[151] N. Sunderaraman et al., (1979), "Air quality and airport operations", *J. APCA*, **29,** 109-132.

[152] A.C. Szkarlat and S.M. Japar, (1983), "Optical and chemical properties of particle emissions from on-road vehicles", *J. APCA*, **33,** 592-597.

[153] J.M. Tims, (1983), "Benzene emissions from passenger cars", *CONCAWE Report* No. 12/83, 27 p.

[154] H.M. Tosine and R.E. Clément, (1986), "Dioxin furan news", 6th Int. Symp.on Chlorinated Dioxins, Fukuoka, Japan, 16/19 September 1986, *Chemosphere*, **18,** N5.

[155] A. Truchot et al., (1984), "Contribution of petroleum refineries to emissions of nitrogen oxides", *CONCAWE Report* No. 9/94, 56 p.

[156] T.J. Truex et al., (1980), “Sulfate in Diesel exhaust”, *E.S.&T.*, **14,** 1118-1121.

[157] T.J. Truex et al., (1987), “The chemistry and control of $H_2S$ emissions in three-way catalysts”, *SAE Paper* No. 872162, 10 p.

[158] K. Tsuchiya and S. Hirano, (1975), “Characteristics of 2-stroke motorcycle exhaust HC emission and effects of air/fuel ratio and ignition timing”, *SAE Paper* No. 750908, 13 p.

[159] L.C. van Beckhoven and C.J. Sliggers, (1987), “Air pollution by road traffic in the Netherlands”, *Paper* No. C338/87, *IMechE Conference “Vehicle Emissions and Their Impact on European Air Quality”*, London, 3.5 November, pp. 119-130.

[160] E. van Veen, (1986), *VOC emissions inventory and control of emissions from gasoline distribution systems, ENCLAIR '86 Proceedings*, Taormina, Italy, 28/31 October, pp. 271-280.

[161] A. Wadge and M. Hutton, (1987), “The cadmium and lead content of suspended particulate matter from a UK refuse incinerator”, *Sci. Tot. Environm.*, **67,** 91-95.

[162] F.J. Washabaugh, (1986), EMCOR 66 ultra short fibers for asbestos-free friction materials, SAE Paper No. 860630, 8 p.

[163] C.S. Weaver, (1989), “Feasibility of emissions control for off-highway Diesel engines”, *SAE Paper* No. 890169, pp. 123-135.

[164] J. Weissmann et al., (1970), *Carburants et combustibles pour moteurs à combustion interne*, Technip, Paris, 703 p.

[165] R. Westerholm et al., (1988), “Some aspects of the distribution of polycyclic aromatic hydrocarbons (PAH) between particles and gas phase from diluted gasoline exhausts generated with the use of a dilution tunnel and its validity for measurement in ambient air”, *Atmosph. Environm.*, **22,** 1005-1010.

[166] J.J. White et al., (1991), “Emission factors for small utility engines”, *SAE Paper* No. 910560 (SP-863), pp. 113-134.

[167] D.J. Williams et al., (1989a), “Particulate emissions from ‘in-use’ motor vehicles, 1 Spark ignition vehicles”, *Atmosph. Environm.*, **23,** 2639-2645.

[168] D.J. Williams et al., (1989b), “Particulate emissions from ‘in-use’ motor vehicles, 2 Diesel vehicles”, *Atmosph. Environm.*, **23,** 2647-2661.

[169] R.L. Williams and S.J. Swarin, (1979), “Benzo(a)pyrene emissions from gasoline and Diesel automobiles”, *SAE Paper* No. 790419, 6 p.

[170] R.W. Wood, (1988), “Identifying neurobehavioral effects of automotive emissions and fuel components”, in: *Air pollution, the automobile and public health*, A.Y Watson, National Academic Press, Washington, pp. 631-657.

[171] D.E. Zinger and L.H. Hecker, (1979), “Gaseous emissions from unregulated mobile sources”, *J. APCA*, **29,** 526-527.

[172] R.B. Zweidinger et al., (1988), “Detailed hydrocarbon and aldehyde mobile source emissions from roadway studies”, *E.S.&T.*, **22,** 956-962.

[173] J.M. Dash, (1992), “Nitrous oxide emissions from vehicles”, *J. Air Waste Managem. Assoc.*, **42,** 63-67.

# A ir pollution and health 4

*"The lungs, the lungs, I tell you."*
Molière
'The Hypochondriac', Act III, Scene X

Each day, over 12 $m^3$ (15 kg) of air pass through the lungs of the average individual. This amount varies with a person's age and level of physical activity. The quality of respiration affects the functioning of the body's cellular metabolism and hence, the health of the individual.

The acute toxic effects of automotive exhaust gases have been known since the advent of the internal combustion engine. Engines release sufficient carbon monoxide to cause mortal intoxication when run in confined spaces (garages, etc.). This is why CO emissions were the target of the earliest regulations. Apart from its acute toxic effects, automotive pollution is blamed for long-term harmful effects that are caused by the presence of other chemical compounds in the emissions. These compounds are both organic and inorganic.

These long-term effects are very difficult to identify and today one can still raise the question asked by US Representative David Stockman:

*"Will the reduction in auto pollution actually improve ambient air quality significantly, and will better air actually improve public health?"* [104].

Respiratory diseases now rank fourth among the causes of human death [102]. Airborne pollutants enter the human body primarily through the respiratory system. This chapter begins by reviewing the respiratory system's main characteristics and the respiratory disorders that result from pollutants. These pollutants also continue on past the lungs to enter the circulatory system and can therefore affect other physiological functions.

## 4.1 Characteristics of the respiratory system

The respiratory system consists of the upper airways (nose, pharynx, larynx, trachea) and intrathoracic passages (bronchi or bronchial tubes, bronchioles) and the lungs containing the pulmonary alveoli, which are minute air sacs that allow contact between the inhaled air and the blood circulating through the pulmonary epithelium. The pulmonary system is responsible for gaseous exchanges: the reoxygenation of the blood to feed cell metabolism and the removal of the $CO_2$ that is the product of this metabolism.

The respiratory system satisfies the body's need for air: from 6 liters/min at rest to more than 60 liters/min during stress[1]. Oxygen enters the blood through the alveolar epithelia, which are laminae of cytoplasm about 50 nm thick that carpet the 50 $m^2$ of alveoli. The 300 million alveoli measure 0.1 to 0.3 mm and serve as the air terminations of the pulmonary system. These alveoli are the terminations for about 32,000 capillaries—each one 0.5 mm in diameter—that form a total cross-section of 113 $cm^2$. Oxygen affixes to blood hemoglobin (1.34 ml $O_2$/g) and is conveyed to the tissues in the form of oxyhemoglobin. In return, $CO_2$ is conveyed towards the lung by the hemoglobin or the blood plasma in the form of $NaHCO_3$.

### 4.1.1 Defense mechanisms of the respiratory system

The respiratory system is open to the exterior and is extremely vulnerable. It is menaced by every conceivable type of aggressor and pollutant: gases, dust and inert particles, and living corpuscles (bacteria, viruses, mushroom spores, pollen grains), which are all suspended in the inhaled air.

Fortunately, the respiratory system is equipped with defense systems adapted to deal with these intruders. These defense systems are triggered by and develop in contact with an aggressor. This is when they demonstrate their full effectiveness. However, in the case of massive or prolonged attack they may be overrun, leaving the aggressor to act freely. A particular pollutant may also inhibit these natural defenses and open the system up to other aggressions.

Different pulmonary defense mechanisms are involved: physical, immunological, and biochemical [17]:

- **Mechanical defenses:** these defenses act differently in the two sections of the respiratory system. The upper respiratory tract acts on the larger particles with short retention times (filtration in the nasal fossae), while the inner lung acts on the smaller particles with longer retention times that have crossed the first barrier. The defenses are provided by a set of cellular elements that adjust the movements of the fluids transporting the deposited particles: this is the rising 'rolling carpet' of the cilia coating the walls of the respiratory passages and the special cells that actuate with unidirectional pulsations to raise the loaded mucus to the exterior for its expulsion by coughing and spitting. The particles are trapped in the inner lung on the surfactant film that keeps the pulmonary alveoli open. In this case, the rate of purification is much slower. The lung system is also physically defended by the dissolution of water-soluble gases ($O_3$ and $SO_2$) in the secretions impregnating the mucous membranes.

1. By way of comparison, a racer running at 12 km/h, a cyclist doing 30 km/h and an automobile consuming 8 liters of gasoline per 100 km use respectively 60, 24 and 6 liters of pure oxygen per km.

- **Cellular defenses:** 'large' cells (alveolar macrophages) present in the alveoli exhibit considerable phagocytic power, then migrate with their load to be eliminated by deglutition or passage into the lymphatic system. These macrophages are included in the alveolar surfactant film, which thus facilitates their mobility.
- **Immunological defenses:** the alveolar macrophages have a highly varied enzymatic arsenal (e.g., antiproteases acting on oxidants, benzopyrene hydrolase acting on B(a)P, etc.), which can attack many organic structures and thus promote their detoxification.

## 4.2 Diseases of the respiratory system

We will emphasize the diseases specifically related to air pollution by inert particles. We shall therefore ignore viral, microbial, and allergic ailments such as those induced by pollen. It should nevertheless be kept in mind that the pollutants conveyed by inhaled air can attack the tissues and make them more vulnerable to microbial pathologies and totally or partially inhibit the defense mechanisms mentioned above, thus facilitating such ailments. The diseases of the pulmonary system are distinguished by a decrease in pulmonary function: e.g. breathing capacity [63 and 90].

### 4.2.1 Chronic bronchitis

Chronic bronchitis is characterized by persistent coughing and spitting [96], which are characteristic manifestations, particularly in cigarette smokers [5]. An excess of particles inhibits the mucociliar process. The accumulation of mucus slows down the cleaning rate [88] and the permanent or intermittent increase in bronchial mucus leads to spitting. The bronchial walls tend to thicken, with swelling of the mucous membranes and cellular desquamation, which causes a shrinking of the respiratory passages. This can lead to chronic inflammatory reactions (tracheo-bronchitis). Chronic bronchitis can be sustained by chemical irritation caused chiefly by cigarette smoke and certain airborne pollutants.

### 4.2.2 Pulmonary emphysema

Emphysema is the destruction of the alveoli walls that results from the abnormal swelling of the bronchioles and it reduces the flow of the air/blood exchange, and hence the intensity of oxygenation.

Inflammations occur simultaneously in the bronchiole wall, narrowing the air passages. Due to the higher aerodynamic resistance, breathing demands greater muscular effort.

### 4.2.3 Pneumoconiosis and pulmonary fibrosis

Depending on their size, 'inert' airborne particles can, to varying degrees, penetrate into the respiratory tree. The finer particles reach the alveoli, where the macrophages try to phagocyte them and 'metabolize' them. However, this is futile if the particles are inorganic. The corresponding hypersecretion of the macrophages creates fibrosis. Collagen fibers make up the skeleton of the pulmonary cells. Any abnormal development of these fibers in the alveolar interstices reduces their volumetric capacity and their elasticity. The fibroblasts that generate the excess collagen [5] are stimulated by macrophage secretions in response to external attack, like that induced by ozone [62].

These manifestations occur primarily in very dusty environments (silicosis in miners). Hence they do not concern ambient pollution. However, the particles can carry organic compounds (such as PAH) into the alveoli, where they are adsorbed, and where they exert mutagenic and carcinogenic effects.

### 4.2.4 Asthma

Asthma is characterized by 'attacks of breathlessness' that occur as spasms of varying intensity, separated by periods of normal breathing [96]. Fortunately, this temporary obstruction of the respiratory passages is reversible [9]. One type of asthma results from allergic causes. It is nevertheless not always easy to establish a direct relationship between the recrudescence of asthma attacks and episodes of air pollution [41].

### 4.2.5 Cancer of the respiratory passages

Cancer is characterized by the anarchical and rampant growth of certain cells that have escaped the control mechanisms of the body. It is an epigenetic phenomenon: the substitution of elements of the genetic code, a duplication error of these elements, a shift in the deoxyribonucleic acid (DNA) sequences[2], etc. The daughter cells produced by the division of the transformed cells exhibit the same defects as the mother cell [51] and contribute to the formation of malignant tumors.

Apart from genetic factors (reasons why individuals placed in the same conditions do not contract the same diseases), cancer can be caused by physical (radiation), biological (viruses), and chemical agents.

2. DNA, the acid that plays a central genetic role and enters into the composition of the chromosomes, as a support of the genetic information according to the sequence of the associated organic bases.

Chemical carcinogenesis, with which we are concerned here, acts through complex mechanisms. Typically, cancer appears in tissues that are in the course of growth or regeneration. In cells undergoing proliferation, the DNA that is in the course of replication (mitosis) is vulnerable. Without inducing changes in the chemical composition of DNA, reproduction errors of the organic base sequences (adenine, guanine, thymine, cytosine) can occur, with transformation of the genetic information. The inability of the error repair mechanisms to react and prevent the development of tumors, incurs the risk of cancer [58].

Chemical carcinogens can cause different types of DNA damage: splitting of chromosomes in sensitive places, shifts in the organic base sequence, addition or inhibition of some segments of the sequence, inversion of segments in the sequence, exchanges of sequences between different chromosomes, etc.

Exposure to genotoxic products is not the only factor in the development of cancer. It is acknowledged that carcinogenesis occurs in two steps: initiation, which transforms a normal cell into a tumoral cell, and promotion, which allows the reproduction of the latent tumoral cells into real tumors. The initiating product may be a carcinogen applied in subliminal doses and the promoter may be a product that is not in itself carcinogenic.

Many carcinogens are inert in their initial form as present in the atmosphere and require prior enzymatic transformation into active metabolites. This is the case with benzo(a)pyrene, of which a minority fraction is converted to mutagenic and water-soluble epoxy-diol. Most of it, which remains inert due to its insolubility in organic liquids, is naturally excreted [58].

Other 'co-carcinogens' multiply the effects of the carcinogens in various ways such as interfering with gene repair mechanisms or purification mechanisms of the respiratory system. Smoking, for example, can exacerbate the effect of diesel particles and vice versa. Genetic predispositions, eating habits, and alcoholism can exert promotional effects.

The respiratory system is not the only area affected by carcinogenesis. Recent epidemiological studies have also cast suspicion on the cause of the increased cases of bladder cancer in subjects who have occupational contact with diesel emissions [64 and 86]. Other studies contradict this result [106].

### 4.2.6 Susceptibility to infection

As already pointed out, the weakening of the physiological defenses can leave the door open to microbial, fungal, and viral respiratory infections [81], which are liable to leave permanent after-effects if contracted during infancy. If poorly treated and repetitive, these ailments can represent additional risk factors. Epidemiological studies must attempt to clarify these risks [25].

## 4.3 Diseases of other physiological organs

### 4.3.1 Cardiovascular diseases

The penetration of the pulmonary interface by airborne pollutants, especially CO, is a well-known cause of the development of athersclerosis and coronary heart disease in cigarette smokers [18]. Airborne or tobacco-generated CO increases the death rate in patients affected by angina pectoris [90].

### 4.3.2 Neuropsychic effects

Sensory ailments can result from exposure to airborne pollutants. This includes the lachrymogenic effects of irritants such as aldehydes and ozone, migraines caused by small CO intake, and losses of attention and vigilance, which are dangerous for drivers [59]. The unpleasant odor from diesels also causes sensory disturbances.

## 4.4 Methods for characterizing health effects

Many methods are used to investigate the effects of airborne pollutants on health. They include the experimental (*in vitro, in vivo,* and *ex vivo*) and anthropical (clinical case studies, controlled exposures, and epidemiological investigations) methods.

### 4.4.1 Epidemiologic investigations

#### 4.4.1.1 General

Epidemiology analyzes the possible relationship between disease and short and long term exposure to various pollutants. It serves to establish a direct relationship between man and air pollution.

The prolonged exposure of humans in exposure cells is unethical and therefore impossible. Short exposures are possible but only for investigations with rapid and reversible effects [7 and 75].

Epidemiology helps to directly observe the effects of pollutants on human populations. It takes into account the variety of environmental conditions and individual differences in sensitivity to the pollutants [107]. The inability to control the 'experimental' conditions, especially the lack of exposure indicators, presents an enormous handicap in using the results. These results reflect a large number of uncontrolled parameters (confusion factors), which can completely distort their interpretation.

Other problems are: keeping the population being examined in its initial condition, finding, for a given pollutant, a control population sheltered from the pollution being investigated, and determining the dose/effect relationship [25].

Apart from episodes of acute pollution that have demonstrated a relationship between mortality and airborne pollution, studies are directed, for practical reasons, at specific categories of the population (for example, children, the elderly, pregnant women, and asthmatics) [7]. Attempts have been made to identify the relationship between observed respiratory ailments and certain pollutants, such as $NO_x$ [38]. The main difficulty resides in the evaluation of the sensitivity thresholds of the respiratory system to airborne pollutants.

#### 4.4.1.2 Automotive effluents

Many studies have attempted to determine the relationship between diesel engine emissions and the development of lung cancer in occupationally-exposed subjects (bus drivers, garage employees), without successfully demonstrating any irrefutable direct relationship.

The studies show that smoking is the dominant factor causing lung cancer, but atmospheric pollution and particles can add a synergistic effect [28] and a multiplying effect—rather than an additive effect [37]. Depending on the number of cigarettes smoked per day, the age at which the smoker began the habit, and the number of years smoked, the number of cancers appearing in smokers and non-smokers respectively vary by a factor of 10 [51]. Fig. 4.1, which compares smokers in urban and rural environments, shows the synergistic effect between smoking and air pollution [31].

### 4.4.2 *In vivo* experimental investigations

In addition to epidemiological investigations, which are difficult to perform and yield results that are hard to interpret, US, Japanese, European, and German laboratories are pursuing investigations on living animals. Investigations are conducted by inhalation, instillation in the trachea, or coating of the skin by products derived from engine exhaust gases or diesel particulate extracts [64 and 82]. Hamsters, rats, and mice are placed in exposure chambers [12]. The tests performed so far, with concentrations much higher than environment values (700 to 7000 $\mu g/m^3$ for 24 to 30 months) [16 and 34], have induced tumors in rats after two years. Extrapolation of the results from rats (hamsters do not react) to humans, which are subjects not initially susceptible to contracting lung cancer, would have required many years exposure to diesel particle concentrations much higher than those found in city streets [35 and 60].

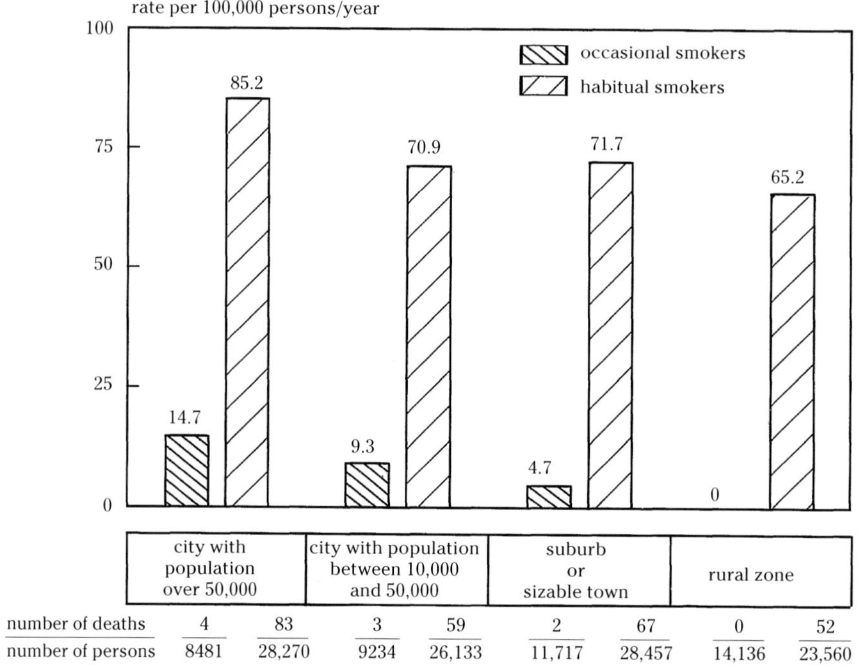


**Fig 4.1** Frequency of appearance of bronchial carcinoma compared between smokers and non-smokers residing in rural and urban areas [31] (with correction for age)

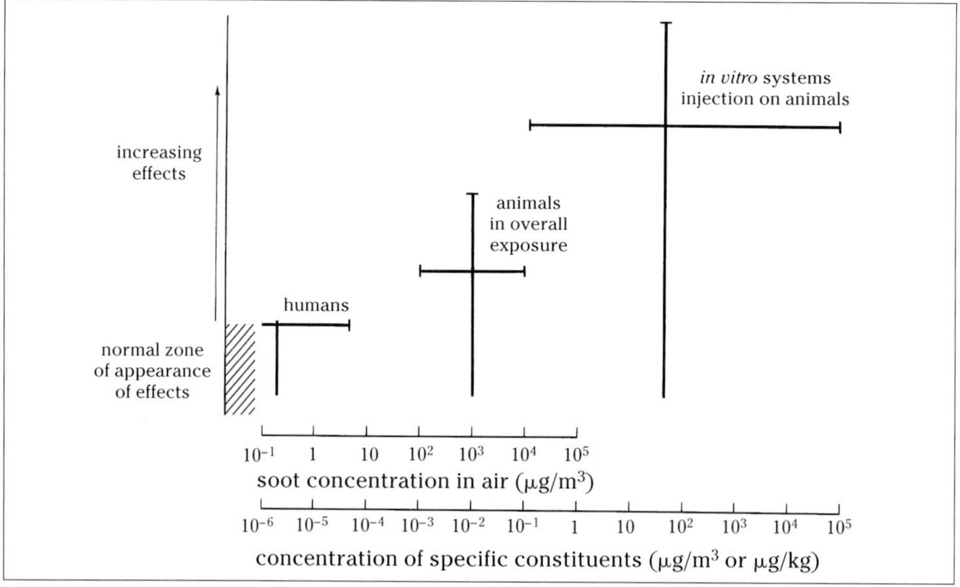


**Fig 4.2** Areas of interest of various experimental methods for persons exposed to diesel effluents [69]

Figure 4.2 [69] illustrates the difficulties encountered in toxicity studies in which, to have visible effects, it is necessary to use *in vitro* and, to a lesser degree, in vivo concentrations considerably higher than those to which the populations are normally exposed.

### 4.4.3 *In vitro* experimental investigations

Epidemiological and experimental investigations *in vivo* are costly. They have not yet provided clear answers to the risks to human health from automotive effluents. A simpler approach is to use batteries of *in vitro* biotests employing bacteria[3], specialized animal or human cells (for example, alveolar macrophages, lymphocytes), or plant organisms. These tests would determine the effects of the pollutants and the dose/response relationship [22, 23, and 101].

Carcinogenesis, which is still not fully understood, develops over several years and may pass through stages of mutagenesis. Most carcinogens are mutagens, but it is unclear whether all mutagens are carcinogens. The study of the mutagenic activity of airborne pollutants tends to imply their carcinogenic potential.

Recent tests, based on direct exposure to pollutants, have identified the direct mutagenic effect of diesel exhaust gases on bacteria and also on human and animal cells, even if the active compounds are not filtered or extracted from these gases, that is, in conditions similar to those of inhalation [22, 24, 35, 76, and 97].

## 4.5 Effects of the different pollutants

### 4.5.1 Short-term toxicity illustrated by the case of CO

The toxicity of CO is relatively well known. It is mortal above 1000 ppm [13]. It can also act in much lower concentrations, due to its affinity for blood hemoglobin, which is 240 times greater than that of oxygen [103]. This blocking of the hemoglobin (reversible, although with considerable difficulty) reduces the oxygen supply to the

3. One of the most popular biotests is the Ames test [2 and 23]. It consists in determining the mutagenic activity of a chemical agent in vitro, from mutant strains of the Salmonella typhimurium bacteria, incapable of developing in the absence of histidine. The reversed mutants, spontaneous or induced by a mutagenic agent, restore the ability to produce histidine and hence of growth in the absence of histidine, and can therefore develop on a histidine-free medium, as opposed to the original bacteria. The bacteria are seeded on a nutrient agar (free of histidine) in the presence of the mutagen to be tested. After residence for 48 h at 37°C, the colonies appearing are counted and the slope at the origin of the dose/effect curve represents the mutagenic power of the test product. To take account of the enzymatic transformations occurring in the products that have penetrated into the organism, a rat liver extract ($S_9$ mix) is also added to the test product, in order to convert the pro-mutagenic agents into active mutagens.

tissues. This situation is aggravated when combined with cardiovascular problems (for example angina pectoris, athersclerosis). Asphyxiation often occurs in closed garages. Fortunately, catalytic converters reduce the risk.

Carbon monoxide may also display long-term toxicity. 'Chronic' intoxication is manifested by non-specific symptoms, such as headaches, dizziness, and nausea [55], which occurs when CO blocks 25% of the hemoglobin [52]. Loss of consciousness, which is dangerous for drivers [72), can occur if the CO rate reaches 50%, and death occurs when the rate reaches 70%. The WHO recommends a maximum of 2.5 to 3% COHb in non-smoking subjects [35] (this rate varies between 5 and 15% in a smoker).

### 4.5.2 Effect of nitrogen oxides

Nitric oxide (NO) is by itself non-toxic. The suspected effects concern its fixation to hemoglobin (the link is 1000 times stronger than with CO) and slight modifications of the emphysema type. These effects are unconfirmed in animal tests [55] and are not manifested below 15 to 20 ppm [103].

The essential effect of NO stems from its role as an $NO_2$ precursor. Nitrogen peroxide is insoluble, and can penetrate deeply into the pulmonary system [78]. It acts on the pulmonary alveoli and impairs their structures (going as far as causing emphysema), inhibits the pulmonary defenses (modifying the 'mobility' of bronchial mucus), and has a cytotoxic effect on the alveolar macrophages [100]. It stimulates their activity in low doses and then weakens the defenses of the body, thus causing other complications (infection, etc.). Nitrogen peroxide can thus cause the death of specific cells in the lungs and impair the regulation of the pulmonary functions [74 and 98]. The symptoms of the toxic action of $NO_2$ are insomnia, coughing, panting, and impairment of the mucous membranes. Japan recommends an environmental limit of 0.04 ppm of $NO_2$ [52].

### 4.5.3 Effect of ozone and oxidants

Like $SO_2$, ozone displays toxic effects similar to those of $NO_2$, but in much lower concentrations [21]. However, its lower stability and greater solubility limit its depth of penetration. The human body reacts by a shrinkage of the respiratory passages as soon as the $O_3$ concentration exceeds 0.1 ppm [103]. Physical activity also diminishes tolerance to these pollutants. Other symptoms are irritations of the eyes and mucous membranes, headaches with coughing and reflexive inhibition of breathing, as well as reduced lung capacity [9]. $O_3$ can trigger attacks of asthma, followed by acute inflammation and pulmonary edema [93]. Ozone causes oxidation of proteins and peroxidation of fatty acids [33], especially unsaturated fatty acids [95]. Anti-oxidants, like vitamin E, can counteract its action. The WHO recommends an ozone limit of 200 $\mu g/m^3$ (0.1 ppm) over 1 h and 65 $\mu g/m^3$ (0.03 ppm) over 24 h.

Ozone strongly affects the pulmonary functions of asthmatics. Its carcinogenic or mutagenic action has not been demonstrated.

Apart from its mutagenic effects, peroxyacetylnitrate (PAN) is a powerful irritant of the eyes [43]. The WHO also recommends a PAN limit of 300 μg/m$^3$ over 1 h and 80 μg/m$^3$ over 8 h [33].

### 4.5.4 Effect of hydrocarbons

Human health is mainly affected by unsaturated hydrocarbons. The olefins are liable to undergo partial metabolic conversion, converting them to genotoxic epoxides [4].

#### 4.5.4.1 Monocyclic aromatic hydrocarbons

Benzene is a well-known haematotoxic and occupational exposure to it can cause leukemia [73]. However, these leukemias only occur with concentrations over 40 ppm [50]. They affect the bone marrow by inhibiting the formation of red blood corpuscles. The white corpuscles are also destroyed (*leucopaenia*) as well as the blood platelets. Benzene is a suspect in other haematological disorders, such as Hodgkin's disease and lymphoma, and may cause chromosomic anomalies. The metabolites of benzene responsible for these biological effects are still poorly known, although phenols and epoxides are often mentioned as resulting from the enzymatic oxidation of benzene [50].

In high concentrations (>1 g/m$^3$) (cleaning of tanks, for example), the inhalation of benzene causes disturbances of the central nervous system and, sometimes, liver ailments.

Toluene and xylenes are less toxic. Up to 1400 ppm, toluene has no effect on rats, apart from a loss of auditory capacity [84]. The authorized limits are 375 mg/m$^3$ for toluene and 435 mg/m$^3$ for xylenes [20 and 30].

#### 4.5.4.2 Polycyclic aromatic hydrocarbons, PAH and derivatives

In the late eighteenth century, the carcinogenic activity of soot was identified in chimney-sweeps who were in contact with compounds in the soot, particularly PAH. Around 1930, the responsibility of PAH as carcinogenic components of tars was firmly established. For diesel engine emissions, the responsibility of PAH is less clearly demonstrated. However, their presence in cigarette smoke, at the rate of 1 to 50 ng/cigarette, is universally acknowledged as the major contribution to lung cancer [48], which demonstrates their possible contribution to the development of other cancers. Each of the PAH detected in exhaust emissions has at least some mutagenic and carcinogenic activity (Tables 4.1 and 4.2). The compounds with four or more aromatic rings may be carcinogenic [46].

**Table 4.1** Carcinogenic and mutagenic activity of some PAH (adapted from [47, 54, 57, 66 and 89] Key: E, vehicle exhaust. D, diesel exhaust. C, combustion gas. U, spent oil. V, grilled meats. P, fish. T, tobacco smoke.
Effect: 0, none. (+), very weak. +, weak.. ++, moderate. +++, strong. ++++, very strong.

| Compound | Number of rings | Carcinogenesis | Mutagenesis | Tumor initiation | Detection |
|---|---|---|---|---|---|
| naphthalene | 2 | 0 | 0 | 0 | |
| fluorene | 3 | 0 | 0 | 0 | |
| anthracene | 3 | 0 | 0 | 0 | ECPVDT |
| phenanthrene | 3 | 0 | 0 | 0 | ECPVDT |
| naphthacene | 4 | 0 | 0 | 0 | |
| triphenylene | 4 | 0 | 0 | 0 | |
| pyrene | 4 | 0 | 0 | 0 | ECTVPD |
| benz(a)anthracene | 4 | + | + | + | ECPVDT |
| 1-methylbenz(a)anthracene | 4 | 0 | + | + | UT |
| 7-methylbenz(a)anthracene | 4 | + | + | + | UT |
| 12-methylbenz(a)anthracene | 4 | + | + | + | UT |
| 7,12-dimethylbenz(a)anthracene | 4 | + | + | + | |
| 4,12-dimethylbenz(a)anthracene | 4 | 0 | 0 | 0 | |
| benzo(c)phenanthrene | 4 | ++ | ++ | + | ECVPT |
| fluoranthene | 4 | 0 | 0 | 0 | EVPD |
| chrysene | 4 | 0 | + | + | ECVPDT |
| methylchrysenes | 4 | (+) | + | + | ECVDT |
| picene | 5 | 0 | 0 | + | |
| benzo(a)pyrene | 5 | + | + | + | ECVPDT |
| benzo(e)pyrene | 5 | 0 | + | 0 | ECVPDT |
| cyclopenta(cd)pyrene | 5 | + | + | + | ECVPT |
| benzo(j)fluoranthene | 5 | +++ | +++ | + | ECVPDT |
| benzo(b)fluoranthene | 5 | ++ | ++ | + | ECVPDT |
| benzo(a)fluoranthene | 5 | 0 | + | 0 | EPTU |
| benzo(ghi)fluoranthene | 5 | 0 | + | 0 | ECPTD |
| benzo(k)fluoranthene | 5 | + | ++ | + | ECVPDT |
| dibenz(a,c)anthracene | 5 | + | + | + | ECVPT |
| dibenz(a,h)anthracene | 5 | + | + | + | ECVPD |
| dibenz(a,j)anthracene | 5 | (+) | + | (+) | ECVPDT |
| benzo(b)chrysene | 5 | 0 | 0 | 0 | DCV |
| benzo(c)chrysene | 5 | ++ | + | (+) | DCV |
| 3-methylcholanthrene | 5 | + | + | + | |
| dibenzo(a,e)pyrene | 6 | + | + | + | ECT |
| dibenzo(a,i)pyrene | 6 | + | + | + | ECTP |
| dibenzo(a,l)pyrene | 6 | + | + | + | CTP |
| dibenzo(e,l)pyrene | 6 | 0 | 0 | 0 | CT |
| dibenzo(a,h)pyrene | 6 | + | + | + | CTV |
| indeno(1,2,3,cd)pyrene | 6 | + | ? | + | ECVPDT |
| benzo(ghi)perylene | 6 | 0 | + | 0 | ECVPDT |
| dibenzo(def,p)chrysene | 6 | + | + | + | |
| dibenzo(b,def)chrysene | 6 | + | + | + | |
| dibenzo(fg,op)naphthacene | 6 | 0 | 0 | 0 | |
| benzo(rst)pentaphene | 6 | + | + | + | |
| benzo(c)pentaphene | 6 | 0 | 0 | 0 | |
| anthanthrene | 6 | + | + | 0 | ECVPDT |
| naphtho(1,2,3,4-def)chrysene | 6 | + | + | + | |
| dibenzo(b,k)chrysene | 6 | 0 | 0 | 0 | |
| coronene | 7 | | | | |

**Table 4.2** Carcinogenic and mutagenic activity of some PAH derivatives (adapted from [47, 54, 57, 66 and 89]
Key: E, vehicle exhaust. C, combustion gas. T, tobacco smoke. B, crude oil. U, spent oil.
Effect: 0, none. (+), very weak. +, weak.

| Compound | Number of rings | Carcinogenesis | Mutagenesis | Tumor initiation | Detection |
|---|---|---|---|---|---|
| carbazole | 3 | 0 | 0 | 0 | CTP |
| benzo(a)carbazole | 4 | 0 | 0 | 0 | CTP |
| benzo(b)carbazole | 4 | 0 | 0 | 0 | T |
| benzo(c)carbazole | 4 | 0 | (+) | 0 | CT |
| 10-aza-benzo(a)pyrene | 5 | 0 | + | 0 | C |
| benzo(b)naphtho(2,1,d)thiophene | 4 | 0 | + | 0 | ECBU |
| benzo(b)naphtho(1,2,d)thiophene | 4 | 0 | 0 | 0 | CB |
| benzo(b)naphtho(2,3,d)thiophene | 4 | 0 | 0 | 0 | CB |
| phenanthro(4,5,b,cd)thiophene | 4 | 0 | (+) | 0 | CB |

Mutagenic PAH, whose activity depends closely on the steric structure (B(a)P is carcinogenic, unlike B(e)P), which requires prior enzymatic conversion to active metabolites.

The degree of substitution can increase the carcinogenic activity and the location of the substituents in the molecule plays a decisive role in this activity [47]. Enzymatic activation is unnecessary to make some PAH derivatives mutagenic. These include polynuclear amines and amides [47], nitrated [48] and especially dinitrated PAH, of which the original PAH, with fewer than four rings, are not recognized as carcinogens. These dinitro-PAH are converted by enzymatic reduction to mutagenic polyaromatic amines [53]. The role of nitro-PAH in the genesis of human cancer remains to be clarified.

Polyaromatic nitrophenols detected in diesel engine exhausts have been recognized as mutagenic metabolites of nitro-PAH [79]. However, the mutagenicity of polyaromatic ketones and quinones [15 and 85] remains to be positively established.

### 4.5.4.3 Motor fuels and lubricants

The toxicity of inhaling motor fuels [8] is essentially due to their benzene content, whose toxicity has already been mentioned. Among paraffinic hydrocarbons, n-hexane, which is present in gasolines at a content of about 5%, is toxic to the nervous system; above 1000 ppm, n-octane causes attention loss [39]. In an occupational atmosphere, its content in the air must not exceed 50 ppm [27]. In rats and mice exposed to over 2000 ppm of unleaded gasoline vapors, tumors of the liver and kidney appear, in addition to kidney disorders and accumulations of alveolar macrophages [67].

Motor fuels can be particularly toxic in contact with the skin, which allows benzene and tetraethyl lead to penetrate through the epidermis. Hence, hand-washing with gasoline should be avoided. Unlike industrial or household solvents, these products are not labeled to inform consumers of their toxicity [14].

Engine lubricants are non-volatile and can therefore be virtually ignored as airborne pollutants. New refined oils, in the usual additive concentrations, are neither carcinogenic nor toxic [91]. On the other hand, spent oils tend to be enriched with PAH and their derivatives. Handling these oils could incur risks, essentially through contact with the skin [45]. Gloves should therefore be worn when replacing crankcase oil.

### 4.5.5 Effect of aldehydes

Aldehydes are irritants and their toxicity increases with lower molecular weight. This effect is reinforced by the presence of double bonds. The substances resulting from automotive pollution are mainly formaldehyde (HCHO), acetaldehyde ($CH_3CHO$), and acrolein ($CH_2{=}CHCHO$).

Formaldehyde, which irritates the ocular mucous membranes in low concentrations, irritates the throat and bronchial tubes as the concentration rises. Although its toxicity is much lower than that of formaldehyde, acetaldehyde also causes eye and skin irritation and increases heart activity. In the longer term, it lowers the count of leucocytes and erythrocytes [52].

Acrolein is the most toxic of all. Its toxicity threshold is lower than the olfactory threshold. It exerts cytotoxic action on the alveolar macrophages [23] and irritates the eyes and nasal mucous membranes at concentrations of 0.5 ppm. In an occupational atmosphere this exposure must not exceed 5 minutes.

The maximum permissible contents for continuous exposure in occupational surroundings are:

- 2 ppm for HCHO
- 100 ppm for $CH_3CHO$
- 0.1 ppm for $CH_2{=}CHCHO$.

Formaldehyde is also reproached for genotoxic and carcinogenic properties [32]. Mutagenesis has been proved on bacteria but not confirmed on mammals. By contrast, formaldehyde could be an initiator or promoter of carcinogenesis and has proved to be carcinogenic in rats (naso-pharynx cancer).

### 4.5.6 Effect of alcohols

In high concentrations, all alcohols exert narcotic action on the nervous system [87].

Among the alcohols considered as components of motor fuels and liable to reach the atmosphere in the form of exhaust vapors or by evaporation, methanol raises by far the most concern. Methanol causes serious intoxication by respiration or ingestion. Its enzymatic oxidation in the liver converts it to highly toxic formic acid.

Symptoms of intoxication are headaches, dizziness, cyanosis, nausea, impaired vision, apathy, and finally coma [68].

The fact that the ingestion of ethyl alcohol is recommended in a case of poisoning by methanol, due to the competition of the enzymatic oxidations to acetic and formic acids in the liver, reveals a sharp difference in toxicity between methanol and ethanol. In Brazil, it is also estimated that the toxicity of ethanol motor fuel is much lower than that of conventional gasoline [71].

### 4.5.7 Effect of sulfur compounds

Sulfur dioxide ($SO_2$) is a moderate irritant, strongly hydrophilic and hence easily dissolved in the nasal mucous membranes, with little risk of affecting the lungs [93]. In the tissues, it is transformed into bisulfite and after enzymatic oxidation, it is eliminated by the kidneys in sulfate form. However, it acts on the defense mechanisms and can thus contribute to the effects caused by other pollutants ($NO_2$, PAH, metals). During peak episodes of industrial pollution, it can therefore act on high-risk individuals. After oxidation to $H_2SO_4$, $SO_2$ can also form particles of ammonium sulfate that penetrate into the lung.

Apart from these pollution peaks, the environmental concentrations, in which traffic plays a minor role, can be considered to have little direct effect on public health [61].

### 4.5.8 Effect of diesel particulates

The effects attributable to PAH, which 'impregnate' the carbonaceous particles and soot emitted by combustion systems and diesel engines, have been mentioned earlier.

Added to these specific effects is the general effect of particles, which is to mechanically overload the lungs with dust of all types. This can impair the purification mechanisms of the pulmonary 'ducts' and thus facilitate the carcinogenic action of other compounds [13]. An effect may be observed on rats, when the particle concentration in air exceeds 8 $mg/m^3$.

### 4.5.9 Mineral particles

In addition to the organic particles that have already been discussed and which originate in combustion, airborne dust contains mineral particles. Some inorganic compounds such as asbestos fibers, particularly the chrysotile structure, cause the formation of tumors in the pleura after very long latency periods (about 40 years), which is probably synergistic with other carcinogens [92] such as tobacco [37]. These effects, due more to occupational conditions than to the environment, have been confirmed on rodents by interpleural injections of chrysotile.

#### 4.5.9.1 Metallic compounds and the case of lead

The question of the health effects of airborne pollution by lead, used as an anti-knock additive in motor fuels, was the subject of considerable debate [3, 36, 44, 56 and 70] and the subject of several publications a few years ago. The fears aroused by automotive-generated airborne lead are based on the extrapolation to the environment of the observations made in occupational surroundings [26] (Saturnism) and on young children.

The controversy is essentially due to the fact that a hazardous threshold for blood lead poisoning is still poorly identified. It appears to vary between 200 and 250 μg/liter in a child. The long-term effects of prolonged exposure to contents considered harmless in occupational surroundings concern the psychic development of the child. Lead happens to be one of the rare metals to have absolutely no biological utility as a trace element.

Lead enters the body from breathing in fine particles, essentially automotive generated (more than 51% [10]), that reach the alveoli. Lead also enters by the digestive tract (beverages contaminated by lead pipes, foods in contact with metallic packings, etc.). Automotive exhausts could also be involved in food lead-poisoning due to the redeposition of lead fines on crops.

Lead from automotive traffic occurs mainly in the form of fine inorganic particles (oxides, sulfates, and halogenides), and in a very small proportion in organic form, as it is added to the gasoline ($<1\%$) [49].

Lead tetra-alkyls, which are fuel additives, are lipophilic and hence easily absorbed by the skin [56]. They are also rapidly absorbed in the pulmonary alveoli and despite partial exhalation, 30 to 40% is retained in the blood stream. It is dealkylated in the liver to trialkyl compounds, whose toxicity is connected with the disturbance of ion exchange mechanisms in the brain [56]. Lead also tends to inhibit enzymatic biosynthesis that forms blood hemoglobin [6]. However, this demands a minimum level of lead poisoning [87].

Inorganic lead compounds also act on the nervous system, retarding psychic development in children exposed to lead. It is estimated that 94% of the lead ingested is retained in the bones (average residence time 30 years), with the rest divided among the brain, the muscles, the liver, the kidneys (2%), and the blood (4%) [87].

The decision to progressively eliminate lead in motor fuels should reduce the average lead poisoning of adults by 20 to 30% [26], but this will not achieve a significant improvement in health. However, for some sensitive subjects, especially children, this reduction could be decisive.

#### 4.5.9.2 Other metals: zinc, cadmium, nickel, manganese, precious metals

Automotive traffic emits these metals in infinitesimal amounts by comparison with present lead emissions.

Zinc is generally ignored as a toxic element in the concentrations routinely found in the air, and it could even inhibit the toxic effect of metals like cadmium and copper [55]. Cadmium itself is a very toxic element [99], but fortunately virtually absent from automotive emissions. Copper is not recognized as a toxic element [29].

Manganese, as an element or an inorganic derivative, is one of the least toxic products to mammals and birds [77]. In high doses, as in manganese mines, it can cause pneumonia and impairment of the central nervous system. Its derivative MMT (Section 11.1.5) is highly toxic, but concerns only a limited population exposed to occupational hazards [65].

Nickel is considered to be a carcinogen, playing the role of initiator and promoter, causing cancer of the sinus, the nasal fossae, and the bronchial tubes in highly-exposed subjects. The relationship of lung cancer with nickel has not been demonstrated [94]. Other problems observed chiefly concern skin allergies and the teratogenic effect of nickel carbonyl.

Chromium displays certain analogies with nickel. It acts on the liver and the kidneys and it is also a carcinogen [29].

The precious metals used in automotive catalysts (Pt, Pd and Rh) are generally not considered toxic in the metal state, and the risk of methylation by microorganisms is infinitesimal, according to the National Academy of Sciences [11]. Only their salts, of which certain chlorinated complexes can cause allergies [19], display physiological action [83] and have been employed in pharmacology [40 and 80].

## 4.6 Conclusion

In conclusion, the question can be asked whether the current transformations of the environment, particularly the changes in the air we breathe caused specifically by the spread of the automobile, represent a menace to human health.

The progress of medicine, which has been spectacular if one considers the huge increase in life expectancy over the past century, has revealed diseases of 'civilization'. Their previous existence was virtually obscured by the mortality of infectious diseases, either microbial or viral, which have been virtually eliminated today.

The contribution of automotive pollution to overall air pollution cannot be ignored, nor can its potentially harmful consequences on high-risk people (asthmatics, the elderly, young children, pregnant women). It is important to remember that pollution acts synergistically with other causes of death [42] like smoking, alcoholism, and obesity. These are all factors that tend to reduce a person's capacity to react to the aggressions of airborne pollution. Measures to reduce these causes of mortality must therefore be taken simultaneously.

Measures to reduce the individual emissions of individual vehicles are unfortunately liable to do no more than stabilize the total amount of pollutants emitted. Moreover, the addition of aromatics to motor fuels to offset the elimination of lead is liable to raise other health problems. The reduction of emissions is certain to be 'overcompensated' for by the growth of the world's population and the developing countries' access to the 'automobile civilization.'

In any case, it must not be forgotten that Nature emits products that are dangerous to human health, especially carcinogenic products. Fortunately, these products are only slightly active most of the time [105]. Furthermore, although unrelated to atmospheric pollution, highway accidents still represent the principal effect of automotive traffic on human health.

## REFERENCES

[1] Anon., (1978), "Can air pollutants cause chronic lung diseases?", *E.S.&T.*, **12,** 1356-1359.

[2] B.N. Ames, (1979), "Identifying environmental chemicals causing mutations and cancer", *Science*, **204,** 587-593.

[3] M. Behaghel, (1984), "Le plomb atmosphérique, point de vue de l'industrie automobile", *Poll. Atmosph.* (July/September), 203-205.

[4] P.M. Berglund and G. Petersson, (1990), "Hazardous petrol hydrocarbons from refuelling with and without vapour recovery", *Sci. Tot. Environm.*, **91,** 49-57.

[5] J. Bignon, (1986), "Cibles cellulaires et réponses pathologiques aux aérosols inhalés", *Poll. Atmosph.*, 132-136.

[6] C. Boudène, (1980), "Récentes acquisitions sur la toxicité du plomb", *Poll. Atmosph.* (85), 62-70.

[7] E.A. Bresnitz and K.M. Rest, (1988), "Epidemiologic studies of effects of oxidant exposure on human populations", in: *Air pollution, the automobile and public health*, A.Y. Watson, Nat. Acad. Press, Washington, pp. 389-413.

[8] P.E. Bright, (1985), "Health aspects of petroleum fuels", General principles, *CONCAWE Report* 2/85, 20 p.

[9] P.A. Bromberg, (1988), "Asthma and automotive emissions", in: *Air pollution, the automobile and public health*, A.Y. Watson, Nat. Acad. Press, Washington, pp. 465-498.

[10] E. Caplun et al., (1984), "Le plomb dans l'essence", *La Recherche*, **15,** 270-280.

[11] P.M. Carey, (1988), *Air toxic emissions from motor vehicles, EPA/AA/TSS/PA-86-5 Report* (PB88-115001), 108 p.

[12] M. Chevrier et al., (1983), *CCMC's health effects research program, 6e Congrès Mondial pour la Qualité de l'Air*, Paris, 16/20 May, pp. 137-144.

[13] M. Chevrier, (1987), *Toxicité comparée des gaz d'échappement Diesel et essence, SIA Conference, "Moteurs Diesel pour véhicules automobiles et utilitaires"*, Lyon, 13/14 May, pp. 36-42.

[14] M. Chiron, (1990), “Les carburants automobiles resteront-ils le dernier repaire du benzène?”, *Recherche transports sécurité*, **25,** 49-54.

[15] D.R. Choudhury, (1982), “Characterization of polycyclic ketone and quinone particulates by gas chromatography/mass spectrometry”, *E.S.&T.*, **16,** 102-106.

[16] I. Chouroulinkoff and N. Bogetto, (1987), “Intérêt des études in vitro pour la caractérisation biologique des émissions Diesel”, *Poll. Atmosph.*, Special Issue, November, pp. 124-134.

[17] J. Chretien, (1985), “Toxicologie pulmonaire du tabac, Rappel de quelques mécanismes physiopathologiques”, *Bull. Ordre* No. 287, October, pp. 947-952.

[18] T.B. Clarkson, (1988), “Evaluation of automotive emissions as risk factors for the development of atherosclerosis and coronary heart disease”, in: *Air pollution, the automobile and public health*, A.Y. Watson, Nat. Acad. Press, Washington, pp. 605-629.

[19] M.J. Cleare, (1977), “Immunological studies on platinum complexes and their possible relevance to autocatalysts”, *SAE Paper* No. 770061, 12 p.

[20] D.T. Coker et al., (1987), “A survey of exposures to gasoline vapour”, *CONCAWE Report* 4/87, 39 p.

[21] A.V. Colucci, (1982), “Comparison of the dose/effect relationship between $NO_2$ and other pollutants”, in: *Air pollution by nitrogen oxides*, T. Schneider and L. Grant, Elsevier Science Publications, Amsterdam, pp. 427-440.

[22] Y.A. Courtois et al., (1987), “Étude des effets mutagènes induits lors de l’exposition directe de systèmes biologiques aux émissions automobiles”, *Poll. Atmosph.*, Special Issue, November, pp. 143-154.

[23] Y.A. Courtois, et al., (1988), “Exposition des citadins à la pollution atmosphérique en région parisienne, Intérêt des bio-essais toxicologiques”, *Poll. Atmosph.* (120), 411-418.

[24] Y.A. Courtois, et al., (1990), “Effets biologiques des effluents Diesel, Données expérimentales”, *Paper* No. 90052, SIA Int. Conf., Lyon, 13/14 June, pp. 101-108.

[25] Dab and Abenhaim, (1987), “Intérêts et limites des méthodes épidémiologiques pour l’étude des effets de la pollution atmosphérique chez l’homme”, *Poll. Atmosph.* (October/December), 330-335.

[26] S. Dally and P.E. Fournier, (1984), “Le plomb atmosphérique, Aspects médicaux”, *Poll. Atmosph.* (July/September), 195-198.

[27] J.P. Derrien, (1988), *Toxicité des carburants moteurs (avant combustion) et des lubrifiants neufs et usés, Précautions d’emploi, SIA Int. Conf., “Le Moteur à Allumage Commandé de la Prochaine Décennie”*, Strasbourg, 18/19 May, 7 p.

[28] R. Doll, (1978), “Atmospheric pollution and lung cancer”, *Environ. Health Perspectives*, **22,** 23-31.

[29] E. Di Ferrante, (1978), *Trace metals, Exposure and health effects*, Pergamon Press, Oxford, 262 p.

[30] A.R. Eyres, (1987), “Health aspects of toluene and xylene exposures associated with motor gasoline”, *CONCAWE Report* 7/87, 10 p.

[31] Fat, (1980), “Tierexperimentelle und epidemiologischen Untersuchungen zur biologischen Wirkung von Abgasen aus Verbrennungsmotoren (Otto und Diesel)”, *Schriftenreihe* No. 14, 194 p.

[32] B. Festy, (1984), “Le formaldehyde, un modèle de contaminant environnemental à la nocivité discutée”, *Poll. Atmosph.*, pp. 176-181.

[33] B. Festy, (1986), “Nocivité des oxydants photochimiques”, *Poll. Atmosph.* (April/June), 139-141.

[34] B. Festy and I. Chouroulinkov, (1988), *Études biologiques des émissions de moteur Diesel, Données bibliographiques et étude expérimentale française, 5e Symposium sur la Recherche en Matière de Pollution Atmosphérique*, Strasbourg, 22/25 March, 34 p.

[35] B. Festy, (1988), *La pollution atmosphérique d'origine automobile, Quelques données concernant ses effets potentiels sur la santé, SIA Int. Conf., “Le Moteur à Allumage Commandé de la Prochaine Décennie”*, Strasbourg, 18/19 May, 4 p.

[36] R. Fiat, (1984), *Commentaires sur la Note IRT No. 29*, 11 July, 14 p.

[37] P. Freour and J.F. Tessier, (1988), “Est-il possible de faire la part du tabagisme dans l'action de la pollution aérienne sur l'appareil respiratoire?”, *Poll. Atmosph.* (120), 419-427.

[38] M. Gervois et al., (1988), “Difficultés et enseignements des enquêtes épidémiologiques actuelles sur l'influence de la pollution atmosphérique urbaine en pathologie respiratoire aiguë”, *Poll. Atmosph.* (120), 395-399.

[39] J.R. Glowa and M.E. Natale, (1982), “Behavioral toxicity of volatile fuel components”, in: *The toxicology of petroleum hydrocarbons*, H.N. McFarland et al., API, Washington, pp. 354-357.

[40] Gmelins, (1939), *Handbuch der anorganische Chemie*, Platin, Teil A Lf 2, pp. 275-276.

[41] I.F. Goldstein and E.M. Dulberg, (1981), “Air pollution and asthma, Search for a relationship”, *J. APCA*, **31,** 370-377.

[42] M. Gough, (1989), “Estimating cancer mortality”, *E.S.&T.*, **23,** 925-930.

[43] T.E. Graedel, (1988), “Ambient levels of anthropogenic emissions and their atmospheric transformation products”, in: *Air pollution, the automobile and public health*, A.Y. Watson, Nat. Acad. Press, Washington, pp. 133-160.

[44] P. Grandjean, (1983), *Health aspects of petrol lead additives, Bureau Européen des Unions de Consommateurs*, Bruxelles, 10/11 May, 12 p.

[45] G. Grimmer et al., (1982), “Untersuchungen über die carcinogene Wirkung von gebrauchtem Motorenschmieröl aus Kraftfahrzeugen”, *Erdöl und Kohle*, **35**, 466-472.

[46] G. Grimmer, et al., (1987), “Contribution of polycyclic aromatic hydrocarbons and nitro derivatives to the carcinogenic impact of Diesel engine exhaust condensate evaluated by implantation into the lungs of rats”, *Cancer Lett.*, **37,** 173-180.

[47] R.G. Harvey, (1985), “Polycyclic hydrocarbons and carcinogenesis”, *ACS Symp. Series* No. 283, Washington, 406 p.

[48] S.S. Hecht, (1988), “Potential carcinogenic effects of polynuclear aromatic hydrocarbons and nitroaromatics in mobile source emissions”, in: *Air pollution, the automobile and public health*, A.Y. Watson, Nat. Acad. Press, Washington, pp. 555-578.

[49] B. Henderson-Sellers, (1984), *Pollution of our Atmosphere*, Bristol, Adam Hilger Limited, 210 p.

[50] H. Hermann, (1980), “Evaluation of benzene toxicity in man and animals”, *DGMK Research Report* 174-6, June, 209 p.

[51] M. Herman, (1978), "Le cancer et l'environnement", *Inst. Franç. du Pérole Report* No. 26051, 58 p.

[52] O. Hirao and R.K. Pefley, (1988), *Present and future automotive fuels*, J. Wiley and Son, New York, 570 p.

[53] N. Ishinishi et al., (1986), *Carcinogenic and mutagenic effects of Diesel engine exhaust*, Elsevier Science Publications, New York, 539 p.

[54] J. Jacob et al., (1984), "Polycyclic aromatic compounds of environmental and occupational importance, Their occurrence, toxicity and the development of high purity certified reference materials, Part 1", *Fresenius Z. für Anal. Chemie*, **317,** 101-114.

[55] R. Joumard et al., (1982), "Effets des polluants atmosphériques sur la santé", *INRETS Report* No. 23, 114 p.

[56] R. Joumard et al., (1983), "Le dossier du plomb, Additif des carburants automobiles", *IRT Note* No. 29, 68 p.

[57] W. Karcher et al., (1985), *Spectral atlas of polycyclic aromatic compounds including data on occurrence and biological activity*, Reidel Pub., Dordrecht, 818 p.

[58] D.G. Kaufman, (1988), "Assessment of carcinogenicity, Generic issues and their application to Diesel exhaust", in: *Air pollution, the automobile and public health*, A.Y. Watson, Nat. Acad. Press, Washington, pp. 519-553.

[59] J.N. Kirkpatrick, (1987), "Occult carbon monoxide poisoning", *West. J. Med.*, **146**, 52-56.

[60] H. Klingenberg and H. Winneke, *Studies on health effects of automotive emissions, How dangerous are Diesel emissions?, 3rd Int. Symp., "Highway Pollution"*, München, 18/22 September, 11 p.

[61] F. Krainik, (1986), "Les effets sur la santé de la pollution aux oxydes de soufre", *Poll. Atmosph.* (April/June), 137-138.

[62] J.A. Last, (1988), "Biochemical and cellular interrelationships in the development of ozone induced pulmonary fibrosis", in: *Air pollution, the automobile and public health*, A.Y. Watson, Nat. Acad. Press, Washington, pp. 415-440.

[63] M. Lippmann, (1988), "Health significance of pulmonary function responses to airborne irritants", *J. APCA*, **38,** 881-887.

[64] B. Lopez, (1987), "État des connaissances actuelles sur la toxicité des émissions Diesel", *UTAC Note* No. 77.16, 23 March, 26 p.

[65] D.R. Lynam et al., (1989), *Environmental assessment of MMT fuel additive, 3rd Int. Symp., "Highway Pollution"*, München, 18/22 September, 8 p.

[66] J. McCann et al., (1975), "Detection of carcinogens in the Salmonella/microsome test, Assay of 300 chemicals", *Proc. Nat. Acad. Sci.*, **72,** 5135-5139.

[67] H.N. McFarland, (1982), "Chronic gasoline toxicity", in: *The toxicology of petroleum hydrocarbons*, H.N. McFarland, et al., API, Washington, pp. 78-86.

[68] P.A. Machiele, (1987), "Flammability and toxicity trade-offs with methanol fuels", *SAE Paper* No. 872064, 13 p.

[69] R.O. McClellan, (1986), "Toxicological effects of emissions from Diesel engines", in: *Carcinogenic and mutagenic effects of Diesel engine exhaust*, N. Ishinishi, et al., Elsevier Science Publications, New York, pp. 3-8.

[70] R. Mansillon, (1984), "Le plomb atmosphérique, point de vue de l'industrie du pétrole", *Poll. Atmosph.* (July/September), 199-202.

[71] E. Massad, et al., (1986), "Toxicity of prolonged exposure to ethanol and gasoline autoengine exhaust gases", *Environ. Res.*, **40,** 479-486.

[72] L.W. Mayron and J.J. Winterhalter, (1976), "Carbon monoxide, A danger to the driver?", *J. APCA*, **26,** 1085-1088.

[73] M.A. Mehlman, (1983), *Carginogenicity and Toxicity of Benzene*, Princeton Sci. Publ., Princeton, 128 p.

[74] D.B. Menzel, (1982), "Non-respiratory functions of the lung, Pharmacological effects", in: *Air pollution by nitrogen oxides*, T. Schneider and L. Grant, Elsevier Science Publications, Amsterdam, pp. 417-426.

[75] V. Mohsenin, (1988), "Airway responses to 2.0 ppm nitrogen dioxide in normal subjects", *Arch. Environ. Health*, **43,** 242-246.

[76] B. Molinier-Vanrel, et al., (1991), *Influence des conditions de fonctionnement d'un moteur Diesel sur les effets mutagènes de ses effluents, Int. Symp., "Transports et Pollution de l'Air"*, Avignon, 10/13 September, 10 p.

[77] W. Moore et al., (1975), "Toxicologic evaluations of fuel additive, methylcyclopentadienyl manganese tricarbonyl (MMT)", *SAE Paper* No. 750927, 8 p.

[78] M.G. Mustafa, et al., (1979), "Effects of nitrogen dioxide on lung metabolism", in: *Nitrogenous air pollutants, Chemical and biological implications*, D. Grosjean, Ann Arbor Science, Ann Arbor, pp. 165-178.

[79] M.G. Nishioka et al., (1988), "Detection of hydroxylated nitro aromatic and hydroxylated nitro polycyclic aromatic compounds in an ambient air particulate extract using bioassay directed fractionation", *E.S.&T.*, **22,** 908-915.

[80] P. Pascal, (1956), *Traité de Chimie Minérale*, Vol. XIX.

[81] J.E. Pennington, (1988, "Effects of automotive emissions on susceptibility to respiratory infections", in: *Air pollution, the automobile and public health*, A.Y. Watson, Nat. Acad. Press, Washington, pp. 499-518.

[82] W.E. Pepelko and W.B. Peirano, (1983), "Health effects of exposure to Diesel engine emissions", *J. Am. Coll. Toxicology*, **2,** 253-306.

[83] E.R. Plunkett, (1976), *Handbook of Industrial Toxicology*, Chemical Publ. Co., New York.

[84] G.T. Pryor et al., (1982), "Transient cognitive deficits and high frequency hearing loss in weanling rats exposed to toluene", in: *The toxicology of petroleum hydrocarbons*, H.N. McFarland et al., API, Washington, pp. 305-313.

[85] T. Ramdahl, (1983), "Polycyclic aromatic ketones in environmental samples", *E.S&T.*, **17,** 666-670.

[86] H.A. Risch et al., (1988), "Occupational factors and the incidence of cancer of the bladder in Canada", *Br. J. Ind. Med.*, **45,** 361-367.

[87] A. Roussel et al., (1983), "Impact médical des pollutions d'origine automobile", *Poll. Atmosph.*, Supplement 99 (July/September), 1-30.

[88] R.B. Schlesinger, (1988), "Biological disposition of airborne particles, Basic principles and application to vehicular emissions", in: *Air pollution, the automobile and public health*, A.Y. Watson, Nat. Acad. Press, Washington, pp. 239-298.

[89] R. Schoental, (1964), "Carcinogenesis by polycyclic aromatic hydrocarbons and by certain other carcinogens", in: *Polycyclic hydrocarbons*, E. Clar, Academic Press, London, pp. 134-160.

[90] C.M. Shy et al., (1978), *Health effects of air pollution*, American Lung Association, 48 p.

[91] J.D. Smith, (1987), "Health aspects of lubricants", *CONCAWE Report* 5/87, 43 p.

[92] H.E. Stokinger and D.L. Coffin, (1968), "Biologic effects of air pollution", in: *Air pollution*, A.C. Stern, Academic Press, New York, pp. 446-546.

[93] M.J. Suess et al., (1985), *Ambient air pollutants from industrial sources, A Reference Handbook*, Elsevier Science Publications, Amsterdam, 843 p.

[94] F.W. Sunderman, (1984), *Nickel et environnement humain*, INSERM, Paris, 518 p.

[95] B.E. Tilton, (1989), "Health effects of tropospheric ozone", *E.S.&T.*, **23,** 257-263.

[96] R. Touraine, (1986), "La place de la pollution atmosphérique urbaine dans la bronchite chronique et l'asthme", *Poll. Atmosph.*, pp. 144-146.

[97] B. Vanrel, (1989), *Caractérisations biologique et physico-chimique des gaz d'échappement Diesel, Étude des extraits particulaires et mise au point d'un protocole d'exposition directe d'un système bactérien*, Doctoral Dissertation, Université René Descartes (Paris V), Paris, 5 June, 227 p.

[98] T. Veninga et al., (1982), "Comparison of biological effects of $NO_2$, $O_3$ and combinations of both oxidants", in: *Air pollution by nitrogen oxides*, T. Schneider and L. Grant, Elsevier Science Publications, Amsterdam, pp. 441-445.

[99] A. Viala and F. Gouezo, (1988), "Action, sur la santé de l'Homme, des métaux lourds (Pb, Cd, V, Hg) en suspension aérienne aux faibles concentrations", *Poll. Atmosph.* (120), 389-394.

[100] C. Voisin, (1980), "Approche in vitro de l'action des polluants gazeux d'origine automobile sur la défense phagocytaire de l'appareil respiratoire", *Poll. Atmosph.* (85), 44-49.

[101] C. Voisin et al., (1987), "Effets in vitro sur les macrophages alvéolaires", *Poll. Atmosph.*, Special Issue, November, pp. 135-142.

[102] C. Voisin, (1988), "Les effets de la pollution atmosphérique sur la santé respiratoire, Enjeux et modalités d'approche", *Poll. Atmosph.* (120), 364-365.

[103] H. Wagner, (1984), "Probleme beider hygienische Bewertung von Luftschadstoffen, Wirkung einiger Primär- (CO, NO) und Sekundärprodukte ($NO_2$, $O_3$) aus Kfz-Emissionen", *Staub*, **44,** 390-395.

[104] A.Y. Watson et al., (1988), *Air Pollution, The automobile and public health*, Nat.Acad. Press, Washington, 704 p.

[105] E.K. Weisburger, (1979), "Natural carcinogenic products", *Environ. Sci. Techn.*, **13,** 278-281.

[106] E.L. Wynder et al., (1985), "A case control of Diesel exhaust exposure and bladder cancer", *Environ. Res.*, **37,** 475-489.

[107) D. Zmirou, (1987), "Approches épidémiologiques appliquées à la pollution de l'air par les transports", *Poll. Atmosph.*, Special Issue, November, pp. 155-162.

# Air pollution and the environment

# 5

*In addition to its effects on human health, air pollution affects the physiology of plants and the integrity of the minerals used in man-made structures.*

*Combined with natural causes (for example, volcanic eruptions and biomass emissions), air pollution caused by humans is blamed for the acidification of lakes, for 'acid rain' in North America and Scandinavia, and for the 'death of the forests' in Germany and Central Europe.*

*Before examining the involvement of automotive emissions in these situations, this chapter describes the symptoms and possible causes of pollution damage.*

## 5.1 Acid rain

The acidic gases $SO_2$, $NO_x$, and HCl are emitted by sources of airborne pollution and are converted by oxidation in the atmosphere to secondary pollutants such as sulfuric and nitric acids. When solubilized in rainfall, snow, fog, and dew, these acids precipitate and are deposited on vegetation, soils, and the materials of monuments and other structures.

Due to the presence of atmospheric $CO_2$ and the chemical equilibrium between $CO_2$ and bicarbonate, 'pure' rain is not a neutral aqueous solution in the chemical sense of the term, but is an electrolyte with a pH of 5.6 [10 and 32]. The pH records at several localities have been kept since 1850. In 1872, R.A. Smith introduced the concept of 'acid rain' in his book The beginnings of chemical climatology, which was based on the observations made by Frenchman J.I. Pierre around 1860 [10]. The disparity in the sampling conditions used over a time interval longer than one century nonetheless makes accurate comparisons difficult [12].

Systematic observation networks of the EACN type have revealed the acidification of rainfall in regions far from the industrial centers (such as Scandinavia and Canada), whereas the values observed in the neighborhood of industries barely increased [12]. Only 25% of the stations sampled showed a significant increase in acidity [22]. In Germany, lower acidity was observed at the urban stations rather than at the rural stations [10]. The same findings were reported in France on the EMEP and BAPMON networks, despite increased systematic acidification from west to east [17]. Other observations in Berlin reveal very slight reductions of pH, from 0.1 to 0.3 units over a 50-year period (1930 to 1980) [24].

The natural fluctuations of rain pH in different localities, which are not suspected of being affected by industrial emissions (Fig. 5.1), makes it difficult to identify the anthropogenic influences affecting the acidity of rainfall [10]. If the acidification of rain is not often flagrant, an increase is nevertheless systematically found in the sulfate and nitrate contents of the rain, with an increase in nitrates in comparison with sulfates, reflected by a rise in the N/S ratio [17, 21, and 22].

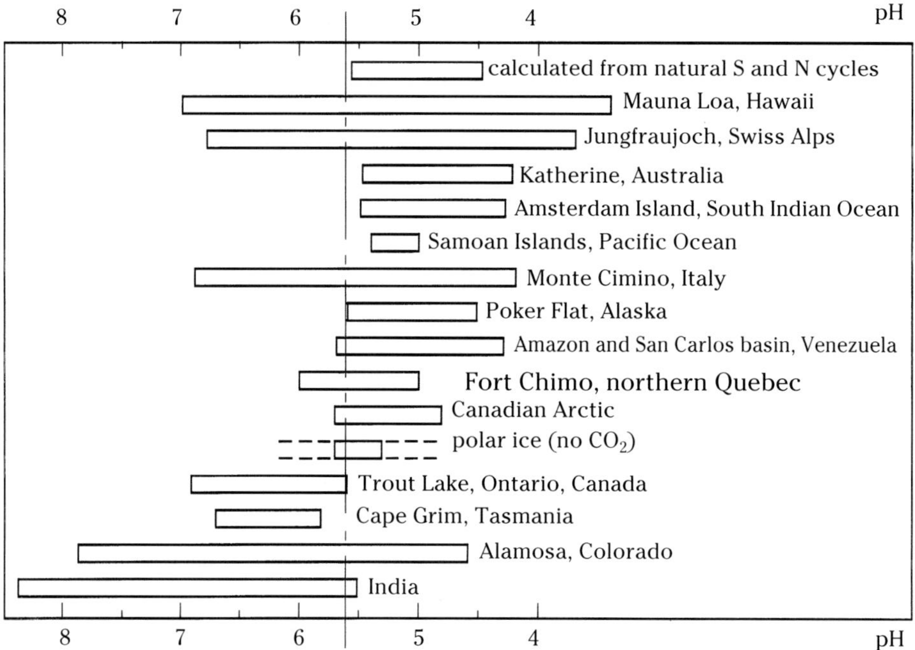


**Fig 5.1** pH of rain in different stations far from sources of industrial pollution [10]

## 5.2 Acidification of lakes and waterways

The acidification of rain appears to be a highly variable occurrence in time and in space. In countries whose granitic and siliceous soils of primary origin are relatively thin and exhibit mainly acidic reactions (Scandinavia, Canada, and Scotland), pH is found to drop in the waterways and lakes [1]. The areas concerned are often relatively far from pollution sources, which means that pollution is transported over very long distances.

The effects of the acidification of a lake, from pH 6.8 to pH 5.1 in successive steps spread over five years [15], are the following:

| Year | pH | Effects observed |
|---|---|---|
| **1976** | 6.8 | |
| **1977** | 6.1 | growing bacterial activity,<br>increase in invertebrates, predators of larvae of fish, insects and crustaceans,<br>increase in green algae,<br>decrease in brown algae. |
| **1978** | 5.8 | disappearance of a first type of crustacean,<br>reproduction accident in the minnow,<br>higher mortality of lake trout embryos. |
| **1979** | 5.6 | increased lake bottom vegetation,<br>development of algae carpet on the shore,<br>disappearance of fresh water shrimp, food of lake trout,<br>weakening of mechanical strength of crayfish shells,<br>severe decline in the minnow population,<br>decrease in the trout population. |
| **1980** | 5.4 | disappearance of a second type of crustacean,<br>parasites infesting crayfish,<br>decline of crayfish,<br>increase in vendace,<br>reproduction accidents in lake trout. |
| **1981** | 5.1 | reproduction accidents in sucker fish. |

The following is generally observed [14]:

- reduction or disappearance of trout and salmon
- reduction or disappearance of amphibians
- modification of phytoplankton and zooplankton
- growth of peat moss, prevalent in small lakes
- substitution of bacteria by fungus as the main decomposition agent

These observations were made in Norway, Sweden, Scotland, and North America (Ontario and Adirondacks).

Figure 5.2 shows the relationship observed between water acidity and the living conditions of aquatic fauna.

Acidification of water also leads to the dissolution of heavy metals, which normally remain insoluble at higher pH levels, causing mercury, cadmium, lead, and copper to pass into the food chain. These metals, introduced into drinking water, can have repercussions on human health. Aluminum and magnesium also affect the development of vegetation and trees.

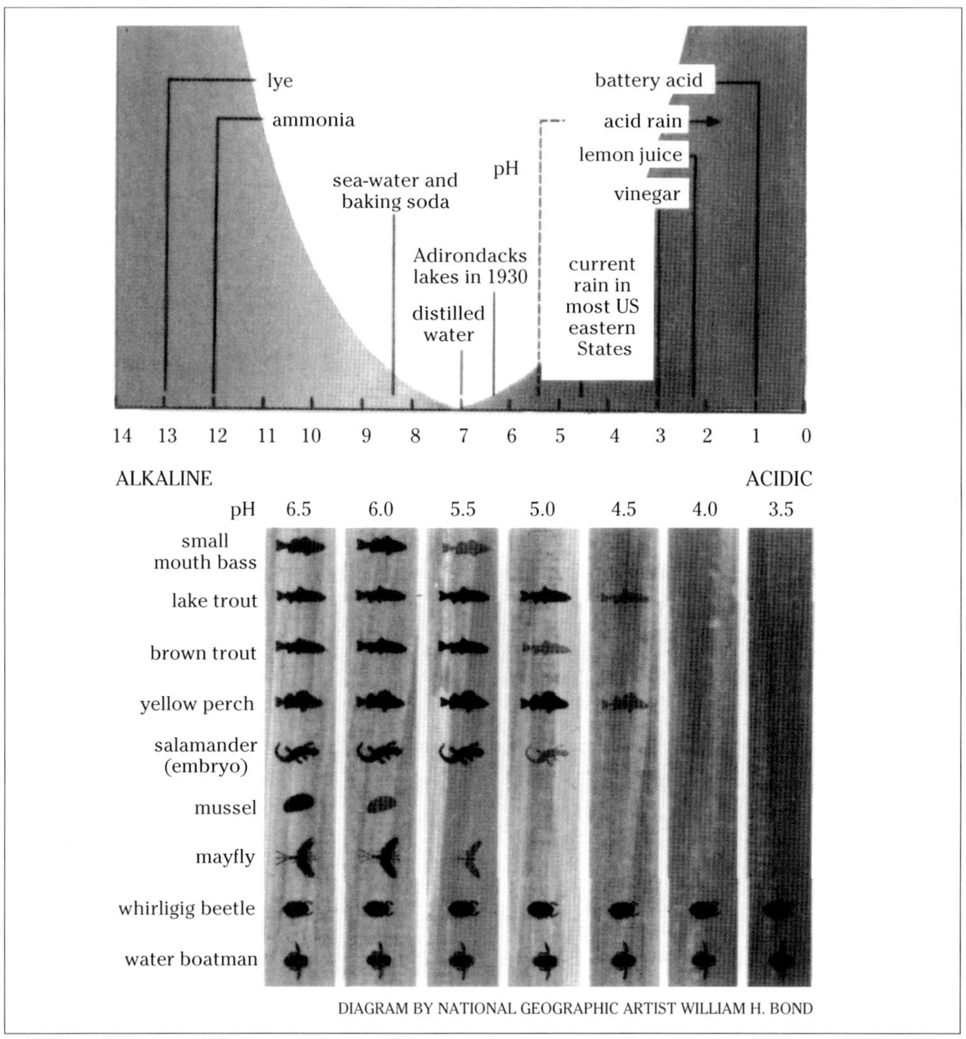


**Fig 5.2** Relationship between acidity and life of aquatic fauna [23]
After William H. Bond, National Geographic Society

## 5.3 The 'death' of the forests

The acidification of lakes and waterways highlighted the problem of long-distance transportation of pollutants. However, it was forest damage that sparked the awareness of the general public and the media about the problem of air pollution.

The damage caused to the forests by industrial pollution is not a new phenomenon. In the neighborhood of the chemical plants of La Maurienne in the Alps and Pierrefitte in the Pyrénées, the damage caused to the flora by hydrofluoric acid emissions generated by the treatment of aluminum ores was reported many years ago [19]. Similarly, in Bohemia, southern Poland and the ex-East Germany, where high sulfur lignites are burned in the industrial power plants, whole forests have disappeared (more than 500,000 hectares or 2.2 million acres in Czechoslovakia) [41].

More recently, tree damage has been found in forests very far from sources emitting both urban and industrial airborne pollutants. The trees growing in the cities are actually healthier than the forests of the mountain ranges of western and central Europe (Black Forest, Vosges, Harz, etc.). Transported pollutants have been identified as the cause of the acidification of the lakes.

### 5.3.1 Damage reported

A cry of alarm rang out in the mid-1970s when, in Baden-Württemberg and Bavaria [33], the damage to the fir forests was found to have accelerated. A subjective method of visually inspecting the damage was set up. The affected trees were subdivided into areas of observation with scaling factors applied to the damage observed [37]. This scale, which was extended to other conifers that were subsequently affected (spruce, Douglas fir, Norway pine) and also to deciduous species (beech), was copied and applied in the other countries with tree damage, such as Switzerland, Belgium, and France. Table 5.1 shows the scale of evaluation used in France in the DEFORPA programs [26].

**Table 5.1** Damage grading scale [11]

| State observed | Grade allocated |
|---|---|
| **treetop** | |
| healthy: deficit <10% | 1 |
| slightly damaged: deficit 10 to 25% | 2 |
| highly damaged: deficit 25 to 60% | 3 |
| dying: deficit 60 to 100% | 4 |
| dead, dry: deficit 100% | 5 |
| tree disappeared | 9 |
| **foliage color** | |
| normal color | 1 |
| abnormal color without quantification | 2 |
| abnormal color on 0 to 25% of foliage | 3 |
| abnormal color on 25 to 60% of foliage | 4 |
| abnormal color on 60 to 100% of foliage | 5 |
| **foliage size** | |
| normal size | 1 |
| abnormally small size | 2 |
| **trunk appearance** | |
| healthy trunk | 1 |
| trunk exhibiting cankers, rot, sweating, detached bark etc | 2 |

The following symptoms are observed [16 and 33]:

- The 'Christmas garland symptom', which appears as a lack of vigor of the second-order branches in spruce, reduced growth of crown shoots in fir, and the forming a 'stork's nest' crown, is usually a characteristic of senescent trees.
- Conifers drop their needles. Beech trees begin to drop leaves in June, develop fewer branches, and tend to be dry.
- There is pronounced discoloration of the needles of young spruce and of fir at any age. Only the needles of the last year remain green.
- A gradual yellowing of appearance and dropping of needles that spreads from the interior to the exterior of the crown and from the base of the tree towards the top.
- Increased photosensitivity is reflected by yellowing of the needles directly exposed to light.
- There is a deficiency of nutrients in the needles, especially magnesium, but also calcium and zinc.
- Pollutants in low concentrations are found in the needles, in areas far from pollution sources; for example, sulfur concentrations that are close to the nutrient deficiency levels for this element, as well as low concentrations of heavy metals were found.
- There is intensified growth of lichens in the middle altitude regions.

## 5.3.2 Evolution of the damage

Observations in the different Länder[1] of the former West Germany demonstrated a rapid acceleration of the death of the trees or, more precisely, of 'new damage to the forests'. Fig. 5.3 shows the very rapid decline of the health of the fir and spruce forests in the *Land* of Baden-Württemberg between 1980 and 1984. According to the criteria described above, at the end of 1984 more than 90% of the firs were diseased, 5% were dead, and 80% of the spruce were considered to be diseased [33]. Fortunately, this catastrophic situation subsequently improved, both in France and in Germany, where the degradation slowed down from 1985 onwards. The trend reversed in 1986 [8], and the vigor of the Vosges firs was found to be better than a century earlier [5].

## 5.3.3 Causes

Using the pollution hypothesis, Germany, in the early 1980s, placed an emphasis on research into the causes of the damage observed in the forests. Among other consequences, this research sharply accelerated the decision to rapidly reduce automotive emissions by requiring catalytic mufflers and unleaded fuels.

1. Each of the States of the German Federal Republic.

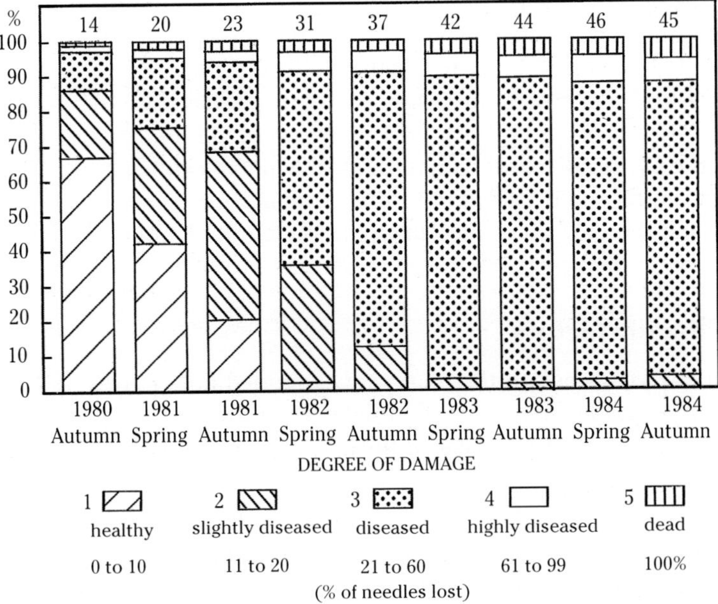


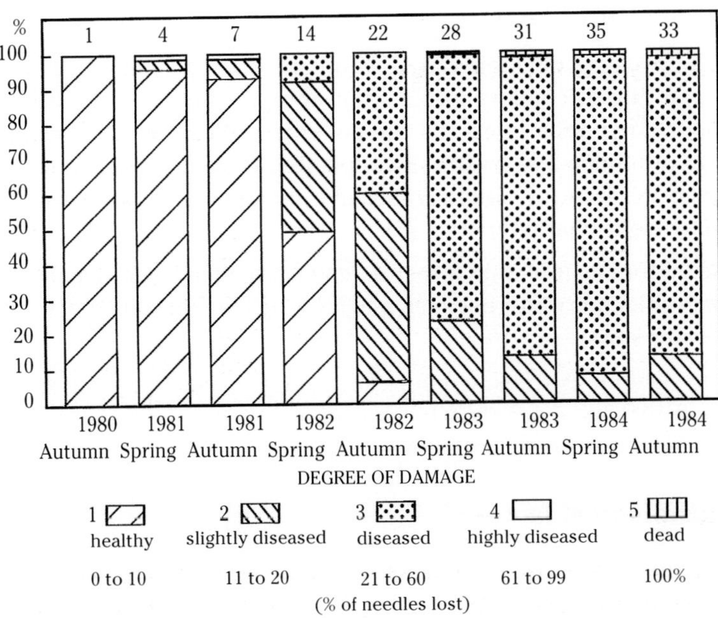


**Fig 5.3** State of firs (top) and spruce (bottom) between 1980 and 1984 in the *Land* of Baden-Württemberg [33]

Fluctuations in the growth rates of trees were observed in past centuries by the technique of dendroclimatology[2] , which was developed in Germany by Professor Bruno Huber of München in the years 1950/1960. The results of this technique, which identifies dry and wet years, are well correlated with the early and late vine harvesting dates in France [27]. By 1957, there were 200 publications in Germany dealing with the causes of forest damage. More than two centuries ago, descriptions of damage to the fir could be found in the German forestry archives [25]. In fact, without ignoring the part played by air pollution and its automotive component, it appears that forest damage can actually be ascribed to several factors.

#### 5.3.3.1 Climatic factors

In 1976, a few years before the alarm was sounded in the early 1980s, a severe drought took place. The analysis of the thickness of the growth rings of the Vosges firs, which were corrected for the age of the tree [6], revealed a relationship between the lack of water and the growth of the tree since 1890 , with a degree of hysteresis. Tree growth returned to normal in 1983, the year of the greatest anxiety [8].

In certain forest areas, like the Belgian Ardennes, periods of late frost also occurred in July [20]. These also had damaging effects on the forest, although the 'late frost' factor is not recognized as decisive in the Vosges [40].

#### 5.3.3.2 Silvicultural factors

The search for maximum yields from woodland stands inclined silviculturalists towards the planting of conifers in soils not always suited to their survival. One example of poor adaptation concerns the pedunculate oak, which was introduced into the center of France by foresters who planted it in the midst of native sessile oaks [4]. Unlike the latter, it failed to survive in soils with unfavorable physico-chemical and hydrous characteristics [8].

One of the factors aggravating forest damage is higher stand density [6], which sharpens competition for water between neighboring trees in soils that often have an unfavorable water supply.

Contrary to deciduous trees, conifers keep their leaves in winter and are more sensitive to acid mist and oxidants, which occur at a time when deciduous trees offer a minimum surface to airborne irritants.

#### 5.3.3.3 Pathological factors

The ecological modifications of trees in mid-growth can cause changes in the growth rates of the organisms associated with the vegetation, both for parasites and for microorganisms living in symbiosis.

This offered one explanation for the reddening of leaves by fungal attack [33].

2. Analysis of climates from the thickness of the annual growth rings of trees.

Acidification of the soil or water depletion can favor certain pathogenic species, such as Armillaria [28], a fungus that might have developed prior to the effects of the drought. These pathogenic species proliferate at the expense of the bacteria that are indispensable to the roots. Two such bacteria are rhizobium [29], which fixes the atmospheric nitrogen indispensable to the plants, and mycorhizal fungi, whose action is central to the supply of the roots with water and mineral salts.

The modifications made to the cuticle of the leaves and needles can also predispose plants to attack by predatory insects.

#### 5.3.3.4 Chemical factors

These factors involve airborne pollution that includes industrial $SO_2$ emissions, automotive $NO_x$ emissions, and ozone, which is a secondary pollutant derived from unburned hydrocarbons.

The acidity of rain, mist, and dew affects the cuticles of leaves and needles by altering their wettability and permeability. After prolonged contact (in which mist is more harmful than rain), the leaf structure is modified, opening the door to other attacks by microbes, fungi, and insects. However, it has been very difficult to demonstrate experimentally any increase in cuticular permeability [34]. A destruction of the foliage chloroplasts can also cause yellowing of the needles.

The acidic medium—nitric, sulfuric, or ozone— inhibits the opening and closing mechanism of the stoma of the foliage, which are responsible for thermal and water regulation. This acidic medium can cause unpredictable opening and closing of the stoma, giving rise to accelerated drying or penetration of pollutants at night, when the stoma are normally closed [9]. This also weakens frost resistance.

In low doses ($NO_2$ or $SO_2$ $<40$ ppb), these pollutants have a rather beneficial effect by their sulfur and nitrogen input to the vegetation, affording ammonium sulfate. Above this level the effects are negative. The pollutants also act synergistically. $NO_2$ and $SO_2$, which have no effect in isolation, exert a harmful effect when present together. Ozone also reinforces the action of these binary mixtures [9].

Gaseous pollutants also act on the enzymatic processes. Phytotoxic molecules, by inducing the synthesis of anti-oxidants, polyamines, etc., modify enzymatic activities, such as inhibiting the function of nitrite reductase, which reduces $NO_2$ to $NH_3$. These modifications also favor the development of fungi or attacks by parasitic insects. They also change the ratio between the foliate mass and the root mass at the expense of the latter, thus reducing the ability of the trees to find water. The roots remain close to the soil surface and are unable to reach the deeper water table in times of drought.

Rain acidity causes leaching of the elements calcium, potassium, and magnesium from the soil, which are necessary for plant metabolism (magnesium deficiencies cause yellowing of leaves). In an acidic soil, elements like manganese and aluminum, once in solution, can become toxic for root systems [7].

### 5.3.4 Possible degradation mechanisms

Given the many possible effects of different agents on vegetation, it is still difficult today to propose a definitive explanation of the mechanisms observed in the 'death of the forests'. Fig. 5.4 briefly summarizes the different processes liable to interact in causing the weakening and death of trees [26]. Undoubtedly past droughts, particularly in 1976, have played a role in the occurrences manifested in the 1980s [7]. The consequences of air pollution merely reinforced their effects. Acid snow and mist combined with ozone to inhibit the retro-action mechanisms of trees and thus facilitated attacks by predators (such as insects, fungi, and bacteria).

Despite the alarming information of the early 1980s and the prevailing pessimism about the future of the European forests, the situation has since taken a turn for the better. This may be the result of an enforcement of the pollution control measures concerning both industrial $SO_2$ emissions and the $NO_x$ emissions from industry and automotive traffic. These measures have combined with a favorable climatic change. The 'greenhouse effect', associated with the slow warming of the climate and increasing $CO_2$ content, favors photosynthesis and could perhaps be an explanation for the increased productivity of today's fir forests [8].

## 5.4 Effect of precipitation on materials

Buildings and their constituent materials have always suffered the ravages of time and of atmospheric conditions, which are linked to the physical state of the atmosphere and its composition.

The aging of buildings is an ever-present phenomenon. In general, local experience takes account of this in the selection of building materials appropriate to the local environment.

However, degradation has accelerated since the advent of the industrial age. Monuments like the Parthenon and other structures of marble and limestone materials are damaged at a startling rate, after having satisfactorily withstood the centuries. It is estimated that erosion and pollution remove from 0.06 to 0.08 mm per year from Saint Paul's cathedral in London [39]. Metal structures are increasingly unable to withstand atmospheric corrosion and reinforced concrete deteriorates rapidly.

### 5.4.1 Physical actions

Abrasion represents the simplest physical action and is normally due to silica particles transported by wind (the case of the Sphinx), but which can also be set in motion by traffic.

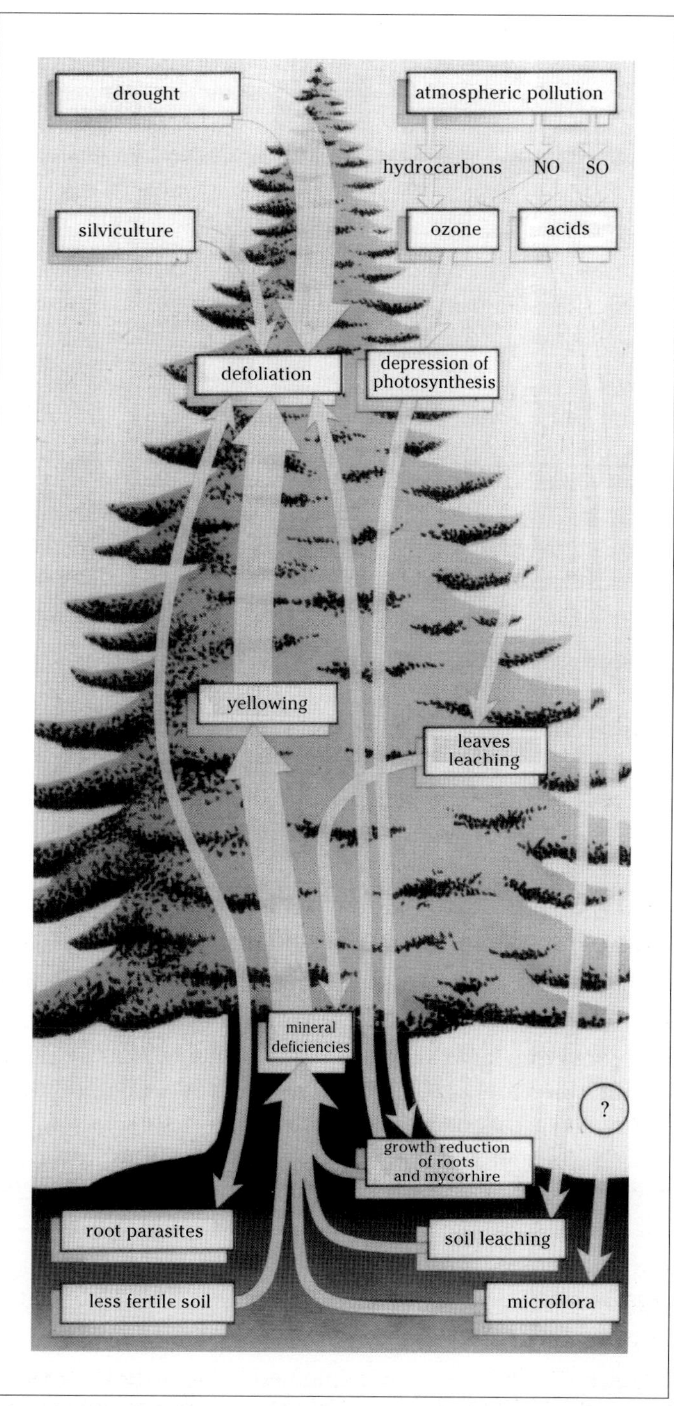


**Fig 5.4** Various actions affecting the life of trees [26]

Atmospheric water also plays an important role during periods of frost by applying mechanical expansion stresses to materials. This varies with the properties of the material (porosity, wettability): granites and metals are not porous, but certain soft limestones can have up to 45% porosity. The salts dissolved in the water cause similar damage when they crystallize as the water evaporates. Defects at the joints in masonry structures allow the penetration of water and begin the degradation process.

Dust is also a factor. Soiling of building façades results from airborne particles set in motion by traffic. The blackening of façades is felt to be an important matter and is ranked immediately after health problems in public opinion polls [38].

It was the burning of coal in the eighteenth century that initially soiled the monuments of the United Kingdom, Belgium, and northern France. Coal soot was subsequently supplanted by particulates from the burning of home-heating oil and diesel engine emissions. Today, diesel engines represent the primary sources of soiling particles in the large cities [31]. On average, the deposition of dust measured in Fribourg is 2 to 3 $g/m^2$ [38]. It depends on the inclination of the receiving surface, its roughness, and the properties of the fallout (greasy soot or dry particles). The oily and adhesive qualities of diesel particles increase their soiling power.

Thus, in London, it was estimated that diesel particles were three times more soiling than coal soot and seven times more soiling than emissions from gasoline vehicles [3].

Soiling also tends to retain the pollutants conveyed by rain, thus favoring chemical attack.

### 5.4.2 Chemical action

Although building stone also tends to corrode in dry climates (as at the Acropolis in Athens), the physical effects of water are intensified when it is acidified by the pollutants $NO_2$ and $SO_2$.

Limestone is converted into calcium sulfate (plaster) or nitrate (saltpetre). These compounds, which are more watersoluble than the initial calcium carbonate, migrate to the surface through dissolution and crystallization. Blending with silicates causes the formation of harder layers on the surface, which display poor adhesion with the underlying support. These crusty scales ultimately drop off (stone 'leprosy') [30].

In concrete, the dissolution of portlandite $Ca(OH)_2$ by acid rain causes the formation of blooms. Airborne $CO_2$ gradually converts the hydroxide to the carbonate, reducing the resistance of the concretes to acid attack.

Accelerated attack could also be explained by threshold effects of pollutant concentrations attacking the materials [14], but this has not been positively demonstrated.

## 5.5 Effect on atmospheric visibility

Another effect of air pollution on the environment is reduced visibility. It is generally agreed that it is now virtually impossible to see the Milky Way over large cities. This effect is in addition to the effects on the Earth's climate and the ongoing changes discussed in Chapter 2.

Visibility is directly proportional to the clarity of the atmosphere. Reduced visibility is detrimental to a large number of tourist landmarks [18].

Natural causes (volcanic eruptions, fog, sea spray, and sand storms) can reduce visibility, but unlike those of anthropogenic origin, their effects are not permanent.

Particulate-emitting industries (steel, cement, thermal power plants) increase the atmospheric load of particles that diffract light. Diesel traffic is also a major factor in the darkening skies. In California, it is estimated that if 20% of the vehicles were diesel this would cause a 20 to 25% reduction in visibility [3]. In the Netherlands it was reported that carbon particles reduced visibility by 4%, with sulfate and nitrate particles having the strongest effect [13].

## 5.6 Conclusion

The major environmental concerns are acid rain and the 'death of the forests'.

A combination of climatic effects, pathological factors, and forest management practices, combined with an increase in air pollution (partly of automotive origin) has increased the attack on plant life.

The media and political treatment given to these questions by 'ecology' movements led to the enactment of regulations that were initially conceived for different reasons: the image of Bohemian forests that were destroyed by other forces (the neighboring combustion of high-sulfur lignites) served as a model to represent 'what was going on' and it was used to raise people's concerns [35 and 36].

In retrospect, the decisions taken no longer correspond to the initial objectives. The destruction of the forests could continue despite the decrease in industrial and automotive pollution. New industrial processes are being set up to satisfy the new regulations and these in turn mark the advent of new industrial activities.

In any case, less toxic levels of pollution will benefit human health, if increasing traffic levels does not counteract this advantage.

## REFERENCES

[1] C.E. Asbury, et al., (1989), "Acidification of Adirondack lakes", *E.S&T.*, **23,** 362-365.

[2] H.Babich and G. Stotzky, (1972), "Ecologic ramifications of air pollution", *SAE Paper* No. 720630, 16 p.

[3] D.J. Ball, (1987), "Particulate carbon emissions and Diesel vehicles", IMechE Conf., "Vehicle Emissions and Their Impact on European Air Quality", London, 3/5 November, *Paper* No. C337/87, pp. 83-88.

[4] M. Becker and G. Lévy, (1983), "Le dépérissement du chêne, Une leçon d'écologie", *La Recherche*, **14,** 534-536.

[5] M. Becker, (1987), "Santé de la fôret, Le sapin témoigne", *La Recherche*, **18,** 1096-1098.

[6] M. Becker, (1988), *Tendances à long terme et crises de vitalité de la sapinière vosgienne, Rôle du climat, des déficits d'alimentation en eau et de la structure des peuplements*, Journées DEFORPA, Nancy, 24/26 February, pp. 2-50 to 2-65.

[7] M. Bonneau, (1988), *Impact sur le milieu naturel de la pollution atmosphérique, SIA Int. Conf., "Le Moteur à allumage commandé de la prochaine décennie"*, Strasbourg, 18/19 May, 6 p.

[8] M. Bonneau and G. Landmann, (1988), "De quoi la forêt est-elle malade?", *La Recherche*, **19,** 1543-1553.

[9] J. Bonté and P. Louguet, (1988), *Effets de la pollution de l'air sur les plantes herbacées des milieux naturels et cultivés, 5e Symp. sur la Recherche en Matière de Pollution Atmosphérique*, Strasbourg, 22/25 March, 12 p.

[10] C.J. Brandt, (1983), *Säurehaltige Niederschläge, Entstehung und Wirkungen auf terrestrische Ökosysteme, VDI Verlag "Reinhaltung der Luft"*, 277 p.

[11] M. Buffet, (1987), *Le réseau de surveillance sanitaire des forêts, Description, Problématique*, DEFORPA Programme, First Report, GREF, Nancy, pp. 11-16.

[12] R.J. Delmas, (1984), *Évolution temporelle de l'acidité des précipitations, Livre blanc sur les pluies acides*, Min. Environn., 20 June, pp. 161-170.

[13] H.S.M.A. Diederen et al., (1985), "Visibility reduction by air pollution in the Netherlands", *Atmosph. Environm.*, **19,** 377-383.

[14] Energy Resources Limited, (1983), *Acid Rain, A review of phenomenon in the EEC and Europe*, Graham Trotman, London, 159 p.

[15] Environment Canada, (1984), *The Acid Rain Story*, 15 p.

[16] J.P. Garrec, (1986), "De la forêt polluée à la forêt dépérissante", *Poll. Atmosph.*, pp. 142-143.

[17] C. Hennequin et al., (1984), *La surveillance des retombées atmosphériques humides en France, Livre blanc sur les pluies acides*, Min. Environn., 20 June, pp. 145-160.

[18] A.E. Hudson, (1980), "Air pollution and visibility", *J. APCA*, **30,** 117-146.

[19] M-J. Husset, (1974), *Épurer l'atmosphère, Science et Vie*, Special Issue "Environnement", pp. 78-91.

[20] R. Impens and M.E. Laitat, *Surveillance du dépérissement des forêts en Belgique, APPA Symp., "Pluies Acides et Dépérissements Forestiers en France et en Europe"*, Nancy, 7 December.

[21] D. Jost and S. Beilke, (1983), "Trend saurer Depositionen", in: *Saure Niederschläge, Ursachen und Wirkungen*, J. Löbel und W.R. Thiel, VDI Berichte, No. 500, pp. 135-139.

[22] A.S. Kallend et al., (1983), "Acidity of rain in Europe", *Atmosph. Environm.*, **17,** 127-137.

[23] A. La Bastille, (1981), "Acid rain, How great a menace?", *National Geographic*, **160,** 652-681.

[24] E. Lahmann and W. Fett, (1983), "Regenwasseruntersuchungen in Berlin, 1932 bis 1982", in: *Saure Niederschläge, Ursachen und Wirkungen*, J. Löbel und W.R. Thiel, VDI Berichte, No. 500, pp. 155-158.

[25] G. Landmann, (1988), *Évaluation de l'incidence des conditions écologiques sur le dépérissement et premiers résultats d'une approche symptômatologique*, Journées DEFORPA, Nancy, 24/26 February, pp. 2-07 to 2-48.

[26] I. Leclercq, DEFORPA, (1987), *A la recherche du mal des forêts*, Min. Environn., 40 p.

[27] E. Le Roy Ladurie, (1983), *Histoire du climat depuis l'an mil, champs*, Flammarion, Paris, 2 Vol., 541 p.

[28] F. Le Tacon, (1988), *Aspects microbiologiques du dépérissement de sapin pectine (Abies alba Mill.) et de l'épicéa commun (Picea excelsa Link) dans les Vosges*, Journées DEFORPA, Nancy, 24/26 February, pp. 5-03 to 5-36.

[29] R. Linthurst, (1983), "Effects of acid deposition on vegetation, An overview", in: *Saure Niederschläge, Ursachen und Wirkungen*, J. Löbel und W.R. Thiel, *VDI Berichte*, No. 500, pp. 175-185.

[30] M. Mamillan and A. Bouineau, (1984), *Effets des polluants de l'air sur l'altération des bâtiments, Livre blanc sur les pluies acides*, Min. Environn., 20 June, pp. 217-237.

[31] T.A. Mansfield, (1988), *The sources and rates of building soiling in the urban environment, Short course on Diesel particulates*, Leeds, April, 10 p.

[32] M. Martin, (1984), *L'acidité atmosphérique, Livre blanc sur les pluies acides*, Min. Environn., 20 June, pp. 103-117.

[33] B. Prinz and G.H. M. Krause, (1987), "Le dépérissement des forêts en République Fédérale d'Allemagne", *Poll. Atmosph.* (113), 45-53.

[34] O. Queiroz, (1988), *Recherches sur le métabolisme foliaire d'épicéas sains ou dépérissants en forêt et d'épicéas soumis à pollution contrôlée*, Journées DEFORPA, Nancy, 24/26 February, pp. 4-33 to 4-77.

[35] P. Roqueplo, (1988), "Expertise scientifique, Le cas des pluies acides", *La Recherche*, **19,** 1553-1556.

[36] P. Roquelpo, (1989), "Le statut social des pluies acides", in: *Man and his Ecosystem*, L.J. Brasser, Elsevier Science Publications, Amsterdam, Vol. 2, pp. 305-310.

[37] H. Schröter, (1983), "Mehrjährige Untersuchungen zum Tannensterben in Baden-Württemberg", in: *Saure Niederschläge, Ursachen und Wirkungen*, J. Löbel und W.R. Thiel, *VDI Berichte* No. 500, pp. 241-247.

[38] M.N. Terrat, (1985), "La salissure due au trafic automobile", Note bibliographique, *INRETS/CERNE Report NNP* 83, 27 p.

[39] S.T. TrudgilL et al., (1990), "Rates of stone loss at St Paul's cathedral, London", *Atmosph. Environm.*, **24B,** 361-363.

[40] C. Vignal, (1988), *Dépérissement forestier dans les Vosges, Étude des paramètres climatiques pertinents*, Journées DEFORPA, Nancy, 24/26 February, pp. 2-67 to 2-87.

[41] G. Wetstone and S. Foster, (1983), "Acid precipitation, What is it doing to our forests?", *Environment*, **25,** 10-12 and 38-40.

# Laws and regulation 6

## 6.1 Historical background

Automotive exhaust emissions are covered by regulations in most of the industrial countries. Through the years, the number of regulated pollutants has steadily increased, the statutory limits have become more severe, and the countries involved more numerous. The first requirements remained quite vague, such as the West German law of 3 February 1910 [39] stating that: *"vehicles must be safe and built so as to preclude any nuisance for the public, by smoke or odor"*. The first regulations in the United States, which were enacted in California in 1959, eliminated crankcase emissions (*blow-by*) and limited CO and HC [78].

The first federal standards under the *Clean Air Act,* which applied to 1968 model vehicles, were published in the Federal Register in 1966 [54]. These standards corresponded roughly to the values set in California in 1960.

Successive amendments in 1968, 1970, etc., converted the standards from pollutant concentration values to pollutant mass values. These values were expressed as masses emitted per unit distance traveled, based on an imposed driving cycle. The Constant Volume Sample (CVS) method [101] was used to accumulate the emissions corresponding to the driving cycle.

The standards, which initially covered carbon monoxide and unburned hydrocarbon emissions, were then extended to nitrogen oxides and particulates, which subsequently covered diesel engines.

In Europe [45] in 1956, the *VDI* (*Verein Deutscher Ingenieure*) was asked to draft pollution directives. Around 1961, a Franco-German committee focused its attention on the reduction of CO and unburned HC emissions. In France, exhaust fumes have been regulated since 1963 [3], crankcase gas emissions since 1964 [4], and idling CO emissions since 1969 [5]. Since traffic conditions in European cities are significantly different from those in American cities a different driving cycle was adopted, which was based primarily on Paris traffic conditions.

Furthermore, given the diversity of the types of vehicles driven in Europe (size and motor drive systems), the statutory limits were adjusted in accordance with the weight of the vehicles affected.

In Japan [88], the first measures concerning CO were enacted in 1966 and then extended to HC and $NO_x$ in 1973. These standards involve both concentration and mass emission limits relative to driving cycles specific to Japan.

Other countries are collaborating in drafting standards on automotive pollution, particularly the participants of the *Economic Commission for Europe* (*ECE*) Working Group W29 in Geneva, which is made up of the *EEC*, the other European countries including the Eastern Bloc countries, the United States, and Canada. The regulations developed by this body are only applicable according to the wishes of each of the member countries [80].

Retracing the history of standards on automotive pollution in the different countries of the world is not the objective of this chapter. Statutory limits tend to become increasingly severe from year to year. Accordingly, the rest of this chapter discusses the present and foreseeable state of regulations for major pollutants in various countries. Distinctions are drawn between the different types of vehicles concerned (passenger cars, trucks, buses, motorcycles, etc.).

The first step is to examine the different procedures use to verify and ensure conformance to the various standards.

## 6.2 Regulatory test procedures

To be able to check the application of the regulations in measurement conditions that are as reproducible as possible, it was necessary to develop standard running procedures for the vehicles to be checked. These procedures were associated with analytical methods that were also regulated. Analytical methods are discussed in the next chapter. The same cycles are also used to measure the specific fuel consumption of the vehicles. The cycles correspond to a sequence of speeds as a function of time carried out on a chassis dynamometer (Section 7.1.1).

So far, unfortunately, the parties have not been unanimous in adopting universally applicable procedures and several types of test cycles are in use, for which no correlation exists for converting from one to the other. The test cycles are summarized in Table 6.2. Table 6.1 compares different parameters relative to these test cycles [71].

### 6.2.1 American driving cycles

#### 6.2.1.1 FTP-72 or LA-4 cycle

The FTP (Federal Test Procedure) cycle, also called the UDDS (Urban Dynamometer Driving Schedule) [102], Swedish A10, or CVS (Constant Volume Sampler) cycle from the name of the gas sampling apparatus, simulates an urban route 12.07 km long with frequent stops, a speed range of 0 to 91.2 km/h, and an average speed of 31.5 km/h. It lasts 22 min 52 s, and 17.8% of the time is allocated to idling, which corresponds to stops at urban traffic lights or in rush-hour traffic

**Table 6.1** Comparative parameters of driving cycles [71]

| Parameter | Unit | ECE | Calif. | FTP 72 | FTP 75 | Japan 10 modes | Japan 11 modes |
|---|---|---|---|---|---|---|---|
| **average speed** | (km/h) | 18.7 | 35.6 | 31.5 | 34.1 | 17.7 | 30.6 |
| **average speed** (non-idling) | (km/h) | 27.1 | 41.7 | 38.3 | 41.6 | 24.1 | 39.1 |
| **average acceleration** | ($m/s^2$) | 0.75 | 0.68 | 0.60 | 0.67 | 0.54 | 0.64 |
| **average deceleration** | ($m/s^2$) | 0.75 | 0.66 | 0.70 | 0.71 | 0.65 | 0.60 |
| **average time** of a sequence from start | (s) | 45 | 117 | 66 | 70 | 50 | 94 |
| **average number** of acceleration/ deceleration changes and *vice versa* during one sequence | | 1 | 3 | 5.6 | 6 | 2 | 5 |
| **idling** | (% time) | 30.8 | 14.6 | 17.8 | 18.0 | 26.7 | 21.7 |
| **accelerations** | (% time) | 18.5 | 31.4 | 33.5 | 33.1 | 24.4 | 34.2 |
| **constant speed** | (% time) | 32.3 | 21.9 | 20.1 | 20.4 | 23.7 | 13.3 |
| **decelerations** | (% time) | 18.5 | 32.1 | 28.6 | 28.5 | 25.2 | 30.8 |

**Table 6.2** Main characteristics of driving cycles [44]

| Cycle | Maximum speed (km/h) | Average speed (km/h) | Type of traffic | Starting conditions | Countries concerned |
|---|---|---|---|---|---|
| **ECE 15** | 50 | 18.7 | slow and fluid urban | cold+ 40 s idling | EEC |
| **FTP 72** | 91.2 | 31.5 | fluid urban | cold | Sweden |
| **FTP 75** | 91.2 | 34.1 | fluid urban | cold | USA<br>California<br>Norway<br>Switzerland<br>Canada<br>Australia |
| **HWFET** | 96.4 | 77.4 | fast road, slow expressway | warm | California<br>Sweden<br>Switzerland |
| **10 modes** | 40 | 17.7 | fluid urban | warm | Japan |
| **11 modes** | 60 | 30.6 | fluid urban, slow road | cold+ 25 s idling | Japan |

(Fig. 6.1). It derives from itinerary No. 4 examined in Los Angeles [70].

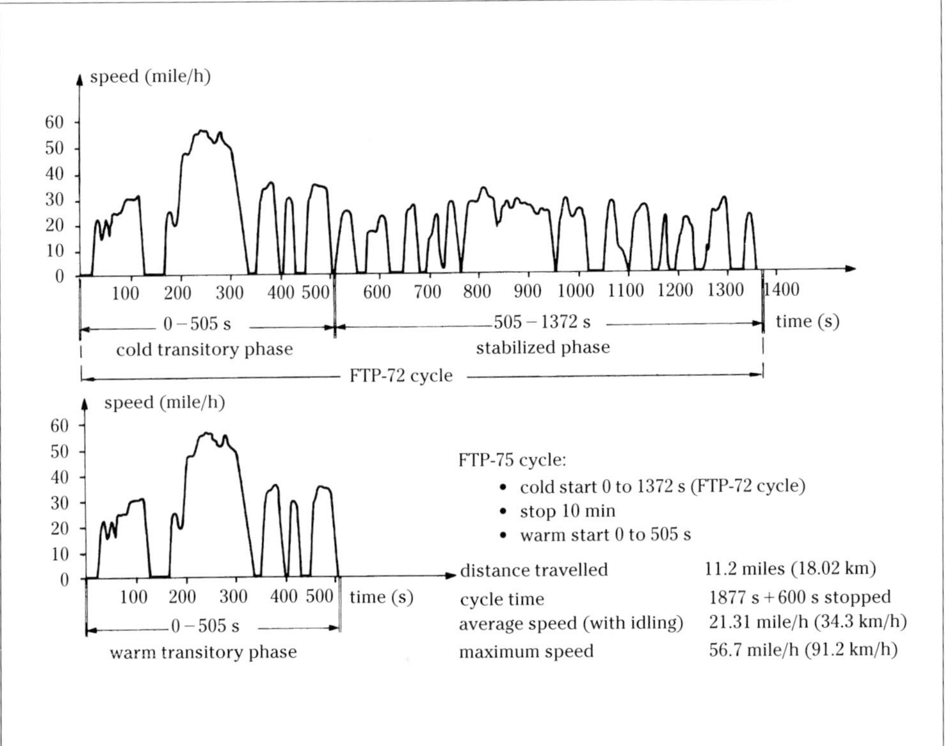


**Fig 6.1** FTP-72 and FTP-75 cycles [97]

The cycle consists of two phases of which the first is 505 s (5.78 km at 41.2 km/h average) and the second 867 s. The vehicle begins the first phase with a cold start after overnight parking at an ambient temperature of 20°C [63]. The two phases are separated by stopping the engine for 10 minutes. The weighting factors applied are 0.43 for the first phase and 0.57 for the second to take into account an average of 4.1 starts per day in the United States [96].

This cycle is referred to in Australia as the ADR 27 (Australian Design Rules) cycle [116]. In Sweden, both phases keep the same weighting factor in evaluating the pollutants.

#### 6.2.1.2 FTP-75 cycle

This cycle adds the following to foregoing cycle: after a ten-minute shutdown with the hood closed, a third phase of 505 s, identical to the first phase of the FTP-72 cycle, but with a warm start (Fig. 6.1).

The distance traveled is 17.86 km and the average speed 34.3 km/h. The emissions corresponding to the three phases are accounted for separately and the mass values of the pollutants (expressed as g/mile) are adjusted by different weighting factors: 0.43 for the cold phase, 1.00 for the second phase, and 0.57 for the last phase.

The gear shift conditions during the cycle are not imposed by the standard, but are recommended for each type of vehicle by the manufacturer [97]. This cycle is referred to in Australia as the ADR 37 (Australian Design Rules) cycle [116]. A fourth phase is to be added to the FTP-75 cycle in the near future that will require higher speeds and accelerations.

#### 6.2.1.3 HWFET or HFET highway cycle

The HWFET (HighWay Fuel Economy Test) inter-urban cycle, also called the 'countryside' road cycle in Switzerland, simulates continuous traffic conditions (idling time 1%) on road or expressway, with a warm engine (Fig. 6.2). It lasts 12 min 45 s for a distance of 16.45 km traveled at an average speed of 77.4 km/h (maximum speed 96.4 km/h). This cycle is carried out twice and the measurement is made on the second cycle.

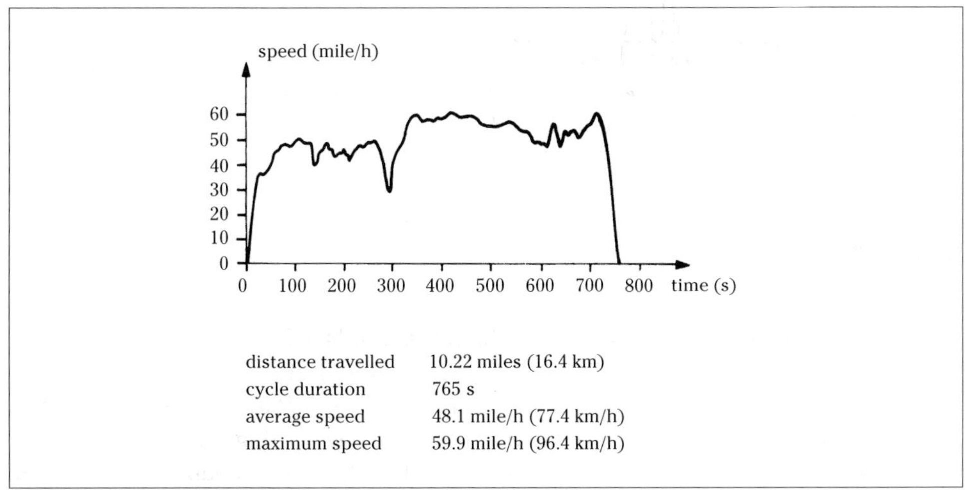


**Fig 6.2** HWFET cycle [97]

#### 6.2.1.4 CUE or SET cycle

The CUE (Crowded Urban Expressway) cycle, also called the SET (Sulfate Emission Test) cycle [28], is a 21.72 km cycle. It was designed by the *EPA* to simulate driving conditions causing maximum sulfate emissions, as in driving on a crowded urban expressway. It lasts 23 min with an average speed of 56.32 km/h and a maximum speed of 91.73 km/h. The idling time is 2.3%. It comprises 44% acceleration, 40% deceleration, and 16% cruising speed [63].

#### 6.2.1.5 LSC cycle

The LSC (Low-Speed Cycle) is a cycle lasting about 10 min with a maximum speed of 45 km/h [47]. Fig. 6.3 shows the variation in speed during this cycle.

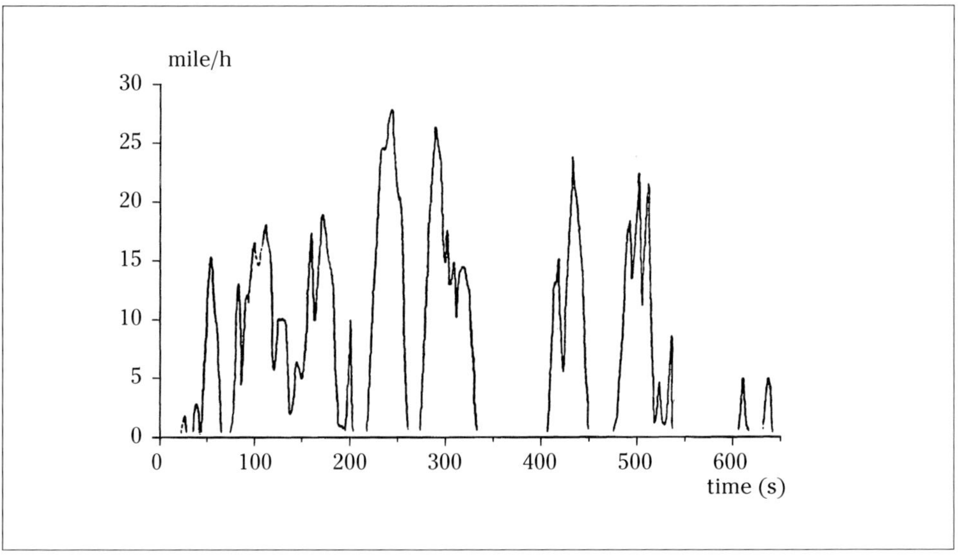


**Fig 6.3** LSC cycle: speed changes [47]

#### 6.2.1.6 Californian cycle

This cycle is an early cycle designed in 1968. It consists of seven identical sequences (Fig. 6.4), separated by idling, with a total duration of 16 min 19 s. It imposes a cold start after preconditioning for at least 12 h in ambient conditions [65]. The average speed is 38 km/h [24]. This cycle was abandoned in 1972 in favor of the FTP-72 cycle.

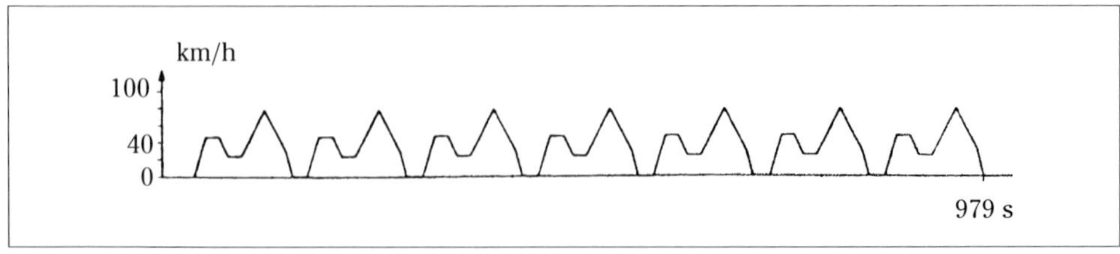


**Fig 6.4** Californian cycle [71]

#### 6.2.1.7 NYCC cycle

The NYCC (New York City Cycle) represents 'flea jumping' urban traffic. It lasts 10 min with a distance of 1.8 km that is traveled at an average speed of 11.4 km/h [43].

#### 6.2.1.8 US 9-mode cycle

This cycle is designed to measure gaseous pollutants from gasoline-powered vehicles weighing more than 2.7 t or transporting more than 12 passengers [95]. Since 1981, this cycle has been replaced, like the Diesel 13-mode cycle, by the transient cycle. Table 6.3 lists the main characteristics. The weighting factors employed in California were different from those in the table [79].

**Table 6.3** 9-mode cycle for gasoline-fuelled trucks
Constant speed 2000 rpm

| Mode | Speed | Induction pipe vacuum (kPa) | Duration (s) | Cumulative time (s) | Weighting Factor |
|---|---|---|---|---|---|
| 1 | idling | 54 | 70 | 70 | 0.232 |
| 2 | level | 34 | 23 | 93 | 0.077 |
| 3 | uphill in partial load | 54 | 44 | 137 | 0.147 |
| 4 | level | 54 | 23 | 160 | 0.077 |
| 5 | downhill in partial load | 64 | 17 | 177 | 0.057 |
| 6 | level | 54 | 23 | 200 | 0.077 |
| 7 | full load | 10 | 34 | 234 | 0.113 |
| 8 | level | 54 | 23 | 257 | 0.077 |
| 9 | throttle valve closed | – | 43 | 300 | 0.143 |

#### 6.2.1.9 DDS cycle

The DDS (Durability Driving Schedule) cycle is used as a mileage accumulation endurance cycle for pollution control devices, particularly for catalytic converters. It has eleven modes, each covering 5.95 km with a maximum speed that ranges from 48 to 112 km/h, depending on the mode. During each of the first nine modes, there are four stops of 15 s and five decelerations from nominal speed to 32 km/h, followed by re-accelerations up to the nominal speed. The tenth mode is traveled at a constant speed of 88.5 km/h and the eleventh starts from full acceleration up to 112 km/h [2]. Another cycle has been developed for catalyst engine bench tests: IIEC-2 (Catalyst Deterioration Cycle) [117].

#### 6.2.1.10 US 13-mode cycle

This cycle was designed to measure pollutants from diesel engines on the engine test bench, because the wide disparity of diesel engines used in light-duty trucks, heavy-duty trucks, and buses precludes measurement on a chassis dynamometer. It was introduced in California in 1971 for application in 1973 [24].

It consists of thirteen stabilized driving modes, of which the experimental conditions and weighting factors are given in Table 6.4. For each mode, the mass emissions are determined from the concentrations measured for each pollutant and from the measurements of the power and the corresponding exhaust gas flow rate. The results are tied to the horsepower developed by the engine to avoid penalizing more powerful engines. They are expressed in g/bhph (1 bhph brake horsepower hour = 0.7457 kWh).

**Table 6.4** USA and ECE 13-mode cycles

| Mode No. | Speed | Loading rate (%) | Weighting factors | | |
|---|---|---|---|---|---|
| | | | USA | ECE | (1) |
| **1** | idling | – | 0.20/3 | 0.25/3 | 0.151 |
| **2** | maximum torque speed | 10 | 0.08 | 0.08 | 0.023 |
| **3** | | 25 | 0.08 | 0.08 | 0.062 |
| **4** | | 50 | 0.08 | 0.08 | 0.044 |
| **5** | | 75 | 0.08 | 0.08 | 0.060 |
| **6** | | 100 | 0.08 | 0.25 | 0.017 |
| **7** | idling | – | 0.0667 | 0.25/3 | 0.151 |
| **8** | maximum horsepower speed | 100 | 0.08 | 0.10 | 0.069 |
| **9** | | 75 | 0.08 | 0.02 | 0.074 |
| **10** | | 50 | 0.08 | 0.02 | 0.094 |
| **11** | | 25 | 0.08 | 0.02 | 0.073 |
| **12** | | 10 | 0.08 | 0.02 | 0.031 |
| **13** | idling | – | 0.0667 | 0.25/3 | 0.151 |

(1) Simulation of transient cycle from US 13-mode cycle.

#### 6.2.1.11 Transient cycle

This transient cycle was substituted for the foregoing cycle in the United States to take into account the variety of heavy-duty truck traffic and buses in American cities, including traffic in and around the cities on roads and expressways. It consists of four phases: the first is a NYNF (New York Non Freeway) [20] phase typical of light urban traffic with frequent stops and starts, the second is a LANF (Los Angeles Non Freeway) phase typical of crowded urban traffic with few stops, the third is a LAFY (Los Angeles FreewaY) phase simulating crowded expressway traffic in Los Angeles, and the fourth phase repeats the first NYNF phase. It comprises a cold start after parking overnight, followed by idling, acceleration and deceleration phases, and a wide variety of different speeds and loads sequenced to simulate the running of the vehicle that corresponds to the engine being tested. There are few stabilized running conditions, and the average load factor is about 20 to 25% of the maximum horsepower available at a given speed. The cycle is carried out twice and the second repetition is made with a warm start after a stop of 20 min on completion of the first cycle. It requires the availability of a specially programmed electric dynamometer capable of driving the combustion engine [106].

The equivalent average speed is about 30 km/h and the equivalent distance traveled is 10.3 km for a running time of 20 min. The variation of speed and torque with time is shown as a percentage of nominal values in Fig. 6.5.

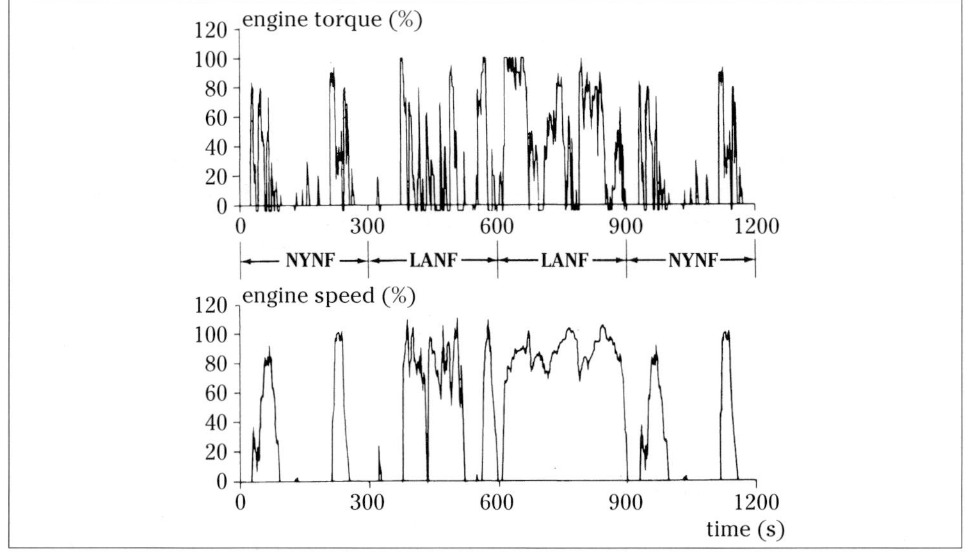


**Fig 6.5** US transient cycle [20]

An approximation of the results given by the 'transient' cycle is obtained by applying special weighting coefficients to the data supplied by the 13-mode cycle: these coefficients are given in Table 6.4. The correlation between the American transient cycle and the European stabilized cycle, first established with respect to gaseous emissions, has been extended to particulate emissions [42]: the *UBA*[1] and the *CCMC* [37] have accordingly concluded that the introduction of a European transient cycle is unnecessary. However, the United Kingdom plans to apply the American transient test to trucks to measure $NO_x$ and particulates.

### 6.2.1.12 8-mode cycle

This cycle was developed to simulate the American 'transient' cycle. It helps to obtain a good correlation with this cycle, particularly for particulate and $NO_x$ emissions [30 and 87]. Fig. 6.6 describes it in a speed/load diagram.

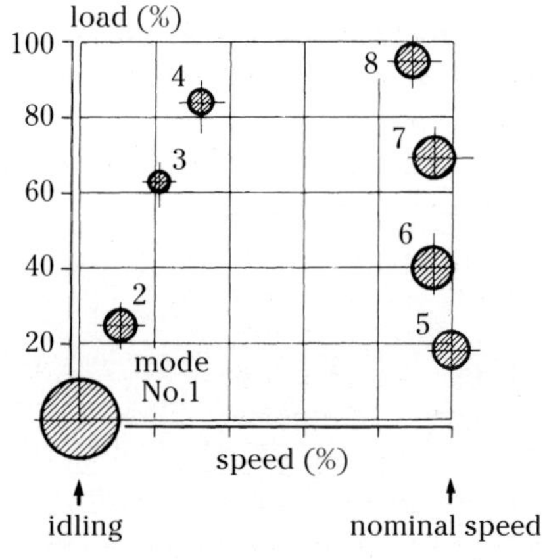


**Fig 6.6** 8-mode cycle simulating the transient cycle [30]

1. Umweltbundesamt: German Federal Environmental Administration.

#### 6.2.1.13 ADB cycle

The ADB (Advanced Design Bus) cycle is a transient cycle used to characterize bus traffic [46]. The cycle lasts about 47 min for a total travel distance of 22.5 km. It consists of three phases:

- A CBD (Central Business District) phase comprising 14 accelerations to 32 km/h, each one followed by a 20 s segment at this speed, a deceleration at 2.06 m/s$^2$, and an idle for 7 s. The distance covered is 3.2 km.
- An ART (ARTerial) phase with four accelerations to 64 km/h, each one followed by a 20 s segment at this speed, a deceleration, and a 7 s idle. This phase covers 3.2 km.
- A COMM (COMMuter) phase with a single acceleration to 88.5 km/h, speed held for 200 s, a deceleration, and a 20 s idle. This phase covers 6.5 km.

#### 6.2.1.14 Cycle for small service engines

This cycle consists of 16 modes selected according to the apparatus being tested (lawnmower, chainsaw, motor tiller, hedge cutter, etc.) [48 and 103].

### 6.2.2 European cycles

#### 6.2.2.1 ECE urban cycle

This cycle was developed around 1962 by the *UTAC* [25] and is based on Paris traffic conditions, which are quite different from the Californian conditions first used as the basis for test cycles [45]. It was adopted in 1960 at the United Nations in Geneva by the *ECE* (*Economic Commission for Europe*) as a European cycle. The cycle, which is repeated four times, is shown in Fig. 6.7. with speed indicated as a function of time along with mandatory gear changes [17]. The total distance represents 4.052 km and emissions are measured after idling for 40 s.

#### 6.2.2.2 EUDC extra-urban cycle

The ECE cycle was recently supplemented with a phase representing extra-urban traffic at higher speed (up to 120 km/h) [11]. It lasts 400 s to cover a distance of 6.955 km at an average speed of 62.6 km/h. This phase also appears in Fig. 6.7. It is carried out after the ECE cycle and begins by idling for 20 s [17]. Emissions are legally expressed in g/km instead of g/test. The change was adopted under pressure from the Netherlands, which showed that over 70% of European mileage was driven at more than 70 km/h, conditions that lead to 40% of HC emissions and 80% of $NO_x$ emissions [110]. It represents a compromise between the West German and British proposals and that of the consultative Committee of Manufacturers of the Common Market (*CCMC*). This phase is carried out after the ECE cycle. For vehicles less powerful than 30 kW, the maximum speed of the last phase is limited to 90 km/h [38].

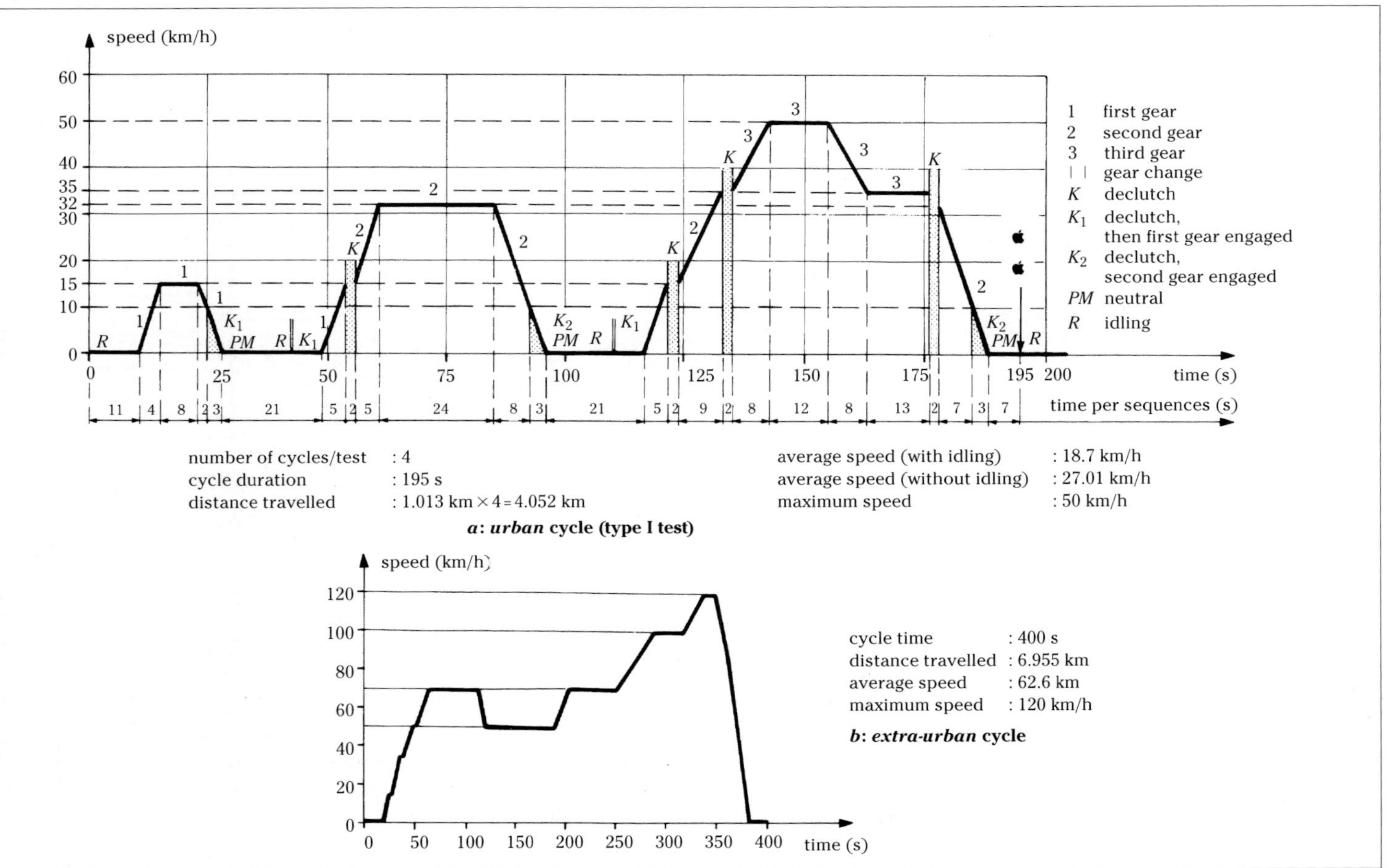


**Fig 6.7** ECE urban and extra-urban cycles [97]

#### 6.2.2.3 UBA cycle

This cycle, recently developed by *TÜV Rheinland* at the request of *UBA*, also reaches a maximum speed of 120 km/h and is presumed to represent a compromise between the varieties of traffic on the different types of roads [52] (Fig. 6.8).

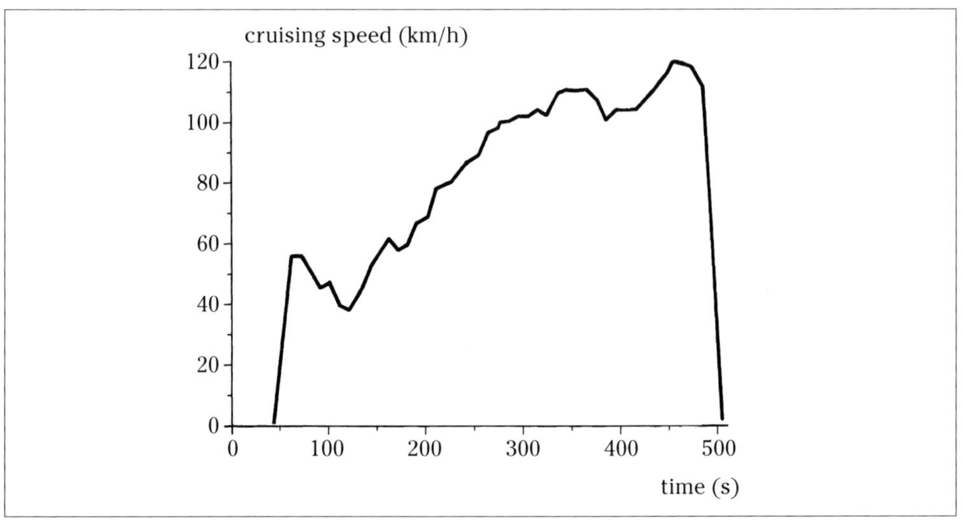


**Fig 6.8** UBA cycle [52]

#### 6.2.2.4 Berlin urban cycle

This cycle, developed in 1985 using a Volkswagen Rabbit being driven in Berlin, covers a route of 8.828 km with 15 stops lasting from 1 to 43 s [111] (Fig. 6.9).

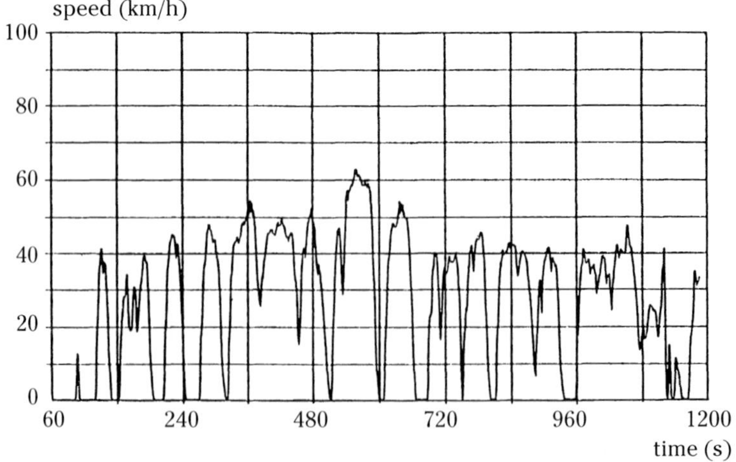


**Fig 6.9** Berlin urban cycle [111]

### 6.2.2.5 German bus cycle

This cycle, developed at the *Technische Hochschule Braunschweig (Advanced Technical School)* and called *Stochastischer Fahrzyclus für Stadt-Linien Omnibusse*, lasts 29 min over a distance of 11 km with a maximum speed of 58.2 km/h and an average speed of 22.9 km/h [115].

### 6.2.2.6 European 13-mode cycle

This cycle, adapted to diesel engines, was introduced by ECE Regulation No. 49 [8] and then adopted by the *EEC* [12]. It consists of tests run on an engine test bench under stabilized running conditions, similar to those of the American 13-mode cycle. Only the weighting factors are different (Table 6.4). This cycle was slightly modified to measure the efficiency of particulate filters by avoiding excessively high exhaust temperatures that induce accidental regenerations [19].

### 6.2.2.7 Two-wheel cycles

For motorcycles, ECE Regulation No. 40 [6] introduced a 15-mode cycle to be performed on a chassis dynamometer, with 15 modes at a maximum speed of 50 km/h (Fig. 6.10).

This 15-mode cycle [84] is repeated four times, lasting a total of 13 min. Samples are taken after two preparatory cycles. Fig. 6.10 shows the performance of this cycle.

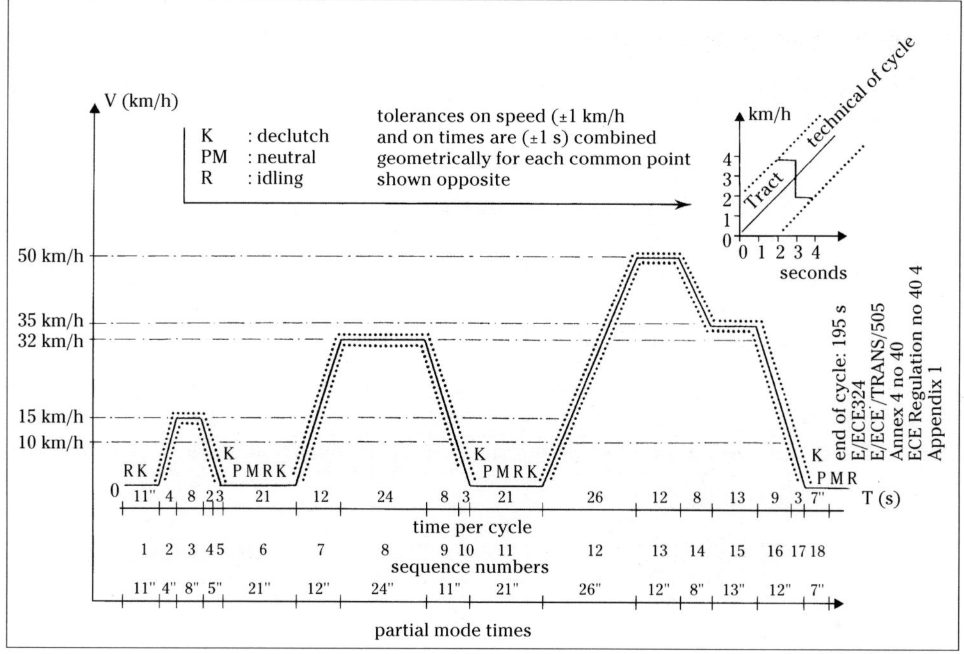


**Fig 6.10** R40 15-mode cycle [6]

For pedal motorcycles—defined as vehicles with an unloaded weight less than 400 kg, a swept volume under 50 $cm^3$, and an inability to exceed 50 km/h—the cycle to be followed is defined by ECE Regulation No. 47 [7]. This cycle, whose features are listed in Table 6.5, has seven modes and is repeated four times for a total time of 448 s. Regulations R40 and R47 are not applied in the *EEC* countries for the time being, except for R40 in Germany [72].

**Table 6.5** 7-mode driving cycle for pedal motorcycle

| Mode No. | Speed | Acceleration ($m/s^2$) | Speed (km/h) | Duration (s) | Cumulative time (s) |
|---|---|---|---|---|---|
| 1 | idling | – | – | 8 | 8 |
| 2 | acceleration | full throttle | 0 to max | | – |
| 3 | stabilized speed | full throttle | max | } 57 | – |
| 4 | deceleration | −0.56 | max to 20 | | 65 |
| 5 | stabilized speed | – | 20 | 36 | 101 |
| 6 | deceleration | −0.93 | 20 to 0 | 6 | 107 |
| 7 | idling | – | – | 5 | 112 |

### 6.2.2.8 European endurance cycle

This aging cycle, like the American DDS cycle, tests the durability of pollution control devices. It has three phases at stabilized speeds of 70 km/h, 100 km/h, and at 80% of the maximum speed (limited to 130 km/h) that last 5, 5, and 10 min respectively [17]. Idling for 15 s is inserted between two consecutive phases. The accelerations and decelerations prescribed between the phases are 1.5 $m/s^2$, or, if not possible, the maximum acceleration capability of the vehicle. This cycle is repeated until 30,000 km is completed and allows necessary stops for refueling and adjustments.

### 6.2.2.9 European durability cycle

This endurance program, designed to check the durability of pollution control systems, features eleven cycles of 6 km carried out with accelerations and speeds up to 113 km/h [17]. These eleven cycles are repeated up to a total distance of 80,000 km.

### 6.2.2.10 European railroad cycle

To evaluate emissions of diesel rail vehicles (locomotives, rail cars, etc.), the Research Department of the *Union Internationale des Chemins de Fer* (*UIC, International Railway Union*) has developed the cycle shown in Table 6.6 [41 and 69].

**Table 6.6** UIC test cycle

| Engine speed | Power (%) | Weighting factor |
|---|---|---|
| nominal speed | 100 | 0.2 |
| intermediate speed 1 | 50 | 0.1 |
| intermediate speed 2 | 25 | 0.1 |
| idling speed | 5 | 0.6 |

#### 6.2.2.11 ICOMIA marine cycle

The ICOMIA cycle (Marine Duty Cycle) has five modes including one idling mode [16 and 32] with weighting factors. This cycle is gradually being abandoned in favor of a more general-purpose ISO Duty Cycle with five modes derived from the R49 13-mode cycle [85].

### 6.2.3 Japanese cycles

A 4-mode cycle that was first used in Japan between 1966 and 1974 to limit the volumetric concentrations of CO emitted by vehicles fueled with gasoline or LPG [88]. It was replaced by the 10- and 11-mode cycles.

#### 6.2.3.1 6-mode cycles

Two 6-mode cycles are used in Japan for heavy-duty vehicles weighing more than 2.5 t or transporting more than ten passengers: one cycle for gasoline or LPG-fueled vehicles and one cycle for diesel vehicles. Tables 6.7 and 6.8 list the characteristics of these two cycles. Total emissions are determined by weighting the concentrations corresponding to each mode using the factors given in the tables and expressing the results as volumetric concentrations (ppm). Diesel passenger cars are tested by the 10-mode cycle described below.

**Table 6.7** Japanese 6-mode cycle for diesel vehicles [62]

| Mode No. | Speed (% of nominal speed) | Loading rate (%) | Weighting factor |
|---|---|---|---|
| **1** | idling | | 0.355 |
| **2** | 40 | 100 | 0.071 |
| **3** | 40 | 25 | 0.059 |
| **4** | 60 | 100 | 0.107 |
| **5** | 60 | 25 | 0.122 |
| **6** | 80 | 75 | 0.286 |
| duration of each mode: 3 min | | | |

**Table 6.8** Japanese 6-mode cycle for heavy-duty vehicles (gasoline or LPG)

| Mode No. | | Speed (rpm) | Induction pipe vacuum (kPa) | Weighting factor |
|---|---|---|---|---|
| **1** | idling | | | 0.125 |
| **2** | stabilized | 2000 | 17 | 0.114 |
| **3** | stabilized | 3000 | 17 | 0.277 |
| **4** | stabilized | 3000 | 27 | 0.254 |
| **5** | stabilized | 2000 | 56 | 0.139 |
| **6** | deceleration throttle valve closed in 10 s | from 2000 to 1000 | 56 | 0.091 |
| duration of modes 1 to 5: 3 min | | | | |

### 6.2.3.2 10-mode cycle

This cycle reproduces urban driving after a warm start. It corresponds to a distance of 0.664 km at an average speed of 17.7 km/h and lasts 135 s. The cycle is performed six times after warming the vehicle at 40 km/h for 15 min. The emissions measured in the last five cycles are expressed in g/km (Fig. 6.11). It therefore represents a route of 3.32 km, carried out in 675 s, at a maximum speed of 40 km/h, with 26.4% of the time at idle.

### 6.2.3.3 11-mode cycle

This cycle simulates driving on an urban expressway after a cold start. It includes starting the engine at a temperature of 20 to 30°C. After an idling period of 25 s, a distance of 1.021 km is traveled at an average speed of 30.6 km/h for 120 s. The emissions measured in this cycle are expressed in g/test (Fig. 6.11).

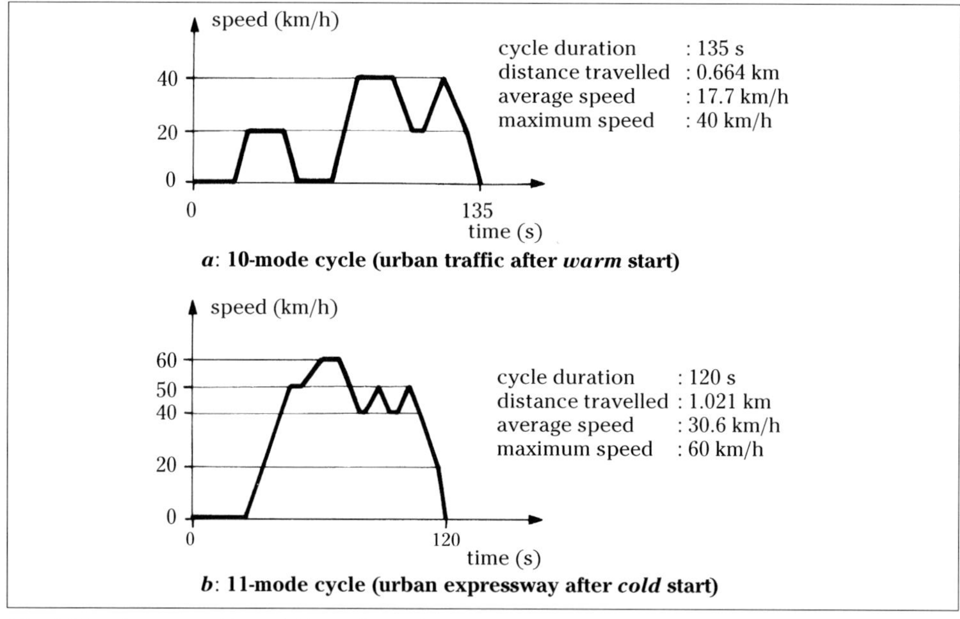


**Fig 6.11** Japanese 10- and 11-mode cycles

### 6.2.3.4 New 10- to 15-mode cycle

The previous 10-mode cycle, limited to 40 km/h, was extended at a maximum speed of 70 km/h (Fig. 6.12). It represents a distance of 4.16 km, completed in 660 s at an average speed of 22.7 km/h, with 31.4% of the time idling [109]. This test is applicable to new gasoline and diesel vehicles manufactured after November 1991. It has been applied since October 1993 to test vans under 2.5 t and the results are expressed in g/km instead of ppm.

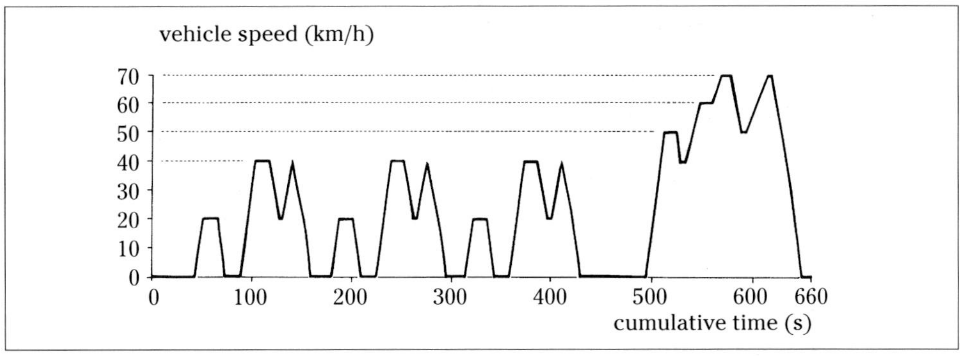


**Fig 6.12** New Japanese 10- to 15-mode cycle [109]

### 6.2.3.5 New 13-mode cycle for heavy-duty vehicles

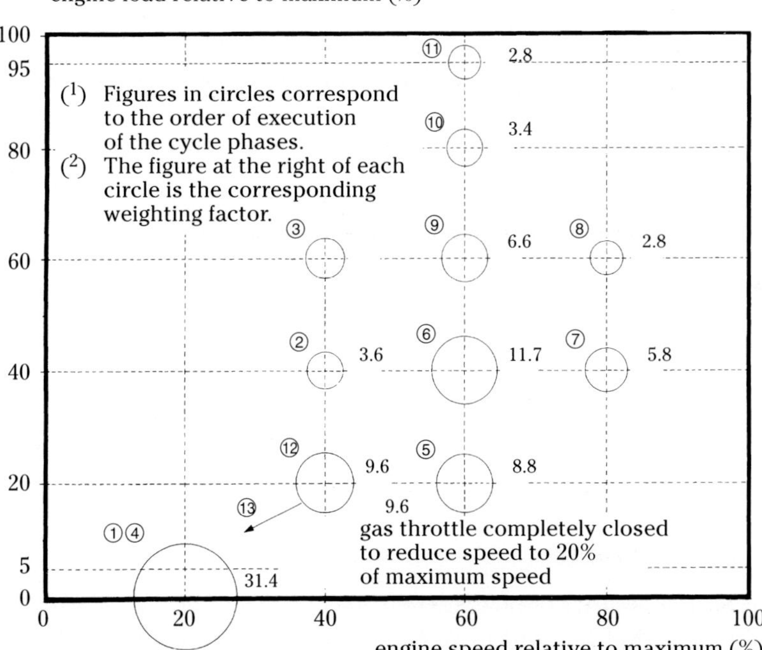


**Fig 6.13** New Japanese gasoline 13-mode cycle [109]

The previous 6-mode cycle for the same types of vehicle is replaced by a 13-mode cycle carried out in stabilized conditions and the measured values are expressed in g/kWh instead of volumetric concentrations [109]. This new cycle, which emphasizes low-speed driving, is identical for gasoline and diesel vehicles. Only the weighting factors applied to each mode are different (Figs. 6.13 and 6.14).

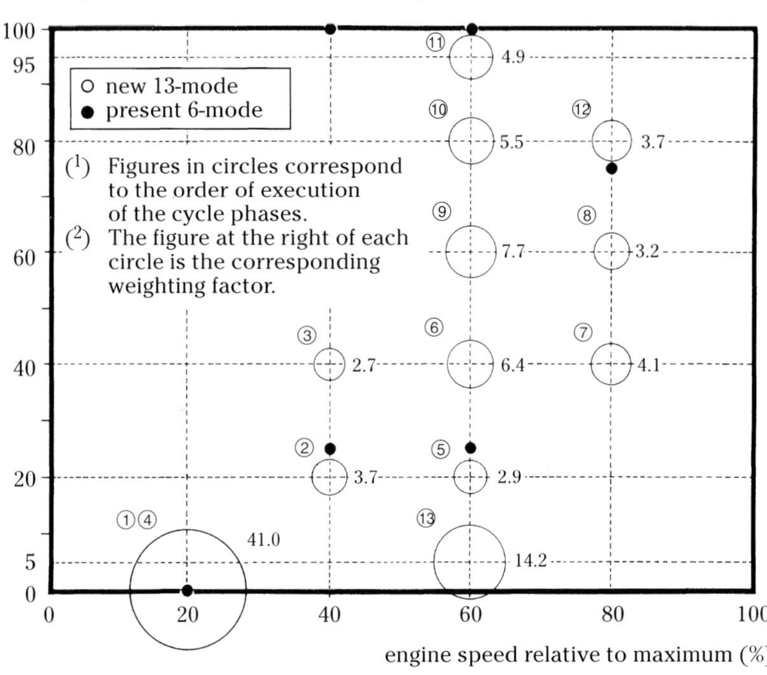


**Fig 6.14** New Japanese diesel 13-mode cycle [109]

## 6.2.4 Other cycles

### 6.2.4.1 9-mode cycle

This cycle is used in Australia to test light-duty vehicles [22] equipped with spark ignition engines.

### 6.2.4.2 Fork-lift cycle

A cycle with a number of phase repetitions of 10 s of lifting followed by 20 s of unloaded travel that is used in Germany to estimate diesel pollution in the workplace [64].

### 6.2.4.3 EPA landing/take-off cycle

To estimate the pollutant emissions of aircraft around airports, the *EPA* has developed a special 5-mode cycle [56], representative of the running conditions specific to each type of engine mounted on today's aircraft. As a function of the type of engine, Table 6.9 gives the duration and horsepower developed during each mode.

This cycle concerns emissions generated below 900 m (3000 ft). It has two different idle/taxi segments because the starting sequence takes place on a cold engine, contrary to the return sequence. The descent phase is not taken into account (as opposed to the approach phase), except for supersonic aircraft.

**Table 6.9** 5-mode take-off/landing cycle

| Category(1) | T1, P2 | | T2, T3, T4 | | T5 | |
|---|---|---|---|---|---|---|
| **Mode** | **Time (min)** | **Power (%)** | **Time (min)** | **Power (%)** | **Time (min)** | **Power (%)** |
| idling/taxi (departure) | 19 | (a) | 19 | (a) | 19 | (a) |
| take-off | 0.5 | 100 | 0.7 | 100 | 1.2 | 100 |
| climb | 2.5 | 90 | 2.2 | 85 | 2.0 | 65 |
| descent | n/a | n/a | 1.2 | n/a | n/a | 15 |
| approach | 4.5 | 30 | 4.0 | 30 | 2.3 | 34 |
| idling/taxi (return) | 7.0 | (a) | 7.0 | (a) | 7.0 | (a) |

(1) Categories:
- T1 turbofan/turbojet, thrust <35.6 kN
- T2 turbofan/turbojet, thrust >35.6 kN
- T3 JT3D engine (B707, DC-8)
- T4 JT8D engine (B727, B737, DC-9)
- T5 supersonic cruise engine
- P1 piston engine
- P2 turboprop engine

(a) Power recommended by manufacturer.

#### 6.2.4.4 LHD and MTU cycles

The LHD (load, haul, dump) cycle was developed to simulate the work of mining vehicles: traveling with an empty bucket to the ore heap to be loaded, loading the bucket, retreating from the pile with the loaded bucket, traveling to dump site, raising and dumping the load, and returning empty to the original heap. The cycle has six modes to which the weighting factors in Table 6.10 are applied [40 and 55].

**Table 6.10** LHD cycle: mine vehicles

| Mode | Torque speed | Load (%) | Torque (Nm) | Time weighting factor |
|---|---|---|---|---|
| 1 | maximum | 50 | 190 | 0.04 |
| 2 | maximum | 75 | 285 | 0.07 |
| 3 | maximum | 100 | 382 | 0.17 |
| 4 | nominal | 75 | 260 | 0.22 |
| 5 | nominal | 100 | 135 | 0.05 |
| 6 | nominal | 50 | 173 | 0.45 |

The MTU cycle developed for the same purpose has only four modes characterized by the engine speed and the control rod position [107].

It simulates four operating steps:

(1) travel to the ore heap located at the cutting face
(2) frontal loading of the bucket
(3) exit from ore heap
(4) transport from the cutting face to unloading point, tipping, and returning to cutting face

### 6.2.5 Idling pollutant measurements

These measurements are included in Type II tests in the ECE regulations. The CO content of the exhaust gas is determined immediately on completion of the Type I test, with the engine idling and the choke de-activated [97]. To take into account the dilution of the exhaust gas by ambient air during sampling, both CO and $CO_2$ are measured. The CO concentration, to be compared with the statutory limits, is given by the formula:

$$C_{CO} \text{ corrected} = \frac{15}{C_{CO} + C_{CO_2}}$$

in % volume if: $C_{CO} + C_{CO_2} < 15\%$

### 6.2.6 Exhaust smoke opacity measurements

#### 6.2.6.1 European techniques

Two types of tests are recommended by the *ECE* according to Regulation No. 24.

- A stabilized speed test on the full-load curve: six speeds are uniformly distributed between maximum speed at full load and the highest of the following speeds:
    - 45% of speed at maximum horsepower
    - 1000 rpm
    - minimum speed imposed by the regulator

  For each of these speeds, the nominal flow rate G (expressed in liters/s) is defined as:

  $G = V \times \frac{n}{60}$ for two-stroke engines

  $G = V \times \frac{n}{120}$ for four-stroke engines

  where:

    - $V$ (liters) = total swept volume of the engine
    - $n$ (rpm) = engine speed

- A free acceleration test: this test is conducted on a warm engine, after the previous stabilized speed test. A series of engine no-load accelerations is carried out, between idling speed and full-load speed, and an average value is taken of the absorption coefficient corresponding to four successive non-dispersed values. For supercharged engines, the value selected is the maximum value of the absorption coefficient measured at stabilized speeds, plus 0.5 $m^{-1}$ [97].

### 6.2.6.2 American USPHS smoke cycle

The USPHS (United States Public Health Service) cycle, shown in Fig. 6.15, is conducted on an engine test bench [36].

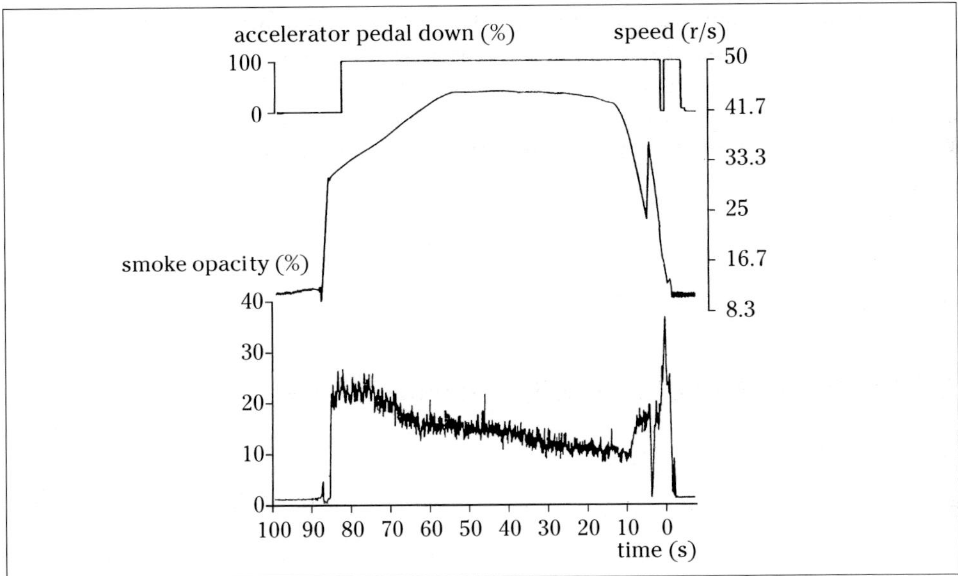


**Fig 6.15** Diesel smoke, American federal regulations [36]

It includes the following phases: one idling, one full throttle, one rapid deceleration, a second acceleration to the nominal speed of the engine, braking to 60% of the nominal speed by increasing the load, and return to idling. This cycle, which lasts about 3 min, is repeated three times. The smoke is tested continuously by a total flow opacimeter whose plot is shown in Fig. 6.15.

### 6.2.6.3 Japanese 3-mode cycle

This cycle, established in 1972 to measure diesel smoke, is shown in Table 6.11 [36 and 62].

**Table 6.11** Japanese 3-mode cycle for diesel smoke

| Mode No. | Speed (% of speed at maximum horsepower) | Loading rate (%) |
|---|---|---|
| 1 | 40 | 100 |
| 2 | 60 | 100 |
| 3 | 100 | 100 |

## 6.2.7 Blow-by emission measurements

### 6.2.7.1 ECE Type III test

To ensure that the crankcase ventilation system prevents any emission of gases into the atmosphere, this test verifies that the pressure prevailing in the crankcase remains lower than atmospheric pressure under three vehicle running conditions [97]: a no-load idling condition and a stabilized speed of 50 km/h for each of two horsepower outputs (the power absorbed by the dynamometer in the Type I test and that same fig. multiplied by 1.7).

### 6.2.7.2 Other procedures

Countries that do not employ the ECE Type III test recommend that the pressure in the crankcase should never exceed atmospheric pressure.

## 6.2.8 Measurements of evaporative emissions

Evaporative losses, which may be generated by the entire feed circuit of gasoline-fueled vehicles from the fuel tank to the carburetor (Chapter 11), are determined using either an activated charcoal canister or more frequently by the SHED (Sealed Housing for Evaporative Determination) method. The corresponding experimental techniques are described in detail in Chapter 7. In both cases, the emissions are measured during a laboratory test sequence simulating the running of the vehicle on an urban circuit during the summer months.

### 6.2.8.1 Trap technique

This is the only method that enables the measurement of running losses. It is based on the measurement of the gain in weight of activated charcoal canisters. After having been calibrated, the oven-dried canisters are connected to the assumed locations of vapor emissions. If the vehicle has a system for controlling evaporative losses, it is first loaded by running the car until it reaches equilibrium in the mass of hydrocarbons retained in the system. The vehicle is then allowed to rest, with the engine shut off, for 11 to 16 h. The tank is then emptied and refilled to 40% with fresh reference fuel at a temperature between 10 and 14.4°C. The traps are inserted immediately afterward [10].

The first phase involves 1 h at rest that represents a daily cycle during which the temperature of the fuel tank is raised from 15.6 to 28.9°C. The vehicle is then pushed onto the chassis dynamometer to carry out 12.1 km, within 10 min of finishing the first phase. A rest period of 1 h with the hood closed, starting within the 3 min following the shutdown of the engine, helps to add the hot soak losses. The canisters are re-weighed. This technique is no longer applied today, except in Japan and Taiwan.

#### 6.2.8.2 SHED technique

This technique is being universally adopted today even though it is incapable of measuring running emissions, which are considered to be less important than the others. It requires the use of a sealed enclosure, which consists of a material impermeable to hydrocarbons, to house the vehicle during the test. Apart from the replacement of canister weighing by an FID analysis in the sealed enclosure, the technique employed is approximately equivalent to the one described in the trap technique. European authorities are now proposing a variant slightly different from that adopted in the United States [9].

After a prior rest period with the engine shut off, lasting between 11 and 16 h at a temperature of 20 to 30°C, the tank is emptied and then re-filled to 40% of its capacity with fresh reference fuel. The vehicle is then pushed into the enclosure to measure the diurnal losses and the tank temperature is raised from 15.6 to 28.9°C in 1 h. The content in the enclosure is measured before the vehicle is taken out and driven a distance of 17.9 km on a chassis dynamometer, from a cold start. The engine is kept idling during the purging of the enclosure and then, with the engine shut off, the vehicle is re-introduced into the enclosure, which is closed within the 2 min following the engine shutoff. The vehicle remains there for an hour with the hood closed and the windows and trunk open, after which the hydrocarbon concentration is measured. The results are expressed as the mass of hydrocarbons evaporated, taking into account the C/H ratio of the fuel used.

The proposed European procedure makes the following changes:

- tests a vehicle that has run for at least 3000 km, steam cleaned if necessary
- preconditions the systems for controlling evaporative losses: canisters are purged by nitrogen at ambient temperature then loaded by two diurnal cycles, which are carried out by heating in 1 h from 16 to 30°C, and then the vehicle is conditioned (new purge of the system) by carrying out four ECE cycles and two EUDC cycles
- rests the vehicle between 20 and 30°C for 10 to 36 h
- drains the tank and re-fills to 40% with fresh fuel at temperatures between 10 and 14°C
- tests diurnal losses by raising the tank temperature from 16 to 30°C in 1 h
- removes the vehicle from the enclosure, then places it on the chassis dynamometer and runs one ECE cycle followed by one EUDC cycle
- as in the American procedure, re-introduces the vehicle into the enclosure to measure hot soak losses, with the temperature in the enclosure remaining within the range 23 to 31°C

The losses are calculated with predetermined C/H ratios: 2.33 for breathing losses from the tank and 2.30 for hot soak losses.

The SHED procedure is also proposed in the United States to evaluate tank refueling emissions.

#### 6.2.8.3 Collision losses

A safety requirement also states that after collision or overturning the contents of the tank must not spread and evaporate. MVSS test No. 301 in the United States simulates a vehicle collision followed by roll-over. The fuel loss must not exceed 28 g during a one-minute interval [89].

## 6.3 Exhaust gas pollutants

Legal limits on emissions are regulated in some thirty countries throughout the world using the procedures discussed above [36]. Given the disparity in the severity of the regulation cycles and the measurement techniques—although in most of the tables below the limits have been expressed in consistent units, either g/km or g/kWh—it is impossible to compare the limits applicable in countries using different cycles as a basis.

### 6.3.1 Statutory values in the United States

These values are expressed in g/mile measured by the FTP-75 cycle. The latest limits were imposed in the United States in 1987 on passenger cars and in 1988 on utility vehicles (Table 6.13). The current standards must be met at 80,000 km (50,000 miles) for passenger cars and 192,000 km (120,000 miles) for utility vehicles, taking into account the deterioration factors in Table 6.14.

The *Clean Air Act,* amended in 1990, anticipates increasingly severe federal legislation harmonized with the limits set by California.

The Bill applies the California laws with a delay of one year. The maximum values applicable at 50,000 miles (80,000 km) and 100,000 miles (160,000 km) will respectively apply in 1994 to 40%, in 1995 to 80%, and in 1996 to 100% of a manufacturer's production of passenger vehicles, light-duty vehicles (<1.7 t), and medium-duty vehicles (1.7 to 2.6 t). They will be set for non-methanic hydrocarbon (NMHC), CO, $NO_x$, and particulates (Table 6.12).

**Table 6.12** Draft Federal legislation (values in g/mile)

| | 50,000 miles | | | | | 100,000 miles | | | | |
|---|---|---|---|---|---|---|---|---|---|---|
| | NMHC | CO | $NO_x$ (1) | $NO_x$ (2) | Part | NMHC | CO | $NO_x$ (1) | $NO_x$ (2) | Part |
| passenger vehicle | 0.25 | 3.4 | 0.4 | 1.0 | 0.08 | 0.31 | 4.2 | 0.6 | 1.25 | 0.10 |
| light duty | 0.25 | 3.4 | 0.4 | 1.0 | 0.08 | 0.31 | 4.2 | 0.6 | 1.25 | 0.10 |
| medium duty | 0.32 | 4.4 | 1.0 | | 0.08 | 0.4 | 5.5 | – | – | – |

(1) gasoline vehicles, (2) diesel vehicles

**Table 6.13** American statutory levels [23, 65 and 97] Federal legislation (49 States) Gaseous pollutants

| Year / Cycle | CO | | HC | | $NO_x$ (Town) | | $NO_x$ (Road) | |
|---|---|---|---|---|---|---|---|---|
| | FTP 75 | | | | | | HWFET | |
| | **Light passenger cars**(1) | | | | | | | |
| | (g/mile) | (g/km) | (g/mile) | (g/km) | (g/mile) | (g/km) | (g/mile) | (g/km) |
| 1960(1) | 84 | 52.2 | 10.6 | 6.58 | 4.1 | 2.54 | – | – |
| 1976(1) | 3.4 | 2.11 | 0.41 | 0.25 | 0.4 | 0.25 | – | – |
| 1968-69 | 51 | 31.7 | 6.3 | 3.91 | – | – | – | – |
| 1970-71 | 34 | 21.12 | 4.1 | 1.60 | – | – | – | – |
| 1972 | 28 | 17.4 | 3.0 | 1.86 | – | – | – | – |
| 1973-74 | 28 | 17.4 | 3.0 | 1.86 | 3.1 | 1.92 | – | – |
| 1975-76 | 15 | 9.32 | 1.5 | 0.93 | 3.1 | 1.92 | – | – |
| 1977-79 | 15 | 9.32 | 1.5 | 0.93 | 2.0 | 1.24 | – | – |
| 1980 | 7.0 | 4.35 | 0.41 | 0.25 | 2.0 | 1.24 | – | – |
| 1983 | 3.4 | 2.11 | 0.41 | 0.25 | 1.0 | 0.62 | 1.22 | 0.76 |
| 1994 | 3.4 | 2.11 | 0.25 | 0.15 | 0.4 | 0.25 | 0.48 | 0.30 |
| | **Light-duty trucks**(5) | | | | | | | |
| | (g/mile) | (g/km) | (g/mile) | (g/km) | (g/mile) | (g/km) | (g/mile) | (g/km) |
| 1984-87 | 10 | 6.21 | 0.8 | 0.5 | 2.3 | 1.43 | 2.94 | 1.83 |
| 1988 <1.7 t | 10 | 6.21 | 0.8 | 0.5 | 1.2 | 0.74 | 1.54 | 0.96 |
| 1988 >1.7 t | 10 | 6.21 | 0.8 | 0.5 | 1.7 | 1.05 | 2.18 | 1.35 |
| future | 5.0 | 3.10 | 0.5 | 0.31 | 0.5 | 0.31 | 0.64 | 0.40 |
| | **Trucks and buses** | | | | | | | |
| | (g/bhph) | (g/kWh) | (g/bhph) | (g/kWh) | (g/bhph) | (g/kWh) | (g/bhph) | (g/kWh) |
| 1988(3) | 15.5 | 20.8 | 1.3 | 1.74 | 10.7 | 14.35 | – | – |
| 1990(3) | 15.5 | 20.8 | 1.3 | 1.74 | 6 | 8 | – | – |
| 1991-94(3) | 15.5 | 20.8 | 1.3 | 1.74 | 5 | 6.7 | – | – |
| 1998 | 15.5 | 20.8 | 1.3 | 1.74 | 4 | 6.7 | – | – |

(1) Estimation.
(2) Limits initially planned by the *Clean Air Act*.
(3) Transient cycle.
(4) Fewer than 12 passengers, unlimited weight.
(5) Weight >3.5 t or more than 12 passengers or 4×4 all-terrain vehicles.

**Table 6.14** US deterioration factors

| Vehicle | CO | HC | $NO_x$ |
|---|---|---|---|
| gasoline vehicles, 3-way catalyst | 1.2 | 1.3 | 1.1 |
| diesel vehicles | 1.2 | 1.0 | 1.0 |
| gasoline utility vehicles, 3-way catalyst | 1.5 | 1.7 | 1.2 |
| diesel utility vehicles | 1.2 | 1.0 | 1.0 |

Private cars will also have to emit less than 10 g/mile (6.23 g/km) of CO at a temperature of −7°C (20°F) and less than 3.4 g/mile at a temperature of +20°C (68°F), starting with 1993 models. At intermediate temperatures the variation in the limit is linear [27].

In a second phase (from 2003) the limits would be halved to 0.125 g/mile HC, 1.7 g/mile CO, and 0.2 g/mile $NO_x$ for passenger and light-duty vehicles. They would also have to be met after 100,000 miles or after ten years.

At the same time as the enforcement of these regulations the *EPA* anticipates the introduction of 'clean' alternative motor fuels [27]:

- 'reformulated' gasoline (maximum benzene content 1%, aromatics 25%, no heavy metals, 15% reduction of volatile organic compounds, and toxicity compared with the present situation without any increase in $NO_x$)
- 'reformulated' diesel fuel
- compressed natural gas (CNG)
- liquefied petroleum gases (LPG)
- hydrogen
- fuels containing at least 85% alcohol (e.g. M85 or E85)

Special limits will be imposed on vehicles running on these fuels (Table 6.15). A limit on formaldehyde emissions will be set. Moreover, hydrocarbons will be differentiated by means of the NMOG (Non Methanic Organic Gases) concept, taking into account the differences in atmospheric reactivity of the emitted chemical derivatives using the following equation:

$$\text{NMOG} = \text{NMHC} \times \text{RF} + \sum_{n=1}^{m} (\text{carbonyl})_n \times (\text{RF})_n$$

where:

- NMOG = non methanic organic gases
- NMHC = non methanic hydrocarbons
- RF = reactivity factor
- $m$ = number of carbonyl derivatives present in the exhaust

**Table 6.15** Limits applicable to 'clean' vehicles

| Pollutant | Enforcement date | 50,000 miles (g/mile) | 100,000 miles (g/mile) |
|---|---|---|---|
| **NMOG** | 1996 | 0.125 | 0.156 |
| | 2001 | 0.075 | 0.090 |
| **CO** | 1996 | 3.4 | 4.2 |
| | 2001 | 3.4 | 4.2 |
| **$NO_x$** | 1996 | 0.4 | 0.6 |
| | 2001 | 0.2 | 0.3 |
| **particulates** | 1996 | – | 0.08(1) |
| | 2001 | – | 0.08(1) |
| **HCHO** | 1996 | 0.015 | 0.018 |
| | 2001 | 0.015 | 0.018 |

(1) Only for diesel

These clean vehicles will be introduced progressively at first in captive fleets of at least ten units that can be supplied from the same refueling point and that travel in areas of the country suffering from acute air pollution problems. Subsequently, the program will cover 30% of all vehicles produced in 1998, rising to 70% by the year 2000 [27].

The limits planned for trucks and buses are listed in Table 6.16.

**Table 6.16** Future limits on trucks and buses

| Vehicle | Pollutant | Dates | (g/mile) | (g/km) |
|---|---|---|---|---|
| **light trucks** | NMHC | from 1995 | 0.32 | 0.2 |
| 1.7-2.6 t | HC | from 1995 | 0.38 | 0.24 |
| | $NO_x$ | from 1995 | 0.7 | 0.435 |
| | CO | from 1995 | 4.4 | 2.73 |
| **light trucks** | NMHC | from 1995 | 0.39 | 0.24 |
| 2.6-3.8 t | HC | from 1995 | 0.46 | 0.29 |
| | $NO_x$ | from 1995 | 1.1 | 0.68 |
| | CO | from 1995 | 5.0 | 3.1 |
| | particulates | from 1995 | 0.12 | 0.075 |
| | | | **(g/bhph)** | **(g/kWh)** |
| **heavy-trucks** | $NO_x$ | from 1996 | 4.0 | 5.36 |
| | particulates | 1991-93 | 0.25 | 0.34 |
| | particulates | from 1994 | 0.10 | 0.13 |
| **busses** | particulates | from 1991 | 0.1 | 0.13 |
| **off road Diesel machines** | $NO_x$ | ? | 6.9 | 9.25 |

Table 6.17 summarizes the history of California legislation, also adopted from 1993 by New York State. It also imposes a limit on non-methanic HC. In this case the corresponding value is 0.39 g/mile (0.24 g/km) instead of 0.41 g/mile as in the table for total HC. It imposes more severe limits earlier on HC and $NO_x$, especially on light-duty vehicles, while remaining more liberal on the limits for CO.

Several alternatives are available: A, B, C, and D (Table 6.17).

- A = endurance and warranty for 80,000 km or 5 years
- B = endurance of 80,000 km and warranty for 120,000 km or 7 years
- C/D = endurance and warranty for 160,000 km or 10 years specific requirements for maintenance and overhaul

The deterioration factors are looser for alternatives A and B and more stringent for alternatives C and D. They differ according to C and D. California also plans to limit benzene exhaust emissions from vehicles equipped with three-way catalysts and to advocate benzene-free fuels. First measured by the 13-mode cycle, truck and bus emissions expressed in g/bhph are currently measured by the transient cycle. The California limits are also more severe in this case or come into force earlier than the federal limits.

**Table 6.17** American statutory levels [23, 65, 97] Californian legislation: gaseous pollutants

| Year | CO | | HC | | $NO_x$ (Town) | | $NO_x$ (Road) | |
|---|---|---|---|---|---|---|---|---|
| Cycle | FTP 75 | | | | | | HWFET | |
| | **Light passenger vehicles** | | | | | | | |
| | (g/mile) | (g/km) | (g/mile) | (g/km) | (g/mile) | (g/km) | (g/mile) | (g/km) |
| 1971(8) | 23 | 14.3 | 2.2 | 1.37 | 4.0 | 2.5 | – | – |
| 1972(8) | 23 | 14.3 | 1.5 | 0.93 | 3.0 | 1.86 | – | – |
| 1973 | 39 | 24.2 | 3.2 | 1.99 | 3.0(8) | 1.86 | – | – |
| 1974 | 39 | 24.2 | 3.2 | 1.99 | 2.0 | 1.24 | – | – |
| 1975-76 | 9.0 | 5.6 | 0.9 | 0.56 | 2.0 | 1.24 | – | – |
| 1977-78 | 9.0 | 5.6 | 0.41 | 0.25 | 1.5 | 0.93 | – | – |
| 1986 option A(1) | 7.0 | 4.35 | 0.41 | 0.25 | 0.4 | 0.25 | 0.53 | 0.33 |
| 1986 option B(1) | 7.0 | 4.35 | 0.41 | 0.25 | 0.7 | 0.43 | 0.93 | 0.58 |
| 1986 option C(1) | 7.0 | 4.35 | 0.41 | 0.25 | 1.0 | 0.62 | 1.33 | 0.83 |
| 1986 option D(1) | 8.3 | 5.16 | 0.46 | 0.29 | 1.0 | 0.62 | 1.33 | 0.83 |
| 1994 | 7.0 | 4.35 | 0.41 | 0.25 | 0.4 | 0.25 | 0.53 | 0.33 |
| 1993(9) (10) | 3.4 | 2.11 | 0.25 | 0.16 | – | – | – | – |
| | **Light utility vehicles** | | | | | | | |
| | (g/mile) | (g/km) | (g/mile) | (g/km) | (g/mile) | (g/km) | (g/mile) | (g/km) |
| 1975 | 20 | 12.5 | 2.0 | 1.24 | 2.0 | 1.24 | – | – |
| 1976-77 | 17 | 10.5 | 0.9 | 0.56 | 2.0 | 1.2 | – | – |
| 1986-89(2) | 9 | 5.6 | 0.41 | 0.25 | 0.4 | 0.25 | 0.8 | 0.5 |
| 1986-89(3) | 9 | 5.6 | 0.5 | 0.31 | 1.0 | 0.62 | 2.0 | 1.24 |
| 1986-89(4) | 9 | 5.6 | 0.6 | 0.37 | 1.5 | 0.93 | 3.0 | 1.86 |
| 1993(9)(11) | 3.4 | 2.11 | 0.25(10) | 0.16 | – | – | – | – |
| 1993(9)(12) | 3.4 | 2.11 | 0.32(10) | 0.20 | – | – | – | – |
| 1995-96(2)(14)(17) | 3.4 | 2.11 | 0.25(10) | 0.16 | 0.4 | 0.25 | – | – |
| 1995-96(3)(14)(17) | 4.4 | 2.74 | 0.32(10) | 0.20 | 0.7 | 0.44 | – | – |
| 1995-96(4)(4)(17) | 5.0 | 3.12 | 0.39(10) | 0.24 | 1.1 | 0.69 | – | – |
| 1995-96(15)(14)(17) | 5.5 | 3.43 | 0.46(10) | 0.29 | 1.3 | 0.81 | – | – |
| 1995-96(16)(17)(14) | 7.0 | 4.36 | 0.60(10) | 0.37 | 2.0 | 1.25 | – | – |
| | **Trucks and buses** | | | | | | | |
| | (g/bhph) | (g/kWh) | (g/bhph) | (g/kWh) | (g/bhph) | (g/kWh) | (g/bhph) | (g/kWh) |
| 1983(6) | 25 | 33.5 | 1.5 | 2.0 | 10(7) | 13.4(7) | – | – |
| 1986(6) | 25 | 33.5 | 0.5 | 0.67 | 4.5(7) | 6(7) | – | – |
| 1988(5) | 15.5 | 20.8 | 1.3 | 1.74 | 6.0 | 8.0 | – | – |
| 1991-94(5) | 15.5 | 20.8 | 1.3 | 1.74 | 5.0(13) | 6.7 | – | – |

(1) See text. (2) <1.8 t. (3) 1.8 to 2.7 t. (4) 2.7 to 3.85 t. (5) Transient cycle.
(6) 13-mode cycle. (7) Value corresponding to HC $+NO_x$. (8) Californian cycle.
(9) 80,000 km draft (limits ×1.24 at 160,000 km). (10) Non-methanic HC. (11) <3.75 t.
(12) 3.75 to 5.75 t. (13) 2.5 in 1996. (14) Vehicles: 50% in 1995, 100% in 1996. (15) 3.85 to 4.53 t.
(16) 4.53 to 6.35 t. (17) 80,000 km values: 160,000 km limits ×1.44 (HC), 1.47 (CO), 1.38 ($NO_x$).

New proposals for light-duty vehicles have been made in California and would be enforceable in 1995 on the basis of a lifetime of 120,000 miles (192,000 km). Table 6.18 gives the details.

**Table 6.18** Californian proposals for light-duty vehicles

| Payload (t) | HC (g/km) | CO (g/km) | $NO_x$ (g/km) | Particulates (g/km) |
|---|---|---|---|---|
| 0-1.7 | 0.22 | 3.1 | 0.34 | 0.05 |
| 1.7-2.6 | 0.29 | 4.0 | 0.61 | 0.05 |
| 2.6-3.85 | 0.35 | 4.54 | 0.95 | 0.06 |
| 3.85-4.54 | 0.41 | 5.0 | 1.12 | 0.07 |
| 4.54-6.35 | 0.53 | 6.4 | 1.72 | 0.09 |

As of 1996, California also wants to reduce the $NO_x$ emitted to 0.2 g/mile (0.125 g/km) and wants to gradually reach (Table 6.19) a 'zero pollution level' in several steps.

- From 1994 to 1996, 10% of the TLEV (Transitory Low Emission Vehicles) produced should emit less than 0.125 g/mile (0.077 g/km).
- From 1997, LEV (Low Emission Vehicles) should emit less than 0.075 g/mile HC (0.047 g/km) and less than 0.2 g/mile $NO_x$ (0.12 g/km). The corresponding production levels should reach 25% in 1997 and 98% in 2000.
- ULEV (Ultra Low Emission Vehicles) are expected in 1995, emitting less than 0.040 g/mile HC (0.025 g/km). Their production should reach 2% of sales in 2000 and 15% by 2003.
- ZEV (Zero Emission Vehicles) are then anticipated, using primarily electric propulsion.

**Table 6.19** Californian proposals for light-duty vehicles

| | NMHC | | NMOG | | CO | | $NO_x$ | | Part. | | HCHO | |
|---|---|---|---|---|---|---|---|---|---|---|---|---|
| **Vehicle** | (1) | (2) | (1) | (2) | (1) | (2) | (1) | (2) | (1) | (2) | (1) | (2) |
| **present** | 0.39 | 0.46 | – | – | 7.0 | 8.3 | 0.4 | 1.0 | 0.08 | – | 0.015 | – |
| **after 1993** | 0.25 | 0.31 | – | – | 3.4 | 4.2 | 0.4 | 1.0 | 0.08 | – | 0.015 | – |
| **TLEV** | – | – | 0.125 | 0.156 | 3.4 | 4.2 | 0.4 | 0.6 | – | 0.08 | 0.015 | 0.018 |
| **LEV** | – | – | 0.075 | 0.090 | 3.4 | 4.2 | 0.2 | 0.3 | – | 0.08 | 0.015 | 0.018 |
| **ULEV** | – | – | 0.040 | 0.055 | 1.7 | 2.1 | 0.2 | 0.3 | – | 0.04 | 0.008 | 0.011 |

Values in g/mile: (1) at 50,000 miles, (2) at 100,000 miles.

## 6.3.2 Statutory values in the EEC

The statutory regulations have been imposed with increasing severity since 1972 [90]. Community directives have been published by the Brussels Commission based on regulations set in Geneva by the *Economic Commission for Europe* (*ECE*) of the United Nations. ECE Regulation 15 has been subjected to various amendments over the years and the fourth amendment is currently in force. These regulations were applied optionally and voluntarily by each of the member states that could not prohibit access to its territory by a vehicle not meeting these standards. Subsequently, in accordance with the latest agreements reached in Luxembourg on 27 July 1985, the application of the new directives became mandatory in each of the member states. Fig. 6.16 shows the changes over the years in regulated CO and $HC+NO_x$ emissions for a medium-powered car, based on the values measured for the same vehicle in 1970, before regulations. The regulations first set separate limits for HC and $NO_x$, and then in 1984, set a combined limit for both pollutants.

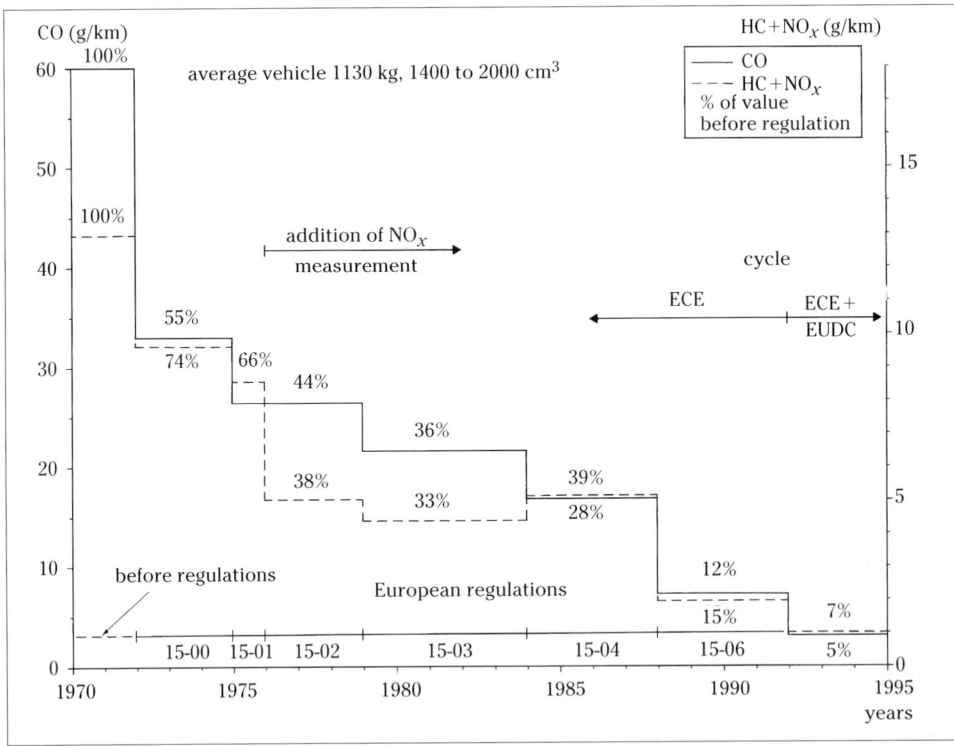


**Fig 6.16** Changes in emission limits in Europe

The European limits were officially expressed in g/test by the ECE cold start cycle. Present statutory limits corresponding to the introduction of the EUDC extra-urban cycle are expressed in g/km. Table 6.20 gives the successive statutory values

**Table 6.20** EEC statutory values: gaseous pollutants
Type I test of *ECE*
Regulation No. 15-04 [97]

| **Reference weight (t)** | | <075 | 0.75 to 0.85 | 0.85 to 1.02 | 1.02 to 1.25 | 1.25 to 1.47 | 1.47 to 1.7 | 1.7 to 1.93 | 1.93 to 2.15 | >2.15 |
|---|---|---|---|---|---|---|---|---|---|---|
| ***Equivalent inertia* (t)** | | 0.68 | 0.8 | 0.91 | 1.13 | 1.36 | 1.59 | 1.81 | 2.04 | 2.27 |
| **Original regulation: Directive 70/220, enforced in 1972** | | | | | | | | | | |
| **CO** | | 100 | 109 | 117 | 134 | 152 | 169 | 186 | 203 | 220 |
| | (g/km) | 24.7 | 26.9 | 28.9 | 33.1 | 37.5 | 41.7 | 45.9 | 50.1 | 54.3 |
| **HC** | (g/test) | 8.0 | 8.4 | 8.7 | 9.4 | 10.1 | 10.8 | 11.4 | 12.1 | 12.8 |
| | (g/km) | 1.97 | 2.07 | 2.14 | 2.32 | 2.49 | 2.66 | 2.81 | 2.99 | 3.16 |
| **Amendment 01: Directive 74/290, enforced in 1975** | | | | | | | | | | |
| **CO** | (g/test) | 80 | 87 | 94 | 107 | 122 | 135 | 149 | 162 | 176 |
| | (g/km) | 19.7 | 21.5 | 23.2 | 26.4 | 30.1 | 33.3 | 36.8 | 40 | 43.4 |
| **HC** | (g/test) | 6.8 | 7.1 | 7.4 | 8.0 | 8.6 | 9.2 | 9.7 | 10.3 | 10.9 |
| | (g/km) | 1.68 | 1.75 | 1.83 | 1.97 | 2.12 | 2.27 | 2.39 | 2.54 | 2.69 |
| **Amendment 02: Directive 77/102, enforced in 1976** | | | | | | | | | | |
| **CO** | (g/test) | 80 | 87 | 94 | 107 | 122 | 135 | 149 | 162 | 176 |
| | (g/km) | 19.7 | 21.5 | 23.2 | 26.4 | 30.1 | 33.3 | 36.8 | 40 | 43.4 |
| **HC** | (g/test) | 6.8 | 7.1 | 7.4 | 8.0 | 8.6 | 9.2 | 9.7 | 10.3 | 10.9 |
| | (g/km) | 1.68 | 1.75 | 1.83 | 1.97 | 2.12 | 2.27 | 2.39 | 2.54 | 2.69 |
| **$NO_x$** | (g/test) | 10 | 10 | 10 | 12 | 14 | 14.5 | 15 | 15.5 | 16 |
| | (g/km) | 2.47 | 2.47 | 2.47 | 2.96 | 3.45 | 3.58 | 3.70 | 3.83 | 3.95 |
| **Amendment 03: Directive 78/665, enforced in 1979** | | | | | | | | | | |
| **CO** | (g/test) | 65 | 71 | 76 | 87 | 99 | 110 | 121 | 132 | 143 |
| | (g/km) | 16 | 17.5 | 18.8 | 21.5 | 24.4 | 27.1 | 29.9 | 32.6 | 35.3 |
| **HC** | (g/test) | 6.0 | 6.3 | 6.5 | 7.1 | 7.6 | 8.1 | 8.6 | 9.1 | 9.6 |
| | (g/km) | 1.48 | 1.55 | 1.60 | 1.75 | 1.87 | 2.0 | 2.12 | 2.25 | 2.37 |
| **$NO_x$** | (g/test) | 8.5 | 8.5 | 8.5 | 10.2 | 11.9 | 12.3 | 12.8 | 13.2 | 13.6 |
| | (g/km) | 2.1 | 2.1 | 2.1 | 2.52 | 2.94 | 3.04 | 3.16 | 3.26 | 3.36 |
| **Amendment 04: Directive 83/351, enforced in 1984** | | | | | | | | | | |
| **CO** | (g/test) | 58 | 58 | 58 | 67 | 76 | 84 | 93 | 100 | 110 |
| | (g/km) | 14.3 | 14.3 | 14.3 | 16.5 | 18.8 | 20.7 | 23 | 24.7 | 27.1 |
| **HC** | (g/test) | 19 | 19 | 19 | 20.5 | 22 | 23.5 | 25 | 26.5 | 28 |
| **+$NO_x$** | (g/km) | 4.69 | 4.69 | 4.69 | 5.06 | 5.43 | 5.8 | 6.17 | 6.54 | 6.91 |

corresponding to the different vehicle weight categories. These limit values must be met by the vehicle models presented for type approval without distinction between gasoline and diesel engines. To account for the statistical dispersion of the performance of vehicles leaving the assembly line, tolerances in the verification of production conformity measured on a random sampling of several vehicles have been set: 120% for CO and 125% for ($HC+NO_x$) in ECE regulation 15-04.

The Luxembourg agreement went on to replace the vehicle categories based on displaced weight by three categories identified by the swept volume of the vehicle engine, distinguishing between spark ignition and diesel (Table 6.21).

**Table 6.21** Community Directive proposed by the Luxembourg Agreements (Directives 88/76/EEC and 89/458/EEC): gaseous pollutants Passenger vehicles ≤2.5 t, ≤6 passengers, ECE cycle

| Vehicle category *V = total displacement* | Maximum mass of pollutants (1) | | | | | | Enforcement date (2) |
|---|---|---|---|---|---|---|---|
| | CO | | $HC+NO_x$ | | $NO_x$ | | |
| | (g/test) | (g/km) | (g/test) | (g/km) | (g/test) | (g/km) | |
| **gasoline** *V > 2.0 l* | 25 | 6.17 | 6.5 | 1.6 | 3.5 | 0.86 | NM: 01-10-1988<br>VN: 01-10-1989 |
| **gasoline** *1.41 ≤ V ≤ 2.0 l* | 30 | 7.4 | 8 | 1.97 | not prescribed | *not prescribed* | NM: 01-10-1991<br>VN: 01-10-1992 |
| **gasoline** *V < 1.4 l* | 45 | 11.09 | 15 | 3.7 | 6 | 1.48 | NM: 01-10-1990<br>VN: 01-10-1991 |
| | 19 | 4.6 | 5 | 1.23 | | | NM: 01-07-1992<br>VN: 31-12-1992 |
| **diesel** *>2 l* | 30 | 7.4 | 8 | 1.97 | not prescribed | *not prescribed* | NM: 01-10-1988<br>VN: 01-10-1989 |
| **diesel** *1.41 ≤ V ≤ 2.0 l* | 30 | 7.4 | 8 | 1.97 | not prescribed | *not prescribed* | NM (IID): 01-10-1988<br>VN (IID): 01-10-1993<br>NM (ID): 01-10-1994<br>VN (ID): 01-10-1996 |
| **diesel** *V < 1.4 l* | 45 | 11.09 | 15 | 3.7 | 6 | 1.48 | NM: 01-10-1990<br>VN: 01-10-1991 |
| | 19 | 4.6 | 5 | 1.23 | | | NM: 01-07-1992<br>VN: 31-12-92 |

(1) Maximum type approval values.
For production conformity, multiply by 1.2 for CO, 1.25 for $NO_x$ and $HC+NO_x$, then by 1.16.
For automatic transmission, multiply by 1.3 for $NO_x$ and 1.2 for $HC+NO_x$.
(2) NM, new models. VN, new vehicles. ID, direct injection. IID, indirect injection.

Earlier enforcement deadlines have been planned for newly designed models, as opposed to new production vehicles whose design existed before the regulations entered into force. There is generally a difference of one year between the two cases. Moreover, for the intermediate category, which are vehicles with a total displacement between 1.4 and 2 liters, a second more severe step has been set with a delay of one year. Also for diesel engines in this intermediate category, a distinction is made between pre-chamber and direct injection engines, with the latter subjected to the same regulation but becoming effective three years later. The production conformity factors have the same values as noted previously, 20 and 25%.

An appendix to the Luxembourg directive states that, at the manufacturer's request, for total displacements over 1.4 liters the 1983 federal limits can be substituted for the European limits by using the US procedure and the FTP-75 cycle. Tax incentives, in the form of lower vehicle purchase taxes, have been proposed in Germany, Sweden, Austria, Italy, the Netherlands, Denmark, and Luxembourg, for buyers of vehicles meeting these US standards in anticipation of the European regulations.

The more severe regulation passed by the Strasbourg Parliament on 12 April 1989 lowers the maximum values and advances the enforcement dates. A range of ±10% for compliance with the limits is nevertheless permitted for type approval.

The new Community standard includes the EUDC extra-urban cycle. The regulatory limits are based on mileage emissions and no longer on values measured by tests. The latest proposals advanced by the *European Commission for the Environment* and the *ACEA* are shown in Table 6.22. To these limits, which are

**Table 6.22** Present and planned European standards for all light vehicles (ECE + EUDC cycle: values in g/km)

| **Pollutant** | **NM 01.07.1992** | | **NM 01.01.1993** |
|---|---|---|---|
| | **VN 01.01.1993** | | **VN 01.01.1997** |
| | (1) | (2) | (1) |
| **CO** | 2.72 | 3.16 | 2.2(3)-1.0(4) |
| **HC + $NO_x$** (gasoline) | 0.97 | 1.13 | 0.5 |
| **HC + $NO_x$** (diesel IDI ) | 0.97 | 1.13 | 0.7 |
| **HC + $NO_x$** (diesel DI) | 0.97 | 1.13 | 0.9 |
| **particulates** (diesel) | 0.14 | 0.18 | 0.08(5)-0.10(6) |

(1) Type approval, (2) production conformity,
(3) Gasoline, (4) diesel,
(5) IDI diesel, (6) DI diesel

different for type approval and production with a durability of 80,000 km, the Parliament proposes to add a limit of 250 g/km on $CO_2$ emissions from 1996. Gasolines will also be limited to a maximum of 1% benzene. Diesel fuels will have to have a maximum of 0.05% sulfur, a cetane number of 50, and a 90% distillation point under 340°C.

For small utility vehicles, the present regulation applies Directive 15-04 (Table 6.20) according to the inertia classes and based on the ECE cycle. The EEC plans to enforce the limits in Table 6.23 in the future, applicable to ECE+EUDC cycle on 1 October 1993 for new vehicles (NV) and 10 October 1995 for new models (NM).

After having recommended the limits of ECE Regulation No. 49 since 1982, the recent European Directive concerning trucks and buses is much more severe. After weighting, it expresses the emissions in g/kWh measured on the engine test bench by the European 13-mode cycle (Table 6.24).

**Table 6.23** Future *EEC* regulation for small utility vehicles. Enforcement date: 01.10.1993 (NM), 01.10.1994 (NV)

| **Inertia (kg)** | **≤1251** | **1250-1790** | **1701-3500** |
|---|---|---|---|
| **CO (g/km)** | 2.72 | 5.17 | 6.9 |
| **$HC+NO_x$ (g/km)** | 0.97 | 1.4 | 1.7 |
| **particulates (g/km)** | 0.14 | 0.19 | 0.25 |

NM: New Models, New Vehicles

**Table 6.24** Community Directive (Directive 88/77/*EEC*) Trucks and buses >3.5 t, Regulation 49. Gaseous pollutants

| **Maximum weight of pollutants (g/kWh)** | | | **Enforcement date** |
|---|---|---|---|
| **CO** | **HC** | **$NO_x$** | |
| 14 | 3.5 | 18 | 1982 |
| 11.2 | 2.4 | 14.4 | 01-04-1988 NM |
| 11.2 | 2.4 | 14.4 | 01-10-1990 VN |
| 4.5 | 1.1 | 8.0 | 01-07-1992 NM(1) |
| 4.9 | 1.23 | 9.0 | 01-07-1992 NM(2) |
| 4.5 | 1.1 | 8.0 | 01-10-1993 VN(1) |
| 4.9 | 1.23 | 9.0 | 01-10-1993 VN(2) |
| 4.0 | 1.1 | 7.0 | 01-10-1995 NM |
| 4.0 | 1.1 | 7.0 | 01-10-1996 VN |
| <4.0 | <1.1 | 5.0 | 01-10-1998 |

(1) Type approval. (2) Production conformity. NM, new models. VN, new vehicles.

## 6.3.3 Statutory values in Central Europe and Scandinavia

After having initially adopted the ECE regulations a number of countries that remained outside the European Community decided, at a meeting in Stockholm in July 1985, to adopt the 1983 American limits as well as the corresponding FTP-75 cycle (Stockholm Agreement). The enforcement dates vary in different countries [13 and 14]. Table 6.25 summarizes the limits and their enforcement dates. Denmark, an EEC member, did not sign the Luxembourg compromise agreement and is strongly tempted to follow the example of the other Scandinavian countries that signed the Stockholm Agreement.

For trucks and buses some countries such as Sweden [92 and 93] are beginning to shift from the European 13-mode cycle and Regulation R49 to the American transient cycle, while continuing to express the values in g/kWh (Table 6.25).

**Table 6.25** Central and Northern Europe
Statutory values-Gaseous pollutants

| Country | Year | Cycle | CO | HC | $NO_x$ |
|---|---|---|---|---|---|
| | | | (g/km) | (g/km) | (g/km) |
| **Passenger cars and utility vehicles with maximum load ≤2.5 t** | | | | | |
| **Switzerland** | 01-10-1987 | FTP 75 | 2.1 | 0.25 | 0.62 |
| | id | HWFET | – | – | 0.76 |
| **Austria** | 01-10-1987 | FTP 75 | 2.1 | 0.25 | 0.62 |
| **Sweden** | model 88(1) | FTP 75 | 2.1 | 0.25 | 0.62 |
| | model 89 | FTP 75 | 2.1 | 0.25 | 0.62 |
| | id | HWFET | – | – | 0.76 |
| **Norway** | 01-10-1989 | FTP 75 | 2.1 | 0.25 | 0.62 |
| | id | HWFET | – | – | 0.76 |
| **Finland** | 1981 | ECE | 21.5(2) | 1.75(2) | 2.52(2) |
| | 1986 | ECE | 16.5(2) | 5.06(2)(4) | |
| | 01-10-1992 | FTP 75 | 2.1 | 0.25 | 0.62 |
| **Light-duty vehicles** (3) | | | | | |
| **Switzerland** | 1987 | ECE | 16.5(2) | 5.06(2)(4) | |
| | 01-10-1988 | FTP 75 | 6.2 | 0.5(4) | 1.4 |
| | 01-10-1990 | FTP 75 | 6.2 | 0.5 | 1.1 |
| **Austria** | 1987 | ECE | 16.5(2) | 5.06(2)(4) | |
| | 01-10-1989 | FTP 75 | 6.2 | 0.50 | 1.43 |
| **Sweden** | projects 1990 | FTP 75 | 6.2 | 0.5 | 1.1 |
| **Norway** | projects 1991 | FTP 75 | 6.2 | 0.5 | 1.1 |
| **Trucks and buses** | | | | | |
| | | | (g/km) | (g/km) | (g/km) |
| **Switzerland** | 1987 | R49-13 modes | 8.4 | 2.1 | 14.4 |
| | 1991 | id | 4.9 | 1.2 | 9.0 |
| **Austria** | 1991 | id | 4.9 | 1.2 | 9.0 |
| **Sweden** | 1990 | R49-13 modes | 4.9 | 1.2 | 9.0 |
| | 1995 | "transient" | 4.9 | 1.2 | 9.0 |
| **Norway** | projects 1993 | R49-13 modes | | | 7.0 |
| **Finland** | 1989 | R49-13 modes | 14 | 3.5 | 18 |

(1) Voluntary contribution.
(2) Translation of values measured in g/test (ECE-15-03) for 1130 kg vehicle.
(3) In Switzerland: >9 passengers or payload >0.76 t or 4 × 4 all-terrain vehicle.
In Austria: >7 passengers or payload >0.76 t or 4×4 all-terrain vehicle.
(4) HC + $NO_x$.
(5) For payload >1.4 t, 30% reduction (1989 and 1990).

### 6.3.4 Statutory values in Eastern Europe

The *Economic Commission for Europe (ECE)* of the *United Nations* includes most Eastern European countries among its members including the ex-Czechoslovakia, Hungary, Romania, the ex-Yugoslavia, the ex-USSR, and the ex-Democratic Republic of Germany. These participating states can accordingly apply the ECE regulations domestically as they wish. They also agree to refrain from prohibiting the importation of vehicles meeting these regulations. Hungary plans to adopt EEC limit values as of 1994.

### 6.3.5 European railroad limits

The following statutory limits have been announced by the *Union Internationale des Chemins de Fer* (UIC, *International Railway Union*) [69].

| Pollutant (g/kWh) | Before 1 January 1982 | After 1 January 1982 |
|---|---|---|
| $NO_x$ | 24.0 | 20.0 |
| CO | 12.0 | 8.0 |
| HC | 4.0 | 2.4 |

### 6.3.6 Statutory values in Japan

Following the first limits introduced in 1973, based on the 10-mode cycle (Fig. 6.11), Japanese regulations became increasingly severe and demanded control systems comparable in complexity to those required to satisfy California standards. While they use the standard CVS system, the Japanese driving cycles are specific to the country.

In addition to the limit values given in Tables 6.26 and 6.27, Japan imposes average values that must be complied with by vehicles manufactured or imported in quantities of more than 2000 per year. The test is performed on a sample representing 1% of production. These regulated average values generally represent 70 to 75% of the limit values, but they may fall to nearly 50% for $NO_x$ [97]. A special regulation exists for gasoline or LPG-fueled vehicles and for diesel vehicles. For the latter, the 11-mode cycle is replaced by a 6-mode cycle (Table 6.7) that expresses the limits in the form of concentrations (% or ppm). A similar 6-mode cycle exists for gasoline or LPG-powered trucks, but the weighting factors applied to each of the modes are different (Table 6.8).

Changes in Japanese regulations concerning gaseous pollutants pertain mainly to nitrogen oxides [109]:

- In all cases for all pollutants, even for the unchanged limits, the new cycles described above are applicable from 1 November 1991.

- For all diesel commercial vehicles and for gasoline vans >2.5 t, the limits are lowered by 35% in an initial period (1992/1994), and subsequently lowered by 65% (before 1999).
- The distinction between diesel IDI and DI vehicles is eliminated and the stricter limit concerning pre-combustion chamber engines prevails.
- For trucks >2.5 t, the limits in g/kWh become 9.2 for CO, 3.8 for HC and 7.8 (DI) and 6.8 (IDI) for $NO_x$ for new models as of 1 October 1992 and for all vehicles produced from 1 September 1993.

**Table 6.26** Japanese statutory limit values [97]
Gaseous pollutants (passenger vehicles)

| Year | Fuel | CO | | | HC | | | $NO_x$ | | |
|---|---|---|---|---|---|---|---|---|---|---|
| **Light passenger vehicles <1.7 t** | | | | | | | | | | |
| **cycle** | | 10 modes | 11 modes | | 10 modes | 11 modes | | 10 modes | 11 modes | |
| | | **(g/km)** | **(g/test)** | **(g/km)** | **(g/km)** | **(g/test)** | **(g/km)** | **(g/km)** | **(g/test)** | **(g/km)** |
| **1973** | gasoline | 26 | – | – | 3.8 | – | – | 3.0 | – | – |
| **1973** | LPG | 18 | – | – | 3.2 | – | – | 3.0 | – | – |
| **1975** | gasoline/LPG | 2.7 | 85 | 20.81 | 0.39 | 9.5 | 2.33 | 1.6 | 11 | 2.7 |
| **1976** | gasoline/LPG | 2.7 | 85 | 20.81 | 0.39 | 9.5 | 2.33 | 0.84(1) | 8(1) | 1.96 |
| **1976** | gasoline/LPG | 2.7 | 85 | 20.81 | 0.39 | 9.5 | 2.33 | 1.2(2) | 9(2) | 2.20 |
| **1978** | gasoline/LPG | 2.7 | 85 | 20.81 | 0.39 | 9.5 | 2.33 | 0.48 | 6 | 1.47 |
| **1988(10)** | gasoline/LPG | 2.7 | 85 | 20.81 | 0.39 | 9.5 | 2.33 | 0.25 | 6 | 1.47 |
| **cycle** | | 10 modes | 6 modes | | 10 modes | 6 modes | | 10 modes | 6 modes | |
| **1974** | diesel | – | 680 ppm | | – | 670 ppm | | – | 590(5)ppm | |
| **1977** | diesel | – | 680 ppm | | – | 670 ppm | | – | 500(6)ppm | |
| **1979** | diesel | – | 680 ppm | | – | 670 ppm | | – | 450(7)ppm | |
| **1982** | diesel | – | 680 ppm | | – | 670 ppm | | – | 390(8)ppm | |
| **1983** | diesel | – | 680 ppm | | – | 670 ppm | | – | 610(9)ppm | |
| **1987** | diesel | 2.7 | – | | 0.62 | – | | 0.98(3) | – | |
| **1987(11)** | diesel | 2.7 | – | | 0.62 | – | | 1.26(4) | 0.6 g/km(12) | |

(1) Vehicle weight <1 t.
(2 Vehicle weight >1 t.
(3) Vehicle weight <1.25 t.
(4) Vehicle weight >1.25 t.
For DI engine: (5) 1000 ppm. (6) 850 ppm. (7) 700 ppm. (8) For DII engine. (9) For DI engine
(10) from 1991, 10-15 mode cycle replaced 10-mode cycle.
(11) from 1994, 10-15 mode cycle replaced 10-mode cycle.
(12) from 1999, 0.4 g/km.

**Table 6.27** Japanese statutory limit values [97]
Gaseous pollutants (utility vehicles)

| Year | Fuel | CO | | | HC | | | $NO_x$ | | |
|---|---|---|---|---|---|---|---|---|---|---|
| **Light-duty vehicles < 2.5 t** | | | | | | | | | | |
| **cycle** | | 10 modes | 11 modes | | 10 modes | 11 modes | | 10 modes | 11 modes | |
| | | (g/km) | (g/test) | (g/km) | (g/km) | (g/test) | (g/km) | (g/km) | (g/test) | (g/km) |
| **1973** | gasoline | 26 | – | – | 3.8 | – | – | 3.0 | – | – |
| **1973** | LPG | 18 | – | – | 3.2 | – | – | 3.0 | – | – |
| **1975** | gasol./LPG | 17 | 130 | 31.83 | 2.7 | 17 | 4.16 | 2.3 | 20 | 4.9 |
| **1979(10)** | gasol./LPG | 17 | 130 | 31.83 | 2.7 | 17 | 4.16 | 1.4 | 10 | 2.45 |
| **1979(11)** | gasol./LPG | 17 | 130 | 31.83 | 2.7 | 17 | 4.16 | 1.6 | 11 | 2.69 |
| **1981(10)** | gasol./LPG | 17 | 130 | 31.83 | 2.7 | 17 | 4.16 | 0.84 | 8 | 1.96 |
| **1981(11)** | gasol./LPG | 17 | 130 | 31.83 | 2.7 | 17 | 4.16 | 1.26 | 9.5 | 2.33 |
| **1988** | gasol./LPG | 17 | 130 | 31.83 | 2.7 | 17 | 4.16 | 0.7 | 9.5 | 2.33 |
| **1974-87** | diesel | **Idem, diesel passenger vehicles** | | | | | | | | |
| **cycle** | | 10 modes | 6 modes | | 10 modes | 6 modes | | 10 modes | 6 modes | |
| **1988** | diesel DI | 2.7 | 680 ppm | | 0.62 | 670 ppm | | 1.26 | 380 ppm | |
| **1988** | diesel | 2.7 | 680 ppm | | 0.62 | 670 ppm | | 1.26 | 260 ppm | |
| **Trucks and buses > 2.5 t** | | | | | | | | | | |
| **cycle** | | 10 modes | 11 modes | | 10 modes | 11 modes | | 10 modes | 11 modes | |
| **1973** | gasoline | – | 1.6% | | – | 520 ppm | | – | 2200 ppm | |
| **1973** | LPG | – | 1.1% | | – | 440 ppm | | – | 2200 ppm | |
| **1977** | gasol./LPG | – | 1.6% | | – | 520 ppm | | – | 1350 ppm | |
| **1982** | gasol./LPG | – | 1.6% | | – | 520 ppm | | – | 990 ppm | |
| **1989** | gasoline | – | 1.6% | | – | 520 ppm | | – | 650 ppm | |
| **1974-87** | diesel | **Idem, diesel passenger vehicles** | | | | | | | | |
| | | 10 modes | 6 modes | | 10 modes | 6 modes | | 10 modes | 6 modes | |
| **1988-90** | diesel DI | 2.7 | 980 ppm | | 0.62 | 670 ppm | | 1.26 | 610 ppm | |
| **1989** | diesel IDI | 2.7 | 980 ppm | | 0.62 | 670 ppm | | 1.26 | 520 ppm | |

(10) Light vehicles.
(11) Medium-weight vehicles.

## 6.3.7 Legislation in other countries

A number of extra-European countries (Table 6.28) apply the ECE regulations, such as Hong Kong, Israel, the Philippines, and New Zealand. New Zealand tends to adopt Australian regulations. Argentina plans to approach the ECE regulations, but other countries of the Americas (Canada, Mexico, Brazil) are adopting the United States regulations or intend to do so. Canada plans to adopt, for models sold in 1994, the limits imposed by California for 1993.

**Table 6.28** Other countries, Statutory values
Gaseous pollutants [22, 31, 75, 81, 82, 97 and 104]
Passenger cars (1)

| Country | Year | Cycle | CO | HC | $NO_x$ |
|---|---|---|---|---|---|
| | | | (g/km) | (g/km) | (g/km) |
| **Canada** | 1975 | FTP 75 | 15.33 | 1.24 | 1.92 |
| | 01-09-1987 | FTP 75 | 2.11 | 0.25 | 0.62 |
| | 1994 | FTP 75 | 2.11 | 0.15 | 0.25 |
| **Australia and New Zealand** | 01-07-1976 | FTP 72 | 24.2 | 2.1 | 1.9 |
| | 01-01-1982 | FTP 72 | 22 | 1.91 | 1.73 |
| | 01-01-1986 | FTP 75 | 9.3 | 0.93 | 1.9 |
| **Taiwan** | | | | | |
| **VN** (2) | 01-07-1987 | ECE | 14.31 | 4.69 | |
| **NM** (2) | 01-07-1988 | ECE | 14.31 | 4.69 | |
| | 1989 | FTP 75 | 2.11 | 0.25 | 0.25 |
| **Singapore** | 01-10-1986 | ECE Regulation 15-04 | | | |
| **South Korea** | 1980-83 | 10-m | 26 | 3.8 | 3.0 |
| | 01-07-1984 | 10-m | 18 | 2.8 | 2.5 |
| (3) | 01-07-1987 | FTP 75 | 8 | 2.1 | 1.5 |
| (4) | 01-07-1987 | FTP 75 | 2.11 | 0.25 | 0.62 |
| **Mexico** | 1989 | FTP 75 | 21.9 | 1.99 | 2.29 |
| | 1990 | FTP 75 | 18.52 | 1.79 | 1.99 |
| | 1991 | FTP 75 | 6.96 | 0.70 | 1.39 |
| | 1993 | FTP 75 | 2.11 | 0.25 | 0.62 |
| **Brazil** | 01-06-1988 | FTP 75 | 24 | 2.1 | 2.0 |
| | 01-01-1992 | FTP 75 | 12 | 1.2 | 1.4 |
| | 01-01-1997 | FTP 75 | 2.0 | 0.3 | 0.6 |
| **Israel** | 01-10-1986 | ECE Regulation 15-04 | | | |
| **Saudi Arabia** | 01-10-1986 | ECE Regulation 15-04 | | | |

(1) <2.7 t.
(2) Translation of measured values into g/test (ECE-15-03) for vehicle weighing 1130 kg.
(3) Vehicle engine <800 $cm^3$.
(4) Engine >800 $cm^3$ but <2.5 t.

### 6.3.8 Idling emissions

This measurement concerns only spark ignition engines. Idling CO emissions were among the first to be controlled, because they require no particular heavy equipment. Subsequently, controls were extended to include unburned hydrocarbons emitted while idling. In the United States, five control tests are available below 80,000 km to check the CO and HC volumetric concentrations from light vehicles at idle (Table 6.29).

The EEC regulation (Regulation 15 Type II) specifies a limit with the engine adjusted and an upper limit that the user must not be able to exceed by manipulating the available adjustment instruments. In Switzerland, the CO and HC limits differ according to the vehicle payload. For HC emissions, Japan distinguishes between two-stroke engines and four-stroke engines.

## 6.4 Particulate pollutants (Passenger vehicles and trucks)

Since these emissions are rather specific to diesel combustion, mass particulate emissions were regulated later than gaseous emissions. An excessive reduction of the statutory limits will raise the problem of the reliability of the present measurement procedure (Chapter 7), when the value to be measured reaches the order of magnitude of the measurement errors.

### 6.4.1 European statutory values

The EEC imposes the same limits, with the same schedule, for passenger cars and light-duty vehicles (Table 6.31). The directive limits emissions to 0.19 g/km for certification (0.24 g/km for production conformity) measured on the combined ECE+EUDC cycle. For trucks, the EEC Council of 19 March 1991 set the limits shown in Table 6.30.

Germany proposed to limit particulate emissions initially from 1992 to 0.36 g/kWh for engine power >85 kWh and 0.63 g/kWh for lower power, and then to 0.15 g/kWh in the 1995/1996 period [18]. European countries that tend to adopt American limits plan more severe restrictions. Among these, only Switzerland and Sweden currently plan limits for trucks and buses.

### 6.4.2 American statutory values

As in the case of gaseous emissions, California is in advance of the federal regulations. Buses are also covered by early limits when compared with those applicable to trucks (Table 6.32).

**Table 6.29** Idling emissions, Statutory values

| Country | Vehicle | Pollutant | Test | Limit |
|---|---|---|---|---|
| **EEC** | passenger car | CO | type II all cases | 3.5% 4.5% |
| | two-wheeled vehicle | CO | type II | 4.5% |
| | car with catalyst | CO | idling | 0.5% |
| | car with catalyst | CO | 2000 rpm | 0.3% |
| **Switzerland** | light vehicles (1) | CO | | 0.5% vol. |
| | light vehicles (1) | HC | | 100 ppmV |
| | vehicle (2) | CO | | 1% vol. |
| | vehicle (2) | HC | | 200 ppm |
| | motorcycles | CO | type II | 3.5% vol. |
| | pedal motorcycles | CO | type II | 0.1 g/min |
| | pedal motorcycles | HC | type II | 0.1 g/min |
| **Austria** | **Identical EEC** | | | |
| **Sweden (Norway)** | light vehicles | CO | | 0.5% |
| | light vehicles | HC | | 100 ppmV |
| **USA** | light vehicles | CO | (3) | 1.2% |
| | light vehicles | HC | (3) | 220 ppmV |
| | light vehicles | CO | (4) | 1.0% |
| | light vehicles | HC | (4) | 220 ppmV |
| | light vehicles | CO | (5) | 0.5% vol. |
| **Canada** | light vehicles | CO | | 0.5% |
| **Japan** | light vehicles | CO | | 4.5% |
| | four-stroke engine | HC | | 1200 ppmV |
| | two-stroke engine | HC | | 7800 ppmV |
| | special engine | HC | | 3300 ppmV |
| **South Korea** | light vehicles | CO | | 4.5% |
| | | HC | | 1200 ppmV |
| **Taiwan** | light vehicles | CO | type II | 3.5% |
| | | HC | type II | 900 ppmV |
| **Brazil** | 1988-NM | CO | | 3% |
| | 1990-VN | CO | | 3% |
| | 1992-all | CO | | 2.5% |
| | 1997-all | CO | | 0.5% |

(1) <9 passengers or payload <0.76 t. (2) >9 passengers or payload >0.76 t.
(3) Choice of one of the following tests under 80,000 km:
- test at 2500 rpm, idling,
- test at 2500 rpm, idling after engine restart,
- idling test after engine restart,
- idling test,
- load test.

(4) Idling test at two speeds, under 80,000 km. (5) Recent regulation.

New California proposals for light-duty vehicles become enforceable in 1995 on the basis of a durability of 120,000 miles (192,000 km) (Table 6.18).

**Table 6.30** European limits for trucks

| Enforcement date | Power (kW) | Limit (g/kWh) | Remarks |
|---|---|---|---|
| 01.07.1992 | <85 | 0.63 | NM approval |
| 01.07.1992 | >85 | 0.36 | NM approval |
| 01.07.1992 | <85 | 0.70 | NM production conformity |
| 01.07.1992 | >85 | 0.40 | NM production conformity |
| 01.07.1993 | <85 | 0.63 | VN approval |
| 01.07.1993 | >85 | 0.36 | VN approval |
| 01.07.1993 | <85 | 0.70 | VN production conformity |
| 01.07.1993 | >85 | 0.40 | VN production conformity |
| 01.10.1995 | <85 | 0.15 | NM approval |
| 01.10.1995 | >85 | 0.15 | NM approval |
| 01.10.1996 | <85 | 0.15 | VN approval |
| 01.10.1996 | >85 | 0.15 | VN approval |
| 01.10.1998 | all types | 0.10 | |

## 6.4.3 Japanese statutory values

Japan has so far not planned to limit mass particulate emissions. It is planned to introduce a limitation of 0.34 g/km for diesel vehicles from 1 October 1994 for new models and from 1 September 1995 for all cars produced [109]. This limit will be lowered in 1999 to 0.08 g/km. The same limits will be applied to utility vehicles weighing <1.7 t for new models as of 1 November 1991.

For utility vehicles weighing between 1.7 and 2.5 t the limit is set at 0.43 g/km (ultimately reducible to 0.09 g/km) on 1 October 1993 for new models and on 1 September 1994 for all vehicles produced. For trucks >2.5 t, the limit will be 0.96 g/kWh (scheduled to drop to 0.25 g/kWh in the long term) on 1 October 1994 for new models and on 1 September 1995 for all vehicles produced.

Taiwan has proposed a limit value of 0.12 g/km as of 1 July 1995 for passenger vehicles and a limit of 0.94 g/kWh for trucks, measured on the transient cycle. The latter figure would be reduced to 0.34 g/kWh in 1997.

## 6.4.4 Smoke opacity limits

Again for reasons of convenience of measurement, smoke emissions of diesel engines were regulated much earlier than mass particulate emissions. In accordance with the cycle described above (Fig. 6.15), the American federal regulation imposes

**Table 6.31** European statutory values [23, 65 and 97] Mass diesel particulate emissions

| Country | Year | Category | Cycle | Limit value | |
|---|---|---|---|---|---|
| **Light passenger vehicles (< 12 passengers, no weight limit)** | | | | | |
| | | | | **(g/test)** | **(g/km)** |
| **EEC** | 01-10-1988(2) | NM | ECE fd | 1.1 | 0.27 |
| | 01-10-1989(2) | VN | ECE fd | 1.1 | 0.27 |
| | 01-07-1992(6) | NM | ECE fd + EUDC | – | 0.14 |
| | 01-01-1993(7) | VN | ECE fd + EUDC | – | 0.14 |
| | 01-01-1996(7) | NM | ECE fd + EUDC | – | 0.10 |
| | 01-10-1997(7) | VN | ECE fd + EUDC | – | 0.10 |
| | 01-10-1996(8) | NM | ECE fd + EUDC | – | 0.06 |
| **Switzerland** | 01-10-1987 | all | FTP 75 | – | 0.37 |
| | 01-10-1988 | all | FTP 75 | – | 0.124 |
| **Austria** | 01-01-1987 | all | FTP 75 | – | 0.37 |
| **Sweden** | models 88 | all | FTP 75 | – | 0.124 |
| **Norway** | 01-01-1989 | all | FTP 75 | – | 0.124 |
| **Finland** | 01-01-1992 | all | FTP 75 | – | 0.37 |
| **Light utility vehicles (2)** | | | | | |
| | | | | **(g/test)** | **(g/km)** |
| **EEC** | 01-10-1988 | NM | ECE fd | 1.1 | 0.27 |
| | 01-10-1989 | VN | ECE fd | 1.1 | 0.27 |
| | 01-10-1994(8) | NM(3) ⩽1130 kg | ECE fd + EUDC | – | 0.14 |
| | 01-10-1994(8) | NM(3) 1360-1590 kg | ECE fd + EUDC | – | 0.25 |
| | 01-10-1994(8) | NM(3) ⩾1810 kg | ECE fd + EUDC | – | 0.35 |
| **Switzerland** | 01-10-1988 | all | FTP 75 | – | 0.37 |
| | 01-10-1990 | all | FTP 75 | – | 0.16 |
| **Austria** | 01-10-1989 | all | FTP 75 | – | 0.37 |
| **Sweden** | 1990 projects | all | FTP 75 | – | 0.16 |
| **Trucks and buses** | | | | | |
| | | | | | **(g/kWh)** |
| **EEC** | 01-07-1992 | NM(4) | R49 13-mode | – | 0.63 |
| | 01-10-1993 | VN(4) | R49 13-mode | – | 0.63 |
| | 01-07-1992 | NM(5) | R49 13-mode | – | 0.36 |
| | 01-10-1993 | VN(5) | R49 13-mode | – | 0.36 |
| | 01-10-1995 | NM | R49 13-mode | – | 0.15 |
| | 01-07-1996 | VN | R49 13-mode | – | 0.15 |
| | 1998(9) project | VN | R49 13-mode | – | 0.10 |
| **Switzerland** | 1990 projects | | R49 13-mode | – | 0.7 |
| | 01.01.1993 | | R49 13-mode | – | 0.4(10) |
| **Austria** | 1991 | | R49 13-mode | – | 0.7 |
| **Sweden** | 1995 | | "transient" | – | 0.4-0.5 |
| **Norway** | 1993 projects | trucks | R49 13-mode | – | 0.35 |
| | 1993 projects | buses | R49 13-mode | – | 0.14 |

(1) Weight <3.5 t or >12 passengers or 4×4 all-terrain vehicles. (2) Luxembourg Agreement.
(3) VN from 01.10.1995. (4) <0.85 kW. (5) >0.85 kW.
(6) EEC 70/220. (7) ACEA. (8) Ripa di Meana.
(9) UBA proposal. (10) trucks >85 kW.

**Table 6.32** American statutory values [23, 65 and 97]
Mass diesel particulate emissions

| Year | Cycle | Vehicle | | | |
|---|---|---|---|---|---|
| | | Federal law (49 States) | | Californian law | |
| **Light passenger vehicles** (1) | | | | | |
| | | (g/mile) | (g/km) | (g/mile) | (g/km) |
| 1983 | FTP 75 | 0.60 | 0.37 | | |
| 1986 option A(3) | FTP 75 | | | 0.20 | 0.12 |
| 1986 option B(3) | FTP 75 | | | 0.20 | 0.12 |
| 1986 option C(3) | FTP 75 | | | 0.40 | 0.25 |
| 1986 option D(3) | FTP 75 | | | 0.40 | 0.25 |
| 1987 | FTP 75 | 0.20 | 0.12 | | |
| 1994 | FTP 75 | | | 0.08 | 0.05 |
| projects | – | 0.08 | 0.05 | | |
| **Light utility vehicles** (2) | | | | | |
| | | (g/mile) | (g/km) | (g/mile) | (g/km) |
| 1984 | FTP 75 | 0.60 | 0.37 | | |
| 1986 | FTP 75 | | | 0.20 | 0.12 |
| 1987-89 | FTP 75 | 0.26 | 0.16 | | |
| 1989 | FTP 75 | | | 0.08 | 0.05 |
| projects | – | 0.08 | 0.05 | | |
| **Trucks** | | | | | |
| | | (g/bhph) | (g/kWh) | (g/bhph) | (g/kWh) |
| 1988 | "transient" | 0.60 | 0.80 | 0.60 | 0.80 |
| 1991 | "transient" | 0.25 | 0.34 | 0.25 | 0.34 |
| 1994 | "transient" | 0.10 | 0.13 | 0.10 | 0.13 |
| **Buses** | | | | | |
| | | (g/bhph) | (g/kWh) | (g/bhph) | (g/kWh) |
| 1988 | "transient" | 0.60 | 0.80 | 0.60 | 0.80 |
| 1991 | "transient" | 0.10 | 0.13 | 0.10(4) | 0.13 |

(1) Fewer than 12 passengers, unlimited weight.
(2) Weight <3·5 t or more than 12 passengers or 4×4 all-terrain vehicles.
(3) See text.
(4) 0·05 in 1996.

an opacity limit of 20% during acceleration, 15% during braking, and never exceeding 50% at any point during the cycle [36]. The *EEC* statutory limit values corresponding to Regulation 24 (Directive 72/306/EEC) are listed in Table 6.33 and illustrated in Fig. 6.17 for the stabilized speed test at full load. It limits the opacity of exhaust gases at full load and stabilized speed, from 1000 rpm (or 45% of maximum speed), with the measurement taken at six uniformly distributed points. The opacimeter is mounted in series or on a by-pass and the limit is given by a curve versus the theoretical engine exhaust flow.

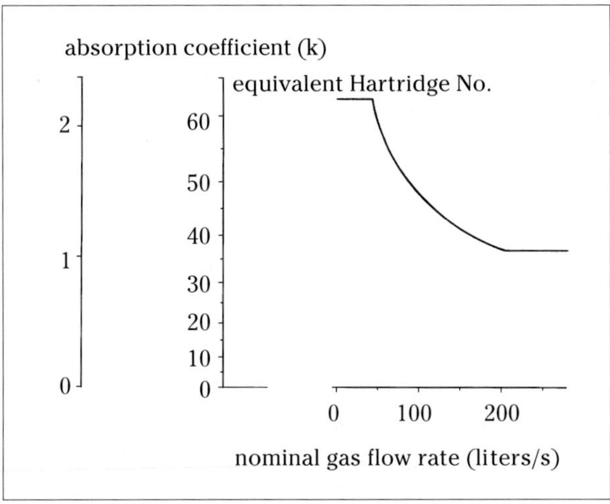


**Fig 6.17** Diesel smoke: European regulations [36]

**Table 6.33** Diesel smoke opacity, ECE Regulation No. 24: Tests in stabilized speed at full load

| **Limit optical absorption coefficient k as a function of nominal gas flow G** | | | | | |
|---|---|---|---|---|---|
| **G (1/s)** | **k ($m^{-1}$)** | **G (1/s)** | **k ($m^{-1}$)** | **G (1/s)** | **k ($m^{-1}$)** |
| ⩽42 | 2.26 | 95 | 1.535 | 150 | 1.225 |
| 45 | 2.19 | 100 | 1.495 | 155 | 1.205 |
| 50 | 2.08 | 105 | 1.465 | 160 | 1.19 |
| 55 | 1.985 | 110 | 1.425 | 165 | 1.17 |
| 60 | 1.90 | 115 | 1.395 | 170 | 1.155 |
| 65 | 1.84 | 120 | 1.37 | 175 | 1.14 |
| 70 | 1.775 | 125 | 1.345 | 180 | 1.125 |
| 75 | 1.72 | 130 | 1.32 | 185 | 1.11 |
| 80 | 1.665 | 135 | 1.30 | 190 | 1.095 |
| 85 | 1.62 | 140 | 1.27 | 195 | 1.08 |
| 90 | 1.575 | 145 | 1.25 | ⩾200 | 1.065 |

In France, using the free acceleration test applicable to vehicles that have traveled more than 3000 km, the maximum opacity is set (Law of 3 January 1978) at the following values:

- 2 $m^{-1}$ for passenger cars
- 2.5 $m^{-1}$ for other vehicles

In the EEC, in the same test, the limits are set at the following:

- 2.5 $m^{-1}$ for atmospheric diesel engines
- 3.0 $m^{-1}$ for supercharged diesel engines

Regulation 24 is also applied in Switzerland, Austria, Finland, Australia, and Brazil (Table 6.34). Sweden uses the Bosch blackening index instead of the opacimeter. Japan now also uses the Bosch index in combination with the corresponding 3-mode 'smoke' cycle (Table 6.11). South Korea uses the same cycle with the opacimeter. Japan now also uses the Bosch index in combination with the corresponding 3-mode 'smoke' cycle (Table 6.11). South Korea uses the same cycle with the opacimeter.

**Table 6.34** Diesel smoke opacity: limit values in different countries [23, 65, 74, 81, 82, and 97]

| Country | Year | Test | Limit values |
|---|---|---|---|
| **EEC** | 01-01-1982 | regulation 24 (1) | |
| | 1972 | free acceleration | <0.5 $m^{-1}$ |
| **Switzerland** | 1972 | regulation 24 (1) | |
| **Sweden** | – | acceleration with load | <3.5 *Bosch* units (2) |
| **Finland** | 1980 | regulation 24 (1) | |
| **Austria** | 1972 | regulation 24 (1) | |
| **USA** | 1981 | smoke cycle | (see text) |
| **Japan** | 01-07-1972 | full load | 50% opacity |
| | 01-01-1975 | no load acceleration | 50% opacity |
| | 1981 | 3-m cycle | 5 *Bosch* units |
| | 1984 | 3-m cycle | 4 *Bosch* units |
| **South Korea** | 1980 | 3-m cycle | 50% opacity |
| **Australia** | – | regulation 24 (1) | |
| | – | or US Regulation | |
| **Brazil** | 1972 | regulation 24 (1) | |

(1) Table 6.33. (2) <2.5 units for buses carrying over 30 passengers.

## 6.5 Limit values of evaporative emissions

In 1970, California was the first to impose quantity limits on evaporative emissions that were followed by the federal administration. Japan then quickly enacted similar measures and recently the non-EEC European countries imposed the same limits. The *EEC* tends to impose the same figures on evaporative losses. The limits universally adopted are 2 g/test, according to the SHED or trap method. However, California plans to lower the limits to 1 g/test. Table 6.35 summarizes the existing situation in the different countries concerned.

**Table 6.35** Evaporative emissions: limit values in different countries [23, 65, 74, 81, 82, and 97]

| Country | Year | Test | Limit value (g/test) | | |
|---|---|---|---|---|---|
| Category | | | A | B | C |
| **EEC** | project | SHED | 2 | – | – |
| **Switzerland** | 01-10-1987 | SHED | 2 | – | – |
| | 01-10-1988 | SHED | – | 2 | – |
| **Austria** | 01-10-1989 | SHED | 2 | 2 | – |
| **Sweden** | 88 models | SHED | 2 | – | – |
| | 1992 ? | SHED | – | 2 | – |
| **Norway** | 01-01-1989 | SHED | 2 | – | – |
| **Finland** | 01-01-1992 | SHED | 2 | – | – |
| **USA** | 1971 | trap | 6 | 6 | – |
| | 1972 | trap | 2 | 2 | – |
| | 1978 | SHED | 6 | 6 | – |
| | 1981 | SHED | 2 | 2(3) | – |
| | 1985(1) | SHED | – | – | 3 |
| | 1985(2) | SHED | – | – | 4 |
| **California** | 1970 | trap | 6 | 6 | – |
| | 1972 | trap | 2 | 2 | – |
| | 1978 | SHED | 6 | 6 | – |
| | 1980 | SHED | 2 | 2 | – |
| | project | SHED | 1 | – | – |
| **Canada** | 01-09-1987 | SHED | 2 | – | – |
| **Brazil** | 01-01-1990 | – | 6 | — | |
| **Australia** | 01-07-1976 | trap | 2 | – | – |
| | 01-01-1982 | SHED | 6 | 6 | – |
| | 01-01-1988 | SHED | 2 | 2 | – |
| **Japan** | 01-07-1972 | trap | 2 | – | – |
| **South Korea** | 01-07-1987 | SHED | 4(4) | – | – |
| | 01-07-1987 | SHED | 2(5) | 2(6) | 4(7) |
| **Taiwan** | 01-07-1988 | trap | 2 | – | – |

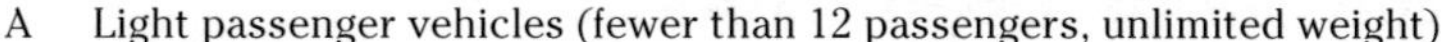

A Light passenger vehicles (fewer than 12 passengers, unlimited weight).
B Light utility vehicles (weight 3.5 t or more than 12 passengers, or 4×4 all-terrain vehicles).
C Trucks and buses.
(1) 3.8 to 6.35 t. (2) >6.35 t. (3) 2.6 g/test at altitude. (4) <800 $cm^3$.
(5) >800 $cm^3$. (6) <2.7 t. (7) >2.7 t.

Vehicle refueling emissions will also be limited shortly, under an American federal plan, to 0.10 g/gallon (0.026 g/liter or 0.035 mg/g) of fuel delivered. Starting in 1990, this EPA regulation will require the installation of large activated carbon canisters on vehicles to absorb refueling emissions [81 and 82]. In Germany, the *UBA* in Berlin plans to set a limit shortly on refueling evaporative emissions. From January 1993 all newly-built service stations must be equipped with vapor recovery systems. California also plans to include running losses in the SHED test with a limit of 0.05 g/mile of HC. The EPA plans to limit refueling flow rates to 10 gal/min (37.9 l/min).

## 6.6 Blow-by emissions

Discussions concerning the limitation of blow-by gas emissions from engine crankcases began in the 1950s in California and Europe [25]. Imitating California, where this regulation was set as early as 1960, most countries impose zero emissions from engine crankcases. The corresponding French law dates from 1964.

## 6.7 Two-wheeled vehicles and two-stroke engines

The classification of this type of vehicle varies in different countries, according to the weight of the unit and its driver, and according to the engine total displacement and the type of engine, either two-stroke or four-stroke. Table 6.36 summarizes the legislation of the various countries. Japan, the world's leading two-wheeled vehicle manufacturer, imposes no national regulation. Two-stroke three- or four-wheeled vehicles are covered by general regulations (Table 6.26), but two-stroke engines require less severe idling levels (Table 6.29). The Economic Commission for Europe has issued Regulation No. 40 for motorcycles [6] and Regulation No. 47 for mopeds [7].

The *EEC* does not yet enforce these regulations and Austria is the only country doing so today. Switzerland also applies them but imposes less severe limits and, along with Taiwan, is one of the rare countries to have a limit on $NO_x$ emissions. In Switzerland and Japan, idling emissions of two-wheeled vehicles are also regulated (Table 6.29).

## 6.8 Regulation of other pollutants

The legislation does not only demand the observance of the statutory limits. The *American Clean Air Act* requires vehicle and engine manufacturers to identify and measure all the pollutants present in the exhaust to make sure that compliance with

**Table 6.36** Statutory values for motorcycles: gaseous pollutants [36, 72, and 97]

| Reference weight (1) | Type | Test cycle | CO | HC | $NO_x$ | Enforcement date |
|---|---|---|---|---|---|---|
| | | | (g/km) | | | |
| **EEC Regulations Nos. 40 and 47** | | | | | | |
| <100 kg | 4-stroke | ECE | 17.5 | 4.2 | – | Not enforced in EEC. |
| 100-300 kg | 4-stroke | ECE | $17.5 + 17.5\,\frac{M-100}{200}$ | $4.2 + 1.8\,\frac{M-100}{200}$ | – | |
| >300 kg | 4-stroke | ECE | 35 | 6 | – | |
| <100 kg | 2-stroke | ECE | 12.8 | 8 | – | |
| 100-300 kg | 2-stroke | ECE | $12.8 + 19.2\,\frac{M-100}{200}$ | $8 + 4\,\frac{M-100}{200}$ | – | |
| >300 kg | 2-stroke | ECE | 32 | 12 | – | |
| <400 kg (2) | 2-stroke | 7-m | 8 | 5 | – | |
| <400 kg (3) | 2-stroke | 7-m | 15 | 10 | – | |
| **Austria, Regulations Nos. 40 and 47** | | | | | | |
| motorcycles | 4-stroke | ECE | 13.0 | 3.0 | 0.3 | 01-10-1990 |
| motorcycles | 2-stroke | ECE | 8.0 | 7.5 | 0.1 | 01-10-1990 |
| **Taiwan, Regulation No. 40** | | | | | | |
| motorcycles | – | ECE | 4.5 | 3.0(6) | | 01-10-1991 |
| motorcycles | – | ECE | 2.11 | 0.875(6) | | 1993 |
| **Switzerland, Regulations OEV 3 (motorcycles) and OEV 4 (pedal motorcycles)** | | | | | | |
| motorcycles | 4-stroke | ECE | 13.0 | 3.0 | 0.30 | 01-10-1987 |
| motorcycles | 2-stroke | ECE | 8.0 | 3.0 | 0.10 | 01-10-1990 |
| mopeds | 2-stroke | 7-m | 0.5 | 0.5 | 0.10 | 01-10-1988 |
| **Reference total displacement (4)** | **Type** | **Test cycle** | **CO** | **HC** | **$NO_x$** | **Enforcement date** |
| | | | **(g/km)** | | | |
| **United States, federal law** | | | | | | |
| 50-170 $cm^3$ | – | FTP 75 | 17 | 5.0 | – | 1978 |
| 170-750 $cm^3$ | – | FTP 75 | 17 | $5 + 0.0155 \times (V - 170)$ | – | 1978 |
| >50 $cm^3$ | – | FTP 75 | 17 | 14 | – | 1978 |
| all | 2-stroke/ 4-stroke | FTP 75 | 12 | 5 | – | 1980 |
| all | 2-stroke/ 4-stroke | FTP 75 | 12 | 4.75(5) | – | 1983 |
| **United States, Californian law** | | | | | | |
| <280 $cm^3$ | – | FTP 75 | 12 | 1 | – | 1982 |
| >280 $cm^3$ | – | FTP 75 | 12 | 2.5 | – | 1982 |
| **Japan, no regulation** | | | | | | |

(1) Reference weight = motorcycle weight + 75 kg.
(2) Two-wheeled vehicle.
(3) Three-wheeled vehicle.
(4) Piston displacement V.
(5) Non-methanic HC proposal.
(6) HC+$NO_x$.

the legal limits of regulated pollutants does not result in the emission of other pollutants liable to incur an unacceptable risk for public health or well-being [36]. The term 'pollutant' covers diesel particles, nickel, MMT combustion products, ammonia, sulfates, hydrogen sulfide, hydrogen cyanide, ruthenium combustion products, nitrosamines, and any other pollutant that could be emitted.

The latest Clean Air Act Amendment concerns toxic air pollutants, i.e. benzene, 1-3 butadiene, formaldehyde, acetaldehyde, and polycyclic organic matter (POM), the total content of which must be reduced by 15% in 1995.

Aldehydes, for example, form part of these still non-regulated pollutants. However, plans for regulations concerning methanol-fueled vehicles are emerging in California [15]. Table 6.37 gives the recommended values for formaldehyde emissions. The *EPA* also plans to enact a legal limit before 1 October 1992 on emissions from methanol-fueled vehicles. The figure proposed is 0.015 g/mile of formaldehyde for vehicles not emitting more than 0.25 g/mile of HC.

Brazil has also set future standards for aldehyde emissions (formaldehyde + acetaldehyde) for alcohol-fueled vehicles: based on the FTP-75 cycle and measured by the DNPH method, 0.15 g/km on 1 January 1992 and 0.03 g/km from 1997.

**Table 6.37** Formaldehyde emission standards, Californian proposals

| Vehicle | Type approval After 1990 | | Conformity | | Enforcement date |
|---|---|---|---|---|---|
| | (mg/mile) | (mg/km) | (mg/mile) | (mg/km) | |
| **passenger** | 15 | 9.32 | 23 | 14.3 | 1990-1993 |
| **trucks < 1.7 t** | 15 | 9.32 | 15 | 9.32 | after 1994 |
| **trucks 1.7 to 2.6 t** | 18 | 11.2 | 27 | 16.8 | 1990-1993 |
| | 18 | 11.2 | 18 | 11.2 | after 1994 |
| **trucks > 2.6 t** | 22 | 13.7 | 33 | 20.5 | 1990-1993 |
| | 22 | 13.7 | 22 | 3.7 | after 1994 |
| | **(g/bhph)** | **(g/kWh)** | **(g/bhph)** | **(g/kWh)** | |
| **heavy trucks** | 0.05 | 0.067 | 0.1 | 0.134 | 1990-1993 |
| | 0.05 | 0.067 | 0.05 | 0.134 | after 1994 |

## 6.9 Cold climates

In all the countries concerned, the regulations apply to the running of vehicles at temperatures ranging between 20 and 30°C. The use of the same vehicles in regions where the temperature is generally colder (Canada, Scandinavia, etc.) implies the use of the choke for longer periods or a colder air intake, which influence the level of emissions, primarily CO and unburned HC [108], since the presence of the choke delays the formation of $NO_x$ during the warm-up period [73]. To get a sufficient fuel-vapor/air ratio, it is necessary to have a significant liquid-fuel/air ratio, with greater unburned HC as a consequence.

For example, according to the FTP-75 cycle with the same fuel and vehicles equipped with catalytic converters, as the temperature drops from 21.1 to 4.4°C CO emissions are multiplied by a factor of 1.9 and HC emissions by 1.8. A new drop from 4.4 to −6.7°C increases them by 1.36 and 1.6 respectively [108]. Under the same conditions, $NO_x$ emissions are boosted by a factor of 1.23 in the former case and 1.1 in the latter. For an average temperature drop of 11°C, earlier records [29] on vehicles with catalytic converters indicate overall increases of 300% in CO and 275% in HC, which appeared mainly in the cold part of the FTP-75 cycle. $NO_x$ remained practically unchanged.

The *EPA* plans to reduce low-temperature CO emissions, limiting emissions at −7°C to 6.23 g/km (10 g/mile) for 40% of vehicles in 1993, 80% in 1994, and 100% in 1995.

## 6.10 Inspection of vehicles in circulation

The statutory limits discussed in this chapter concern primarily the models offered to customers or samples of new vehicles taken from the end of the assembly line. The question arises whether, on the basis of measurements taken during type approval, it is possible to predict the quantity of actual emissions of vehicles in circulation. In other words, can the regulatory cycles be extrapolated to actual traffic conditions and to what extent does the state of the vehicle, as measured for type approval, deteriorate during the life of the vehicle?

### 6.10.1 Influence of actual traffic conditions

Although the different standard driving cycles developed throughout the world are based on an actual type of traffic at the time of their development, they cannot claim to represent all types of traffic because their essential aim is to compare the emission performance of the vehicles produced in relatively simple measurement conditions. It is therefore conceivable that vehicles that are specially adjusted to meet the standards may, in contrast, generate much more pollution in actual traffic than off-standard vehicles.

To estimate the total emissions from a fleet of vehicles in circulation at a given time it is necessary to have an accurate breakdown by model, quantity, and age, and to know the actual traffic conditions encountered by these vehicles.

A French study on the actual use of vehicles (EUREV) [100] involved the selection of a number of typical vehicles (make, model, age) based on vehicle registration records and monitoring the conditions of use imposed by the owners [1]. This study helps to construct four new cycles representing slow urban, fast urban, road, and expressway traffic, which, unlike the ECE cycles, incorporate variable accelerations and decelerations [57 and 61]. In fact, these transitory phases have a strong influence on emission levels. Furthermore, higher average speed significantly increases $NO_x$ emissions [58] except for vehicles with small total displacements where the enrichment required for the carburetted mixtures tends to hinder the formation of $NO_x$. In addition, the fact that in France 27% of the average vehicle mileage is traveled with a cold engine [46], below the 70°C coolant set point, has a substantial effect on the level of actual emissions.

## 6.10.2 Influence of vehicle maintenance

Even in the United States, where the laws require compliance with the standards after 80,000 km (50,000 miles), this provision is only checked on vehicles in good working order, presented by the manufacturers or monitored by the competent authorities. In the hands of consumers, the engine settings can be changed and anti-pollution systems can be modified, tampered with, or disabled by misfuelling (Chapter 11). It was estimated in 1980 in the United States that out of 2000 vehicles tested, only 33% were in good working order, 18% had been tampered with, 47% were improperly adjusted, and the remaining 2% were accidentally defective [112].

Inspection and maintenance programs are difficult to set up because the statutory test procedures are complicated and demand costly equipment (chassis dynamometers), handled by competent staff [113]. The low degree of reproducibility of the measurement makes it difficult, if not impossible, to compare the results of single measurements taken on different dates or by different laboratories [68].

The technique used in the United States to monitor vehicles in circulation consists of taking a statistical sampling of the vehicles [50 and 51]. The problem lies within the competence of each state and not of the federal authorities. If over 50% of the vehicles fail to satisfy the test requirements covering CO, HC, $NO_x$, and diesel particulate levels, the manufacturer of the vehicles must investigate the problem, find the cause of the defects, and propose remedial action to the authorities [26]. If the defects are systematic or basic, the manufacturer is obliged to recall the affected vehicles. In a promising method tested in Los Angeles, the exhaust from in-use vehicles is passed through an infrared beam that is used to calculate the $CO/CO_2$ ratio at the exhaust and thus detect faulty settings or inoperative catalytic converters [76].

To inspect the state of maintenance of vehicles, simplified procedures, which vary in the different states, are based on idling [94] and no-load (2500 rpm)

Added to the gaseous pollutants is a visible smoke index measured by an SAE method. For gas turbines for automotive applications, the statutory limits are the same as for piston engines, measured by the FTP-75 cycle (Table 6.13).

For off-road diesel engines as of 1996, California proposes to apply the same limit values applicable to road diesel vehicles in 1990: 9.2 g/kWh $NO_x$ and 0.53 g/kWh particulates. After the year 2000, the figures will be lowered to 7.73 g/kWh for $NO_x$ and 0.21 g/kWh for particulates.

## REFERENCES

[1] M. André, (1985), "Utilisations réelles des véhicules particuliers", *TEC* No. 73/74, pp. 34-38.

[2] Anon., (1977), "Control of air pollution from new motor vehicles and new motor vehicle engines", *Fed. Register*, **42** (124), 32906-33004.

[3] Anon., (1963), *Arrêté du 12 Novembre 1963 relatif aux émissions de fumées à l'échappement*, Journal Officiel, p. 10305.

[4] Anon., (1964), *Arrêté du 28 Juillet 1964 relatif aux émissions de gaz de carter*, Journal Officiel, p. 7446.

[5] Anon., (1969), *Arrêté du 31 Mars 1969 relatif à la limitation de la teneur en CO des gaz d'échappement des véhicules automobiles*, Journal Officiel, pp. 4929-4930.

[6] Anon., (1981), "United Nations, E/ECE/324, E/ECE/TRANS/505", *Rev.1/Add. 39, Regulation* No. 40, 21 April, 26 p.

[7] Anon., (1981), "United Nations, E/ECE/324, E/ECE/TRANS/505", *Rev.1/Add. 46, Regulation* No. 47, 1 November, 32 p.

[8] Anon., (1982), "United Nations, E/ECE/324, E/ECE/TRANS/505", *Rev.1/Add. 48, Regulation* No. 49, 5 April, 26 p.

[9] Anon., (1982), "Measurement of fuel evaporative emissions from gasoline powered passenger cars and light duty trucks using the enclosure technique", *SAE Recommended Practice* J171, June, 10 p.

[10] Anon., (1983), "Measurement of fuel evaporative emissions from gasoline powered passenger cars and light duty trucks by the trap method", *SAE Recommended Practice* J170, June, 6 p.

[11] Anon., (1987), *Draft MVEG proposal for an extra urban driving cycle*, EEC Bruxelles, 16 November, 10 p.

[12] Anon., (1988), "EEC Directive 88/77", *EEC Journal Officiel* No. L36, 8 February, p. 61.

[13] Anon., (1986), *Ordonnance sur les émissions de gaz d'échappement des voitures automobiles légères, OEV1, Office Fédéral de la Protection de l'Environnement*, 4 Hallwylstrasse, 3003 Berne, Switzerland, 183 p.

[14] Anon., (1986), *Ordonnance sur les émissions de gaz d'échappement des voitures automobiles lourdes, OEV2, Office Fédéral de la Protection de l'Environnement*, 4 Hallwylstrasse, 3003 Berne, Switzerland, 44 p.

[15] Anon., (1988), *La proposition du CARB pour les véhicules fonctionnant au méthanol, Automobile emission control by catalysts*, Newsletter, 11 June.

[16] Anon., (1989), "Katalysatortechnik für V8 Ottomotoren im Bootbetrieb", *MTZ*, **50**, 205-206.

[17] Anon., (1990), "Directive 90/C81/01", *EEC Journal Officiel* No. C81, 30 March, p. 110.

[18] Anon., (1991), "Unser Ziel ist die Null-Emission", *VDI Nachrichten*, No.13 (29 March), p. 3

[19] A. Balzotti et al., (1990), "Italian city buses with particulate traps", *SAE Paper* No. 900114 (SP-816), 79-96.

[20] R.A. Baranescu, (1988), "Influence of fuel sulfur on Diesel particulate emissions", *SAE Paper* No. 881174, 11 p.

[21] K.G. Badertscher, (1987), "Abgasuntersuchungen von im Verkehr befindlichen Fahrzeugen, Gegenwart und Zukunft", *Schweiz, VDI Berichte*, (639), 27-34.

[22] G.J. Barnes and R.J. Donohue, (1985), "A manufacturer's view of world emission regulations and the need for harmonization of procedures", *SAE Paper* No. 850391, 10 p.

[23] G.J. Barnes, (1986), *Development of US vehicle regulations, technologies and costs, "Enclair 86" Proceedings*, OECD, Taormina, pp. 83-92.

[24] R.C. Bascom and G.C. Hass, (1970), "A status report on the development of the 1973 California Diesel emissions standards", *SAE Paper* No. 700671, 14 p.

[25] W. Berg, (1985), "Evolution of motor vehicle emission control legislation in Europe, Leading to the catalyst car?", *SAE Paper* No. 850385 (SP-614), pp. 17-38.

[26] W. Berg, (1987), "Verfahren der Feldüberwachung in den USA und Kalifornien", *VDI Berichte*, No. 639, pp. 87-125.

[27] W. Berg, (1991), "Die neue "Abgas-Gesetzgebung" der USA", *VDI Fortschritt-Berichte*, No. 150, pp. 154-239.

[28] J.N. Braddock and P. A. Gabele, (1977), "Emission patterns of Diesel powered passenger cars, Part II", *SAE Paper* No. 770168, 11 p.

[29] J.N. Braddock, (1981), "Impact of low temperature on 3-way catalyst car emissions", *SAE Paper* No. 810280, 28 p.

[30] W. Cartellieri et al., (1989), "Erfüllung der Dieselabgasgrenzwerte von Nutzfahrzeug, Dieselmotoren der 90er Jahre", *MTZ*, **50,** 440-451.

[31] B-H. Cho and S.A. Tamplin, (1985), "The motor vehicle emissions control program in Korea", *SAE Paper* No. 852231, 8 p.

[32] S.W. Coates and G.G. Lassanske, (1990), "Measurement and analysis of gaseous exhaust emissions from recreational and small commercial marine craft", *SAE Paper* No. 901597 (SP-835), pp. 25-39.

[33] L.T. Collin, (1978), INCOLL, "A new technology in emission testing", *SAE Paper* No. 780618, 19 p.

[34] L.T. Collin, (1985), INertia COLLection, "A simplified dynamic engine test method", *SAE Paper* No. 850132, 22 p.

[35] L.T. Collin, (1987), "A high efficient short test for vehicle emission", *SAE Paper* No. 872099, 16 p.

[36] D. Collins, (1982), *Sources of emissions and worldwide legislation, Symp. on engine and vehicle exhaust emissions*, Shoreham, Sussex, 21/22 April, 44 p.

[37] G.M. Cornetti et al., (1988), "US transient cycle versus ECE R49 13-mode cycle", *SAE Paper* No. 880715, 14 p.

[38] C. Cucchi and M. Hublin, (1989), "Evolution of emission legislation in Europe, and impact on technology", *SAE Paper* No. 890487, 16 p.

[39] K.F. Ditsch, (1987), "Abgasuntersuchungen von im Verkehr befindlichen Fahrzeugen, Gegenwart und Zukunft, Bundesrepublik Deutschland", *VDI Berichte*, No. 639, pp. 75-85.

[40] W.M. Draper et al., (1987), "Impact of a ceramic trap and manganese fuel additive on the biological activity and chemical composition of exhaust particles from Diesel engines used in underground mines", *SAE Paper* No. 871621, 18 p.

[41] M. Duflot et al., "Pollution de l'atmosphère par les gaz d'échappement", *Report* No. B13/RP21/F (1977), et: "Limites d'émission de polluants dans les gaz d'échappement des moteurs Diesel", *Report* No. 22 (1978), Office de Recherches et d'Essais of the Union Internationale des Chemins de Fer, Utrecht.

[42] G. Fränckle and H.J. Stein, (1988), "Instationäre oder stationäre Abgasprüfverfahren für Nutzfahrzeug-Dieselmotoren?", *ATZ*, **90,** 15-22 and 85-92.

[43] P.A. Gabele et al., (1981), "Exhaust emission patterns from two light duty Diesel automobiles", *SAE Paper* No. 810081, 14 p.

[44] Y. Georgiades et al., (1988), "Establishment of atmospheric pollution standards for motor vehicles", *Sci. Tot. Environm.*, **77,** 215-230.

[45] H.R. Glatz, (1987), "The historic development, the political background and the future perspectives of motor emission control and emission control regulation in Europe", *Paper* C358/87, *IMechE Conf. "Vehicle Emissions and Their Impact on European Air Quality"*, London, 3.5 November, pp. 1-8.

[46] W.A. Goetz et al., (1988), "Performance and emissions of propane, natural gas, and methanol fueled bus engines", *SAE Paper* No. 880494, 12 p.

[47] M.D. Gurney and J.R. Allsup, (1989), "Predictability of emissions from in-use vehicles at low ambient temperature and alternative driving cycle based on standard tests", *SAE Paper* No. 890625, 9 p.

[48] C.T. Hare and J.J. White, (1990), "A next generation emission test procedure for small utility engines, Part 1 Background and approach", *SAE Paper* No. 901595 (SP-835), pp. 1-8.

[49] H.M. Haskew et al., (1987), "I/M effectiveness with today's closed loop systems", *SAE Paper* No. 871103, 29 p.

[50] H.M. Haskew and J.J. Gumbleton, (1988), "GM's in-use emission performance, past, present, future", *SAE Paper* No. 881682, 29 p.

[51] H.M. Haskew et al., (1989), "GM's results, The EPA/industry cooperative test program", *SAE Paper* No. 890185, 22 p.

[52] H. Heitland et al., "Einfluss des zukünftigen Pkw Verkehrs auf die $CO_2$ emission", *MTZ*, **51,** 66-72 (199).

[53] H.E. Hilger, (1987), "Emissionsminderung Automobilgase, Abgas-Sonderuntersuchung-Feldüberwachung, Nuremberg Conference", 7/9 April, *VDI Berichte*, No. 639, p. 453.

[54] T.A. Huls, (1973), "Evolution of federal light-duty mass emission regulations", *SAE Paper* No. 730554, 21 p.

[55] J.H. Johnson et al., (1981), "The engineering control of Diesel pollutants in underground mining", *SAE Paper* No. 810684, 46 p.

[56] R.E. Jones, (1978), "Gas turbine engine emissions, Problems, progress and future", *Prog. Energy Comb. Sci.*, **4,** 73-113.

[57] R. Joumard, (1986), *Séquences, cinématiques représentatives du trafic automobile français*, Rech. Transp. Sécurité, December, pp. 17-20.

[58] R. Joumard, (1987), "Influence of speed limits on road and motorways on pollutant emissions", *Sci. Tot. Environm.*, **59,** 87-96.

[59] R. Joumard, (1989), *Émissions réelles de polluants du trafic automobile en France*, Thesis, Université de Savoie, 149 p.

[60] R. Joumard and M. André, (1989), *Cold start emissions of the traffic, "Highway pollution", 3rd Int. Symp.*, München, 18/22 September, 8 p.

[61] R. Joumard and L. Paturel, (1989), "Mesure sur cycles représentatifs des émissions unitaires de CO, HC, $NO_x$ et HAP des véhicules légers essence et diesel", in: *Man and his Ecosystem*, J.L. Brasser, Vol. 4, Elsevier Science Publications, Amsterdam, pp. 417-422.

[62] M. Kagami et al., (1984), "The influence of fuel properties on the performance of Japanese automotive Diesels", *SAE Paper* No. 841082, 15 p.

[63] J.M. Kawecki, (1978), "Emission of sulfur-bearing compounds from motor vehicles and aircraft engines, A report to Congress", *EPA Report* 600/9-78-028, 436 p.

[64] H. Kleine, (1989), "Dieselabgase im Arbeitsumfeld, Möglichkeiten der Gefahrenbeseitigung", *Die BG*, **9,** 1-4.

[65] H. Klingenberg, (1978), "Harmonization of testing procedures for automotive exhaust gas", *SAE Paper* No. 780647, 29 p.

[66] H. Klingenberg and D. Schürmann, (1985), "Eine Idee zur Uberprüfung der Effizienz von Abgas Katalysatoren in Personenwagen", *MTZ*, **46,** 261-262.

[67] H. Klingenberg and R.H. Müller, (1986), "Vorschlag und Uberprüfung der Effizienz von Abgas Katalysatoren in Personenwagen ohne Rollenprüfstand", *MTZ*, **47,** 181-183.

[68] H. Klingenberg, (1987), "Grundprinzipien und Grenzen de Abgassonderuntersuchung", *VDI Berichte*, No. 639, pp. 127-138.

[69] O. Kruggel, (1985), "Untersuchungen zur Stickoxidminderung an Großdieselmotoren", "Emissionsminderung Automobilabgase, Dieselmotoren", *VDI Berichte* No. 559, pp. 459-478.

[70] R.E. Kruse and T.A. Huls, (1973), "Development of the federal urban driving schedule", *SAE Paper* No. 730553, 7 p.

[71] M. Kuhler and D. Karstens, (1978), "Improved driving cycle for testing automotive exhaust emissions", *SAE Paper* No. 780650, 16 p.

[72] F.J. Laimböck, (1991), "The potential of small loop scavenged spark ignition single cylinder engines", *SAE Paper* No. SP-847, 74 p.

[73] J. Laurikko et al., (1987), "Automotive exhaust emissions at low ambient temperature", *Technical Report* No. 496, Technical Research Centre of Finland, Espoo, 38 p.

[74] J. Laurikko, (1989), "Motor vehicle exhaust emissions and control in Finland", *SAE Paper* No. 890584, 8 p.

[75] J.J. Lawson, (1986), *Costs of vehicle emission standards in Canada*, "Enclair 86" Proceedings, OECD, pp. 103-124.

[76] D.R. Lawson et al., (1990), "Emissions from in-use motor vehicles in Los Angeles, A pilot study of remote sensing and the inspection and maintenance program", *J. Air Waste Managem. Assoc.*, **40,** 1096-1105.

[77] H.P. Lenz and E. Pucher, (1987), "Abgasuntersuchungen von im Verkehr befindlichen Fahrzeugen, Gegenwart und Zukunft, Österreich", *VDI Berichte*, (639), 59-74.

[78] J.A. Maga and J.R. Kinossian, (1966), "Motor vehicle emission standards, Present and future", *SAE Paper* No. 660104, 10 p.

[79] J.A. Maga and G.C. Hass, (1969), "Present and future emission standards for heavy-duty vehicles", *SAE Paper* No. 690765, 5 p.

[80] J.L. Marduel, (1987), *Les réglementations européennes et américaines relatives aux émissions de polluants et aux niveaux sonores des véhicules fonctionnant au gazole, SIA Conference, "Moteurs diesel pour véhicules automobiles et utilitaires"*, Lyon, 13/14 May, pp. 36-42.

[81] J.S. McArragher et al., (1988), "Trends in motor vehicle emission and fuel consumption regulations, 1988 update", *CONCAWE Report* 4/88, 65 p.

[82] J.S. McArragher et al., (1989), "Trends in motor vehicle emission and fuel consumption regulations, 1989 update", *CONCAWE Report* 6/89, 86 p.

[83] W.H. Megonnel, (1971), "Regulation of pollutant emissions from aircraft, Today and tomorrow", *SAE Paper* No. 710337, 4 p.

[84] J.K.H. Menzl, (1984), "Das Emissionsverhalten von Zweitakt Otto-Kleinmotoren", *VDI Berichte*, No. 531, "Emissionsminderung Automobilgase, Ottomotoren", pp. 237-244.

[85] G. Monnier et al., (1991), "IAPAC compressed air assisted fuel injection for high efficiency low emission marine outboard two-stroke engines", *Japan SAE Paper* No. 911251, 16 p.

[86] E.J. Morgan and R.H. Lincoln, (1990), "Duty cycle for recreational marine engines", *SAE Paper* No. 901596 (SP-835), pp. 9-24.

[87] F.X. Moser et al., (1990), "Zur Partikelemmission von Nutzfahrzeug Dieselmotoren", *MTZ*, **51,** 186-193.

[88] Y. Mori and K. Wadachi, (1986), "Motor vehicle exhaust emission control in Japan", *"Enclair 86" Proceedings*, OECD, pp. 237-263.

[89] G.S. Musser et al., (1990), "Improved design of onboard control of refueling emissions", *SAE Paper* No. 900155, 29 p.

[90] K.H. Neumann and F. Barthel, (1989), *National and international emission regulations in Europe for passenger cars, 3rd Int. Symp., "Highway Pollution"*, München, 18/22 September, 14 p.

[91] C. Nordgren, (1987), "Abgasuntersuchungen von im Verkehr befindlichen Fahrzeugen, Gegenwart und Zukunft, Schweden", *VDI Berichte*, (639), 35-46.

[92] L. Olsson, (1986), "Exhaust emission control technology, Benefits and costs, Light-duty vehicles and trucks and heavy-duty vehicles", *"Enclair 86" Proceedings*, OECD, pp. 135-144.

[93] L. Olsson, (1987), "Motor vehicle control and regulations for Sweden", *SAE Paper* No. 871081, 6 p.

[94] J. Panzer, (1972), "Idle emissions testing", *SAE Paper* No. 720937, 46 p.

[95] B. Raynal, (1978), *Contrôle de la pollution atmosphérique due aux véhicules automobiles, Techn. de l'Ing.*, Booklet B 429, 10 p.

[96] B. Raynal, (1982), *Moteurs thermiques et pollution atmosphérique, Contrôle des Véhicules automobiles, Techn. de l'Ing.*, Booklet B 378/2, 8 p.

[97] B. Raynal, (1988), *Moteurs thermiques et pollution atmosphérique, Réglementation des véhicules automobiles, Techn. de l'Ing.*, Booklet B 378/2, 17 p.

[98] R.C. Rijkeboer et al., (1988), *Steekproefcontroleprogramma, onderzoek naar luchtverontreining door voertuigen in het verkeer (Statistical control program, Study of air pollution from vehicles in circulation)*, 1987/1988 Annual Report, VROM Lucht 79, November, 63 p.

[99] R.C. Rijkeboer and W.J. Zwalve, *Car emissions in the field, 3rd Int. Symp. "Highway Pollution"*, München, 18.22 September, 8 p.

[100] J.P. Roumegoux, (1985), "Comportement des conducteurs et utilisation réelle des véhicules, implications énergétiques", *IRT/CERNE* Study Day 18 September, 21 p.

[101] SAE Recommended Practice, (1978), "Constant volume sampler system for exhaust emission measurement", *SAE* J1094a, 24 p.

[102] SAE Information Report, (1988), "Emission test driving schedules", *SAE* J1506, 8 p.

[103] SAE Recommended Practice, (1983), "Test procedure for the measurement of exhaust emissions from small utility engines", *SAE* J1088, 6 p.

[104] V. Shantora and J.A. Libman, (1985), "Review of the new vehicle emission standards in Canada", *SAE Paper* No. 850393 (SP-614), pp. 91-96.

[105] R.J. Sommerville et al., (1987), "Evaluation of the California smog check program", *SAE Paper* No. 870624.

[106] K.J. Springer, (1988), *Diesel lube oils, 5th dimension of Diesel particulate control, AGELFI Symp.*, Bordeaux, 13/14 October, pp. 297-309.

[107] A. Stawsky et al., (1984), "Evaluation of an emission control strategy for underground Diesel mining equipment", *SAE Paper* No. 840176 (P-140), pp. 139-160.

[108] F. Stump et al., (1989), "The influence of ambient temperature on tailpipe emissions from 1984-1987 model year light duty gasoline motor vehicles", *Atmosph. Environm.*, **23,** 307-320.

[109] H. Umino, (1991), "Legislation in Japan, Connected with vehicle emission and fuel economy regulations", *VDI Fortschritt-Berichte*, (150), 130-153.

[110] L. Van Beckhoven, (1987), "An appraisal of the proposals for the further development of EEC legislation on automotive emissions", *SAE Paper* No. 871077 (SP-718), 6 p.

[111] B. Voß, (1990), "Zeitweise Motorabschaltung, Kritische Zeiten bezüglich Schadstoffemission und Kraftstoffverbrauch", *ATZ*, **92,** 526-532.

[112] M.P. Walsh, (1980), "Future trends in the control of emissions from motor vehicles", *SAE Paper* No. 801359, 10 p.

[113] M.P. Walsh, (1985), "Global trends in motor vehicle air pollution control, the significance for developing countries", *SAE Paper* No. 852221, 13 p.

[114] M.P. Walsh, (1989), "Global trends in motor vehicle air pollution control, A 1988 perspective", *SAE Paper* No. 890581, 13 p.

[115] R. Westerholm et al., (1986), "Chemical analysis and biological testing of emissions from a heavy duty Diesel truck with and without two different particulate traps", *SAE Paper* No. 860014, 11 p.

[116] D.J. Williams et al., (1989), "Particulate emissions from 'in-use' motor vehicles, 1 Spark ignition vehicles", *Atmosph. Environm.*, **23,** 2639-2645.

[117] W.T. Wotring et al., (1978), "50,000 mile vehicle road test of three-way and $NO_x$ reduction catalyst systems", *SAE Paper* No. 780608, 21 p.

[118] W. Zwalve, (1987), "Abgasuntersuchungen von im Verkehr befindlichen Fahrzeugen, Gegenwart und Zukunft, Niederlände", *VDI Berichte*, (639), 47-57.

# Methods of characterization and analysis

# 7

## 7.1 Sampling

In any analysis, the sample must be uniform and representative of the product analyzed. Analytical sampling must correspond to the actual emissions of the vehicle or the engine according to the standard driving cycles described in the previous chapter.

To meet these cycles, vehicles are placed on chassis dynamometers located in premises that allow some control of the ambient conditions (temperature, relative humidity) and permit the sampling of a fraction of the exhaust emissions without disturbing the vehicle running conditions.

For trucks and buses, where the drive power and the rolling weight can vary considerably, the use of chassis dynamometers becomes very difficult [67]. Therefore, tests are performed on the engine itself, which is removed from its vehicle and mounted on an engine test bench equipped to reproduce the standard running cycles, with a sampling system that does not disturb the engine.

### 7.1.1 Chassis dynamometer tests

The chassis dynamometer reproduces the load and inertia of the vehicle when driven on the road. The mechanical energy transmitted to the rollers by the drive wheels of the vehicle is absorbed in one of the following ways.

- By hydraulic braking using a rotor integral with the rollers and pushed by a stream of pressurized water. A scoop adjusts the thickness of the water ring in the brake by varying the water level. The inertia of the vehicle during acceleration and deceleration is simulated by the coupling of a number of flywheels to the rollers.
- By electromagnetic braking using the eddy currents dissipated in a rotor driven by the rollers and cooled by a water stream. These currents are generated by a magnetic field created by an adjustable dc winding. The inertia is provided by flywheels as above.

- By electric braking using a dc or asynchronous electric machine [14]. The current produced can be returned to the grid after passage through a thyristor. The machine can also drive the vehicle during decelerations. Programming helps to adjust the load applied as a function of speed in accordance with the actual characteristics of the vehicle obtained on a road circuit

For truck and bus engines, which are tested on an engine test bench, a hand-controlled brake is sufficient for the US and European 13-mode cycles. For the 'transient' cycle, however, a dc or asynchronous electric machine, which can both absorb and supply power, is necessary.

### 7.1.2 CVS method and dilution tunnels

Since 1982, despite the drawback of having to analyze dilute gases that may need to be reconcentrated, all countries have adopted the CVS procedure as a sampling method. With this method, the exhaust gases are diluted with filtered ambient air to maintain a constant total flow rate (exhaust+air) under all running conditions [52]. This helps to approach the dilution conditions of the exhaust in the ambient air at the tail pipe exit. The total flow rate is determined by the following:

- either by calculating the total rotations of a positive-displacement pump with known characteristics that draws the mixture (PDP)
- or by making the mixture flow through a venturi at critical conditions (CFV)

Figure 7.1 shows a complete installation including a chassis dynamometer and a sampler for a lightweight vehicle. Throughout the test a set of pumps is used to continuously collect constant fractions of exhaust gas and dilution air [48] in fluorocarbon plastic bags and to cumulate the emissions over the duration of the sequence. The regulated pollutants (CO, HC and $NO_x$) are analyzed at the end of each sequence, both in the bags containing the exhaust gas and in the dilution air, by the analytical methods described below.

With diesel engines, the risk of condensation of the heavier hydrocarbons in the bags necessitates continuous analysis of the HC. The dilute gases are therefore transferred to the analyzer by a line heated to 190°C and an integrator is used to calculate the cumulative emissions over the cycle time. The diesel vehicle test includes the measurement of particulate emissions. Since the particles are retained on a filter the exhaust cannot be totally filtered, because the resulting back-pressure would alter the operation of the engine and the corresponding emissions. It is therefore necessary to sample a known and representative fraction of the exhaust emitted by the engine. To do this, a dilution 'tunnel' of sufficient length is used to homogenize the aerosol/dilution air mixture of the CVS system before the sampling probe designed to measure particulates (diagram (b) in Fig. 7.1).

To measure actual on-road emissions, onboard systems of the mini-CVS type have been developed that use a plug with 55 or 112 identical tubes (*splitter*) placed on the

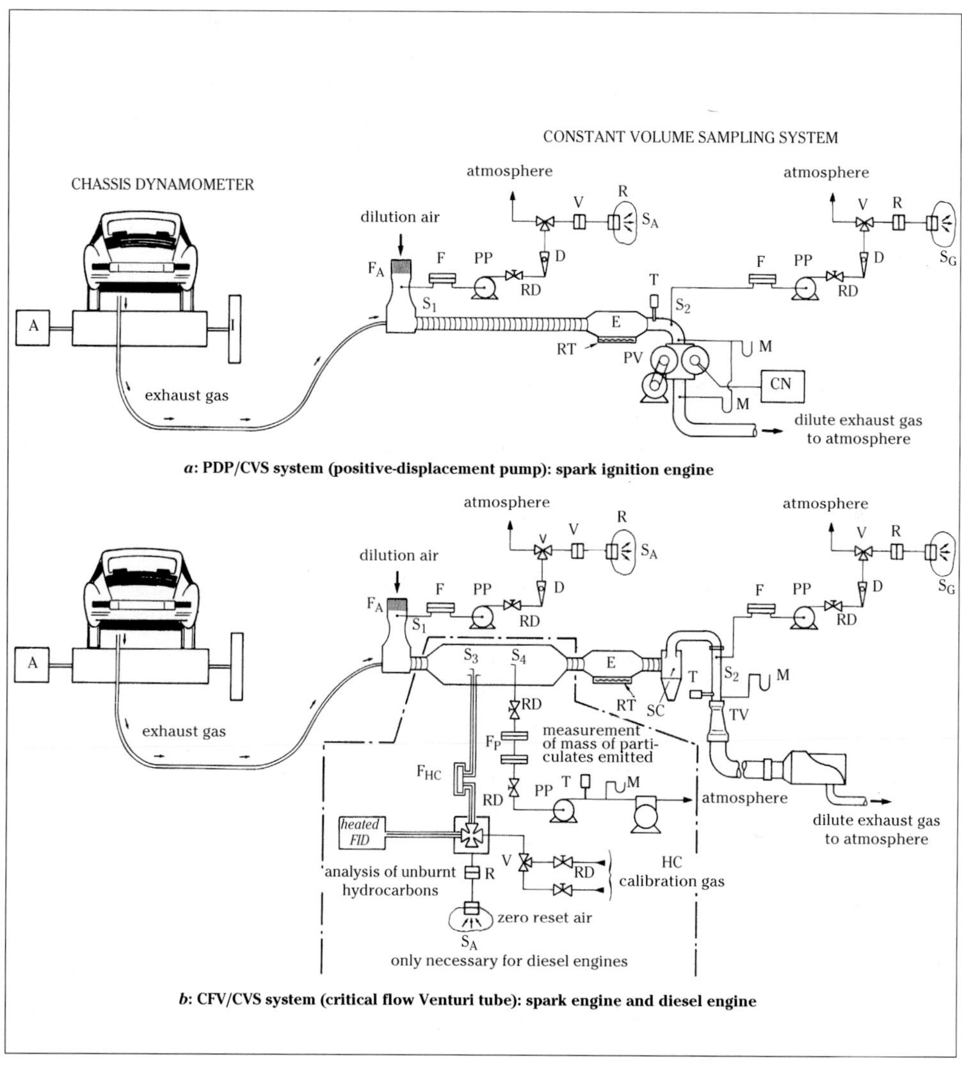


| | | | |
|---|---|---|---|
| A | power absorption system | PP | sampling pump |
| CN | cumulative numerical counter of pump rotations | PV | positive-displacement pump |
| D | low meter | R | quick-lock fitting |
| DT | cumulative flow meter | RD | flow controller |
| E | heat exchanger | RT | temperature controller |
| F | filter | $S_1$ | to $S_4$ sampling probes |
| $F_A$ | dilution air filter | $S_A$ | dilution air collecting bag |
| $F_{HC}$ | heated filter on hydrocarbon analysis circuit | $S_G$ | dilute exhaust gas collecting bag |
| $F_P$ | measurement filters for mass of particulates emitted | SC | cyclone separator |
| I | flywheel | T | temperature sensor |
| M | pressure gauge | TV | Venturi tube |
| PA | suction pump for dilute exhaust gas mixture | V | quick-action valve |

**Fig 7.1** Pollutant testing system [48]

vehicle exhaust pipe, of which only one tube is used to sample a known fraction of the exhaust. Their performance has been compared with measurements taken on chassis dynamometers [46]. The same system was applied to diesel engines, adding a mini-tunnel to measure particulates [26 and 45]. Another system does not use a splitter but performs an in-line analysis of the gaseous pollutants and particulates without dilution, using a fraction of the exhaust whose mass flow rate is calculated from the measured volumetric flow rate and the analysis of $CO_2$, HC, and $O_2$ gases [54, 55, 56, 61 and 62]. The exhaust gases can be extracted and diluted by means of an air pump [65].

To test vehicles while running the INCOLL test, already mentioned in Chapter 6, is proposed [11 and 13]. It does not require a chassis dynamometer, but during accelerations it uses the inertia of the moving parts inside and downstream of the engine (flywheel, transmission, gearbox in neutral) as a load during accelerations [12]. The intensity of the load is identified by the position of the throttle valve [34 and 35]. This method is similar to the free acceleration test, which is currently the only regulation test for measuring smoke emissions, but whose results are virtually unrelated to full-load soot emissions. To overcome this drawback, it has been proposed that a load be applied to diesel engines by using the brakes of the drive axle of the vehicle while running on a freely rotating roller and measuring the emissions using the Bosch technique [28].

### 7.1.3 Precautions

Many precautions must be observed during the tests in order to obtain measurement results that are reliable and reproducible. Apart from possible analytical interference and artefacts[1] that are liable to appear during emission trapping, the state of the vehicles to be tested is extremely important as is the condition of the analytical system. It is therefore indispensable to precondition the vehicles before testing. Every standard procedure imposes this type of treatment in order to start with a clearly-defined thermal state for the engine and to purge the exhaust systems and trapping lines. This ensures that the results will not depend on the previous record of the vehicle and of the engine. This pretreatment is indispensable, for example, for measuring particulates. On a vehicle that has been idle for a long period, the oxide particles lining the exhaust system are likely to be detached and thus abnormally increase the mass of 'particulates' measured, accounting for between 5 and 95% of the total mass collected on the filters [36].

The type and composition of the exhaust may also vary along the route through the exhaust and trapping manifolds [76]. This applies in particular to diesel exhaust

1. Accidental mechanisms identified during an experiment.

that drops in temperature as it passes through the manifolds. Accordingly, the initial hydrocarbons in the vapor phase are progressively condensed on the particulates, increasing their weight and SOF content [1]. This condensation of hydrocarbons that were originally in a gas phase also occurs on the filters required for the weight analysis of the particles. Particles collected on an electro-filter have a lower SOF content than those collected on a fiber-glass filter [9]. Also, in the dilution tunnels the oxidation reactions occurring may give rise to the additional formation of formaldehyde and acetaldehyde, up to fifteen times the contents measured in the undiluted gases [74].

It is important to check the possible selective absorptions and adsorptions of certain products on the walls of the connecting pipes, which are liable to cause significant holdup. This applies, for example, to benzene and PAH on glass [31]. Prior saturation of the surfaces with the offending compound can nevertheless cause positive errors. The walls of metal tubes may also exert catalytic effects and convert the products to be measured, especially if the transfer tubes are hot.

Diffusion of the gases to be analyzed through the plastic transfer tubes may also be a source of error. Complex structures combining metals and plastics can reduce these effects.

For exhausts that are liable to contain particulates with a substantial hydraulic diameter, sampling must be isokinetic. Diesel particulates are nevertheless sufficiently small for the exhaust to behave like a gas and this precaution can be disregarded. However, it is important to make sure that the Reynolds No. in the dilution tunnels is sufficiently high to guarantee turbulent flow and that the distribution of the species to be measured is uniform throughout the tunnel cross-section.

Blanks are indispensable in each test. The dilution air must be analyzed under the same conditions, as fresh filters may already display some mutagenicity [29]. However, this mutagenic effect does not seem to depend on the type of filter and the collecting artefacts, if any, must occur very quickly from the onset of trapping [21].

The removal of interfering compounds can cause a holdup of the compounds to be analyzed. This applies to the trapping of steam by desiccants of the $CaCl_2$ type, which are necessary in infrared measurements to prevent the dissolution of the alkaline earth halogenide windows. The water retained can dissolve soluble compounds like $SO_2$ and $NO_2$. Water vapor diffusion across a selective semi-permeable membrane, renewed from time to time, overcomes this drawback [43].

The make-up of the measuring instruments is also very important and the results obtained may vary according to the type of instrument, the manufacturer, and its degree of calibration or maintenance. For FID instruments, it may be important to specify the materials of the detector, its operating parameters (gas flow rates, pressure, temperature, bias voltage) and its internal geometry [36]. Calibration by suitable gas mixtures is also crucially important.

With the dilution tunnels employed for measuring diesel particulates, instead of stressing the indispensable isokinetic conditions, it would be more effective to impose stricter standards on the tunnel materials, their internal surface roughness, their geometric dimensions, the positions and dimensions of the probes installed, and the narrow temperature ranges to be applied at the different points [36].

#### 7.1.3.1 Possible interference

In the different analytical techniques employed, other compounds present in the exhaust can generate a response in the range corresponding to the compound being tested for.

For NO analyzed by chemiluminescence, nitrogen compounds other than $NO_2$ ($NH_3$, HCN, amines, etc.) can be converted to NO [40 and 75] and 'inert' molecules ($O_2$, $N_2$, $CO_2$ and $H_2O$, etc.) can discharge by colliding with the $NO_2$ species excited without light emission and thus yield false readings. $H_2O$ displays the most serious interference [68]. Its removal by condensation eliminates its discharge effect and maintains correct values for NO, which is insoluble in water, but conversely it absorbs $NO_2$ before measurement, thus yielding lower $NO_2$ values. Lowering pressure, raising the temperature above the dew-point, or removing the water by diffusion across a semi-permeable membrane overcomes these drawbacks. However, an excessive temperature increase in the sampling lines can cause the reduction of $NO_2$ to NO by the hydrocarbons that are present, which are catalyzed by the metals used in the lines, thus distorting the $NO/NO_2$ ratio [57].

In high concentrations ($>10\%$) CO also causes luminescence, yielding overvalued NO figures.

### 7.1.4 Sampling techniques

Various techniques are available [30 and 37] for trapping airborne contaminants and automotive effluents.

- Bubblers containing a suitable solvent, offer a simple and convenient method for sample transport and recovery, but are subject to artefacts, contamination, and to the limited absorption capacity of the solvent, which depends on the compound being analyzed.
- Cryogenic traps, which are indispensable for highly-volatile but non-selective compounds, are inconvenient to handle and accumulate large quantities of water. They can be employed in the form of a capillary tube, immersed in liquid argon, directly at the top of the chromatographic column. The water trapped is not a problem if desorption is sufficiently slow [64].
- Teflon[2], Tedlar[3], and Mylar[4] bags [44] are capable of holding from 10 to 100 liters of gas, but are delicate, difficult to clean, and liable to lose important compounds by permeation. Tedlar is usually recommended [38].

2. Polytetrafluoroethylene.
3. Polyvinyl fluoride.
4. Polyterephthalate.

- Glass containers, which are easy to clean and firmly store their contents, are fragile and have limited volumes.
- Spherical and cylindrical metal cartridges are used after prior vacuum. They are easy to clean and serve for several analyses with the same sampling [73].

Wet sampling generally consists of the absorption of the compounds analyzed in a suitable solvent. The exhaust gas is bubbled through a wash-bottle containing the solvent. The flow rate is set to collect the maximum of compound in the minimum time, thus preventing a part of the compound from passing through without being absorbed and from exceeding the absorption capacity of the volume of solvent selected.

To eliminate problems of pressure drops and the simultaneous collection of particulates the gases are washed in diffusion scrubbers with solvent trickling on the walls [15].

Gaseous pollutants are trapped on solid supports made of silica gels, activated charcoal, or organic polymers such as Tenax[5] [73], Tenax-GC[6] [25], or XAD-2[7] [7 and 32] on which specific substituents can be grafted, which are adapted to a particular compound. The retention capacities of Tenax have been determined for different compounds [41 and 42] and the *INRS* has compiled a list of usable adsorbents for the compounds to be analyzed as well as the adsorption capacity of activated charcoals for different compounds [8]. A comparison between cryogenic trapping and XAD-2 cartridges shows that the retention capacity of these systems varies with the compounds analyzed. XAD-2 is better for light aromatics and polyaromatics and for aldehydes but the cryogenic trap is preferable for phenols and aromatic ketones [63].

## 7.2 Review of analytical principles employed

### 7.2.1 Spectroscopic methods

Absorption spectroscopy is based on the measurement of the effects created by the interaction of electromagnetic radiation with the internal energy states of molecules. A molecule, which must in this case have a magnetic or electric dipole moment, absorbs specific energy quanta in the incident radiation, depending on the wavelength, while it undergoes energy transitions from the basic state to the higher energy levels permitted. This excitation of the higher energy levels can affect the electrons of the molecule, the interatomic vibrations, or the rotations of the molecule about different axes.

5. Poly(oxy-m-terphenyl-2',5'-ylene).
6. Polymer of 2,6-diphenyl-p-phenylene oxide.
7. Styrene/divinylbenzene copolymer.

Each gas displays characteristic wavelengths for which it absorbs the electromagnetic radiation that excites the molecules concerned. This is reflected by an absorption spectrum of the gas. Spectroscopic methods, which are used for continuous gas analysis, use absorption in the visible, the ultraviolet, and the infrared wavelengths, based on the Beer-Lambert law. This law expresses the relationship between the radiation intensity $I$ passing through a vessel of length $l$ transparent to radiation and containing an absorbent substance in concentration $c$:

$$I = e^{-kcl}$$

where $k$ is the absorption coefficient of the substance to be analyzed.

#### 7.2.1.1 Absorption in the infrared

The molecules formed of at least two different atoms (CO, NO, $CO_2$, $NO_2$, $H_2O$, etc.), unlike the gases consisting of identical atoms ($H_2$, $O_2$, $N_2$, $Cl_2$, etc.), absorb infrared radiation by converting the light energy received into vibration/rotation energy of the molecules, which can be detected in the form of heat.

The spectral range used is the near and middle infrared (from 0.75 to 30 μm). For combustion gases, especially automotive exhausts, analyzers without spectral dispersion are used, which are called NDIR and are better for industrial tests. Instead of using a monochromator (prism or grating) to separate the light, NDIR instruments use the total absorption over a given wavelength [6].

The infrared emitters are heated filaments that act like black body radiators over a wide range of wavelengths. The detection receiver is a volume of gas identical to the one to be measured in the gaseous mixture to be analyzed. This receiver thus remains insensitive to absorption by other chemicals, if their absorption ranges do not overlap. Single-beam instruments are available in which the output signal from the detector, either continuous or modulated, is proportional to the infrared radiation transmitted by the cell containing the gas to be analyzed. Most of the instruments use twin beams generated by two identical infrared sources (metal wires heated by the Joule effect) and are equipped with a differential detector of which the signal is proportional to the attenuation of the infrared radiation across the absorption cell. The incident infrared beams are modulated by a rotating modulator. In positive-filter instruments, one beam passes through an absorption cell containing the gas to be analyzed and the second crosses a cell containing a non-absorbent reference gas (such as nitrogen) and the two beams then each pass through a chamber filled with the gas to be measured in its pure state, thus comprising a differential sensor (Fig. 7.2). Negative-filter instruments do not have a reference cell, but only one cell containing the gas to be analyzed, which is crossed by both beams. At the output, the first beam passes through a compensation cell and the second beam passes through a cell filled with the gas to be analyzed and then both reach a type of differential sensor.

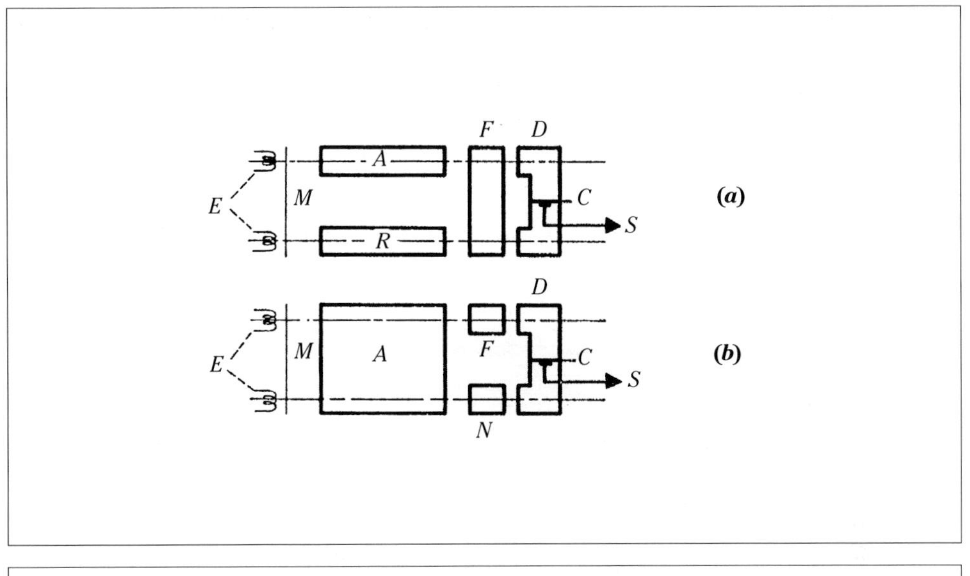


| | (a) | | (b) |
|---|---|---|---|
| *A* | absorption cell | *A* | absorption cell |
| *C* | diaphragm of capacitive sensor | *C* | diaphragm of capacitive sensor |
| *D* | detector | *D* | detector |
| *E* | IR emitter | *E* | IR emitter |
| *F* | compensation cell | *F* | compensation cell |
| *M* | rotating modulator | *M* | rotating modulator |
| *R* | reference cell | *N* | cell containing gas to be analyzed |
| *S* | differential measurement signal | *S* | differential measurement signal |
| **(*a*)** | **Positive-filter analyzer** | **(*b*)** | **Negative-filter analyzer** |

**Fig 7.2** NDIR positive- and negative-filter analyzers [23]

The differential sensor is the Golay pressure sensor. It consists of two identical chambers containing the gas to be measured in its pure state, which are separated by a diaphragm that moves between the plates of a capacitor. The difference in heat received in each chamber, due to the presence of the gas to be analyzed on the path of one of the half-beams, causes an overpressure on one side of the diaphragm, which is modulated by the rotation of an upstream rotary modulator turning at a frequency of about 10 Hz. The capacitance variations of the system are electronically amplified. To compensate for the influence of variations in ambient temperature, the two chambers are connected by a capillary tube in some instruments, thus avoiding the movement of the membrane during a slow variation in temperature.

Other single-beam instruments (which avoid the drifts caused by the presence of two independently aging infrared sources or any fouling between the emitter and the receiver) have a modulator that causes the beam to pass alternately through the reference cell and the analysis cell. The chambers of the differential detector are superposed in this case. The same pressure sensor is used (Fig. 7.3). The cells have gilt walls to avoid absorption of the radiation by the walls and have transparent alkaline earth halogenide windows at the ends, thus requiring thorough drying of the gas to be analyzed. The use of cells of different lengths helps to vary the concentration range of the gas to be measured.

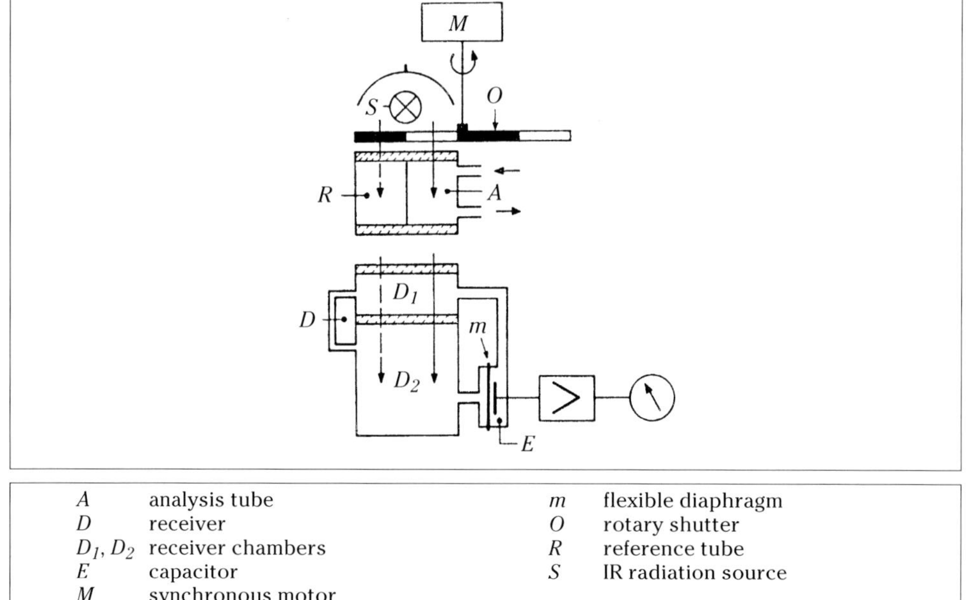


**Fig 7.3** Unor type NDIR analyzer [23]

To eliminate any possible interference caused by the presence of foreign gases absorbable in the same infrared range, these gases are introduced into the reference cell to absorb all the radiation in their absorption zone. Hence their variable content in the gas to be measured no longer disturbs the measurement.

Another method for eliminating the effect of interfering gases is to make them act in the same way on the measurement channel and on the reference channel. This is achieved in correlation analyzers [33]. A 'correlation wheel' driven by a synchronous motor has two cells in the form of filled segments, one with nitrogen and the second with the pure gas to be measured. A multi-reflection measurement chamber is also used to enhance the sensitivity of the measurements (Fig. 7.4).

NDIR analyzers can be used to measure many gases, including CO, $CO_2$, $CH_4$, NO, $SO_2$, HCl, and hydrocarbons. In automotive pollution, they are mainly used for CO and $CO_2$. They were formerly used to measure exhaust hydrocarbons but delivered poor results [47] because, for an instrument calibrated with n-hexane, aliphatics yield nearly 100% response while olefins and aromatics do not. Table 7.1 gives the percentage responses of different hydrocarbons in comparison with n-hexane as a

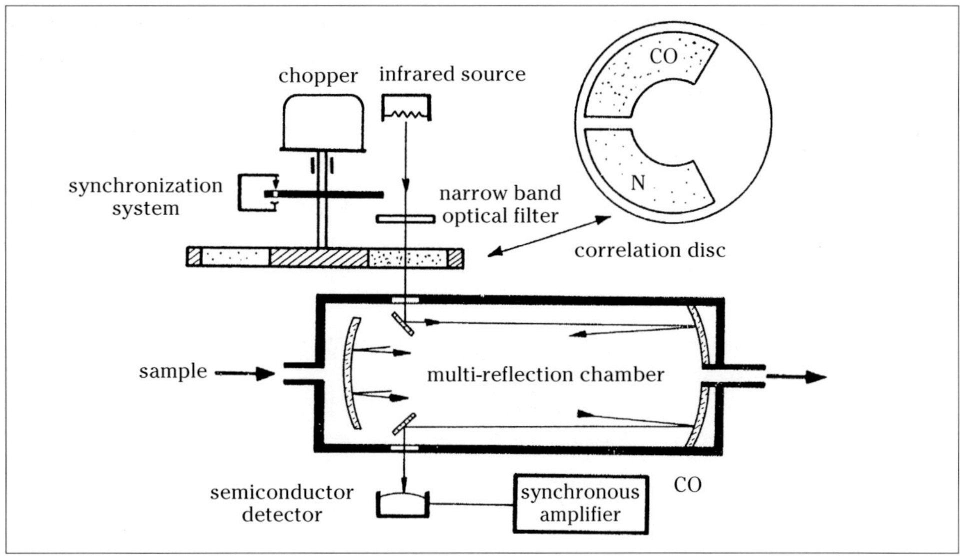


**Fig 7.4** Correlation analyzer [33]

**Table 7.1** Relative responses of NDIR and FID instruments: calibration with n-hexane [17]

| Hydrocarbon | Average relative responses based on carbon | |
|---|---|---|
| | NDIR | FID |
| **paraffins:** | | |
| • methane | 30 | 110 |
| • ethane | 100 | 102 |
| • propane | 103 | 100 |
| • i-butane | 101 | – |
| • n-butane | 106 | 100 |
| • i-pentane | 99 | 100 |
| • n-pentane | 104 | 102 |
| • n-hexane | 100 | 100 |
| • n-heptane | 97 | 101 |
| **olefins:** | | |
| • ethylene | 9 | 100 |
| • propylene | 31 | 100 |
| • 1-butene | 53 | – |
| • 1-pentene | 57 | – |
| • 1-hexane | 61 | – |
| **aromatics:** | | |
| • benzene | 2 | 98 |
| • toluene | 13 | 98 |
| **acetylenics:** | | |
| • acetylene | 1 | 99 |
| • methylacetylene | 16 | 99 |
| • ethylacetylene | 32 | 99 |

reference, for an NDIR instrument and an FID instrument, with the average values depending on the type and setting of the instruments (cell lengths in NDIR, flame adjustment in FID, etc.).

### 7.2.1.2 Laser spectroscopy with semiconducting diodes

Unlike the above system, lasers (Fig. 7.5) by their very principle emit virtually monochromatic radiation in an extremely narrow band, 100 to 1000 times smaller than the gas absorption band. Semiconducting laser diodes are generally made from lead salts (e.g. $PbS_{1-x}Se_x$). When the diode current reaches a certain level laser radiation is emitted in the middle infrared. The wavelength can be adjusted by altering the operating temperature [58, 63 and 66].

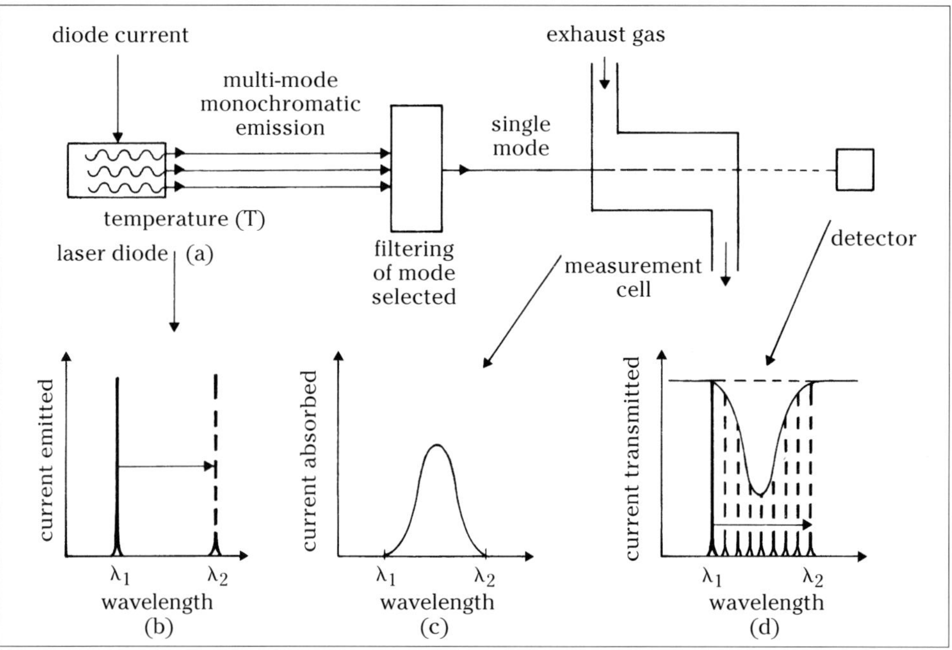


(a) Schematic representation of a laser spectrometer. The laser emits on a number of near and discrete frequencies (modes) and the mode is selected by filtering.
(b) The laser emission is scanned from $\lambda_1$ to $\lambda_2$.
(c) Absorption band.
(d) Signal detected: current transmitted when the laser emission varies between $\lambda_1$ and $\lambda_2$.

**Fig 7.5** Laser diode spectrometry [58]

The small diode dimensions (about 1 mm) makes it possible to install many diodes over a short length. The ms sweep time of a laser diode helps to scan the gas absorption band by measuring its profile and the intensity absorbed. The position of the band is a characteristic of the chemical being measured and the intensity of the absorption is proportional to the concentration.

A multi-diode system thus allows:

- simultaneous measurement of several components
- real-time measurement (measurement cycle $<1$ s)
- direct measurement in the gas stream

These systems, which are still expensive, are currently in the development stage [27, 66, and 70].

#### 7.2.1.3 Fourier transform systems

The radiation of a wide-band source (continuous spectrum) is applied to a Michelson interferometer. The wavelengths making up the continuous spectrum pulsate between each other in the interferometer when the length of the optical path taken by the radiation varies. To do this the interferometer divides the radiation into two beams: one is reflected on a fixed mirror and the second on a vibrating mirror. When recombined the two beams give interference fringes (interferogram) (Fig. 7.6). The interferogram represents the intensity distribution of the spectral components of the incident radiation as a function of the difference in optical path caused by the mobile mirror and contains all the information on the spectral distribution of the radiation during the time that it crosses the mobile mirror. If the radiation leaving the interferometer is sent into a gas mixture (exhaust gas), the spectral components corresponding to the absorption spectra of the different gases are absorbed. The light intensity distribution is attenuated by the absorption of these chemicals. The resulting interferogram is recorded by the detector whose signal represents the concentration distribution of the different chemicals in the gas mixture to be measured. This distribution is obtained *simultaneously*.

Information on this distribution in the mixture depends on the difference in optical path (diagram (b) in Fig. 7.6). The mathematical Fourier transform, run on a computer, helps to obtain the equation giving the intensity distribution as a function of wavelength from the distribution as a function of the optical path. The spectral resolution depends on the distance traveled by the vibrating mirror, which has to oscillate at several cm/s. The accuracy of the conservation of planeity of the mirror during its movement must be such that the variations remain small in comparison with the wavelengths of the infrared radiations and therefore must not exceed a few nm. The computer must input the data, sort them, and execute the Fourier transform in less than a second. Under these conditions, Fourier transform spectroscopy allows [58, 63, and 77]:

- simultaneous and selective analysis of the different components of the mixture
- real-time measurement (measurement cycle $<1$ s response time $<7$ s)
- direct measurement in the engine effluent

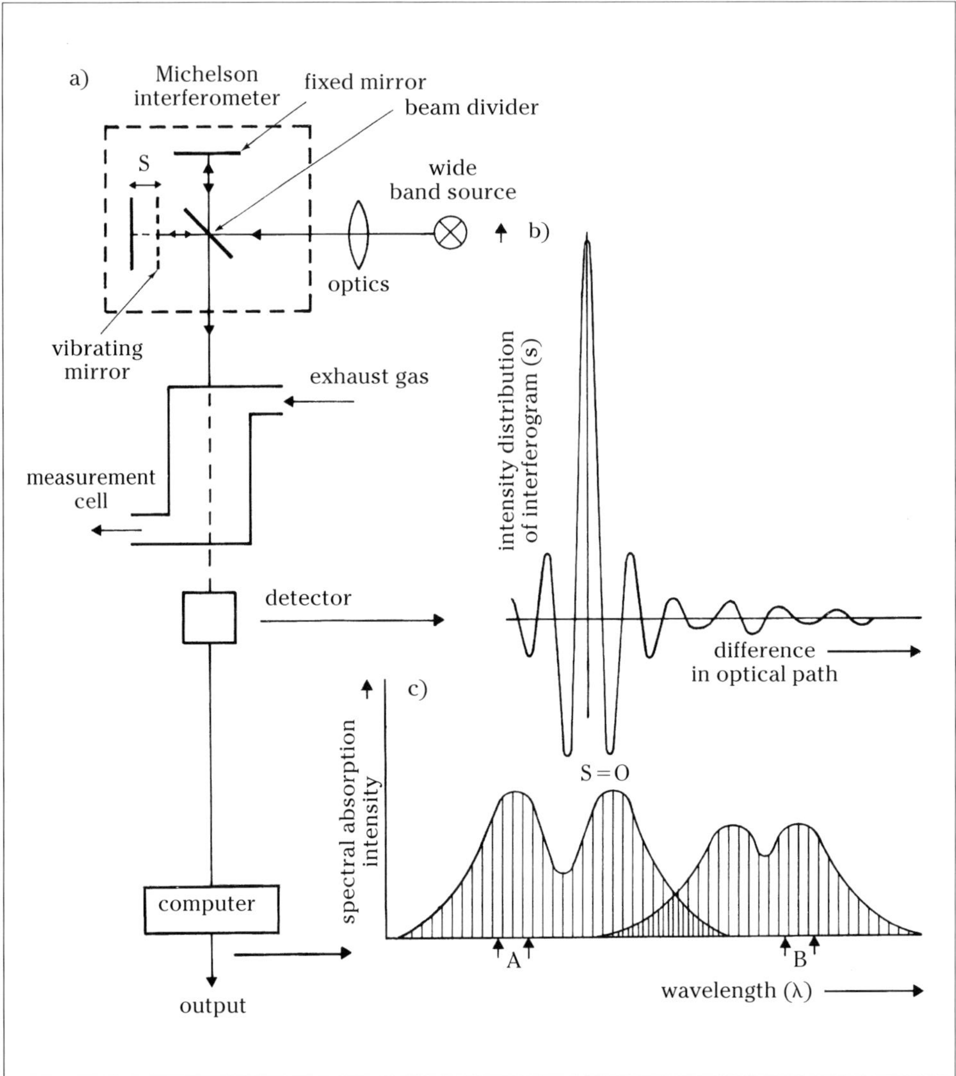


(a) Schematic representation of the spectrometer.
(b) Resulting interferogram.
(c) Spectrum of a hypothetical binary gas mixture obtained by Fourier transform of the interferogram:
- inhibition of source emission
- spectrum in the form of absorption spectrum
- the vertical lines indicate the rotation structure
- A and B have a narrow common region within the spectrum

The interferogram (b) and spectrum (c) have no direct relationship.

**Fig 7.6** Fourier transform interferometer [58]

### 7.2.1.4 Absorption in the ultraviolet

The same principle of using a non-dispersed radiation was applied in the ultraviolet band, particularly to measure $NO_2$ [47] at a wavelength of about 400 nm. This technique has been discarded today in favor of chemoluminescence.

### 7.2.1.5 Analysis by chemoluminescence

A number of chemical reactions are accompanied by the emission of light energy. This happens during the spontaneous return to the normal state of excited nitrogen peroxide molecules formed by the reaction of ozone with nitric oxide, with photon emissions in the 0.6 to 3 μm band:

$$NO + O_3 \Rightarrow NO_2^{\bullet} + O_2$$
$$NO_2^{\bullet} \Rightarrow NO_2 + h\upsilon$$

The gas to be analyzed is introduced into the reaction chamber with ozone produced by a high-voltage discharge in oxygen [22]. For measuring NO the light energy is filtered to eliminate interference by other gases, such as CO and $SO_2$ and ethylenic hydrocarbons, and is then amplified by photomultiplier to yield a signal proportional to the NO concentration. $NO_2$ is measured by thermal decomposition to NO at 600 to 650°C in a stainless steel furnace:

$$2NO_2 \Rightarrow 2NO + O_2$$

or around 300 to 400°C in a molybdenum furnace, which reacts less with the interfering compounds. The $NO_2$ concentration is obtained from the difference between the measurements across or bypassing the furnace.

## 7.2.2 Ionization methods

The introduction of carbon compounds into a non-ionized hydrogen flame generates ions that can be detected in the form of an electric current between an electrode raised to between 100 and 300 V and the burner representing the second electrode [23 and 60]. This is the basis of the flame ionization FID analyzer and the FID detectors used in chromatography. The current, in the range of 10 pA, is a function of the number of carbon atoms passing through the flame. It crosses a high resistance where the voltage across the terminals is amplified and measured. Fig. 7.7 shows an FID burner and Fig. 7.8 a complete analyzer [18 and 47].

The gas to be analyzed is introduced into the air/hydrogen diffusion flame. The air and hydrogen flow rates are set to obtain the maximum response from the analyzer. The FID analyzer is unaffected by the presence of water vapor in the gas to be analyzed, but it is influenced by any oxygen that could accompany the sample. This effect is minimized by replacing pure hydrogen by a 40% $H_2$/60% He mixture and, for the zero and reference gases, by using mixtures in which the $O_2$ content is close to that of the gas to be measured.

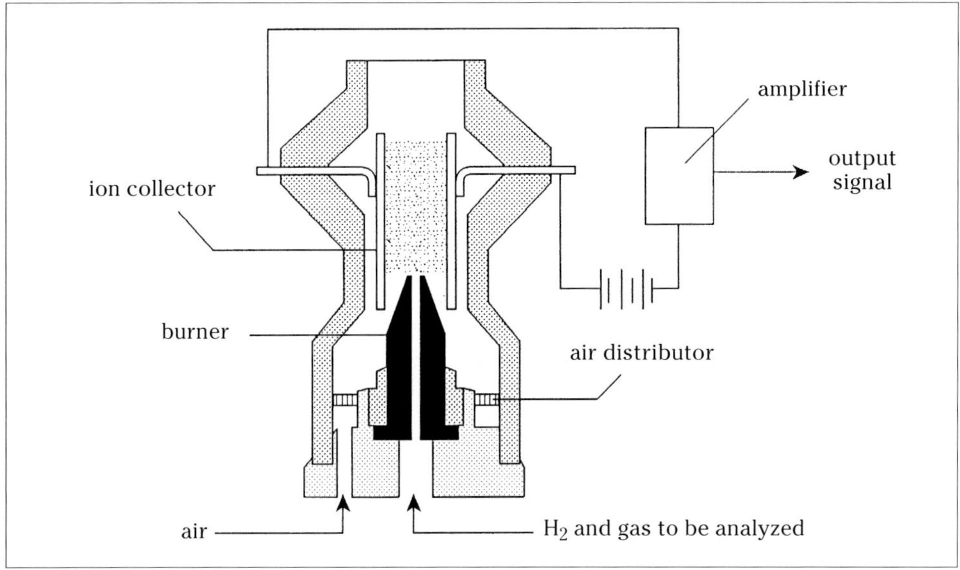


**Fig 7.7** Burner of an FID instrument [47]

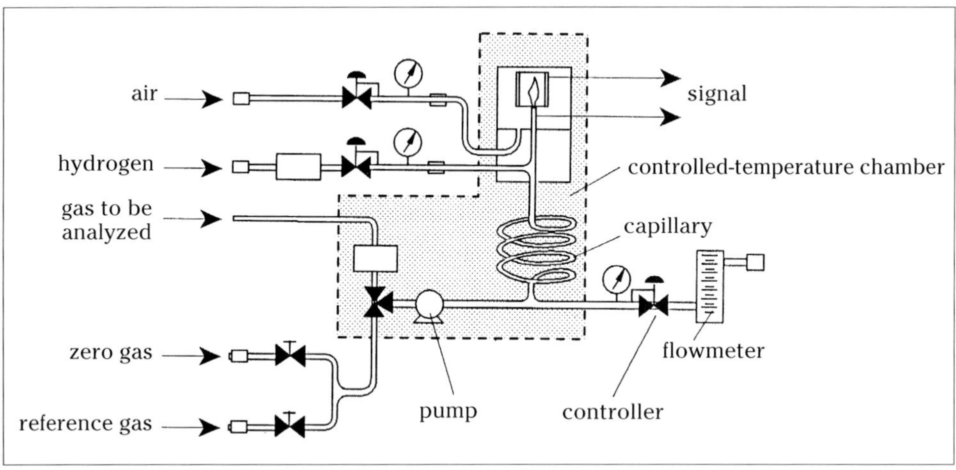


**Fig 7.8** FID hydrocarbon analyzer [47]

The FID analyzer is used to measure 'hydrocarbons', including carbon compounds, reported as ppm by volume of carbon (ppmC) measured in comparison with an aliphatic hydrocarbon reference (propane or hexane). Although incomparably better than that of the NDIR method (Table 7.1), the FID response of organic compounds may deviate from 1 in passing from alkenes to arenes and especially to oxygenated compounds (alcohols, aldehydes, and ethers) (Tables 7.2 and 7.3) [20].

**Table 7.2** Relative responses of FID instruments
Calibration with n-heptane [17]
A, real number of carbon atoms
B, apparent number of carbon atoms

| Substance | A | B | Substance | A | B |
|---|---|---|---|---|---|
| **normal paraffins** | | | | | |
| methane | 1 | 1.0 | pentane | 5 | 5.0 |
| ethane | 2 | 2.0 | hexane | 6 | 6.1 |
| propane | 3 | 3.0 | heptane | 7 | 7.0 |
| n-butane | 4 | 3.8 | octane | 8 | 7.8 |
| i-butane | 4 | 3.8 | nonane | 9 | 8.8 |
| **branched paraffins** | | | | | |
| 2-methylpropane | 4 | 3.8 | 2,2,4-trimethylpentane | 8 | 8.0 |
| 2,2-dimethylpropane | 5 | 4.7 | 3-methyleptane | 8 | 8.1 |
| 2-methylbutane | 5 | 5.3 | 2,2-dimethylhexane | 8 | 8.1 |
| 2,2-dimethylbutane | 6 | 6.1 | 2,5-dimethylhexane | 8 | 8.1 |
| 3-methylpentane | 6 | 6.3 | 4-methylheptane | 8 | 8.1 |
| 2-methylpentane | 6 | 6.3 | 2,2,3-trimethylpentane | 8 | 8.1 |
| 2,3-dimethylpentane | 7 | 6.9 | 2,3,5-trimethylhexane | 9 | 8.6 |
| 2-methylhexane | 7 | 7.1 | 2,2-dimethylheptane | 9 | 8.7 |
| 3-methylhexane | 7 | 7.1 | 2,2,4-trimethylhexane | 9 | 8.9 |
| 2,2-dimethylpentane | 7 | 7.1 | 2,2,5-trimethylhexane | 9 | 8.9 |
| 2,4-dimethylpentane | 7 | 7.1 | 2,3,3,4-tetramethylpentane | 9 | 8.9 |
| 3-ethylpentane | 7 | 7.1 | 2,3,3-trimethylhexane | 9 | 9.0 |
| 2,2,3-trimethylbutane | 7 | 7.1 | 3,3-diethylpentane | 9 | 9.0 |
| 3,3-dimethylpentane | 7 | 7.2 | 2,2,3,3-tetramethylpentane | 9 | 9.0 |
| 2-methylheptane | 8 | 7.7 | 2,2,3-trimethylhexane | 9 | 9.0 |
| 2-methyl-3-ethylpentane | 8 | 7.8 | 2,2,4-trimethylhexane | 9 | 9.0 |
| 2,3-dimethylhexane | 8 | 7.9 | 3,3,5-trimethylpentane | 10 | 9.8 |
| 2,4-dimethylhexane | 8 | 7.9 | 2,2,4,5-tetramethyhexane | 10 | 9.9 |
| 3,4-dimethylhexane | 8 | 7.9 | 2,2,3,3-tetramethylhexane | 10 | 10.1 |
| 3-ethylhexane | 8 | 8.0 | | | |
| **cyclanes** | | | | | |
| cyclopropane | 3 | 2.9 | cic-1,2-dimethylcyclohexane | 8 | 7.4 |
| cyclopentane | 5 | 4.7 | trans-1,4-dimethylclohexane | 8 | 7.4 |
| methylcyclopentane | 6 | 5.7 | cis-1,2-trans-4-trimethylcyclopentane | 8 | 7.4 |
| cyclohexane | 6 | 5.8 | 1-methyl-cis-2-ethylcyclopentane | 8 | 7.5 |
| ethylcyclopentane | 7 | 6.5 | 1-methyl-cis-3-ethylcyclopentane | 8 | 7.5 |
| cis-1,2-dimethylcyclopentane | 7 | 6.5 | trans-1,2-cis-3-trimethylcyclopentane | 8 | 7.5 |
| trans-1,3-dimethylcyclopentane | 7 | 6.5 | trans-1,2-dimethylcyclohexane | 8 | 7.6 |
| cis-1,3-dimethylcyclopentane | 7 | 6.5 | 1-methyl-trans-2-ethylcyclopentane | 8 | 7.6 |
| methylcyclohexane | 7 | 6.6 | ethylcyclohexane | 8 | 7.6 |
| trans-1,2-dimethylcyclopentane | 7 | 6.6 | 1,1-dimethylcyclohexane | 8 | 7.7 |
| 1,1-dimethylcyclopentane | 7 | 6.7 | 1,1,2-trimethylcyclopentane | 8 | 7.7 |
| 1-methyl-trans-3-ethylcyclopentane | 8 | 7.3 | 1,1,3-trimethylcyclopentane | 8 | 7.8 |
| n-propylcyclopentane | 8 | 7.3 | 1-methyl-cis-4-ethylcyclohexane | 9 | 8.1 |
| trans-1,2-cis-4-trimethylcyclopentane | 8 | 7.3 | 1-methyl-trans-4-ethylcyclohexane | 9 | 8.3 |
| cis-1,2-trans-3-trimethylcyclopentane | 8 | 7.3 | isopropylcyclohexane | 9 | 8.3 |
| isopropylcyclopentane | 8 | 7.3 | 1,1,2-trimethylcyclohexane | 9 | 8.6 |

**Table 7.3** Relative responses of FID instruments

| Substance | A | B | Substance | A | B |
|---|---|---|---|---|---|
| **olefins** | | | | | |
| acetylene | 2 | 2,6 | 2-butene | 4 | 3.7 |
| ethylene | 2 | 1.9 | 1.3-butadiene | 4 | 3.8 |
| propene | 3 | 2.9 | dimethylbutadiene | 6 | 5.8 |
| 1-butene | 4 | 3.8 | | | |
| **aromatics** | | | | | |
| benzene | 6 | 5.8 | 1-methyl-4-ethylbenzene | 9 | 8.4 |
| toluene | 7 | 7.0 | 1-methyl-3-ethylbenzene | 9 | 8.5 |
| p-xylene | 8 | 7.4 | n-propylbenzene | 9 | 8.5 |
| o-xylene | 8 | 7.6 | 1-methyl-2-ethylbenzene | 9 | 8.6 |
| ethylbenzene | 8 | 7.6 | n-butylbenzene | 10 | 9.2 |
| m-xylene | 8 | 7.7 | 1-methyl-2-isopropylbenzene | 10 | 9.3 |
| 1,2,3-trimethylbenzene | 9 | 8.2 | 1-methyl-4-isopropylbenzene | 10 | 9.3 |
| isopropylbenzene | 9 | 8.1 | sec-butylbenzene | 10 | 9.4 |
| 1,2,3-trimethylbenzene | 9 | 8.2 | 1-methyl-3-isopropylbenzene | 10 | 9.5 |
| 1,3,5-trimethylbenzene | 9 | 8.2 | tert-butylbenzene | 10 | 9.6 |
| **substituted polyaromatics [69]** | | | | | |
| PAH | x | 0.93 x | oxy-PAH | x | 0.82 x |
| S-PAH | x | 0.81 x | nitro-PAH | x | 0.68 x |
| dinitro-PAH | x | 0.48 x | | | |
| **alcohols** | | | | | |
| methanol | 1 | 0.77 | sec-butanol | 4 | 3.3 |
| ethanol | 2 | 1.8 | tert-butanol | 4 | 3.8 |
| n-propanol | 3 | 2.6 | hexanol | 6 | 5.3 |
| i-propanol | 3 | 2.2 | octanol | 8 | 7.7 |
| n-butanol | 4 | 3.5 | decanol | 10 | 9.4 |
| i-butanol | 4 | 3.6 | | | |
| **aldehydes** | | | | | |
| formaldehyde | 1 | 0 | heptanal | 7 | 6.3 |
| isobutanal | 4 | 3.0 | decanal | 10 | 8.7 |
| **ethers** | | | | | |
| diethylether | 4 | 3.0 | diisopropylether | 6 | 5.0 |
| **ketones** | | | | | |
| acetone | 3 | 2.1 | 2-butanone | 4 | 3.2 |
| **esters** | | | | | |
| methyl acetate | 3 | 1.0 | n-butyl acetate | 6 | 4.8 |
| ethyl acetate | 4 | 2.4 | 2-methylbutyl acetate | 7 | 5.6 |
| n-propyl acetate | 5 | 3.8 | | | |
| **acids** | | | | | |
| acetic acid | 2 | 1.0 | hexanoic acid | 6 | 5.1 |
| propionic acid | 3 | 2.0 | heptanoic acid | 7 | 5.6 |
| butyric acid | 4 | 3.0 | octanoic acid | 8 | 6.6 |
| **miscellaneous** | | | | | |
| carbon disulfide | 1 | 0.01 | acetonitrile | 2 | 1.3 |

### 7.2.3 Magnetic methods

A gas subjected to a heterogeneous magnetic field undergoes a force directed towards increasing fields if the gas is paramagnetic and decreasing fields if it is diamagnetic. Most gases are diamagnetic and only a few are highly paramagnetic. The latter include oxygen and to a much lesser degree nitrogen oxides, which exhibit a magnetic susceptibility representing 44% and 29% of that of oxygen respectively for NO and $NO_2$.

Due to these differences in susceptibility, if a complex gas mixture (exhaust gas) penetrates into a magnetic field a force is exerted virtually exclusively on the paramagnetic molecules. The force created is identified and measured in different ways:

- By exploiting the decrease in magnetic susceptibility with rising temperature: two parallel tubes are subjected alternately to a field created by a rotating magnet and heated by an electric coil. The periodic replacement of warmer $O_2$ by colder $O_2$ in the offset phase in the two tubes causes variations in cyclic pressure in a diaphragm capsule of the same type as the one employed in NDIR. The pressure variation is proportional to the magnetic field and to the $O_2$ content of the gas. The modulation caused by the rotating field can be amplified.
- By creating a 'magnetic wind', which also exploits the variations in susceptibility with temperature. The gas to be analyzed circulates in an annular chamber of which the two branches are connected by a horizontal tube with three successive zones: a cold zone in the field of a permanent magnet, a zone heated by a filament placed alongside in the same field, and a third zone heated by a second filament outside the field. The oxygen molecules of the gas to be analyzed are attracted to the magnetic field and are heated in the zone heated by the filament. Their paramagnetism decreases and they are expelled by the colder molecules with greater susceptibility, creating a 'magnetic wind' inside the tube. The corresponding flow rate is measured by the imbalance of a Wheatstone bridge incorporating the above two filaments.
- Using a rotating mobile accessory where the rotation is caused by a variation in oxygen partial pressure. The return torque of the mobile device, counterbalanced by an electrostatic field or an electromagnetic effect, is detected by optical effect.

### 7.2.4 Electrochemical methods

Coulometric methods based on electrolysis have been recommended, especially to determine $SO_2$ [4]. Conductimetry is also used if the compound to be determined causes a change in the electrical resistivity of the absorption solution [5]. This applies to the determination of acidic and basic gases.

The polarographic method is based on differences in redox potentials specific to the various chemical reactions. For oxygen, this potential is reduced to a lower potential than the other reducible compounds present in the exhaust gases, namely $SO_2$ and NO, which are also present in lower concentrations than $O_2$. Hence this technique allows a measurement of the $O_2$ partial pressure in the gas. The sensitive element, kept at about 45°C and combined with an amplifier, consists of a gold cathode and a silver anode separated by cellulose gel impregnated with KCl to form the electrolyte [53]. A voltage of 0.8 V is applied between the anode and cathode. The oxygen in the gas to be analyzed diffuses towards the cathode across a PTFE diaphragm where is it reduced to the state of $OH^-$ ions by liberating four electrons. The current thus generated is proportional to the number of molecules of $O_2$ involved.

Another electrochemical technique, not used for quantitative analysis, is a potentiometric technique. It is applied in the λ oxygen sensor used to maintain the fuel/air ratio of 1 upstream of the three-way catalytic mufflers. It exploits the property of certain refractory oxides such as zirconia to exhibit an ionic conductivity at high temperature (>300°C) due to the mobility of the $O^{--}$ ions. The probe is generally in the form of a glove finger of zirconia stabilized by CaO or $Y_2O_3$, and lined internally and externally with porous platinum. The ceramic seals off the gas mixture to be analyzed, at the exterior of the probe, from a reference mixture of which the oxygen partial pressure is stable, usually consisting of the surrounding air reaching the center of the probe. If the $O_2$ concentrations are different on both sides of the zirconia an electrochemical concentration cell is created whose electromotive force corresponds to the Nernst law. A variation in the oxygen concentration causes a change in the voltage across the terminals of the cell. The presence of platinum rapidly brings the composition of the gas mixture in contact with it to thermodynamical equilibrium. When the $O_2$ concentration rises sharply, at the time of the transition from the rich mixture to the lean mixture, a sudden voltage rise is observed (about 500 mV in less than 20 ms), which is used to control the fuel/air ratio of the carburetted mixture around stoichiometric proportions. More recent solutions based on strontium titanate films obtained by vaporization allow operation up to 1000°C with response times of a few ms to variations in oxygen partial pressure.

### 7.2.5 Mass spectrography

This method, which is still considered to lie in the domain of the research laboratory, is nevertheless finding increasing use in the real world of air pollution research because, combined with chromatographic methods, it serves to identify compounds that are otherwise difficult to characterize, especially in the PAH range.

Mass spectrometry is concerned with the ionization of molecules and the splitting of bonds between atoms under the effect of a high-energy source. This leads to the formation of positive ions by stripping electrons using ionization by gas-phase electron impact under high vacuum. The electrons needed are produced by thermo-ionic emission (heating of a filament) and accelerated by a potential difference (about 70 *e*V) between the anode and the filament and then collide with the molecules to be identified, causing their ionization and splitting. The molecular ion initially formed can then decompose into positive fragment ions and neutral fragments. With propane, for example, the following is observed:

$$CH_3-CH_2-CH_3+e \Rightarrow CH_3-CH_2-CH_3^+ + 2e$$

$$CH_3-CH_2-CH_3^+ \Rightarrow CH_3-CH_2^+ + CH_3$$

etc.

The spectrometer then separates the positive ions as a function of their mass and charge according to the characteristic $M/e$ ($M$ mass of the ion, $e$ electron charge), which gives a characteristic position of the molecule on the spectrum. The discharge intensity of these ions gives a quantitative estimate of each of the ions. The analysis is performed in a magnetic field under low pressure. A charged particle in motion in a magnetic field describes a circular path of which the radius depends on the intensity of the field and the ratio $M/e$. By varying the magnetic field, the entire mass spectrum is thus scanned. The quality of the resolution, allowing for the separation of ions of neighboring mass, requires relatively long scanning times and depends on the system used for separation [2]:

- single-focus magnetic field
- superposed magnetic and electric fields
- continuous field and high-frequency field (quadri- or single-pole filters)
- space without field (time-of-flight spectrometer)

Quadripole instruments have higher scanning rates and, despite lower resolution, are better for coupling with chromatography.

The presence of characteristic ions and the relative abundance of natural isotopes of many elements help to obtain valuable information on the presence of specific functional groups. Spectrum libraries are available for a rapid identification of the formulation of the compounds analyzed. Portable instruments are used today to apply this technique in-line by direct coupling to the sampling tube [24].

### 7.2.6 Atomic absorption spectrometry

This method is essentially concerned with inorganic elements. For automotive emissions these include metals like lead and catalytic elements. The target element is dissociated from its chemical bonds and placed in a 'fundamental' state [31] and this dissociation is usually carried out in a flame. The element is accordingly capable of absorbing radiations over discrete wavelengths characteristic of the narrow bandwidth. This technique concerns all metals and metalloids, with the exception of sulfur, carbon, halogens, and gases.

### 7.2.7 Chromatographic methods

Chromatography is not in itself an analytical method but a method for separating the components of a mixture, a method that does not destroy the elements of the mixture as opposed to other methods such as distillation. It is based on the differential migration of the components of the mixture to be separated, which is conveyed in a suitable substrate [71] representing the stationary phase. The quality of separation depends on the distance traveled in the substrate and on the relative affinity of the components for the substrate. At the outlet of the system the isolated components must be detected, identified, and quantified by measuring a particular physical or chemical property specific to the components to be measured. The responses of the detector are plotted on the chromatogram. Three parameters are involved in chromatography:

- *elution time,* which is set for a given system and a given compound: this helps to characterize a compound
- *peak area,* which serves to determine the component in the mixture
- *peak width,* whose narrowness characterizes the quality of separation of the components of the mixture

One of the advantages of this separation method is that minimal fractions of samples are required.

Two main categories of methods are employed to analyze air pollution using substrates contained in a tube or 'column'.

- **Gas phase chromatography** (GC), carried out on gaseous or volatilized products. This is the only feasible method for permanent gases. The transport vehicle is a gas whose the pressure can be selected. The temperature to which the column is raised can be kept constant or programmed and is usually lower than 300°C to avoid cracking. After having used columns filled with the stationary phase [3] GC now increasingly uses capillary columns (very small diameter of 0.1 to 0.5 mm, and very long, several dozen meters in length), which are more effective, exhibit greater permeability and better selectivity, and allow faster analyses. In this case, the stationary phase coats the wall of the column or is 'grafted' to it. The types of stationary phase and filling recommended differ according to the types of product to be analyzed [72].
- **Liquid-phase chromatography** (HPLC), carried out at lower temperature but requiring high pressures (up to 50 to 60 MPa) to convey the mixture to be separated and the liquids allowing selective desorption of the adsorbed components. The desorption solvent can maintain a constant composition (isocratic regime) or have a composition gradient as a function of time to improve the separations. Fig. 7.9 shows the components of a liquid phase chromatograph.

Added to these two main types is supercritical chromatography, which employs $CO_2$ for example as a carrier gas in supercritical conditions. This promising technique

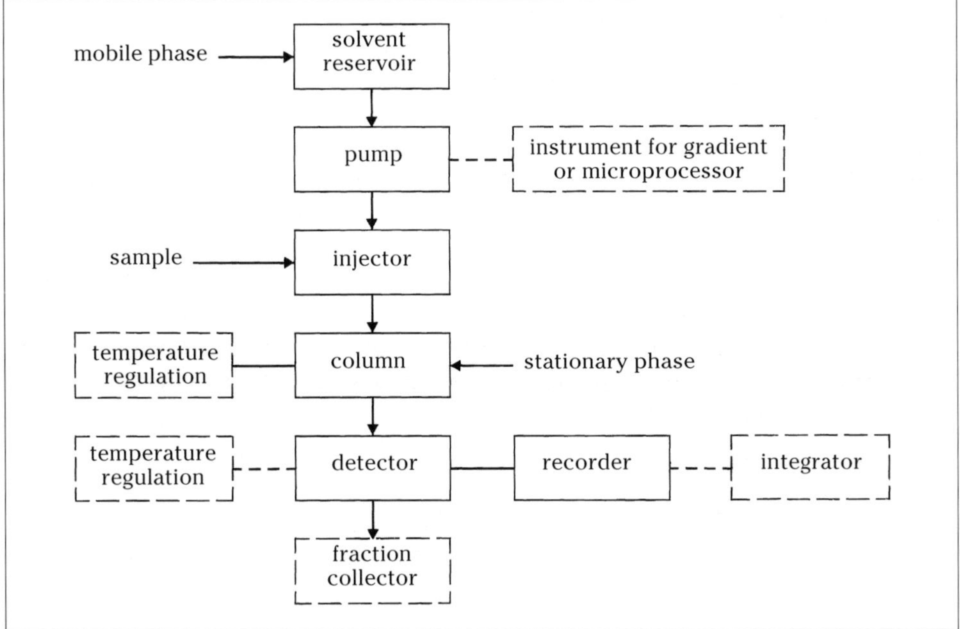


**Fig 7.9** Principle of liquid-phase chromatograph [51]

is used to analyze high-molecular weight pollutants. The detector is one of the essential components of GC and HPLC chromatographs. Multi-purpose detectors are used in GC:

- **Catharometer,** which makes a continuous comparison of the heat flux conveyed by the pure carrier gas to the flux removed on the passage of the molecules of a component of the mixture. The heat flux is generated by an electric resistor [72]. This detector has low sensitivity.
- **Flame ionization detector** (FID), as described above, is more sensitive but destroys the molecules of the component as they pass through the hydrogen flame. It only detects molecules containing carbon.
- **Electron capture detector** (ECD), which is highly selective and which measures the ionization current on the passage of molecules displaying an affinity for the free electrons emitted by the free electron source. It detects electro-negative compounds, such as halogen and nitrogen derivatives, with high sensitivity.
- **Thermo-ionic detector,** also called NPD (nitrogen phosphorus detectors), is highly selective. This detector is highly sensitive for measuring nitrogen and phosphorus derivatives.
- **Flame photometry detector** (FPD), is highly selective and filters the light emitted by the combustion of the component in a hydrogen flame and measures the intensity of the light emitted. This detector is highly sensitive for use in measuring sulfur compounds [32].

These detectors can be used simultaneously for complex analyses [19].

The use of other analytical systems in combination with chromatographic separation helps to augment the detection and quantification capacity: mass spectrometry, cryogenic matrix analyzed by infrared, placed at the column outlet [10 and 50]. In this technique, the successive fractions eluted are trapped on the different portions of a cryogenically cooled disc to analyze them in-line by infrared spectrometry. It is excellent for identifying PAH and their oxygen derivatives.

HPLC is not marked by multi-purpose detectors or specific high-sensitivity detectors. The following are employed:

- **Spectrometric detectors,** which measure the intensity at a wavelength absorbed on the passage of the component in the optical path of the detector. They have a fixed wavelength (e.g. 254 or 280 nm) or an extended spectrum for simultaneous measurement over a wide range of wavelengths.
- **Fluorimetric detectors,** which are highly selective and sensitive, but only apply to specific cases.
- **Differential refractometers** measure the variation in refractive index between the mobile phase and the column effluent. This is a multi-purpose but relatively insensitive detector, which also demands perfect temperature control of the mobile phase.
- **Electrochemical detectors** are limited to conducting effluents. Ammetric detectors, adapted to cells with small dead volumes, are generally used.

In liquid chromatography, it is usually necessary to calibrate the system with a known composition of the compounds to be analyzed. Most detectors are also sensitive to the concentration of the solute and flow rate variations of the eluent phase hence tend to modify the areas of the elution peaks. Quantitative analysis therefore demands pumps discharging at constant delivery [51].

## 7.2.8 Ionic chromatography

In ion exchange chromatography, a variant of liquid phase chromatography, the stationary phase is an ion exchanger, a solid support onto which the functional groups carrying positive and negative charges are grafted. Electro-neutrality is guaranteed by the presence of ions of opposite sign, cations or anions, which can be exchanged in equivalent numbers with those of the same sign in the solution to be analyzed.

Hence this technique is used to analyze electrolytic solutions, especially if the compounds concerned cannot be subjected to gas phase chromatography due to their excessive volatility. In automotive pollution, for example, this concerns the determination of carboxylic acids, sulfates and $SO_2$ [16 and 39]. In view of the specific conductivity of the solutions to be analyzed, conductimetric detectors lend themselves well to this type of analysis.

# REFERENCES

[1] M.K. Abbass et al., (1989), "Diesel particulate composition changes along an air-cooled exhaust pipe and dilution tunnel", *SAE Paper* No. 890789, 15 p.

[2] AFNOR, (1974), "Analyse des gaz par spectrométrie de masse, Détermination de leur composition chimique", *Standard X* 20-302, 6 p.

[3] AFNOR, (1974), "Analyse des gaz par chromatographie en phase gazeuse", *Standard X* 20-303, 4 p.

[4] AFNOR, (1974), "Analyse des gaz par coulométrie en continu", *Standard X* 20-304, 5 p.

[5] AFNOR, (1975), "Analyse des gaz par conductimétrie électrique", *Standard X* 20-305, 5 p.

[6] AFNOR, (1978), "Méthode d'analyse de gaz par absorption d'un faisceau de radiations infrarouges non dispersé", *Standard X* 20-301, 4 p.

[7] I. Alfheim et al., (1985), "Sampling ambient air for mutagenicity testing by high volume filtration on glass fibre filters and on XAD-2", *Environm. Int.*, **11,** 111-118.

[8] Anon., (1984), "Prélèvement et analyse de polluants organiques gazeux, Méthode utilisée par l'INRS", *Cahiers de notes documentaires*, (114), 55-61.

[9] C. Beckmann et al., (1988), "Investigation of Diesel particle characteristic during sampling and conditioning", *J. Aerosol Sci.*, **19,** 1001-1004.

[10] J.W. Childers et al., (1988), "Identification of semivolatile compounds in selected air sample extracts by gas chromatography/matrix isolation infrared spectrometry", in: *Proc. EPA/APCA International Symposium "Measurement of Toxic and Related Pollutants"*, R.K.M. Jayanty, Research Triangle Park, North Carolina, pp. 15-20.

[11] L.T. Collin, (1978), INCOLL, "A new technology in emission testing", *SAE Paper* No. 780618, 19 p.

[12] L.T. Collin, (1985), INertia COLLection, "A simplified dynamic engine test method", *SAE Paper* No. 850132, 22 p.

[13] L.T. Collin, (1987), "A high efficient short test for vehicle emission", *SAE Paper* No. 872099, 16 p.

[14] J.A. Colwill, (1980), "Regenerative dynamometers using d.c. machines", *SAE Paper* No. 800410, 5 p.

[15] P.K. Dasgupta et al., (1988), "Continuous liquid phase fluorimetry coupled to a diffusion scrubber for the real time determination of atmospheric formaldehyde, hydrogen peroxide and sulfur dioxide", *Atmosph. Environm.*, **22,** 949-963.

[16] P. Degobert, (1987), "Caractérisation physico-chimique des émissions d'une voiture diesel, présentation générale", *Poll. Atmosph.*, Special Issue November, pp. 90-99.

[17] J.G. Dobson et al., (1966), "Anwendung von FID Detektoren für die Analyse kontinuirlischer Prozesse", *Archiv für Technisches Messen*, **361,** R25-R44.

[18] R. Dutta, (1984), "Abgasmessungen an Ottomotoren, Probenahme und Analytik", *VDI Berichte*, No. 531, "Emissionsminderung Automobilabgase-Ottomotoren", pp. 403-427.

[19] R.F. Earp and R.D. Cox, (1984), "Identification and quantification of organics in ambient air using multiple gas chromatographic detection", in: *Identification and analysis of organic pollutants in air*, L.H. Keith, Butterworth Publications, Boston, pp. 159-169.

[20] S.A. Espinola and R.K. Pefley, (1982), *Alternate fuel influence on emission test procedure, ACS Symp., "Chemistry of Oxygenates in Fuels"*, Kansas City, September 12-17, pp. 955-969.

[21] D.R. Fitz et al., (1984), "Investigation of filtration artifacts when sampling ambient particulate matter for mutagenic assay", *Atmosph. Environm.*, **18,** 205-213.

[22] F. Gourdon, "Mesure des oxydes d'azote par chimiluminescence", *Nuisances et environnement*, December 1973, pp. 33-37

[23] H. Guérin, Analyse des gaz, Techn. de l'Ing., Vol. P2.229, 12 pp.

[24] R.E. Hague et al., (1988), "Results from the environmental response team's preliminary evaluation of a direct air sampling mass spectrometer (the Bruker MM-1)", in: *Proc. EPA/APCA International Symposium "Measurement of toxic and related pollutants"*, R.K.M. Jayanty, Research Triangle Park, North Carolina, pp. 750-764.

[25] R.L. Hanson et al., (1984), "Comparison of Tenax-GC and XAD-2 as polymer adsorbents for sampling combustion exhaust gases", in: *Identification and analysis of organic pollutants in air*, L.H. Keith, Butterworth Publications, Boston, pp. 79-93.

[26] N. Hirakouchi et al., (1989), "Measurement of Diesel exhaust emissions with mini-dilution tunnel", *SAE Paper* No. 890181, 12 p.

[27] J.C. Hill and R.F. Majkowski, (1980), "Time resolved measurement of vehicle sulfate and methane emissions with tunable diode lasers", *SAE Paper* No. 800510, 8 p.

[28] H. Holtei, (1985), "Neuere Meßverfahren zur Ermittlung dieselmotorischer Emission", *VDI Berichte*, No. 559, "Emissionsminderung Automobilgase, Dieselmotoren", pp. 319-334.

[29] V.S. Houk et al., (1987), "Mutagenicity of Teflon-coated glass fiber filters, A potential problem and solutions", *E.S.&T.*, **21,** 917-920.

[30] R.K.M. Jayanty, (1989), "Evaluation of sampling and analytical methods for monitoring toxic organics in air", *Atmosph. Environm.*, **23,** 777-782.

[31] M. Katz, (1977), *Methods of air sampling and analysis, American public health Association (Intersociety Committee)*, Washingon, 984 p.

[32] M. Katz, (1980), "Advances in the analysis of air contaminants", *A critical review, J. APCA*, **30**, 528-557 and 983-997.

[33] M. Klein and F. Gourdon, (1982), "Une nouvelle méthode de mesure du monoxyde de carbone dans l'air ambiant, Corrélation par filtre gazeux en infrarouge", *Poll. Atmosph.* (July/September), pp. 193-199.

[34] H. Klingenberg and D. Schürmann, (1985), "Eine Idee zur Überprüfung der Effizienz von Abgas Katalysatoren in Personenwagen", *MTZ*, **46,** 261-262.

[35] H. Klingenberg and R.H. Müller, (1986), "Vorschlag und Überprüfung der Effizienz von Abgas Katalysatoren in Personenwagen ohne Rollenprüfstand", *MTZ*, **47,** 181-183.

[36] G. Lach and G. Winckler, (1988), “Specific problems of sampling and measuring Diesel exhaust particulates”, *SAE Paper* No. 881763, 12 p.

[37] S.I. Lamb et al., (1980), “Organic compounds in urban atmospheres”, A review of distribution, collection and analysis, *J. APCA*, **30,** 1098-1115.

[38] D.A. Levaggi et al., (1988), “The use of Tedlar bags for integrated gaseous toxic sampling, The San Francisco Bay area experience”, in: Proc. *EPA/APCA International Symposium “Measurement of toxic and related pollutants”*, R.K.M. Jayanty, Research Triangle Park, North Carolina, pp. 313-323.

[39] B. Lopez et al., (1987), “Émissions Diesel, Analyse des polluants non réglementés”, *Poll. Atmosph.*, Special Issue November, pp. 113-123.

[40] R.D. Matthews et al., (1977), “Interferences in chemiluminescent measurement of NO and $NO_2$ emissions from combustion systems”, *E.S.&T.*, **11,** 1092-1096.

[41] J.F. Pankow, (1988), “Review of gas phase retention volume behavior of organic compounds on Tenax-GC and other sorbent materials”, in: *Proc. EPA/APCA International Symposium “Measurement of toxic and related pollutants”*, R.K.M. Jayanty, Research Triangle Park, North Carolina, pp. 765-768.

[42] J.F. Pankow, (1988), “Gas phase retention volume behavior of organic compounds on the sorbent poly(oxy-m-terphenyl-2’,5’-ylene)”, *Anal. Chem.*, **60,** 950-958.

[43] R. Perret, (1986), “Techniques de mesures des polluants gazeux à l’émission”, *Poll. Atmosph.* (109), 43-51.

[44] J.C. Polasek and J.A. Bullin, (1978), “Evaluation of bag sequential sampling technique for ambient air analysis”, *E.S.&T.*, **12,** 708-712.

[45] C.J. Potter et al., (1985), “The development and validation of an on-board Diesel particulate sampler”, *WSL Report* No. LR.549(AP)M, 40 p.

[46] C.J. Potter et al., (1988), “The measurement of gaseous and particulate emissions from light duty and heavy duty motor vehicles under road driving conditions”, *SAE Paper* No. 880313, 11 p.

[47] B. Raynal, (1983), “Les essais de moteurs à combustion interne, ENSPM Course”, *Inst. Franç. du Pétrole Report* No. 31469, 78 p.

[48] B. Raynal, (1980), *Moteurs thermiques et pollution atmosphérique, Réglementation des véhicules automobiles,* Techn. de l’Ing., Vol.B 378,2, 17 p.

[49] A.R. Reading and G. Greeves, (1980), “Measurement of Diesel exhaust odorants and effect of engine variables”, *SAE Paper* No. 800424, 13 p.

[50] G.T. Reedy et al., (1979), “Gas chromatography/infrared matrix isolation spectrometry”, *Anal. Chem.*, **51,** 1535-1540.

[51] R. Rosset et al., *Chromatographie en phase liquide sur colonnes, Techn. de l’Ing.*, Vol. P 1455, 40 p.

[52] SAE, (1978), Recommended Practice, “Constant volume sampler system for exhaust emission measurement”, *SAE* J1094a, 24 p.

[53] SAE, (1984), Recommended Practice, “Instrumentation and techniques for exhaust gas measurement”, *SAE* J254, 14 p.

[54] D. Schürmann and J. Staab, (1987), "Messung von Automobilabgasen bei Straßen fahrten", *MTZ*, **48,** 35-39.

[55] D. Schürmann and J. Staab, (1988), "Émissions à l'échappement lors d'un parcours routier, Les conditions sont plus réelles", *Revue Automobile (Berne)*, Nos. 37/38, September.

[56] D. Schürmann and J. Staab, (1989), *On the road measurements of automotive emissions, 3rd Int. Symp., "Highway Pollution"*, München, 18/22 September, 18 p.

[57] J. Scott McDonald et al., (1984), "Status of Diesel particulate measurement methods", *SAE Paper* No. 840345, 20 p.

[58] J. Staab et al., (1983), "Strategy for the development of a new multicomponent exhaust emission measurement technique", *SAE Paper* No. 830437, 37 p.

[59] J. Staab and H. Klingenberg, (1984), "Prototyp eines neuen Vielkomponenten Abgasmeßgerätes", *VDI Berichte*, No. 531, "Emissionsminderung Automobilabgase-Ottomotoren", pp. 429-447.

[60] J. Staab et al., (1981), "Improving the method of hydrocarbon analysis", *SAE Paper* No. 810427, 21 p.

[61] J. Staab and D. Schürmann, (1987), "Measurement of automobile exhaust emissions under realistic road conditions", *SAE Paper* No. 871986, 6 p.

[62] J. Staab et al., (1988), *Ein kompaktes Abgasmeßsystem zum Einbau in Personenkraftwagen für Messungen bei Straßenfahrten*, Automobil Industrie (1/88), 39-47.

[63] U. Stenberg et al., (1985), "Enrichment of gaseous compounds from diluted gasoline exhausts, A comparison between adsorption and cryogenic condensation", *Environm. Int.*, **11,** 119-124.

[64] E.R. Stephens, (1989), "Valveless sampling of ambient air for analysis by capillary gas chromatography", *J. APCA*, **39,** 1202-1205.

[65] J. Suzuki et al., (1985), "Development of dilution mini-tunnel and its availability for measuring Diesel exhaust particulate matter", *SAE Paper* No. 851547, 11 p.

[66] M. Tacke and R. Grisar, (1988), "Quantitative Analysen durch Spektroscopie mit IR-Laserdioden", *VDI Berichte*, (677), 417-421.

[67] E.D. Thompson et al., (1990), "A truck and bus chassis dynamometer developed for fuel and lubricant research", *SAE Paper* No. 900211 (SP 839), 13-25.

[68] R.J. Tidona et al., (1988), "Reducing interference effects in the chemiluminescent measurement of nitric oxides from combustion systems", *J. APCA*, **38,** 806-811.

[69] H.Y. Tong and F.W. Karasek, (1984), "Flame ionization detector response factors for compound classes in quantitative analysis of complex organic mixtures", *Anal. Chem.*, **56,** 2124-2128.

[70] J.C. Tracy, (1980), *Laser applications to combustion product analysis, Review of research at General Motors Research Laboratories, ACS Meeting, Div. Pet. Chem.*, Houston, 23/28 March, pp. 116-124.

[71] J. Tranchant, *Chromatographie, Introduction, Techn. de l'Ing.*, Vol. P 1445, 6 p.

[72] J. Tranchant, *Chromatographie en phase gazeuse, Techn. de l'Ing.*, Vol. P 1485, 30 p.

[73] R.W. Tripp et al., (1988), "Comparison of evacuated flasks and Tenax® for detection of selected compounds under controlled conditions", in: *Proc. EPA/APCA International Symposium "Measurement of toxic and related pollutants"*, R.K.M. Jayanty, Research Triangle Park, North Carolina, pp. 324-330.

[74] P. Tritthart, (1984), "Organische Verbindungen im Abgas von Dieselmotoren", *MTZ*, **45,** 125-128.

[75] G.S. Turner and M. Neti, (1974), "Eliminating errors in chemiluminescence $NO_x$ determination in automobile exhaust", *SAE Paper* No. 741032, 4 p.

[76] R.L. Williams et al., (1985), "A review of sampling effects on polynuclear aromatic hydrocarbons (PAH) from heavy-duty Diesel engines", *SAE Paper* No. 852081, 18 p.

[77] M. Adachi et al., (1992), "Automotive emission analyses using FTIR spectrophotometer", *SAE Paper* No. 920723, pp. 133-140.

# Analysis of pollutants 8

# Carbon and nitrogen compounds

## 8.1 CO and $CO_2$

Many methods are available for determining $CO_2$ in gases [5]. In automotive pollution, the NDIR technique described in Chapter 7 is used practically everywhere for $CO_2$ and for CO [3 and 4]. The accuracy of measurement is essentially governed by proper calibration [83 and 92]. Since the method is sensitive to pressure, this parameter must remain unchanged during the analysis or the calibration.

## 8.2 Nitrogen oxides $NO_x$

Historically, $NO_2$ was first analyzed by the wet method using the Griess-Saltzmann technique [1]. With this method, the gas is bubbled through a solution of *N* (1-naphthyl) ethylene diammonium dichloride in p-amino benzenesulfonic acid, which after development in the presence of $NO_2$, yielded a diazo dye measured by spectrophotometry. Despite the changes made (trapping on filter impregnated with triethanolamine [2 and 13], this method lacks accuracy and reliability. A specific spectrophotometric method for $NO_2$ is based on the formation of a yellow diazo compound, which measured at 460 nm and was produced by reaction with p-rosaniline and bisphenol A. This method is valid in the absence of sulfides and sulfites [88].

Another very lengthy but more accurate wet method uses phenol disulfonic acid [83 and 93]. It measures all oxide derivatives of nitrogen (from NO to $NO_3H$) with the exception of $N_2O$. After trapping in an oxidizing solution of $H_2O_2$+$H_2SO_4$, the addition of phenyl disulfonic acid (prepared by dissolving phenol in fuming $H_2SO_4$) produces a color measured by spectrophotometry at 400 nm [53]. The only significant interference is caused by halogenides, which are minimal in automotive effluents.

Electrochemical methods have also been proposed (coulometry, ammetry) [34]. While sensitive, these methods lack specificity. Ultraviolet spectrometry (NDUV) is suitable for $NO_2$, but requires the prior removal of water vapor [34]. The NDIR method was tried [34 and 93], but it suffers from the same interference with $H_2O$ and even CO and $CO_2$.

The chemoluminescence technique described above is now used universally[1] [6]. Instruments are available for operating under atmospheric pressure and reduced pressure [92]. To eliminate the different drifts of the detectors [110] the gas passes alternately through or around the $NO_2 \Rightarrow NO$ conversion furnace. These furnaces may be catalytic ($t<400°C$) or thermal ($t>600°C$) and made of stainless steel [93]. However, this metal presents the drawback of converting $NH_3$, $CH_3NH_2$, and HCN to NO [54].

## 8.3 Nitrous oxide

The most widely-used method employs gas phase chromatography with electron capture detectors [86 and 89]. Since $N_2O$ also absorbs in the infrared band, a prototype analyzer is currently being developed based on 7.8 μm [72] with interfering $SO_2$ and $NO_2$ being eliminated by scrubbing in sodium carbonate and sulfite.

Precautions must be observed when sampling to measure $N_2O$. Nitrous oxide formation, as an artifact, appears in the sampling containers in the simultaneous presence of $NO_x$ and $SO_2$ [74]. Water accelerates the conversion [67]. To avoid this, it is necessary to eliminate $SO_2$ before trapping or to increase the pH in the container.

## 8.4 Nitric acid

Nitrate aerosols can be collected on a quartz fiber filter and then extracted by a carbonate/bicarbonate solution for analysis by ionic chromatography [76].

## 8.5 Ammonia and amines

Ammonia can be measured by chemoluminescence in the form of NO, after thermal oxidation [54]. Another method collects the ammonia on a filter and develops migration rings that are detected by a specific solution of o-phthaldicarboxylaldehyde [100]. Ammonia can also be measured by ionic chromatography [109]. This is the method recommended by the *EPA* after trapping in dilute sulfuric acid.

Amines have been trapped in exhausts by absorption in an acidic solution or on glass wool impregnated with oxalic acid. The solutions obtained are then analyzed spectroscopically by iodometry or chromatographically by GC with a thermo-ionic detector calibrated on nitrogen [18]. However, these methods are not sensitive enough to detect the very low contents present in the exhausts. In the EPA method [24] trapping is performed in dilute sulfuric acid. The solution obtained is

1. The analytical results are expressed in mass of $NO_2$.

measured by GC with specific detection of nitrogen. Ionic chromatography can also be employed [17].

## 8.6 Nitrosamines and nitrites

Alkyl nitrites can be trapped in the bags of the CVS system. They are then measured by GC on a suitable column with an electron capture detector [26]. This measurement must be carried out rapidly to prevent the formation of artifacts in the bags by the reaction between the trapped alcohols and the nitrogen oxides.

Nitrosamines can be analyzed by the Fourier transform infrared method [40]. They have been detected in exhausts after dilution with nitrogen to prevent the oxidation of NO to $NO_2$, which could lead to the formation of nitrosamine as an artifact. Trapping is then carried out on a Tenax GC [102]. The analysis is performed by GC/MS. For crankcase emissions, trapping is carried out on a Chromosorb cartridge protected by a bed of sulfamic acid absorbing amines, to inhibit the external formation of nitrosamine by reaction with $NO_2$. Another trap consists of an absorber containing a buffer solution of citrate and phosphate [33]. Analysis is continued by GC with specific detection of nitrosamines by a TEA detector [59 and 113]. This detector causes the nitrosyl radical obtained by pyrolysis of the nitrosamines to react with $O_3$. It also measures the infrared radiation that is emitted by the excited $NO_2$ formed during the reaction, when it returns to its fundamental state (chemoluminescence) [31].

## 8.7 Hydrogen cyanide

Cyanides and HCN, after wet trapping in an alkaline solution, are generally determined by GC with specific detection by electron capture (ECD) [71] or analyzed with a specific cyanide electrode [53 and 91]. The latter method requires the prior removal of sulfides that poison the electrode. The method recommended by the *EPA* [24] is to trap HCN and $(CN)_2$ in a potassium hydroxide solution, and to treat the solution with chloramine T and potassium phosphate. The cyanogen chloride obtained is determined by GC with an electron capture detector.

## 8.8 'Hydrocarbons'

### 8.8.1 Total hydrocarbons

Given the shortcomings of the NDIR method (Table 7.1) [50], the technique usually employed is FID [92]. It offers the advantage of responding only to carbon compounds (the results are expressed in ppmC) but the presence of oxygen in the samples disturbs the measurements by partially converting the diffusion flame into a premixed flame [104]. To overcome this drawback the calibration mixtures must have an oxygen content identical to that of the gases to be measured (dilution by synthetic air) and the flame must be fed with an $H_2$/He mixture. Special care must be taken in calibration, which must be performed with several different gas mixtures. The construction details and geometry of the different instruments available on the market are becoming increasingly important as the regulated values become smaller. These requirements essentially concern the characteristics of the burner (shape, materials, electrodes, and bias voltage) [104]. Total hydrocarbons of gasoline-powered vehicles are sampled in the bags of the CVS system. For diesel vehicles, whose the heavier hydrocarbons would remain condensed in the bags, a line heated to 190°C conducts the gases sampled in the tunnel to an FID analyzer combined with an integrator covering the duration of the test cycle [94].

### 8.8.2 Non-methane hydrocarbons

One technique is to pre-concentrate the hydrocarbons other than methane by cryogenic trapping before carrying out conventional analysis by FID [22]. Problems will continue due to the more or less rapid vaporization of the hydrocarbons when the trap is heated.

They are therefore generally measured by chromatographic separation and detection by FID and the desired value is then obtained by subtracting methane from the total hydrocarbons [112]. The Methane Analytical System developed by the *EPA* uses a chromatographic column with a controlled-temperature molecular sieve that traps hydrocarbons heavier than $CH_4$ and removes them by backflushing, before elution of $O_2$, $CH_4$, and CO [47]. Another method had previously involved a specific burner oxidizing hydrocarbons other than methane before the FID measurement [87]. Partial combustion of the $CH_4$ in the burner is offset by the passage of the reference gases in the burner. GC is also used to determine the detailed composition of non-methane hydrocarbons [75]. After trapping on Tenax and Soxhlet extraction, the analysis can be performed by GC/MS [39]. Paraffins and olefins from $C_2$ to $C_6$ are determined on different chromatographic columns [23]. Another method is the collection of the exhaust gases, sampled during standard driving cycles, in small Tedlar bags [10 and 11], either in the dilution tunnel or inside large CVS system bags. The contents of the Tedlar bags are then sent to a flushing loop placed at the head end of a gas phase chromatograph equipped with two capillary columns adapted to the compounds being analyzed with FID detection ,[80]. One column is used for the rapid separation of the methane and the second allows the total separation of the other $C_1$ to $C_4$ compounds.

The Fourier transform infrared technique is also used to obtain a detailed real-time (3 s) inventory of the lightest hydrocarbons ($C_1$ to $C_4$), with simultaneous measurement of the other pollutant gases (CO, $CO_2$, $NH_3$, NO, HCN, and $SO_2$, etc.) [15 and 16].

Another technique for measuring methane emissions selectively, without interference and in real time, uses an infrared laser, set to the 1300.65 $cm^{-1}$ peak where $CH_4$ has an absorption coefficient of $3.5 \cdot 10^{-6}$ $ppm^{-1} \cdot cm^{-1}$ [46].

## 8.8.3 Hydrocarbon families: paraffins, olefins and aromatics

Differences in toxicity, harmfulness, and atmospheric reactivity of the hydrocarbon families present in motor fuels and in exhaust emissions justify the search for overall methods designed to measure the share contributed by each of these hydrocarbon groups.

Traps that selectively capture these families have been developed by *UTAC* [30]. Two types of trap, made by the deposition of metallic salts in a sulfuric medium on a refractory support, have been developed. One is based on mercuric sulfate and retains the olefins by chelation. The second is based on palladium sulfate and retains the light monoaromatics. These traps are placed, alone or in combination, at the head end of a GC chromatograph with FID detection and the results are obtained by subtracting the different chromatograms obtained. The traps are not easily regenerable and their frequent replacement has stopped the development of this method in favor of mass spectrometry techniques that are employed to analyze petroleum cuts by families [19]. The use of specialized columns and pre-columns allows the separate analysis of the three families detected by GC/FID [37].

Most analytical methods consider the molecular proportion of aromatics and the ring alone has the same importance as a derivative with a high rate of substitution by alkyl chains. Only NMR spectrometry indicates the atomic percentage of aromatic carbons [99].

### 8.8.3.1 Benzene and aromatics

After the inaccurate gravimetric methods [103], few spectroscopic methods using absorption in the ultraviolet band, specific to aromatic compounds have been developed [53], apart from the use of this technique in rapid response probes for detecting aromatics [25].

Most methods employ capillary GC with FID detection, which generally allows the separation of hydrocarbons with more than six carbons. However, the choice of the adsorbent trap is crucial: activated carbon eluted by carbon disulfide (NIOSH and VDI method) [114], Tenax GC [90], Chromosorb 104, or Porapak Q, whose contents are transferred by 'flash' thermal desorption [90]. The use of molten silica columns grafted chemically by a polar phase of polyethylene glycol allows the separation of many aromatic compounds with the same elementary composition [45, 55, and 78].

Benzene and toluene are also analyzed by packed column gas chromatography [119].

#### 8.8.3.2 Halogen derivatives of hydrocarbons

The derivatives 1,2-dibromoethane and 1,2-dichloroethane have been measured by GC with suitable separation columns and electron capture detection [108] as well as GC/MS [73]. Total chlorine and bromine have been determined by neutron activation after trapping on Chromosorb [44].

#### 8.8.3.3 Polynuclear aromatic hydrocarbons (PAH)

*A. Collection of the products to be analyzed*

Depending on the engine or the molecular weight of the PAH, the PAH to be analyzed are adsorbed on soot particles (diesel engine) or they are present in the gas phase (gasoline and diesel engines). Dilution in the tunnel also increases the size of the fraction adsorbed on the particles, especially for PAH with four rings such as fluoranthene and pyrene, of which 90% remain on the diesel particles [26]. Most of the PAH with three rings remain in the gas phase for gasoline engines and 50% of them for diesel engines, and more than 99% of PAH with five rings or more are retained on the particles.

The adsorbed compounds are hence collected from the dilution tunnel [41] during filtration of the particles and the PAH are found in the SOF fraction. The type of filter can affect the analytical results of PAH and fiber-glass filters are liable to 'catalyze' the oxidation of the PAH [61]. Teflon/glass fabrics of the 'Pallflex' type are therefore preferred. The temperature of the filter must also be kept as low as possible to prevent losses by re-entrainment of the PAH with low vapor pressure and to avoid chemical conversions of the PAH that occur rapidly from 260°C [115]. This filtration can be followed by adsorption of the compounds remaining in the gas phase on polymer supports (polyurethane buffer, Bondapak C18 [63], Porapak PS [36], Tenax-GC, Chromosorb 102, and Amberlite XAD-2). Another method initially recommended by Grimmer [35] takes the entire exhaust into a train of condensers with dry ice and liquid nitrogen and subsequently into a particle filter [25 and 56]. This system, which is too complicated for generalized use, has been discarded in favor of polymers. Among these polymers Amberlite XAD-2 has generally been adopted [49] since its capacity is higher than that of Tenax-GC for low boiling point compounds. Tenax itself has a tendency to decompose into diphenyl quinones when in contact with hot exhaust gases [60].

*B. Extraction of trapped products*

Particulates and polymer adsorbents are then extracted by Soxhlet [79] using organic solvents to give an SOF fraction. Acetone, benzene [14], toluene [9], chloroform, methanol, petroleum ether, tetrahydrofuran, dichloromethane DCM, and the benzene/methanol mixture have been used by different authors. The results obtained differ slightly according to the type of solvent. Benzene is highly effective for most of the PAH concerned, but in comparison with cyclohexane it presents the drawback of extracting a greater number of other products that are of no concern. In the extraction of diesel soot, toluene offers greater extraction efficiency than methanol, cyclohexane and DCM for PAH with five rings or more [115]. Extraction with toluene after DCM recovers about 60% of benzo(a)pyrene and 40% of benzo(ghi)perylene [36]. It also extracts fewer polar products than the benzene/methanol mixture, which also causes oxidation of the PAH during extraction [115]. The addition of an alcohol to the aromatic solvent increases the total mass extracted but favors inorganic compounds (e.g. sulfates) and polar organic compounds [61]. The Soxhlet extractors are enveloped in aluminum foil to protect the samples from the influence of light.

However, in the analysis of PAH present in exhaust emissions of gasoline and diesel engines or adsorbed on diesel particulates, DCM has been adopted by most experimental workers because it is suitable both for analyzing PAH and for mutagenicity tests [7, 32, 79, 101, and 105].

In addition to Soxhlet extraction, extraction is also carried out with an ultrasonic bath [7]. This is faster, and the extraction yields are approximately the same, but it has the drawback of destroying the filter and thus requiring additional filtration in the rest of the treatment [32]. Furthermore, it does not allow the measurement of the mass of SOF by the difference in mass before and after extraction making it necessary to use the mass of extract measured after solvent evaporation [61].

*C. Fractionation of organic extracts*

The composition of organic extracts is extremely complex, containing hydrocarbons, oxygenated organic compounds, PAH, sulfur and nitrogen organic heterocyclic compounds, as well as inorganic compounds derived from fuel additives and lubricants. The treatment differs according to the final destination of the extracts, i.e. detail chemical analysis or overall mutagenicity tests (Section 4.4.3).

The first operation is designed to remove the solvent that has been used for extraction. It is first evaporated under a nitrogen stream in a rotary evaporator placed in a water-bath at low temperature ($\approx 30°C$). To avoid overheating at the end of the operation the last 5 $cm^3$ is placed in a small flask and evaporation is completed at ambient temperature with entrainment by a nitrogen stream to a residual volume of less than 1 ml.

To analyze PAH by HPLC satisfactorily, with a minimum of interfering chromatographic peaks, it is necessary to isolate a fraction by selecting the PAH fraction. Complex methods have been used; some of them requiring up to five fractionation steps, and employing acid scrubbing, taking up with cyclohexane, partitioning with dimethyl formamide, and separating on an aminosilane column [70]. In addition of the amount of time spent on them, the complexity of these methods can lead to product losses during the operation.

A much simpler method yields satisfactory results. After the dichloromethane has been transferred to the hexane, the extracts are passed through mini-columns filled with polar stationary phase ('Sep-PAK' silica type) [79]. These mini-columns retain the highly polar products. A first slow elution with hexane allows the non-polar products (aliphatic hydrocarbons) to leave and a second elution by a 50/50 mixture of DCM and hexane carries off the PAH, the medium-polar fraction. This fraction is then transferred to acetonitrile. This technique can be used to simultaneously treat a large number of samples and to analyze the other two recovered fractions (aliphatics and monoaromatics).

To perform the Ames tests, the evaporated extracts are taken up with dimethyl sulfoxide DMSO for direct measurement of their mutagenicity without trying to isolate the PAH fraction [111].

*D. Determination of PAH in the isolated fraction*

The earliest techniques employed chromatography on acetylated hydrophobic paper [56, 57, 60, and 61] with ultraviolet light as a detector. Besides its tedious operating mode and its shortcomings in terms of reproducibility, resolution, and quantification, this procedure degrades the PAH during analysis. Chromatography on an alumina plate is much faster, but the possibilities of degradation remain in the presence of the ultraviolet light use for detection [60].

The methods currently used are HPLC and GC, usually combined with mass spectrometry. Both methods yield equivalent results [27 and 28].

The HPLC method is suitable for non-volatile compounds such as PAH, which can be analyzed at ambient temperature. The separation column is a column packed with an inverse phase on grafted supports specifically for PAH [79]. Elution is carried out with a binary water/acetonitrile mixture [118] that is progressively enriched with acetonitrile and detection is usually carried out by fluorescence at 360, 420, and 460 nm after excitation to 290 nm. Other wavelength pairs can be selected to obtain higher sensitivity for a particular PAH. This technique allows the perfect separation of sixteen PAH and two to six aromatic rings and helps to keep seven of them perfectly measured on an actual diesel exhaust. It is coupled with a detector that simultaneously records the visible ultraviolet spectrum [43, 48] and distinguishes the compounds that are difficult to detect on a single wavelength. This method is also applied to the fluorescence spectrum. However, the spectra in liquid solution usually display a broadened appearance and the spectra of the alkyl derivatives of the PAH may not always be different from those of the PAH itself [60]. This difficulty can be circumvented by using low-temperature luminescence, particularly the Shpol'skii effect [81 and 82]. The PAH fraction is crystallized at 10K in a polycrystalline matrix of octane to measure the fluorescence spectrum in the form of fine lines. This process is reserved for well-equipped laboratories due to its complexity, which demands both rapid freezing to prevent differential migration of the PAH in the octane during setting as well as accurate maintenance of the temperature to within 0.8K to stabilize the spectrum [116 and 117].

Ideal gas phase chromatography uses capillary columns which offer both sensitivity and high resolution [56, 58, and 77] with FID detection, or even better, coupling with GC/MS mass spectrometry [84]. Another technique involves the catalytic reduction of the nitrogen derivatives to the corresponding amines, which are then analyzed.

No method measures the total PAH. More than 75 different PAH, composed exclusively of carbon and hydrogen, have been identified in a diesel exhaust [107]. The results depend on the individual PAH taken into account and the summation by the various authors to express the 'PAH fraction': 7 PAH in the AFNOR standards [7], 11 in the CRC round-robin tests [27], 16 in the VDI Directive [48], and 17 in the CEC procedure.

*E. Nitrogen, oxygen and halogen derivatives of PAH*

After fractionation of the extracts collected by extraction of particulates or gases collected on an XAD-2 type polymer support, these derivatives are found in the polar fractions, separated on silica and Sephadex columns, and eluted by different solvents [42 and 98]. The nitrogen derivatives are identified in GC by NPD detectors [66] or by mass spectrometry [51], which is more sensitive than ultraviolet detection [21]. This is also carried out by HPLC with detection by fluorimetry [106]. The formation of these compounds can take place in the form of artifacts by reaction between gaseous $NO_2$ and the PAH retained on the filter, the reaction being facilitated by the presence of water vapor and ozone [64]. $NO_2$ alone promotes the formation of ketones, aldehydes, and quinones. The influence of the type of filter on the reaction remains debatable [65] and this nitration has little time to occur during a test on an FTP or ECE cycle with passage through the dilution tunnel [62].

Aldehydes, anhydrides, quinones, etc., are determined by GC with FID detection on a column designed to avoid the simultaneous outlet of the phthalic esters. Identification is carried out by GC/MS [8, 12, 20, 52, and 98] and by the Fourier transform infrared technique [29]. Another technique separates them from a benzene solution by thin-layer chromatography on polyamide detected by fluorescence spectrophotometry [85].

The halogen compounds of PAH, probably formed from dichloro- and dibromoethanes of the scavengers, are found in the extracts obtained by Soxhlet extraction. After purification by HPLC, they are analyzed by GC and MS by negative ions [38].

## 8.9 Volatile compounds and evaporative losses

Evaporative losses result from the fuel stored on the vehicle or circulating in the engine feed system. Added to these are refueling losses at the service station.

The following are generally distinguished on board the vehicle:

- running losses, when the vehicle is driven from one point to another
- diurnal losses by respiration of the fuel tank, which expands and shrinks thermally due to daily temperature variations

- hot soak losses from a parked vehicle when the engine turned off after a period of running, especially from the carburetor chamber or the float bowl, which is heated by the engine
- resting losses, which occur when the vehicle is parked for long periods

These losses are measured by suitable means: canisters for running losses and the SHED method for diurnal and hot soak losses. The SHED technique is currently preferred because it accounts for all the emissions from the vehicle concerned.

## 8.9.1 Canister technique

This method, which is of historical significance for the measurement of total losses, is nevertheless necessary for measuring running losses. The canister recommended is a cylindrical tank of about 300 ml, fitted with two inlet and outlet tubes. It contains about 150 g of 2 mm granules of activated carbon with a BET[2] specific surface area of at least 1000 $m^2/g$ that are retained between glass wool pads and have been stored in a drying oven [96]. It is located at the outlet of all the vent tubes that are likely to place the fuel circuit in contact with the atmosphere. The inlet tube is vented to the atmosphere through a drying canister. For vehicles with a single system vented through the air filter, the canister is placed on the air filter itself. For vehicles without systems for monitoring evaporative losses, several similar canisters must be used simultaneously to avoid saturating them. The canisters are tared by weighing before the test and re-weighed at the end of the test. On modern vehicles, the development of fuel injection engines and the generalized installation of loss control canisters that recycle all the running losses to the engine (Section 10.12) have considerably reduced the advantage of this system, which is only valid for these types of running losses.

## 8.9.2 SHED technique

This method, which was developed in the United States around 1968 [69], consists of placing the vehicle to be tested in a hermetically-sealed enclosure and performing the recommended test sequences on it. The evaporative losses are evaluated by measuring the hydrocarbon concentration in the enclosure by FID. The enclosure [95], with a volume of 40 to 50 $m^3$, must be able to accommodate all types of vehicles. It is built of a material impermeable to hydrocarbons, which neither absorbs them nor desorbs them (coated with Tedlar if necessary). The doors must be sealed by an inflatable seal or any other system. One of the sides of the enclosure is preferably of a flexible material to serve as a safety valve in case of an explosion and to absorb slight fluctuations in internal pressure without causing losses from the enclosure by thermal respiration. The walls must offer a minimum of resistance to the passage of

2. Determination by monomolecular adsorption of nitrogen at the temperature of liquid nitrogen.

heat and they must allow cooling to avoid an excessive rise in the internal temperature during the testing of hot soak losses [95]. The enclosure is equipped with several thermocouples to monitor the internal temperature, a fan to homogenize the atmosphere, and an FID analyzer.

The vehicle's fuel tank must also be equipped with an adjustable heating element (e.g. a 2000 W heater) that is applied to the walls below the liquid level and which avoids local overheating of the fuel.

### 8.9.3 Procedures employed

The US procedure developed in 1970 differs slightly from the European procedure currently being developed by Working Group PF-11 of the *CEC*, though both are based on the SHED. The Europeans are inclined to emphasize hot soak losses, which they consider to be higher than diurnal losses since the temperature variations during the day are smaller in Europe than in the United States [68].

One of the common precautions is to ensure that the volatile compounds measured do actually originate in the fuel feed system and are not from other sources (vehicle paint, grease and oil stains, cooling circuit, upholstery). A blank test in the enclosure is therefore performed on a clean vehicle (cleaned with steam if necessary) with the fuel lines purged and the tank and carburetor removed [95]. The results obtained are deducted from the corresponding measurements.

The US procedure first measures diurnal losses. The vehicle tank is first filled to 40% of its capacity (rounded off to the nearest gallon). The vehicle is placed in the enclosure with the engine turned off and kept at ambient temperature (20 to 30°C) for more than 11 h. The tank temperature is raised from 16 to 29°C in 1 h, with the internal temperature of the enclosure remaining between 20 and 30°C. After measuring the FID concentration obtained, the vehicle is removed from the enclosure to undergo an FTP-72 cycle on the chassis dynamometer. At this point the canisters for measuring running losses are connected if necessary. The vehicle is then returned to the enclosure with the hood shut and the engine idling. The engine is turned off when the SHED is closed. After 1 h in the enclosure, where the temperature must be held between 24 and 32°C, the FID content is measured.

The European procedure also measures diurnal losses by raising the fuel tank from 16 to 30°C in 1 h. The vehicle is then removed from the enclosure for an ECE 15 cycle followed by an EUDC peri-urban cycle on the chassis dynamometer. Returned to the enclosure, the vehicle then undergoes the test for hot soak losses by residing for 1 h in the SHED, where the ambient temperature must remain in the range 23 to 31°C.

Preparation and pre-conditioning of the vehicle are essential to ensure quality results. The vehicles used should have just gone through an FTP-72 cycle (USA) or about 3000 km (*CEC*) to bring the canisters that limit evaporative losses to equilibrium.

The *CEC* tends to recommend loading the test canisters to the maximum limit by first purging them with nitrogen at ambient temperature and then carrying out in succession two temperature buildups of the 'hot soak losses' test (14 from 16) with the selected reference fuel, followed by an ECE 15 cycle and two EUDC cycles. The vehicle is then allowed to rest for one night at ambient temperature.

The fuel tank must be purged before the test and then filled to 40% of its capacity with the reference fuel at a temperature between 10 and 14°C.

The European procedure is not yet definitively set. The measurement of running losses is still not finalized because these losses are judged to be virtually negligible. Actual measurement with the SHED procedure would require the introduction of a chassis dynamometer into the enclosure, which is currently being attempted in the United States. To do so on a chassis dynamometer introduced into the SHED (170 $m^3$), California recommends a running phase for 1 h and 15 min comprising three FTP-72 (LA-4) cycles. This phase then leads directly to the measurement of hot soak losses.

The measurement of refueling losses is still not subject to regulations, but a measurement technique that places a vehicle and a refueling nozzle in an SHED is now proposed in the United States [97]. After drainage, the vehicle fuel tank is filled to a quarter of its capacity with the fuel concerned and then raised to 35°C. Using a nozzle, the tank is then filled to the maximum with fuel at 28°C. The indication of the FID analyzer is recorded up to its stabilized value.

## REFERENCES

[1] AFNOR, (1973), "Teneur de l'air atmosphérique en dioxyde d'azote (Méthode de Griess-Saltzmann)", *Standard X* 43-009, 6 p.

[2] AFNOR, (1976), "Teneur de l'air atmosphérique en dioxyde d'azote (Méthode de dosage par piégeage sur filtre imprégné de triéthanolamine)", *Standard X* 43-015, 4 p.

[3] AFNOR, (1974), "Analyse des gaz par spectrométrie de mass, Détermination de leur composition chimique", *Standard X* 20-302, 6 p.

[4] AFNOR, (1976), "Dosage du monoxyde de carbone, Méthode d'absorption d'un faisceau de radiations infrarouges non dispersé", *Standard X* 20-361, 2 p.

[5] AFNOR, (1979), "Analyse des gaz, Dosage du dioxyde de carbon, Guide pour le choix des méthodes de dosage", *Standard X* 20-380, 10 p.

[6] AFNOR, (1980), "Mesure des oxydes d'azote par chimiluminescence", *Standard X* 43-018, 7 p.

[7] AFNOR, (1988), "Détermination des hydrocarbures polycycliques", *Standard NF X* 43-025, 18 p.

[8] Y. Alsberg et al., (1985), "Chemical and biological characterization of organic material from gasoline exhaust particles", *E.S.&T.*, **19,** 43-50.

[9] Anon., (1989), “Messen von PAH an stationäre industriellen Anlagen, Verdünnungsmethode (RWTÜV-Verfahren), Gaschromatographische Bestimmung”, *VDI Richtlinie* 3873 (provisional), 22 p.

[10] J.C. Bailey et al., (1989), *Speciated hydrocarbon emissions from a sample of UK vehicles, 3rd Int. Symp., “Highway Pollution”*, München, 18/22 September, 8 p.

[11] J.C. Bailey et al., (1990), “Speciated hydrocarbon emission from vehicles operated over the normal speed range on the road”, *Atmosph. Environm.*, **24A,** 43-52.

[12] J.M. Bayona et al., (1988), “Characterization of polar polycyclic aromatic compounds in a heavy duty Diesel exhaust particulate by capillary column gas chromatography and high resolution mass spectrometry”, *E.S.&T.*, **22,** 1440-1447.

[13] P. Bourbon et al., (1977), “Dosage du NO atmosphérique sur support sec”, *Atmosph. Environm.*, **11,** 485-488.

[14] B.A. Bricklemeyer and R.S. Spindt, (1978), “Measurement of polynuclear aromatic hydrocarbons in Diesel exhaust gases”, *SAE Paper* No. 780115, 8 p.

[15] J.W. Butler et al., (1981), “On-line characterization of vehicle emissions by FTIR and mass spectroscopy”, *SAE Paper* No. 810429, 10 p.

[16] J.W. Butler et al., (1985), “A system for on-line measurement of multicomponent emissions and engine operating parameters”, *SAE Paper* No. 851657, 13 p.

[17] S.H. Cadle et al., (1979), “Measurements of unregulated emissions from General Motors’ light duty vehicles”, *SAE Paper* No. 790694, 21 p.

[18] S.H. Cadle and P.A. Malawa, (1980), “Low molecular weight aliphatic amines in exhaust from catalyst-equipped cars”, *E.S.&T.*, **14,** 718-723.

[19] H. Castex et al., (1983), “Analyse des kérosènes et des gas oils moyens par spectrométrie de masse à moyenne résolution”, *Revue Inst. Franç. du Pétrole*, **38,** 523-532.

[20] D.R. Choudhury, (1982), “Characterization of polycyclic ketone and quinone particulates by gas chromatography/mass spectrometry”, *E.S.&T.*, **16,** 102-106.

[21] P. Ciccioli et al., (1989), “Evaluation of nitrated polycyclic aromatic hydrocarbons in anthropogenic emission and air samples”, *Aerosol Sci. Techn.*, **10,** 296-310.

[22] J.S. Craig, (1988), “Field comparison study of the combustion engineering 8202A and integrated grab sample preconcentration direct flame ionization detection for ambient measurements of non-methane hydrocarbons”, in: *Proc. EPA/APCA International Symposium “Measurement of toxic and related pollutants”*, R.K.M. Jayanty, Research Triangle Park, North Carolina, pp. 793-798.

[23] R.A. Cudney et al., (1977), “A fast gas chromatographic method for measuring $C_2$-$C_6$ alkanes and alkenes in air”, *J. APCA*, **27,** 468-470.

[24] H.E. Dietzmann et al., (1979), “Analytical procedures for characterizing unregulated emissions from motor vehicles”, *EPA Report* No. 600/2-79-017, p. 481.

[25] A.M. Douaud et al., (1988), “Potential des moteurs à mélange pauvre face aux moteurs actuels à réglage stoechiométrique, Consommation, émissions, exigence en octane”, *Revue Inst. Franç. du Pétrole*, **43,** 111-123.

[26] K.E. Egebäck and B.M. Bertillson, (1983), "Chemical and biological characterization of exhaust emissions from vehicles fueled with gasoline, alcohol, LPG and Diesel", *Report* Nos. nv pm 1635, National Swedish Environment Board.

[27] W.C. Eisenberg et al., (1983), "Polycyclic aromatic hydrocarbon analysis round-robin study", *NTIS Report* No. PB84-194869, 60 p.

[28] W.C. Eisenberg et al., (1984), "Cooperative evaluation of methods for the analysis of PAH in extracts from Diesel particulate emissions", *SAE Paper* No. 840414, 11 p.

[29] M.D. Erickson et al., (1979), "Identification of alkyl-9-fluorenones in Diesel exhaust particulate", *J. Chromat. Sci.*, **17,** 449-454.

[30] M. Favennec, (1980), "Méthode de séparation par familles des hydrocarbures", *Poll. Atmosph.*, **85,** 27-31.

[31] D.H. Fine et al., (1977), "Determination of dimethylnitrosamine in air and water by thermal energy analysis, Validation of analytical procedures", *E.S.&T.*, **11,** 577-580.

[32] E.F. Funkenbusch et al., (1979), "The characterization of soluble organic fraction of Diesel particulate matter", *SAE Paper* No. 790418, 21 p.

[33] E.U. Goff et al., (1980), "Nitrosamine emissions from Diesel engine crankcases", *SAE Paper* No. 801374, 8 p.

[34] F. Gourdon, (1973), *Mesure des oxydes d'azote par chimiluminescence, Nuisances et Environnement*, December, pp. 33-37.

[35] G. Grimmer et al., (1972), "Probenahme und Analytik polycyclisher aromatischer Kohlenwasserstoffe in Kraftfahrzeugabgasen", *Erdöl und Kohle*, **25,** 442.

[36] G. Grimmer, (1988), "Qualitätssicherung bei der Probenhme von Stoffen am Beispiel der polycyclischen aromatischen Kohlenwasserstoffen (PAH)", *Staub*, **48,** 401-404.

[37] D. Gruden, (1988), *Aromaten im Abgas von Ottomotoren, Verlag TÜV Rheinland, Köln*, 126 p.

[38] PP. Haglung et al., (1987), "Analysis of halogenated polycyclic aromatic hydrocarbons in urban air, snow, and automobile exhaust", *Chemosphere*, **16,** 2441-2450.

[39] C.V. Hampton et al., (1982), "Hydrocarbon gases emitted from vehicles on the road, 1 A qualitative gas chromatography/mass spectrometry survey 2 Determination of emission rates from Diesel and spark ignition vehicles", *E.S.&T.*, **16,** 287-298 and E.S.&T., **17**, 699-708.

[40] P.L. Hanst et al., (1977), "Atmospheric chemistry of N-nitroso dimethylamine", *E.S.&T.*, **11,** 403-405.

[41] A. Hartung et al., (1982), "Messung polycyclischer aromatischer Kohlenwasserstoffe im Abgas von Dieselmotoren", *MTZ*, **43,** 263-266.

[42] A. Hartung et al., (1986), "Quantitative Bestimmung polycyclischer aromatischer Kohlenwasserstoffe (PAK) und ihrer Oxy Derivate (Oxy PAK) in Diesekpartikel Extrakten unter besonderer Berücksichtigung der Artefakt Bildung während der Probenahme", *VW Forschungsbericht* No. FMT 8604 V/5, 33 p.

[43] A. Hartung and K.H. Lies, (1990), "Schnellverfahren zur Bestimmung der PAK Werte", *MTZ*, **51,** 12-17.

[44] E. Häsänen et al., (1979), "On the occurrence of aliphatic chlorine and bromine compounds in automobile exhaust", *Atmosph. Environm.*, **13,** 1217-1219.

[45] E. Häsänen et al., (1981), "Benzene, toluene and xylene concentrations in car exhaust and in city air", *Atmosph. Environm.*, **15,** 1755-1757.

[46] J.C. Hill and R.F. Maajkowski, (1980), "Time resolved measurement of vehicle sulfate and methane emissions with tunable diode lasers", *SAE Paper* No. 800510, 8 p.

[47] J.S. Hoffman et al., (1987), "A gas chromatograph based system for measuring the methane fraction of Diesel engine hydrocarbon emissions", *SAE Paper* No. 870340, p. 11, *NTIS Report* No. PB87-174850, 28 p.

[48] L. Huber et al., (1987), "Bestimmung von polyzyklischen Aromaten mit HPLC, UV/VIS Diodenarray und Fluoreszenzdetektion", *Staub*, **47,** 22-27.

[49] R.B. Jacko and M.L. Holcomb, (1984), "Simplified measurement technique for polycyclic aromatic hydrocarbons using the EPA method 5 sampling train", *J. APCA*, **31,** 156-157.

[50] M.W. Jackson, (1966), "Analysis for exhaust gas hydrocarbons, Non-dispersive infrared versus flame ionization", *J. APCA*, **11,** 697-702.

[51] T.E. Jensen et al., (1986), "1-nitropyrene in used Diesel engine oil", *J. APCA*, **36,** 1255.

[52] R.M. Kamens et al., (1989), "The behavior of oxygenated polycyclic aromatic hydrocarbons on atmospheric soot particles", *E.S.&T.*, **23,** 801-806.

[53] M. Katz, (1977), *Methods of air sampling and analysis, American public health association (Intersociety Committee)*, Washington, 984 p.

[54] M. Katz, (1980), "Advances in the analysis of air contaminants", A critical review, *J. APCA*, **30,** 528-557 and 983-997.

[55] A. Kluge and G. Schulz, (1983), *Messung der Benzoexposition bei Umschlag und Produktion von Ottokraftstoffen*, DGMK Forschungsbericht 250, October, 196 p.

[56] J. Kraft and K.H. Lies, (1981), "Polycyclic aromatic hydrocarbons in the exhaust of gasoline and Diesel vehicles", *SAE Paper* No. 810082, 11 p.

[57] J. Kraft et al., (1982), "Determination of polycyclic aromatic hydrocarbons in diluted and undiluted exhaust gas of Diesel engines", *SAE Paper* No. 821219, 15 p.

[58] H. Kurosaki and E. Kitajima, (1984), "Chromatographic analysis on capillary columns of PAH and nitro-PAH from automotive vehicle exhaust particulates", *Niigata Rikagaku*, (10), 8-13.

[59] S.I. Lamb et al., (1980), "Organic compounds in urban atmospheres, A review of distribution, collection and analysis", *J. APCA*, **30,** 1098-1115.

[60] M.L. Lee et al., (1981), *Analytical Chemistry of Polycyclic Aromatic Compounds, Academic Press*, New York, 462 p.

[61] F.S-C. Lee and D. Schuetzle, (1983), "Sampling, extraction and analysis of polycyclic aromatic hydrocarbons from internal combustion engines", in: *Handbook of polycyclic aromatic hydrocarbons*, A. Bjørseth, Marcel Dekker, New York, pp. 27-94.

[62] K. Levson et al., (1988), "Artifacts during the sampling of nitro PAHs of Diesel exhaust", *Fresenius' Z. Anal. Chem.*, **330,** 527-528.

[63] J.L. Lindgren et al, (1980), "A comparison of two techniques for the collection and analysis of polynuclear aromatic compounds in ambient air", *J. APCA*, **30,** 166-168.

[64] A. Lindskog et al., (1985), "Transformation of reactive PAH on particles by exposure to oxidized nitrogen compounds and ozone", *Environm. Int.*, **11,** 125-130.

[65] A. Lindskog et al., (1987), "Chemical transformation of PAH on airborne particles by exposure to $NO_2$ during sampling, A comparison between two filter media", *Sci. Tot. Environm.*, **61,** 51-57.

[66] B. Lopez et al., (1987), "Emissions diesel, Analyse des polluants non réglementés", *Poll. Atmosph.*, Special Issue November, pp. 113-123.

[67] R.K. Lyon and J.A. Cole, (1989), "Kinetic modeling of artefacts in the measurement of $N_2O$ from combustion sources", *Comb. Flame*, **77,** 139-143.

[68] J.S. McArragher et al., (1988), "Evaporative emissions from modern European vehicles and their control", *SAE Paper* No. 880315, 9 p.

[69] S.W. Martens, (1969), "Evaporative emission measurements with the SHED, A second progress report", *SAE Paper* No. 690502, 11 p.

[70] W.E. May et al., (1984), "Characterization of polycyclic aromatic hydrocarbons in air particulate extracts by liquid gas chromatographic methods", in: *Identification and analysis of organic pollutants in air*, L.H. Keith, Butterworth Publications, Boston, pp. 159-169.

[71] N. Metz, (1987), "Round-robin testing for selected unregulated exhaust emissions", *SAE Paper* No. 871987, 14 p.

[72] T.A. Montgomery et al., (1989), "Continuous infrared analysis of $N_2O$ in combustion products", *J. APCA*, **39,** 721-726.

[73] M.D. Müller and H.R. Buser, (1986), "Halogenated aromatic compounds in automotive emissions from leaded gasoline additives", *E.S.&T.*, **20,** 1151-1157.

[74] L.J. Muzio et al., (1989), "Errors in grab sample measurements of $N_2O$ from combustion sources", *E.S.&T.*, **39,** 287-293.

[75] P.F. Nelson and S.M. Quigley, (1984), "The hydrocarbon composition of exhaust emitted from gasoline fuelled vehicles", *Atmosph. Environm.*, **18,** 79-87.

[76] W.K. Okamoto et al., (1983), "Nitric acid in Diesel exhaust", *J. APCA*, **33,** 1098-1100.

[77] B.S. Olufsen and A. Bjørseth, (1983), "Analysis of polycyclic aromatic hydrocarbons by gas chromatography", in: *Handbook of polycyclic aromatic hydrocarbons*, A. Bjørseth, Marcel Dekker, New York, pp. 257-300.

[78] M. Pasquereau and P. Degobert, (1986), "Mesure des émissions individuelles d'hydrocarbures aromatiques dans les gaz d'échappement d'automobiles", *Inst. Franç. du Pétrole Report* No. 34098, 43 p.

[79] M. Pasquereau and P. Degobert, (1987), "Analyse des hydrocarbures aromatiques polycycliques (HAP) présents dans la phase particulaire des échappements des moteurs diesel", *Inst. Franç. du Pétrole Report* No. 35056, 46 p.

[80] M. Pasquereau and R. Dozière, (1989), "Mesure des émissions de méthane et des hydrocarbures oléfiniques légers dans les gaz d'échappement d'automobiles", *Inst. Franç. du Pétrole Report* No. 37346, 23 p.

[81] L. Paturel et al., (1985), “Réalisation d’un dispositif expérimental pour le dosage des hydrocarbures aromatiques polynucléaires par spectrofluorimétrie Shpol’skii à 10 K”, *Anal. Chim. Acta*, **147,** 293-302.

[82] L. Paturel et al., (1986), “Mesures de HAP par spectrofluorimétrie Shpol’skii dans les effluents gazeux d’une unité de fabrication d’électrodes réfractaires”, *Poll. Atmosph.* (109), 54-64.

[83] J.M. Perez, (1972), “Cooperative evaluation of techniques for measuring nitric oxide and carbon monoxide”, *SAE Paper* No. 720104, 9 p.

[84] B.A. Petersen et al., (1982), “Analysis of PAH in Diesel exhaust particulates by high resolution capillary column gas chromatography/mass spectrometry”, *SAE Paper* No. 820774, 13 p.

[85] R.C. Pierce and M. Katz, (1976), “Chromatographic isolation and spectral analysis of polycyclic quinones, Application to air pollution analysis”, *E.S.&T.*, **10,** 45-51.

[86] M. Prigent and G. de Soete, (1989), “Nitrous oxide $N_2O$ in engine exhaust gases, A first appraisal of catalyst impact”, *SAE Paper* No. 890492, 11 p.

[87] A. Prostak and G.D. Reschke, (1977), “Analyzers for methane in exhaust gas”, *SAE Paper* No. 770143, 7 p.

[88] V. Raman, (1989), *Spectrometric determination of nitrogen dioxide (nitrite), 3rd Int. Symp., “Highway Pollution”*, München, 18/22 September, 6 p.

[89] B. Raynal, (1988), “Moteurs thermiques et pollution atmosphérique, Réglementation des véhicules automobiles”, *Techn. de l’Ing.*, Vol. B378,2, 17 p.

[90] J.M. Roberts, (1984), “Sampling and analysis of monoterpene hydrocarbons in the atmosphere with Tenax gas chromatographic porous polymer”, in: *Identification and analysis of organic pollutants in air*, L.H. Keith, Butterworth Publications, Boston, pp. 371-387.

[91] D.J. Roberton et al., (1979), “HCN content of turbine engine exhaust”, *J. APCA*, **29,** 50-51.

[92] SAE Recommended Practice, (1984), “Instrumentation and techniques for exhaust gas measurement”, *SAE* J254, 14 p.

[93] SAE Recommended Practice, (1982), “Measurement of carbon dioxide, carbon monoxide, and oxides of nitrogen in Diesel exhaust”, *SAE* J177, 11 p.

[94] SAE Recommended Practice, (1988), “Continuous hydrocarbon analysis of Diesel emissions”, *SAE* J215, 4 p.

[95] SAE Recommended Practice, (1982), “Measurement of fuel evaporative emissions from gasoline powered passenger cars and light trucks using the enclosure technique”, *SAE* J171, 9 p.

[96] SAE Recommended Practice, (1983), “Measurement of fuel evaporative emissions from gasoline powered passenger cars and light trucks by the trap method”, *SAE* J170, 6 p.

[97] SAE Recommended Practice, (1973), “Instrumentation and techniques for vehicle refueling emission measurement”, *SAE* J1045, 5 p.

[98] J. Schulze et al., (1986), "Identifizierung von sauerstoffhaltigen Polycyclischen AromatischenKohlenwasserstoffeninDieselrußextraktenmittels Kapillargaschromatographieund Kapillargaschromatographie/Massenspektrometrie", *VW Forschungsbericht*, No. FMT 8504 V. 5, 24 p.

[99] D.E. Seizinger and S.K. Hoekman, (1984), "Aromatic measurements of Diesel fuel, A CRC round-robin study", *SAE Paper* No. 841363, 10 p.

[100] A.D. Shendrikar and J.P. Lodge, (1975), "Microdetermination of ammonia by the ring oven technique and its application to air pollution studies", *Atmosph. Environm.*, **9,** 431-435.

[101] S.A. Shimpi and M.L. Yu, (1981), "Determination of a reliable and efficient Diesel particulate hydrocarbon extraction process", *SAE Paper* No. 811183, 7 p.

[102] R.J. Slone et al., (1980), "Nitrosamine emissions from Diesels", *SAE Paper* No. 801375, 8 p.

[103] C.A. Snyder, (1977), *Analytical techniques*, J. Toxicol. *Environm.Health*, 5-22 and 107-119.

[104] J. Staab et al., (1981), "Improving the method of hydrocarbon analysis", *SAE Paper* No. 810427, 21 p.

[105] F. Stump et al., (1982), "Trapping gaseous hydrocarbons for mutagenic testing", *SAE Paper* No. 820776, 19 p.

[106] S.B. Tejada et al., (1982), "Analysis of nitroaromatics in Diesel and gasoline car emissions", *SAE Paper* No. 820775, 8 p.

[107] H.Y. Tong and F.W. Karasek, (1984), "Quantitation of polycyclic aromatic hydrocarbons in Diesel exhaust particulate matter by high performance liquid chromatography fractionation and high resolution gas chromatography", *Anal. Chem.*, **56,** 2129-2134.

[108] E. Tsani-Bazaca et al., (1981), "Concentrations and correlations of 1,2-dibromoethane, 1,2-dichloroethane, benzene and toluene in vehicle exhaust and ambient air", *Environ. Techn. Lett.*, **2,** 303-316.

[109] C.M. Urban and R.J. Garbe, (1979), "Regulated and unregulated exhaust emissions from malfunctioning automobiles", *SAE Paper* No. 790696, 18 p.

[110] H.J. van de Wiel, (1977), "Device to eliminate erroneous output in cyclic chemiluminescent nitrogen dioxide monitoring", *Atmosph. Environm.*, **11,** pp. 93-94.

[111] B. Vanrel, (1989), *Caractérisations physico-chimiques et biologiques des émissions Diesel, Étude des extraits particulaires et mise au point d'un protocole d'exposition directe d'un système bactérien*, Thesis, Université René Descartes, Paris, 227 p.

[112] P.O. Warner, (1976), *Analysis of Air Pollutants*, John Wiley and Son, New York, 329 p.

[113] M.A. Warner-Selph and J. de Vita, (1989), "Measurements of toxic exhaust emissions from gasoline powered light duty vehicles", *SAE Paper* No. 892075, 11 p.

[114] B.M. Wathen, (1983), "Measurements of benzene, toluene and xylenes in urban air", *Atmosph. Environm.*, **17,** 1713-1722.

[115] R.L. Williams et al., (1985), "A review of sampling effects on polynuclear aromatic hydrocarbons (PAH) from heavy-duty Diesel engines", *SAE Paper* No. ,852081, 18 p.

[116] M. Wittenberg et al., (1984), "Analyse quantitative des hydrocarbures aromatiques polynucléaires par spectrofluorimétrie Shpol'skii à 10 K, Utilisation de la raie de mercure excitatrice diffusée par la matrice comme intensité lumineuse de référence", *Anal. Chim. Acta*, **160,** 185-196.

[117] M. Wittenberg et al., (1985), "Analyse quantitative des hydrocarbures aromatiques polynucléaires dans l'environnement par spectrofluorimétrie Shpol'skii à 10 K, Méthodes de prélèvement et d'extraction des échantillons, Résultats quantitatifs", *Analysis*, **13,** 249-260.

[118] K. Yamane et al., (1988), "Measurement of particulate and unburnt hydrocarbon emissions from Diesel engines", *SAE Paper* No. 880343, 10 p.

[119] E.G. Sweeney et al., (1992), "Composition of gasoline vehicle emissions, An analytical speciation program", *SAE Paper* No. 922253 (SP 938), 225-239.

# Analysis of pollutants: other products

9

## 9.1 Oxygen

Oxygen is routinely measured by the magnetic methods described in Chapter 7 [6]. The most important interference in the use of these methods is the presence of NO in the gas to be analyzed, which makes the method inaccurate for low levels of $O_2$ (2000 ppm NO equivalent to 0.1% $O_2$). The accuracy of the instruments is ±1% of full scale, but their relatively long response time is a handicap when attempting to measure sudden changes in $O_2$ content. The polarographic method described in Chapter 7 is also used [7 and 8] and its response is directly proportional to the partial pressure of the oxygen [133].

## 9.2 Ozone

Ozone is not measured directly in connection with automotive emissions, but is measured in the environment after the side reactions of automotive pollutants.

Manual methods are based on iodometry according to the following reaction:

$$3I^- + O_3 + 2H^+ \Rightarrow I_3^- + O_2 + H_2O$$

The iodate formed in the reaction is then reduced by thiosulfate and measured directly by colorimetry. The resulting iodine is stained, unlike the other iodine compounds. The detection limit is 10 ppb.

Automatic methods are based on ultraviolet spectrometry at 254 nm or on chemoluminescence according to the same principle as the one used for nitrogen oxides.

## 9.3 Carboxyl compounds

Several methods [35 and 117] have been employed in succession to determine aldehydes in the air and particularly in automotive effluents. One of the difficulties in determining aldehydes stems from their very high reactivity. Hence, the preferable methods of detection are those that rapidly convert aldehydes to more stable derivatives [67]. Among the many methods applied after trapping the gases, only the DNPH method [111, 122, and 123] survives, despite recent proposals for competing methods [35]. The following techniques are worth mentioning:

- The chromotropic acid method[1] specific to formaldehyde gives a violet end-point in an acidic medium measured at 570 nm by spectrophotometry. Development is rapid but not very sensitive and high HCHO concentrations are needed. Unsaturated hydrocarbons interfere with this method [23].
- A highly sensitive fluorimetric method, characteristic of acrolein, which is based on its reaction with o-aminobiphenyl. The acrolein is first trapped on molecular sieves [144].
- The bisulfite method, which yields aldehyde derivatives that can be determined by gas chromatography, or determined overall by iodometry. This method is cheap but non-specific. GC does not allow for the consideration of formaldehyde or the separation of propanal, acetone, and acrolein [155].
- The pararosaniline method that slowly develops (>90 min), in the presence of sodium sulfite and pararosaniline[2], a red color that is measured by spectrometry at 560 nm [23]. High $SO_2$ concentrations destroy the color.
- The Hantzsch reaction, which is a fluorimetric method based on the reaction between formaldehyde and acetylacetone in the presence of ammonia, yields a yellow product (3,5 diacetyl 1,4 dihydrolutidine) with a greenish-yellow fluorescence that is measured at 510 nm [29].
- A fluorimetric method based on the enzymatic catalysis of a reaction of HCHO with b-nicotamide adenine dinucleotide [88].
- Direct ultraviolet spectroscopy with second-order derivation at 284 nm, which is the wavelength at which the hydrocarbons do not interfere. This method can be applied continuously for formaldehyde in exhaust gases, but is difficult to calibrate [23 and 76].
- FID detection after catalytic oxidation of HCHO to methane with prior separation on chromatographic column of $CO_2$ and CO that can undergo the same methanation reaction [27 and 115]. This method offers the advantage of an in-line measurement, but with response times from 10 to 30 min.
- The use of mass spectrometry [117] with chemical ionization is an expensive but rapid method that helps to monitor changes in the emissions of the various aldehydes during the test cycles. The interference in the measurement of unsaturated aldehydes, which is caused by hydrocarbons, is reduced in the presence of ammonia [48].
- The formation of derivatives with oximes: o-benzyloxime aldehydes, which are obtained by trapping them in a solution of benzoyloxyamine hydrochlorate and sodium acetate in methanol and then heating for 30 min at 60°C, provide stable,

1. 4,5-dihydroxynaphthalene-2,7 disulfonic acid.
2. Aminophenyl-aminotolyl carbinol.

non-volatile derivatives, which can be determined by gas chromatography with selective NPD detection of nitrogen [97].

- Capture of aldehydes in an oxidizing alkaline solution of hydrogen peroxide from which carboxylic acids are obtained then analyzed by ionic chromatography [41]. The alcohols tend to interfere with this method.
- The MBTH method that forms, in an acidic medium with carbonyl compounds, an azine and a dark blue diazo cation determined by colorimetry at 650 nm. This cation is unstable, its absorption coefficient varies with the aldehyde concerned, and it is affected by the presence of $SO_2$. The addition of sulfamic acid [109 and 114] decreases the interference of $SO_2$ [110]. This method accounts only for aliphatic aldehydes. Direct trapping of the exhaust gases in a vacuum flask containing the MBTH solution prevents changes in the aldehydes in the lines, but does not eliminate the drawbacks listed [148]. This method has nevertheless been used as a derivative method for selective ultraviolet detection of aldehydes at 640 nm, leaving HPLC analyzing aqueous aldehyde solutions [75].
- The use of Girard's reagent T[3], which is dissolved in an absorption medium buffered to pH 4.5. The derivatives obtained can be separated on an ion exchange column and detected by ultraviolet light (HPLC) at 312 nm [63] or measured by polarography [117].
- Ionic chromatography has also been applied to the measurement of formaldehyde. The HCHO is trapped on activated carbon impregnated with an oxidant that converts it to the formate. After desorption in the presence of hydrogen peroxide, the analysis is performed by ionic chromatography [85].
- The DNPH method, in which hydrazones are formed in an acidic medium with all the carbonyl compounds.

Trapping demands careful monitoring of the temperatures of the sampling lines, because the high solubility of the aldehydes in any condensed water seriously distorts the measurements. Trapping for the DNPH method can be achieved in various ways:

- Absorption of the gases in an aqueous acidic solution of DNPH [53]. The low solubility of the hydrazones created requires filtration of the mixture obtained, which is then taken up in a solvent (pentane then toluene) and sent to gas chromatography with FID detection. This technique does not separate the $C_3$ compounds (propanal, acrolein, acetone).
- The hydrazone precipitate can be taken up in chloroform and the solution that is obtained is injected in HPLC [92, 108, and 145]. Elution by a water/methanol mixture with a concentration gradient separates the $C_3$ compounds. HPLC also offers the advantage over gas chromatography of operating at ambient temperature, thus avoiding thermal degradation of the hydrazones [43].

3. N,N,N-trimethyl ammonium acetyl hydrazine.

- Absorption of the gases in a solution of DNPH in acetonitrile [90, 101, and 104] helps to achieve perfect dissolution of the hydrazones. The solution obtained can be injected directly into an HPLC chromatograph with ultraviolet detection at 365 nm. This technique serves to separate the $C_3$ compounds, but the absorption solution changes very rapidly [118] and demands HPLC analysis immediately upon sampling due to the apparent conversion of acrolein and acetone to propanal, in an acidic medium and in the presence of excess DNPH. To overcome this drawback, the remedy is to employ the minimum amount of DNPH and to neutralize the excess immediately by adding an aldehyde not present in the exhaust, which does not interfere with the others and which has a retention time that is not too long. Isovaleraldehyde is ideal for this purpose [119]. This method is currently the most convenient for exhaust emission analyses.
- The use of a different hydrazine from DNPH, such as DNSH, also allows perfect separation of the $C_3$ compounds [79] in HPLC with fluorimetric detection.
- The simultaneous adsorption and formation of hydrazone derivatives by passage over a solid adsorbent on which the DNPH is grafted or impregnated can also be used. A number of supports have been used:
  - Amberlite XAD-2 [55] eluted by ether with gas chromatography analysis and detection by electron capture [15] or HPLC analysis [14]
  - silica gel eluted by acetonitrile with HPLC analysis [13, 24, and 88]: Sep-PAK cartridges allow prolonged storage of the samples, although the acrolein and crotonaldehyde tend to change in favor of an unidentified compound [147]
  - glass beads, treated or untreated by hydrofluoric acid before impregnation by a phosphoric solution of DNPH are then eluted by dichloromethane before HPLC analysis [57 and 62]
  - Sep-PAK $C_{18}$ (SP)[4] silica cartridges impregnated with phosphoric acid and DNPH [86 and 91] and eluted by acetonitrile: these cartridges offer the advantage of avoiding interference due to the high ozone concentrations encountered with silica gel cartridges that have not been treated with acid [21]
  - magnesium silicate (Fluorisil), which is placed in polyethylene cartridges [102] impregnated with a solution of DNPH in dichloromethane and eluted by dichloromethane before HPLC analysis
  - unbonded fiberglass filters impregnated with the same solution [95 and 96]

For solid absorbents impregnated with DNPH, it may be useful to place an unimpregnated absorbent cartridge upstream to avoid interference from reactions that tend to modify the DNPH derivatives. In addition to the wet methods based on DNPH, Fourier transform infrared spectrometry is used to measure formaldehyde and acetaldehyde [64, 117, and 163]. Despite lower sensitivity, this method allows a real-time determination of HCHO, to the detriment of the other aldehydes.

4. Waters Associates, Milford, Massachusetts.

## 9.4 Alcohols

Methanol and ethanol are essentially the alcohols detected in automotive exhaust emissions. The method consists in passing the gases trapped in CVS system bags [126] through gas chromatography with FID detection. The detector is calibrated with the corresponding alcohol to account for the lack of response of the FID (Table 7.3).

Another procedure is to trap the dilute gases sampled in a dilution tunnel in an absorber:

- containing distilled water: the alcohol is measured by GC/FID [125]
- containing distilled water buffered in an alkaline medium [55]

The alcohols are then analyzed by gas chromatography in the form of the corresponding nitrous esters obtained by mixing the acidified solution obtained with sodium nitrite.

An electron capture detector is used to enhance sensitivity.

The FTIR technique is also used for methanol [163].

## 9.5 Carboxylic acids

The most widely-used method is to trap the organic acids in a cooled alkaline solution of sodium carbonate. The solution obtained is then analyzed by ionic chromatography with electrochemical detection [104]. Other methods perform the analysis by gas chromatography of acetonyl esters obtained by reaction between carboxylic acids and chloracetone [105] or by HPLC with ultraviolet detection using derivatives obtained with nitrobenzyl bromide [130]. Another derivative that is used for formic acid, which is trapped on activated carbon and desorbed by dimethylformamide, is p-bromophenacyl formiate measured by HPLC with ultraviolet detection [152].

## 9.6 Phenols

One method is to trap the phenols in an alkaline hydroxide solution forming sodium or potassium phenates. After acid hydrolysis followed by steam entrainment [81] or ether extraction [112], the phenols are analyzed by gas chromatography on a capillary column with FID detection [158]. Another technique traps them on a solid support impregnated with caustic soda, after which the derivatives obtained by reaction with p-nitrobenzenediazonium tetrafluoborate are separated by liquid phase chromatography [93].

## 9.7 $SO_2$ and sulfates

Several methods are available for measuring $SO_2$ [5 and 132]. *AFNOR* Standard X 20-350 describes their advantages, drawbacks, and fields of application.

A first wet method consists in trapping the $SO_2$ in a solution of potassium chloromercurate $K_2HgCl_4$ and developing a color by various reagents. However, trapping is imperfect at low $SO_2$ concentrations. To avoid the mercury salts of the West-Gaeke method, the $SO_2$ can be trapped in morpholine (p-oxazine) and the complex colorimetrically determined with p-rosaniline hydrochlorate [127]. The other trapping methods oxidize $SO_2$ to $SO_4^{2-}$ by bubbling in 3% hydrogen peroxide $H_2O_2$ or on a filter impregnated with a solution of glycerol and sodium carbonate. The sulfate ion is then measured by one of the following methods:

- liquid chromatography (HPLC): the sulfate, by reacting with barium chloranilate ($C_6BaCl_2O_4$), liberates chloranilic acid[5] that is detected by ultraviolet light [83 and 132]; this method has been discarded because the hydrocarbons and additives can interfere
- colorimetric titration in the presence of barium perchlorate ($BaClO_4$) with thorin[6] as indicator [4]
- ionic chromatography with a neutralization column coupled with a conductimetric detector: this sensitive, rapid (direct injection of the sample), and fairly selective method is the one most widely used today [69]

Standard instruments used ultraviolet fluorescence [107] and flame photometry, which are both standardized by *AFNOR* [10 and 11]. The measurement of low $SO_2$ concentrations exploits the reaction:

$$Hg_2^{2+} + H_2O + SO_2 \Rightarrow HgSO_3H^+ + Hg$$

The mercury that is liberated is measured on a gold film conductimetric sensor whose resistivity is modified by the presence of mercury [72]. Other methods being developed are based on pulsed fluorescence and second-derivative ultraviolet spectroscopy [132].

Sulfur derivatives ($SO_2$, $H_2S$, COS, and $CS_2$) can also be analyzed directly by gas chromatography with flame spectrometry detection after cryogenic trapping at −186°C [68].

Particulate sulfates, essentially present in diesel particulates, are sampled on filters. The filter is then treated with ammonia to form ammonium sulfate $(NH_4)_2SO_4$ which is extracted with a water/isopropanol mixture. An ion exchange resin is then used to separate the anions and to measure the resulting sulfuric acid, using the methods described for $SO_2$, particularly ionic chromatography. Another treatment is to disintegrate the filters by ultrasound in a solution of $NaHCO_3$ and $Na_2CO_3$ to analyze the solution obtained by ionic chromatography [122 and 123], or in an

5. Dichloro-3,6-dihydroxy-2,5-p-benzoquinone.
6. Disodium salt of (arsonophenylazo-2)-1-hydroxy-2-naphthalene-disulfonic-3,6 acid.

aqueous solution of isopropanol to perform the analysis with barium perchlorate and thorin [138]. Methyl sulfates are also measured by ionic chromatography, after trapping the corresponding particles and elution by sodium bicarbonate [66 and 142].

During filter sampling, it is important to make sure that the basicity of the filter (for untreated fiberglass filters) does not lead to the production of sulfate as an artifact from gaseous $SO_2$.

A filter covered with an electrolytic gel has been proposed for the evaluation of the sulfuric acid aerosol generated by a catalytic oxidation converter. The electrical resistivity of the surface would be used as a measurement. However, further developments have not ensued [26].

An elegant but costly method to measure sulfuric acid emissions, in real time and without interference, employs monochromatic laser radiation at 1231.1 $cm^{-1}$ directed into the diesel aerosol, which is kept between 160 and 200°C [71].

## 9.8 Hydrogen sulfide

Several methods have been recommended for measuring $H_2S$ in automotive exhaust emissions [124]:

- Colorimetry, as recommended by the *EPA*, absorbs the gas is in a solution of zinc acetate before developing the methylene blue color [53]. This is a slow and demanding method, sensitive to interference by $NO_x$.
- Gas phase chromatography that is conducted on a specific column with a flame spectrometry detector. This method is selective but has a rather long response time.
- Catalytic oxidation by oxygen that is combined with an analysis of the resulting $SO_2$ by either NDIR or fluorescence. It is necessary to take into account pre-existing $SO_2$ and dilution above the dew-point or drying of the gas is essential.
- Gas phase ultraviolet spectrometry through a heated cell is a continuous method with a rapid response. The interfering gases must be subtracted.
- Liquid phase spectrophotometry that is conducted after extraction in an ammonia solution using spectrophotometric measurement of the resulting sulfur. This continuous and selective method incurs the risks of $H_2S$ retention by adsorption in the many tubes.
- The potentiometric method in which the gas diffuses in an electrolytic cell, causing a variation in potential on the passage of $H_2S$. This method may be sensitive to interference.
- The thin film sensor, which is selective for $H_2S$, has a slow response.
- The resistance sensor: the electrical resistance of a gold film changes on the passage of an $H_2S$ stream and is proportional to its concentration [124]. This semi-continuous method has a shorter response time, but demands dilution of the exhaust to avoid water condensation.

Although the latter method displays interference with $O_2$, $O_2$, and $H_2S$ are not simultaneously present in exhaust gases [124].

## 9.9 Mercaptans (thiols) and sulfides

After the removal of $H_2S$ and $CS_2$ on silica impregnated with diethanolamine, mercaptans can be analyzed by a flame photometry detector specific to sulfur [151 and 153]. Sulfides (COS, mono- and disulfides of methyl and ethyl) are analyzed according to the *EPA* [53] by gas chromatography and flame photometry detection, after trapping on Tenax GC with upstream elimination of the $SO_2$ by an alkaline trap. Thiophene may interfere with this measurement.

Another spectrophotometric method is based on the red color developed at 500 nm by the complex obtained in the reaction of a solution of N,N-dimethyl-p-phenylenediamine and ferric chloride with the mercaptans trapped in an aqueous solution of mercuric acetate and acetic acid [81]. The disulfides interfere very little, because they are not retained by the trapping solution.

## 9.10 Metals (Pb, Mn, Zn, Cd, Pt, Pd, etc.)

The metals concerned are collected on a filter along with the particulates emitted in the exhaust. The analysis is then performed by atomic absorption spectroscopy [80] using specific wavelengths of each metal [81], for example: 228.8 nm (Cd), 357.9 nm (Cr), 324.7 nm (Cu), 248.3 nm (Fe), 217.0 nm (Pb), 279.5 nm (Mn), 232.0 nm (Ni), 318.4 nm (V), and 213.8 nm (Zn). This technique has been standardized for lead in air [12], which can also be determined by X-ray using the PIXE method [34]. Atmospheric lead alkyls have been measured, after cryogenic trapping, by gas chromatography associated with atomic absorption spectrometry [70].

Precious metals (Pt, Pd) have been analyzed in dust by acid leaching, mineralization, anion exchange, and atomic absorption spectroscopy [73].

Nickel carbonyl in exhaust emissions is determined in bags filled during CVS cycles. The sample collected is mixed with an equal volume of pure CO and then sent to a chemoluminescence analyzer where $Ni(CO)_4$ reacts with $O_3$ and CO to yield a light-emitting species [53]. Interfering compounds are eliminated by suitable optical fibers. Another method performs trapping in an alcoholic solution of iodine and then measures the nickel by atomic absorption [33].

## 9.11 Particulates

### 9.11.1 Weight method

Weighting the mass of particulates emitted is the current method underlying the regulations in all applicable countries [17 and 18]. By definition, it considers 'particulates' as anything deposited on Teflonated fiberglass filters from the dilute exhaust gases sampled at a temperature lower than 52°C. Filters with the Pallflex trademark have been selected for this purpose. From among 54 types of filters, they represent the best compromise for mechanical strength, efficiency, minimum absorption of moisture and organic vapors, density, and pressure drop [121]. In this method, an aliquot flow rate is sampled in the dilution tunnel connected with the chassis dynamometer and sent to the above filters. These filters are tared and re-weighed after sampling on a precision balance (to within 1 or 10 μg) placed in a controlled-temperature enclosure with controlled relative humidity [122]. A test duration of between 4 and 80 h at 40 to 60% relative humidity has been recommended [25].

Preconditioning the vehicle is indispensable in order to guarantee better repeatability of the results [18 and 99]. For powerful truck and bus engines, which are evaluated by the 'transient' method, a secondary dilution tunnel is associated with the primary dilution tunnel to ensure sampling in the required temperature conditions.

The $\beta$ gauge technique [3], applied routinely to measure the weight of particles in industrial stacks [31] has not been applied to automotive exhausts. The mass of particulates deposited on a filter is determined from the attenuation of a $\beta$ radiation received on the other side of the filter by a Geiger-Müller counter. Its response time, which is better than that of the official weight method, is nevertheless too long to allow instantaneous in-line measurements.

## 9.11.2 Particle size analysis

This analysis is designed to determine the shapes and dimensional distributions of the particles making up the aerosols [129]. Various instruments are available for determining these parameters [94 and 106].

- **Cascade impactors** [103] send the aerosol stream through an orifice on an impaction plate, which forces the stream to suddenly change direction by 90 degrees. Particles with sufficient inertia cannot follow the current lines and impact against the plate. Conversely, the smaller particles follow the current lines and are not captured. However, they can be captured in the next stage if the air is conveyed to a second and smaller orifice, which imparts a higher speed to the flow. Several successive stages can be used to classify the particulates by decreasing size. Deposits at each stage are then weighed. To accelerate the acquisition of the results by avoiding the weighing operations, it has been proposed that a single-pole charge be applied to the particles upstream. Electrometers would then be used to measure the charges collected at each stage, with the corresponding plates being electrically insulated from each other [149]. Cascade impactors help to obtain the mass particle size distribution between 0.3 and 10 μm.

- **Diffusion batteries:** Aerosols, while larger than gaseous molecules, are subject to Brownian motion. When carried by the gas stream in a small-section duct, the particles are fixed to the walls [106]. By placing filters downstream of tubes of different cross-sections, the fraction of the aerosol that has not been stopped by the corresponding tube diameter can be measured. Processing algorithms then give the mass distribution [30]. Diffusion tubes can be formed simply by beds of beads of the same diameter, placed in parallel.

  The combination of an impactor and diffusion batteries helps to cover the particle size range from 0.01 to 10 μm by the use of the SDI 2000 inertial and diffusional spectrometer [30]. This spectometer consists of an eight-stage cascade impactor followed by a battery of five bead beds in parallel [52].
- **Electrical mobility analyzers** charge the particles by passing them through a cloud of ions and then attracting them into a higher electric field. This classifies the aerosols according to the electrical mobility of the particles. The knowledge of the relationship between mobility and size makes it possible to determine the latter. Commercial systems (AEA) rapidly give the numerical particle size distribution of an aerosol between 0.01 and 1 μm [106]. For automotive exhausts [61], they require prior dilution of the tunnel effluent, thus lengthening the response time of the system [52].
- **Photon correlation spectroscopy** [154] is a technique concerned with fluctuations in the light intensity diffused by the particles in an aerosol. A laser beam passes through the diesel aerosol present in the dilution tunnel and the statistical analysis of the fluctuations of the light diffused by the particles serves to obtain their diameter by auto-correlation. Their number is also obtained from the value of the total intensity diffused during the short measurement interval (1 to 10 s). An assumption of the density of soot allows an evaluation of the mass of soot present in the measurement volume. Because of its very short response time, this method helps to monitor changes in particulate emissions during standard test cycles, as well as their particle size distribution.

### 9.11.3 Optical analysis and smoke meters

These methods are based on the light absorption coefficient of the carbon portion of the diesel soot, of which the value is around 9.0 $m^2/g$ for a wavelength of 550 nm [39 and 137].

Two measurement principles are applied to evaluate smoke, particularly diesel smoke:

- *Optical measurement of the absorption of a light beam by a smoke plume* [16]
  - The Ringelmann method [1] makes a subjective comparison of the plume with standard grey scales.
  - The US PHS smoke-meter, placed at the exhaust exit point in the air, causes the entire plume of US engines (of which the exhaust tip is usually vertical) to pass through the beam of an incandescent bulb collected on a photoelectric

cell [134]. The result is indicated in percentage opacity. This instrument is recommended by the *EPA*.

- The Celesco smoke-meter is placed in-line on the exhaust manifold. It uses a pulsed photodiode as a light source.
- To increase the sensitivity of this type of smoke-meter, which is placed for example at the exit of a particle filter, the optical path can be stretched to 0.80 m [39] or 1.5 m [77], or a series of transceiver pairs can be placed in-line, with their signals being added together to decrease the background noise [135]. The same type of opacimeter has been installed in the dilution tunnel [59]. The results have been correlated to within 10% with weight measurements on 13-mode cycles as long as the SOF fraction remained between 9 and 20%. Hence, this smoke-meter represents a good develop ment tool, without claiming to rival the weight measurement for certification purposes.
- The Hartridge smoke-meter uses only a portion of the exhaust stream and requires the placing of a pressure drop on the exhaust to force the flow through the instrument [134]. It compares the absorption in the smoke tube with a zero obtained by the passage of a light beam through an air-filled tube. The response time in transient conditions is longer than that of the Celesco and the PHS.

- *Measurement of the blackening index of a paper that has filtered a known volume of the exhaust gas to be evaluated*
  - The Bosch smoke-meter sucks a given exhaust volume through a filter paper. The blackening of the paper is evaluated on a photoelectric cell by the quantity of light emitted by an incandescent bulb and reflected by the blackened paper. The result is given on a 'Bosch' index scale from 1 to 10.
  - The AVL instrument is an automated version of the Bosch system.
  - The Bacharach method [2] uses the same sampling technique but makes a subjective comparison with 10 grey scales. The process is not used for automotive smoke.

Attempts at correlations [60] between the different optical measurement methods and weight measurements have been made several times and conversion charts have been published [134]. Their validity is far from universal, but their use helps to monitor tendencies during parametric studies. The difficulty of correlation is connected with the composition of the diesel particles, which includes a fraction of black, opaque elemental carbon, combined in variable proportions with a sulfate fraction and a liquid hydrocarbon fraction that is partially opaque and exerts a lesser effect on opacity [139].

For measuring white smoke, which essentially consists of an aerosol of unburnt diesel fuel droplets from a recently started diesel engine that is taking in very cold air, a specific optical method has been developed [146]. The cooled engine exhaust is sampled in a line heated to 200°C and is diluted in a tube with cold air at 0°C to measure the light absorption of the mixture.

## 9.11.4 Other measurement methods

The objective of these methods, which are currently under study, is to achieve a real-time measurement of particulate emissions.

The electric charge acquired by the particles at the exit of the combustion chamber has been proposed as a means for measuring the particle flux density and has been correlated with the Bosch index [42]. The positive or negative charges of the particles are approximately balanced [87], but the slight excess of negative charges can be detected by the sensor. However, the practical problem that subsists is the maintenance of clean measurement electrodes, which are easily grounded by particle deposits [74]. Once fully developed, the use of this sensor in a closed loop would help to eliminate gusts of smoke during accelerations [74].

The spectrophone or photo-acoustic spectroscope [77 and 78] is a technique whose principle is also applied to the measurement of various gaseous pollutants [28]. The process consists in sending the green radiation of an argon laser, modulated to an audible frequency, through the diesel aerosol flowing in an enclosure of which one wall consists of a microphone diaphragm. The absorption of the radiation energy by the particles and its retransmission in the form of heat causes an increase in pressure (acoustic wave modulated at the same frequency). The signal obtained is measured after amplification. It offers an advantage over other optical systems by being proportional to the mass of particles, independently of their size, if the wavelength selected is larger than the average particle diameter [84]. It provides real-time information on particulate emissions. This highly sensitive system, whose results are correlated to within 10% with weight measurements of elemental carbon, is nevertheless a costly and sophisticated system [77 and 139]. A variant of this system uses a $CO_2$ laser as the source [56 and 116] and uses a twin-cell system to eliminate the interference due to absorption by $CO_2$, CO, and $H_2O$.

The simultaneous optical measurement of particulates and adsorbed hydrocarbons has been carried out in a spectral domain in which the diffusion of light is negligible [84]. In a narrow wavelength range, infrared absorption depends only on graphitic carbon and the hydrocarbon absorption bands are found in another region. Hence, this technique uses the modulated radiation of an infrared source and measures the absorption of the incident radiation by the diesel aerosol at two wavelengths: 3.45 nm (caused by the combination of carbon+PAH) and 3.95 nm (caused by carbon alone). The difference gives an evaluation of the adsorbed PAH concentration [156].

Light absorption by soot was measured in the combustion chamber of a diesel engine [40]. The choice of a narrow wavelength band coupled with a powerful light emitter in this band helps to overcome the continuous radiation specific to the flame.

Measurement of the pressure drop across a filter while collecting particulates has been proposed to estimate the mass deposited on the filter [139]. This simple, inexpensive system provides real-time information, but the results depend on the size of the particles and the extractable content. The correlation with weight measurements is relatively good in the presence of 'dry' soot but poor with greasy soot [84].

The tapered element oscillating microbalance (TEOM) [120] consists of a tapered tube with its large-section end firmly fixed and its slender end free. The slender end has a filter on it of the type used for weight measurements, which is crossed by the aerosol stream to be measured [157]. This tapered tube is placed between the plates of an electrostatically-charged capacitor. A retroactive loop system keeps the tube and its filter in oscillation. The oscillation frequency varies with the mass of particles deposited on the filter. This frequency is converted into a modulated electric signal by cutting the light beam that is emitted by a light-emitting diode and which is received on a photodiode before amplification. The system thus allows the real-time measurement of the mass of particles emitted and the measurement range extends from a mg to a g. Due to the possible evaporation of the volatile fractions during measurement cycles at variable load, negative changes in mass may appear [161] due to the desorption of hydrocarbons or even water [136 and 141] during the decelerations that follow the periods of adsorption under more severe conditions. The TEOM thus appears to be a useful development tool, but correlations with official weight measurements are still not good enough to substitute for the latter [141].

### 9.11.5 Chemical analysis and extractible materials

The organic fraction adsorbed on SOF diesel particulates is generally measured after extraction of the filters containing the particles in a Soxhlet extractor, which is protected from the ambient light by packing in an aluminum foil [122]. The results obtained may differ according to the choice of the solvent, which is in most cases dichloromethane (DCM), the method recommended by the EPA. The use of other solvents (benzene/ethanol or benzene/methanol mixtures) can alter the relative shares of the compounds extracted. Extraction using toluene, for example, may favor the extraction of heavy PAH when compared with extraction using DCM, and accordingly alter the mutagenicity of the extracts. The addition of an alcohol to the solvent mixture also leads to the extraction of sulfates [121]. The toluene/ethanol azeotrope with a higher boiling point helps to obtain a fraction denoted TOE on the Soxhlet [122]. In comparison with the SOF, the TOE contains an additional 5 to 10% in the form of highly oxidized polar compounds.

The SOF fraction has also been measured by vacuum sublimation, a much faster method, which gives the organic fraction by the difference in mass [140], but does not allow chemical analysis or a study of the biological effects of this fraction [65]. Precautions must be observed concerning the thorough cleaning of the sublimation furnace. This technique also presents the drawback of counting as hydrocarbons the fraction of water and sulfates adsorbed on the particles.

Two-step combustion at 340 and 1100°C also serves to measure organic carbon and elemental carbon in soot [32].

Supercritical $CO_2$ fluid at 250 atm has also been used for the measurement of SOF.

Thermogravimetry yields a volatile fraction slightly larger than that extracted by solvent [44]. This method can also replace solvent extraction by sending the effluents from the thermobalance to a gas phase chromatograph, thus considerably shortening the analysis time. This principle has been used to carry out the thermodesorption of the volatile fraction by placing the fiberglass filter covered with particles directly into an injector heated to 390°C and placed at the top of the column [45]. This system is currently available on the market [160]. It permits a rapid analysis of the SOF fraction, but the absence of liquid extracts prevents the separation of fractions in the liquid phase on the column.

*Soluble fraction attributable to lubricant*

A method has been proposed to separate the proportion due to lubricating oil from the SOF fraction [36]. It relies on the fact that the distillation intervals of diesel fuel and oil are relatively well separated. It also presumes that combustion does not alter the molecular composition of the oil and the fuel. The technique involves performing a 'simulated analytical distillation' by gas phase chromatography of the SOF extract that is redissolved in the $CS_2$ solvent (which does not respond to FID). The 50% distilled point is calculated and then compared with a calibration curve of the 50% distilled point = f (% oil in SOF) that is obtained by 'simulated distillation' of the mixtures in variable proportions of the lubricant and the fuel used for the test.

## 9.12 Odors

### 9.12.1 Olfactometric analysis

The sensory characteristics of the odors to be measured concern the olfactory thresholds of detectability and recognition, the quality of the odor, and its hedonistic character (pleasant or unpleasant). Today, no physicochemical instrument is capable of performing these measurements. Olfactory measurements are performed by olfactometry, which is based on test panels of humans using their noses to rate odors. Olfactometers, which are instruments used for controlled dilution of the odoriferous gaseous effluents to be evaluated, are used to present the odors to be measured to the various panelists in reproducible conditions and in comparison with suitable standards [51]. The measurement of olfactory thresholds is the subject of an *AFNOR* Standard in France [9] and *VDI* Directives in Germany. The olfactory intensity is measured by psychophysical methods for estimating values or for classification in categories [19], and the hedonistic aspect is assessed according to a pleasant/unpleasant value scale [20].

In the automotive world, diesel engine exhausts have been the subject of odor measurements [38]. After exhaust measurements at the dilution threshold [89, 100, and 131] human panelists have been employed [49] to determine both its odor intensity and its hedonistic character. In a specially-arranged cabin (with a reproducible and climate-controlled ambiance), a dozen subjects periodically sniff the dilute exhaust from a diesel engine through funnels placed in front of them. They issue a comparative judgment based on a series of bottles containing rising concentrations of an odorant such as pyridine [49]. Other measurements have used the technique of odor profiles by grading the sensations perceived in accordance with different standards of quality that were previously supplied. The Turk kit [150] was prepared for this purpose and has standards of four different qualities: smoky-burnt odor, oily odor, acrid/acid odor, and aldehyde or aromatic odor. The standards are mixtures of chemical compounds or specific natural compounds. The A.D. Little profile has only three standards: smoky-burnt typical of substituted phenols and indanols and indenones, oxidized oil typical of unsaturated aldehydes and heavy alcohols, and kerosene typical of aromatic compounds of the class of indanes, tetralines and alkylbenzenes [82]. It also indicates the possible irritation of the nose or eyes.

The MacLeod differential olfactometer has been used to improve the accuracy of the intensity values obtained, but by its design, it only takes into account the actual odor, to the detriment of the irritant effect (affecting the trigeminal nerve, distinct from the olfactory nerve). The results obtained, when compared with the data acquired from the previous panel, have shown that it only partly accounts for the effect produced on human subjects [50].

## 9.12.2 Physicochemical analyses

Faced with the cost of olfactometric measurements, an attempt was made to supplant them by determining odorant concentrations using possible correlations between the results of physicochemical measurements and the corresponding assessments of a human panel. This is the case of the DOAS[7] system [98, 111, and 128], which analyzes the diesel exhaust trapped on Chromosorb 102 by HPLC and determines an odorant intensity from a numerical relationship based on oxygenated aromatic compounds. This equation has been validated on US medium-power engines. The correlation is far inferior on truck engines [38] and is especially poor on European designed engines [49]. The instrument has nevertheless been used without olfactometric comparison for studies on the repercussions of the engine or fuel parameters on the odors [37 and 38].

The odorants emitted in diesel exhaust gases have also been analyzed by gas chromatography [54] using an apolar column at the outlet of which a human, who has

7. Arthur D. Little Inc.

been trained in qualification using the Turk kit, places his nose next to the FID detector. When an odorant emission is detected, in order to improve separations, it is sent to a polar column [46 and 47], which is also followed by the human subject and a mass spectrometry detector.

The difficulty encountered in the substitution of olfactometric analysis by physicochemical analysis stems from the fact that the relationships between perceived olfactory sensation and corresponding odorant concentration are mathematical power expressions (psychophysical law of Stevens [143]). Furthermore, the odorant mixtures may exhibit substantial synergistic or masking effects. The reduction of odorant emissions by a factor of 10 never means a reduction of the sensation perceived in the same proportion.

So far, irritants in exhaust emissions have not been measured by sensory analysis techniques. Since the number of irritants is much smaller than the number of odorants, the physicochemical analysis of light aldehydes, $NO_2$, and sulfuric acid provides an idea of the irritant power of the exhaust.

## 9.13 Repeatability and reproducibility of measurements

As already mentioned earlier in this chapter, the quality of the measurements depends on several factors:

- the model and the make of the measuring instrument
- its state of maintenance and cleanliness
- its calibration and the mixtures used to calibrate it
- the quality and length of the transfer lines to the analyzer
- the temperature and pressure condition in the transfer lines
- the possible presence of interfering compounds and the manner in which they are dealt with
- compliance with the recommended driving cycle (correct adjustment for the inertia of the vehicle while running the chassis dynamometer, choice of the type of chassis dynamometer, and electric or electromagnetic braking)
- the condition of the vehicle to be tested and the record of its use preceding the test, hence the type and duration of preconditioning used before the test

The cold periods of test cycles tend to reduce the accuracy of the results in comparison with hot starting cycles. Many round-robin tests are routinely performed to systematize the experimental procedures and to identify the most important factors in the above non-comprehensive list, which is currently based above all on regulated pollutants. On the reference gas cylinders, reproducibilities range between 1 and 2% [58]. However, the overall reproducibilities observed on an ECE 15 cycle are about 5% for CO and $NO_x$, between 15 and 20% for diesel particulates, and about 25%

on unburnt hydrocarbons. The same orders of magnitude are found for measurements of pollutants on trucks and buses with the transient cycles [22]. For unregulated pollutants, the figures recorded are in the range of 25% maximum for individual hydrocarbons, 50 to 70% for light aldehydes, 20 to 40% for PAH, 65% on sulfates, 12 to 15% on SOF, and 50 to 150% on phenols [113].

## 9.14 Conclusion

The analysis of automotive pollutants has undergone considerable development as a result of the progressive imposition of regulations and the need to have increasingly reliable and varied data to assess the potential changes in the atmosphere and their repercussions on the environment and on human health.

The instrumentation, which was originally rudimentary, is making increasing use of the latest and most sophisticated physicochemical techniques. Today, the environmental and automotive industry laboratories have qualified technicians and analysts capable of deriving maximum benefit from modern analytical tools. The routine testing of an ever-increasing number of chemicals broadened the market for analyzers and should lead to a lowering of prices and a demand for reliable measurement systems with minimal maintenance requirements.

## REFERENCES

[1] AFNOR, (1973), "Gaz de combustion, Indice de noircissement par opacité d'un panache de fumée (Méthode Ringelmann)", *Standard AF X* 43-008, 3 p.

[2] AFNOR, (1973), "Gaz de combustion, Indice de noircissement par filtration sur papier (Méthode Bacharach)", *Standard AF X* 43-002, 3 p.

[3] AFNOR, (1976), "Matières particulaires en suspension, Méthode de mesure de la concentration en masse au moyen d'un appareil séquentiel à jauge $\beta$", *Standard X* 43-017, 3 p.

[4] AFNOR, (1977), "Détermination de la concentration en masse du dioxyde de soufre dans l'air ambiant, Analyse par la méthode spectrophotométrique au thorin", *Standard X* 43-013, 8 p.

[5] AFNOR, (1974), "Analyse des gaz, Dosage du dioxyde de soufre, Guide pour le choix des méthodes de dosage", *Standard X* 20-350, 10 p.

[6] AFNOR, (1980), "Méthode d'analyse de l'oxygène basée sur les propriétés paramagnétiques de ce gaz", *Standard X* 20-377, 7 p.

[7] AFNOR, (1979), "Dosage de l'oxygène, Méthode électrochimique à électrolyte solide", *Standard X* 20-378, 4 p.

[8] AFNOR, (1979), "Dosage de l'oxygène, Méthodes électrochimiques à électrolyte liquide ou gélifié", *Standard X* 20-379, 6 p.

[9] AFNOR, (1986), "Méthode de mesurage de l'odeur d'un effluent gazeux, Détermination du facteur de dilution au seuil de perception", *Standard X* 43-101, 13 p.

[10] AFNOR, (1983), "Dosage du dioxyde de soufre dans l'air ambiant, Méthode par fluorescence UV", *Standard X* 43-019, 6 p.

[11] AFNOR, (1983), "Dosage du soufre total gazeux ou du dioxyde de soufre seul dans l'air ambiant, Méthode par spectrométrie de flamme", *Standard X* 43-020, 6 p.

[12] AFNOR, (1989), "Détermination du plomb dans les aérosols", *Standard X* 43-026 (provisional), 11 p.

[13] AFNOR, (1990), "Détermination du formaldehyde", *Standard X* 43-264 (draft), 19 p.

[14] K. Andersson et al., (1981), "Chemosorption sampling and analysis of formaldehyde in air", *Scand. J. Work Environm. Health*, **7,** 282-289.

[15] G. Andersson et al., (1979), "Chemosorption of formaldehyde on Amberlite XAD-2 coated with 2,4 dinitrophenylhydrazine", *Chemosphere*, **10,** 823-827.

[16] Anon., (1976), "Véhicules routiers, Dispositif pour le mesurage de l'opacité des gaz d'échappement des moteurs Diesel", *ISO Technical Report* No. 4011, 15 June, 18 p.

[17] Anon., (1980), "Standard for emission of particulate regulation for Diesel-fueled light duty vehicles and light duty trucks", *Federal Register*, **45** (45), 14496-14525.

[18] Anon., (1988), "Limitation des émissions de particules polluantes par les moteurs Diesel", *EEC Directive* 88/436, J. Officiel des Communautés Européennes; L. 214, 6 August, 17 p.

[19] Anon., (1986), "Olfaktometrie, Bestimmung der Geruchintensität", *VDI Richtlinien*, No. 3882, Blatt 1, 29 p.

[20] Anon., (1986), "Olfaktometrie, Bestimmung der hedonischen Geruchswirkung", *VDI Richtlinien*, No. 3882, Blatt 2, 23 p.

[21] R.R. Arnts and S.B. Tejada, (1989), "2,4 dinitrophenylhydrazine coated silica gel cartridge method for determination of formaldehyde in air, Identification of an ozone interference", *E.S.&T.*, **23,** 1428-1430.

[22] N.J. Barsic, (1984), "Variability of heavy-duty Diesel engine emissions for transient and 13-mode steady-state methods", *SAE Paper* No. 840346, 22 p.

[23] G. Baumbach, (1983), "Meßverfahren für Aldehyd Emissionen Verbrennungsabgasen", *Staub*,**43,** 95-101.

[24] R.K. Beasley et al., (1980), "Sampling of formaldehyde in air with coated solid sorbent and determination by high performance liquid chromatography", *Anal. Chem.*, **52,** 1110-1114.

[25] C. Beckmann et al., (1988), "Investigation of Diesel particle characteristics during sampling and conditioning", *J. Aerosol Sci.*, **19,** 1001-1004.

[26] M. Beltzer, (1979), "Real time, continuous measurement of automotive sulfuric acid emissions", *J. APCA*, **29,** 57-59.

[27] K. Bergmann and W. Schneider, (1982), "Gas chromatographic method to determine formaldehyde traces in automobile exhaust gases", *Chromatographia*, **15,** 631-634.

[28] D. Bicanic et al., (1989), "Recent developments in photoacoustic sensing of the atmospheric pollution by infrared lasers", in: *Man and His Ecosystem*, Vol. 3, L.J. Brasser, Elsevier Science Publications, Amsterdam, pp. 663-668.

[29] P. Bisgaard et al., (1983), "Quantitative determination of formaldehyde in air using the acetylacetone method", *Anal. Lett.*, **16,** 1457-1468.

[30] D. Boulaud and M. Diouri, (1988), "A new inertial and diffusional device (SDI 2000)", *J. Aerosol Sci.*, **19,** 927-930.

[31] K.W. Bühne, (1987), *Manuelle und automatische Verfahren zur Messung partikelförmiger Emissionen*, Messtechnik im Umweltschutz, pp. M28-M38.

[32] H. Cachier et al., (1989), "Thermal separation of soot carbon", *Aerosol Sci. Techn.*, **10**, 358-364.

[33] S.H. Cadle et al., (1979), "Measurements of unregulated emissions from General Motors' light duty vehicles", *SAE Paper* No. 790694, 21 p.

[34] A. Caridi et al, (1989), "Determination of atmospheric lead pollution of automotive origin", *Atmosph. Environm.*, **12,** 2855-2856.

[35] P. Carlier et al., (1986), "The chemistry of carbonyl compounds in the atmosphere, A review", *Atmosph. Environm.*, **20,** 2079-2099.

[36] W. Cartillieri and P. Tritthart, (1984), "Particulate analysis of light duty Diesel engines (IDI and DI) with particular reference to the lube oil particulate fraction", *SAE Paper* No. 840418, 16 p.

[37] N.P. Cernansky et al., (1978), "Diesel odor sampling and analysis using the Diesel odor analysis system (DOAS)", *SAE Paper* No. 780223, 12 p.

[38] N.P. Cernansky, (1983), "Diesel exhaust odor and irritants, A review", *J. APCA*, **33,** 97-104.

[39] S. Cha et al., (1988), "Continuous measurement of Diesel particulate emission", *J. APCA*, **38,** 252-257.

[40] E. Chambon et al., (1990), "Méthodes de mesure des suies et des températures dans la chambre de combustion d'un moteur Diesel IDI", SIA Int. Conf., Lyon, 13/14 June, *Paper* No. 90092, pp. 177-183

[41] J.L. Cheney and C.L. Walters, (1982), "Applications of aldehyde detection methods for source emission measurements", *Anal. Lett.*, **15,** 621-641.

[42] N. Collings et al., (1986), "Real time smoke sensor for Diesel engines", *SAE Paper* No. 860157, 5 p.

[43] G. Creech et al., (1982), "A comparison of three different high pressure liquid chromatographic systems for the determination of aldehydes and ketones in Diesel exhaust", *J. Chromat. Sci.*, **20,** 67-72.

[44] R.D. Cuthbertson et al., (1979), "The use of a thermogravimetric analyzer for the investigation of particulates and hydrocarbons in Diesel engine exhaust", *SAE Paper* No. 790814, 18 p.

[45] R.D. Cutherbertson et al., (1987), "Direct analysis of Diesel particulate-bound hydrocarbons by gas chromatography with solid sample injection", *SAE Paper* No. 870626, 12 p.

[46] H.L. Daudel et al., (1979), "Detection and instrumental analysis of Diesel engine exhaust gas odorants, A new approach to an old problem", *SAE Paper* No. 790489, 14 p.

[47] H.L. Daudel et al., (1983), "Progress in instrumental analysis of exhaust odorants", *SAE Paper* No. 830117, 14 p.

[48] A.G. Day, (1971), "Improved instrumentation for determination of exhaust gas oxygenate content", *NTIS Report* No. PB-210-251, 45 p.

[49] P. Degobert, (1978), "Pollution odorante par les moteurs diesel", *Revue Inst. Franç. du Pétrole*, 49-55. *Diesel exhaust odor measurements, Proc. 4th Int. Symp. on Automotive Propulsion Systems*, NATO, Washington DC, Vol. 2, pp. 566-581.

[50] P. Degobert, (1980), "Diesel odor offensive effect, True odor or irritancy?", *SAE Paper* No. 800423.

[51] P. Degobert, 1981, *Evaluation of Diesel odorous emissions, CEC Int. Symp.*, Roma, 3/5 June, 12 p.

[52] P. Degobert, (1988), *Emissions Diesel, Aspects physico-chimiques, 5ème Symp. Sur la Recherche en Matière de Pollution Atmosphérique*, Strasbourg, 22/25 March, 13 p.

[53] H.E. Dietzmann et al., (1979), "Analytical procedures for characterizing unregulated emissions from motor vehicles", *EPA Report* No. 600/2-79-017, 481 p.

[54] A. Dravnieks et al., 1970, "Chemical species in engine exhaust and their contribution to exhaust odor", *NTIS Report* No. PB-198072, 90 p.

[55] K.E. Egebäck and B.M. Bertillson, (1983), "Chemical and biological characterization of exhaust emissions from vehicles fueled with gasoline, alcohol, LPG and Diesel", *Report* No. snv pm 1635, National Swedish Environment Board.

[56] F.R. Faxwog and D.M. Roessler, (1979), "Optoacoustic measurements of Diesel particulate emissions", *J. Appl. Phys.*, **50,** 7880-7882.

[57] K. Fung and D. Grosjean, (1981), "Determination of nanogram amounts of carbonyls as 2,4 dinitrodiphenylhydrazones by high performance liquid chromatography", *Anal. Chem.*, **53,** 168-171.

[58] R.C. Geib, (1988), "Progress in measurement of vehicle exhaust components", *J. APCA*, **38,** 280-282.

[59] D.H. Gerke, (1983), "Real time measurement of Diesel particulate emissions with a light extinction opacity meter", *SAE Paper* No. 830183, 4 p.

[60] G.L. Green and D. Wallace, (1980), "Correlation studies of an in-line, full-flow opacimeter", *SAE Paper* No. 801373, 18 p.

[61] P.J. Groblicki and C.R. Begeman, (1979), "Particle size variation in Diesel car exhaust", *SAE Paper* No. 790421, 8 p.

[62] D. Grosjean and K. Fung, (1982), "Collection efficiencies of cartridges and microimpingers for sampling aldehydes in air as 2,4-dinitro phenyl hydrazones", *Anal. Chem.*, **54,** 1221-1224.

[63] M.J. Grubic et al., (1979), *Sampling and analysis of aldehydes and ketones in air by an HPLC derivative method, 178th ACS Meeting*, Washington, 9/14 September, 9 p.

[64] L.P. Haack et al., (1986), "Comparison of Fourier transform infrared spectroscopy and 2,4 dinitrophenylhydrazine impinger techniques for the measurement of formaldehyde in vehicle exhaust", *Anal. Chem.*, **58,** 68-72.

[65] R. Halsall et al., (1987), "An improved method for determining the hydrocarbon fraction of Diesel particulates by vacuum oven sublimation", *SAE Paper* No. 872136, 16 p.

[66] L.D. Hansen et al., (1986), "Determination of gas phase dimethyl sulfate and monomethyl hydrogen sulfate", *E.S.&T.*, **20,** 872-878.

[67] M.S. Harrenstien et al., (1979), "Determination of individual aldehyde concentrations in the exhaust of a spark ignited engine fueled by alcohol/gasoline blends", *SAE Paper* No. 790952, 10 p.

[68] W. Haunold et al., (1989), "Neuartiger Gaschromatograph zur Messung von $SO_2$ und reduzierten Schwefelgasen in Reinluftgebieten", *Staub*, **49,** 191-193.

[69] P. Herger et al., (1990), "Einsatz der Ionenchromatographie zur Immissionsanalyse von $SO_2$", *Staub*, **50,** 13-15.

[70] C.N. Hewitt and P.J. Metcalfe, (1989), "Sampling of gaseous alkyllead compounds using cryotrapping validation and field results", *Sci. Tot. Environm.*, **84,** 211-221.

[71] J.C. Hill and R.F. Majkowski, (1980), "Time resolved measurement of vehicle sulfate and methane emissions with tunable diode lasers", *SAE Paper* No. 800510, 8 p.

[72] Y. Hisamatsu et al., (1989), "Measurement of trace levels of atmospheric sulfur dioxide with a gold film sensor", *J. APCA*, **39,** 975-980.

[73] V.F. Hodge and M.O. Stallard, (1986), "Platinum and palladium in roadside dust", *E.S.&T.*, **20,** 1058-1060.

[74] G. Hong et al., (1987), "Diesel smoke transient control using a real time smoke sensor", *SAE Paper* No. 871629, 6 p.

[75] M. Igawa et al., (1989), "Analysis of aldehydes in cloud and fogwater samples by HPLC with a postcolumn reaction detector", *E.S.&T.*, **23,** 556-561.

[76] K. Ito and T. Yano, (1979), *Formaldehyde emissions from a spark ignition engine using methanol, 3rd Int. Symp. on Alcohol Fuel Technology*, Asilomar, California, 28/31 May, 12 p.

[77] S.M. Japar and A.C. Szkarlat, (1981), "Real time measurements of Diesel vehicle exhaust particulate using photoacoustic spectroscopy and total light extinction", *SAE Paper* No. 811184, 8 p.

[78] S.M. Japar and A.C. Szkarlat, (1981), "Measurement of Diesel vehicle exhaust particulate using photoacoustic spectroscopy", *Comb. Sci. Techn.*, **24,** 215-219.

[79] L. Johnson et al., (1981), "Determination of carbonyl compounds in automobile exhausts and atmospheric samples", *Int. J. Environm. Anal. Chem.*, **9,** 7-26.

[80] B. Juguet et al., (1984), "Étude de la fraction minérale de l'aérosol urbain à Paris, Bilan d'une surveillance prolongée", *Poll. Atmosph.*, 3-12.

[81] M. Katz, (1977), *Methods of air sampling and analysis*, American Public Health Association (Intersociety Committee), Washington, 984 p.

[82] D.A. Kendall, (1974), "Diesel exhaust odor analysis by sensory techniques", *SAE Paper* No. 740215, 12 p.

[83] N.J. Khatri et al., (1978), "The characterization of the hydrocarbon and sulfate fractions of Diesel particulate matter", *SAE Paper* No. 780111, 24 p.

[84] J.G. Killmann et al., (1985), "Instationäre Meßverfahren für Dieselabgase, Emissionsminderung Automobilgase, Dieselmotoren", *VDI Berichte*, (559), 297-317.

[85] W.S. Kim et al., (1980), "Solid sorbent tube sampling and ion chromatographic analysis of formaldehyde", *Am. Ind. Hyg. Assoc. J.*, **41,** 334-339.

[86] P. Kirschmer, (1989), "Aldehydmessungen in der Außenluft", *Staub*, **49,** 263-266.

[87] D.B. Kittelson and N. Collings, (1987), "Origin of the response of electrostatic particle probes", *SAE Paper* No. 870476 (SP. 693), 11 p.

[88] T.E. Kleindienst et al., (1988), "An intercomparison of formaldehyde measurement techniques at ambient concentration", *Atmosph. Environm.*, **22,** 1931-1939.

[89] A. König and H. Rohlfing, (1984), "Geruchsbelästigung durch Kfz-Abgase", *Staub*, **44,** 396-398.

[90] R. Kuntz et al., (1980), "Rapid determination of aldehydes in air analyses", *Anal. Lett.*, **13,** 1409-1415.

[91] K. Kuwata et al., (1983), "Determination of aliphatic aldehydes in air by liquid chromatography", *Anal. Chem.*, **55,** 2013-2016.

[92] K. Kuwata et al., (1979), "Determination of aliphatic and aromatic aldehydes in polluted airs as their 2,4 dinitrophenylhydrazones by high performance liquid chromatography", *J. Chromat. Sci.*, **17,** 264-268.

[93] K. Kuwata and S. Tanaka, (1988), "Liquid chromatographic determination of traces of phenols in air", *J. Chromatogr.*, **442,** 407-411.

[94] L. Le Bouffant, "Pollution atmosphérique (par les aérosols solides ou liquides), Appareils de prélèvement et de mesure", *Techn. de l'Ing.*, Vol. P.4.316, 16 p.

[95] J-O. Levin et al., (1985), "Determination of sub part per million levels of formaldehyde in air using active or passive sampling on 2,4 dinitrophenylhydrazine coated glass fiber filters and high performance liquid chromatography", *Anal. Chem.*, **57,** 1032-1035.

[96] J-O. Levin et al., (1989), "Monitoring of parts per billion levels of formaldehyde using a diffusive sampler", *J. APCA*, **39,** 44-47.

[97] S.P. Levine et al., (1981), "O-alkyloxime derivatives for gas chromatography and gas chromatographic mass spectrometric determination of aldehydes", *Anal. Chem.*, **53,** 805-809.

[98] P.L. Levins et al., (1974), "Chemical analysis of Diesel exhaust odor species", *SAE Paper* No. 740216, 11 p.

[99] K.H. Lies et al., (1983), "Particulate emissions from Diesel engines, Evaluation of measurement and results", *SAE Paper* No. 830455, 13 p.

[100] R.H. Linnell and W.E. Scott, (1962), "Diesel exhaust composition and odor studies", *J. APCA*, **12,** 510-515.

[101] F. Lipari and S.J. Swarin, (1982), "Determination of formaldehyde and other aldehydes in automobile exhaust with an improved 2,4 dinitrophenylhydrazine method", *J. Chromatogr.*, **247,** 297-306.

[102] F. Lipari and S.J. Swarin, (1985), "2,4 dinitrophenylhydrazine coated Fluorisil sampling cartridges for the determination of formaldehyde in air", *E.S.&T.*, **19,** 70-74.

[103] W.H. Lipkea et al., (1978), "The physical and chemical character of Diesel particulate emissions, Measurement techniques and fundamental considerations", *SAE Paper* No. 780108 (SP.430), 51 p.

[104] B. Lopez et al., (1987), "Emissions Diesel, Analyse des polluants non réglementés", *Poll. Atmosph.*, Special Issue November, pp. 113-123.

[105] D.V. McCalley et al., (1984), "Analysis of carboxylic acids by gas chromatography, Derivatization using chloroacetone", *Chromatographia*, **18,** 309-312.

[106] G. Madelaine, (1985), *Métrologie des aérosols submicroniques, 2ème Journées d'Études sur les Aérosols*, GAMS/COFERA, Paris, 5/6 November, 9 p.

[107] G. Maffiolo et al., (1988), "Development and testing of short response time $SO_2$, $NO_x$ and $O_3$ analyzers", *J. APCA*, **38,** 36-38.

[108] M.P. Maskarinec et al., (1981), "Determination of vapor phase carbonyls by high pressure liquid chromatography", *J. Liquid Chromatogr.*, **4,** 31-39.

[109] T.G. Matthews and T.C. Howell, (1981), "Visual colorimetric formaldehyde screening analysis for indoor air", *J. APCA*, **31,** 1181-1184.

[110] K.T. Menzies et al., (1982), "Comparison of aldehyde methods", *SAE Paper* No. 820965, 9 p.

[111] K.T. Menzies et al., (1984), "Development of sampling and analytical methods for toxicants in Diesel exhaust streams", *NTIS Report* No. PB84-196625, 155 p.

[112] N. Metz, (1984), "Personenwagen Abgasemissionen im Spurenbereich", *ATZ*, **86,** 425-430.

[113] N. Metz, (1987), "Round-robin testing for selected unregulated exhaust emissions", *SAE Paper* No. 871987, 14 p.

[114] G.J. Nebel, (1981), "Determination of total aliphatic aldehydes in auto exhaust by a modified 3 methyl 2 benzothiazolone hydrazone method", *Anal. Chem.*, **53,** 1708-1709.

[115] A. Obuchi et al., (1988), *The analysis of oxygen-containing compounds emitted from a Diesel powered engine fueled by low concentration methanol mixed fuel, 8th Int. Symp. on Alcohol Fuels*, Tokyo, 13/16 November, pp. 461-466.

[116] H. Osada et al., (1982), "Real time measurement of Diesel particulate emissions by the PAS method using a $CO_2$ laser", *SAE Paper* No. 820461 (P.107), 11 p.

[117] R. Otson and P. Fellin, (1988), "A review of techniques for measurement of airborne aldehydes", *Sci. Tot. Environm.*, **77,** 95-131.

[118] M. Pasquereau et al., (1983), "Détermination du formaldéhyde et des autres aldéhydes légers par chromatographie liquid haute performance (HPLC), Application au dosage dans les échappements de moteurs à combustion interne", *Inst. Franç. du Pétrole Report* No. 31 244, 18 p.

[119] M. Pasquereau and P. Degobert, (1984), "Améliorations apportées à la méthode HPLC de dosage des aldéhydes", *Inst. Franç. du Pétrole Report* No. 31 888, 5 p.

[120] H. Pataschnick and G. Rupprecht, (1980), *A new real time monitoring instrument for suspended particulate mass concentration, The TEOM, 179th ACS Meeting*, Div. Pet. Chem., Houston, 23/28 March, pp. 188-193.

[121] J.M. Perez et al., (1980), "Informational report on the measurement and characterization of Diesel exhaust emissions", *CRC Report* No. 517, 275 p.

[122] J.M. Perez et al., (1984), "Cooperative development of analytical methods for Diesel emissions and particulates, Solvent extractables, aldehydes, and sulfate methods", *SAE Paper* No. 840413, 20 p.

[123] J.M. Perez et al., (1987), "Chemical methods for the measurement of unregulated Diesel emissions, Carbonyls, aldehydes, particulate characterization, sulfates, PAH, $NO_2$PAH", *NTIS Report* No. PB88-107768, 60 p.

[124] R.S. Petrow et al., (1989), "Vehicle and engine dynamometer studies of $H_2S$ emissions using a semi-continuous analytical method", *SAE Paper* No. 890797, 10 p.

[125] C.B. Prakash and C. Wachmann, (1988), *Measurement of methanol emissions from automobiles using methanol/gasoline blend fuels, 8th Int. Symp. on Alcohol Fuels*, Tokyo, 13/16 November, pp. 467-472.

[126] C.J. Raible and F.W. Cox, (1979), "Chromatographic methods of analysis for methanol and ethanol in automotive exhaust", *SAE Paper* No. 790690, 7 p.

[127] V. Raman et al., (1986), "Morpholine as an absorbing agent for the determination of sulphur dioxide", *Analyst*, **111,** 189-192.

[128] A.R. Reading and G. Greeves, (1980), "Measurement of Diesel exhaust odorants and effect of engine variables", *SAE Paper* No. 800424, 13 p.

[129] A. Renoux, (1988), "Les aérosols dans notre environnement, Quelques idées sur leur mesure", *Poll. Atmosph.* (July/September), pp. 277-283.

[130] I. Roorda et al., (1982), "Dérivation précolonne d'acides carboxyliques à chaîne courte, Détection UV et électrochimique", *Analysis*, **10,** 409-412.

[131] F.G. Rounds and H.W. Pearsall, (1957), "Diesel exhaust odor, its evaluation and relation to exhaust gas composition", *SAE Trans.*, **65,** 608-627.

[132] SAE Recommended Practice, (1980), "Determination of sulfur compounds in automotive exhaust", *SAE* J1280, 19 p.

[133] SAE Recommended Practice, (1984), "Instrumentation and techniques for exhaust gas measurement", *SAE* J254, 14 p.

[134] SAE Information Report, (1978), "Diesel engine smoke measurement", *SAE* J255a, 8 p.

[135] K. Saito, (1988), "Development of Diesel opacimeter for real time measurement of low concentration smoke", *SAE Paper* No. 881319, 9 p.

[136] K. Saito and O. Shinozaki, (1990), "The measurement of Diesel particulate emissions with a tapered element oscillating microbalance and an opacimeter", *SAE Paper* No. 900644, 5 p.

[137] H.C. Scherrer et al., (1981), "Light absorption measurements of Diesel particulate matter", *SAE Paper* No. 810181, 7 p.

[138] D. Schuetzle et al., (1981), "Determination of sulfates in Diesel particulates", *Anal. Chem.*, **53,** 837-840.

[139] J. Scott McDonald et al., (1984), "Status of Diesel particulate measurement methods", *SAE Paper* No. 840345, 20 p.

[140] S.A. Shimpi and M.L. Yu, (1981), "Determination of a reliable and efficient Diesel particulate hydrocarbon extraction process", *SAE Paper* No. 811183, 7 p.

[141] P.R. Shore and R.D. Cuthbertson, (1985), "Application of a tapered oscillating microbalance to continuous diesel particulate measurement", *SAE Paper* No. 850405, 14 p.

[142] T. Smith-Palmer et al., (1989), "The identification of alkyl sulfates and sulfonates in atmospheric samples by ion chromatography", *Sci. Tot. Environm.*, **83,** 185-190.

[143] S.S. Stevens, (1948), "Sensation and phychological measurement", in: *Foundations of Psychology*, E.G. Boring, J. Wiley and Son, New York, Chapter 11.

[144] Y. Suzuki and S. Imai, (1982), "Determination of traces of gaseous acrolein by collection on molecular sieves and fluorimetry with o-aminobiphenyl", *Anal. Chim. Acta*, **136,** 155-162.

[145] T. Tanaka et al., (1981), *Measurement of aldehydes in automotive exhaust using high performance liquid chromatography, CRC Workshop*, Dearborn, Michigan, 4 March, 15 p.

[146] T. Tanaka et al., (1989), "Development of a measuring meter and a control device for Diesel white smoke", *SAE Paper* No. 892044, 9 p.

[147] S.B. Tejada, (1986), "Evaluation of silica gel cartridges coated in situ with acidified 2,4 dinitrophenylhydrazine for sampling aldehydes and ketones in air", *Int. J. Environm. Anal. Chem.*, **26,** 167-185.

[148] P. Tritthart and W. Cartillieri, (1977), "Ein Beitrag zur zuverlassigen Messung der aliphatischen Aldehyde in Motorabgasen", *MTZ*, **38,** 55-57 and 121-125.

[149] R.J. Tropp et al., (1980), "A new method for measuring the particle size distribution of aerosols", *Rev. Sci. Instr.*, **51,** 516-520.

[150] A. Turk, (1967), "Selection and training of judges for sensory evaluation of the intensity and character of Diesel exhaust odors", *Public Health Service Publication* No. 999-AP-32, 45 p.

[151] C.M. Urban and R.J. Garbe, (1979), "Regulated and unregulated exhaust emissions from malfunctioning automobiles", *SAE Paper* No. 790696, 18 p.

[152] S. Vainiotalo et al., (1983), "Sensitive liquid chromatographic method for the determination of formic acid in air samples", *J. Chromatogr.*, **258,** 207-211.

[153] P. Vanderstraeten et al., (1988), "A continuous quantitative detection method for total mercaptans, organic sulphides, $H_2S$ and $CS_2$ for odoriferous emissions", *J. APCA*, **38,** 1271-1274.

[154] F. Vanhobel et al., (1990), "Mesures de taille et de concentration massique de suies et particules générées par un véhicule diesel au cours d'un cycle normalisé", SIA Int. Conf., Lyon, 13/14 June, *Paper* No. 90089, pp. 109-114

[155] C. van Waas, (1978), "De gaschromatografische bepaling van $C_2$-$C_5$ alkanalen in lucht met gebruikmaking van een isolatie- en concentrieringsmethode op basis van bisulfiet-adductvorming", *TNO Report* No. H.399, 28 p.

[156] H. Wancura et al., (1986), "New dynamic particulate measuring system", *Document AVL DYPA* 480, 38 p.

[157] J.C.F. Wang et al., (1980), "A new real time isokinetic dust mass monitoring system", *J. APCA*, **30,** 1018-1021.

[158] M.A. Warner-Selph and J. de Vita, (1989), "Measurements of toxic exhaust emissions from gasoline powered light duty vehicles", *SAE Paper* No. 892075, 11 p.

[159] R. Whitby et al., (1985), "Second generation TEOM filters, Particulate mass comparisons between TEOM and conventional filtration techniques", *SAE Paper* No. 850403, 17 p.

[160] P.T. Williams et al., (1988), "A comparison of exhaust pipe, dilution tunnel and roadside Diesel particulate SOF and gaseous hydrocarbon emissions", *SAE Paper* No. 880351, 10 p.

[162] M. Wittenberg et al., (1985), "Analyse quantitative des hydrocarbures aromatiques polynucléaires dans l'environnement par spectrofluorimétrie Shpol'skii à 10 K, Méthodes de prélèvement et d'extraction des échantillons, Résultats quantitatifs", *Analysis*, **13,** 249-260.

[163] M. Adachi et al., (1992), "Automotive emission analyses using FTIR spectrophotometer", *SAE Paper* No. 920723, pp. 133-140.

# Mechanisms of pollutant formation in engines 10

## How to solve the problem

## 10.1 Introduction

Until recently, carbon dioxide was not considered a pollutant. Inside an engine, the complete combustion of motor fuels composed exclusively of carbon and hydrogen, would only generate $CO_2$ and $H_2O$, to the exclusion of any other harmful product. However, the very short time allowed for chemical oxidation processes to take place in combustion chambers, the lack of homogeneity in the carburetted mixtures, and the heterogeneity and rapid variations in temperature never allow the state of ideal thermodynamic equilibrium to be reached. This means that products of incomplete combustion are present in the exhaust, as well as sulfur compounds from the sulfur-bearing residues remaining in motor fuels. Added to these combustion products are nitrogen oxides formed by the high-temperature oxidation of the inert nitrogen present as a diluent in the air.

The pollutants emitted by internal combustion engines of the type listed in Chapter 3 are the same irrespective of the type of combustion considered, either spark ignition or compression ignition. However, the diesel engine, which operates by compression ignition, emits carbonaceous particulates that are virtually absent in gasoline-fueled engines.

Only the relative quantities emitted vary with the type of engine, its design, its internal geometry, and its running conditions. The orders of magnitude of the quantities emitted are given in Table 10.1 [111]. Two additional pollutants are sulfur oxides, which vary directly with the sulfur content (Chapter 11) of motor fuels, and aldehydes, which result from the use of alcohol fuels.

**Table 10.1** Average order of magnitude of pollutants emitted

| Pollutant | Concentration (ppm) | Relative quantity emitted (g/kg of motor fuel) |
|---|---|---|
| $NO_x$ | 500 to 1000 | 20 |
| CO | 10,000 to 20,000 | 200 |
| HC (ppm C) | 3000 | 25 |
| particulates | – | 2 to 5 |

Given the very short combustion period during an engine cycle and the heterogeneities of temperature and composition of the combustion mixture, the pollutant concentrations in the exhaust differ substantially from the values that can be calculated assuming that thermodynamic equilibrium is reached.

Table 10.2 compares the volumetric concentrations measured on a spark ignition engine with the same values for complete combustion at a fuel/air ratio of 1, which were calculated at equilibrium for two temperatures. For some pollutants (CO, organic compounds, particulates), destructive reactions take place simultaneously and in competition with the formative reactions, even in the combustion chamber.

**Table 10.2** Equilibrium concentrations and actual concentrations

| Product | Equilibrium r = 1 500°C | Equilibrium r = 1 800°C | Engine r = 1 |
|---|---|---|---|
| CO (%) | $2.6 \cdot 10^{-10}$ | $2.6 \cdot 10^{-5}$ | 0.5 to 1 |
| HC (ppm) | 0 | 0 | 200 to 700 |
| NO (ppm) | $3 \cdot 10^{-3}$ | 0.13 | 800 to 2000 |

The most important variable governing pollutant emissions is the air/fuel ratio or its inverse, the fuel/air ratio of the carburetted mixture, which directly affects the relative emissions of CO, NO, aldehydes, and unburnt hydrocarbons (Fig. 10.1). Lean mixtures generate low emissions of CO and HC, provided that lean burning does not cause such a deterioration in combustion that misfiring allows the unburnt fuel to leave the exhaust system unchanged.

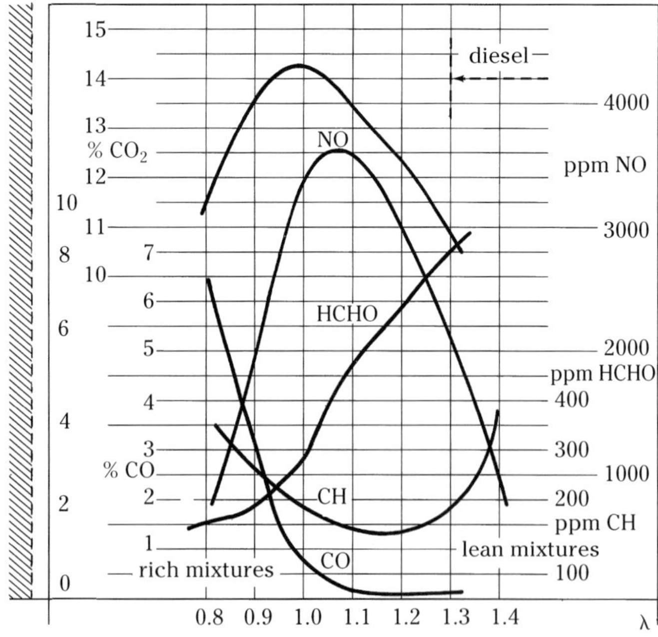


**Fig 10.1** Pollutants as a function of air/fuel ratio

## 10.2 Formation of nitrogen oxides

Nitric oxide (NO) and nitrogen dioxide ($NO_2$) are usually grouped together as $NO_x$, in which NO largely predominates. The main source of NO is molecular nitrogen in the air used as a comburent feeding the engine. Gasoline and diesel fuels contain too little nitrogen for their contribution to NO formation to be significant. Only heavy fuel oils can emit a small proportion of 'fuel NO' in the exhaust [192]; they may contain a few thousandths of parts of nitrogen by mass and are used in marine diesel engines. The mechanism of NO formation from atmospheric nitrogen is that of Zeldovitch. In the neighborhood of stoichiometry, the main reactions leading to the formation (and destruction) of NO are the following:

$$O + N_2 \Leftrightarrow NO + N \tag{10.1}$$

$$N + O_2 \Leftrightarrow NO + O \tag{10.2}$$

$$N + OH \Leftrightarrow NO + H \tag{10.3}$$

This reaction (10.3) takes place mainly in a very rich mixture. NO is formed both in the flame front and in the gas leaving the flame. In engines, where combustion takes place under high pressure, the reaction zone in the flame is very thin (about 0.1 mm) and short-lived. Moreover, the pressure in the cylinder rises during combustion, with the effect of raising the burnt gases to a higher temperature than the one reached immediately after combustion. This is why, except in areas with a high fuel/air ratio, only a small part of the NO is generated in the flame and most of it is formed in the gases leaving the flame. Hence, the NO combustion and formation processes occur independently. Except with very high dilutions, one can therefore ignore NO formation in the flame in favor of its formation in the burnt gases [111].

The formation of NO depends very strongly on the temperature, as shown by Fig. 10.2, which gives, for different temperatures, the degree of advancement of the reaction:

$$N_2 + O_2 \Rightarrow 2NO \tag{10.4}$$

based on the time scale of an engine [221]. The NO formation reactions are in all cases slower than the combustion reactions, which explains the non-equilibrium values of the concentrations measured in the exhaust. It is also highly dependent on the oxygen concentration.

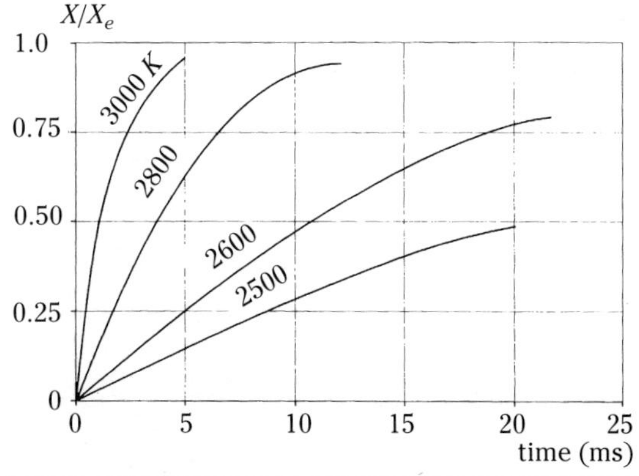


**Fig 10.2** Effect of temperature on advancement of the reaction $N_2 + O_2 \Leftrightarrow 2NO$ [221]

Accordingly, a high temperature and high oxygen concentration increase the quantities of NO produced [111].

## 10.2.1 Formation of nitrogen dioxide

The chemical equilibrium calculations indicate that, in the burnt gases, with the temperatures routinely prevailing in the flames, the $NO_2$ concentration should be negligible in comparison with NO [111]. This is effectively the case in spark ignition engines. In diesel engines, however, up to 30% of the $NO_x$ is found in the form of $NO_2$ [114]. One explanation of the persistence of $NO_2$ is that the NO formed in the flame can be converted rapidly to $NO_2$ by reactions of the type:

$$NO + HO_2 \Rightarrow NO_2 + OH \tag{10.5}$$

$NO_2$ is then reconverted to NO by the reaction:

$$NO_2 + O \Rightarrow NO + O_2 \tag{10.6}$$

unless the $NO_2$ formed in the flame is quenched by mixing with a colder fluid. Prolonged idling of a gasoline engine thus produces a great deal of $NO_2$ [157]. This also occurs at low load in the diesel engine, when many cold zones exist that can inhibit the reconversion of $NO_2$ to NO [114]. The dioxide is also formed in the exhaust at low speed where the gases reside longer in the presence of oxygen [158]. Fig. 10.3 shows the percentage of $NO_2$ with respect to total $NO_x$ in a diesel exhaust as a function of speed and load. This percentage depends on the speed and it is also higher at low load. In the spark ignition engine, for a fuel/air ratio of 0.85, this ratio does not exceed 2%.

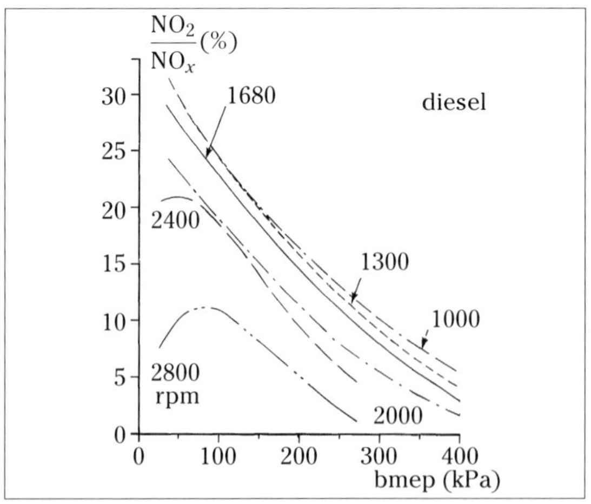


**Fig 10.3** Proportion of $NO_2$ emitted by a diesel engine at different loads and speeds [111]

### 10.2.2 Formation of nitrous oxide

In the gas phase, nitrous oxide ($N_2O$) is formed mainly from the intermediates NH and NCO when they react with NO [56]:

$$NH + NO \Rightarrow N_2O + H \tag{10.7}$$

$$NCO + NO \Rightarrow N_2O + CO \tag{10.8}$$

Hence, this formation mechanism is limited to the oxidation zone. The hydrogen atom concentration there is always high and causes intense destruction of the nitrous oxide by the following reactions:

$$N_2O + H \Rightarrow NH + NO \tag{10.9}$$

$$N_2O + H \Rightarrow N_2 + OH \tag{10.10}$$

This is why the combustion of the premixed gas mixture in a spark ignition engine emits very little $N_2O$, around 3 to 8 ppmV [217]. Diesel engines produce nitrous oxide emissions of the same order of magnitude.

### 10.2.3 Spark ignition engine

The most widespread spark ignition engine types are characterized by the presence in the combustion chamber of a mixture of fuel and air (possibly with the addition of recycled burnt gases), which is homogenized in the intake system during the intake phase. During the pressure increase caused by combustion, the concentrations of NO formed in the burnt gas zones at high temperature are fixed. However, when the temperature drops due to expansion, the concentrations of NO rise to a value far above the equilibrium values corresponding to the exhaust conditions. The actual concentrations are in the neighborhood of the NO concentration peak appearing during expansion, but these values are influenced by the operating conditions of the engine and also by delayed or early combustion of the mixture. In lean mixtures, freezing occurs early in the expansion stroke and little NO decomposition occurs. With rich mixtures, freezing occurs later in the expansion stroke after the charge is fully burned and substantial NO decomposition occurs. As a result, $NO_x$ emissions are generally less sensitive to changes in engine operating conditions with rich mixtures than they are with lean mixtures [141].

The highest NO contribution results from the fractions that are the first to burn. In the absence of strong turbulence, the highest NO concentrations are created in the neighborhood of the spark plug. An NO concentration gradient can thus be observed in the combustion chamber, corresponding to the temperature gradient.

The most important factors governing NO emissions are the fuel/air ratio, the fraction of burnt gases within the unburnt mixture in the cylinder, and the ignition timing. Compared with these parameters, the usual variations in the properties of the fuel make only a negligible contribution.

### 10.2.3.1 Effect of fuel/air ratio

Figure 10.1 has already illustrated the effect of variations in fuel/air ratio on NO emissions. The maximum temperatures of the burnt gases correspond to a fuel/air ratio of about 1.1, a slightly rich mixture. In these conditions, however, the oxygen concentrations are low. As the fuel/air ratio drops, the effect of the increase in the oxygen partial pressure counteracts the temperature drop of the burnt gases, which tends to reduce the formation of NO. The NO emission peak thus appears for a fuel/air ratio of about 0.9, which is a slightly lean mixture. However, if the excess air increases and the mixture becomes leaner to beyond the maximum NO, the drop in the flame temperature slows down the rates of the formation reactions (10.1) and (10.2), as well as the formation of atomic nitrogen from molecular nitrogen. This explains the decrease in $NO_x$ emissions in a lean mixture [85].

During expansion the NO concentrations are frozen more rapidly in a lean mixture, whereas, in a rich mixture, significant decomposition of NO occurs from the maximum concentration peak.

### 10.2.3.2 Effect of the 'burnt gases' fraction

Before combustion, the mixture in the combustion chamber contains air, vaporized fuel, and burnt gases. These burnt gases are residual gases from the previous combustion cycle, or burnt gases intentionally recycled to control the $NO_x$ emissions. The value of the residual gas fraction depends on the load, the valve settings, and particularly on the valve overlap. A higher overlap increases the dilution of the feed and decreases the NO emissions [17]. To a lesser extent, the residual gas fraction also depends on the engine speed, the fuel/air ratio, and the volumetric compression ratio. The reduction of the latter also causes a drop in NO emissions [17].

The burnt gases act as a diluent for the carburetted mixture and the temperature reached after combustion varies inversely with the quantity of burnt gases. This is why increasing the fraction of burnt gases reduces $NO_x$ emissions. However, the combustion rate is simultaneously reduced and an excessively large burnt fraction causes running instabilities.

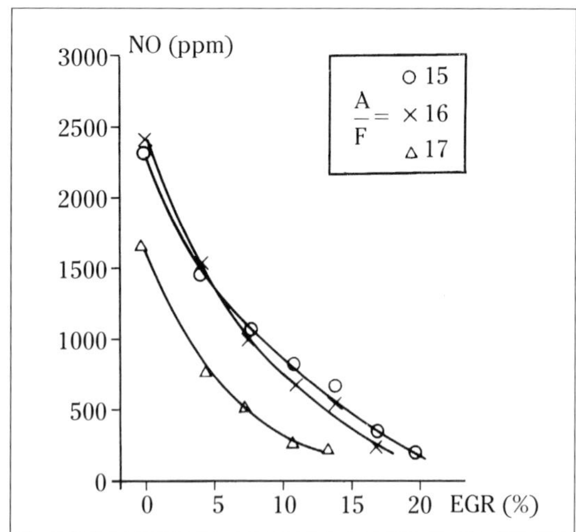


**Fig 10.4** NO concentration in the exhaust as a function of % EGR, Spark ignition engine, 1600 rpm, Volumetric efficiency 50%, Minimum advance for the best torque [111]

Figure 10.4 shows the effect of the burnt gas recirculation rate, commonly called the EGR, on the NO concentration at the exhaust for different fuel/air ratios. Significant reductions are achieved in emissions up to 15 to 20% EGR, a maximum permissible rate for an engine under partial load. The cause of the reduction of the flame temperature resulting from dilution by burnt gases is the increase in the heat capacity of the feed present in the cylinder at the temperature prevailing during combustion. The reaction of the mass of $NO_x$ emitted at the exhaust increases with the volumetric specific heat of the diluent gas selected, around 300°C, from $CO_2$, water vapor to argon, while the exhaust gases lie slightly below the latter two [218].

However, excessive dilution deteriorates combustion quality resulting in partial combustion and even misfiring. While complying with a minimum specific fuel consumption, the lowest NO emissions are obtained for stoichiometric carburetted mixtures, with the maximum EGR compatible without deteriorating combustion quality. Hence, electronic control of the optimal EGR percentage for each engine running configuration is the ideal solution.

#### 10.2.3.3 Effect of ignition timing

Ignition timing strongly influences the level of NO emissions. Increasing the advance causes combustion earlier in the cycle and raises the value of the pressure peak. This is because a larger fraction of the fuel is burned before top dead center and the pressure peak approaches TDC where the cylinder volume is smaller. Higher peak cylinder pressures result in higher peak temperatures for burned gas and the burnt gases remain longer at high temperature. These two conditions promote the formation of NO [117]. By contrast, a decrease in advance reduces the height of the pressure peak, because most of the fuel burns after the top dead center.

Thus, ignition advance favors NO emissions. Under average engine speed and load conditions, on a mass-produced engine, an advance reduction of 10 crankshaft degrees can cut NO emissions at constant power by about 20 to 30% [221]. This is shown in Fig. 10.5 for different fuel/air ratios.

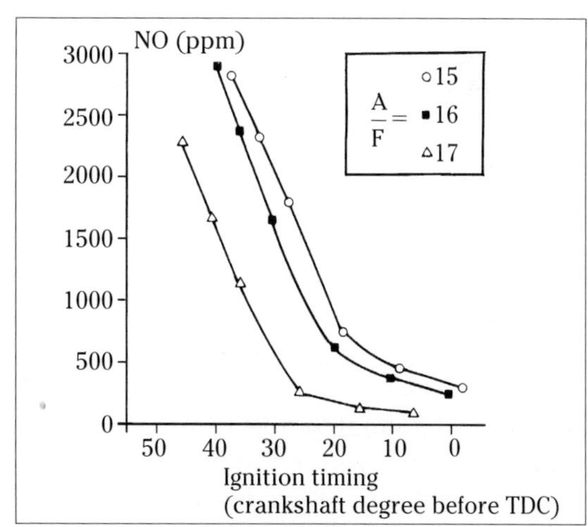


**Fig 10.5** NO concentration at the exhaust as a function of spark retard, Spark ignition engine, 1600 rpm, Volumetric efficiency 50%, Minimum advance for the best torque for the points on the left-hand end of the curves [111]

On the ECE cycle, variations in emissions of 0.3 g/test of NO per crankshaft degree were measured [173]. The ignition delay, by increasing the exhaust temperature, also favors the post-combustion of the hydrocarbons, but to the detriment of consumption and specific power [196].

### 10.2.4 Diesel engine

The difference from the spark ignition engine stems from the fact that the fuel is injected into the cylinder just before combustion is initiated and the heterogeneous distribution of the fuel during combustion gives rise to a heterogeneity of temperature and composition in the burnt gases. Diesel combustion comprises two phases: a combustion phase in a pre-mixed flame, immediately after the ignition delay, followed by a diffusional flame phase. In a pre-mixed flame, the composition of the mixture varies considerably about stoichiometry. In the diffusional flame, the mixture remains closer to stoichiometry.

As in the case of the spark ignition engine, the maximum temperature reached governs the formation of NO. The proportion of the mixture that burns earliest in the combustion process has a great influence, because, when it is subsequently compressed it is raised to a higher temperature and thus increases the NO that formed. These gases are then expanded in the power stroke phase and mixed with air or colder burnt gases, which freeze the NO concentrations formed. The presence of cold air in the combustion chamber is specific to diesel combustion and explains why the quenching of the NO compositions occurs faster in diesel than in spark ignition and why the NO there shows a lesser tendency to decompose.

The measurements show that nearly all the NO is formed in the 20 crankshaft degrees that follow the initiation of combustion. When injection is delayed, combustion starts later, together with NO formation. The concentrations reached are, in this case, lower, because the temperature peak is lower. This delayed injection is applied to large stationary engines to meet regulation limits by halving the NO emissions at the cost of slightly higher consumption [144]. The nitrogen oxide concentrations also increase with the average fuel/air ratio (Fig. 10.6). This decrease in the levels of NO with fuel/air ratio is less than that for a spark ignition engine due to the non-uniform distribution of the fuel in diesel combustion. In diesel combustion, since the fuel/air ratio increases directly with the quantity of fuel injected, the NO emissions are roughly proportional to this quantity of fuel [111]. At high load, which implies higher pressure peaks, the NO level rises.

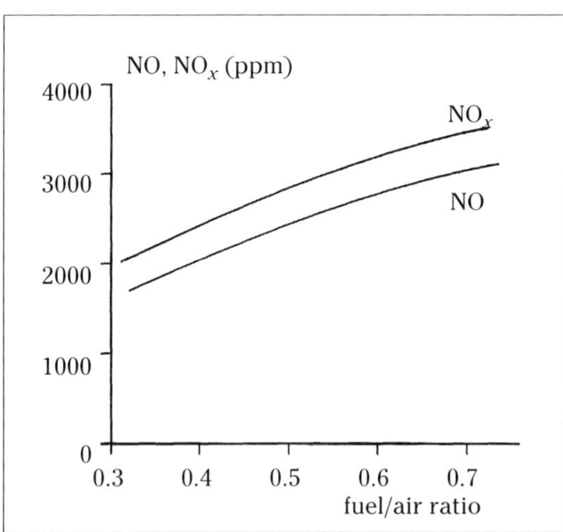


**Fig 10.6** $NO_x$ and NO concentrations in the exhaust as a function of overall equivalence ratio, Direct injection diesel engine, 1000 rpm, Ignition timing 27 degrees before top dead center [111]

The modeling of an indirect injection engine [171] shows that a small proportion of NO is formed in the main chamber (≈35%) and most (≈65%) in the pre-combustion chamber. Except at low load, combustion takes place in an overall rich medium, causing the formation of additional NO at the time when the rich combustion products are diluted [171]. Substantial decomposition has little time to occur in the rich mixture of the pre-combustion chamber, because the NO is then transferred to the main combustion chamber, where the NO conversion reactions are rapidly frozen upon the rapid mixing with cold air. This quenching of the concentrations occurs at about 15 crankshaft degrees after the top dead center.

As with the spark ignition engine, the diluents—especially the EGR—reduce the NO emissions by lowering the temperature of the burnt gases. In the diesel engine, however, this effect depends more on the load. At high load, the exhaust contains a large proportion of $CO_2$ and water vapor, substances with high heat capacity, whereas at low load, mainly atmospheric nitrogen is produced, with lower specific heat.

On the other hand, an increase in the partial pressure causes a rise in the flame temperature and hence NO emissions. This occurs in turbo-charged engines.

## 10.3 Formation of carbon monoxide

The formation of CO is an essential intermediate step in the hydrocarbon oxidation process leading to the final product $CO_2$ [221]:

$$RH \Rightarrow R \Rightarrow RO_2 \Rightarrow RCHO \Rightarrow RCO \Rightarrow CO \tag{10.11}$$

where R represents the hydrocarbon radical. The CO formed is then oxidized at a slower rate to $CO_2$ by the reaction:

$$CO + OH \Leftrightarrow CO_2 + H \tag{10.12}$$

The fuel oxidation rate depends on the available oxygen concentrations, the temperature of the gases, and the time left for the reaction to take place, that is on the engine speed.

The main parameter governing CO emissions is the fuel/air ratio of the carburetted mixture (Fig. 10.1). In a rich mixture, the CO concentrations increase steadily with the fuel/air ratio and the lack of oxygen causes incomplete combustion. A first approximation of the CO concentration in the gases is given by the equilibrium of the 'water gas' reaction:

$$CO + H_2O \Leftrightarrow H_2 + CO_2 \tag{10.13}$$

for a temperature of about 1600 to 1700 K. The freezing of the reaction at these temperatures corresponds to an equilibrium constant:

$$K = \frac{[CO][H_2O]}{[CO_2][H_2]} \tag{10.14}$$

of about 3.5 to 3.8 [221]. In a lean mixture, the CO concentrations are low and vary only slightly with the fuel/air ratio, but they are nevertheless higher than those predictable by kinetic models [111]. This could be due to incomplete oxidation during the expansion phase of the hydrocarbons desorbed from the deposits, the oil films, or the crevices of the combustion chamber [111].

### 10.3.1 Spark ignition engine

Spark ignition engines run at partial load near a fuel/air ratio of 1 and in a rich mixture at full load and when starting if the choke is used. Under these conditions, CO emissions are significant. However, the CO levels in the spark ignition engine exhaust are always lower than the maximum values present in the combustion chamber.

The means applied so far to reduce CO emissions consist in improving the uniformity of the composition of the carburetted mixture and in making the intake mixture leaner. In multi-cylinder engines in particular, the dispersion in the fuel/air ratio between cylinders is one cause of increased CO emissions. In addition, during the transient acceleration and deceleration phases, more accurate control of the quantity of fuel introduced reduces the CO emitted.

### 10.3.2 Diesel engine

Since the diesel engine always runs on an overall lean mixture, CO emissions are much lower than those of the gasoline engine. However, due to the heterogeneity of the mixture, i.e. local oxygen deficiencies, temperature levels or residence times that are insufficient to complete the combustion in the form of $CO_2$ can cause CO emissions. This could occur at low load and at maximum loads at high speed.

## 10.4 Formation of unburnt hydrocarbons

The emission of unburnt hydrocarbons, or organic substances in general, results from the incomplete combustion of the hydrocarbons. Contrary to CO and $NO_x$, which are formed in a homogeneous phase at high temperature in the fluid, the hydrocarbons result from heterogeneous effects in the mixture and in the neighborhood of the cylinder walls, hence at lower temperature. As already shown in Chapters 3 and 8, they are expressed as total hydrocarbons in ppm carbon as indicated by FID instruments.

Unburnt hydrocarbons include a wide variety of hydrocarbons (Table 10.3) which are harmful at varying degrees to human health (Chapter 4) or have different reactivities in the tropospheric chemical conversions. In particular, unburnt HC contains a large proportion of methane, which is inert in this respect. Added to these actual hydrocarbons are oxygenated compounds that are often more reactive, aldehydes, ketones, phenols, alcohols (methanol, ethanol), nitromethane, and esters (methyl formate). While carbonyl compounds account for only a few percent of the HC emissions of a spark ignition engine, aldehydes can range to up to 10% of HC emissions in diesel engines and among these aldehydes, formaldehyde represents 20% of the total carbonyl compounds.

**Table 10.3** Example of distribution of hydrocarbon classes in exhaust gases [111]

| Carbon, percent of total HC | | | |
|---|---|---|---|
| **paraffins** | **olefins** | **acetylenics** | **aromatics** |
| 33 | 27 | 8 | 32 |

The residues left by the flame after combustion of the carburetted mixture do not represent the major source of unburnt hydrocarbons measured in the exhaust. As shown by Fig. 10.7, which represents the concentrations of different classes of HC measured at the wall of a single-cylinder engine as a fraction of crankshaft rotation as soon as the flame has passed, the concentrations fall far below the values measured at the exhaust. Later in the cycle, these concentrations rise, suggesting that, while the carburetted mixture near the walls is totally oxidized, other sources of fuel, which have escaped the main combustion reaction, contribute to the emissions [168].

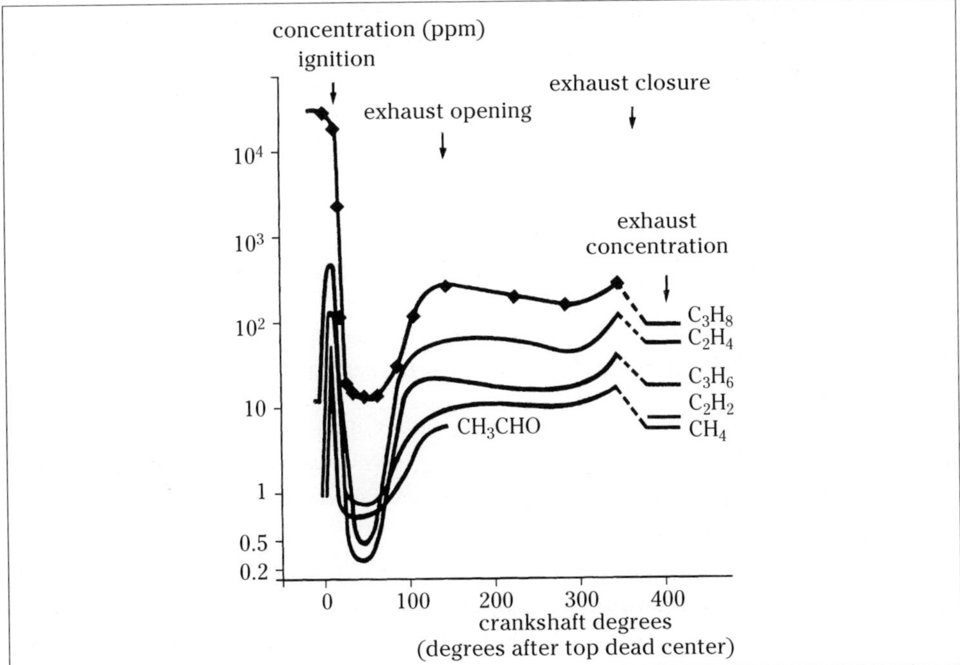


**Fig 10.7** Concentrations of unburnt hydrocarbons during the cycle [168]

### 10.4.1 Flame quench mechanism

The quenching of the combustion flame or its extinction occurs on the walls of the combustion chamber. The cylinder liners, cooled by the liquid of the cooling system, act like a well absorbing the heat of the gaseous mixture and recombining the free radicals generated in the flame. Quenching of the flame can occur under various conditions: the flame may be propagated perpendicularly or obliquely with respect to the chamber wall and it may also be 'jammed' at the inlet of a crevice (a small dead volume communicating with the combustion chamber via a bottleneck, like the top-land volume lying between the piston crown and the cylinder wall) (Fig. 10.8).

When the flame is quenched, it abandons a thin layer of unburnt or partially burnt mixture on the different surfaces present (cylinder head, piston, cylinder, valves) and in the crevices (e.g. groove of first ring, piston crown).

The thickness of this quench zone depends on various factors: temperature and pressure of the gas mixture, density, flame propagation speed, thermal conductivity, specific heat, surface texture and presence of deposits, wall temperature. Empirical correlations help to calculate, at least for light hydrocarbons, the minimum dimensions of the crevices that still allow the flame to propagate [111].

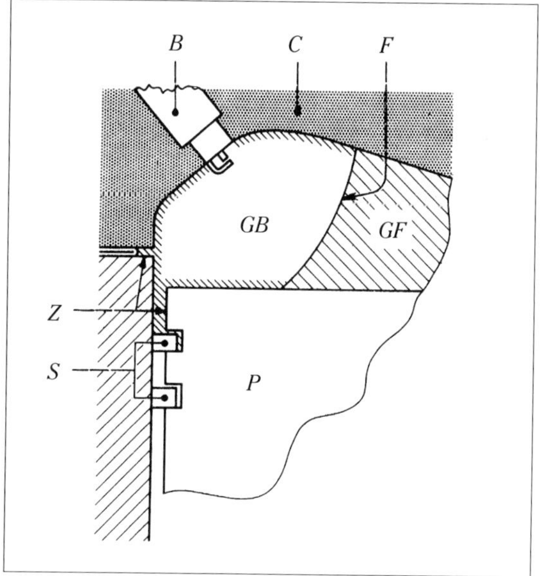


| | | | |
|---|---|---|---|
| *B* | spark plug | *GF* | fresh gases |
| *C* | cylinder head | *P* | piston |
| *F* | flame front | *S* | rings |
| *GB* | burnt gases | *Z* | flame jamming zones |

**Fig 10.8** Formation of unburnt hydrocarbons by quenching at the wall [221]

Flame quenching involves two steps. In the first phase, the flame is extinguished when the heat absorbed by the walls balances the heat generated by the flame. A few ms after quenching, the chemical species thus 'frozen' are diffused and oxidized, reducing the concentrations far below their values reached during quenching. Moreover, the hydrocarbons that have escaped the primary oxidation process, due to jamming of the flame, will still be able to undergo subsequent oxidation during the expansion and exhaust strokes.

The oil layer coating the walls of the chamber will also be able to trap hydrocarbons, especially those of the fuel before inflammation, and to desorb them in the burnt gases at the time of expansion. This absorption/desorption mechanism could be a substantial source of exhaust hydrocarbons.

## 10.4.2 Chemical mechanisms of the formation of unburnts

Oxidation of the hydrocarbons up to $CO_2$ requires a number of elementary steps, which involve the radicals resulting from oxygen and hydrocarbons and which generate incomplete oxidation products [115]. The alkyl radicals ($R^\bullet$), which are important factors in the propagation of free radical chains, are formed by splitting of the C−C and C−H bonds of the hydrocarbons. The oxygen behaves as a bi-radical to form a hydroperoxide radical ($HO_2^\bullet$):

$$R{-}H + {}^\bullet O{-}O^\bullet \Rightarrow R^\bullet + HO_2^\bullet \tag{10.15}$$

The alkyl radicals ($R^\bullet$) react easily with oxygen to give the alkyl peroxide radical:

$$R^\bullet + O_2 \Rightarrow RO_2^\bullet \tag{10.16}$$

This is the initial step in the formation of a chemical bond between the hydrocarbons and the oxygen. The following steps involve a number of repeated free radical reactions which, combined with various dehydrogenation and isomerization reactions, ultimately produce the different forms of oxygenated organics.

### 10.4.2.1 Formation of aldehydes

The $RO_2^\bullet$ radical undergoes hydrogen migration, followed by decomposition to a hydroxy radical and aldehyde:

$$RCH_2OO^\bullet \Rightarrow RC^\bullet HOOH \Rightarrow RCHO + {}^\bullet OH \tag{10.17}$$

The alcoxy radical ($RO^\bullet$) formed during the thermal decomposition of a peroxide of the ROOH type gives an aldehyde in the case of a secondary radical, by splitting of a C−C bond and rearrangement:

$$RR'CHO^\bullet \Rightarrow RCHO + R'^\bullet \tag{10.18}$$

and, in the case of a primary alcoxy radical, an aldehyde radical that can react with oxygen:

$$RCH_2O^\bullet + O_2 \Rightarrow RCHO + HO_2^\bullet \tag{10.19}$$

### 10.4.2.2 Formation of ketones

If, in a reaction similar to reaction (10.17), a secondary $RO_2^\bullet$ radical is involved, a ketone is obtained:

$$RR'CHOO^\bullet \Rightarrow RC^\bullet OOH \Rightarrow RR'C{=}O + {}^\bullet OH \tag{10.20}$$

and, in the case of a tertiary radical:

$$RR'R''COO^\bullet \Rightarrow RR'C{=}O + R''O^\bullet \tag{10.21}$$

#### 10.4.2.3 Formation of alcohols

The $RO^{\bullet}$ radicals can abstract a hydrogen from a hydrocarbon to form an alcohol:

$$RO^{\bullet} + R'H \Rightarrow ROH + R'^{\bullet} \tag{10.22}$$

#### 10.4.2.4 Formation of organic acids

The acyl radical ($RCO^{\bullet}$) is formed by the removal of hydrogen and direct decomposition of the aldehydes. Although it decomposes easily to give CO and an $R^{\bullet}$ radical, it can combine with oxygen to give an acid radical:

$$RCO^{\bullet} + O_2 \Rightarrow RCO_3^{\bullet} \tag{10.23}$$

This peroxide radical ($RCO_3^{\bullet}$) can give peracids by abstracting a hydrogen from a hydrocarbon:

$$RCO_3^{\bullet} + R'H \Rightarrow RCO_3H + R'^{\bullet} \tag{10.24}$$

The peracid can be decomposed to a carboxyl radical ($RCO_2^{\bullet}$):

$$RCO_3H \Rightarrow RCO_2^{\bullet} + {}^{\bullet}OH \tag{10.25}$$

which, by abstracting a hydrogen from a hydrocarbon, gives a carboxylic acid:

$$RCO_2^{\bullet} + R'H \Rightarrow RCO_2H + R'^{\bullet} \tag{10.26}$$

### 10.4.3 Spark ignition engine

Gasoline engine exhausts routinely contain 1000 to 3000 ppmC. This corresponds to about 1 to 2.5% of the fuel fed to the engine [111]. As shown by Fig. 10.1, HC emissions increase rapidly with rising fuel/air ratio. If the mixture is too lean, however, HC emissions increase as the fuel/air ratio decreases sharply due to deteriorated combustion and even misfiring of a number of engine cycles. Several mechanisms, illustrated in Fig. 10.9, contribute to the formation of unburnt HC in a spark ignition engine:

- Quenching of the flame on the walls of the combustion chamber leaves a layer of unburnt carburetted mixture on their surface.
- The carburetted mixture filling the crevice volumes escapes the primary combustion process when the flame is jammed at the inlet of the corresponding crevice.
- The fuel vapors absorbed during the intake and compression strokes, which are in the film coating the walls of the chamber, are desorbed in the form of vapor during expansion and exhaust.
- Incomplete combustion occurs in a fraction of the engine cycles (partial combustion or ignition defect) when combustion is deteriorated due to fuel/air ratio, ignition timing, or EGR maladjustments, in particular during accelerations and decelerations.

Deposits in the combustion chamber can also further increase emissions by altering the above mechanisms. All these processes (except ignition defects) yield high concentrations of unburnt HC near the walls and not throughout the volume of the chamber. In the exhaust phase, two successive HC concentration peaks can be observed, the first corresponding to the expulsion of most of the HC with the main mass of burnt gases, and the second appearing at the end of the exhaust phase, upon the desorption of the final traces of HC in a gas stream that has become very small [111].

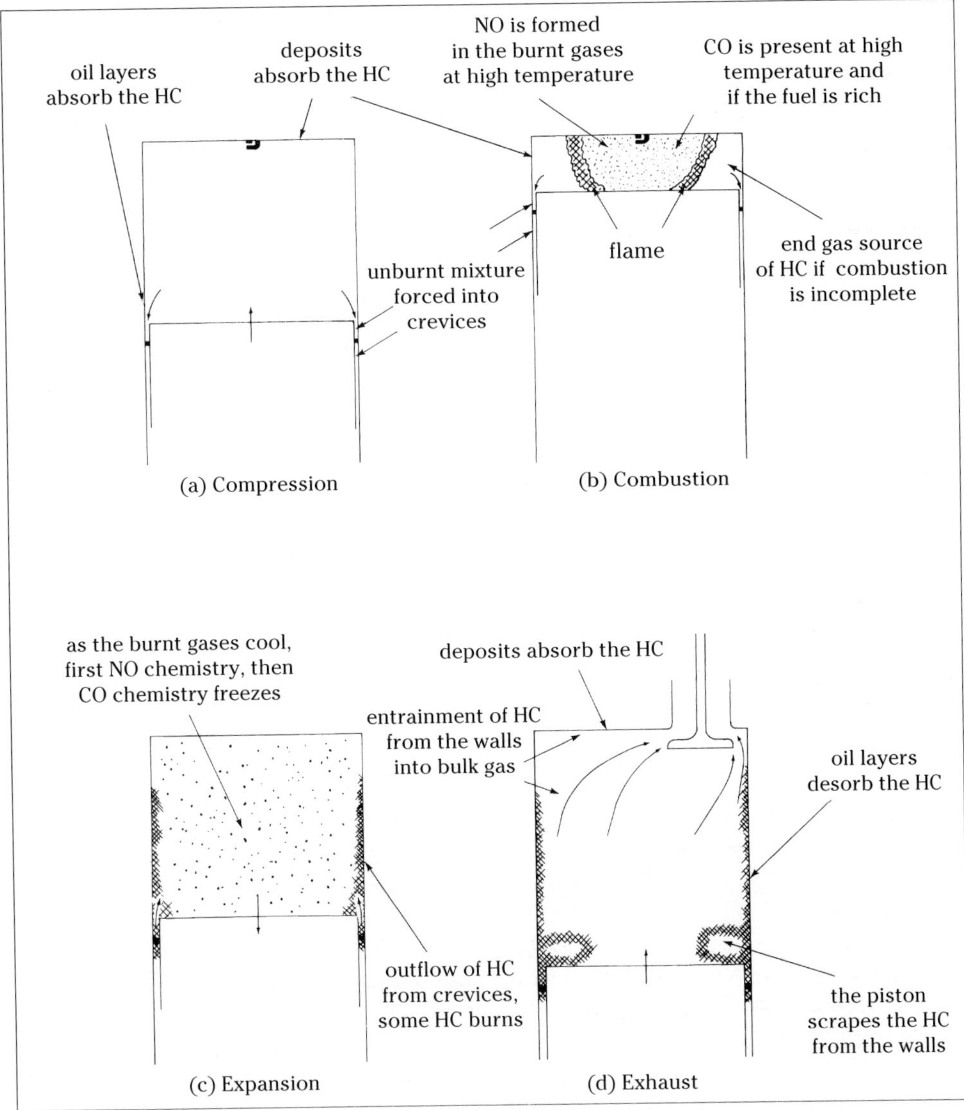


**Fig 10.9** Schematic sources of HC, NO and CO in a four-stroke spark ignition engine [111]

### 10.4.3.1 Flame quenching on the walls

The thickness of the flame quench layer varies between 0.05 and 0.4 mm and is thicker at low load. It contains aldehydes, such as HCHO and $CH_3CHO$, indicating that it is the seat of an oxidation reaction at low temperature. However, these species diffuse into the mass of burnt gases where they are mostly oxidized. The surface texture of the walls of the combustion chamber can affect the level of unburnt HC. Polishing the cylinder walls can cut HC emissions by 14%, compared with those obtained with as-cast walls [272]. The deposits have a similar effect to these rough-textured walls.

### 10.4.3.2 Influence of crevices

Crevices are considered to be the main source of unburnt HC [47 and 193]. The main interstitial volumes (Fig. 10.10) are found between the piston, the rings, and the cylinder wall. Other dead volumes are found in the threads of the spark plug screw pitch, in the space around the central electrode of the spark plug, around the intake and exhaust valve heads, and in the head gasket cutout [206]. When the pressure rises during the compression phase, the carburetted mixture is forced into the crevices. Since these spaces have a large surface/volume ratio, the entering gas is very rapidly cooled by heat exchange with the walls. During the combustion phase, the pressure continues to rise and a new fraction of carburetted mixture enters the crevices. When the flame reaches the level of each crevice, it can either penetrate

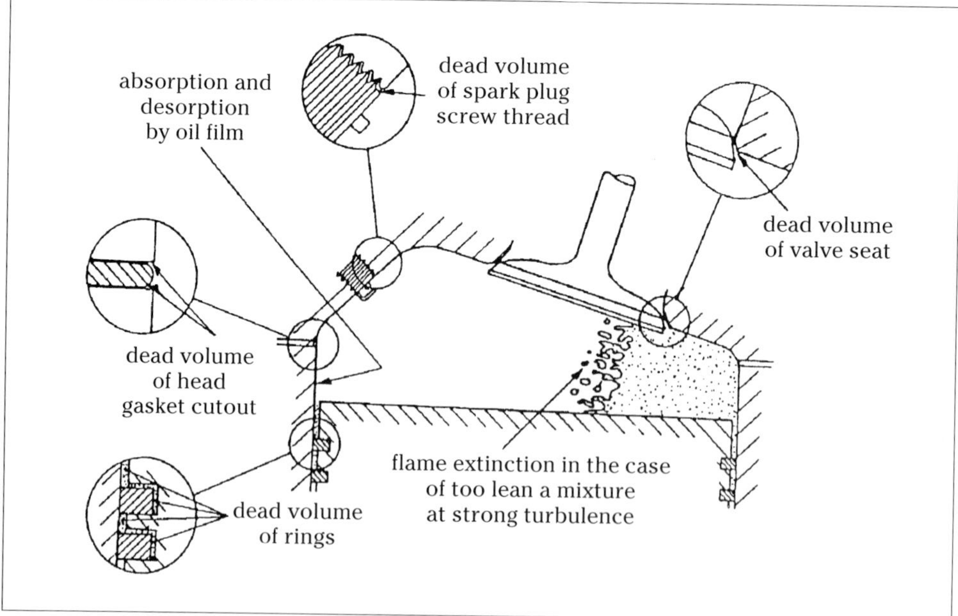


**Fig 10.10** Cylinder head showing possible sources of unburnt HC [206]

therein and burn all or part of the mixture lying there, or be quenched at the orifice of the crevice. The latter possibility depends on the geometry of the crevice entrance (tests have shown that quenching occurs when the space between the piston and the liner is lower than 0.18 mm [100]), on the composition of the unburnt mixture, and on its thermodynamic state. After the flame arrives and is quenched, the burnt gases penetrate in turn into the crevices until the pressure begins to fall in the cylinder. When the pressure in the crevice becomes higher than that of the cylinder (about 15 degrees after top dead center), the trapped gases flow back towards the cylinder.

Zone Z in Fig. 10.8 shows the most important of these crevices, the volume lying between the piston, the rings, and the cylinder wall. It includes a series of volumes connected by cross-section restrictions such as the ring clearance and the ring interval, of which the geometry changes as the ring moves in its groove to seal off the top and bottom of the ring area. They can trap 5 to 10% of the cylinder charge, which thus escapes the primary combustion process. During the expansion phase, when the flow returns to the cylinder, more than 50% of this carburetted mixture can exit unchanged. Simulation in a combustion bomb, although not directly transposable to the multi-cylinder engine, has shown that the volumes of the ring arrangements accounted for 80% of the emissions, the head gasket crevice for 13%, and the spark plug for 2%. The experimental raising of the fire ring as close as possible to the piston head has demonstrated HC emission reductions on a mass-produced engine ranging between 47 and 74% [271], depending on the engine running conditions. This occurs to the detriment of the longevity of the system and at the risk of clogging the rings.

The position of the spark plug can also affect HC emissions. If it is close to the crevice, the crevice is likely filled with burnt gases. Conversely, if it is far away, the crevice is filled with the fresh mixture. The difference is about 20% in most cases [270].

Blowby gases, transferred from the cylinder to the crankcase through the ring clearances during the compression and combustion phases are a source of unburnt HC emissions in the case of direct discharge to the atmosphere. Today, they are recycled to the engine intake. In these new conditions, an increase in the blowby gas volume, recycled to the inlet and thus reburnt, would be one means to reduce HC emissions. This could be obtained by reducing the tightness of the rings, and preventing the return to the cylinder of the mass of unburnt gas trapped in the crevice. However, this is detrimental to engine performance.

Designs of combustion chambers, pistons, and rings that take into account the need to reduce the size of these crevices, and a suitable choice of gaskets and spark plug position, should reduce the participation of the crevices in unburnt HC emissions.

#### 10.4.3.3 Absorption and desorption in oil films

HC emissions increase with the addition of oil to the fuel, as in two-stroke engines, which are lubricated by the fuel. These emissions essentially represent hydrocarbons, whether cracked or not, that originate in the fuel rather than in the oil.

The addition of 5% oil to the fuel of a clean engine can double or triple HC emissions in 10 min, and the addition of 0.6 $cm^3$ of oil to the fuel at the piston head increases the exhaust concentration of unburnt HC by 1000 ppm [168]. The results of these bomb tests are nevertheless contradicted by tests on multi-point injection engines. In these tests, the addition of oil to the fuel only results in slight increases in HC emissions, which are also unchanged if the oil is replaced by a lubricant that does not dissolve the fuel [266].

The following mechanism appears to be involved: During the intake phase, the oil film coating the walls is saturated with hydrocarbon vapors from the fuel at ambient pressure. This dissolution continues at higher pressure during the compression and combustion phases. When the concentration in the carburetted mixture falls to zero in the chamber due to combustion, desorption towards the burnt gases is initiated and continues during the expansion and exhaust phases. Part of the desorbed vapors is mixed with the combustion products at high temperature and is then oxidized. The remainder is mixed with the cold gases, thus escaping oxidation and participating in the hydrocarbon emissions. This effect is proportional to the solubility of the fuel in the oil and is virtually non-existent with gaseous fuels [168], which are insoluble. Moreover, an increase in lubricant temperature, which also decreases this solubility, reduces the participation of oil in HC emissions. This is why higher emissions of unburnt hydrocarbons are observed in starting, in conditions in which, inter alia, the lubricant has not yet had time to warm up [5].

The presence of extensive oil films in the combustion chamber is one factor in HC emissions, which show a tendency to increase with oil consumption. Suitable ring profiles designed to reduce oil consumption also help to lower HC emissions [273].

One measure aimed at reducing the participation of a lubricant in unburnt emissions consists in the use of synthetic oils which have a lower solvent effect with gasoline. Another measure is the division of the cooling circuit in a way that cools the piston heads normally while allowing the temperature of the cylinder walls to rise to higher values [168].

#### 10.4.3.4 Deterioration of combustion quality

The extinction of the flame in the chamber before the flame front reaches the walls is one source of HC in certain engine running conditions. The flame can be extinguished if the pressure and temperature fall too rapidly. This occurs while idling or at low load, when the engine speed is slow and the residual gas fraction is large (high dilution by excessive EGR or carburetted mixture that is too lean) with a pronounced ignition delay. Even if the settings are correct in stabilized operation, this flame extinction can occur in transient conditions (acceleration or deceleration).

Engine cycles without combustion send the carburetted mixture directly to the exhaust as it had entered at the intake. The installation of two spark plugs in the ignition chamber makes it possible, in the case of difficult combustion with a high proportion of EGR to reduce $NO_x$, and to avoid the erratic occurrence of cycles without combustion [149].

#### 10.4.3.5 Effect of deposits

The formation of deposits (lead oxides with leaded fuels or carbonaceous deposits with excessively rich mixtures), which appear in the combustion chambers after a few thousand miles, is known to increase HC emissions. Cleaning away the deposits immediately achieves a temporary reduction in HC.

Their action mechanism may be fairly complex. The absorption/desorption of the hydrocarbons acts like the oil films. The deposits in the crevices should reduce the penetration of the carburetted mixture and thus reduce the HC emitted, but they simultaneously reduce the inlet cross-sections by favoring the quenching of the flame and thus increase the emissions.

#### 10.4.3.6 Post-oxidation of hydrocarbons

The hydrocarbons that have escaped the main combustion process during the engine combustion phase fortunately do not appear entirely as such in the exhaust. When, after freezing in the quench layer, they rediffuse in the mass of burnt gases at high temperature they are rapidly oxidized, at least partially, and quite easily if oxygen is available (for a lean mixture). To oxidize the hydrocarbons in the gas phase, a residence time of at least 50 ms at 600°C is necessary, a temperature routinely encountered at the exhaust valve. The HCs emitted are thus a mixture of unburnt fuel and partial oxidation products, where the hydrocarbons from the fuel account for about 40% of the total. The hydrocarbons are also oxidized in the exhaust line. A few per cent to 40% of the hydrocarbons leaving the cylinder are converted at this point. The engine operating conditions which produce the highest temperatures in the exhaust (mixture at stoichiometry, high speed, delayed ignition, low volumetric ratio) and the longest residence times (low load) offer the highest reductions in HC. The ignition delay raises the temperature of the burnt gases at the time of exhaust, thus favoring post-combustion [117]. Another method to favor this secondary oxidation is to reduce the heat losses at the valves and at the exhaust manifold by increasing the cross-sections and by insulating the walls, for example by the application of a ceramic coating.

Table 10.4 lists the different parameters contributing to the formation of unburnt HC and to their emission in the exhausts of spark ignition engines.

### 10.4.4 Formation of aldehydes

Besides the conditions favoring aldehydes already mentioned (flame quenching, slow combustion at lower temperature), variations in fuel/air ratio represent the most important factor governing aldehyde emissions. As already shown in Fig. 10.1,

**Table 10.4** Critical factors and engine variables in HC emission mechanisms [111]

| **Formation of HC** | **In-cylinder mixing and oxidation** |
|---|---|
| *Crevices:*<br>• crevice volume<br>• crevice location (with respect to spark plug)<br>• load<br>• crevice wall temperature<br>• mixture composition (1)<br><br>*Oil layers:*<br>• oil consumption<br>• wall temperature<br>• speed<br><br>*Incomplete combustion:*<br>• burn rate and variability<br>• mixture composition (1)<br>• load<br>• spark timing (2)<br><br>*Combustion chamber walls:*<br>• deposits<br>• wall roughness<br><br>**Fraction HC flowing out of cylinder**<br>*Residual fraction:*<br>• load<br>• exhaust pressure<br>• valve overlap<br>• direct short-circuiting (2-stroke)<br>• compression ratio<br>• speed<br><br>*In-cylinder flow during exhaust stroke:*<br>• valve overlap<br>• exhaust valve size and location<br>• combustion chamber shape<br>• compression ratio<br>• speed | *Mixing rate with bulk gas*<br>• speed<br>• swirl ratio<br>• combustion chamber shape<br><br>*Bulk gas temperature during expansion and exhaust:*<br>• speed<br>• spark timing (2)<br>• mixture composition (1)<br>• compression ratio<br>• heat losses to walls<br><br>*Bulk gas oxygen concentration:*<br>• equivalence ratio<br><br>*Wall temperature:*<br>• high if HC source near wall<br>• for crevices, value depends on geometry<br><br>**Oxidation in exhaust system**<br>*Exhaust gas temperature:*<br>• speed<br>• spark timing (2)<br>• mixture composition (1)<br>• compression ratio<br>• secondary air flow<br>• heat losses in cylinder and exhaust<br><br>*Oxygen concentration:*<br>• valve overlap<br>• secondary air flow and addition point<br><br>*Residence time:*<br>• speed<br>• load<br>• volume of critical exhaust system component |

(1) Fuel/air equivalence ratio and burnt gas fraction (residual plus recycled exhaust gas).
(2) With respect to MBT timing.

aldehydes essentially appear in a lean mixture, due to incomplete oxidation of the hydrocarbons. This effect of the fuel/air ratio is clearly demonstrated in the case of methanol fuel [253]. The aldehydes, an intermediate oxidation product of methanol, are mainly formed in the expansion stroke [220] during the mixture of the warm air with the unburnts present on the walls in the quenched layer. A higher compression ratio in a lean mixture [209], an increase in ignition advance [220], deposits present in the combustion chamber, the absorbtion of methanol at compression and its desorbtion at expansion, all favor the formation of formaldehyde.

### 10.4.5 Diesel engines

Due to the operating principle of the diesel engine, the fuel resides in the combustion chamber for a shorter time than in spark ignition and is accordingly subjected for a shorter time to the mechanisms that form unburnts, which were described earlier. This partly explains the lower level of unburnts in diesel emissions.

Since diesel fuel contains hydrocarbons with a higher boiling point, hence with higher molecular weight, some pyrolysis already occurs when the fuel is atomized. This contributes to the greater complexity of the unburnt or partially burnt hydrocarbons found in diesel exhausts, and which cover a wider spectrum of molecular compositions. Moreover, most of the heavier hydrocarbons are adsorbed on the soot particles in the form of SOF as indicated in Chapter 9.

Diesel combustion is a complex process marked by the simultaneous occurrence of fuel evaporation, mixing between the air, the fuel, and burnt and unburnt products, and combustion itself. The diesel combustion process can be divided into four phases:

- The ignition delay, which is the time elapsed between the start of injection and ignition. During this ignition delay, it is assumed that preliminary oxidation compounds are formed of the peroxide and aldehyde type [106].
- Combustion in a pre-mixed flame, which concerns the fuel that is mixed with air within the ignition limits during the previous phase, facilitated by the presence of peroxides.
- The combustion phase by diffusion, in which the combustion rate depends on the rate of mixing of the fuel injected with the air within the ignition limits.
- The delayed combustion phase in which energy continues to be liberated at lower speed during the mixing of the residual fuel with excess oxygen.

Two conditions enable the fuel to elude the normal combustion process. The air/fuel mixture may be too lean or too rich to auto-ignite or propagate the flame. In this case the fuel is partially consumed in the thermal oxidation reactions later in the expansion phase after mixing with additional air. The rest remains unburnt due to incomplete mixing or quenching of the oxidation process.

If the fuel is injected during the ignition delay, the mixtures obtained are too lean because incorporation is too fast, or too rich by excessively slow incorporation with the air present in the chamber. In this case, it is mainly the presence of excessively lean mixtures that causes the formation of unburnts [101], since very rich mixtures are ultimately burned during a subsequent mixing with air.

If the fuel is injected after the ignition delay, rapid oxidation of the fuel or of its pyrolysis products occurs during penetration into the air that is raised to high temperature. However, insufficient mixing can lead to excessively rich mixtures, or quenching of combustion can yield incomplete combustion products that are found in the exhaust.

Diesel engine emission levels vary considerably with the running conditions. At idling or low load, they are higher than at full load. Rapid load variations, which cause substantial changes in the combustion conditions, can also give rise to HC emissions by the erratic appearance of cycles without combustion.

#### 10.4.5.1 Emissions by too lean mixtures

The start of injection of the fuel into the cylinder is accompanied by a distribution of the local fuel/air ratios as shown in Fig. 10.11. In this swirling flow, ignition occurs in a zone with a fuel/air ratio that is slightly below stoichiometry. The fuel close to the edge of the injected jet has already passed the lower flammability limit and cannot auto-ignite or maintain a rapid flame front. It can only be the location of slow oxidation reactions which remain incomplete. Found in this zone are unburnt fuel, decomposition products of the fuel, and partial oxidation products (carbon monoxide, aldehydes, and other oxygenated compounds), part of which eventually reaches the exhaust. The amount of unburnt hydrocarbons originating in these lean

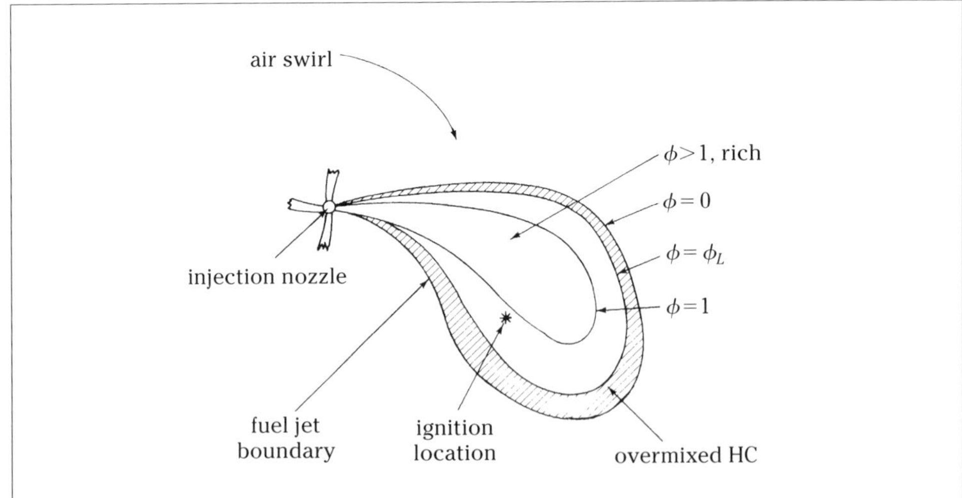


**Fig 10.11** Distribution of local fuel/air ratios $\phi$ at the time of injection, $\phi_L$ is the limit fuel/air ratio corresponding to the lower flammability limit ($\approx 0.3$), and the cross-hatched area contains a mixture with fuel/air ratio $< \phi_L$ [111]

areas depends on the quantity injected during the ignition delay, the mixing rate with air during this period, and the auto-ignition conditions prevailing in the cylinder.

Hence a correlation exists between HC emissions and the ignition delay, i.e. the cetane number (Section 11.2.3) of the fuel. If, due to variations in engine running conditions, the ignition delay increases, HC emissions rise sharply.

#### 10.4.5.2 Emissions by too rich mixtures

There are two causes for HC emissions from too-rich mixtures, i.e. deficient mixing with air. The first stems from the fuel which leaves the nozzle tip at low speed, often late in the combustion process. The main source of this is the nozzle sack volume (Fig. 10.21), but secondary injections due to uncontrolled needle lift also contribute. The second cause is an excess of fuel which can invade the combustion chamber.

At the end of the injection period, the injector sack volume (small volume left at the tip of the needle downstream of its seat, to which the volume of the nozzle holes is added) remains full of fuel. During the combustion and expansion phases, this heated fuel is partly vaporized and, liquid or gaseous, penetrates into the cylinder at low speed through the holes of the nozzle, while slowly mixing with the air, thus escaping the main combustion process. At the minimum ignition delay for a direct injection engine, the HC emissions are thus directly proportional to the nozzle sack volume [87]. However, the entire dead volume fortunately does not escape in the form of unburnt HC. By way of comparison on a given engine [87], 1 $mm^3$ of dead volume gives about 350 ppmC, whereas 1 $mm^3$ of fuel would give 1660 ppmC. Part of the heavier hydrocarbons remains in the nozzle and some oxidation occurs to the part escaping. The same tendency is observed in precombustion chamber engines, but to a lesser degree.

In direct injection engines, exhaust smoke problems limit the fuel/air ratio at full load to about 0.7. At low load, injection at low speed of very small amounts of fuel causes insufficient mixing and locally high fuel/air ratios. In transient conditions of acceleration, excessive injection of fuel can occur, and this also causes high local fuel/air ratios during the expansion and exhaust phases, although the overall air/fuel mixture remains lean. A fuel/air ratio which locally exceeds 0.9 causes a sudden increase in HC emissions. A similar effect is found in precombustion chamber engines [87]. However, this mechanism only has an effect during acceleration, and, in any case, causes less HC emissions than a too-lean mixture at idling and at low load.

#### 10.4.5.3 Flame quenching and misfire

As for the spark ignition engine, flame quenching at the walls is one source of HC emissions, which depends in particular on the impact of the fuel jet on the walls of the chamber.

Ignition deficiencies, which give rise to high HC emissions, are rare with engines that run normally. They only occur at low compression rates and with abnormally delayed injection.

These ignition defects nevertheless occur during cold starting of diesel engines with the formation of "white smoke", essentially consisting of a mist of microdroplets of unburnt fuel.

## 10.5 Formation of particulates

### 10.5.1 Spark ignition engine

In this type of engine particulates have three distinct origins: lead in leaded fuels, sulfates from sulfur in the fuels, and soot.

Sulfate emissions mainly concern vehicles equipped with post-combustion oxidation catalysts. The sulfur from the fuel converted to $SO_2$ in combustion is oxidized to $SO_3$ by the catalyst in the exhaust. It then combines with water molecules to give a mist of $H_2SO_4$. Hence, the emission levels depend directly on the fuel's sulfur content.

With leaded fuels, particulate emissions in the range of 100 to 150 mg/km for a fuel containing 0.15 g/liter of lead, contain 25 to 60% of their mass in the form of lead. This type of particulate is formed by condensation of the lead salts emitted at the exhaust. Emissions in terms of weight are therefore higher during cold starting. Since they are also condensed on the walls of the exhaust system, they can be emitted erratically and quickly during sudden increases in the exhaust flow rate, which detaches them from the walls together with rust and scale. Thus, on an FTP cycle [154] it is observed that vehicles running on leaded and unleaded gasoline respectively emit 6 and 20 times less particulates than the corresponding diesel vehicles.

Soot emissions are abnormal in properly-adjusted spark ignition engines, because they occur only with excessively rich carburetted mixtures.

### 10.5.2 Diesel engine

As already pointed out in Chapter 9, diesel particulates are composed of a carbonaceous material (soot) generated during combustion, on which various organic species (SOF) are adsorbed, consisting of molecules condensed on the soot in the phases following combustion, which themselves may be precursors of soot formation during the combustion phase. This SOF contains unburnt hydrocarbons, oxygenated derivatives (ketones, esters, aldehydes, lactones, ethers, organic acids) and polycyclic aromatic hydrocarbons accompanied by their nitrogen and oxygen derivatives. Added to these are a few inorganic derivatives ($SO_2$, $NO_2$, sulfates).

The composition of these particles depends on the engine running conditions and, in particular, on the exhaust temperature. Above 500°C they are aggregates of carbon spherules, with approximate individual dimensions of 15 to 30 nm, with a small proportion of hydrogen. Below this temperature, these particles are coated with the SOF phase described earlier. Along the exhaust line, an increase in size of the particles is thus observed with an increase in their PAH content due to the progressive condensation on the particles of the organic compounds present in the vapor phase.

Soot particles are primarily produced from the carbon contained in the fuel and depend on the type of fuel, the number of carbons in the molecule, and the C/H ratio [250]. Starting with molecules containing 12 to 22 carbon atoms and an H/C ratio of about 2, the spherules obtained contain some $10^5$ atoms of carbon with an H/C ratio of about 0.1. Despite considerable basic research on soot formation, the formation mechanisms in diesel combustion are still poorly understood [274] because they concern non-reproducible processes occurring at high temperature and high pressure, with a complex fuel composition, in a very turbulent mixture, and in three-dimensional space. For reasons of experimental convenience, research on the genesis of soot has mainly concerned premixed flames [241] and the few investigations conducted on diesel engines have been concerned with direct injection engines [3], because the mechanisms involved in precombustion chamber engines are even more complex [88]. However, the types of soot corresponding to the rich pre-mixed flames and to diesel combustion are different [241]. In the former case they consist of well-formed particles with residence times of about 100 ms, which are usually in the form of chains of aggregates. The much shorter residence time in diesel combustion (4 to 10 ms) [29] and the high pressure and high mixing rate in diesel engines, give rise to higher growth rates and coagulation, yielding a soot in the form of more or less spherical aggregates of individual spherical particles. The formation of particles by polymerization and pyrolysis in liquid droplets is practically non-existent in diesel combustion.

Thus the genesis of soot takes place in the gas phase in diesel combustion processes occurring between 1000 and 2800 K at pressures of 1 MPa, with sufficient excess air to guarantee complete combustion of the fuel. Soot appears in diffusion flames between 2000 and 2400 K, with a maximum at 2100 K. Below and above this range, the soot concentrations are negligible [256]. The time available for the formation of solid soot particles from a fraction of fuel is only a few ms. Once ignition has been completed, the soot appears in less than 1 ms in all parts of the fuel jet [101].

Soot emissions from diesel engines thus arise from three processes occurring partly in parallel [119]:

- formation reactions of soot from fuel and air, primarily in the first combustion phase
- reactions of soot formation from the fuel in the burnt gases, mainly in the second combustion phase
- oxidation of the soot formed, after mixing in oxygen-rich zones

Diesel soot, which is composed of the carbon phase and of associated extractable compounds (SOF), originates in various sources during combustion. The main paths of formation of PAH and soot may be the following [165]:

- the flame itself, which generates PAH and leads to the moderate or slight formation of soot
- pyrolysis at high temperature, which generates PAH and leads to intense soot formation
- pyrolysis at lower temperature, which generates PAH and oxygenated products with slight formation of soot
- vaporization of the fuel and lubricants, which adds components of these products without forming soot.

The contribution of combustion in a premixed flame to soot formation is slight in comparison with that of the diffusion flame [198]. Fig. 10.12 illustrates the different zones of formation of these products in a turbulent diffusion flame.

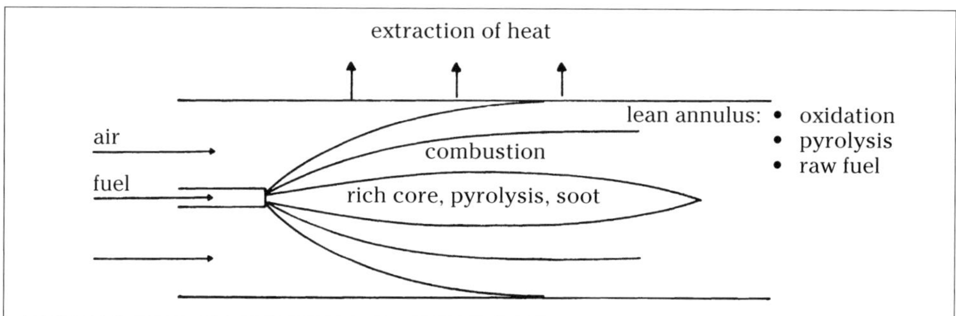


**Fig 10.12** Turbulent diffusion flame, sources of soot and extractible material [165]

Two stages are generally distinguished in the formation and development of soot.

- A stage of particle formation, which is an induction period during which the first condensed phase is initiated from the fuel molecules through the intermediary of their oxidation and/or pyrolysis products. Among these products are different unsaturated hydrocarbons, particularly acetylene and its higher homologues ($C_{2n}H_2$), and polycyclic aromatic hydrocarbons (PAH). The first condensed particles are very small ($d<2$ nm) [103], and are composed of a large number of individual cells ($10^3$ to $10^4$), with an average size of about 20 to 30 Å [71], called crystallites. Even their large number does not represent a high weight factor in their zone of formation, the most active regions of the flame [103].
- A particle enlargement stage, which includes the phases of surface growth, coagulation, and aggregation. Surface growth involves the bonding to the particle surface of species originating in the gas phase, followed by their incorporation. However, since these additions do not lead to H/C ratios corresponding to those of soot, it is necessary to include dehydrogenation

reactions. Surface growth does not change the number of particles, but increases the mass fraction of soot. On the contrary, coagulation causes particle growth by collision, thus decreasing the number of particles. Aggregation of the particles thus formed then causes the formation of chains and aggregates. In a diesel engine, this stage of elementary particle aggregation often occurs simultaneously with oxidation (Section 10.5.2.1) in air of the particles formed. These two antagonistic processes can oppose the enlargement of the particles [167].

The kinetics of soot formation is very fast. In the precombustion chamber of an indirect injection engine, the soot concentration is a maximum around 10 to 20 degrees of crankshaft rotation after the TDC and then decreases. In the precombustion chamber, a large quantity of soot particles is formed in the first instants of combustion, which are then partially burned when the oxygen concentration exceeds a few per cent (⩾5%) [80].

In fact, at each stage of the process the products formed can still evolve differently from the pattern described earlier. Oxidation by air or oxidizing species can convert the soot or soot precursors to gaseous compounds like CO and $CO_2$. The soot particles formed in the precombustion chamber enter through the transfer duct into the main chamber, diffuse into the air, and are partly burned. Thus the particle sizes found in the chamber are smaller than in the precombustion chamber [80].

Soot emissions in the exhaust depend on the balance of the soot formation and oxidation reactions. It was found empirically that the carbon/oxygen (C/O) ratio is the essential factor at the time of soot formation. Soot is formed when in reaction [103]:

$$C_mH_n + yO_2 \Rightarrow 2yCO + \frac{n}{2}H_2 + (m-2y)C_s \tag{10.27}$$

$m$ becomes larger than $2y$, i.e. when $C/O>1$. The corresponding fuel/air ratio is given by:

$$\varnothing = 2\left(\frac{C}{O}\right)(1+\delta) \tag{10.28}$$

where $\delta = n/(4m)$. $\delta$ is 3 for $C/O=1$, with $n/m=2$. The critical values of C/O for soot formation are lower than 1. Depending on the fuel composition and the experimental rig, they vary between 0.5 and 0.8. This critical value of the C/O ratio rises with temperature, but is independent of pressure. However, as soon as the critical value of 5 is reached, the production of soot (more the size of the particles than their number) increases very rapidly with the value of C/O and is strongly favored by the pressure [103]. At high pressure, the limit fuel/air ratio for soot formation shifts towards leaner mixtures [162].

The mixing mechanisms between air and fuel are crucially important for the genesis of soot. Variations in emissions as a function of engine speed and load can be interpreted as variations in air/fuel mixing quality, because the kinetics of soot formation in a precombustion chamber engine appears to be independent of the speed and overall fuel/air ratio [212].

Figure 10.13 shows the importance of the temperature and fuel/air ratio factors on the genesis of soot. With diesel combustion, one drop of fuel at point **A** represents the core of the jet near the nozzle orifice. A few drops (≈5%) follow path **A** → **B** during the mixing of the fuel with air and at ignition reach point D without any soot being formed. In fact, very little soot is observed to form during ignition [274]. After ignition, the fuel continues to enter at point **A**, but the drops now take route **A** → **C** representing combustion at the diffusion flame front with high soot formation. The boundary between the "soot" and "no soot" zones depends on the molecular structure of the fuel, and the aromaticity of the fuel is a factor that promotes the production of soot.

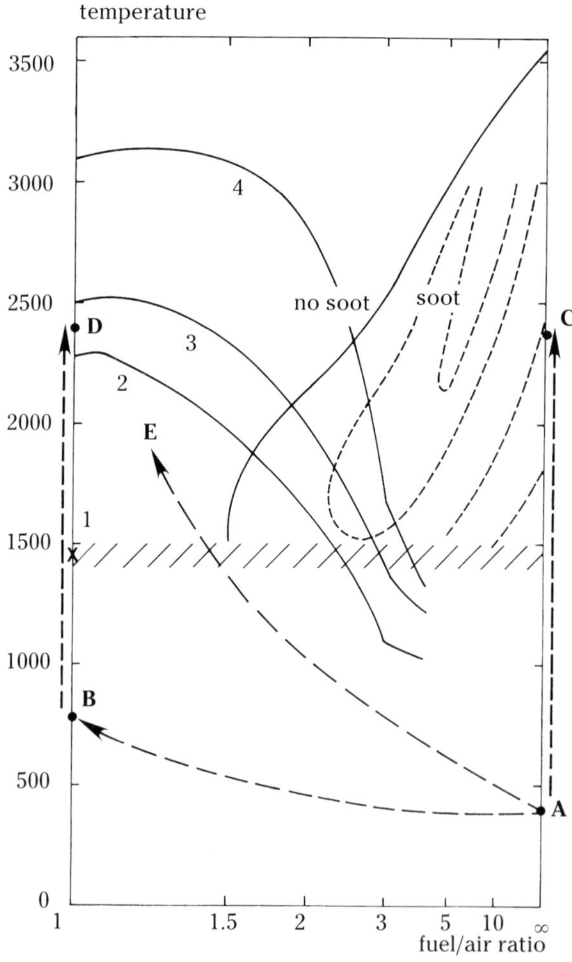


**Fig 10.13** Route of a fuel droplet in the temperature fuel/air ratio diagram [118]

The formation of soot is not a balanced process. The detail mechanisms are not yet fully understood. Three different paths appear to exist, only the first two of which concern diesel. At the lowest temperatures (⩽1700 K), only aromatics or highly unsaturated aliphatics with high molecular weights form soot by pyrolysis. At the medium temperature typical of diffusion flames (⩾1800 K), the usual hydrocarbon motor fuels produce soot, while they burn in a sufficiently rich mixture. At the higher temperatures, outside the diesel field, the nucleation process involves carbon vapor.

Depending on the temperature, below or above 1800 K, two different mechanisms are involved. The first exclusively concerns aromatics, which, by a fast condensation reaction on the aromatic ring, produce polyaromatics followed by soot. The second concerns both aromatics and aliphatics, which, by slower ring and chain splitting reactions form fragments that are then polymerized to yield soot precursors (polyunsaturates of the polyacetylenic type). The partial pressure of these macromolecules increases up to saturation and their condensation forms growth nuclei for soot. Around these nuclei, the macromolecules remaining in the gas phase condense and the particles continue to grow.

During these condensation, fragmentation, nucleation, and aggregation processes, the H/C ratio steadily and simultaneously decreases with the increase in particle size [131]. Another process that contributes to particle growth is the retention of soot on the cylinder walls (where it is attracted by thermophoresis) [137] and its entrainment in the exhaust after continued particle crystallization.

In the burning of liquid fuels of the diesel type, the size of the droplets and hence the quality of spraying are extremely important because the formation of soot increases with droplet size [274].

#### 10.5.2.1 Oxidation of soot

At all stages in the formation of soot oxidation can occur, whether on the precursors, the condensation nuclei, or the particles. The PAH themselves are already decomposed or oxidized when they leave the combustion chamber. Their concentration may be 200 times lower at the exhaust pipe exit and their mutagenicity is also reduced at the exhaust despite their oxidation (or nitration) that should, on the contrary, increase their mutagenicity [102]. A large part of the soot formed is fortunately oxidized before the exhaust stroke begins. It is this combustion of the incandescent particles at high temperature that makes the flame bright. Many chemical species present in the flame ($O_2$, O, OH, $CO_2$ and $H_2O$) can take part in the heterogeneous particle combustion reactions in competition with the formation reactions mentioned earlier. Water is a highly effective agent. A diesel emulsion containing 25% by volume of water cuts particle emissions in half [105]. In lean flames, where oxygen is a significant oxidizing agent, the number of particles increases through the break-up of the aggregates. In rich flames the OH radical is the chief oxidizing agent [212], which acts with high reactivity without breaking the aggregates [57]. As a surface reaction, particle oxidation is favored by a large surface/volume ratio and aggregation makes combustion more difficult. Oxidation also demands a minimum temperature level (at least 700 to 800°C) [39]. The soot oxidation reactions are confined to the combustion chamber because they are rapidly quenched during the cooling of the gases brought in by expansion during the exhaust phase and upon the opening of the exhaust valve [116]. Oxidation occurs very quickly at high pressure. A first post-oxidation phase of about 3 ms can oxidize 90% of the soot formed initially. The rest of the oxidation depends on the rate of mixing with air and is slowed down by expansion [101]. The heterogeneous oxidation product of soot is mainly CO, rather than $CO_2$ [28]. The soot emitted is therefore the resultant of the total soot formed, less the quantity oxidized before the exhaust. Fortunately, the soot emitted usually only accounts for a small percentage ($\leq$10%) of the amount present at any given time in the combustion chamber [34, 39, 137 and 215]. One cause suggested to explain the negative influence of EGR on particulate emissions is that the added diluents slow down the oxidation of the soot [116].

#### 10.5.2.2 Incorporation of SOF in the particles

The final process of particle formation, measured by standard techniques (Section 9.11), consists of the condensation and adsorption of the heavy organic compounds making up the SOF onto the soot aggregates produced by combustion. As the temperature decreases and the vapor pressure of the chemical species in the gas phase rises above their saturation vapor pressure, these species condense on the soot particles with high specific surface area.

This condensation primarily involves the heavy hydrocarbons that occur at the tail-end of the fuel distillation process, the unburnt hydrocarbons pyrolysed during combustion, and the heavy hydrocarbons present in the lubricating oil.

Table 10.5 summarizes the parameters that favor diesel particular emissions [33].

## 10.6 Formation of PAH and nitrated derivatives

Polynuclear aromatic compounds play an essential role in the first stages of soot formation, and they also participate in the composition of the phase adsorbed on the particles. Tests in a stabilized flame with sampling within the flame reveal the presence of a PAH concentration peak immediately before the soot concentration peak, while the PAH nearly disappear as the soot formation begins [121]. The alkylated derivatives of the PAH could be the first precursors of soot formation, which is formed by ionic or free radical polymerization of these species [120].

Samplings and analyses made at atmospheric pressure on flames of simple fuels (ethylene) with a fuel/air ratio close to the one corresponding to soot formation (C/O=0.79) [153] reveal the appearance of light unsaturated structures (acetylene

**Table 10.5** Main characteristics influencing particulate formation [33]

| |
|---|
| **Formation of insoluble fraction favored by:** |
| • elevated temperature |
| • high pressure |
| • absence of oxygen |
| **Oxidation of the insoluble fraction favored by:** |
| • elevated temperature |
| • high pressure |
| • presence of oxygen |
| **Formation of HC particles favored by:** |
| • lean mixture zones |
| • temperatures below the flammability limit |
| • hydrocarbon layers on the walls of the bowl |
| • fuel droplets seeping at the nozzle tip |
| **Sources of particles from the lubricant:** |
| • surface of cylinder liners |
| • valve stem gaskets |
| • turbo-compressor gaskets |
| • recycle of crankcase gases to inlet |

and butadiene) or aromatic structures (e.g. toluene) depending on the residence time in the flame, as well as their disappearance in favor of more stable structures (benzene, phenylacetylene and styrene) and heavier PAH (pyrene and cyclopentapyrene).

At the high temperatures in the flames, the saturated structures present in the fuels can give rise to dehydrogenation reactions or C−C bond splitting with the production of free radicals. For example, methane gives the carbene radical ($:CH_2$) with the simultaneous production of hydrogen radicals $H^\bullet$, and ethylene forms the vinyl radical ($CH_2{=}C^\bullet H$) that is easily converted to acetylene by dehydrogenation. By polyaddition, acetylene yields polyacetylenes, through the ethenyl radicals ($CH{\equiv}C^\bullet$):

$$CH{\equiv}C\bullet \Rightarrow CH{\equiv}C{-}CH{=}C\bullet H \Rightarrow CH{\equiv}C{-}CH{=}CH{-}CH{=}C_\bullet H \tag{10.29}$$

This radical can undergo intramolecular cyclization that converts it to the phenyl radical ($C_6H_5^\bullet$).

By reacting with the methyl and ethyl radicals, this phenyl radical yields alkyl derivatives of benzene: e.g. toluene and xylenes. The addition of two acetylene molecules to this radical and the removal of an $H^\bullet$ radical gives rise to a naphthalene molecule. The continuation of this mechanism allows the creation of more condensed aromatics: some with three rings such as anthracene, phenanthrene, etc.; some with four rings such as naphthacene and pyrene; and some with five rings or more [115].

These mechanisms also produce a panoply of the different PAH, ranging up to the formation of the first soot particles.

The molecular structure of the initial hydrocarbon affects the ease with which the PAH and particles of carbon black are formed. In pyrolysis between 900 and 1200 °C with an absence of oxygen, the production of PAH and carbon black increases in the following order: paraffin, napththene, aromatics [94]. As the temperature rises, carbon formation also increases at the expense of PAH.

Although they have different molecular weights, with the lightest concerning gasoline-powered engines, the PAH are emitted in approximately equal quantities by diesel engines and spark ignition engines. The latter emit PAH in the vapor phase, while the soot particles adsorb the heavier PAH from the diesel engines. In cold starting, the PAH emissions of gasoline engines may be significantly higher than those of diesel engines [25]. Measured by fluorescence on a single-cylinder CFR engine [152], PAH emissions increase with ignition advance, knock, and high speeds. A high surface/volume ratio of the combustion chambers (as in the rotary engine) increases PAH emissions.

The presence of nitration agents of the $NO_x$ type in the exhausts causes the formation of nitrated polycyclic aromatic hydrocarbons in the combustion chamber or at its exit. About 200 nitro-PAH have been identified in exhausts [231]. Among them, the derivatives of naphthalene, anthracene, and pyrene are the most frequently found. The derivatives 1-nitropyrene and 1,6 and 1,8-dinitropyrenes have attracted special attention because they are highly mutagenic without prior enzymatic activation (Chapter 4). $NO_2$ appears to be the preferential nitration agent of pyrene. Polynitropyrenes are formed through the reaction of the $N_2O_4$ radicals with the pyrene radical [225]. Most of the nitro-PAH can be synthesized in the combustion chamber and in the exhaust line. Some can be generated during sampling on the particulate sampling filter [230]. It is estimated that 10 to 20% of the 1-nitropyrene collected on the particulates of light-duty diesel vehicles during a 23 min sampling with an exhaust gas containing 3 ppm $NO_2$ are samplings artifacts. The highest $NO_2$ contents found in the undiluted gases lead to even higher proportions of artifacts (Section 8.8.3.3.E). Moreover, truck engines emit less nitro-PAH than light-duty diesel engines [230]. High speed and high load conditions tend to reduce emissions of PAH and nitro-PAH, at the expense of the formation of partially-oxidized nitro-PAH [231].

### 10.6.1 Role of soot inhibitors

Anti-soot additives are routinely added to the fuels feeding boiler burners. They are usually soluble compounds of transition metals (nickel, cobalt, manganese, lead and magnesium naphthenates, ferrocene[1], and MMT) or of alkaline earth metals

1. Iron dicyclopentadienyl.

(barium and calcium) [120]. The same types of additives are added to jet fuels used in aircraft gas turbines. These turbines run on a rich mixture with smoke emissions during takeoff or during the re-ignition of military jet engines at high altitude. Ferrocene appears to be the optimal product [120]. This material decomposes in the flame into iron oxide particles, which act as seeds for the formation of soot. The following reaction then leads to the gasification of the carbon surrounding the iron nucleus [182]:

$$2Fe_2O_3 + 3C \Rightarrow 4Fe + 3CO_2$$

In diesel-fueled engines, apart from water (Section 11.2.5.3) at high concentration, the alkaline earth metals, especially barium, have proven to be the most effective [105], as compared with iron and manganese in burners and gas turbines. Organic additives of the peroxide type or nitrogen compounds in the category of procetane additives (Section 11.2.5.2) may have an effect, especially on reducing PAH, without affecting smoke emissions [183], whereas barium appears to have little effect on the PAH emitted [120].

The action mechanisms of these additives are poorly understood, and only qualitatively. They may promote the aggregation of the soot particles and thus make them less opaque, hence decreasing the opacity of the smoke without affecting the emissions in terms of weight. They may also affect the formation of soot or contribute to its post-oxidation, once it is formed. This could be the case of metals acting at high temperature on the decomposition of the $H_2O$ molecule into hydroxyl radicals OH•. For reasons of experimental convenience, the possible mechanisms have been investigated on laboratory flames and not on diesel combustion itself.

A first possible ionic mechanism involves metals that are easily ionized in the flames. Ions of the $MOH^+$ type [24] react with the ions in the flame to reduce the rate of nucleation or coagulation of the particles. By transferring the electrical charges to the soot particles, this mechanism reduces coagulation due to the repulsion between the particles [174]. This tends to reduce the amount of soot formed or to make the particles smaller, and hence more susceptible to oxidation [120]. This mechanism concerns elements like Na, K, and Cs, and especially Ba, at low ionization potential.

A second mechanism involves additives which, by reacting in a homogeneous phase in the gases of the flame, produce hydroxyl radicals that are capable of eliminating the soot or its gaseous precursors. This effect reduces the radiation in the first zones of the flame. It essentially concerns the alkaline earth metals (Ba, Ca, Sr) which, by their hydroxides, maintain an $OH^•$ concentration that is capable of oxidizing the carbon [120].

The third mechanism concerns the transition metals (Mn, Fe, Co, Ni). It appears belatedly in the flame, in an oxygen-rich zone, causing the acceleration of the soot oxidation reactions by the inclusion of the catalytic metals in the particles. The corresponding additives have no effect on the amount of soot formed in rich flames but they increase the conversion rate in the oxygen-rich zones, particularly by lowering the soot oxidation temperature (Chapter 12): $6.6 \cdot 10^{-3}$ mol/liter of Ca can reduce the ignition temperature by more than 100°C [183].

Although they have no effect on gaseous pollutants, metallic additives added at the rate of $4.83 \cdot 10^{-4}$ mol/liter similarly reduce particulate emissions by 31% for Fe, 30% for Ce, 23% for Cu, and 21% for Mn. Lead is ineffective [174]. The reduction in the weight of the emissions essentially concerns the dry carbonaceous portion with no significant effect on SOF.

Purely organic additives help to reduce smoke emissions. They are totally ash-free and cannot have any action in the mass of particulates emitted. A mixture of this type, composed of a stable organic peroxide, further stabilized by a fatty acid imidazoline of tall oil (extract of pine resin) and an organic acid, is dissolved in an aliphatic solvent and added to the fuel at the rate of 0.6% by weight, which reduces the total particulate emissions by 33% and elemental carbon emissions by 73%, without altering the mass of SOF emitted [72]. A similar additive, containing six different active compounds, including an amine, dissolved in kerosene and added at the rate of 0.2% to the fuel, provides a reduction of the ignition delay corresponding to 5 points of the cetane number and helps to reduce particular emissions by 70 to 80% [6].

Gaseous additives like sulfur hexafluoride ($SF_6$) and dichlorodifluoromethane (Freon 12) also act on soot. The addition of $SF_6$ reduces the luminosity of the flames and hence affects the formation of soot. On the contrary, Freon 12, an electrophilic compound like $SF_6$, shows an inexplicable tendency to sharply increase the production of soot [181].

## 10.7 Odor formation in diesel exhausts

Diesel engine exhaust gases contain more than a thousand organic compounds [61] boiling at less than 260°C and present in concentrations detectable by gas phase chromatography ($>10^{-13}$ g/ml). Most of them only have a slight odor, including paraffinic and olefinic hydrocarbons, participating in the oily odor of the diesel exhaust. Fewer than a hundred compounds have a distinguishable odor in the concentrations found in the exhaust. These include saturated aldehydes from $C_2$ to $C_8$ and $C_{11}$, aldehyde derivatives of benzene, alkylbenzenes, and furans. The alkyl derivatives of benzene, indane, tetraline, and napththalene tend to add an 'acrid' and 'burnt' scent. Olefinic and cyclanic compounds provide a 'burnt' scent. Oxygenated compounds, containing sulfur (such as trimethylthiophene) or highly unsaturated ones, give a nauseating odor. The presence of fatty acids to $C_9$ has also been found to produce an 'acid' scent [61].

Other chromatographic separations [163] indicate that the 'oily and kerosene' scent is provided by naphthalenes, alkylbenzenes and indanes, tetralines and indenes. The 'smoky-burnt' scent is furnished by many compounds: hydroxy- and methoxy-indanones, methyl- and methoxyphenols, furans and alkylbenzaldehydes, alkenones, dienones, hydroxycyclocarbonyls, and hydroxyindanones [164].

Irritants must be added to these specifically odorous compounds. These are saturated light aldehydes (formaldehyde, acetaldehyde) and unsaturated aldehydes (acrolein, crotonaldehyde), sulfur dioxide, sulfuric acid, nitrogen dioxide, and phenol, which add to the sensory irritation felt in the presence of diesel exhaust gases [99]. In fact, the concentrations measured in diesel exhausts for formaldehyde and acrolein often exceed the sensory irritation thresholds. These two compounds must be considered as the main culprits for irritant effects [36].

Odorous and irritant compounds are unburnt organic compounds included in the general category of unburnt 'hydrocarbons'. The formation mechanism of these chemical species was described earlier (Section 10.4.4 and 10.4.5). The higher concentrations of oxygenated products are formed in the slow oxidation reaction zone, which precedes ignition and where many partial oxidation products are generated [222] (lean mixtures, see Fig. 10.11). Increasing the size of the zone below the lean mixture limit raises the odor level [10]. The odorous compounds formed are normally oxidized more thoroughly later, but part of them may survive if they are quenched in cold zones or areas where the fuel/air ratio is too low to ensure combustion. As a rule, direct injection engines have more irritating odorous emissions than precombustion chamber engines [37, 52, and 222]. The 'M' type chamber of MAN [23], which is fuel-economic and features tangential air swirl injection with a high quench effect on the walls [207], turns out to be highly odorous in this respect [98]. However, a well-timed direct injection engine may smell better than a poorly-timed precombustion chamber engine. Modifications of the engine running conditions (speed, charge, injection advance) within normal setting ranges have little effect on the odor levels emitted [36]. However, extreme settings of the corresponding parameters, which tend to deteriorate combustion, do affect odor emissions. One factor with a strong effect on diesel odor emissions is the size of the residual volume (Section 10.4.5.2) (Fig. 10.21) around the nozzle needle, which also causes unburnt emissions. Its reduction tends to decrease the odor level [52]. Yet an excessive reduction of unburnt HC does not necessarily mean a commensurate reduction of odor, because a temperature drop at the exhaust does not favor the afterburning of the odorant compounds [98]. On direct injection engines, greater swirl in the combustion chamber reduces the odorant level [98]. Turbo-charging reduces the odorant level in direct injection engines but has little effect with highly aromatic fuels [52].

The engine temperature influences the odor level. Intense cooling increases the odor while air preheating at the inlet decreases it. This is in accordance with high odor emissions during cold starts [52].

Load generally has a greater influence than speed. The minimum lies around 50% of maximum load [222]. The most intense odors are generated at full load and high speed [227] (incomplete combustion with rich mixture) as well as at partial load and low speed (medium combustion temperature) [51]. The idling odor level is always high [43 and 50]. The injection delay reduces the odor level at high speed and load because delayed ignition raises the temperature at the exhaust and favors afterburning of the odorants [98]. On the contrary, at low load the temperature level at the exhaust always remains too low for post-combustion, and the odor level then increases with the injection delay because the time left to complete combustion in the chamber is shorter [98]. Exhaust gas recirculation (EGR) also has a harmful effect on odor [36]. Transient acceleration and deceleration conditions are also recognized as favoring odor emissions [99], although in an actual driving situation, the movement of the vehicle favors the dispersion of the exhaust and makes these odors less irritating than for a stationary idling vehicle [43].

While in a precombustion chamber engine the cetane number has little effect on odor emission [38], the following measures could reduce the odor levels [222]:

- increasing the temperatures at the end of compression or preheating of the inlet air, which reduce the ignition delay (to the detriment of $NO_x$ emissions)
- optimization of the injection timing according to the load and speed to reduce the ignition delay
- reduction of the residual volume in the injection nozzle

However, the use of diesel catalytic filters to retain and burn the particulates (Chapter 12), which lower somewhat the odorant concentrations but do not affect the concentrations of the irritant light aldehydes [48], has a negligible effect on the overall odor level as assessed by the DOAS method.

The chemical composition of the fuels also has repercussions on the odor levels. Among various parameters (viscosity, distillation temperatures), an aromatics content exceeding 35% by volume raises the odorant level [37 and 51], except in a CFR precombustion chamber engine [38]. The use of lighter fuels (type JP4 kerosenes) reduces the odor level, especially at high load [98]. The sulfur content, while not directly implicated in the odor, can affect the irritant level and adds the harmful presence of $SO_2$.

Without being on the same scale as diesel odorant emissions, spark ignition engines can exhibit odorous exhausts, primarily during the starting period after the appearance of smoke [97]. Based on the measurement of dilutions at the olfactory threshold (Section 9.12), the peak odor is obtained with an air/fuel ratio of $\lambda \approx 1.1$ to 1.2 [89]. A rich mixture reduces the odor level as well as aldehyde emissions (Section 10.4.4, Fig 10.1). Under certain conditions (Chapter 12), the reducing conditions that prevail temporarily in catalytic mufflers may, with sulfur and nitrogen from the fuels, produce harmful hydrogen sulfide or cyanides [36]. However, the exhausts of gasoline engines provided with properly-adjusted catalytic mufflers are totally odorless.

## 10.8 Two-stroke spark ignition engines

The two-stroke engine offers basic advantages over the four-stroke cycle. These advantages are connected with its higher power per liter due to its lower pumping and friction losses and its double combustion frequency. Yet the concepts used so far cause higher specific fuel consumption and prohibitive hydrocarbon emissions in the exhaust gases. The emission levels of two-stroke spark ignition engines mounted on the majority of two-wheelers and a few automobiles [147] are similar to those of four-stroke engines in terms of CO, and lower for $NO_x$ [151 and 251]. The lower level of $NO_x$ emissions is ascribed to the fact [65] that the two-stroke engine with carburetor runs on a very rich mixture (to satisfy transients, because the carburetted mixture passes through the crankcase before reaching the cylinder). This high fuel/air ratio helps to limit the response time in acceleration resulting in low $NO_x$ emissions (Fig. 10.1).

In addition, thanks to its basic advantages described above, the two-stroke engine runs with lower loads than the four-stroke engine. This allows a substantial dilution of the carburetted charge by residual gases, thus lowering the combustion temperatures and hence the $NO_x$ emissions [65].

By contrast, these conditions are detrimental in terms of unburnt emissions. The two-stroke principle is based on the scavenging of the burnt gases by the fresh gases, transferred from the crankcase/pump to the combustion chamber through the transfer duct. Despite the many expedients developed to limit the mixing of fresh and burnt gases, particularly in carburetted engines, scavenging causes the direct passage of part of the fuel into the exhaust without any combustion. The consequences are high hydrocarbon emissions and a corresponding loss of power (higher consumption). Moreover, at partial load this type of engine is subject to combustion and ignition problems, which is another source of unburnt hydrocarbons [252].

One of the solutions suggested to avoid fuel losses by scavenging consists in stratifying the carburetted charge by feeding in mixtures with different fuel/air ratios, so that a lean mixture escapes at the exhaust port [202]. Another solution is mechanical fuel injection once the exhaust port is blocked [147].

The energy required for fuel injection is usually supplied by a pump driven by the engine, which commensurately reduces the power delivered to the drive shaft. Moreover, compared with the four-stroke engine, the very short time subsisting at the end of compression, after closure of the intake and exhaust ports, demands rapid high-speed injection resulting in the projection of part of the liquid against the walls and increased emissions of unburnt hydrocarbons.

A more economical solution is to provide pneumatic fuel injection using the comburent air let in during the compression phase and compressed in the combustion/expansion phase. In the IAPAC[2] engine (Fig. 10.14), a low-pressure

2. Injection Assistée Par Air Comprimé (compressed air assisted fuel injection).

injector located in a small precombustion chamber placed upstream of an injection valve injects a carburetted pre-mixture at high fuel/air ratio, at sufficiently low speed to avoid projecting fuel on the cylinder walls [63 and 64].

By scavenging the burnt gases with fuel-free air, this process helps to minimize unburnt hydrocarbon emissions in the exhaust, cutting the usual levels of two-stroke engines by 80 to 90% [66]. These values are still higher than those of four-stroke engines at low speed and high charge, the conditions in which the jet of carburetted mixture is likely to reach the exhaust port. Although $NO_x$ is slightly higher than in the standard two-stroke engine (due to the higher efficiency and operation with a leaner mixture) [184 and 185], the IAPAC engine's emissions are better than the emissions of conventional four-stroke engines by a factor of between 5 and 10 up to mid-load of the engine (the most frequent operating zone) and by a factor of 2 at full load [65]. Since the IAPAC runs on a lean mixture, it emits little CO and reduces $CO_2$ emissions at a power output equal to a conventional four-stroke engine.

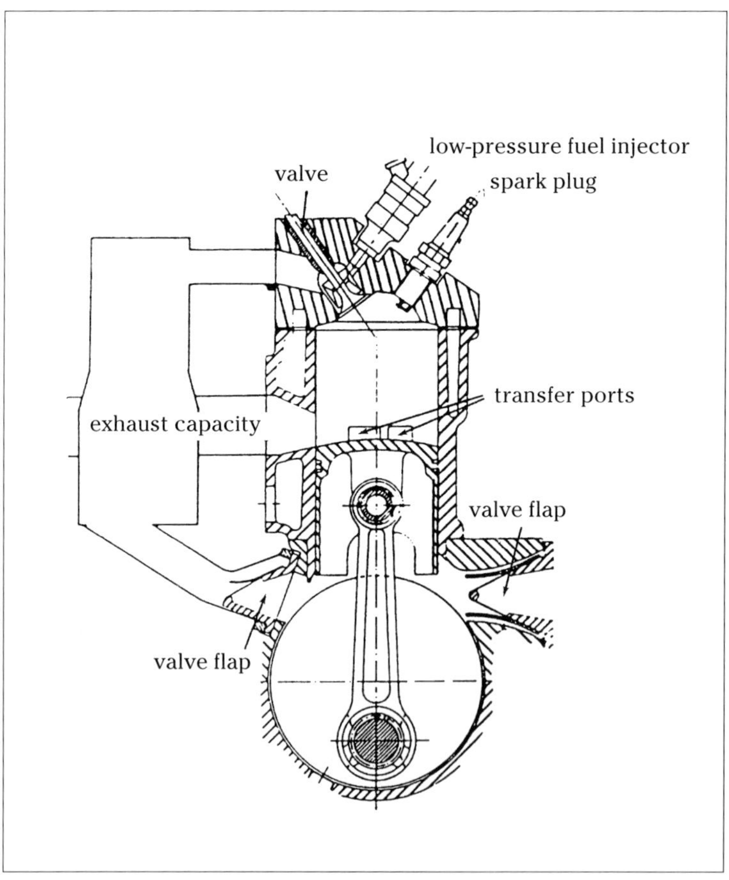


**Fig 10.14** IAPAC two-stroke engine [63]

## 10.9 Pollution control measures inside the spark ignition engine and the lean burn strategy

The promulgation of increasingly stricter statutory limits tends to force the installation of catalytic converters downstream of the engine in all applications, with the effect of reducing emissions below regulation levels. However, catalytic mufflers only offer a sufficient conversion rate once a minimum temperature level is reached (Section 12.9). Most of the emissions measured in standard test cycles (FTP-75 and ECE-15) occur during the cold phases of the cycle and In France, about 27% of automobile driving takes place at a coolant temperature lower than the optimal level. Therefore, a reduction of the emissions upstream of the catalytic mufflers should make it easier to meet stricter standards and to reduce cold start emissions when the catalyst is still cold.

A whole series of engine settings and internal changes help to adjust pollutant emissions. They can be classed in different categories [90 and 200]:

- formation of the carburetted mixture
- ignition
- combustion chamber shape
- volumetric compression ratio
- distribution: valve lift, timing, overlap
- exhaust gas recirculation

Methods for reducing emissions downstream of the engine are discussed in Chapter 12.

### 10.9.1 The lean burn engine

Lean engine intake charges have been recommended and investigated for several years to highlight their superior performance in terms of fuel consumption and efficiency. This reduction in specific consumption also leads to lower emissions of $CO_2$, the "pollutant" that is currently the focus of the most attention [91] in connection with the greenhouse effect (Section 2.3.1).

The overall lean mixture (air/fuel ratio $>1.25$) (Fig. 10.1) also offers the advantage of simultaneously reducing the three major pollutants (CO, HC, and $NO_x$) (Section 10.3.1, 10.4.1, 10.2.2.1). In going from an air/fuel ratio of $= 1.0$ to 1.4, consumption is cut by 7% and $NO_x$ emissions are reduced by 54% or even 85% by delaying ignition [177].

Yet this is only possible if the flame can be initiated at the spark plug and suitably propagated in a fuel/air mixture containing a large excess of air, without the risk of erratically producing no-burn cycles, causing additional emissions of unburnt HC and driveability problems.

The dilution of the carburetted mixture by air (lean mixture) or by exhaust gas recirculation (EGR) has the following results beyond a certain limit [59]:

- a decrease in combustion rates, shifting combustion into the expansion phase, despite the increase in the ignition advance
- cyclic torque irregularities causing unstable operation
- a sharp increase in the frequency of misfires
- an increase in unburnt HC emissions
- higher consumption connected with the deterioration of combustion rates

The parameters that help to run an engine near the lean limit can be classed in three categories [177]:

- measures applied before the inlet into the cylinder: preparation and dosage of the carburetted mixture (carburetor or injection system), feed pipe and mixture adjustment system, design of intake ducts
- measures in the engine: combustion chamber shape, arrangement of the valves (up to four valves per cylinder) [176] and spark plug(s)
- post-engine measures: design and arrangement of the exhaust system, addition of oxidation catalysts to eliminate residual masses of CO and HC leaving the chamber

One solution to reduce these drawbacks is to send a stratified charge into the cylinder, so that, in the neighborhood of the ignition point a richer mixture than the average carburetted mixture permits ignition and combustion propagation. Several stratified charge mixtures have been tested and subsequently abandoned. A distinction is made between precombustion chamber systems (CVCC type) and direct injection systems (PROCO type).

- The Honda CVCC system uses a small precombustion chamber fitted with its own intake valve (Fig. 10.15). A rich mixture is introduced into this precombustion chamber and a very lean mixture enters the main chamber through the classic intake valve. The spark plug ignites the rich mixture, which leaves the precombustion chamber and then burns the lean fraction of the carburetted charge. This type of combustion lowers the temperature peak, thus reducing $NO_x$ while maintaining a sufficient temperature to oxidize the HC and a low fuel/air ratio to avoid emitting CO. Despite its low specific consumption, this system is penalized by its low power per liter of cylinder displacement [42]. The system led to various developments and was then abandoned around 1986. By way of illustration, a system of similar design attempted to replace one of the carburetors by an injector that injects the rich mixture at 3.5 MPa during the compression period in a smaller precombustion chamber near the spark plug. This system reduces the $NO_x$ but this is counterbalanced by an increase in consumption [236].

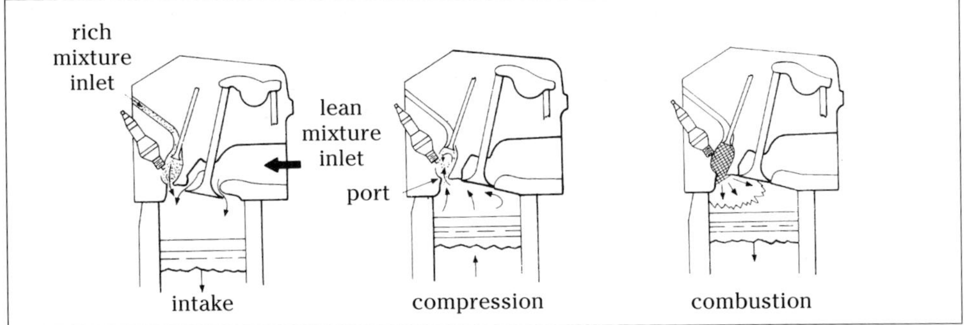


**Fig 10.15** CVCC stratified charge engine [111]

- The Ford PROCO system offers stratification by direct injection (Fig. 10.16). It does not employ a precombustion chamber but a combustion chamber excavated in the piston crown. A very open jet of rich mixture is sent to the center of the cylinder by a low-penetration nozzle [240]. This mixture, which is ignited by the spark plug, is mixed with a leaner mixture and with the excess air at the periphery by a strong swirl as the piston descends.
- The Texaco TCCS system differs from the PROCO [180]. It provides tangential injection aimed at the spark plug and prolonged ignition. The optimal setting of the injection time and the ignition point helps to initiate combustion at the time when the rich mixture reaches the plug. The flame front is maintained as the gyrating air takes in the fuel. This system presents the drawback of the diesel engine (rich heterogeneous mixture) with high particulate emissions, but without the advantages of diesel.

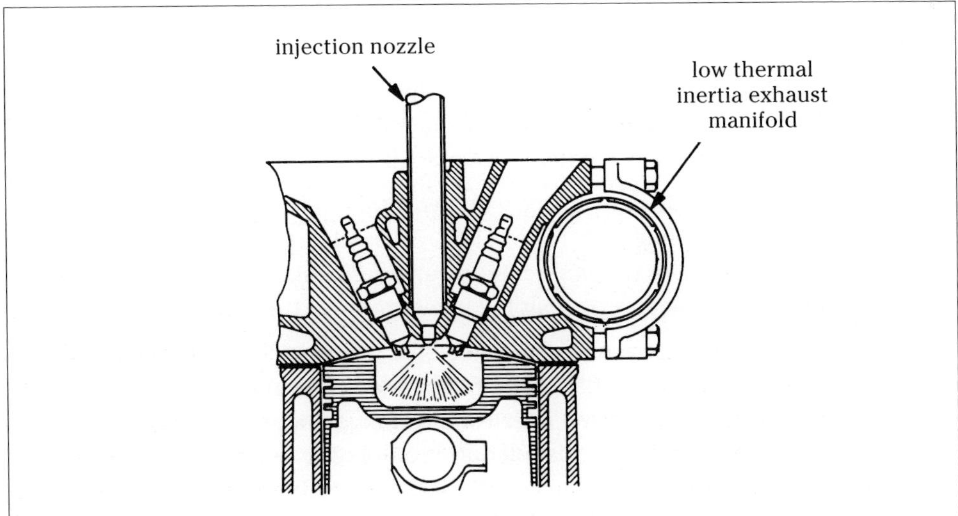


**Fig 10.16** PROCO stratified charge engine [240]

The solutions recommended to overcome ignition defects are the following: using spark plugs with much higher energy (wider electrode spacing, prolonged sparking time), reducing thermal losses at the spark plugs (fine electrodes, diameter reduced from 14 to 10 mm, higher thermal gradient), and shifting or increasing the number of ignition points. The present level of energy developed at the spark (about 40 mJ) is nevertheless sufficient for stable operation and minimal HC emissions [173]. The shifting of the ignition point in the combustion chamber helps to provide for stable operation at lower fuel/air ratio while reducing HC emissions, but to the detriment of spark plug life. Double ignition helps to increase the probability of ignition, the ignition energy, and the combustion rate, without increasing heat losses. However, these solutions also tend to increase the cost, may have a harmful effect on component life, and they are less effective than swirl enhancing devices.

Other attempts were therefore directed at increasing turbulence. By changing the geometry of the combustion chambers, the risks of extinction by quench at the wall were reduced by decreasing the surface/volume ratio and by increasing the turbulence generated by the intake (swirl) to increase the propagation of combustion [85]. The improvements made to combustion chamber shapes help substantially to reduce the pressure peak, with favorable action on the $NO_x$ levels, but the ideal chamber shape has not yet been found, and the variations in shape appear to have little or no effect on HC emissions [90].

Reducing dead volumes helps to achieve gains in unburnt hydrocarbon emissions. A smaller bore in the head gasket improves HC emissions, but raises problems of manufacturing tolerances.

A first solution to increase turbulence is to have a suitable design of the intake pipes (helicoidal pipes) that will increase the swirl of the mixture in the combustion chamber [177]. This increased turbulence helps to reduce the time interval between the spark at the plug (called the "initiation period") and start of combustion, as well as the combustion time. The corresponding values again become of the same order of magnitude as in combustion with a classic fuel/air ratio. The turbulence increases the stability of engine torque and hence driveability.

A second solution equips the engine with two intake valves per cylinder or fits the intake valve with a swiveling "swirl flap" [175]. This valve, which is closed at partial charge, cuts the flow from the main intake valve by aiming it at the second swirl generating line, which remains open at full power to let in the maximum of air [219].

A third solution for increasing turbulence on a multi-point injection engine is to provide a high-speed air jet that is generated in a lower section duct than the main inlet duct [267] and is injected by a nozzle aimed tangentially to the cylinder wall at the level of the inlet valve. This installation requires the addition of a second air intake control flap, with the two flaps controlled differently according to the engine load: idling, low load, and full load [200]. This system offers the advantage of not altering the geometry of the combustion chamber and not demanding dual ignition.

It also enables the engine to idle when hot with a lean mixture, but idling when cold results in excessive HC emissions and requires a richer mixture.

Table 10.6 summarizes the advantages and drawbacks of the systems proposed to increase turbulence.

**Table 10.6** Advantages and drawbacks of turbulence enhancing systems

| System proposed | Advantages | Drawbacks |
|---|---|---|
| **air jet** | power unchanged<br>possible control of turbulence | limited efficiency range |
| **helicoidal pipe** | high swirl level possible<br>simplicity | power drop<br>fixed swirl |
| **two inlet valves** | good swirl level<br>flexibility in turbulence control<br>power gain | cost |
| **swirl flap** | high swirl possible<br>progressive control | complexity<br>industrial feasibility<br>cost<br>power drop |

Increasing turbulence by means of the additional air jet helps to shift the combustion stability limit towards lower fuel/air ratios (from 0.95 to 0.75) and helps to obtain more stable idling operations [200]. By allowing operation at a fuel/air ratio of 0.7 instead of 0.8, it cuts $NO_x$ emissions sixfold and halves CO emissions, but increases HC emissions. Turbulence also facilitates the use of exhaust gas recirculation. For example, it helps to go from 20 to 28% EGR before increasing HC emissions, with the additional consequence of a further reduction of $NO_x$ [173].

Improved preparation of the mixture is achieved by using single-point injection (further upstream from the intake valves) in comparison with multi-point injection (immediately upstream from the valves) because it allows the fuel a longer time to vaporize. Single-point injection reduces HC emissions by 10 to 15% under the same engine running conditions when compared with multi-point injection, while improving operating stability. The carburetted mixture is also better prepared due to an increase in the inlet temperature, which favors vaporization of the fuel. At an equivalent fuel/air ratio, a 20 to 30% reduction in HC emissions is achieved by raising the inlet temperature from 25 to 80°C. On the other hand, $NO_x$ emissions are increased by 35 to 55%. Since 70 to 80% of CO and HC emissions are connected with the first 2 min of the cold start cycles of the FTP-75 type, partial preheating of the inlet manifolds during the period when the catalysts have not yet reached their initiation temperature helps to reduce these emissions. To do so, heating elements at a temperature of 40 and 55°C are placed in each inlet manifold of a multi-point injection engine and the jets are aimed at these heating elements. The electricity supply to these heating elements is gradually reduced and stopped when the coolant reaches 60 to 65°C [123]. The speed of passage of the inlet gases is governed by the diameter of the inlet valve. A reduction in this diameter from 35 to 29 mm decreases HC emissions by 15 to 25%. It also helps to reduce the fuel/air ratio before reaching the operating stability limit, but increases $NO_x$ emissions up to 45% at a fuel/air ratio of 0.9.

With multi-point injection, the position of the injector for a cylinder with two inlet valves has a considerable influence on the level of unburnt HC emitted and on the stability of the output torque. However, the injection position is primarily controlled by the ease of starting. Systems are being designed to improve the preparation of the mixture in multi-point injection: heating of the mixture or hot spots (vaporization), interaction with air at high speed (atomization), or ultrasonic atomization. The quality of atomization can in fact play a major role on emissions due to the fact that the smaller diameter and lighter droplets behave hydrodynamically like the air vector by matching the curves in the manifolds without any risk of coalescence on the walls. A maximum hydraulic diameter of about 10 μm is recommended [159] to overcome these drawbacks and to guarantee optimal distribution of the carburetted mixture between the cylinders. The carburetor helps to obtain a better distribution of the mixture at low charge, but injection proves to be better at high charges [159]. This is because carburetors atomize well at partial charge due to the higher vacuum at the inlet. At full charge, however, carburetors are much poorer than fuel injection. With carburation, the droplet diameter depends on the air speed at the throttle, whereas, with injection, it depends on the injection pressure. Air injection concentric with fuel injection (air mantle injector) further helps to improve atomization.

The distribution timing also influences emissions. It normally represents a compromise between maximum power, low-speed torque, and operating stability at idle with a low charge. An increase in the valve overlap at idle increases emissions and operating instability, but improves engine performance at high speed while reducing NO emissions [58] by recycling burnt gases to the intake manifold during the piston upstroke. This increase in overlap also helps to cut HC emissions by nearly 80%, but the overlap is limited by the operating instabilities that then increase the HC. Unburnt HC exit at the exhaust in two steps [58 and 83]: a first gust corresponds to the dead volumes located near the exhaust valve (valve itself, spark plug threads), and the second gust corresponds to the dead volume further in the system (rings). Higher overlap causes internal recycling of this second type of unburnt HC by inhibiting the second exhaust gust. These emission characteristics vary with engine speed and load. A multi-valve engine with a variable timing camshaft that shifts the intake valve would help to modify the compromise zone according to engine conditions, and thus gain 20% on HC emissions and 25% on $NO_x$ emissions for a hot engine [58].

However, by shortening the combustion time the combustion temperature is also raised, and, depending on the charge, this could have a detrimental effect on $NO_x$ emissions [176 and 178]. Delayed ignition in certain engine running conditions helps to lengthen the combustion time with a drop in combustion temperature that helps to reduce $NO_x$ (by about 0.3 g/test of $NO_x$ per crankshaft degree) [200]. The resulting increase in the exhaust temperature also favors afterburning and reduces the level of unburnt HC [143 and 196].

Increasing the stroke/bore ratio also increases the combustion rate and facilitates ignition, thus helping to run with more excess air. This is advantageous at partial charge but much less so at high charge [178].

Another way to accelerate ignition and flame propagation is to increase the volumetric ratio (up to 18), in conditions where this is feasible without knock, i.e. at partial charge [178]. This provides a compression ratio that varies with charge. An increase in the volumetric ratio tends to increase $NO_x$ emissions but the transition to a lean burn reduces $NO_x$ in higher proportions [90] (Fig. 10.17).

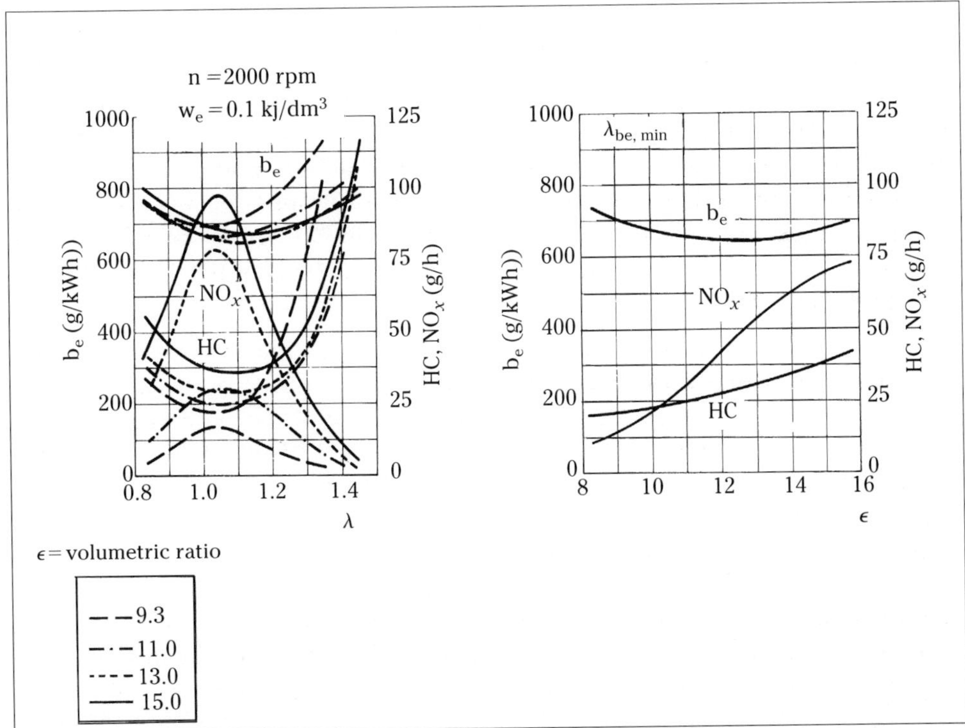


λ = air/fuel ratio, $b_e$ = specific consumption, $w_e$ = work per cycle

**Fig 10.17** Influence of compression ratio on emissions and consumption [90], Four-cylinder, two-liter gasoline engine

Improved preparation of the mixture consists in correctly controlling the fuel/air ratio in each cylinder, even in transient periods, to avoid driveability problems. The recommended solution is multi-point injection, which is individualized injection of the fuel per cylinder, with heating of the injectors and intake pipes to improve cold starting and reduce emissions during the cold start period [178]. Heating the intake ducts prevents fuel films from forming on the walls: these films vaporize during decelerations, excessively enriching the mixture [67].

A subdivision of the cooling circuits of the cylinder and the cylinder head [67] helps to keep the block at a higher temperature than the cylinder head and to raise the temperature of the block at partial charge, with a beneficial effect on both HC and $NO_x$ emissions [178]. This split is obviously eliminated at full charge. Compared with a hot engine (water and oil temperatures at 90°C) at equivalent power output, cold lubricating oil increases HC emissions by 75% at fuel/air ratio 0.9, and by 44% at fuel/air ratio 1, and $NO_x$ emissions rise 85% due to the larger intake charge needed to overcome additional friction losses [5]. Dividing the cooling circuit also ensures faster engine warmup and better preparation of the carburetted mixture in these conditions [67].

The transition to lean burn gives rise to a much wider cyclic dispersion of the indicated mean effective pressures. If, for an air/fuel ratio $\lambda$ of 0.8, the bmep oscillates to a maximum of 20 kPa, this oscillation can reach 140 kPa for $\lambda=1.2$ [268]. Consequently, to improve driveability with a lean burn engine it may be necessary to control the torque oscillations (measured with acceleration sensors placed on the flywheel) by controlling the per-cylinder injection start and duration using a feedback system or a preset engine map [67 and 178] and by monitoring the ignition point of each cylinder while idling [67]. Controlling torque oscillations helps to minimize HC emissions, which increase sharply with dispersion [268].

### 10.9.2 Fuel cutoff in deceleration

To limit unburnt emissions during periods when the engine brakes the vehicle rather than propelling it, it has been suggested that the fuel supply be cut off during these sequences.

However, this measure has two undesirable repercussions [243]:

- an unburnt hydrocarbon emission peak at the moment of cutoff and a second when the fuel feed resumes
- exhaust backfiring and jerky acceleration

Hydrocarbon emissions appear in all cases while abnormal combustion occurs at the exhaust mainly during short deceleration periods.

In the carburetted engine, to avoid stalling on resumption of the driving phase, a storage system is designed to provide additional fuel. This accumulates during the deceleration period in the enriching tube. When this tube is drained at the time of the sudden throttle lift, it helps to compensate for the excessively lean mixture that would otherwise cause a large intake of air due to the high vacuum behind the throttle. The richness of the stored volume affects the intensity of jerky acceleration. As to the hydrocarbon emission peaks, the first corresponds to the sudden evaporation of the fuel coating the exhaust manifold downstream of the throttle, caused by the high vacuum created by its closure. The second results from the incomplete combustion of the fuel stored in the enriching tube, which is fed in when the throttle is reopened.

In the injection engine, a calibrated port placed on the air flow helps to vary the amount of fuel injected as a function of the air flow rate. During deceleration with the throttle closed, a deceleration valve opens to allow the passage of the air bypassing the measurement orifice controlling the fuel injection and the engine thus sucks in a larger volume of air than for normal carburation. The two hydrocarbon emission peaks correspond with those of carburation, but the area wetted by the fuel is much smaller and hydrocarbon emissions are lower.

To overcome these drawbacks, it would be necessary to reduce the fuel films coating the walls and to decrease or prolong the gust of fuel fed at the time of pickup, but this eliminates the possibility of "sporty" driving of the vehicle.

### 10.9.3 Turning off the engine at traffic lights

Turning off the engine at city traffic lights is another way to reduce both pollution and consumption. It appears that the advantageous switch-off time depends closely on the type of vehicle and the pollutant concerned (CO, HC, $NO_x$, diesel particulates). Apart from the consumption aspect, there is no advantage for vehicles equipped with catalytic converters, since the switch-off time is insufficient to cool the catalyst. For other vehicles, which are correctly tuned with a warm engine, stops lasting an average of 50 s offer some advantage to turning off the engine, if this does not shorten the service life of the starter and the battery [260].

## 10.10 Measures in the engine to control diesel emissions

The type of diesel combustion has a direct influence on pollutant emissions. The direct injection engine, which offers specific consumption 10% lower than that of the precombustion chamber engine and less smoke emissions at partial charge [210], is disadvantaged by its emissions of noise and other pollutants ($NO_x$ and HC incorporated with particulates in the form of SOF) and is therefore reserved for trucks and buses. $NO_x$ emissions can be doubled and unburnts and particulates increased by 50% for the same power output on the FTP cycle [255].

The main problem raised by the diesel engine is the striking of a satisfactory compromise in all configurations between $NO_x$ and particulate emissions, i.e. to prevent the air/fuel ratio $\lambda$ both from rising locally above 0.9 (which favors $NO_x$) and from falling below 0.6 (soot formation) [210]. Nevertheless the $NO_x$/particulate trade-off is more favorable in the case of hydrotreated fuels, and the severity of treatment improves performance [285].

### 10.10.1 Effect of ignition advance and optimization of injection systems

The quality of the injection system in terms of emissions is more important in direct injection engines than in precombustion chamber engines, where the quality of the mixture also depends on the transfer duct between the precombustion chamber and the combustion chamber. The injectors used are generally different: hole-type for direct injection and pintle-type nozzles for the other cases.

Variations in injection timing have contrary effects on nitrogen oxide, unburnt, and particulate emissions (Fig. 10.18).

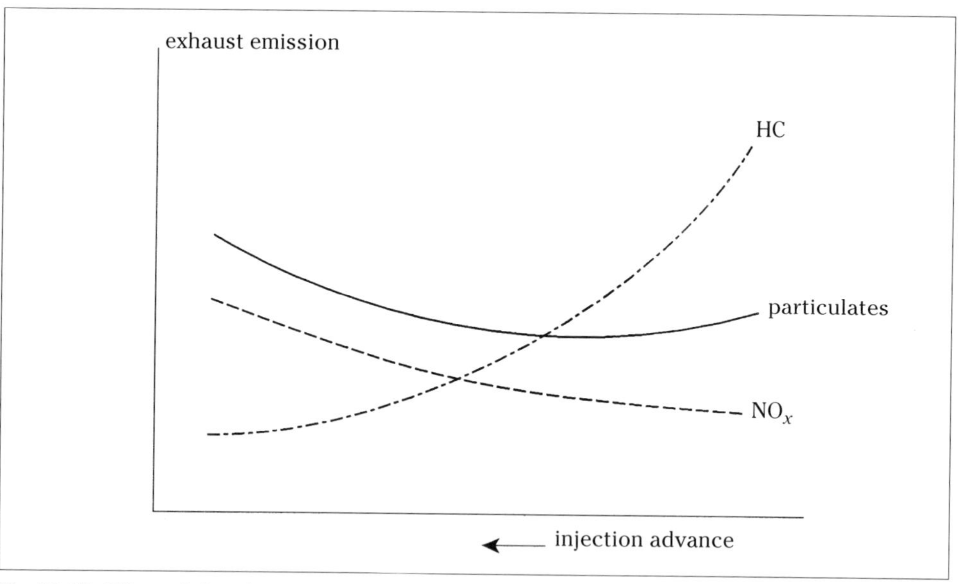


**Fig 10.18** Effect of diesel injection advance on emissions [166]

Increasing the injection advance, which favors the development of maximum pressure and higher combustion temperature, tends to increase NO emissions. Direct injection engines using higher advances have greater NO emissions than precombustion chamber engines [135]. Reducing the advance can therefore be one suitable way to reduce NO emissions [20, 113 and 144], provided injection timing is adjusted according to speed and charge [234] to avoid an excessive increase in specific consumption [283]. By lengthening the ignition delay, the injection advance increases the quantity of premixed fuel and forms a larger proportion of lean mixtures. These mixtures, which are more difficult to ignite, generate more CO [135]. While basically favoring the reduction of HC by facilitating combustion (Fig. 10.19), it can also increase them. During a longer ignition delay in direct injection engines, the injected fuel can hit the chamber walls and provide a source of unburnt HC.

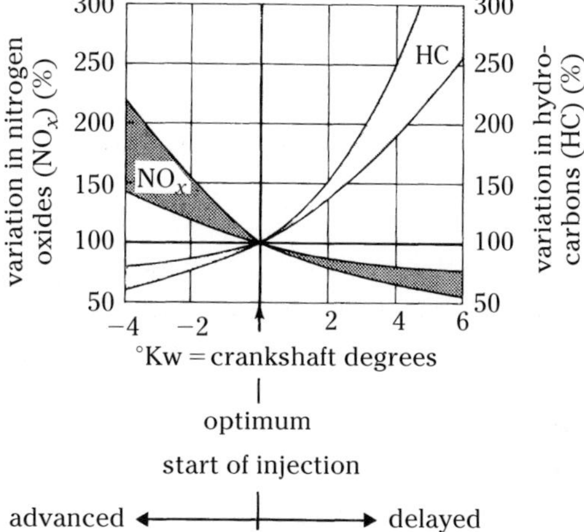


**Fig 10.19** Effect of ignition advance on hydrocarbon and nitrogen oxide emissions. Precombustion chamber engine, FTP-75 cycle [283]

The injection advance mainly affects particulates and smoke. In direct injection, shortening the advance increases smoke to a maximum. The smoke then decreases slightly before the top dead center. Retarding the timing reduces the oxidation of the particles and advancing the timing leads to a higher peak of particle concentrations in the cylinder, but to a lower exhaust mass of particulates [286]. This delay also increases specific consumption but reduces emissions of nitrogen oxides and the SOF fraction, as well as the latter's mutagenicity [30]. However, this delayed injection is applied to large stationary engines to meet statutory emission standards by halving NO emissions at the cost of slightly higher consumption [144]. On a precombustion chamber engine, the injection delay decreases NO emissions, and slightly cuts particulates, mainly at full charge, but increases HC [254]. A timing going from 8 to 23 degrees before the top dead center doubles the level of particulates emitted during an FTP-75 cycle [276] for a precombustion chamber engine for which the nominal advance is 15 degrees. An abnormal advance in fact increases the quantity of soot formed in the precombustion chamber, while an injection delay limits the quantity formed in the prechamber [80], but favors the reduction of SOF [132]. However, the action of the advance is negligible on a direct injection engine. Automatic injection timing devices as a function of speed and charge help to find an acceptable compromise between the reduction of $NO_x$ by injection delay and efficiency and soot formation.

On a precombustion chamber engine, electronic control of the timing according to a speed/charge map [234] helps to cut $NO_x$ emissions by 15% and particulate emissions by 25% on an FTP-75 cycle [166].

A higher injection speed (by increasing the injection pressure) acts on the emissions of a direct injection engine [30]. By increasing the speed of the air/fuel mixture, it increases the proportion of fuel burned in the premixed phase [134], thus increasing $NO_x$ but decreasing particulates, of both the solid fraction and the SOF. An increase in the injection pressure [187] (to over 100 MPa) again increases the particulates emitted on a US transient cycle due to the higher SOF emissions [205]. The use of injectors with more but finer holes (Fig. 10.20) [33] helps to improve air/fuel mixing by spraying finer droplets that ignite more easily and offset the injection delay that reduces nitrogen oxides. At constant $NO_x$ emissions, increasing the number of holes reduces the amount of smoke [210]. The number of holes must be greater if the injector is more central and less inclined with respect to the cylinder axis and if the engine speed is lower [34].

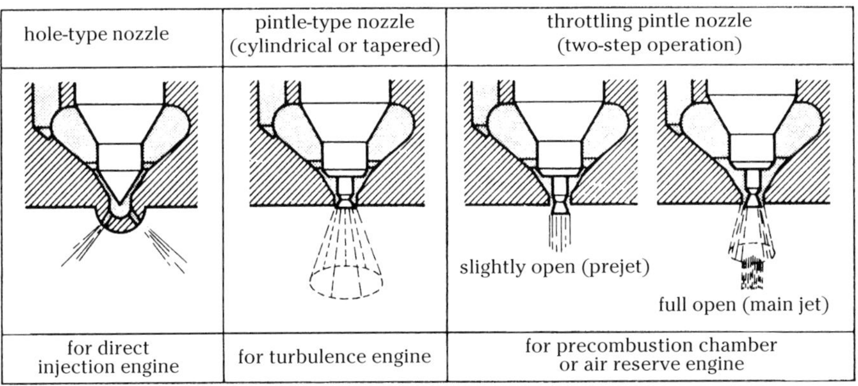


**Fig 10.20** Different types of injector [92]

In this regard, pump-injectors [259], due to the shortening of the high-pressure lines, help to reach higher pressures [108 and 109].

For a given type of injector, an optimal injection pressure exists (between 75 and 100 MPa) which varies with the speed of the direct injection engine. Above this value and at constant $NO_x$ emissions, the particulates emitted decrease but at the cost of an increase in specific consumption and combustion noise [283]. The increase in combustion noise, due to a sudden pressure increase, can be lessened by using a prior pilot jet [237]. The value of the optimal injection pressure on a 4-liter single-cylinder engine at a maximum speed of 2000 rpm (r/min) was found to be around 160 MPa [49] and was used in engine development. The smoke emission decreases steadily as the injection pressure rises, but above this level, $NO_x$ emissions increase too fast. Other types of injectors are being designed to improve the initial mixing of the fuel with the air [203]. Conical fuel jets tend to entrain the hot compressed air more easily into the liquid, while higher pressure pneumatic injections cause the formation of fuel aerosols which also entrain the hot compressed air.

The shape of the injection curve can also affect emissions [84]. Very fast injection at higher pressure speeds up the drainage of the injector and of its residual volume (Fig. 10.21), thus reducing unburnt HC [20]. The elimination of the nozzle sac volume in the injector provides effective action on unburnt emissions [213]. Expected advances in injection pump design are a uniform feed rate and a net cutoff at the end of injection, two-step injection, and zero flow with the accelerator pedal raised. There are also improvements needed regarding the injectors, such as needles unaffected by fouling, an increase in opening and injection pressures, variable-diameter injectors [7] that are easier to install on large engines and which, at low charge, help to cut CO, HC, and particulate emissions by half [108].

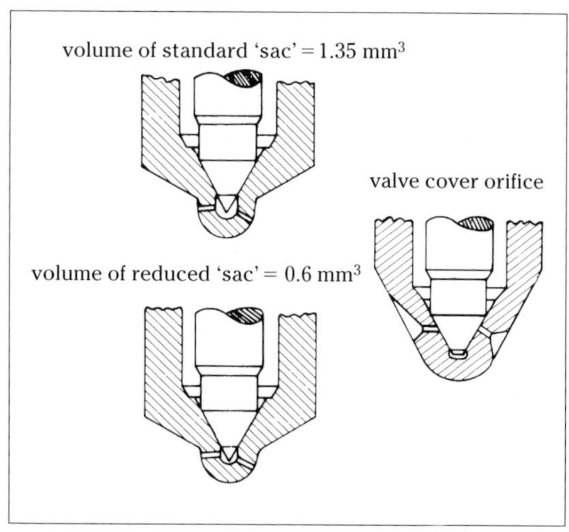


**Fig 10.21** Reduction of dead volume in injector nozzle

Lengthening the injection time helps reduce $NO_x$, HC, and CO emissions at low charge, but at high charge, it penalizes particulates and smoke. One suggestion [108] to overcome this drawback is a system to throttle the injected flow, which is active at low charge but inhibited when the quantity injected exceeds a pre-set threshold. In the precombustion chamber engine, a check valve upstream from the injectors [4 and 41] or a pressure compensation capillary on the injection pump helps to avoid secondary injections by needle rebound (Fig. 10.20), a process that generates increased emissions of unburnts and particulates. With non-detergent diesels, the use of flat-tipped needles, which are less sensitive to fouling, helps to stabilize the injected flow rates over time while maintaining the initial settings [283] (Table 10.7).

**Table 10.7** Effect of modifications to injection pumps on the reduction of pollutant emissions [283], Diesel engine for passenger vehicles

| Modification | Unburnt HC | Nitrogen oxides | Particulates |
|---|---|---|---|
| pressure compensation capillary | • | | • |
| flat-tipped injector needle | (•) | | • |
| electronic regulation of injection start | • | • | • |
| electronic regulation of EGR | (•) | • | (•) |
| total electronic regulation (EGR, start of injection, quantity injected) | • | • | • |

A reduction of the injected flow rate combined with a decrease in the advance can reduce $NO_x$ emissions by 30% on a precombustion chamber engine (measured on FTP-75 cycle), but increases HC emissions by 100%, CO by 70%, and particulates by 150% [74].

Control of the quantities injected during accelerations can also cut particulate emissions by 20% [223]. An accurate monitoring of the fuel flow rate injected in cold starting according to the engine temperature helps to control smoke emissions. [142]. A more sophisticated method uses a $\lambda$ probe in the exhaust, combined with sensors that measure the pressure and temperature of the air intake and the engine speed. This information, transmitted to a computer, offers the possibility of accurate control of the start of injection, precise dosage of the fuel injected by acting on the control rack of the injection pump, and the application of altitude corrections [7]. On trucks in particular, this helps to avoid gusts of smoke at gear changes [142].

### 10.10.2 Effect of combustion chamber geometry

The design of more open chambers should help to eliminate the impact of fuel jets on the walls, which generates unburnt emissions. On direct injection engines, combustion chambers with "recovery ridges", which prevent the injected fuel from being "blown" into the cold zones of the chamber when the piston descends, reduce unburnt emissions [142]. To reduce particulate emissions on a direct injection engine, moderate turbulence generated in the piston bowl associated with multiple-hole injectors has proven to be effective [33]. To prepare an optimal carburetted mixture, the combustion chamber must be designed to obtain the following [34]:

- an obstacle-free fuel-jet route that is as long as possible before reaching the combustion chamber walls
- a large surface area of the piston bowl below the jet impact point to promote spreading along the wall without interfering with the other jets
- intense recirculation of the carburetted mixture in the fuel jet dispersion zone
- maintaining or increasing the level of turbulence in the piston bowl after top dead center (at the start of expansion, when the piston descends)

Although increasing the pressure tends to favor the formation of soot both in a premixed flame and in a diffusion flame [224], an increase in the maximum pressure to 100 to 150 MPa helps to promote the recombustion of the soot by raising the temperature at the exhaust (if the higher efficiency does not lower this temperature), but to the detriment of noise and $NO_x$ emissions [20]. On direct injection engines, a high volumetric ratio is required to facilitate cold starting and to guarantee operation without white smoke. Increasing the compression ratio improves HC emissions and reduces the SOF fraction of the particulates [32], but excessive compression ratios cause higher soot emissions at full load [41 and 210]. Appropriate chamber shapes must also help to increase the air movements favorable to soot recombustion.

Increasing the stroke/bore ratio improves the efficiency and, at constant $NO_x$ emissions, reduces smoke emissions together with the reduction of the dead volume above the fire ring [210].

In direct injection engines, attempts have been made to add a small enclosure [263], a "pre-chamber" which fills with air during the compression period and empties on expansion, facilitating the oxidation of the particulates by its auxiliary air. This addition unfortunately increases the consumption of the engine. This additional air capacity has also been added to the precombustion chamber of precombustion chamber engines with a 40% reduction of particulate emissions, but with 3% higher consumption [262].

In precombustion chamber engines, the increase of the ratio between the precombustion chamber volume and that of the main combustion chamber helps to decrease the formation of soot by reducing the air deficit in the precombustion chamber [210]. The shape of the precombustion chamber, which induces different turbulence intensities in the chamber, acts on the $NO_x$ [4]. The cross-section of the transfer duct controls the turbulence generated at the time of the transfer of the ignited charge. The reduction of the cross-section diminishes particulate emissions at full charge, but increases them at partial charge, so that this value is therefore optimized for full charge [254]. The position of the glow plug in the precombustion chamber may disturb the flows when the engine is hot. By decreasing the protuberance of the glow plug [194], particulate emissions are decreased at full charge, while the effect at partial charge remains negligible [254]. A modification of the geometry of the combustion chamber to a "Ricardo" type precombustion chamber engine (deeper piston bowl, bell-shaped instead of spherical, wider transfer duct, recessed glow plug) helps to reduce HC and particulate emissions, but at the cost of $NO_x$ emissions [254].

Given the importance of the participation of the lubricant in particulate formation, more effective control of oil rising along the valve stems [4], as well as an improvement in the tightness of the rings [261] and the valve stems [161] is a beneficial step.

### 10.10.3 Effect of turbulence

The turbulence generated by the intake has antagonistic effects on efficiency and on $NO_x$, and noise emissions, as well as on unburnt, smoke, and particulate emissions [74 and 146]. To reduce the extent and lifetime of the very rich phases that generate soot in the cylinder, it is advisable to achieve the most effective possible mixing of the fuel injected with the air in the initial ignition phase (increase in the swirl level) [116]. However, this has the drawback of increasing the maximum pressure in the combustion chamber, with higher noise and $NO_x$ emissions [88]. One means to reduce $NO_x$ emissions would therefore be to limit the speed of mixing by decreasing the air swirl movements or the injection speed [20].

The position of the injector in the precombustion chamber helps to adjust the turbulence within the chamber and thus to improve particulate emissions [73, 74, and 188]. This positioning also affects the amount of fuel projected against the walls, which is a source of unburnts and soot [254]. The position of the injector in the precombustion chamber also has an effect on the formation of $NO_x$ [4].

### 10.10.4 Effect of engine speed and transients

The effects of idling are most pronounced on emissions. The transition from idling at 750 rpm to idling at 680 rpm (r/min) reduces the exhaust rate and simultaneously decreases all the pollutants on the FTP-75 cycle: −14% for HC, −2% for CO, −3% for NO, and −5% for particulates [7]. Electronic control of the injection pump is needed to stabilize the speed. But if many electrical accessories are used, this can cause substantial discharge of the battery during prolonged idling stop.

Changes in engine speed (acceleration and deceleration) also tend to increase emissions. In statutory tests on standard cycles and in practice, they are responsible for a large fraction of the emissions. Accelerations are a strong contributor to emissions of diesel particulates [261]. The equivalence ratio is enriched during accelerations and made leaner in decelerations. There is some lag in the increase in the charge pressure in acceleration and its reduction in deceleration. The EGR rate is increased in acceleration and decreased in deceleration. On the US 'transient' cycle for turbo-charged engines, particulate emission peaks are observed when the engine is again loaded after an idling period and the height of these emission peaks is more or less proportional to the idling time [34].

Several measures are available to reduce these effects [7]:

- reduction of moments of inertia (engine, turbo-charger)
- reduction of volumetric capacities (air intake, exhaust)
- cooling system with lowest possible heat transfer capacity (without instability in the case of temperature fluctuations)
- increase in surplus power available

All these measures must shorten the transition phases between the different engine running configurations.

### 10.10.5 Effect of cetane number

Another means to reduce the scale of soot formation is to lengthen the ignition delay by using a fuel with a low cetane number [101]. However, this may present serious drawbacks. Besides, the unacceptable noise already mentioned, if ignition is excessively delayed, droplets of liquid fuel may reach the cylinder walls and form deposits that burn very poorly and generate unburnt hydrocarbons and soot.

### 10.10.6 Influence of temperature

Lowering the inlet temperature helps to lower the maximum combustion temperature and accordingly the $NO_x$ emissions. It has therefore been suggested that the air be cooled at the turbo-charger exit [95] to allow for an inlet temperature not exceeding 50°C [20]. The effect is significant on particulate emissions, essentially at high load and low speed, but less effective at high speed. The advantage is particularly apparent in 13-mode cycles, with specified power values and where the emissions are related to the power [75]. It is less effective on FTP and ECE cycles. Yet this cooling can lengthen the ignition delay with the same drawbacks as discussed earlier (arrival of droplets on the cylinder walls and formation of unburnt HC and soot) [34]. Consequently, especially during the cold starting period, the use of a burner [77] to heat the injector and the combustion chamber, or heating the intake air, would help to reduce emissions of HC and "white smoke" while starting. Intake air heating, by an electric ceramic heater [247] or by the ignition of a small amount of diesel in the inlet air, facilitates the starting of direct injection engines on trucks while reducing starting unburnts and eliminating white smoke. Inlet air combustion is stopped once a temperature of 25°C is reached in the coolant [142]. Control of the coolant temperature, by temporary flow interruptions, also helps to cut HC emissions by 30% in an FTP-75 cycle [7].

The temperature of the exhaust line plays a role in emissions due to deposits of unburnt HC condensed in the line during low load periods and revolatilized when the load is increased [1]. The ceramization of the exhaust structures (e.g. using silicium nitride) should favor the afterburning of the soot and hydrocarbons, but an increase in smoke is normally observed at equivalent $NO_x$ emission [210]. The operation of the direct injection diesel engine in uncooled mode (by ceramization of the cylinder head and valves) helps to reduce emissions at low charge (including particulates), but at high charge, in addition to the expected increase in $NO_x$, particulates are also increased [263], although the thermal insulation of combustion chamber should help to reburn the soot at the end of the cycle. This effect appears to be due, in these conditions, to the transition from the premixed flame combustion mode to the diffusion flame combustion mode (Section 10.5.2).

In precombustion chamber engines, the interlocking of the operation of the glow plugs to the coolant temperature helps to reduce emissions (and noise) in cold starting [188].

### 10.10.7 Effect of supercharging

Since the formation of CO is due to insufficient excess air, especially at high load, supercharging helps to avoid this. The excess air provided by the turbo-charger also tends to favor soot recombustion [20], thus partially compensating for the increase in particulates induced by the EGR installed to reduce $NO_x$. Nitrogen oxides can thus be cut by half without penalizing particulates [284]. The chief improvement is in particulate emissions at high load, but in an operating zone that is not usually considered in the standard test cycles on passenger vehicles [74], since low loads do not require the turbo-charger. Hence supercharging does not appear to be a valid alternative for meeting the statutory limits on ECE and FTP cycles [75].

The advent of variable-geometry turbo-chargers [84] (variation in blade inclination) [284] helps to obtain the excess air on truck engines at low speed, which favors the reduction of soot and unburnt HC, without increasing the pressure and the mechanical loads at high speed [20]. However, it demands effective control in transient periods to minimize particulates [75].

### 10.10.8 Effect of exhaust gas recycling

Despite the harmful effects that excessive EGR may have on the internal pollution of the engine and its wear, recycling, by reducing the combustion temperature, has a beneficial effect on nitrogen oxide emissions. On a direct injection engine fed with intake air between 40 and 60°C (mining operations), initial $NO_x$ emissions can be cut by 30 and 50% respectively [148]. The same figures rise to 50 and 85% respectively if the intake air is humidified, which has the effect of increasing the heat capacity of the carburetted charge. However, recycling has a harmful effect on CO, particulate, and smoke emissions, even if the addition of water limits the increase in particulates [148]. Besides, EGR increases PAH emissions, which are further boosted by the addition of water. The injection of water serves to limit the cracking reactions that generate soot by limiting the combustion temperature. However, on a precombustion chamber engine the soot emissions first increase slowly and then faster with the quantity of water injected, especially if the water is injected into the precombustion chamber. CO and HC emissions follow the same pattern and water only favors the reduction of NO [112]. Since these effects do not have the same importance under the different engine operating conditions, control of the EGR rate according to the load and speed, or a regulation of this rate according to the air/fuel ratio and the speed helps to draw maximum benefit from this alternative [7 and 78]. Electronic control of the recirculation gate according to a preset map helps to exploit EGR more effectively. Recycling is cut off, with the engine cold, and its ratio depends on the coolant temperature, the ambient pressure, the amount of fuel injected, and the engine speed. Besides, it is inhibited in full acceleration according to the pressing of the accelerator pedal to limit smoke gusts [113 and 166]. The optimization of EGR thus helps to cut $NO_x$ emissions by 40% without affecting consumption or HC emissions, and without excessively penalizing CO (+10%) and particulate (+30%) emissions [74]. Combined with supercharging, EGR helps to reduce $NO_x$, unburnt HC, and particulates simultaneously [14]. An inlet throttle valve associated with the EGR gate, both actuated according to the load and speed, helps to reduce $NO_x$ and particulates simultaneously [239].

### 10.10.9 Electronic control of injection and EGR

Given the often contradictory effect of the engine settings on the various pollutants, whose effects fortunately do not have the same intensities at the different engine operating points, only electronic control of the action parameters (mainly the quantity and flow rate injected, fraction of the exhaust recycled) serves to obtain the best compromise at all times on emissions of unburnt pollutants, nitrogen oxides, and particulates.

The electronic control system must meet the following requirements [234]:

- display very high accuracy of monitoring and adjustment, stable over time
- it must incorporate multiple and complex adjustment functions
- it must offer great flexibility for programming the control system to take into account the different operating profiles of a vehicle (to meet the legislative requirements from one country to another)
- the engine running conditions must be identified instantaneously
- the engine must be regulated in accordance with the criteria imposed

The system must also operate in all the possible situations encountered, be protected from interference and failures, and be easy to maintain with a rapid diagnostic system. It must also respond as quickly as possible in transient running conditions, and in this case, open-loop systems may be preferable to closed-loop arrangements, which react more slowly [70].

To operate with the necessary information, the computer receives the data from the following sensors: position of the accelerator, position of the injector needle, tachometer, air, fuel and coolant temperatures, load pressure, and running speed. The actuators adjust the quantity injected, the start of injection, gas recycling, charge pressure, and gearbox ratio. This electronic configuration helps to cut particulate and nitrogen oxide emissions simultaneously in comparison with mechanical regulation, while improving specific consumption [234], and minimizing emissions and consumption [82]. Electronic regulation of injection [187] also helps to reduce (by a factor of 3) the ranges of variation of pollutant emissions according to the timing (Fig. 10.19) and to diminish the effect of manufacturing tolerances on emissions [283].

## 10.11 Re-aspiration of crankcase gases

The legislation in force in the different countries bans emissions from engine crankcases (Section 6.2.7). These gases originate in the combustion gases or in carburetted mixtures sent to the crankcase during the high-pressure phases through the functional clearances that cause leaks in the piston rings and along the distribution components (valve guides, valve push rods). Before the pollution control regulations, these blowdown gases were sent to the atmosphere through a vent called a 'crankcase breather' to avoid pressurizing the crankcase and to eliminate the explosion hazard of fuel vapor.

The solution adopted is to ventilate the crankcase by returning the gases to the engine intake, where they are partly burned and discharged in the exhaust where they undergo afterburning. To do this, the crankcase is equipped with a vent and a suction line terminating upstream and/or downstream of the carburetor and subject to negative intake pressure. This line is usually fitted with a settler to remove engine oil droplets that may be entrained and that can foul the engine as well as an explosion-proof flame-resistant cap to prevent any backfiring from the carburetor to the crankcase.

## 10.12 Control of evaporative losses

The different mechanisms of hydrocarbon emission by fuel evaporation are discussed elsewhere (Section 11.1.3). The main sources of evaporation are the fuel tank and the carburetor bowl, if present.

Losses from the fuel tank, by diurnal respiration or in refueling, are more or less proportional to the size of the vapor phase and hence to the level of the tank [54]. The evaporation rate is inversely proportional to the pressure in the tank. One way to reduce losses is to place the tank under low pressure with tared safety valves, always leaving a free volume to allow for expansion of the liquid during possible heating.

Losses at the carburetor are proportional to the capacity of the bowl(s), to the inlet pressure, and to the temperature of the bowl metal, which could reach 40 to 70°C, in hot soak conditions.

To prevent the vapors emitted from spreading into the air, an absorbent canister, which is usually filled with activated charcoal, is placed on the vehicle [136]. This canister is connected on one side to both the vapor space above the fuel present in the tank and to the carburetor. The other side is connected to the open air (Fig. 10.22). A purge line on the side opposite the air vent terminates downstream of the air filter in the intake manifold.

The design of the canister demands a suitable choice of activated charcoal, which must not only absorb the hydrocarbons (endothermic process) but desorb them easily (exothermic process) to preserve the absorption capacity of the canister. The charcoals selected are usually pyrolysis wood charcoals [170] activated by chemical treatment with phosphoric acid at about 500°C. The specific surface area of the charcoal, the volume and size of the pores of the beads, must be optimized to facilitate both absorption and desorption. A pore volume of 1.5 $cm^3/g$, a BET surface area of 1600 to 1900 $m^2/g$, and a uniform pore distribution between 16 and 40 Å are

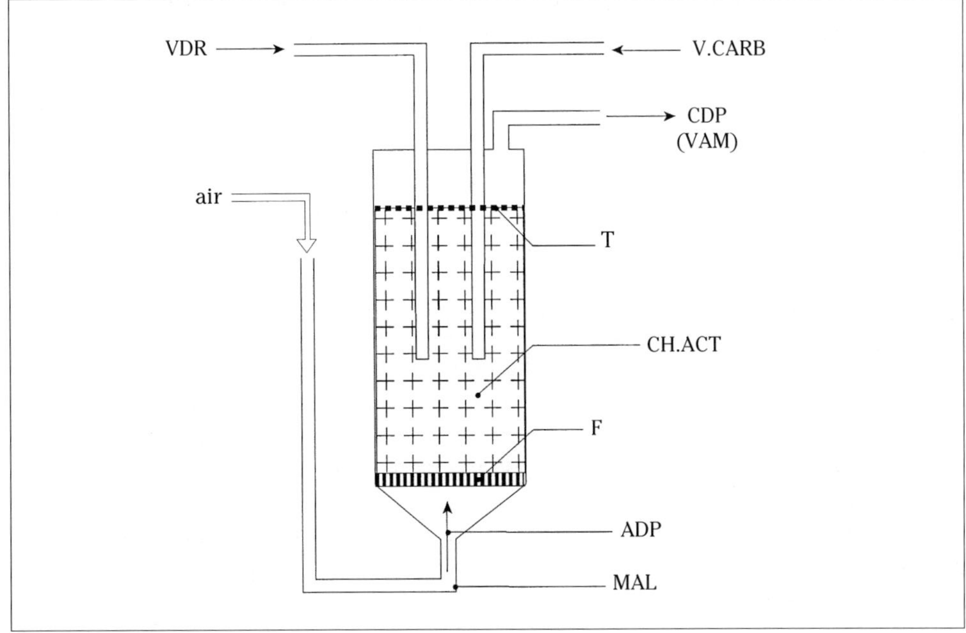


VDR, vapors from tank. V.CARB, vapors from carburettor.
CDP (VAM), purge circuit to engine intake. T, screen.
CH.ACT, activated charcoal. MAL air vent.
F, filter. ADP, purge air.

**Fig 10.22** Vapor recovery canister [65]

generally selected [8]. The type of fuel may affect the absorption capacity of the charcoal. The addition of methanol up to 35% by volume keeps it constant, but reduces it considerably above this figure [277]. The absorption of water vapor before the charcoal is first used must be avoided, because this would reduce its absorption capacity. The volume of charcoal must be sufficient to avoid saturation of the canister, which would then become a source of hydrocarbon vapors. If refueling losses do not need to be recovered, a capacity of 1 liter is normally considered capable of storing about 100 g of hydrocarbons. After conditioning (several absorption/desorption cycles), 100 g of charcoal can store about 5 g of HC [93].

The vapors from the carburetor float chamber are recovered as follows:

- with the engine turned off, a double valve, controlled by the closure of the intake throttle on the carburetted mixture, shuts off the aeration opening of the carburetor chamber and opens the connection of the vapor phase of the chamber with the canister
- with the engine running, the check valve cuts the connection to the carburetor vapor space and the canister and a fraction of the inlet air (about 2%) flows through the canister in countercurrent to purge it

For the fuel tank, the connection between the vapor space of the tank and the canister passes through a gas/liquid separator that returns the droplets to the tank and has a calibrated orifice to prevent rapid saturation of the canister.

Due to the endothermicity of the desorption reaction, it has been proposed for cold climates that the desorption air be heated by an electric heater [21]. On the contrary in warm climates, the absorption efficiency of charcoal is much lower and raises problems when the canister reaches temperatures of 45°C: 10% of the tank capacity can exit in vapor form and 70 kg of activated charcoal would be needed to retain it [150].

Other measures limiting evaporation consist in placing thermal shields around the carburetor chamber or making the chamber of plastic to avoid heat conduction. Thermal shields also protect the tank from the radiation of the exhaust system. To avoid any accidental overflow that could cause evaporation on service station forecourts during refueling, an anti-overflow tube dips into the tank to a certain depth and leaves a free space at its top that forms an expansion volume.

Another solution that is rarely applied, which prevents any loss of vapor from the tank both in operation and during refueling, is to use a flexible membrane inside the enclosure forming a sort of plastic bag containing the fuel (Fig. 10.23). Nevertheless, fuel degasification on refueling remains a problem [150].

The control of fuel vapor losses during refueling in the service station is another suggestion. The canister described earlier offers one alternative to satisfy the *EPA*

**Fig 10.23** Fuel tank with anti-evaporation membrane. *IFP Photo*

recovery program for gasoline vapors emitted during refueling at the pump. US studies estimate that about 0.8 to 1.3 g of HC is sent to the atmosphere per liter distributed [93 and 169] for an average refueling of 45 liters (Section 3.4.1). The mass of vapors emitted is directly proportional to the volume of fuel distributed, independently of the shape and size of the tank and the fuel flow rate [27]. The system obviously demands a tight seal between the nozzle (conventional) and the tank filling tube, which usually consists of a membrane with elastomer lips, that is resistant to hydrocarbons, especially aromatics, and is installed on the filling tube (this membrane would be superfluous if the refueling rate creates an air inlet by "gas-lift" pushing the gasoline vapors inside the tank) [190]. It also demands the installation of a cartridge, connected to the fuel tank vent [190] and with a much larger capacity (3 to 5 times greater) [214] than the one designed merely to absorb diurnal and hot soak losses [93]. This means 3.5 liters of canister for a 56 liter tank [189] and a larger section canister purge line [139]. This system is particularly recommended by the European oil companies [191]. Stage I of the *EPA* Program imposes a system for returning displaced gasoline vapors to the tanker truck during the filling of the service station tanks [11].

*EPA* Stage II proposes total recovery of the vapors throughout the distribution circuit, from the refinery to the vehicle tank [228]. The nozzle is fitted with a bellows concentric with the fuel distribution tube and connected to a second hose that returns the vapors to the storage tank. This system also prevents air from entering the service station reservoir whenever fuel is distributed.

This system has gradually been installed in Sweden since 1986 [18]. It eliminates about 99% of people's exposure to gasoline vapors when filling vehicle fuel tanks. It is also being examined in Germany, in preference to the onboard canister, and its general distribution is planned within five years [214]. Apart from the liability problems for the two industries (canister installed by the vehicle manufacturer and vapor recovery nozzle installed by the motor fuel distributor), each of these alternatives offers specific advantages:

- The large-capacity canister [9], usually installed on a vehicle without the driver's knowledge, recovers the fuel vapor to the driver's benefit, cutting his apparent consumption and recovering about 14 liters per year. It also recovers evaporative losses during operation, in so far as these losses are appreciable (above 40°C) [190]. Given the age distribution of cars in circulation, however, a certain period of time will have to elapse before most of the vehicles are suitably equipped [11]. This also raises problems of safety (debatable) during refueling, or collision due to the increase in the volumes containing gasoline vapors [190].
- The vapor recovery nozzle is less effective (60 to 99% recovery depending on the sources and the quality of the system used) but it is adaptable to relatively old vehicles not equipped with anti-evaporation canisters and the number of service stations to be equipped is much smaller than the number of vehicles.

## 10.13 Influence of speed limits

A review of the different investigations conducted in Germany, the Netherlands, Switzerland, and France [127 and 128] shows that the lowering of speed limits on expressways, roads, and in the city has little effect on the level of pollutants emitted. The following occurs at stabilized speed:

- CO emissions drop to a minimum at around 80 to 90 km/h, with wide variations above and below
- HC emissions decrease up to around 100 km/h and then increase slightly
- $NO_x$ emissions increase slowly up to 70 to 80 km/h and then rapidly afterwards, especially on large engines: the sharp decrease anticipated in the neighborhood of the maximum speeds, due to the higher fuel/air ratio needed to obtain maximum power, only appears with small vehicles whose cylinder displacement $<1.4$ liters

On the other hand, measurements on a test cycle, which are closer to actual traffic conditions, reveal a very slight influence from speed limits. Only a sharp curtailment of these limits, once properly obeyed, would result in a drop of a few per cent in $NO_x$ emissions, accompanied by a slight increase in CO and HC emissions.

However, if the overall effect of speed is to increase emissions due to the turbulence generated at the rear of the vehicle, it tends to disperse the pollutants more rapidly and hence to reduce the local concentrations [68].

A German study [211] shows that, while a small number of vehicles exceed the prescribed speed limit, most of them are driven below a limit threshold on expressways due to the power available. This is 119 km/h for a speed limit of 130 km/h and the average speed drops to 107 km/h for a speed limit of 100 km/h. This variation from 119 to 107 km/h on the expressway network would achieve a drop of 12% in CO emissions, 1.7% in HC emissions, and 10.5% in $NO_x$ emissions. Another experiment, which lowered the speed limit from 100 to 60 km/h on a section of urban expressway [15], showed a 50% reduction in $NO_x$ emissions over a six-month period reducing the nitrogen oxide contents in the environment from 570 to 350 $\mu g/m^3$.

## 10.14 Influence of ambient temperature

Despite the aspiration of denser air at low temperature, which would tend to make the mixture leaner, lowering the ambient temperature causes a sharp increase in CO and HC emissions. This is due to the poor quality of mixing caused by the difficulty of vaporizing gasoline in cold air [204] and to the enrichment (provided by the choke) required to start the engine and to ensure satisfactory driveability, particularly during transients, before reaching running temperature (generally between 80 and 90°C). While it takes 4 min to reach running temperature for the coolant at +20°C, it takes more than 8 min at −20°C [204]. This affects HC emissions by increasing the thickness of the quench layer on the walls of the combustion chamber. It was found in the United States that, for each degree Celsius of temperature drop below ambient temperature, HC emissions from gasoline vehicles rose 0.4% and CO emissions 0.8% [81 and 172]. This has significant consequences for emissions in cold climates, where engine warmup generates high CO emissions [40]. At cold starts, to obtain a proper fuel vapor/air ratio, it is necessary to have a higher fuel liquid/air ratio in cold climates than in temperate climates. This increases the HC emissions.

The effect of low temperatures on starting is magnified by the fact that most drivers travel in short hops. In France, 40% of the routes do not exceed 2 km, which corresponds to 27% of the driving with the choke on [129]. On the ECE cold start cycle at 20°C, 77% of the total HC emissions correspond to the first quarter of the cycle, with the last quarter accounting for only about 3% of the total [173]. This is no longer the case when the vehicle is started with an outdoor temperature at −10°C, because thermal equilibrium is not yet reached at the end of the cycle [265]. In comparison with +20°C, emissions during the first 40 s of the ECE-15 cycle rise 31% at 5°C and 62% at −10°C for HC, and 20°C and 6% respectively for CO. $NO_x$ emissions are relatively unaffected.

At room temperature, with a three-way catalyst, most of the CO and HC is emitted in the first 120 s [216]. On the ECE-15 cycle, on going from +20 to −10°C, CO and HC emissions are doubled, while $NO_x$ emissions are relatively unchanged [265]. In the same tests in stabilized conditions, but with the engine starting warm, the effects of lowering the (outdoor) temperature of the aspirated air are negligible [204]. In fact, a decrease in CO is observed due to the leaner mixture caused by the aspiration of a larger air mass with higher density. On the other hand, preheating the intake air to around 80°C (with the coolant remaining at ambient temperature and the choke closed) helps to reduce CO emissions by about 30% on the ECE cold start cycle [12].

With vehicles equipped with three-way catalysts on the FTP cycle, unburnt HC and CO emissions increase sharply when the ambient starting temperature drops from 21 to 4°C, and then to −7°C [245]. The HC and CO double in g/km on going from 21 to 4°C, and then increase by a factor of about 1.5 on going from 4 to −7°C. In the same conditions, $NO_x$ and formaldehyde vary only slightly with temperature. An increase in the ambient temperature from 24 to 37°C increases NO emissions by about 6% [172]. As for the ECE-15 cycle, most of the HC emissions occur during the first period of the FTP cycle [172] (before catalyst light-off): passage from 0.58 to 3.24 g/km HC when the temperature drops from 21 to −7°C.

Combined with high-altitude driving (Colorado), the lowering of the temperature of an FTP cycle to 5°C instead of between 20 and 29°C to simulate cold starting and winter driving at high altitude leads to particulate carbon emissions more than 50% higher on spark ignition vehicles equipped with catalytic converters [269].

This effect on HC emissions is more pronounced in carburation and single-point injection than in multi-point injection, because with a cold engine, enriched carburation causes much greater wetting of the walls of the intake system than in multi-point injection [159]. On a lean burn engine, this enrichment in the carburetor equipped version leads to operation in the range corresponding to the maximum $NO_x$ emission and this could mean a more than 85% increase in emissions in comparison with warm running [200]. Another cause of greater low-temperature $NO_x$ emissions stems from the fact that, to overcome the higher friction in these conditions, it is necessary to demand greater power from the engine to follow the standard cycle [204]. To reduce the effects of cold starting, it has been proposed that engines be equipped with quick-heat intake manifolds [22]. A thin plate placed in the intake manifold and warmed by a temporary and partial deviation of the exhaust gases (system shut off by a thermostat once the coolant running temperature is reached) allows faster vaporization of the fuel while reducing CO emissions.

For diesel-powered vehicles, temperature appears to have little effect on CO, HC, and particulate emissions between 24 and −7°C [81]. Only the first phase of the FTP cycle reveals slightly higher HC and CO emissions due to hydrocarbon quenching on the cold walls. $NO_x$ emissions rise with the temperature drop for cold start cycles, by 33% in going from 24 to −7°C. The mass of particulates emitted increases slightly when the temperature drops from 28 to 7°C [26]. This is probably due to greater adsorption of the unburnt fuel on the particles formed.

For vehicles powered by various proportions of methanol, formaldehyde and methanol exhaust emissions increase sharply when the temperature drops from 24 to 4.5°C.

## 10.15 Influence of driving style

Independently of the vehicle transmission characteristics, particularly the staging of the gearbox ratios, driver behavior also affects pollutant emissions. Its effect on consumption at equivalent average speed is well known.

It is mainly in urban driving with a warm engine that driving style reveals the sharpest differences through the use of higher gears or long decelerations before stopping at the traffic lights ("wise" driving as opposed to "sporty" driving).

These differences, which are difficult to identify for CO emissions, are abundantly clear for $NO_x$ and HC emissions. In urban driving for the same average speed on an identical vehicle, an increase in consumption of 33% (from 6 to 8 liters/100 km) boosts $NO_x$ emissions by 33% (from 3 to 4 g/km) and HC emissions by 16% (from 0.6 to 0.7 g/km) [229].

On a road, the average speeds vary more with driving style than in the city. $NO_x$ and HC emissions increase with consumption, which is related to distance traveled. On expressways, most drivers use overdrive. In these conditions, due to the enrichment at high load and the reduction of the ignition advance, the faster driver tends to emit less nitrogen oxides, while the effect on HC emissions is much less clear.

## 10.16 Influence of altitude

High altitude operation of a vehicle with a naturally aspirated engine tends to decrease the air mass introduced into the combustion chamber and hence, if remedial measures are not applied, to enrich the carburetted mixture. In carburation systems, compensation is generally achieved by varying the fuel flow rate (needle controlled by an aneroid capsule) [46]. A comparison between the same types of vehicle at sea level and in Colorado (altitude 3000 m) [242] shows that HC and CO increase sharply with altitude (doubling on the average from 0 to 3000 m), whereas nitrogen oxides decrease by half. However, proper setting of the idling fuel/air ratio at altitude reduces idling CO in mountainous areas. The generalized use of fuel injection combined with fuel/air ratio correction using a $\lambda$ probe will nullify the effect of altitude.

With naturally aspirated diesel engines, the fuel/air ratio of the injected mixture rises with altitude, so that smoke emissions also increase with altitude, especially if additional fuel is injected to offset the corresponding power loss. On naturally aspirated engines, injection pumps that are self-correcting by the use of an anemometer capsule help to overcome this drawback [166 and 188]. This problem does not occur on supercharged engines, in so far as the turbo-charger succeeds in maintaining a constant fuel/air ratio up to an altitude limit [55].

## 10.17 Conclusion

How the various pollutants present in engine exhausts are formed is not yet fully understood.

However, the enormous experience gained by automobile manufacturers throughout the world, combined with the experience of the research and development laboratories that cooperate with them, is helping to identify the various engine construction and adjustment factors that affect the output of pollutants.

Unfortunately, the effects of these parameters are sometimes antagonistic, particularly for the reduction of $NO_x$ in comparison with other pollutants. Furthermore, the reduction of pollutants cannot be the only concern of automobile manufacturers. The cost of the vehicle, driving comfort, noise emissions, and fuel savings are factors that are considered along with pollution in the development of a vehicle.

The contribution of automotive electronics is helping to control all these parameters by allowing adjustments in real-time to optimize responses to various demands.

## REFERENCES

[1] M.K. Abbass et al., (1989), "Pyrosynthesis of PAH in a Diesel engine operated on kerosene", *SAE Paper* No. 890827, 15 p.

[2] P. Advenier et al., (1990), "Le Diesel automobile face à la réduction des émissions, évolution des moteurs", *Influence des caractéristiques du gazole, SIA Int. Conf.*, Lyon, 13/14 June, *Paper* No. 90064, pp. 43-53.

[3] C.A. Amman et al., (1980), "Some rudiments of Diesel particulate emissions", *SAE Paper* No. 800251 (P-86), 177-204.

[4] M. Amano et al., (1976), Approaches to low emission levels for light duty Diesel vehicles, *SAE Paper* No. 760211, 15 p.

[5] G.E. Andrews et al., (1989), "The role of cooling water and lubricating oil temperatures on transient emissions during SI engine warm-up", *2nd Int. Conf. "New Developments in powertrain and chassis engineering"*, Strasbourg, 14/16 June, *Paper* No. C382/015, pp. 37-49.

[6] G.E. Andrews and A.M. Nurein, (1990), *A non metallic Diesel fuel additive for the reduction of particulate emissions, IMechE Seminar, "Fuels for automotive and industrial Diesel engines"*, London, 19/29 November, pp. 65-75.

[7] F. Anisits, (1985), "Möglichkeiten zur Beeinflussung der Abgas-Emission", "Emissionsminderung Automobilabgase, Dieselmotoren", *VDI Berichte*, (559), 83-98.

[8] Anon., (1989), *Westvaco European Seminar on evaporative losses for the automotive industry, activated carbon perspectives*, Bruxelles, 19 September, 50 p.

[9] Anon., (1990), "Closing the gasoline system, control of gasoline emissions from the distribution system and vehicles", *CONCAWE Report* No. 3/90, 18 p.

[10] P. Aubertin, (1990), *Les moteurs XUD 11 de PSA, performances, dépollution, SIA Int. Conf.*, Lyon, 13/14 June, *Paper* No. 90056, pp. 185-189.

[11] T.C. Austin and G.S. Rubinstein, (1985), "A comparison of refueling emission control with onboard and stage II systems", *SAE Paper* No. 851204, 30 p.

[12] M.N. Azpiazu et al., (1990), "Effect of air preheating on automotive emissions, water, air and soil pollution", **51,** 231-237.

[13] R. Barbella et al., (1988), "Soot and unburnt liquid hydrocarbon emissions from Diesel engines", *Comb. Sci. Techn.*, **59,** 183-198.

[14] C. Bassoli et al., (1979), "Exhaust emissions from a European light duty turbo-charged engine", *SAE Paper* No. 790316 (SP-442), 19 p.

[15] J. Baumüller and U. Reuter, (1990), "Reduzierung von Stickoxydbelastungen, Tempolimit auf einer Stadtautobahn (B10) in Stuttgart, ein Versuch", *Staub*, **50,** 445-449.

[16] P. Belardini et al., (1989), "The combustion chamber shape parameters and their influence on emissions of a direct injection turbocharged Diesel engine", *2nd Int. Conf. "New developments in powertrain and chassis engineering"*, Strasbourg, 14/16 June, *Paper* No. C382/122, pp. 313-323.

[17] J.D. Benson and R.F. Stebar, (1971), "Effects of charge dilution on nitric oxide emission from a single cylinder engine", *SAE Paper* No. 710008, 12 p.

[18] P.M. Berglund and G. Petersson, (1990), "Hazardous petrol hydrocarbons from refuelling with and without vapour recovery", *Sci. Tot. Environm.*, **91,** 49-57.

[19] M. Bidault, (1980), "Essai d'optimisation d'un moteur Diesel pour poids lourds sur les plans pollution et consommation", *Poll. Atmosph.* (85), 116-121.

[20] M. Bideault, (1990), "La réduction des émissions des moteurs de véhicules industriels", *SIA Int. Conf.*, Lyon, 13/14 June, *Paper* No. 90099, pp. 265-279.

[21] R.P. Bishop and P.G. Berg, (1987), "Vapor canister heater for evaporative emission systems", *SAE Paper* No. 870123, 6 p.

[22] W.D. Bond, (1972), "Quick heat intake manifolds for reducing cold engine emissions", *SAE Paper* No. 720935, 19 p.

[23] Y. Bonnetain et al., (1980), "Le poids lourd, conception et fonctionnement", *IRT Information Sheet* No. 18, 176 p.

[24] P.A. Bonczyk, (1988), "Suppression of soot in flames by alkaline earth and other metal additives", *Comb. Sci.Techn.*, **59,** 143-163.

[25] O. Boulhol, (1990), "Les émissions polluantes du parc automobile français", *Air Environnement*, No. 9, June.

[26] J.N. Braddock, (1982), "Impact of low ambient temperature on Diesel passenger car emissions", *SAE Paper* No. 820278, 17 p.

[27] J.N. Braddock et al., (1986), "Factors influencing the composition and quantity of passenger car refueling emissions, Part 1", *SAE Paper* No. 861558, 15 p.

[28] O. Brandt and P. Roth, (1988), "Measurement of the high temperature oxidation rate of soot particles", *J. Aerosol Sci.*, **19,** 863-866.

[29] D. Broome and I.M. Khan, (1971), *The mechanisms of soot release from combustion of hydrocarbon fuels with particular reference to the Diesel engine, IMechE Conf. "Air pollution control in transport engines"*, London, 9/11 November, 12 p.

[30] J. Campbell et al., (1981), "The effect of fuel injection rate and timing on the physical, chemical and biological character of particulate emissions from a direct injection diesel", *SAE Paper* No. 810996, 35 p.

[31] E.N. Cantwell et al., (1972), A systems approach to vehicle emission control, *SAE Paper* No. 720510, 10 p.

[32] W.P. Cartellieri and W.F. Wachter, (1987), "Status report on a preliminary survey of strategies to meet US 1991 HD Diesel emission standards without exhaust gas aftertreatment", *SAE Paper* No. 870342, 16 p.

[33] W.P. Cartellieri, (1988), *Innermotorische Möglichkeiten zur Partikelminderung bei DE-Dieselmotoren, Tagung "Rußminderung bei Dieselfahrzeugen"*, Essen (Haus der Technik), 24/25 February, 15 p.

[34] W. Cartellieri et al., (1989), "Erfüllung der Dieselabgasgrenzwerte von Nutzfahrzeug-Dieselmotoren der 90er Jahre", *MTZ*, **50,** 440-451.

[35] W. Cartellieri and P.L. Herzog, (1988), "Swirl supported or quiescent combustion for 1990's heavy duty DI Diesel engines, An analysis", *SAE Paper* No. 880342, 23 p.

[36] N.P. Cernansky, (1983), “Diesel exhaust odor and irritants, A review”, *J. APCA*, **33,** 97-104.

[37] N.P. Cernansky and E.D. Petrow, (1985), “A comparison of the odorous emissions from a direct injection and an indirect injection Diesel engine”, *Int. J. Vehicle Design*, **6,** 183-198.

[38] N.P. Cernansky, (1989), “Fuel effect on Diesel odor from an IDI CFR engine”, *Int. J. Vehicle Design*, **10,** 295-309.

[39] E. Chambron et al., (1990), “Méthodes de mesure des suies et des températures dans la chambre de combustion d'un moteur Diesel IDI”, *SIA Int. Conf.*, Lyon, 13/14 June, *Paper* No. 90092, pp. 177-183.

[40] T.Y. Chang and J.M. Norbeck, (1983), “Vehicular CO emission in cold weather”, *J. APCA*, **33,** 1188-1189.

[41] R. Cichocki and W. Cartellieri, (1981), “The passenger car direct injection Diesel, A performance and emissions update”, *SAE Paper* No. 810480, 14 p.

[42] D. Collins, (1978), “The spark ignigion reciprocating gasoline engine”, in: *“Vehicle emissions, fuel consumption and air pollution”*, M.S. Janota, Peter Pelegrinus, Stevenage, Hertfordshire, UK, pp. 18-33.

[43] J.M. Colucci and G.J. Barnes, (1970), “Evaluation of vehicle exhaust gas odor intensity using natural dilution”, *SAE Paper* No. 700105, 10 p.

[44] F.E. Corcione et al., (1991), “Improvement of combustion system of a small DI engine for low exhaust emissions”, *SAE Paper* No. 910481, 11 p.

[45] M.J. Covitch, (1988), “Oil thickening in the Mack T-7 engine test, (2) Effects of fuel compositon on soot chemistry”, *SAE Paper* No. 880259, 23 p.

[46] W.H. Crouse and D.N. Anglin, (1977), *Automotive Emission Control,* McGraw Hill, New York, 278 p.

[47] W.A. Daniel, (1970), “Why engine variables affect exhaust hydrocarbon emission”, *SAE Paper* No. 700108, 25 p.

[48] A.M. Danis et al., (1985), “Effect of ceramic monolith particulate filters on Diesel exhaust odorant and irritant species”, *SAE Paper* No. 850011, 13 p.

[49] R. Decker et al., (1990), “Einfluß der Kraftstoffhochdruckeinspritzung auf die Verbrennung im Dieselmotor”, *MTZ*, **51,** 388-394.

[50] P. Degobert, (1978), “Pollution odorante par les moteurs Diesel”, *Revue Inst. Franç. du Pétrole*, **23,** 453-466.

[51] P. Degobert, (1979), “Odeurs d'échappement diesel, leur importance, méthodes d'appréciation”, *Journées de Conférences GFC*, Paris, 21 March, *Inst. Franç. du Pétrole Report* No. 26864, 44 p.

[52] P. Degobert, (1981), “Evaluation of Diesel odorous emissions”, *CEC Int. Symp.*, Roma, 3/5 June, *Paper* No. EF/3/3, 12 p.

[53] P. Degobert, (1986), “Pollution provoquée par le moteur Diesel, niveaux d'émission, comparaison avec le moteur à allumage commandé”, *Revue Inst. Franç. du Pétrole*, **41,** 687-698.

[54] M. Delanette, (1989), *Les automobiles et la pollution, techniques anti-pollution*, ETAI, Paris, 306 p.

[55] J.W. Dennis, (1971), "Turbocharged Diesel engine performance at altitude", *SAE Paper* No. 710822, 20 p.

[56] G.G. de Soete, (1989), "Cinétique de la formation de polluants gazeux dus à la combustion, un exemple type, l'oxyde et le protoxyde d'azote", *Poll. Atmosph.* (122), 176-183.

[57] J.B. Donnet and J. Lahaye, (1983), "Burning of soot particles", in: *"Soot in combustion systems and its toxic properties"*, L. Lahaye and G. Prado, Plenum Press, New-York, 1983, pp. 259-271.

[58] C. Dopson and T. Drake, (1991), "Emission optimization by camshaft profile switching", *SAE Paper* No. 910838 (SP-863), 195-205.

[59] A.M. Douaud et al., (1988), "Potentiel des moteurs à mélange pauvre face aux moteurs actuels à réglage stoechiométrique, consommation, émissions, exigence en octane", *Revue Inst. Franç. du Pétrole*, **43,** 111-123.

[60] R. Douglas and G.P. Blair, (1982), "Fuel injection of a two stroke spark ignition engine", *SAE Paper* No. 820952, 14 p.

[61] A. Dravnieks et al., (1970), "Chemical species in engine exhaust and their contribution to exhaust odor", *NTIS Report* No. PB-198072, 90 p.

[62] C-J. Du et al., (1984), "Measurements of polycyclic aromatic compounds in the cylinder of an operating Diesel engine", *SAE Paper* No. 840364, 12 p.

[63] P. Duret et al., (1988), *Un nouveau moteur à injection assistée par air comprimé pour applications automobiles, Conf. "Le moteur à allumage commandé de la prochaine décennie"*, Strasbourg, 18/19 May, Ing. Automobile, pp. 220-230.

[64] P. Duret et al., (1988), "A new two-stroke engine with compressed air assisted fuel injection for high efficiency low emission applications", *SAE Paper* No. 880176.

[65] P. Duret et J.F. Moreau, (1989), "The IAPAC two-stroke engine with compressed air assisted fuel injection, Origin and reduction of pollutant emissions", *2nd Int. Conf. "New developments in powertrain and chassis engineering"*, Strasbourg, 14/16 June, *Paper* No. C382/126, pp. 99-108.

[66] P. Duret and J.F. Moreau, (1990), "Reduction of pollutant emissions of the IAPAC two stroke engine with compressed air assisted fuel injection", *SAE Paper* No. 900801, 16 p.

[67] K.D. Emmenthal and I. Geiger, (1989), "Entwicklungsstand eines alternativen Magerssmotors", *Automobil-Industrie*, (3), 279-287.

[68] R.E. Eskridge et al., (1991), "Turbulent diffusion behind vehicles, Effect of traffic speed on pollutant concentrations", *J. Air Waste Managem. Assoc.*, **41,** 312-317.

[69] G. Essig et al., (1990), "Diesel engine emission reduction, the benefits of low oil consumption design", *SAE Paper* No. 900591, 10 p.

[70] G. Felger, (1987), *Engine management systems, A substantial contribution to emission control, IMechE Conf. "Vehicle emissions and their impact on European Air Quality"*, London, 3/5 November, *Paper* No. C346/87, pp. 259-268.

[71] A. Feugier and P. Gateau, (1989), "Formation des polluants particulaires dans la combustion des hydrocarbures", *Poll. Atmosph.* (122), 184-189.

[72] M.S. Filowitz and M. Vataru, (1989), "Diesel particulate control without engine modifications, A cost effective fuel supplement", *SAE Paper* No. 890828, 15 p.

[73] H.J. Förster, (1991), "Entwicklungsreserven des Verbrennungsmotors zur Schonung von Energie und Umwelt, Teil 1", *ATZ*, **93,** 258-272.

[74] M. Fortnagel, (1985), "Gemischbildung Verbrennung und Emission an Dieselmotoren", "Emissionsminderung Automobilabgase, Dieselmotoren", *VDI Berichte* No. 559, 65-81.

[75] M. Fortnagel, (1988), *Die Beeinflussung der Partikelemission von Dieselmotoren für Personenkraftwagen und Leichtnutzfahrzeugen durch innermotorische Maßnahmen, Möglichkeiten und Grenzen, Tagung "Rußminderung bei Dieselfahrzeugen"*, Essen (Haus der Technik), 24/25 February, 25 p.

[76] R.A.C. Fosberry and Z. Holubecki, (1966), "Some considerations of the effect of atmospheric conditions on the performance of automotive Diesel engines", *SAE Paper* No. 660744, 20 p.

[77] G. Fraenkle and H.O. Hardenberg, (1975), "New methods for reducing visible emissions of Diesel engines", *SAE Paper* No. 750772, 8 p.

[78] C.C.J. French and D.A. Pike, (1979), "Diesel engined, light duty vehicles for an emission controlled environment", *SAE Paper* No. 790761, 19 p.

[79] Y. Fujiwara and S. Fukazawa, (1980), "Growth and combustion of soot particulates in the exhaust of Diesel engines", *SAE Paper* No. 800984, 14 p.

[80] Y. Fujiwara et al., (1984), "Formation of soot particulates in the combustion chamber of a precombustion chamber type Diesel engine", *SAE Paper* No. 840417, 10 p.

[81] P.A. Gabele et al., (1986), "Emissions from a light duty Diesel, ambient temperature and fuel effects", *SAE Paper* No. 860618, 10 p.

[82] E. Gaschler, (1985), "Abgasbeeinflussung durch elektrische Einspritzregelung", "Emissionsminderung Automobilabgase, Dieselmotoren", *VDI Berichte* No. 559, 249-260.

[83] B. Gatellier et al., (1990), *The reduction of exhaust emissions (HC and $NO_x$) of a four valve spark ignition engine by means of valve timing, 3rd EAEC Int. Conf.*, Strasbourg, 11/13 June, 7 p.

[84] A.P. Gill, (1988), "Design choices for 1990's low emission Diesel engines", *SAE Paper* No. 880350, 20 p.

[85] A.J. Gomez et al., (1988), "Lean burn, A review of incentives, methods and trade-offs", *SAE Paper* No. 880291, 14 p.

[86] C. Grasas Alsina et al., (1986), "Low pressure discontinuous gasoline injection in two stroke engines", *SAE Paper* No. 860168, 14 p.

[87] G. Greeves et al., (1977), Origins of hydrocarbon emissions from Diesel engines, *SAE Paper* No. 770259, 17 p.

[88] G. Greeves and C.H.T. Wang, (1981), Origins of Diesel particulate mass emission, *SAE Paper* No. 810260, 12 p.

[89] D. Gruden, (1972), "Abgasemission und Abgasgeruch des Viertakt Fahrzeug Ottomotors", *ATZ*, **74,** 180-188.

[90] D. Gruden et al., (1984), "Motorinterne Maßnahmen zur Erfüllung neuer Abgasvorschriften", "Emissionsminderung Automobilabgase, Ottomotoren", *VDI Berichte* No. 531, 169-187.

[91] D. Gruden, (1990), "Anforderungen an Motorenöle der Zukunft, Erdöl, Erdgas", *Kohle*, **106,** 24-28.

[92] J-C. Guibet and B. Martin, (1987), *Carburants et moteurs,* Editions Technip, Paris, 903 p.

[93] J.A. Gunderson and D.K. Lawrence, (1975), "Control of refueling emissions with an activated carbon canister on the vehicle", *SAE Paper* No. 750905, 22 p.

[94] N. Hafiani et al., (1988), *Formation de particules par pyrolyse d'hydrocarbures, GSM Symp.*, Rueil Malmaison, 5 November 1988, Editions Technip, Paris, pp. 225-232.

[95] J.M. Hales and M.P. May, (1986), "Transient cycle emission reduction at Ricardo, 1988 and beyond", *SAE Paper* No. 860456, 12 p.

[96] K. Halupka, (1960), "Das Höhenverhalten abgasturboaufgeladener Viertakt Dieselmotoren", *MTZ*, **21,** 359-363.

[97] H. Hardenberg, (1972), "Untersuchungen zur Entstehung und Beseitigung von Kraftstoffrauch und Abgasgeruch", *MTZ*, **33,** 248-254.

[98] H. Hardenberg and H. Daudel, (1978), *Ergebnisse, Probleme und Grenzen organoleptischer Geruchsbestimmung an Nutzfahrzeugmotoren, 17th FISITA Conf.*, Budapest, pp. 323-331.

[99] C.T. Hare et al., (1974), "Public opinion of Diesel exhaust", *SAE Paper* No. 740214, 22 p.

[100] W.W. Haskell and C.E. Legate, (1972), "Exhaust hydrocarbon emissions from gasoline engines, Surface phenomena", *SAE Paper* No. 720255, 13 p.

[101] A. Haupais, (1988), *Etude expérimentale sur moteur de la formation et de l'oxydation des suies, GSM Symp.,* Rueil Malmaison, 5 November 1988, Editions Technip, Paris, pp. 233-245.

[102] S. Hayano et al., (1985), "Formation of hazardous substances and mutagenicity of PAH produced during the combustion process in a Diesel engine", *Atmosph. Environm.*, **19,** 1009-1015.

[103] B.S. Haynes and H.G. Wagner, (1981), "Soot formation", *Prog. Energy Comb. Sci.*, **7,** 229-273.

[104] E. Heck et al., (1989), "Motorkonzept mit Oxydationskatalysator", *MTZ*, **50,** 101-108.

[105] G. Heinrich et al., (1982), "Spektrometrisches Meßverfahren zur Untersuchung der Rußentwicklung im Dieselmotor", *ATZ*, **84,** 85-90.

[106] N.A. Henein, (1976), "Analysis of pollutant formation and control , and fuel economy in Diesel engines", *Prog. Energy Comb. Sci.*, **1,** 165-207.

[107] H. Henning, (1989), "Der Mercedes-Benz 'Diesel' '89', Eine Alternative zum geregelten Katalysator", *ATZ*, **91,** 212-213.

[108] G. Herdin and T. Sams, (1988), "Motorische Auswirkungen eines theoretisch optimierten Direkteinspritzungverfahrens auf Emissionen und Verbrennungsgeräusch", *VDI Berichte*, No. 714, 205-239.

[109] G. Herdin et al., (1988), "Neue Direkteinspritz Dieselmotorengeneration der Steyr-Daimler-Puch AG, Teil 2 Versuchsergebnisse", *MTZ*, **49,** 351-358.

[110] J.B. Heywood, (1976), "Pollutant formation and control in spark-ignition engines", *Prog. Energy Comb. Sci.*, **1,** 135-164.

[111] J.B. Heywood, (1988), *Internal Combustion Engine Fundamentals,* McGraw Hill, New York, 930 p.

[112] O. Hiemesch and G. Reibold, (1988), *Möglichkeiten zur Begrenzung der Partikelemission bei PKW-Dieselmotoren, Tagung "Rußminderung bei Dieselfahrzeugen"*, Essen (Haus der Technik), 24/25 February, 19 p.

[113] O. Hiemesch et al., (1990), "Das BMW Abgasreinigungskonzept für Dieselmodelle", *MTZ*, **51,** 196-200.

[114] J.C. Hilliard and R.W. Wheeler, (1979), "Nitrogen dioxide in engine exhaust", *SAE Paper* No. 790691, 12 p.

[115] O. Hirao and R.K. Pefley, (1988), *Present and future automotive fuels, Performance and exhaust clarification*, J. Wiley and Son, New York, 570 p.

[116] H. Hiroyasu et al., (1980), "Soot formation and oxidation in Diesel engines", *SAE Paper* No. 800252 (P-86), 205-218.

[117] R. Hofmann, (1984), "Einfluß des Verbrennungsablaufes auf die motorischen Kennwerte", "Emissionsminderung Automobilabgase, Ottomotoren", *VDI Berichte* No. 531, 51-67.

[118] H.S. Homan, (1983), "The dependence of soot yield on flame conditions, A unifying picture", *Comb. Sci. Techn.*, **33,** 1-15.

[119] M. Houben and G. Lepperhoff, (1990), "Untersuchungen zur Rußbildung während der dieselmotorischen Verbrennung", *MTZ*, **51,** 11-16.

[120] J.B. Howard and W.J. Kausch, (1980), "Soot control by fuel additives", *Prog. Energy Comb. Sci.*, **6,** 263-276.

[121] J.B. Howard and J.P. Longwell, (1983), "Formation mechanisms of PAH and soot in flames", in: *"Polynuclear aromatic hydrocarbons, formation, metabolism and measurement"*, M. Cooke et al., (7th Int. Symp.), Battelle Press, Columbus, pp. 27-62.

[122] D.M. Human and T.L. Ullman, (1989), "Simulation of high altitude effect on heavy duty Diesel emissions", *NTIS Report* No. PB90-153867/XAD, 94 p.

[123] D. Hütterbräucker and J. Henke, (1990), "Verringerung der Kaltstartemission durch partielle Saugrohrvorwärmung an der Mercedes-Benz Vierzylinder-Einspritzmotoren", *MTZ*, **51,** 316-317.

[124] R.J. Jakobs and K. Westbrooke, (1990), "Aspects of influencing oil consumption in Diesel engines for low emissions", *SAE Paper* No. 900587, 18 p.

[125] S.H. Jo et al., (1973), "Development of a low emission and high performance 2-stroke gasoline engine", *SAE Paper* No. 730463, 9 p.

[126] H.R. Johnson and R.S. Williams, (1990), "Performance of activated carbon in evaporative loss control systems", *SAE Paper* No. 902119 (SP-839), 20 p.

[127] R. Joumard, (1985), "Emissions de polluants du trafic routier, Influence des limitations de vitesse", *INRETS/CERNE Report*, 50 p.

[128] R. Joumard, (1987), "Influence of speed limits on road and motorway pollutant emissions", *Sci. Tot. Environm.*, **59,** 87-96.

[129] R. Joumard and M. André, (1990), "Cold start emissions of traffic", *Sci. Tot. Environm.*, **93,** 175-182.

[130] R.S. Joyce et al., (1969), "Activated carbon for effective control of evaporative losses", *SAE Paper* No. 690086, 12 p.

[131] T. Kadota and N.A. Henein, (1981), "Time resolved soot paticulates in Diesel spray combustion", in: *Particulate Carbon, Formation During Combustion*, D.C. Siegla and G. W. Smith, Plenum Press, New York, pp. 391-421.

[132] K. Kageyama and N. Kinehara, (1982), "Characterization of particulate emission from swirl chamber type light duty Diesel engine as a function of engine parameters", *SAE Paper* No. 820181, 12 p.

[133] E.W. Kaiser et al., (1982), "The effect of oil layers on the hydrocarbon emissions from spark-ignited engines", *Comb. Sci. Techn.*, **28,** 69-73.

[134] T. Kamimoto et al., (1987), "Effect of high pressure injection on soot formation processes in a rapid compression machine to simulate Diesel flames", *SAE Paper* No. 871610, 9 p.

[135] I.M. Khan and H.C. Grigg, (1971), "Progress of Diesel combustion research", *9th Int. Conf. on Combustion Engines*, Stockholm, 28 p.

[136] J.B. King et al., (1970), "The 1970 General Motors emission control systems", *SAE Paper* No. 700149, 13 p.

[137] D.B. Kittelson et al., (1990), "Particulate emissions from Diesel engines, influence of in-cylinder surface", *SAE Paper* No. 900645, 15 p.

[138] E. Koberstein and H.D. Pletka, (1982), "Exhaust purification with small 2-stroke engines, A challenge for catalytic systems", *SAE Paper* No. 820279, 11 p.

[139] W.J. Koehl et al., (1986), "Vehicle onboard control of refueling emissions, System demonstration on a 1985 vehicle", *SAE Paper* No. 861551, 16 p.

[140] D.N. Koert et al., (1987), "Carbonyl formation from a model Diesel fuel", *APCA Meeting, Paper* No. P. 87/1.2, 22 p.

[141] K. Komiyama and J.B. Heywood, (1973), "Predicting $NO_x$ emissions and effects of exhaust gas recirculation in spark-ignition engines", *SAE Paper* No. 730475, 18 p.

[142] W.D. Korner, (1990), "Les moteurs VI modernes sous l'aspects des émissions à l'échappement", *Problèmes et perspectives d'avenir, SIA Int. Conf.* , Lyon, 13/14 June, *Paper* No. 90094, pp. 281-295.

[143] V. Korte and D. Gruden, (1987), "Possible spark-ignition engine technologies for European exhaust emission legislations", *IMechE Conf. "Vehicle Emissions and Their Impact on European Air Quality"*, London, 3/5 November, *Paper* No. C334/87, pp. 187-196.

[144] O. Kruggel, (1985), "Untersuchungen zur Stickoxidminderung an Großdieselmotoren", "Emissionsminderung Automobilabgase, Dieselmotoren", *VDI Berichte* No. 559, 459-478.

[145] O. Kruggel, (1988), "Untersuchungen zur Stickoxidminderung an schnelllaufenden Großdieselmotoren", *MTZ*, **49,** 23-29.

[146] H.A. Kuck, (1985), "Dieselmotorische Verbrennung", "Emissionsminderung Automobilabgase, Dieselmotoren", *VDI Berichte* No. 559, 45-63.

[147] V. Kuentscher, (1986), "Application of charge stratification, lean burn combustion systems and anti-knock control devices in small two-stroke cycle gasoline engines", *SAE Paper* No. 860171, 9 p.

[148] I. Kurki-Suonio et al., (1988), "Einfluß der Abgasrückführung und des katalytischen Nachbrenners auf die $NO_x$ und Gehalte der Abgase eines Dieselmotors", *MTZ*, **49,** 31-35.

[149] H. Kuroda et al., (1978), "The fast burn with heavy EGR, New approach for low $NO_x$ and improved fuel economy", *SAE Paper* No. 780006, 15 p.

[150] G. Lach and J. Winckler, (1990), "Kraftstoffdampf-Emission von Personenwagen mit Ottomotoren", *ATZ*, **92,** 388-396.

[151] F.J. Laimböck, (1991), "The potential of small loop scavenged spark ignition single cylinder engines", *SAE Paper* No. SP-847, 74 p.

[152] J.L. Laity et al., (1973), "Mechanisms of polynuclear aromatic hydrocarbon emissions from automotive engines", *SAE Paper* No. 730835, 10 p.

[153] F.W. Lam et al., (1988), "The behavior of polycyclic aromatic hydrocarbons during the early stages of soot formation", *22nd Int. Symp. on Combustion*, Seattle, 14/19 August, pp. 323-332.

[154] J.M. Lang et al., (1981), "Characterization of particulate emissions from in-use gasoline fueled motor vehicles", *SAE Paper* No. 811186, 20 p.

[155] P.S. Lee et al., (1989), "Generation of Diesel particles coated with polycyclic aromatic compounds, Evidence suggesting that dinitropyrene formation is a collection artifact", *J. Aerosol Sci.*, **20,** 627-637.

[156] T.J. Lemmons and P.A. Gabele, (1986), "Factors influencing the composition and quantity of passenger car refueling emissions", *NTIS Report* No. PB86-148467/GAR, 34 p.

[157] M. Lenner et al., (1983), "The $NO_2/NO_x$ ratio in emissions from gasoline powered cars, high percentage in idle engine measurements", *Atmosph. Environm.*, **17,** 1395-1398.

[158] M. Lenner, (1987), "Nitrogen dioxide in exhaust emissions from motor vehicles", *Atmosph. Environm.*, 21, 37-43.

[159] H.P. Lenz, (1984), *VDI Berichte* No. 531, 341-357.

[160] G. Lepperhoff, (1985), "Verminderung von Partikeln im Abgas", "Emissionsminderung Automobilabgase, Dieselmotoren", *VDI Berichte* No. 559, 99-115.

[161] G. Lepperhoff, (1988), *Möglichkeiten zur Verminderung der Partikelemission, Schmieröleinfluss und Partikelfilter mit selbsttragender Regeneration, Tagung "Rußminderung bei Dieselfahrzeugen"*, Essen (Haus der Technik), 24/25 February, 17 p.

[162] G. Lepperhoff, (1990), "Formation et oxydation des suies dans les moteurs diesel automobile à préchambre", *SIA Int. Conf.*, Lyon, 13/14 June, *Paper* No. 90097, pp. 55-61.

[163] P.L. Levins et al., (1973), "Chemical analysis of odor components in Diesel exhaust", *ADL Report* No. 74744-5, 80 p.

[164] P.L. Levins et al., (1974), "Chemical analysis of Diesel exhaust odor species", *SAE Paper* No. 740216, 11 p.

[165] J.P. Longwell, (1983), "Polycyclic aromatic hydrocarbons and soot from practical combustion systems", in: *"Soot in combustion systems and its toxic properties"*, L. Lahaye and G. Prado, Plenum Press, New York, pp. 37-56.

[166] G. Lonkai and O. Hiemesch, (1990), "Le concept de dépollution BMW des véhicules automobiles Diesel", *SIA Int. Conf.,* Lyon, 13/14 June, *Paper* No. 90058, pp. 209-215.

[167] L. Luo et al., (1989), "Particle growth and oxidation in a direct injection Diesel engine", *SAE Paper* No. 890580, 11 p.

[168] T.H. Ma et al., (1987), "Tracing the sources of hydrocarbon emissions in engines, A review of several research programmes made over the past five years", *IMechE Conf. "Vehicle emissions and their impact on European Air Quality"*, London, 3/5 November, *Paper* No. C326/87, pp. 229-235.

[169] J.S. McArragher et al., (1988), "Evaporative emissions from modern European vehicles and their control", *SAE Paper* No. 880315, 9 p.

[170] M.J. Manos et al., (1977), "Characteristics of activated carbon for controlling gasoline vapor emissions, Laboratory evaluation", *SAE Paper* No. 770621, 10 p.

[171] S.H. Mansouri et al., (1982), "Divided chamber Diesel engine, Part 1 A cycle simulation which predicts performance and emissions", *SAE Paper* No. 820273, 30 p.

[172] W.F. Marshall and B.H. Eccleston, (1980), "Emissions of off-ambient temperatures", *SAE Paper* No. 800512, 21 p.

[173] F. Martin, (1990), (unpublished results).

[174] B. Martin and B. Herrier, (1990), *Efficiency of fuel additives on Diesel particulate trap regeneration, IMechE Seminar, "Fuels for automotive and industrial Diesel engines"*, London, 19/29 November , pp. 77-84.

[175] S. Matsushita et al., (1984), "Development of the Toyota lean combustion system", *SAE Paper* No. 850044, 10 p.

[176] R.J. Menne and W.H. Adams, (1987), "Lean burn engine induction system optimization as a means to improve the operating characteristics of four-valve spark ignition engines", *IMechE Conf. "Vehicle emissions and their impact on European Air Quality"*, London, 3/5 November, *Paper* No. C357/87, pp. 237-246.

[177] R.J. Menne et al., (1984), "Wege zu niedriegeren Abgaswerten", "Emissionsminderung Automobilabgase, Ottomotoren", *VDI Berichte* No. 531, 131-150.

[178] R.J. Menne, (1988), "Magerkonzepte, Eine Alternative zum Dreiwegkatalysator", *MTZ*, **49,** 421-427.

[179] J.K.H. Menzl, (1984), "Das Emissionsverhalten von Zweitakt Otto-Kleinmotoren", "Emissionsminderung Automobilabgase, Ottomotoren", *VDI Berichte* No. 531, 237-244.

[180] E. Mitchell et al., (1972), "A stratified charge multifuel military engine, A progress report", *SAE Paper* No. 720051, 9 p.

[181] J.B.A. Mitchell and D.J.M. Miller, (1989), "Studies of the effects of metallic and gaseous additives in the control of soot formation in diffusion flames", *Comb. Flame*, **75,** 45-55.

[182] J.B.A. Mitchell et al., (1990), "The use of additives in the control and elucidation of soot formation", *Comb. Sci. Techn.*, **74,** 63-66.

[183] N. Miyamoto et al., (1987), "Characteristics of Diesel soot suppression with soluble fuel additives", *SAE Paper* No. 871612, 7 p.

[184] G. Monnier and P. Duret, (1991), "IAPAC compressed air assisted fuel injection for high efficiency low emission marine outboard two-stroke engines", *SAE Paper* No. 911849 (SP-883), 123-135.

[185] G. Monnier et al., (1991), "IAPAC compressed air assisted fuel injection for high efficiency low emission marine outboard two-stroke engines", *Japan SAE Paper* No. 911251 (STEC), 16 p.

[186] M. Morel, (1987), "Les technologies de dépollution pour les futures normes européennes et applicables aux voitures particulières à essence", *Poll. Atmosph.*, Special Issue November, pp. 25-36.

[187] T. Morimatsu et al., (1988), "Improvement of emissions from Diesel engines", *J. Eng. Gas Turbine Power*, **110,** 343-348.

[188] P. Moser, (1990), "L'avenir des véhicules automobiles à moteurs diesel à préchambre", *SIA Int. Conf.*, Lyon, 13/14 June, *Paper* No. 90057, pp. 193-200.

[189] G.S. Musser and H.F. Shannon, (1986), "Onboard control of refueling emissions", *SAE Paper* No. 861560, 21 p.

[190] G.S. Musser et al., (1990), "Improved design of onboard control of refueling emissios", *SAE Paper* No. 900155, 29 p.

[191] R. Muths, (1989), "Pertes d'hydrocarbures par évaporation", *Poll. Atmosph.* (121), 57-66.

[192] T. Nagai and M. Kawakami, (1989), "Reduction of $NO_x$ emission in medium speed Diesel engines", *SAE Paper* No. 891917, 15 p.

[193] M. Namazian and J.B. Heywood, (1982), "Flow in the piston cylinder ring crevices of a spark ignition engine, effect on hydrocarbon emissions, efficiency and power", *SAE Paper* No. 820088, 25 p.

[194] J.R. Needham, (1989), *Diesel particulates, engine experience and current regulations*, 5th Leeds University Short Course on Diesel Particulates, April, 43 p.

[195] J.R. Needham et al., (1991), "The low $NO_x$ truck engine", *SAE Paper* No. 910731, 10 p.

[196] K.H. Neumann, (1984), "Emissionsminderung durch Motorkonzepte", "Emissionsminderung Automobilabgase, Ottomotoren", *VDI Berichte* No. 531, 109-129.

[197] M. Ning et al., (1991), "Soot formation, oxidation and its mechanism in different combustion systems and smoke emission patterns in DI Diesel engines", *SAE Paper* No. 910230, 16 p.

[198] S.R. Norris-Jones et al., (1984), "A study of the formation of particulates in the cylinder of a direct injection Diesel engine", *SAE Paper* No. 840419, 8 p.

[199] M. Nuti, (1986), "Direct fuel injection, An opportunity for two stroke SI engines in road vehicle use", *SAE Paper* No. 860170, 14 p.

[200] B. Nuttin et al., (1988), *Mise en œuvre d'une stratégie mélange pauvre, Perspectives d'application dans le contexte européen, Conf. "Le Moteur à Allumage Commandé de la Prochaine Décennie"*, Strasbourg, 18/19 May, Ing. Automobile, pp. 159-174.

[201] M. Odaka et al., (1991), "Effects of EGR with a supplemental manifold water injection to control exhaust emissions from heavy duty Diesel powered vehicles", *SAE Paper* No. 910739, 11 p.

[202] S. Onishi et al., (1984), "Multi-layer stratified scavenging (MULS), A new scavenging method for two stroke engines", *SAE Paper* No. 840420, 12 p.

[203] A.K. Oppenheim et al., (1990), "A methodology for inhibiting the formation of pollutants in Diesel engines", *SAE Paper* No. 900394, 11 p.

[204] N. Ostruchov, (1978), "Effect of cold weather on motor vehicle emissions and fuel economy", *SAE Paper* No. 780084, 14 p.

[205] T. Otani et al., (1988), "Effects of fuel injection pressure and fuel properties on particulate emissions from HDDI Diesel engine", *SAE Paper* No. 881255, 8 p.

[206] A. Panesar et al., (1988), "The results of recent experiments on unburnt hydrocarbons", *IMechE Conf. "Combustion in engines,technology and applications"*, *Paper* No. C45/88, pp. 261-271.

[207] K.N. Pattas et al., (1984), "Comparative measurement of the efficiency of catalytic afterburning devices on a heavy duty Diesel engine", *SAE Paper* No. 840171 (P-140), 89-96.

[208] M.J. Pipho et al., (1991), "$NO_2$ formation in a Diesel engine", *SAE Paper* No. 910231, 13 p.

[209] F. Pischinger and K. Kramer, (1979), *The influence of engine parameters on the aldehyde emissions of a methanol operated four stroke otto cycle engine, 3rd Int. Symp. on Alcohol Fuel Technology*, Asilomar, California, 28/31 May, 11 p.

[210] F. Pischinger et al., (1988), "Grundlagen und Entwicklungslinien der Dieselmotorischen Brennverfahren", *VDI Berichte* No. 714, 61-94.

[211] E. Plaßmann et al., (1986), *Einfluß des Fahrverhaltens auf die Abgasemissionen von Personenkraftwagen auf Autobahn, Ergebnisse des Abgas-Grossversuchs in der Bundesrepublik Deutschland, 21st FISITA Conf.*, Belgrade, 2/6 June, 8 p.

[212] S.L. Plee et al., (1981), "Effects of flame temperature and air/fuel mixing on emission of particulate carbon from a divided chamber Diesel engine", in: *Particulate Carbon, Formation During Combustion*, D.C. Siegla and G.W. Smith, Plenum Press, New-York, pp. 477-481.

[213] W. Polach, (1988), *Möglichkeiten der Einspritzanlage zur Schadstoffminderung bei direkteinspritzenden Dieselmotoren, Tagung "Rußminderung bei Dieselfahrzeugen"*, Essen (Haus der Technik), 24/25 February, 19 p.

[214] K. Pollak, (1989), "Maßnahmen zur Reduzierung der KW-Emissionen beim Betanken", *Erdöl, Erdgas, Kohle*, **105,** 249.

[215] M. Pouille, (1990), "La comparaison de la combustion dans le moteur essence et diesel, aspects, performance, consommation et émission", *SIA Int. Conf.*, Lyon, 13/14 June, *Paper* No. 90049, pp. 70-77.

[216] M. Prigent et al., (1989), "Principaux facteurs agissant sur la température de mise en action des catalyseurs d'échappement", *SIA Conf. "Equip Auto"*, Paris, 23/25 October, *Paper* No. SIA 89077, pp. 277-282.

[217] M. Prigent and G. de Soete, (1989), "Nitrous oxide $N_2O$ in engine exhaust gases, A first appraisal of catalyst impact", *SAE Paper* No. 890492, 11 p.

[218] A.A. Quader, (1971), "Why intake charge dilution decreases nitric oxide emission from spark ignition engines", *SAE Paper* No. 710009, 11 p.

[219] F. Quissek et al., (1988), "Passenger car application of the AVL-HCLB engine", *Conf. "Le moteur à allumage commandé de la prochaine décennie"*, Strasbourg, 18/19 May, Ing. Automobile, pp. 145-158.

[220] K.S. Rao et al., (1983), "Mixture maldistribution and aldehyde emission in an alcohol fueled SI engine", *SAE Paper* No. 830511, 12 p.

[221] B. Raynal, (1982), "Moteurs thermiques et pollution atmosphérique, origine de réduction des polluants", *Techn. de l'Ing.*, Vol.B.378, **1**, 26 p.

[222] A.R. Reading and G. Greeves, (1980), "Measurement of Diesel exhaust odorants and effect of engine variables", *SAE Paper* No. 800424, 13 p.

[223] L.A. Reams et al., (1982), "Capabilities of Diesel electronic fuel control", *SAE Paper* No. 820449, 16 p.

[224] K.K. Rink et al., (1987), "The influence of fuel composition and spray characteristics on particulate formation", *SAE Paper* No. 872035, 11 p.

[225] D.S. Ross et al., (1987), "Diesel exhaust and pyrene nitration", *E.S.&T.*, **21,** 1130-1131.

[226] M.N. Saeed and N.A. Henein, (1989), "Combustion phenomena of alcohols in CI engines", *J. Eng. Gas Turbine Power*, **111,** 439-444.

[227] C.W. Savery et al., (1974), "Progress in Diesel odor research", *SAE Paper* No. 740213, 12 p.

[228] C.H. Schleyer and W.J. Koehl, (1986), "A comparison of vehicle refueling and evaporative emission control, methods for long-term hydrocarbon control progress", *SAE Paper* No. 861552, 14 p.

[229] A. Schröer, (1984), "Der individuelle Einfluß des Fahrers auf das Emissionsverhalten des Fahrzeuges", "Emissionsminderung Automobilabgase, Ottomotoren", *VDI Berichte* No. 531, 489-505.

[230] D. Schuetzle and J.M. Perez, (1983), "Factors influencing the emissions of nitrated polynuclear aromatic hydrocarbons (nitro PAH) from Diesel engines", *J. APCA*, **33,** 751-755.

[231] D. Schuetzle et al., (1983), "The identification and potential sources of nitrated polynuclear aromatic hydrocarbons (nitro PAH) in Diesel particulate extracts", in: *"Mobile source emissions including polycyclic organic species"*, D. Rondia et al., Reidel, Dordrecht, pp. 299-312.

[232] H. Schulte et al., (1989), "Preinjection, A measure to influence exhaust quality and noise in Diesel engines", *J. Eng. Gas Turbine Power*, **111,** 445-450.

[233] H. Schulte et al., (1990), "The contribution of the fuel injection system to meet future demand on truck Diesel engines", *SIA Int. Conf.*, Lyon, 13/14 June, *Paper* No. 90071, pp. 251-258.

[234] G. Schwarzbauer and H. Weiss, (1988), "Digitale Diesel-Elektronik beim BMW-Turbodieselmodell 324td", *MTZ*, **49,** 37-41.

[235] G.W. Schweimer, (1990), "The power train of the Volkswagen eco-polo", *SIA Int. Conf.*, Lyon, 13/14 June, *Paper* No. 90068, pp. 217-226.

[236] U. Seiffert et al., (1984), "Auswirkung von Kraftstoff- und Abgasgesetzgebung auf die Ottomotoren Entwicklung in Europa", *SAE Paper* No. 845072, 8 p.

[237] T. Shimada et al., (1989), "The effect of fuel injection pressure on Diesel engine performance", *SAE Paper* No. 891919, 10 p.

[238] M. Shimoda et al., (1991), "Application of heavy duty Diesel engine to future emission standards", *SAE Paper* No. 910482, 8 p.

[239] V.L. Shogren et al., (1986), "Emission controls for a 2.2 liter Diesel engine", *SAE Paper* No. 860417, 14 p.

[240] A. Simko et al., (1972), "Exhaust emission control by the Ford programmed combustion process, PROCO", *SAE Paper* No. 720052, 22 p.

[241] O.I. Smith, (1981), "Fundamentals of soot formation in flames with application to Diesel engine particulates", *Prog. Energy Comb. Sci.*, **7,** 275-291.

[242] D.E. Sorrels et al., (1974), "Impact of altitude on vehicular exhaust emissions", *SAE Paper* No. 741033, 11 p.

[243] U. Spicher and A. Schüers, (1990), "Einfluß der Schubabschaltung auf den Verbrennungsablauf", *MTZ*, **51,** 82-87.

[244] G.S. Springer and D.J. Patterson, (1973), *Engine emissions, pollutant formation and emissions*, Plenum Press, New York, 371 p.

[245] F. Stump et al., (1989), "The influence of ambient temperature on tailpipe emissions from 1984-1987 model year light duty gasoline motor vehicles", *Atmosph. Environm.*, **23,** 307-320.

[246] H. Tanabe et al., (1991), "Effects of cooling water temperature on particulate emissions from a small high-speed DI Diesel engine", *SAE Paper* No. 910740, 8 p.

[247] T. Tanaka et al., (1989), "Development of a measuring meter and a control device for Diesel white smoke", *SAE Paper* No. 892044, 9 p.

[248] T. Toda et al., (1976), "Evaluation of burned gas ratio (BGR) as a predominant factor to $NO_x$", *SAE Paper* No. 760765, 13 p.

[249] W.A.M. den Tonkelaar et al., (1987), "Effect of driving conditions and structure of built-up areas on average levels of air pollution in urban roads", *Sci. Tot. Environm.*, **59,** 233-242.

[250] S. Tosaka et al., (1989), "The effect of fuel properties on particulate formation (The effect of molecular structure and carbon number)", *SAE Paper* No. 891881, 7 p.

[251] K. Tsuchiya and S. Hirano, (1975), "Characteristics of 2-stroke motorcycle exhaust HC emission and effects of air/fuel ratio and ignition timing", *SAE Paper* No. 750908, 13 p.

[252] K. Tsuchiya et al., (1983), "A study of irregular combustion in 2-stroke cycle gasoline engines", *SAE Paper* No. 830091, 12 p.

[253] Y. Tsukasaki et al., (1990), "Study of mileage-related formaldehyde emission from methanol-fueled vehicles", *SAE Paper* No. 900705, 6 p.

[254] D. Überschär, (1988), *Rußminderung bei PKW-Dieselmotoren ohne Sekundärmaßnahmen, Tagung "Rußminderung bei Dieselfahrzeugen"*, Essen (Haus der Technik), 24/25 February, 22 p.

[255] A. Urlaub, (1985), "Direekeinspritzende PKW-Dieselmotoren", "Emissionsminderung Automobilabgase, Dieselmotoren", *VDI Berichte* No. 559, 261-273.

[256] O.A. Uyehara, (1980), "Diesel combustion temperature on soot", *SAE Paper* No. 800969, 28 p.

[257] P. Vanderstraeten et al., (1988), "A continuous quantitative detection method for total mercaptans, organic sulphides, $H_2S$, and $CS_2$ for odoriferous emissions", *J. APCA*, **38,** 1271-1274.

[258] E. Vielledent, (1978), "Low pressure electronic fuel injection system for two-stroke engines", *SAE Paper* No. 780767, 15 p.

[259] T. Visek, (1988), "Neue Direkteinspritz Dieselmotorengeneration der Steyr-Daimler-Puch AG, Teil 1 Aufbau und Konstruktion", *MTZ*, **49,** 47-51.

[260] B. Voß, (1990), "Zeitweise Motorabschaltung, Kritische Zeiten bezüglich Schadstoffemission und Kraftstoffverbrauch", *ATZ*, **92,** 526-532.

[261] W.F. Wachter, (1990), "Analysis of transient data of a model year 1991 heavy duty Diesel engine", *SAE Paper* No. 900443, 12 p.

[262] W.R. Wade et al., (1984), "Combustion, friction, and fuel tolerance improvements for the IDI Diesel engine", *SAE Paper* No. 840515, 26 p.

[263] W.R. Wade et al., (1986), "Future Diesel engine combustion systems for low emissions and high fuel economy", *21st FISITA Conf.*, Belgrade, 2/6 June, *Paper* No. 865012, 9 p.

[264] W.R. Wade et al., (1987), "Reduction of $NO_x$ and particulates in the Diesel combustion process, Trans. ASME", *J. Eng. for Power*, **109,** 426-434.

[265] H. Waldeyer et al., (1984), "Einfluß winterlicher Temperaturen auf das Emissionsverhalten von Personenkraftwagen", "Emissionsminderung Automobilabgase, Ottomotoren", *VDI Berichte* No. 531, 203-216.

[266] S. Wallace and A. Warburton, (1987), "The control of CO, HC and $NO_x$ emissions and the application of lean burn engines", *IMechE Conf. "Vehicle emissions and their impact on European Air Quality"*, London, 3/5 November, *Paper* No. C359/87, pp. 205-212.

[267] P. Walzer, (1986), "Magerbetrieb beim Ottomotor", *ATZ*, **88,** 301-312.

[268] P. Walzer et al., (1988), *Neues ottomotorisches Abgaskonzept, Symp. "Magerkonzepte, Eine Alternative zum Dreiwegkatalysator"*, Essen, 18 May, 20 p.

[269] J.G. Watson et al., (1990), "Chemical source profiles for particulate motor vehicle exhaust under cold and high altitude operating conditions", *Sci. Tot. Environm.*, **93,** 183-190.

[270] J.T. Wentworth, (1968), "Piston and ring variables affect exhaust hydrocarbon emissions", *SAE Paper* No. 680109, 22 p.

[271] J.T. Wentworth, (1971), "The piston crevice volume effect on exhaust hydrocarbon emissio", *Comb. Sci. Techn.*, **4,** 97-100.

[272] J.T. Wentworth, (1972), "More on origins of exhaust hydrocarbons, effects of zero oil consumption, deposit location, and surface roughness", *SAE Paper* No. 720939, 8 p.

[273] J.T. Wentworth, (1982), "Effect of top compression ring profile on oil consumption and blowby with the sealed ring orifice design", *SAE Paper* No. 820089, 10 p.

[274] A. Williams, (1989), *Carbon formation and the influence of hydrocarbon structure*, 5th Leeds University short course on Diesel particulates, April, 19 p.

[275] D.J. Williams et al., (1989), "Particulate emissions from 'in-use' motor vehicles, (1) Spark ignition vehicles", *Atmosph. Environm.*, **23,** 2639-2645.

[276] D.J. Williams et al., (1989), "Particulate emissions from 'in-use' motor vehicles, (2) Diesel vehicles", *Atmosph. Environm.*, **23,** 2647-2661.

[277] R.S. Williams and H.R. Johnson, (1991), "Impact of methanol blends on activated carbon performance", *SAE Paper* No. 910563 (SP-863), 153-162.

[278] T.Wu and K.J. McAuley, (1973), "Predicting Diesel engine performance at various ambient conditions", *SAE Paper* No. 730148, 19 p.

[279] H. Yamaguchi et al., (1991), "A study of particulate formation on the combustion chamber wall", *SAE Paper* No. 910488, 7 p.

[280] H. Yokota et al., (1991), "Fast burning and reduced soot formation via ultra high pressure Diesel fuel injection", *SAE Paper* No. 910225, 9 p.

[281] R.C. Yu and S.M. Shahed, (1981), "Effects of injection timing and exhaust gas recirculation on emissions from a DI Diesel engine", *SAE Paper* No. 811234, 11 p.

[282] M. Zellat and J. Pouille, (1990), "Modélisation tridimensionnelle de la combustion et de la formation de suie dans un moteur à injection indirecte", *Comparaison avec l'experience, SIA Int. Conf.*, Lyon, 13/14 June, *Paper* No. 90048, pp. 63-69.

[283] K. Zimmermann, (1985), "Einspritzausrüstung für schadstoffarme Dieselmotoren", "Emissionsminderung Automobilabgase, Dieselmotoren", *VDI Berichte* No. 559, 157-173.

[284] N. Zloch and B. Engels, (1985), "Abgassturbolader für schadstoffarme Dieselmotoren", "Emissionsminderung Automobilabgase, Dieselmotoren", *VDI Berichte* No. 559, 175-186.

[285] C. Bertoli et al., (1992), "Initial results on the impact of automotive diesel oil on unregulated emissions of DI light diesel engines", *SAE Paper* No. 922189, 9 p.

[286] M.J. Pipho et al., (1992), "Injection timing and bowl configuration effects on in-cylinder particle mass", *SAE Paper* No. 921646 (SP.931), pp. 111-126.

# Influence of fuel properties 11

Engine settings exert a powerful influence on the amount of pollutants emitted because they affect both the formation and destruction of pollutants before exhaust gases are released into the atmosphere.

Motor fuels also play a role in emissions primarily because the fuel/air ratio can be altered by a variation in their physicochemical properties, which is not always offset by an adjustment of the engine parameters. Fig. 11.1 shows the variation in the emissions of various gaseous pollutants as a function of the fuel/air ratio: maximum $NO_x$ in a slightly lean mixture (maximum efficiency), minimum CO and HC in a lean mixture, more aldehydes in a lean mixture, and the appearance of soot in a very rich mixture ($\lambda < 0.6$). These are the conditions encountered in diesel engines around the fuel droplets at the point of combustion.

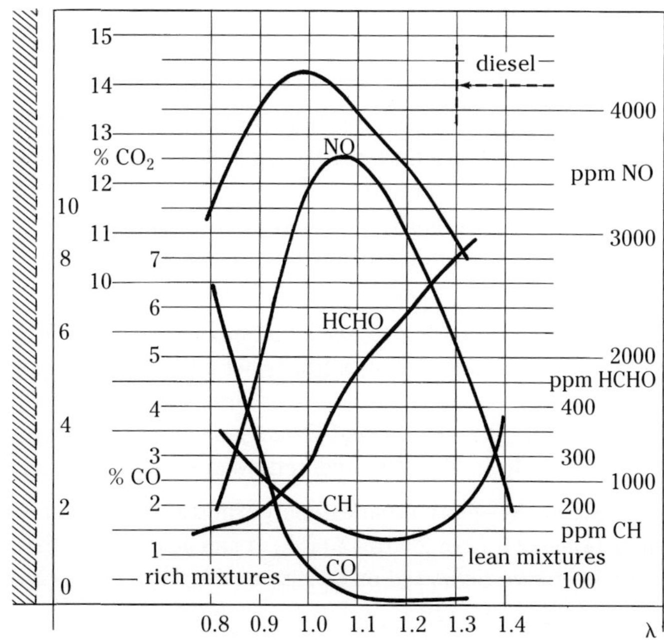


**Fig 11.1** Pollutants as a function of fuel/air ratio

This chapter examines in succession the effects of motor fuels on the pollutants emitted by spark ignition engines, as well as the effect of fuel properties on evaporation losses. This is followed by an examination of the influence of the physicochemical parameters of diesel fuels on the emissions of direct injection and pre-combustion chamber diesel engines. The repercussions of the introduction of alternative fuels (alcohols, and liquefied and compressed petroleum gases) are reviewed and are followed by a discussion of the influence of engine lubricants on emissions.

## 11.1 Effect of motor fuels

The properties of motor fuels, both regular- and premium-grade gasolines, must meet the specifications of the countries imposing limits on their permissible ranges of variation. In France, these specifications are CSR 03-L (1991, regular), CSR 04-N (1991, premium), and CSR 04 bis-D (1991, unleaded premium). The corresponding tables indicate the authorized limits for density, distillation interval, volatility, sulfur content, and additive content.

### 11.1.1 Effect of fuel density

Motor fuel density depends closely on the proportions of the different hydrocarbons making up the blends of regular- and premium-grade gasolines and particularly on the overall carbon/hydrogen atomic ratio.

The maximum variations observed in the different European countries range up to 0.05 for an average figure of 0.75 (or 6%). For reasons of volatility, density variations are also observed between fuels in summer and winter. Since a higher octane number implies enrichment in denser aromatic hydrocarbons (higher C/H ratio), premium-grade gasoline, and especially unleaded premium, has a higher density than regular-grade (maximum 0.770 as compared with 0.765, a difference of 0.6%).

The increase in fuel density tends to make a fuel mixture leaner with a carburetor [35] and richer with injection [51]. Higher altitude, which reduces the density of the air, has the same effect. While sensors (altitude compensators) can help to account for of the density of the intake air, no fuel density sensor is yet available on the market that can actually help to alter the injected quantities accordingly.

However, given the slight relative variations permitted for motor fuel densities (0.02 to 0.03 on an average of 0.77 or 2.5 to 4%) [35], it can be assumed that their effects on the emissions of an engine regulated on a reference fuel are practically negligible.

### 11.1.2 Effect of olefinics and aromatics content

Olefins are produced in several refinery operations. They are used to maximize the gasoline yield from crude and to provide feedstock for other refinery processes. The amount of olefinic hydrocarbons blended into a finished gasoline can range from 5 to 20%. The upper limit is imposed to control the formation of gums [86]. Nevertheless, olefins provide a valuable contribution to a fuel, in particular to the overall octane number.

Olefins have been shown to be more photochemically active than paraffins. Therefore, olefins in the fuel have been a target for control or reduction in regulated reformulated gasoline composition. Low molecular weight olefins found in exhausts have been proven to be partial combustion products of paraffins. Hence, the removal of fuel olefins is no guarantee of low olefin exhaust emissions. Even highly exaggerated olefin concentrations in a fuel do not significantly alter the ozone-forming potential of exhausts, compared with a more conventional paraffinic fuel of the same volatility [86].

Since aromatic hydrocarbons have a Research Octane Number (RON) of more than 100 and a Motor Octane Number (MON) generally greater than 90 [35], the addition of aromatic fractions is one means employed in refining to achieve the knock resistance levels required by modern automotive fuels.

This tendency to increase the fuel aromatics content is currently being reinforced with the prospect of the generalized use of unleaded fuels. In fact, refineries produce aromatics that are cheaper than the branched paraffins produced by isomerization or alkylation. Only benzene, due to its toxicity, is legally limited to under 5% (European Directive 85/210/EEC enforceable from 1 October 1989), after having reached highs of 15% in Germany [35].

Table 11.1 shows, for example, that the aromatic fraction of German motor fuels containing 0.15 g/liter of Pb was higher than that of French premium-grade gasoline containing 0.4 g/liter of Pb, and that the German premium approaches the maximum benzene content of 5%.

As already indicated above, aromatics have a higher C/H ratio, and hence a higher density and a higher output of $CO_2$. This effect is not significant, but their higher heat of combustion per unit volume raises the combustion temperature and consequently the level of $NO_x$ emitted [52]. Fig. 11.2 shows, for an engine running at 1500 rpm and at medium load, the variation in $NO_x$ as a function of the air/fuel ratio for a non-aromatic alkylate and an aromatic premium gasoline, which reveals a 20% reduction of the contents for the alkylate at maximum emission.

It has also been found that reducing fuel aromatics content raises the emissions of 1-3 butadiene and aldehydes [88].

CO emissions are relatively unaffected by the aromaticity of the fuel. On the other hand, aromatics with a more stable structure than paraffins exhibit a slower combustion kinetics, which, under the same conditions, results in higher unburnt hydrocarbon emissions. Emissions are reduced by 16% when going from an aromatic premium to an alkylate (Fig. 11.3).

This stability of the aromatic ring means that the exhaust contains a fraction of the benzene in the fuel. This fraction is directly proportional to the content of the fuel [87]. For example, depending on the type of combustion chamber, 0.03 to 0.15 g/h is emitted per % benzene in the isooctane fueling a single-cylinder 624 $cm^3$ injection engine running at 2000 rpm [33]. The other aromatic hydrocarbons (toluene, xylenes, etc.) are dealkylated before undergoing the process that forms benzene, but it is estimated that these hydrocarbons produce about ten times less benzene at the exhaust than benzene itself.

**Table 11.1** Compositions of European automotive fuels [33 and 35]

| Component | French premium grade | German premium grade | German regular grade |
|---|---|---|---|
| **paraffins** | **44.47** | **43.3** | **47.3** |
| $C_4$ | 1.46 | 3.00 | 1.42 |
| $C_5$ | 11.64 | 22.3 | 14.12 |
| $C_6$ | 12.27 | 11.04 | 10.54 |
| $C_7$ | 11.52 | 4.26 | 9.51 |
| $C_8$ | 4.26 | 1.73 | 6.25 |
| $C_{9+}$ | 0.65 | 0.97 | 5.48 |
| **naphthenes** | **2.67** | | |
| $C_5$ | 0.18 | | |
| $C_6$ | 1.03 | | |
| $C_7$ | 1.41 | | |
| $C_8$ | 0.05 | | |
| **olefins** | **7.36** | **3.9** | **11.7** |
| $C_4$ | 0.59 | 0.89 | 1.43 |
| $C_5$ | 3.16 | 1.88 | 0.70 |
| $C_6$ | 2.09 | 0.57 | 2.66 |
| $C_7$ | 1.40 | 0.28 | 2.67 |
| $C_8$ | 0.12 | 0.10 | 1.41 |
| $C_{9+}$ | – | 0.16 | 2.0 |
| **diolefins** | **0.12** | **–** | – |
| $C_5$ | 0.06 | – | – |
| $C_6$ | 0.06 | – | – |
| **aromatics** | **45.79** | **52.8** | **41.4** |
| $C_6$ | 2.22 | 3.93 | 2.59 |
| $C_7$ | 12.84 | 5.31 | 8.53 |
| $C_8$ | 16.70 | 9.16 | 5.94 |
| $C_9$ | 10.76 | 20.25 | 11.79 |
| $C_{10}$ | 3.08 | 14.14 | 11.18 |
| $C_{11}$ | 0.19 | – | 1.33 |
| **total** | **100.41** | **100.0** | **100.4** |

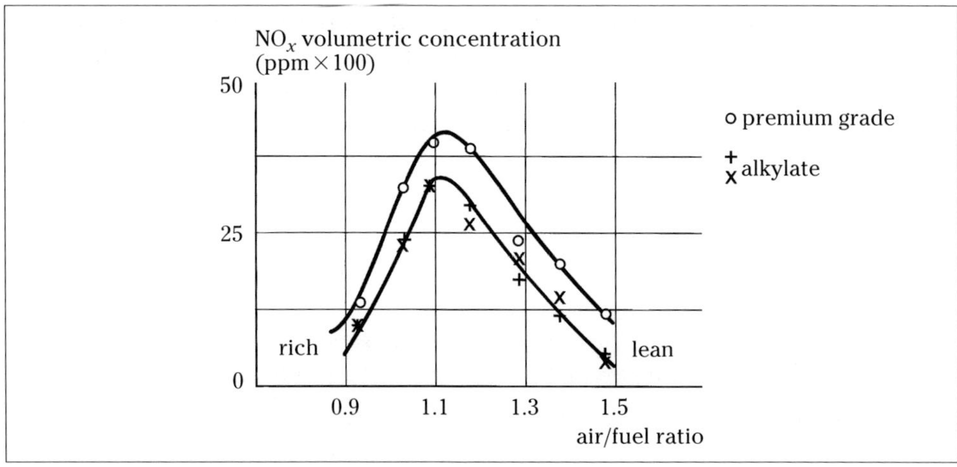


speed: 1500 rpm
brake mean effective pressure (BMEP): 500 kPa
compression ratio: 11

**Fig 11.2** $NO_x$ emissions for two aromatics compositions [52]

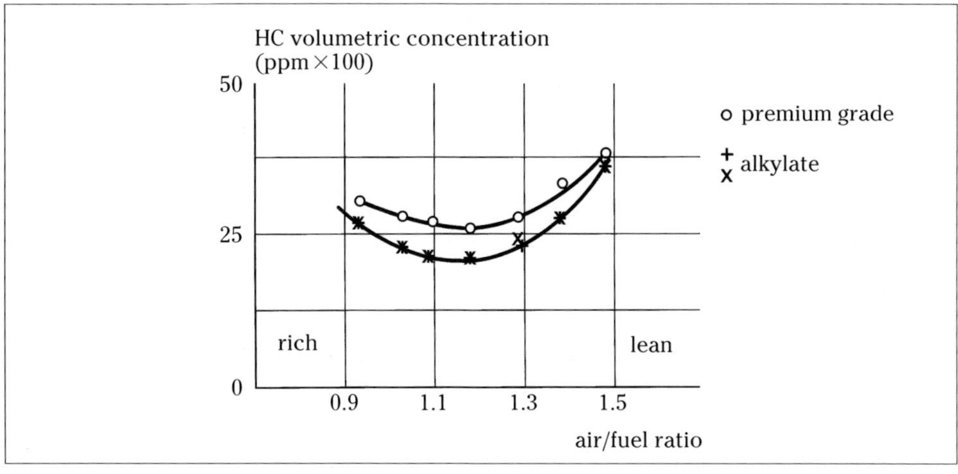


speed: 1500 rpm
brake mean effective pressure (BMEP): 500 kPa
compression ratio: 11

**Fig 11.3** HC emissions for two aromatics compositions [52]

In addition, the aromatics in the fuel play a role in the exhaust emissions of polycyclic aromatic hydrocarbons, phenols, and aromatic aldehydes, which increase with the aromatics, whereas formaldehyde decreases [32 and 37]. The dependence of PAH on the aromatics content in the fuel varies both with the type of PAH concerned and the type of aromatic in the fuel. Benzene has little effect on the PAH formed and it is mainly the light PAH (up to four rings) that increase in direct proportion to the aromatics content, whereas the heavier PAH (more than five rings) are unaffected [63] (Fig. 11.4). The PAH already contained in the fuel also affect the PAH emissions.

### 11.1.3 Effect of volatility

Volatility is generally expressed by the distillation curve and the Reid vapor pressure measured at 37.8°C (RVP).

This is a very important property for engine operation: cold starting time, acceleration performance, operating stability while idling, and warm engine operation (vapor locks and percolation) are indispensable for driving comfort.

Excessively heavy fractions (distilling above 200 to 220°C) may play a role in the emissions of unburnt products due to their poor vaporization. This leads to incomplete combustion, with the formation of aldehydes and an increase in HC. There is a strong correlation between increasing hydrocarbon emissions and the T90 distillation point [87].

Yet it is mainly the lighter fractions demanded for cold starting and running that affect exhaust emissions and, above all, evaporation losses.

The volatility properties vary with climatic conditions and with the seasons. For motor fuels in France:

- $45 \leqslant \text{RVP} \leqslant 79$ kPa (20 June to 9 September)
- $50 \leqslant \text{RVP} \leqslant 86$ kPa (10 April to 19 June, 10 September to 31 October)
- $55 \leqslant \text{RVP} \leqslant 99$ kPa (1 November to 9 April)

The RVP is affected by the more volatile fractions and particularly the butane/pentane cut. This light cut, which is generally a surplus in refining processes, is added to motor fuel up to the top limit authorized, taking full advantage of its excellent octane number (butane RON 94) to offset the decrease in lead content.

Volatility has no effect on $NO_x$ exhaust emissions and only CO and HC emissions rise with the RVP. At the maximum, CO and HC increase by 20% on the FTP cycle when the RVP rises from 65 to 80 kPa [76].

The main effect of fuel volatility is related to fuel evaporation losses on the vehicle and during refueling at the service station (emissions between the refinery and the service station are ignored here).

The following are generally distinguished on board the vehicle:

- running losses in highway driving (somewhat neglected until now, but their importance is increasing)
- diurnal losses by respiration of the fuel tank, which thermally expands and contracts during daily temperature variations
- hot soak losses that occur from a parked vehicle, with the engine turned off after a running period, particularly from the carburetor chamber or the fuel tank, which are heated by the engine

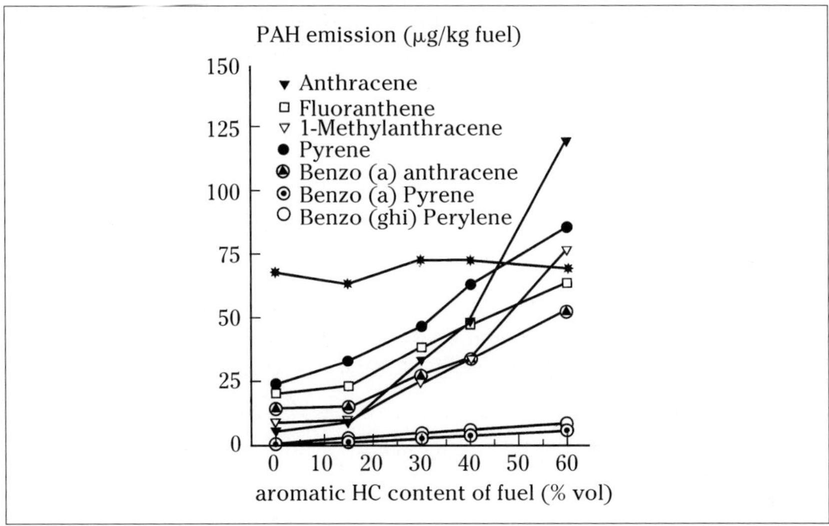


**Fig 11.4** PAH emissions as a function of fuel aromatic content and type [63]

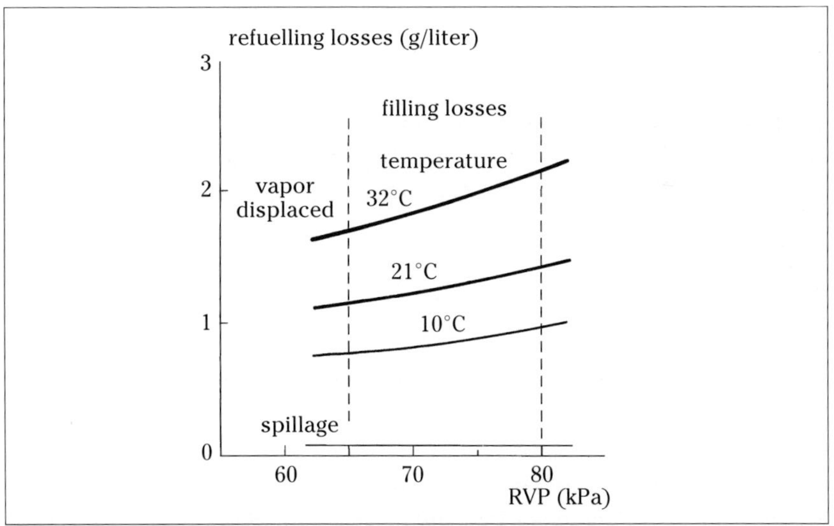


**Fig 11.5** Refuelling losses at different temperatures [76].
Reprinted with permission ©1985 *Society of Automotive Engineers Inc*

These losses are measured (Chapter 7) by appropriate techniques: canisters for running losses, Sealed Housing for Evaporative Determination (SHED) for diurnal losses and hot soak losses.

Refueling losses at the service station depend on the RVP of the fuel distributed and on the ambient temperature [76] (Fig. 11.5). As the RVP rises from 65 to 80 kPa, the losses increase by 38% at 30°C and 36% at 10°C.

Refueling losses include dripping losses, which are independent of temperature and RVP, and which also ultimately evaporate. The effect of volatility on gasoline vapor emissions and their contributions to volatile organic compounds (VOC) depend on the type of feed selected for the engine, either carburation or injection. Since the carburetor chamber has an evaporation surface area that aggravates the losses, it increases them by approximately 4 g/SHED test at different RVP on American vehicles dating from 1978 to 1985 [76] (Fig. 11.6).

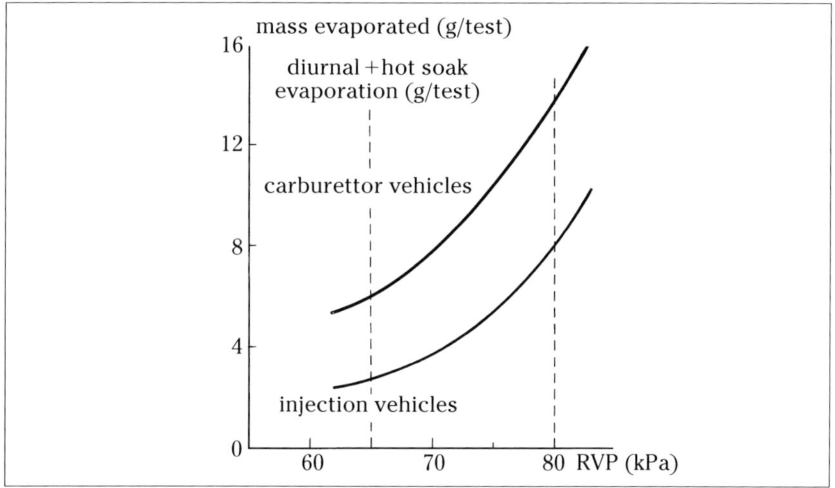


**Fig 11.6** Effect of RVP on diurnal + hot soak evaporation [76]
Reprinted with permission ©1985 *Society of Automotive Engineers Inc*

Figure 11.7 shows, as a function of RVP, and distinguishing between carburation and injection, all the hydrocarbon emissions occurring at the exhaust or by evaporation, which are expressed by weight per distance traveled with vehicles that meet the American standard of 2 g/test. Diurnal losses are the ones that increase the most with rising RVP, but the exhaust always represents the major source of HC emissions.

Apart from the economic implications of the replacement of butanes by branched paraffins produced by isomerization, the reduction of the RVP to around 50 kPa would raise problems for cold starting and driveability [76]. Yet this figure is planned by the *EPA* for 1992 in the southwestern States of the USA [43].

### 11.1.4 Effect of octane number

The octane number has an effect on emissions, particularly on the occurrence of knock. A lower number gives rise to greater knock and increases the $NO_x$ emissions mainly in a lean mixture [37] (Fig. 11.8). In actual fact, however, these knock conditions are fortunately not encountered in reality due to their destructive effect on the engine.

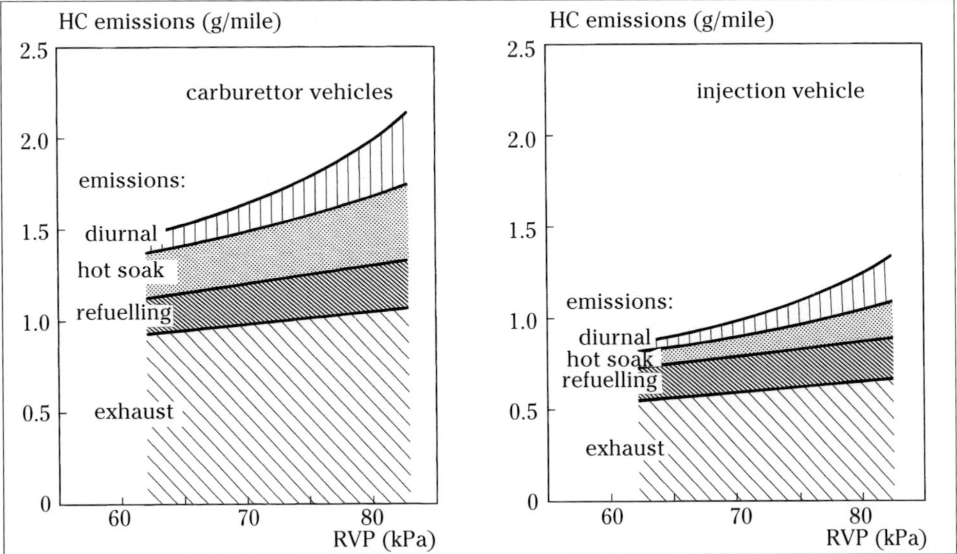


**Fig 11.7** Contribution of different sources to HC emissions [42]

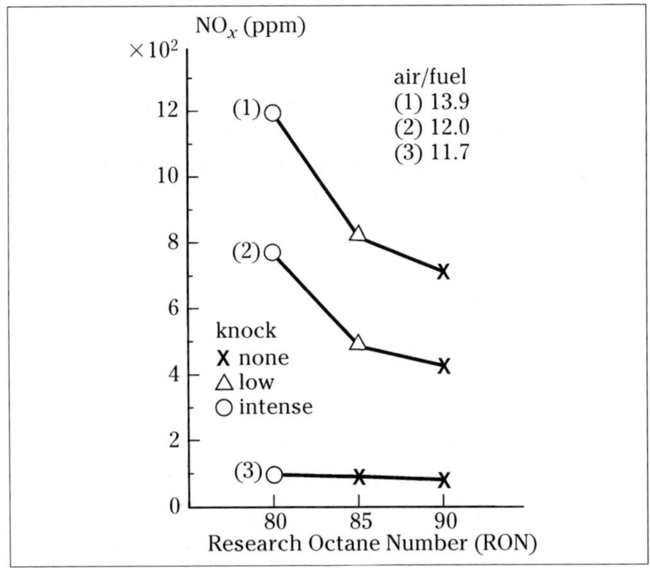


**Fig 11.8** Effect of octane number on $NO_x$ [37]

## 11.1.5 Effect of sulfur content

Although the sulfur content of gasolines is generally low (between 50 and 500 ppm), it may affect the efficiency of tailpipe catalysts and hence increase emissions of HC, CO, and $NO_x$ [89].

Moreover, since sulfur may inhibit the aldehyde-forming reaction in a cold catalyst, reducing the sulfur content could increase aldehyde emissions [90].

### 11.1.6 Effect of additives

Several types of additives are added to automotive fuels:

- octane improvers: lead alkyls, methylcyclopentadienyl manganese tricarbonyl (MMT), ferrocene (iron dicyclopentadienyl) [70], etc.
- anti-oxidant additives, which inhibit olefin polymerization and gum formation: phenylene diamines, aminophenols, and alkylated phenols
- surfactant additives, which help to clean the intake circuits polluted by recycled oil vapors and substances not retained by the oil filter (fatty acid amines, succinimides, etc.)
- anti-freeze additives close to the surfactants already mentioned
- dyes and anti-fraud additives

The chlorine and bromine contents of lead additives, which play the role of scavengers in the form of volatile halogenides, do not always succeed in totally eliminating deposits in combustion chambers. However, the presence of these deposits does not appear to have a significant effect on CO and $NO_x$ emissions, but increase HC emissions [26 and 27]. This increase in HC appears in the first few thousand miles of travel (Fig. 11.9). By contrast, aldehyde emissions appear to be unaffected by lead. On the other hand, manganese additives (MMT) have a harmful effect on hydrocarbon and aldehyde emissions [10 and 61].

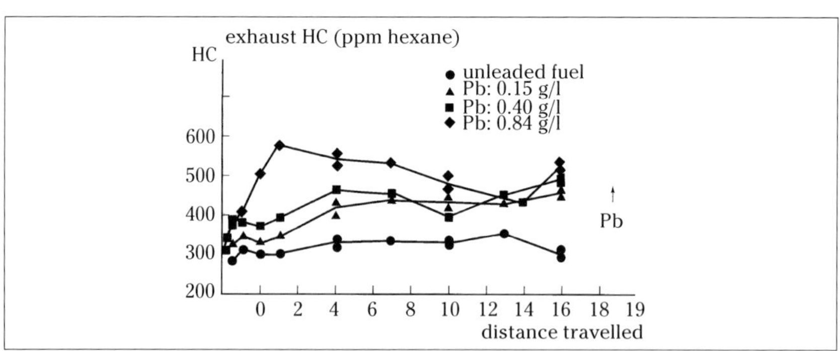


**Fig 11.9** Effect of lead additives [27]
Reprinted with permission ©1969 *Society of Automotive Engineers Inc*

Whereas CO and $NO_x$ emissions are unaffected [10], hydrocarbons increase in direct proportion to the MMT content [39]. Catalytic converters do not always succeed in overcoming this increase [48] and are gradually clogged by $Mn_3O_4$ deposits [40].

Organic and organo-metallic additives added to the fuel to act on combustion reactions do not appear to influence emissions, nor do anti-deposition additives [57].

However, keeping the feed circuits clean helps to preserve the initial settings and to stabilize CO emissions while idling.

### 11.1.7 Effect of mis-fueling

This term applies to the introduction of an unsuitable fuel to an engine, such as diesel to a spark ignition engine. It usually applies to the fueling of an engine equipped with a catalytic converter with leaded gasoline for reasons of price or availability.

The resulting poisoning of the catalyst causes its efficiency to drop, with a commensurate increase in HC and aldehyde contents downstream from the catalytic converters [62]. Fig. 11.10 shows the rapid growth in HC and aldehyde emissions with the introduction of leaded gasoline. Although the level at the exhaust never reaches that obtained without a catalyst, the resumption of fueling with unleaded gasoline fails to restore the initial activity.

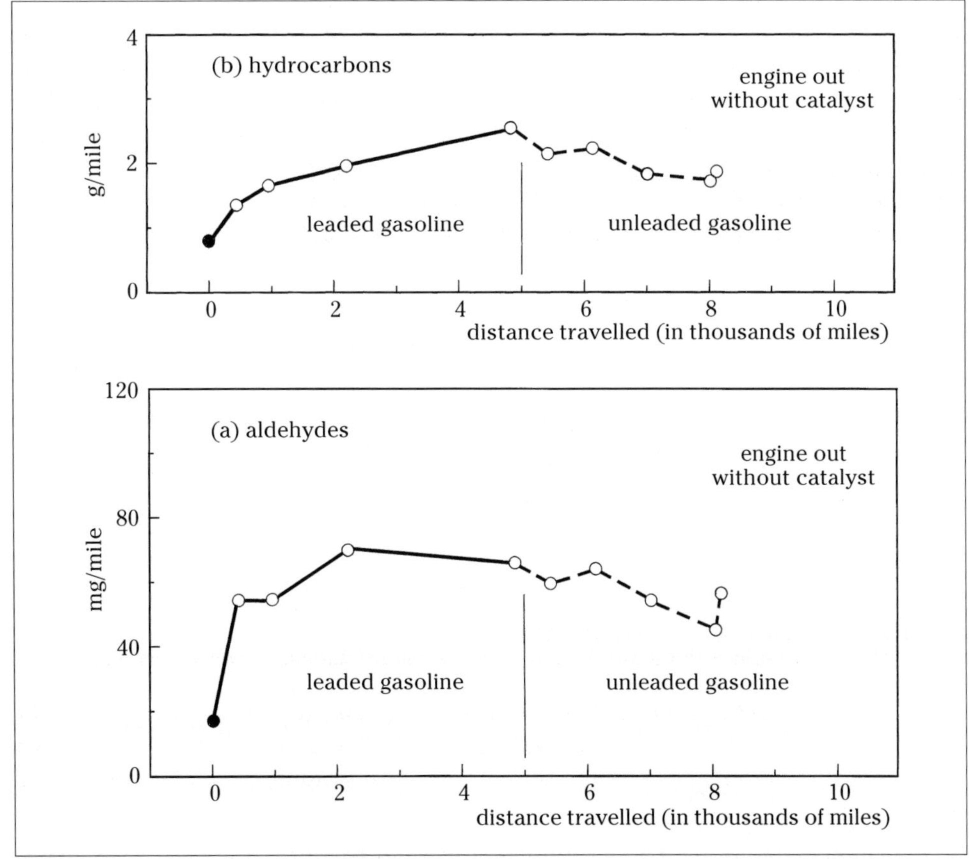


**Fig 11.10** Effect of mis-fueling [62]

## 11.2 Effect of diesel fuels

Diesel fuels are also covered by specifications (in France CSR 09-O and 09 bis-B of 1990) indicating the ranges of values permitted for the various parameters, whose repercussions on emissions we shall now discuss: viscosity, density and distillation interval, cetane number (and indirectly aromatics content), sulfur content, additives, etc.

The pollutants monitored are the same as those connected with motor fuels, with the addition of particles and associated extractable organic compounds (Soluble Oil Fraction, SOF), which are more specific to diesel engines.

Fuel parameters have the equivalent effect on emissions that engine running parameters do [71]. Differences in fuel behavior are observed with direct injection engines used on trucks and buses, and indirect injection pre-combustion chamber engines mounted on automobiles. The former is generally more tolerant of fuel properties than the latter.

In addition, the properties of manufactured diesel fuels are generally closely inter-correlated. Efforts made to totally separate the aromatics, cetane, sulfur content, and 90% distilled point are not always successful [18 and 44].

For example (Fig. 11.11), a thorough disconnection of the % aromatics, the 10% distilled, and the 90% distilled, does not control the percentage of sulfur [36].

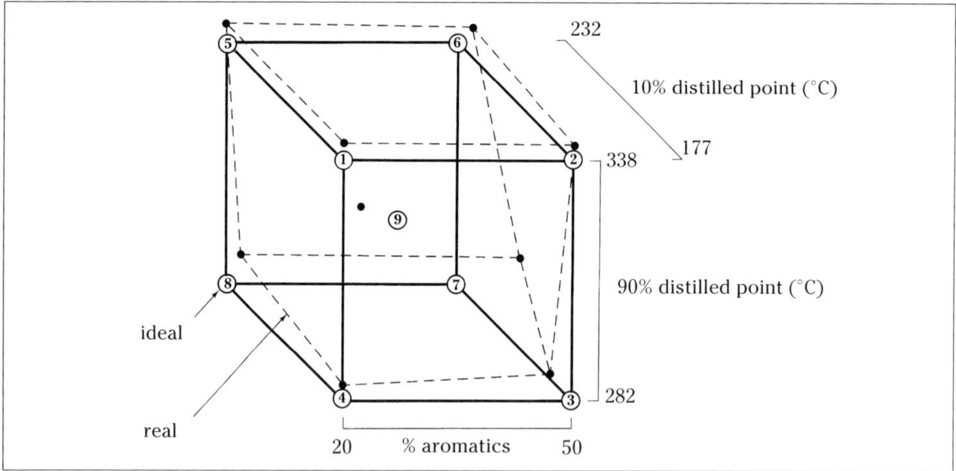


**Fig 11.11** Uncoupling of diesel parameters [36]
Reprinted with permission © *Society of Automotive Engineers Inc*

### 11.2.1 Effect of viscosity, density, and distillation interval

With increasing kinematic viscosity, smoke and unburnt HC emissions increase and $NO_x$ emissions decrease. The kinematic viscosity has little influence on the soluble organic fraction (SOF), but dry soot increases with an increase in kinematic viscosity [91].

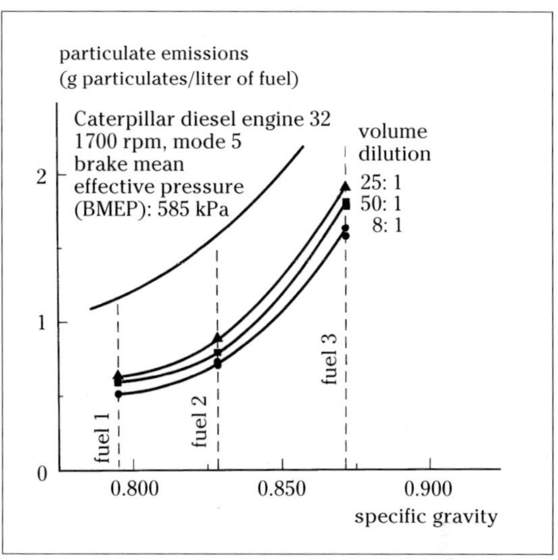


**Fig 11.12** Effect of diesel density [23]
Reprinted with permission ©1979 *Society of Automotive Engineers Inc*

The higher density of diesel results in greater particulate emissions. Fuel densities above the engine calibration range produce an overfueling effect and a sharp increase in emissions [92]. This effect has been observed on the atmospheric or turbo-charged direct-injection engine [23]. Fig. 11.12 illustrates the particle emission factor in g/liter of fuel as a function of density for a 10.4 liter V8 engine running at 1700 rpm and for a 14 liter turbo-charged engine running at 1700 rpm. The % SOF rises simultaneously with the density.

The distillation interval also affects particulate emissions. The French specification demands that the 85% distilled point must be under 350°C and the 65% distilled point above 250°C.

Figure 11.13 shows that, when the size of the fraction distilling above 265°C exceeds 50%, particulate emissions increase rapidly [23].

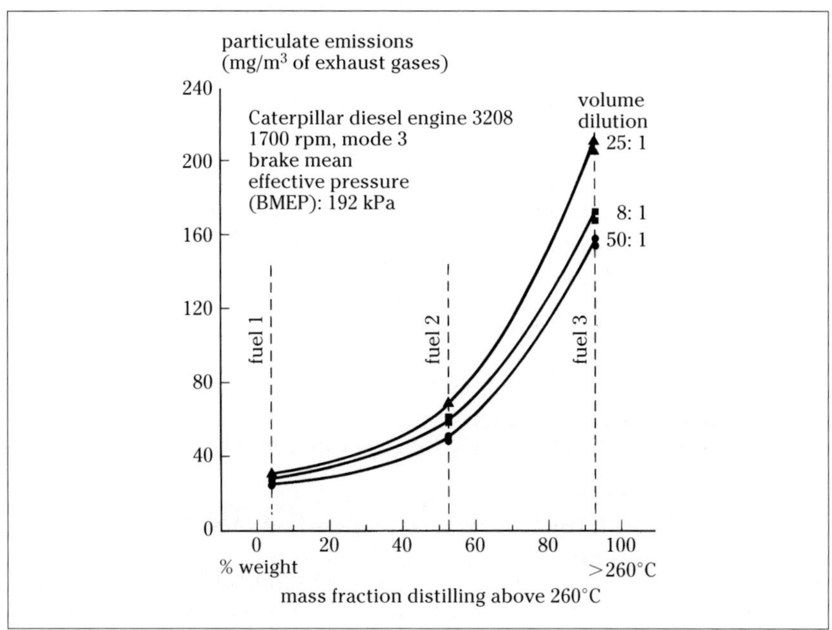


**Fig 11.13** Effect of heavy fractions on particulates [23]
Reprinted with permission ©1979 *Society of Automotive Engineers Inc*

Figure 11.14, which concerns a naturally aspirated eight-cylinder direct injection engine, shows the emissions of the various pollutants as a function of cetane number according to the 'US transient' cycle. It shows that a change from a fuel with a 90% distilled point at 342°C to a fuel at 381°C does not change the gaseous emissions but increases particulate emissions by about 12 to 50% depending on the cetane number [28].

For prechamber engines, a rise in the 10% distilled point from 210 to 216°C has practically no effect on emissions. The same rise in the 90% distilled point from 310 to 316°C may, depending on the vehicle investigated, increase the HC emissions by 5%, particles by 3%, and especially SOF by 8% [36].

On indirect-injection engines at high load, an increase in the 90% distilled point may, contrary to the tendency found at lower loads, cause a decrease in particulate emissions [11]. This may be explained by the fact that the prechamber is the point of a very rich mixture under these conditions. A lighter fuel, which vaporizes faster, causes the formation of more soot nuclei than with heavier fuels. The rapid vaporization of a lighter diesel fuel (kerosene) at the injector outlet reduces the mass of droplets, whose kinetic moment normally gives rise to effective mixing of the air and fuel, causing increased particulate and CO emissions [2]. At the other loads the corresponding fuel/air ratio is lower and this tendency does not occur as it does in direct injection, where the mixing takes place in the main chamber. In any case, these full-load running conditions are rarely encountered with pre-combustion chamber engines.

## 11.2.2 Effect of aromatics content

The aromatics content of diesel fuel directly affects the cetane number. The two parameters are antagonistic. Only the addition of procetane additives helps to break the relationship.

Unburnt hydrocarbons, particles, and the extractable SOF fraction increase with the aromatics content [74]. Increasing the aromatics content of the fuel from 25 to 45% could cause a threefold increase in CO and HC emissions [93]. $NO_x$ is relatively unaffected.

Under the same conditions, the aromatics content has a tenfold stronger effect on pollutant emissions than the 90% distilled factor. However, the addition to diesel of a volatile light aromatic can, by increasing the fraction burning in a pre-mixture flame, tend to offset their tendency to form soot [7].

Figure 11.15 shows the effect of a change from 32.4 to 42.4% aromatics compared with the variations in distillation starts and ends mentioned above [36]. On automobile engines, the effects may be as high as 24% particles, 63% HC, and 42% SOF.

On a light-duty prechamber engine, transient operation enhances the influence of fuel characteristics on pollutants. CO, HC, and particulate emissions increase with

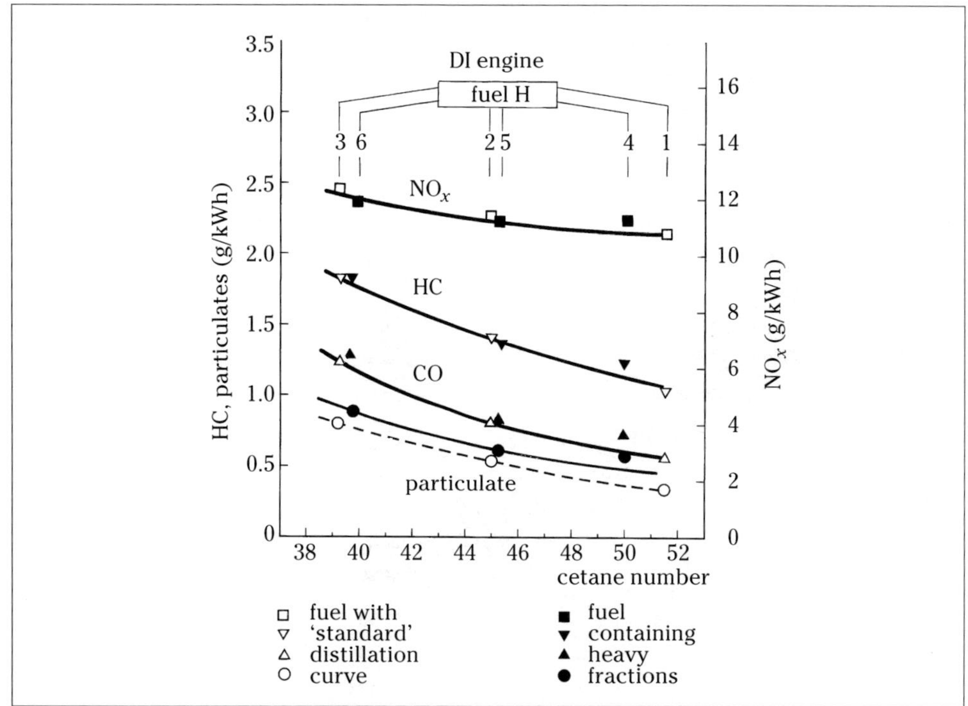


**Fig 11.14** Effect of heavy fractions on emissions [28], with variable cetane number

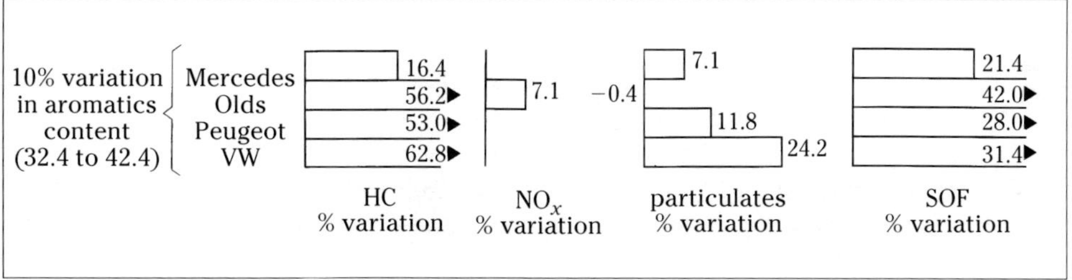


**Fig 11.15** Effect of % aromatics on emissions [36]
Reprinted with permission ©1986 *Society of Automotive Engineers Inc*

the aromatics content. However, for an engine already displaying low emissions [96] and for fuels with a cetane number higher than 50, the effect of fuel quality on pollutants is not pronounced [94].

On a truck direct-injection engine, the effect of the % aromatics is much less clear [31]. Other studies [53, 94 and 96] on a DI engine reveal the preponderant effect of diaromatics on PAH particulate emissions and their content of extractable compounds, without establishing relationships with monoaromatics. Fig. 11.16 shows the same tendency on a direct-injection engine with the naturally aspirated V8 engine already mentioned [23]. In this case [95], a decrease in aromatics reduces $NO_x$

emissions, but has no effect on CO and HC and only a slight effect on particulates. A hydrotreated fuel emits a smaller amount of PAH, but aldehyde emissions are unaffected by fuel quality [96].

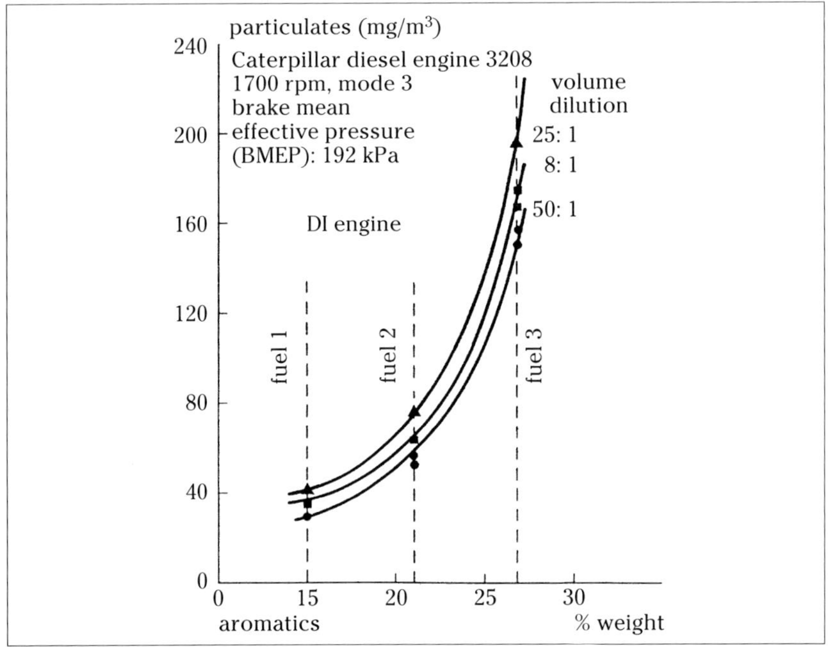


**Fig 11.16** Effect of aromatics content on particulate emissions [23]
Reprinted with permission ©1979 *Society of Automotive Engineers Inc*

## 11.2.3 Effect of cetane number

The lengthening of the ignition delay caused by a drop in the cetane number leads to increased emissions of unburnt hydrocarbons, particulates, SOF, and CO, but decreased emissions of smoke and dry soot [91].

Figure 11.17 shows the effects of the cetane number on the pollutants emitted by a direct-injection engine [28]: the $NO_x$ are the least sensitive to the cetane number. However, it may result in an increase in dry soot emissions as the pre-mixed burnt fraction decreases [96]. An increase in the cetane number results in a decrease in CO, HC, $NO_x$, and SOF, with little effect on particulates [95]. On prechamber engines, the effect of the cetane number essentially concerns the extractable SOF part and the insoluble carbon fraction remains practically unaffected [44].

The cetane number also affects emissions of blue and white smoke, which are exhaust mists consisting of droplets of unburnt diesel produced when starting and at high altitude due to a drop in the barometric pressure. The tendency for this process to occur, as identified by the negative pressure in the manifold when it appears, is greater as the cetane number decreases (Fig. 11.18) [46].

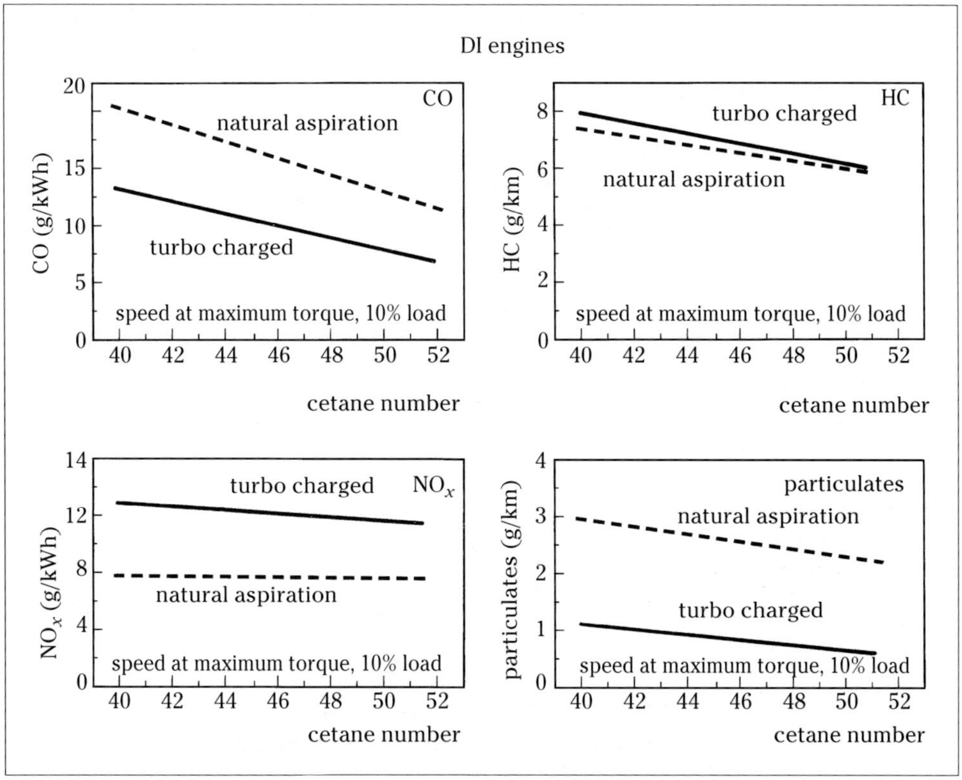

DI engines
CO
natural aspiration
turbo charged
CO (g/kWh)
speed at maximum torque, 10% load
cetane number
HC
turbo charged
natural aspiration
HC (g/km)
speed at maximum torque, 10% load
cetane number
turbo charged
NO$_x$
natural aspiration
NO$_x$ (g/kWh)
speed at maximum torque, 10% load
cetane number
particulates
natural aspiration
turbo charged
particulates (g/km)
speed at maximum torque, 10% load
cetane number

**Fig 11.17** Effect of cetane number on DI engine emissions [28]

white smoke initiation point (mm Hg × 100)
vehicle at 2500 rpm
γ=0.790
cetane number

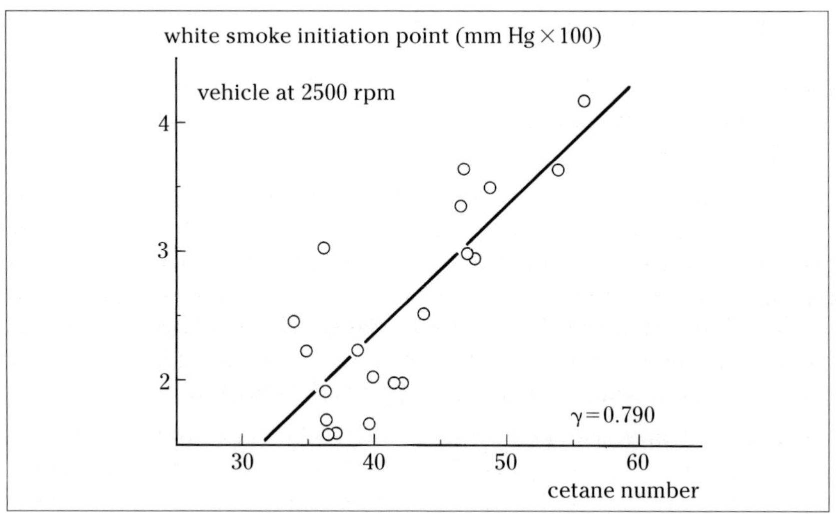

**Fig 11.18** Effect of cetane number on white smoke emissions [46]
Reprinted with permission ©1987 *Society of Automotive Engineers Inc*

### 11.2.4 Effect of sulfur content

The sulfur content is one of the regulated characteristics for diesel fuels. It is currently limited in France to 0.3% and the average figure (0.29) of products distributed corresponds to the European average. In Europe, the sulfur contents found range between 0.05 and 0.65% [21]. Plans are under way to lower it to 0.2%, which represents the Swiss regulation. California is working towards a limit of 0.05%.

Most of the sulfur is in the form of $SO_2$. A diesel fuel containing 0.3% releases about 100 ppm of $SO_2$ at the exhaust [35]. However, part of the $SO_2$ (2 to 3%) is oxidized to $SO_3$ and sulfuric acid ('sulfates') that make a significant contribution to the mass collected on the analytical filters designed to measure 'particulates'. It is estimated that 1 ppm of sulfate corresponds to 8 $mg/m^3$ of particulates [38]. This contribution is due to the following [80]:

- the mass of actual sulfates, which is added to that of carbon and SOF
- the mass of water combined with the sulfates, which are very hygroscopic: at a relative humidity of 50%, the average value in the filter weighing cells, one can expect 1.3 g of water per g of $H_2SO_4$ (0.8 to 3.0 g per g of $H_2SO_4$ for a relative humidity between 20 and 80%): the deposited sulfates thus contain by mass 53% $H_2O$ and 47% $SO_4^=$ [13]
- an increase in organic compounds making up the SOF due to the presence on the filter of sulfuric acid and water, which improves the retention by the filter and condenses any hydrocarbons that otherwise would have remained in the gas phase

A reduction of 10 to 15% in particulate emissions would be achieved by decreasing the sulfur content from 0.3 to 0.05%.

This overall effect appears in Fig. 11.19, which gives the breakdown of particulate emissions for two motor fuels with different sulfur contents, on a turbo-charged direct-injection, six-cylinder 14-liter engine at medium load. The following equation was developed with this engine:

$$\text{PART (g/kWh)} = 10^{-4}\,(18\,(\text{Aro\%}) + 5.6\,(90\%\ \text{dist}) + 5200\,(\text{S\%}) = 400)$$

indicating in this case a sulfur content contribution nearly 300 times higher than that of aromatics and 1000 times higher than that of the 90% distilled. Hence, the reduction of diesel sulfur contents appears to be one of the means available for meeting the very severe future emission standards of 0.7 g/kWh in Switzerland and Sweden, and 0.1 g/kWh in the USA [74 and 81]. In fact, with a fuel containing 0.3% sulfur and particulate emissions of 0.1 g/kWh, it is estimated that sulfates account for 70% [64].

Except on $SO_2$ and SOF, the sulfur content has little influence on the other pollutants [93].

This decrease in sulfur content would also help to reduce the odor levels in diesel exhausts and diminish their nauseating character [66].

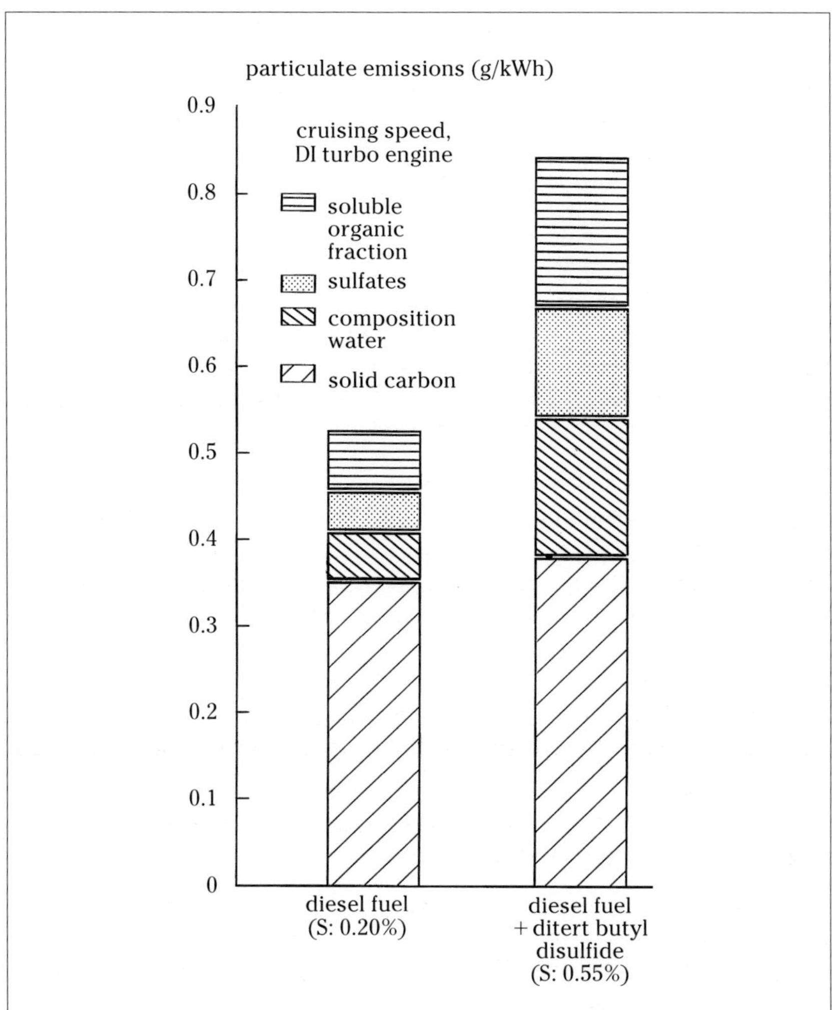


**Fig 11.19** Effect of % sulfur on particulate fractions [80]
Reprinted with permission ©1984 *Society of Automotive Engineers Inc*

## 11.2.5 Effect of additives

### 11.2.5.1 Metallic additives

Metallic additives, in the form of acid salts (naphthenates, stearates, sulfonates, etc.) have been used to reduce diesel smoke emissions characterized by exhaust opacity.

A number of alkaline earth and transition metals have been suggested (Ca, Ba, Mg, Fe, Mn, Cu, Ni). On both the direct injection and indirect-injection prechamber engine, the alkaline earth metals Ba and Ca prove to be the most effective [58].

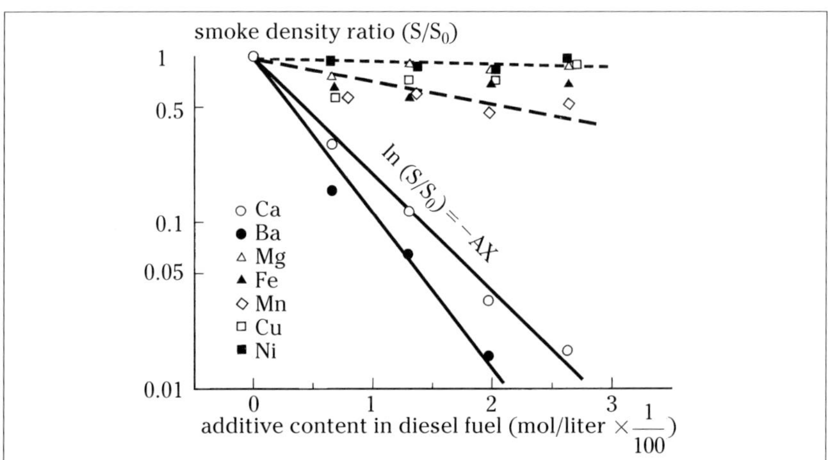


**Fig 11.20** Effect of different metallic additives on smoke [58]
Reprinted with permission ©1987 *Society of Automotive Engineers Inc*

Figure 11.20 shows in log units the ratio between the opacity with additives and the initial opacity, expressed in 'Bosch' units, as a function of additive content.

The type of anion selected has little effect on the results and other pollutants (CO, HC, $NO_x$) are unaffected by the additive. However, since the particles are expressed by weight, a small addition of metal rapidly reduces the emissions. The drop is more rapid for Ba than for Ca. As the metal content increases, the mass of the oxides or sulfates formed counteracts the reduction of carbon particles (Fig. 11.21). This occurs more rapidly with Ba than with Ca. This formation of sulfates depends on the sulfur content of the fuel [6]. Whereas visible smoke is reduced by adding Ba, the weight emissions are increased in most cases, since the additive shifts the grain size distribution of the particles emitted towards the smaller sizes, more characteristic of $BaSO_4$ [47]. For these reasons and due to the toxicity of soluble salts of Ba (such as $BaCO_3$), metallic additives have been abandoned.

### 11.2.5.2 Organic additives

Organic additives are added to diesel fuel for various purposes:

- to shorten the ignition delay (procetane)
- as stabilizers, anti-oxidants, which inhibits the polymerization of unsaturated compounds (gum formation) and thus improve storage stability
- as surfactants to keep the nozzles clean [35 and 59], which is a very important factor in prechamber engines

The various corresponding products are added simultaneously in the form of additive packages [50] or multi-purpose additives.

Figure 11.22 shows that not only does the additive reduce the levels of pollutants emitted to their initial value before deterioration of the injection system by fouling, but also that its removal leads to a rapid return to the previous levels deteriorated by fouling.

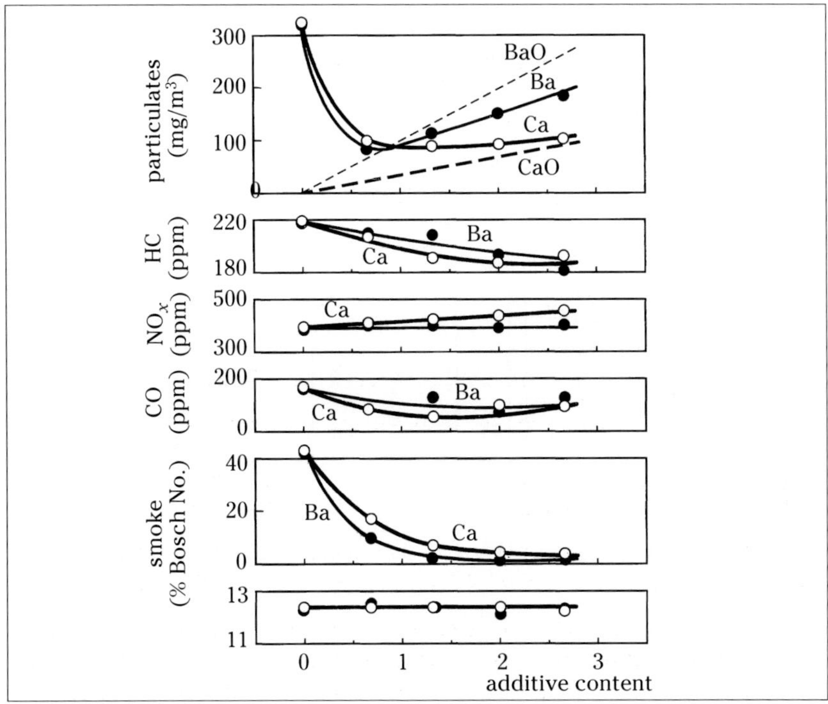


**Fig 11.21** Effect of barium and calcium on different pollutants [58]
Reprinted with permission ©1987 *Society of Automotive Engineers Inc*

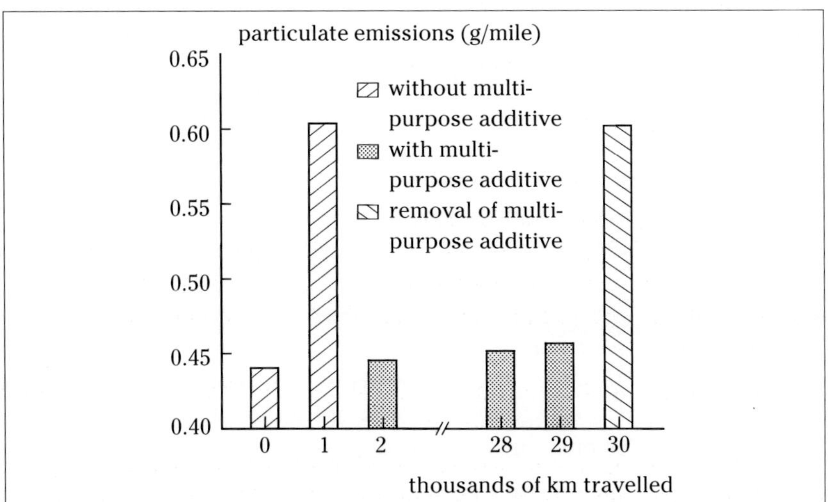


**Fig 11.22** Effect of additive packages on particulates [50]
Reprinted with permission ©1986 *Society of Automotive Engineers Inc*

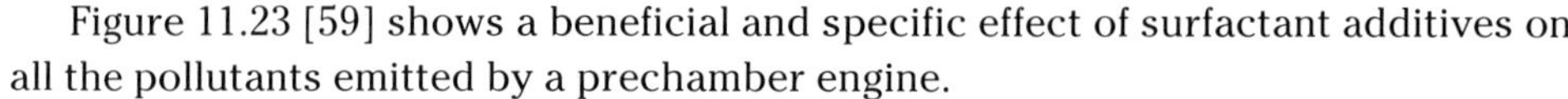

Figure 11.23 [59] shows a beneficial and specific effect of surfactant additives on all the pollutants emitted by a prechamber engine.

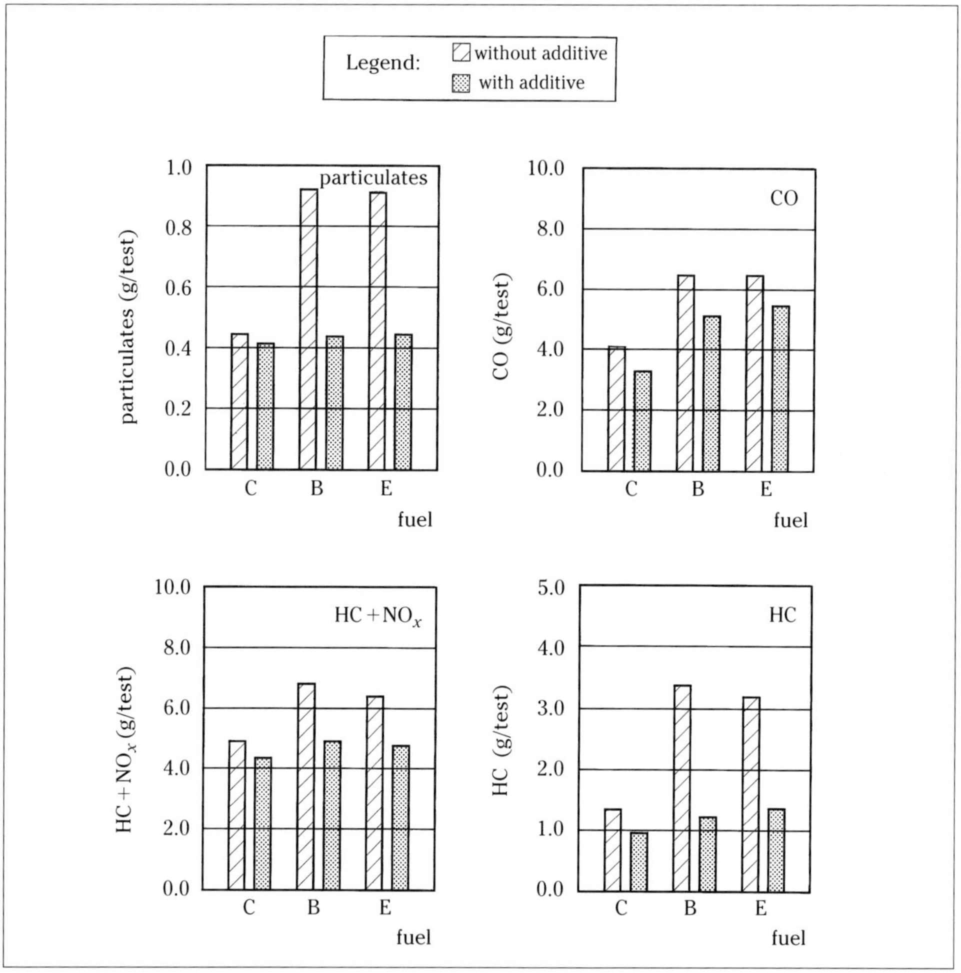

**Fig 11.23** Effect of detergent additives [59]
Reprinted with permission ©1987 *Society of Automotive Engineers Inc*

### 11.2.5.3 Addition of water

The addition of water (Fig. 11.24) has been closely investigated, because it appeared to be one of the rare means of simultaneously reducing particulate emissions and $NO_x$ emissions. The other means generally yielded opposing results.

Several techniques have been proposed: water emulsions in the diesel, direct injection of water into the cylinder, or water spraying (fumigation) into the inlet air [67]. The first alternative appeared to be the most effective.

Since water lowers the flame temperature, it reduces the $NO_x$ emitted. By lengthening the ignition delay, it increases the proportion of fuel burned in the premixing flame and reduces the proportion of soot formed in a diffusion flame [4]. This appears in Fig. 11.24, which gives the percentage reduction of particulate emissions for two water concentrations in the diesel fuel, as a function of load of a direct-injection single-cylinder engine. This shows that a reduction of 70% can be achieved with 10% water.

The SOF fraction adsorbed on the particles also decreases with the proportion of water. This may be due to an analytical artifact, because the water causes condensation of the hydrocarbons on the walls of the sampling lines before precipitation on the carbon particles [4]. In fact, unburnt hydrocarbons increase due to the drop in combustion temperature. However, raising the inlet temperature is not an economic means to offset the increase in HC [3]. It has also been found that the PAH present in the SOF increase with the proportion of water in the diesel [4].

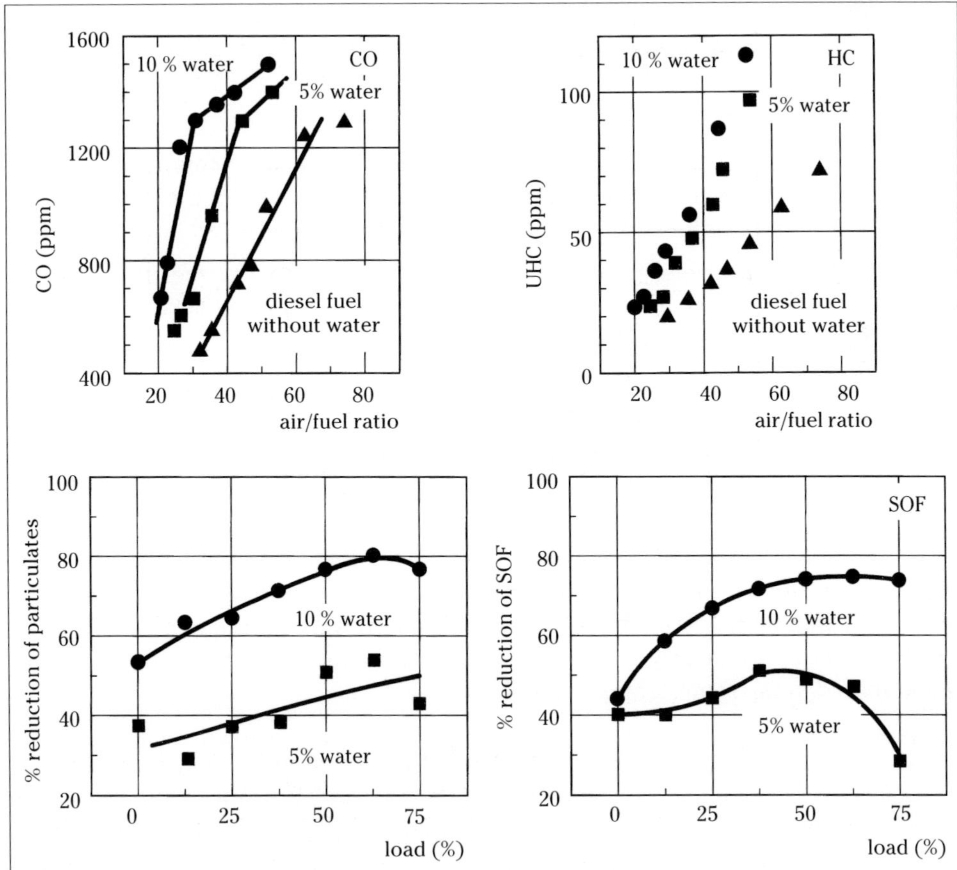


**Fig 11.24** Effect of two water concentrations in diesel [4]
Reprinted with permission ©1988 *Society of Automotive Engineers Inc*

Apart from the fact that it is not a technique compatible with automotive diesel fuel, the addition of water is not a solution for reducing diesel pollutants because, although it decreases $NO_x$, it increases HC and CO emissions, and particulate reduction depends on the load applied to the engine.

## 11.3 Effect of alternative fuels

These are essentially mixtures of alcohols (methanol, ethanol, tert-butanol, etc.), ethers (MTBE, TAME, etc.), ketones (ABE, acetone/butanol/ethanol), vegetable oils or their ester derivatives, and light hydrocarbons (liquefied, LPG, or compressed petroleum gas) [35].

These fuels are added in small proportions to gasoline or in a high proportion for spark ignition and diesel engines, with the requisite transformations.

### 11.3.1 Spark ignition engines

#### 11.3.1.1 Low-content oxygenated compounds

These are fuel blends that contain less than 10% oxygenated compounds. Up to these concentrations, it is not necessary to significantly alter the settings of the engine, which can continue to run on a pure hydrocarbon fuel.

As the mixture becomes poorer due to the oxygen input by the fuel, this helps to reduce CO emissions by 50% on the ECE cold start cycle and by 30% on the same cycle with a warm start [34 and 41].

Unburnt hydrocarbon emissions are relatively unaffected. The reduction is less than 10%, taking into account the fact that the alcohol compounds have a lower response factor to FID analysis than that of the actual hydrocarbons. Methane and lower weight hydrocarbon emissions are increased due to lower exhaust temperatures, which inhibits their post-oxidation [98].

At an equivalent fuel/air ratio, the oxygenated compounds have a lower flame temperature, with a resulting decrease in $NO_x$ emissions. However, this effect is offset by a shift on the $NO_x = f$ (fuel/air ratio) curve towards maximum emissions at a ratio of 0.95. Consequently, total emissions are slightly increased (by about 5%) [41] or decreased in the same proportion [34].

Another consequence of the mixture becoming leaner, as shown in Fig. 11.1, is to favor aldehyde emissions. The formaldehyde contents emitted are proportional to the methanol content of the fuel: for 3% methanol, the HCHO emitted increases by 9 to 10%, and acetaldehyde increases by nearly 100% for 5% ethanol. For these types of mixture, acrolein emissions also increase by about 20%. The addition of MTBE increases the level of formaldehyde emissions, but reduces the emission of 1-3 butadiene [88].

Alcohol emissions depend on the type of alcohol used. Methanol multiplies methanol emissions by a factor of 5 and ethanol increases its own emissions tenfold.

#### 11.3.1.2 High-content oxygenated compounds

Mixtures with a high oxygenated content are generally prepared from methanol or ethanol: M15 indicates 15% methanol in the gasoline and M100 is pure methanol.

These fuels demand heating of the feed circuits due to the higher heats of vaporization of the alcohols and fuel/air ratio settings to prevent the carburetted mixture from becoming too lean.

Under these conditions, CO emissions remain unchanged when going from gasoline to M15 and to M100. This is also true of ethanol and ethers [56]. Unburnt products (hydrocarbons and alcohols) are considerably reduced with M15 and M100 (Fig. 11.25). This apparent reduction must nevertheless be considered with moderation, given the lower response factor of alcohols to FID. However, the possibility of running at partial load with a leaner mixture is favorable in these conditions to the reduction of CO and HC emissions.

The lower combustion temperature and the cooling of the combustion chamber cause a drop in $NO_x$ emissions (Fig. 11.26). However, the possible rise in compression ratios tends to increase these emissions. The passage from a rate of 8.2 with gasoline to a rate of 13 with M100 leaves the emissions unchanged [56]. PAH emissions are obviously sharply reduced when going from gasoline to alcohols.

Aldehyde emissions are considerably higher than with the corresponding gasoline-fueled engines because the mixtures become leaner. M100 increases HCHO emissions by 6.5 on an ECE cold start cycle and M15 increases them by a factor of 2.5 [56]. With ETBE and pure methanol, under the same conditions, formaldehyde emissions are doubled and quadrupled respectively in comparison with isooctane [45]. It should be observed in this case, however, that the aldehydes are easily oxidized by simple catalytic converters.

Using M85 may reduce the ozone-formation potential of the fuel by approximately 40 to 50%, compared with pure gasoline [99].

On two corresponding vehicles, switching from gasoline to M15 increases CO by a factor of 1.98, HC by 1.13, and $NO_x$ by 0.72 [20] when the air/fuel ratio is corrected by the $\lambda$ sensor.

The high volatility of the alcohols used also causes an increase in evaporation losses. The losses rise from 0.1 to 0.68 g/test for diurnal losses and from 0.2 to 0.43 g/test for hot soak losses, when going from gasoline to M90. In this case, 60% of the evaporation losses consist of methanol (instead of 90%) [24 and 25].

Using fuel mixed with methanol produces formic and acetic acids, which pass along with water into the engine oil, causing corrosion and wear [99].

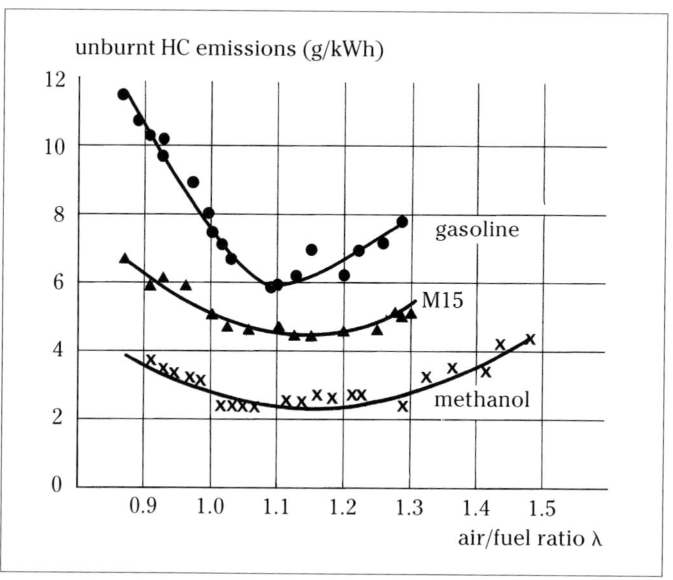


**Fig 11.25** Effect of alcohol content on HC [56]

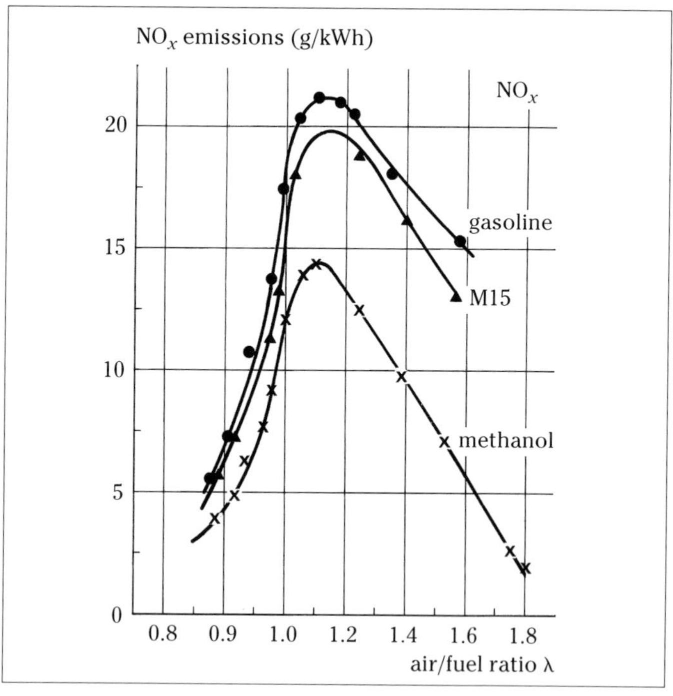


**Fig 11.26** Effect of alcohol contents on $NO_x$ emissions [56]

## 11.3.2 Diesel engines

Contrary to the situation with spark ignition engines, alcohols lend themselves poorly to diesel combustion due to their high volatility and low cetane number.

The low alcohol contents have not found any applications because the problems of alcohol solubility in diesel and the lowering of the flash point of the mixture obtained have made the implementation of these solutions difficult.

### 11.3.2.1 High-content oxygenated compounds

To be able to use pure methanol, diesel engines have been converted to ignite alcohols:

- by replacing glow plugs by spark plugs, thereby converting them into spark ignition engines
- by using a pilot diesel injection (dual-fuel technique) to ignite the alcohol introduced either by spraying into the inlet air (fumigation) or by dual injection

Pollutant measurements taken on a four-stroke dual-fuel engine (Volvo), on a four-stroke supercharged dual-fuel engine (IFP) [29], and on a two-stroke spark plug engine with M100 (Detroit Diesel Allison by General Motors) give the multiplication factors listed in Table 11.2.

**Table 11.2** Emission multiplication factors [29]

| Pollutant | Volvo | DDA | IFP |
|---|---|---|---|
| CO | 3 | 3.23 | 4 |
| HC | 1.38 | 2.0 | 10 |
| $NO_x$ | 0.44 | 3.5 | 0.33 |
| aldehydes | 10 | 3.5 | – |
| particulates | 0.44 | – | – |

The heavy oxygenated molecules obtained by the polymerization of ethylene oxide can also be used as a diesel fuel. These molecules have comparable properties to diesel (cetane number, volatility, viscosity) and help to prevent practically all particulate emissions.

### 11.3.2.2 Vegetable oils and derivatives

A number of vegetable oils, mostly fatty acid triglycerides of European origin (rape, sunflower, etc.) or tropical origin (coconut, palm, etc.), have been suggested and investigated as diesel fuel substitutes [35].

The transesterification of these oils also serves to prepare products (essentially methyl esters) whose properties more closely resemble those of gas oil (cetane number, distillation curve, viscosity). This allows the preparation of 'diester' type mixtures.

The emission factors obtained with the oils and esters [50] show the following results:

- CO emissions are lower with esters, higher with oils
- $NO_x$ emissions are practically the same for gas oil, oils, and esters
- compared with gas oil, unburnt emissions are higher with rapeseed oil, lower with methyl oleate, and identical with rapeseed esters
- aldehyde measurements show an overall multiplication by 4, and by 7 for the specific case of acrolein with rapeseed oil: with esters, aldehyde emissions are comparable to those of diesel
- smoke emissions are reduced compared with diesel, both with oil and with esters

### 11.3.3 Liquefied and compressed gases

Fuel-LPG is a mixture of $C_3$ and $C_4$ carbons in variable proportions in the various user countries. It is distributed in liquid form under pressure.

Fuel natural gas (compressed natural gas, CNG) consists mainly of methane, which has the highest octane number of any commonly-used fuel and is distributed under pressure by compressor stations. Compressed at 250 bar for city buses, it fulfills the future EEC-2000 regulations. Despite the reduced power due to its lower topping-up, it may reduce $CO_2$ emissions by 20% [100]. CNG reduces CO emissions by 50%, keeps the overall $NO_x$ emissions at the same level, but increases the HC emissions due to the difficult oxidation of methane [101].

#### 11.3.3.1 On the spark ignition engine

LPG can fuel specially-designed vehicles or vehicles adapted to dual-carburation (gasoline or LPG).

Table 11.3 gives the multiplication factors measured on several vehicles tested on the FTP-78 cycle (column 2) [20] and the variation with the type of vehicle fueled with dual-fuel systems, on another vehicle with different feed systems [17] tested on the ECE 15-04 cold start cycle (column 3) and on the Extra Urban Driving Cycle (EUDC) (column 4). The wide dispersion of the results shows the predominant importance of the feed systems selected for the vehicles.

**Table 11.3** Emission multiplication factors with LPG [17]

| Pollutant | FTP-78 cycle | ECE-15 cycle | EUDC cycle |
|---|---|---|---|
| CO | 0.23 to 1.03 | 0.16 to 0.33 | 0.50 |
| HC | 0.31 to 0.6 | unchanged | 0.7 to 0.8 |
| $NO_x$ | 0.78 to 1.55 | unchanged | 0.9 |

Table 11.4 gives a number of emission factors recorded on LPG-fueled vehicles in the Netherlands in different traffic conditions [65]. The figures given correspond to

warm engines at stabilized temperatures. When starting from cold, the factors given must be multiplied by 1.3 for the first 4 to 5 km. On fork-lifts supplied with propane, CO emissions are estimated to be ten times greater than diesel emissions [55].

**Table 11.4** Emission factors of LPG-fuelled light vehicles [65]

| | CO | | HC | | $NO_x$ | | Fuel consumption |
|---|---|---|---|---|---|---|---|
| | (g/kg fuel) | (g/km) | (g/kg fuel) | (g/km) | (g/kg fuel) | (g/km) | (g/km) |
| urban cycle average speed 25 km/h | 55 | 3.3 | 23 | 1.36 | 21 | 1.24 | 59 |
| road cycle average speed 50 km/h | 39 | 1.76 | 26 | 1.17 | 29 | 1.3 | 45 |
| freeway cycle average speed 110 km/h | 22 | 1.16 | 20 | 1.04 | 51 | 2.75 | 54 |

#### 11.3.3.2 On the diesel engine

An attempt is being made to apply LPG to urban transit buses to reduce particulate emissions in cities [12 and 14]. The most widely adopted solution is dual-fuel feed[1], with pilot diesel injection igniting the gas mixed with the inlet air. The second alternative converts the diesel into a spark ignition engine [22].

Tests conducted on the dual-fuel system [78] with 30% substitution of diesel by LPG show that CO and $NO_x$ are unchanged. HC are increased, but particulate emissions are reduced by half.

## 11.4 Effect of lubricants

In addition to automotive fuels, lubricating oils also affect emissions, both of hydrocarbons and particulates.

On a spark ignition engine, it is considered that total HC emissions due to the lubricant are negligible [49]. However, the lubricant contributes to unburnt HC emissions by its ability to absorb the fuel during the intake and compression phases, and to discharge it in the exhaust phase. This effect is greater for lean mixtures [69]. It is mainly PAH emissions that have been associated with lubricant combustion [63], as well as particulates from spark ignition engines, of which the weight fraction

1. In this method, also called 'fumigation', the diesel is injected not into the pure air, but into an air/LPG mixture prepared in the intake system, by carburation or by injection [35].

attributable to lubricant is as high as 15% [83]. With low oil consumption, the lubricant is not a dominant factor in PAH emissions. However, the oil accumulates the PAH which would otherwise be discharged at the exhaust. The dispersion into the environment of these highly contaminated oils raises serious problems of soil and water pollution, leading some experts to recommend total loss lubrication instead [79].

With a diesel engine, oil consumption represents a fraction of the particulates emitted. This amount is tending to grow because engine parameters are being more thoroughly controlled to meet increasingly stringent future standards: the lubricant share, estimated in 1988 at 15%, is up to 35% of particulates [84] and will continue to rise if oil consumption is not reduced [73 and 75]. In fact, it is estimated that, of the vehicles produced in 1987, a third of the particulate emissions result from the lubricant and two-thirds from the fuel [15].

Most of this oil fraction is found in the SOF part of the particulates [54]. With gasoline-fueled engines, spent oil accumulates the PAH [1], which are then found in the exhaust in proportions increasing with the age of the oil [82].

## 11.5 Conclusion

While automotive fuels are not major factors in causing emissions from internal combustion engines, their contribution is nevertheless significant.

Perfect, non-polluting fuels have already been tested, such as hydrogen. In this case, however, incompletely solved technical problems persist (storage aboard the vehicle, for example) and cost problems make these solutions unfeasible for the time being.

To meet the pollution standards, the degrees of freedom in the possible variations of automotive fuel parameters are nevertheless relatively limited on account of engine requirements (fuel economy, driving comfort, noise emissions, etc.).

## REFERENCES

[1] M.K. Abbass et al., (1987), "The aging of lubricating oil, The influence of unburnt fuel and particulate SOF contamination", *SAE Paper* No. 872085, 10 p.

[2] M.K. Abbass et al., (1989), "Pyrosynthesis of PAH in a Diesel engine operated on kerosene", *SAE Paper* No. 890827, 15 p.

[3] E.M. Afify et al., (1987), "The effect of air charge temperature on performance, ignition delay and exhaust emissions of diesel engines using W/O emulsions as fuel", *SAE Paper* No. 870555, 13 p.

[4] G.E. Andrews et al., (1988), "The reduction in Diesel particulate emissions using emulsified fuels", *SAE Paper* No. 880348, 9 p.

[5] G.E. Andrews et al., (1990), *Ethanol/Diesel mixtures for reduced $NO_x$ and particulate emissions, IMechE Seminar, "Fuels for automotive and industrial Diesel engines"*, November, pp.107-116

[6] N.D. Apostolescu et al., (1977), "Effects of a barium based fuel additive on particulate emissions from Diesel engine", *SAE Paper* No. 770828, 8 p.

[7] A. Barbella et al., (1989), "Effect of fuel aromaticity on Diesel emission", *Comb. Flame*, **77,** 267-77.

[8] R.M. Bata et al., (1989), "Emissions from IC engines fueled with alcohol gasoline blends, A literature review", *J. Eng. Gas Turbine Power*, **111,** 424-431.

[9] R.M. Bata and V.P. Roan, (1989), "Effects of ethanol and/or methanol in alcohol gasoline blends on exhaust emissions", *J. Eng. Gas Turbine Power*, **111,** 432-438.

[10] J.D. Benson, (1977), "Manganese fuel additive (MMT) can cause vehicle problems", *SAE Paper* No. 770655, 22 p.

[11] S.P. Bergin, (1983), "The influence of fuel properties and engine load upon the carbon and hydrocarbon fractions of particulate emissions from a light-duty Diesel engine", *SAE Paper* No. 831736, 21 p.

[12] E. Bo, (1987), "Contributo dell'autotrazione a GPL al miglioramento della qualità dell'aria nei centri urbani", *La Rivista dei Combustibili*, **41,** 178-183.

[13] F. Brear, (1991), *An introduction to Diesel exhaust aftertreatment technology with special reference to the control of particulates, A short course on Diesel particulates*, University of Leeds, 8/12 April, 38 p.

[14] G. Canal, (1980), "L'autobus urbain et le gaz de pétrole liquéfié", *Poll. Atmosph.* (85), 138-148.

[15] W. Cartellieri et al., (1989), "Erfüllung der Dieselabgasgrenzwerte von Nutzfahrzeug-Dieselmotoren der 90er Jahre", *MTZ*, **50,** 440-451.

[16] J.A. Caton et al., (1991), "Performance and fuel consumption of a single cylinder, direct injection Diesel engine using a platinum fuel additive", *SAE Paper* No. 910229, 11 p.

[17] CPBP, (1986), *Comité professionnel du butane et du propane, essais d'un véhicule bicarburation essence/GPL.*

[18] P. Degobert, (1984), *Les gazoles futurs amèneront-ils une augmentation des polluants et notamment des particules?, Journées Int. SIA*, Lyon, 5/6 June, 35 p.

[19] P. Degobert, (1989), "Influence des propriétés des carburants sur les émissions", *Poll. Atmosph.* (121), 43-56.

[20] K.E. Egebäck and B.M. Bertilson, (1983), *Chemical and biological characterization of exhaust emissions from vehicles fueled with gasoline, alcohol, LPG and Diesel*, snv pm Report 1635, National Swedish Environment Board.

[21] Ethyl, (1988), *Ethyl European Diesel fuel survey*, Winter 1987/1988, 12 p.

[22] J.R. Fellous and P. Tiedema, (1978), "Les gaz de pétrole liquéfiés, carburant pour les transport publics urbains", *Gaz d'Aujourd'hui*, **102,** 283-294.

[23] L.E. Frisch et al., (1979), "Effect of fuels and dilution ratio on Diesel particulate emissions", *SAE Paper* No. 790417 (PT-17), 29 p.

[24] P.A. Gabele et al., (1985), "Characterization of emissions from vehicles using methanol and methanol gasoline blended fuels", *J. APCA*, **35,** 1168-1175.

[25] P.A. Gabele, (1990), "Characterization of emissions from a variable gasoline/methanol fueled car", *J. Air Waste Managem. Assoc.*, **40,** 296-304.

[26] J.C. Gagliardi, (1967), "The effect of fuel anti-knock compounds and deposits on exhaust emissions", *SAE Paper* No. 670128, 25 p.

[27] J.C. Gagliardi and F. Ghannam, (1969), "Effects of tetraethyl lead concentration on exhaust emissions in customer type vehicle operation", *SAE Paper* No. 690015, 19 p.

[28] H. Garthe and H.W. Knuth, (1988), *Influence of changed Diesel fuel parameters on the gas and particulate emissions at steady-state and transient working conditions, AGELFI Symp.*, Bordeaux, 13/14 October, pp. 179-193.

[29] P. Gateau et al., (1982), (unpublished results).

[30] P. Gateau et al., (1985), "Utilisation des huiles végétales et de leurs produits de transestérification comme carburants Diesel", *Revue Inst. Franç. du Pétrole*, **40,** 509-528.

[31] E. Goldenberg, (1988), (unpublished results).

[32] G.P. Gross, (1972), "The effect of fuel and vehicle variables on polynuclear aromatic hydrocarbon and phenol emissions", *SAE Paper* No. 720210, 25 p.

[33] D. Gruden, (1988), *Aromaten im Abgas von Ottomotoren, Verlag TUV Rheinland*, Köln, 126 p.

[34] J-C. Guibet and P. Degobert, (1982), "Les nouveaux carburants pour l'automobile, carburants oxygénés, emploi et émissions", *Revue Inst. Franç. du Pétrole*, **37,** 823-845.

[35] J-C. Guibet and B. Martin, (1987), *Carburants et moteurs*, Éditions Technip, Paris, 903 p.

[36] C.T. Hare and L.R. Smith, (1986), "Light-duty Diesel FTP emissions as a function of fuel volatility and aromatic content", *SAE Paper* No. 861120, 32 p.

[37] O. Hirao and R.H. Pefley, (1988), *Present and future automotive fuels, performance and exhaust clarification*, J. Wiley and Sons, New York, 570 p.

[38] M. Horiuchi et al., (1990), "The effects of flow through type oxidation catalysts on the particulate reduction of 1990's Diesel engines", *SAE Paper* No. 900600 (SP-816), 183-193.

[39] G.A. Hughmark and B.A. Sobel, (1980), "A statistical analysis of the effect of MMT concentration on hydrocarbon emissions", *SAE Paper* No. 800383, 10 p.

[40] R.G. Hurley et al., (1989), "Characterization of automotive catalysts exposed to the fuel additive MMT", *SAE Paper* No. 890582, 11 p.

[41] H. Ing and B. Lopez, (1986), *Pollution par les gaz d'échappement des véhicules automobiles alimentés par des carburants oxygénés*, Journée AFITE, Paris, "Les carburants oxygénés feront-ils courir de nouveaux risques de pollution", 27 May, pp. 73-84.

[42] J.H. Johnson, (1988), "Automotive emissions", in: *Air pollution, the automobile and public health*, A.Y. Watson, National Academic Press, Washington, pp. 39-75.

[43] C.R. Jones and P.R. Watters, (1988), "Coping with lower gasoline volatility, the impact on gas processing", *Energy Progress*, **8,** 143-146.

[44] M. Jourdan, (1987), *Influence des caractéristiques des gazoles sur les émissions des moteurs Diesel d'automobiles, SIA Int. Conf.*, Lyon, May, 15 p.

[45] E.W. Kaiser et al., (1991), "Hydrocarbon and aldehyde emissions from an engine fueled with ethyl-t-butyl ether", *J. Air Waste Managem. Assoc.*, **41,** 196-197.

[46] M. Kato et al., (1987), "The influence of fuel qualities on white smoke emissions from light-duty Diesel engines", *SAE Paper* No. 870341, 7 p.

[47] D.B. Kittelson et al., (1978), "Diesel exhaust particle size distributions, fuel and additive effects", *SAE Paper* No. 780787, 12 p.

[48] D.L. Lenane, (1978), "Effect of MMT on emissions from production cars", *SAE Paper* No. 780003, 20 p.

[49] G. Lepperhoff and J. Schommers, (1986), "Einfluß des Schmieröls auf die PAH-Emissionen von Verbrennungsmotoren", *MTZ*, **47,** 367-371.

[50] P.B. Mabley and A.J. Mills, (1986), "Additives for compression ignition fuels, State of the art", *Paper* No. 865157, *21st FISITA Conf.*, Belgrade, 2/6 June, 6 p.

[51] A. Marhold, (1988), "Vergaserkraftstoffzusammensetzung und Emissionen", *Erdöl, Erdgas, Kohle*, **104,** 368-371.

[52] H. May et al., (1984), "Einfluß von Zündung und Kraftstoff zusammensetzung auf die Schadstoff-Emission", *VDI Berichte* No. 531 "Emissionsminderung Automobilabgase-Ottomotoren", pp. 307-323.

[53] H. May et al., (1986), "Einfluß der Zusammensetzung und des Siedeendes von Dieselfraftstoff auf die Rußemission und die an Ruß angelagerten Stoffe beim Dieselmotor", *BMFT Report* 01 VQ 103 8, 103 p.

[54] W.J. Mayer et al., (1980), "The contribution of engine oil to Diesel particulate emissions", *SAE Paper* No. 800256, 10 p.

[55] D.L. McKinnon et al., (1991), "A Diesel particulate filter system using assisted regeneration for mechanical handling equipment", *SAE Paper* No. 910134 (P-240), pp. 49-62.

[56] H. Menrad and A. König, (1982), *Alkoholkraftstoffe, Springer Verlag*, Wien, pp. 185-198.

[57] L.W. Mixon et al., (1971), "Effect of fuel and lubricant additives on exhaust emissions", *SAE Paper* No. 710295, 13 p.

[58] N. Miyamoto et al., (1987), "Characteristics of Diesel soot suppression with soluble fuel additives", *SAE Paper* No. 871612, 7 p.

[59] X. Montagne et al., (1987), "Fouling of automotive Diesel injectors, test procedures, influence of composition of Diesel oil and additives", *SAE Paper* No. 872118, 9 p.

[60] X. Montagne and B. Martin, (1990), *Influence of Diesel fuel characteristics on pollutant emissions, determination of a criterion used to foresee their emission rate, IMechE Seminar, "Fuels for Automotive and Industrial Diesel Engines"*, London, 19/29 November, pp. 19-26.

[61] J.B. Moran, (1975), "The environmental implications of manganese as an alternative anti-knock", *SAE Paper* No. 750926, 55 p.

[62] G.J. Nebel, (1981), "The effect of misfueling on aldehyde and other auto exhaust emissions", *J. APCA*, **31,** 877-879.

[63] P.S. Pedersen et al., (1980), "Effects of fuel, lubricant and engine operating parameters on the emission of polycyclic hydrocarbons", *E.S.&T.*, **14,** 71-79.

[64] R.R. Richards and J.E. Sibley, (1988), "Diesel engine emissions control for the 1990s", *SAE Paper* No. 880346, 16 p.

[65] R.C. Rijkeboer, (1988), personal paper.

[66] H. Rohlfing and A. König, (1990), "Geruchmeßtechnik", *ErgoMed*, **14,** 78-85.

[67] T.W. Ryan et al., (1981), "The effects of fuel properties and composition on Diesel engine exhaust emissions", *A review, SAE Paper* No. 810953, 12 p.

[68] G.A. Schoonveld and W.F. Marshall, (1991), "The total effect of a reformulated gasoline on vehicle emissions by technology (1973 to 1989)", *SAE Paper* No. 910380, 24 p.

[69] J. Schramm and S.C. Sorenson, (1989), "Effects of lubricating oil on hydrocarbon emissions in an SI engine", *SAE Paper* No. 891622, 16 p.

[70] K.P. Schug et al., (1990), "Effects of ferrocene as a gasoline additive on exhaust emissions and fuel consumption of catalyst equipped vehicles", *SAE Paper* No. 900154, 9 p.

[71] D.E. Seizinger et al., (1982), "Diesel particulates and bioassay effect of fuels, vehicles, and ambient temperature", *SAE Paper* No. 820813, 9 p.

[72] P.R. Shore, (1988), "Advances in the use of tritium as a radiotracer for oil consumption measurement", *SAE Paper* No. 881583, 12 p.

[73] K.J. Springer, (1988), *Diesel lube oils, fourth dimension of Diesel particulate control, AGELFI Symp.*, Bordeaux, 13/14 October, pp. 297-309.

[74] K.J. Springer, (1989), "Low-emission Diesel fuel for 1991-1994", *J. Eng. Gas Turbine Power*, **111**, 361-368.

[75] K.J. Springer, (1989), "Diesel lube oils, fourth dimension of Diesel particulate control", *J. Eng. Gas Turbine Power*, **111,** 355-360.

[76] R.F. Stebar et al., (1985), "Gasoline vapor pressure reduction, an option for cleaner air", *SAE Paper* No. 852132, 25 p.

[77] F.D. Stump et al., (1990), "Seasonal impact of blending oxygenated organics with gasoline on motor vehicle tailpipe and evaporative emissions", *J. Air Waste Managem. Assoc.*, **40,** 872-880.

[78] Totalgaz, (1985), *Influence d'une alimentation "Dual" gazole et GPL sur les émissions de polluants et de particules d'un autobus*, 9 p.

[79] P. Van Donkelaar, (1989), Umweltverträglichkeit von Sumpf-und Verlustschmierung, Tribologie + Schmierungstechnik, **36,** 198-302.

[80] J.C. Wall and S.K. Hoekman, (1984), "Fuel composition effects on heavy-duty Diesel particulate emissions", *SAE Paper* No. 841364, 42 p.

[81] J.C. Wall et al., (1987), "Fuel sulfur reduction for control of Diesel particulate emissions", *SAE Paper* No. 872139, 20 p.

[82] P.T. Williams et al., (1989), "The influence of PAH contamination of lubricating oil on Diesel particulate emissions", *SAE Paper* No. 890825, 9 p.

[83] D.J. Williams et al., (1989), "Particulate emissions from 'in-use' motor vehicles, 1 Spark ignition vehicles", *Atmosph. Environm.*, **23,** 2639-2645.

[84] D.J. Williams et al., (1989), "Particulate emissions from 'in-use' motor vehicles, 2 Diesel vehicles", *Atmosph. Environm.*, **23,** 2647-2661.

[85] R.L. Williams et al., (1990), "Formaldehyde, methanol and hydrocarbon emissions from methanol fueled cars", *J. Air Waste Managem. Assoc.*, **40,** 747-756.

[86] W.M. Studzinski et al., (1992), "Paraffinic versus olefinic refinery streams, an engine exhaust emission investigation", *SAE Paper* No. 922377, 21 p.

[87] N-H. Huynh et al., (1992), "The impact of gasoline formulation on engine performance and exhaust emissions", *SAE Paper* No. 920297 (SP.910), 83-97.

[88] R.A. Gorge et al., (1991), "Toxic air pollutant vehicle exhaust emissions with reformulated gasolines", *SAE Paper* No. 912324, 28 p.

[89] J.D. Benson et al., (1991), "Effects of gasoline sulfur level on mass exhaust emissions, auto/oil air quality improvement research program", *SAE Paper* No. 912323, 14 p.

[90] C.A. Jemma et al., (1992), "Speciation of hydrocarbon emissions from European vehicles", *SAE Paper* No. 922376, 15 p.

[91] N. Miyamoto et al., (1992), "Description of Diesel emissions by individual fuel properties", *SAE Paper* No. 922221, 8 p.

[92] W.C. Betts et al., (1992), "The influence of Diesel fuel properties on particulate emissions in European cars", *SAE Paper* No. 922190, 12 p.

[93] Y. Asaumi et al., (1992), "Effects of fuel properties on Diesel engine exhaust emission characteristics", *SAE Paper* No. 922214, 8 p.

[94] B. Martin and P.H. Bigeard, (1992), "Hydrotreatment of Diesel fuels, its impact on light-duty Diesel engine pollutants", *SAE Paper* No. 922268, 15 p.

[95] C.I. McCarthy et al., (1992), "Diesel fuel property effects in exhaust emissions from a heavy-duty Diesel engine that meets 1994 emission requirements", *SAE Paper* No. 922267, 23 p.

[96] C. Bertoli et al., (1992), "Initial results on the impact of automotive Diesel oil in unregulated emissions of DI light Diesel engine", *SAE Paper* No. 922189, 9 p.

[97] L.C. van Beckhoven, (1991), "Effects of fuel properties on Diesel engine emissions, A review of information available to the EEC/NVEG Group", *SAE Paper* No. 910608 (P.240), 237-249.

[98] F.M. Salih and G.E. Andrews, (1992), "The influence of gasoline/ethanol blends on emissions and fuel economy", *SAE Paper* No. 922378, 15 p.

[99] H. Nishide et al., (1992), "Performance and exhaust emissions of Nissan FFVNX coupé", *SAE Paper* No. 920299, 117-122.

[100] K. Hamai et al., (1992), "Effects of clean fuels (reformulated gasolines, M85, and CNG) on automotive emissions", *SAE Paper* No. 922380, 14 p.

[101] K.S. Varde et al., (1992), "Emissions and their control in natural gas fueled engines", *SAE Paper* No. 922250, 63-76.

# Post-combustion treatments 12

## 12.1 Introduction

Due to the promulgation of increasingly stringent statutory regulations, anti-pollution measures designed to reduce emissions from within an engine (Chapter 10) are no longer sufficient to meet the latest standards (Chapter 6).

Exhaust treatments at the engine exit were first applied to spark ignition engines. The regulations at the time were primarily concerned with carbon monoxide and unburnt hydrocarbons, which demanded a "simple" oxidizer. The initial limits raised no problems for diesel engines, which easily met this type of requirement.

The imposition of increasingly strict limits on $NO_x$ has led to the design and development of three-way catalysts for gasoline-powered vehicles to simultaneously oxidize the oxidizable pollutants and reduce the nitrogen oxides. The imposition of limits on particulate emissions, which are generated chiefly by diesel engines, has also given rise to the development of particulate filters.

The goal of aftertreatment technologies is to adjust the chemicals in the exhaust system to a composition as close as possible to a mixture of water vapor and carbon dioxide, since this compound was considered to be a non-pollutant before the emergence of the "greenhouse effect".

This chapter deals with oxidation catalytic reactors and three-way catalytic reactors as they are applied to spark ignition engines. The oxidation catalysts installed on diesel engines are also examined along with the use of diesel particulate filters and the problems raised by the combustion of the soot trapped in these filters.

## 12.2 Physical conditions and exhaust gas composition before treatment

In a spark ignition engine, the exhaust gas temperature may vary between 300 and 400°C at idling and 900°C at full load. The gas streams flowing through the exhaust system fluctuate considerably in accordance with accelerations and decelerations and, for an average-sized engine, range between 10 and 150 $m^3/h$ according to the engine's speed and load. Depending on the fuel/air ratio on which the engine runs, the exhaust mixture contains some surplus oxygen (lean mixture) or a larger amount of carbon monoxide (rich mixture). This composition also fluctuates with engine operating conditions [297].

The exhaust gas of a spark ignition engine is therefore a relatively complex mixture that contains the following three categories of compounds.

(1) Oxidant chemical compounds

- oxygen: 0.2 to 2% by volume
- nitrogen oxides: NO (0.01 to 0.4%), $N_2O$ (<100 ppm)

(2) Reducing chemical compounds

- carbon monoxide: 0.1 to 6%
- hydrogen: 0.5 to 2%
- unburnt "hydrocarbons": 0.5 to 1%

This category includes actual hydrocarbons and their partial oxidation products (aldehydes, etc.).

(3) Other compounds

- nitrogen: 70 to 75%
- water vapor: 10 to 12%
- carbon dioxide: 10 to 13.5%
- sulfur dioxide: 15 to 60 ppm
- traces of other compounds, usually fuel additives and lubricants, which are liable to deactivate catalysts (lead, phosphorus, zinc)

As already pointed out in Chapter 10, the actual figures above differ significantly from the thermodynamically accessible values at equilibrium (Table 10.2). Consequently, the catalytic acceleration of the potential reactions between the components in the exhaust must be exploited to reduce pollutant concentrations substantially, tending towards the equilibrium compositions.

## 12.3 Catalytic mechanisms

### 12.3.1 CO oxidation mechanism

In the presence of excess oxygen in the exhaust gas, an oxidation catalyst helps to conduct the following overall reaction:

$$CO + 1/2\ O_2 \Rightarrow CO_2 \tag{12.1}$$

The oxidation of CO by oxygen is generally considered to take place in four basic steps:

$$CO_{gas} \Rightarrow CO_{ads} \tag{12.2}$$

$$O_{2,gas} \Rightarrow 2O_{ads} \tag{12.3}$$

$$O_{ads} + CO_{ads} \Rightarrow CO_{2,gas} \tag{12.4}$$

$$O_{ads} + CO_{gas} \Rightarrow CO_{2,gas} \tag{12.5}$$

Reactions (12.4) and (12.5) lead to the formation of $CO_2$. In a rich mixture, however, the high adsorption of CO (highly polar) on noble catalysts [49] would hinder its oxidation by oxygen. A sufficient temperature must be reached (between 100 and 200°C) for the initiation of CO desorption in order to release catalyst sites accessible to oxygen. The oxygen dissociates, reaction (12.3), and the reaction of type (12.4) begins. This reaction releases new sites and the catalytic oxidation of CO is suddenly triggered [297].

On precious metals (Pt and Pd), the CO oxidation rate in steady-state conditions peaks at around 500 K. Consideration of all the reagents present leads to a rate equation of the following form:

$$V_{CO} = \frac{k_1 P_{CO} P_{O_2}}{(1 + k_2 P_{CO} + k_3 P_{HC})^2 \, (1 + k_4 P_{NO}^n)} \tag{12.6}$$

This reveals a first-order kinetics with respect to oxygen and an inhibiting effect of NO. By contrast, $CO_2$ and $H_2O$ exert no influence at all. On rhodium, above 280°C, chemisorbed oxygen tends to inhibit the oxidation of CO to $CO_2$ [369].

### 12.3.2 Hydrocarbon oxidation mechanism

In the presence of surplus oxygen and an oxidation catalyst the following overall reaction is carried out:

$$CxHy + \left(x + \frac{y}{4}\right) O_2 \Rightarrow xCO_2 + \frac{y}{2} H_2O \tag{12.7}$$

The oxidation of hydrocarbons can be described by an expression similar to the one concerning CO. NO and CO tend to exert an inhibiting effect in these reactions [297].

### 12.3.3 Nitrogen oxide reduction mechanism

Except at very high temperatures, the NO molecule is thermodynamically unstable. It is therefore theoretically subject to decomposition into nitrogen and molecular oxygen according to the reaction:

$$NO \Rightarrow \frac{1}{2} N_2 + \frac{1}{2} O_2 \tag{12.8}$$

This exothermic reaction is nevertheless very difficult to carry out, both thermally and in the presence of a catalyst. An effective catalyst capable of reducing NO in the presence of oxygen (as in diesel exhausts) still remains to be discovered.

The problem with various catalyst (precious metals, oxides) is the partial dissociation of the adsorbed NO molecule and the dissociation products that remain strongly adsorbed on the surface of the catalysts. Desorption of the oxygen formed limits the advancement of the reaction. Elevated temperatures or the presence of chemical reducing agents are indispensable to restoration of catalyst activity [297].

These reducing agents can be the species that are present in the exhaust accompanying the NO: CO, $H_2$, and unburnt hydrocarbons. In particular, the hydrogen present may result from the steam reforming of CO ('water shift' reaction) catalysed for example by NiO or $CeO_2$ [52]:

$$CO + H_2O \Rightarrow CO_2 + H_2 \tag{12.9}$$

The reactions leading to the destruction of NO are accordingly:

$$NO + CO \Rightarrow 1/2\ N_2 + CO_2 \tag{12.10}$$

$$NO + H_2 \Rightarrow 1/2\ N_2 + H_2O \tag{12.11}$$

$$NO + (HC) \Rightarrow 1/2\ N_2 + H_2O + CO_2 \tag{12.12}$$

$$2NO + 5CO + 3H_2O \Rightarrow 2NH_3 + 5CO_2 \tag{12.13}$$

$$2NO + CO \Rightarrow N_2O + CO_2 \tag{12.14}$$

$$2NO + 5H_2 \Rightarrow 2NH_3 + 2H_2O \tag{12.15}$$

$$2NO + H_2 \Rightarrow N_2O + H_2O \tag{12.16}$$

For the oxidation of the chemical reducing agents CO, HC, and $H_2$, competition occurs between the oxygen produced by the dissociation of NO and the molecular oxygen present in the exhaust gas. If the partial pressure of the molecular oxygen substantially exceeds the partial pressure of the NO that is present, the rate of elimination of this NO drops considerably (Fig. 12.1). This is why, with the catalysts

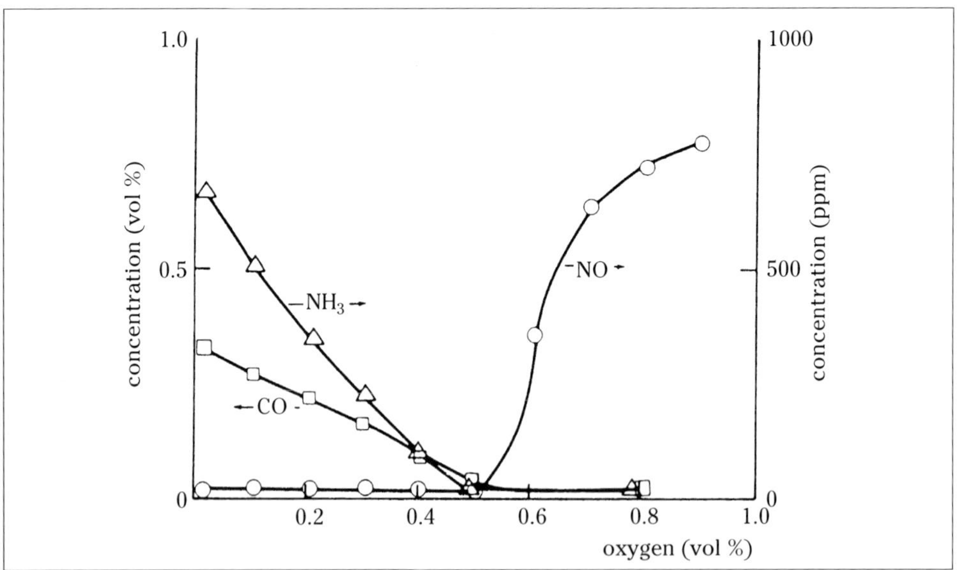


mixture 0.1% NO + 1% CO + 0.3% $H_2$ + 10% $CO_2$ + 0 to 1% $O_2$,
catalyst 0.1% Rh on alumina pellets, 427°C, VHSV = 38,000 $h^{-1}$

**Fig 12.1** Effect of $O_2$ content of gases treated on the conversion rate of CO and NO and on the formation of $NH_3$,

available today, it is impossible to remove all of the NO from the exhaust gases of engines fed with excess air (lean-burn spark ignition engines and diesel engines). This is because the air/fuel ratio reached on a diesel engine, even at full charge, always exceeds $\lambda=1.2$ [191].

On the contrary, in a rich mixture where the chemical reducing agents are present in substantial excess, atomic nitrogen resulting from the dissociation of NO can undergo a more thorough reduction. The main reaction involves the formation of ammonia in one of the following two ways:

$$NO + 5/2H_2 \Rightarrow NH_3 + H_2O \qquad (12.17)$$

$$2NO + 5CO + 3H_2O \Rightarrow 2NH_3 + 5CO_2 \qquad (12.18)$$

### 12.3.4 Dual catalysis

In the above case, where an excess of reducing agents persists with the undesirable formation of ammonia, it is necessary to provide two reactors in series. The first reduces the NO (with a variable production of $NH_3$). The mixture is then sent to a second oxidizer, which eliminates the CO and hydrocarbons by oxidation. To obtain these oxidizing conditions, it is essential to inject additional air between the two reactors (Fig. 12.2). This system is used on large marine spark-ignition engines [11].

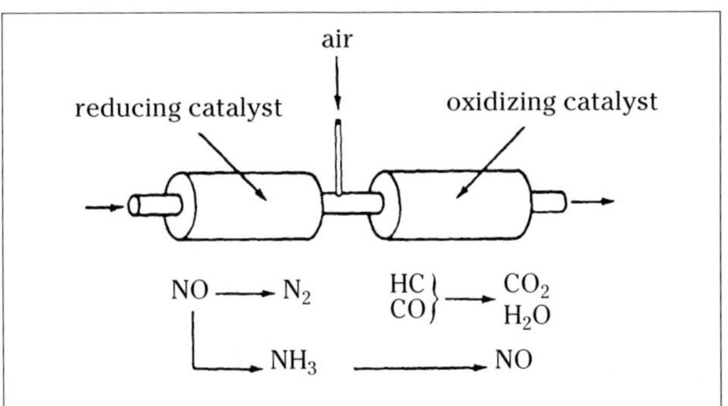


**Fig 12.2** Exhaust gas purification by dual catalysis [297]

This dual catalysis purification technique nevertheless presents drawbacks. To reduce the NO in the first stage, the engine run “rich”, which implies higher fuel consumption. Besides its desirable oxidation to molecular nitrogen by the reaction:

$$NH_3 + 3/4\ O_2 \Rightarrow 1/2\ N_2 + 3/2\ H_2O \qquad (12.19)$$

the ammonia formed in the first stage may undergo more intensive oxidation on the second catalyst, returning it to the initial state of NO:

$$NH_3 + 5/4\ O_2 \Rightarrow NO + 3/2\ H_2O \qquad (12.20)$$

The proportion of ammonia re-oxidized to NO depends on the type of catalyst, the temperature, and the oxygen partial pressure. In some conditions, the NO yield may be very high [297].

### 12.3.5 Three-way catalysis

Because of the drawbacks listed above, dual catalysis was discarded on small engines in favor of 'three-way' catalysis, which—as its name indicates—simultaneously eliminates the three regulated pollutants: CO, HC, and $NO_x$.

When the air/fuel mixture fed to the engine is strictly maintained at stoichiometry, there is no competition between NO and $O_2$ for the oxidation of carbon monoxide, hydrogen, and unburnt hydrocarbons. This is because no relative excess of one or the other of these two categories of compounds exists. A suitable catalyst, called a three-way catalyst, then allows virtually the total elimination of all three pollutants.

If the mixture is not perfectly stoichiometric at the engine intake, the effectiveness of the catalyst decreases (Fig. 12.3):

- for lean mixtures (excess air), the NO elimination efficiency decreases
- in the case of enrichment (excess fuel), the efficiency of oxidation of CO and HC decreases

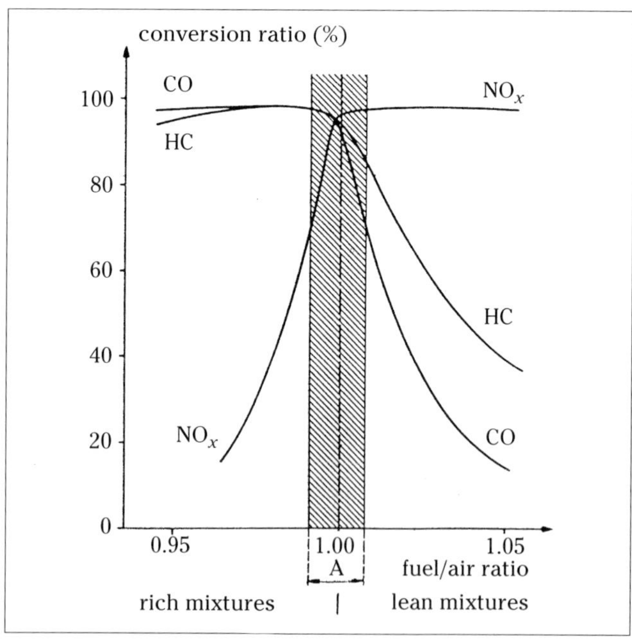


A: setting window

**Fig 12.3** Pollutant conversion rates as a function of variations in fuel/air ratio about stoichiometry [297]

In a rich mixture, once all the available oxygen and NO have been consumed, CO and hydrocarbons can still be eliminated by steam reforming with the water vapor present:

$$CO + H_2O \Rightarrow H_2 + CO_2 \quad (12.21)$$

$$(HC) + H_2O \Rightarrow CO + CO_2 + H_2 \quad (12.22)$$

The narrowness of the "window" (Fig. 12.3) in which the three-way catalyst operates ideally demands permanent regulation and monitoring of the fuel/air ratio of a conventional carburetor. The response time of the closed-loop ratio-regulation system to accelerations and decelerations causes oscillations about the fuel/air ratio of 1, the set-point value. The pulsation frequency varies between 0.5 and 5 Hz about the set-point [90], with an amplitude such that the fuel/air ratio is maintained between 0.93 and 1.07 ($r = 1 \pm 0.07$).

An increase in the pulsation amplitude results in a drop in the maximum efficiency corresponding to the intersection of the curves for NO and for CO and HC (Fig. 12.3). The stoichiometry of the carburetted mixture is monitored permanently in a closed loop by means of an oxygen sensor, which is called the '$\lambda$ sensor' (described in Chapter 7). This sensor is combined with a fuel injection system because carburetors, despite attempts to design complex and fragile ones with a feedback loops [322], have proven to be incapable of guaranteeing, at a competitive price, sufficient reliability in the dosage of the carburetted mixture [299][1]. The signal generated in the oxygen sensor by deviations from stoichiometry controls the dosage of the air/fuel mixture and returns it to the stoichiometric value.

Three-way oxidation converters may cause consumption increases of a few per cent, especially at low speed, due to richer settings than those used on European vehicles not equipped with anti-pollution devices. However, oxidizing catalyst converters, which operate with leaner mixtures, have no effect on consumption [299].

In the absence of a $\lambda$ oxygen sensor, three-way systems have been proposed with delayed and progressive additional air injection [293]. In the first zone of the catalyst bed, the NO is reduced by the reducing species. After the injection of air into a second zone, where the oxygen content is stoichiometric, unburnt HC as well as any ammonia that has formed are oxidized. A third zone containing excess oxygen completes the combustion of unburnt HC. However, the practical installation of air inlet tubes in the monolith raises technical problems whose solutions have not yet been demonstrated by endurance trials. The generalization of oxygen sensors has squelched the interest shown in this type of technique.

Certain additives incorporated with the catalysts help to improve performance in pulsed conditions. By oxidizing rapidly and reversibly, these elements can serve as redox buffers. The surplus oxygen oxidizes these elements to a higher valency and they can then oxidize the unburnt HC in periods of reducing operation.

1. The carburettor solution may still be valid with open-loop' regulation (without $\lambda$ sensor), lowering the efficiency of the elimination of CO and NO, if permitted by regulation limits [298].

## 12.4 Thermal reactors

Carbon monoxide and unburnt hydrocarbons formed in the combustion chamber already undergo partial oxidation during the expansion and exhaust strokes (Section 10.4.3.6). An attempt was therefore made to prolong this oxidation effect of the reducing pollutants by adding a thermal reactor at the exhaust, which consisted of a larger exhaust manifold that was attached directly to the cylinder head [143]. This reactor ensures rapid mixing of hot exhaust gases with injected secondary air (when running on a rich mixture). It improves the uniformity of the mixture in terms of temperature and composition, and increases its hot residence-time for further oxidation of the CO and HC leaving the combustion chamber.

The minimum temperature required to oxidize HC and CO (600°C and 700°C respectively) is much higher than the level required for catalytic conversion. Since this temperature level is not reached in all engine running conditions, the thermal reactor must be designed so as to minimize the heat losses and increase the residence time. It must also exhibit low thermal inertia to benefit from rapid warmup after starting. To do this, a concentric assembly containing a liner of fine refractory steel plate inside a thermally-insulated cast iron cylinder is used to thermally insulate the gases downstream of the exhaust valves (Fig. 12.4).

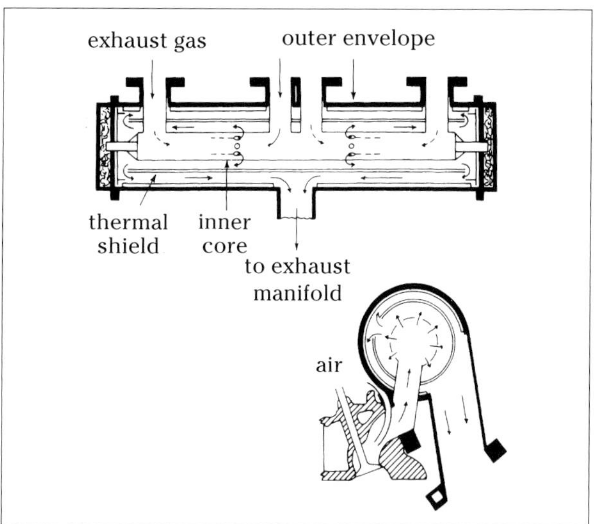


**Fig 12.4** Thermal reactor for oxidation of CO and HC [306]

The effectiveness of the reactor depends on the temperature reached, its capacity, and the oxygen availability of the reaction mixture. The operating temperature depends on the inlet temperature, the heat losses, and the amount of fuel (HC, CO, and $H_2$) to be burned in the reactor. This factor is very important. The combustion of 1% of residual CO causes a temperature rise of about 80°C. This is why the reactor is much more effective on engines running on rich mixtures with additional air injection than on lean mixtures, where the excess air merely ensures complete combustion. In a lean mixture, the core of the reactor is at a temperature about 100°C lower than the temperature found in a rich mixture, making it difficult to oxidize the CO and HC.

With rich mixtures, the mixing of exhaust gases with secondary air is a determining factor. Baffles must be installed in the reactor to break the segregation between the exhaust and the additional air, due to the fact that the air intake is interrupted by the passage of gas on the opening of a valve. Maximum efficiency is achieved with 10 to 20% excess air. Total combustion is never obtained, due to the imperfection of the mixture and to its insufficient residence time.

### 12.4.1 Additional air input devices

A simple system employs an air pump driven by the engine. This is generally a self-lubricated carbon vane pump mounted on an eccentric rotor [177 and 347] and incorporated into a ManAirOx (Manifold Air Oxidation) unit [306] (Fig. 12.5). The compressed air is conveyed to the exhaust valves by metal ducts. This air intake must be interrupted during decelerations, which temporarily create mixtures that are too rich to burn in the cylinder and are therefore liable to explode in the exhaust

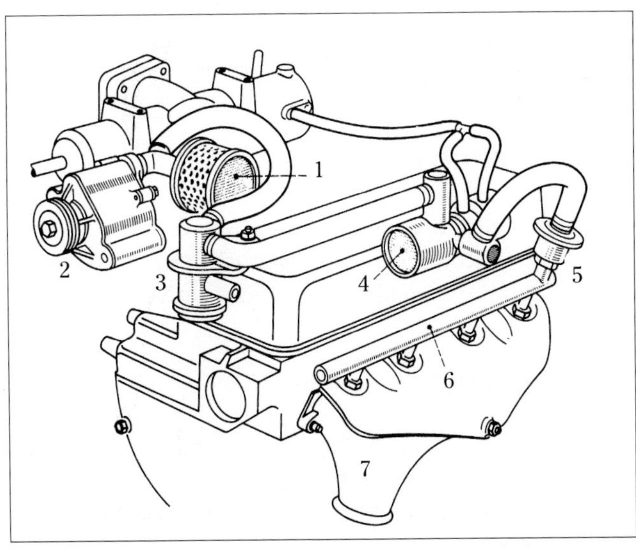


| | | | |
|---|---|---|---|
| 1 | air filter | 5 | check valve |
| 2 | air pump | 6 | distribution bar |
| 3 | discharge valve | 7 | exhaust manifold |
| 4 | bypass valve | | |

**Fig 12.5** Exhaust air injection system

when mixed with the additional air. A diversion valve, which is controlled by the negative pressure at the inlet created by the closure of the throttle during deceleration, sends the additional air to the exterior [177]. The pump itself is protected from exhaust backfire by a check valve.

On some vehicle models, air injection at the exhaust is achieved without an air pump using intake valves (pulsair) that open under the effect of the pressure pulses in the exhaust circuit. Thanks to these very low inertia valves, the pressure oscillations about atmospheric pressure serve to allow the external air to enter the exhaust manifold during negative pressure periods [94]. The effectiveness of this system, which is less expensive than the air pump, is limited at high engine loads [306]. This is because it delivers 60% of the engine air flow while idling, but only 10% while accelerating at high speed [94].

The major drawback of the thermal reactor when applied to rich mixtures stems from the increase in the fuel/air ratio that results in sometimes prohibitive increases in fuel consumption (from 15 to 25%). With a lean mixture, the lower temperatures reached tend to decrease its effectiveness. The ignition delay sometimes applied to raise the exhaust temperature is detrimental to engine performance. The difficulties inherent in thermal reactors (complexity, inadequate efficiency, higher consumption due to operation with a rich mixture, no action on $NO_x$) have led to their complete abandonment in favor of catalytic systems, since their only specific advantage, the ability to accommodate leaded fuels, is disappearing with the widespread use of unleaded fuels.

## 12.5 Catalyst structure

In comparison with conventional catalysts used in the chemical and petrochemical industries, automotive post-combustion catalysts are distinguished by their supports (matrix) and the composition of the active phase (catalyst).

### 12.5.1 Catalyst supports

Since catalytic activity is essentially exerted by the surface atoms, to derive maximum benefit from the activity of the catalysts, which should be used in the smallest possible quantities (especially for precious metals), they must be dispersed on supports. By minimizing contact between catalyst particles these supports prevent sintering, which causes a loss of activity. They also provide the requisite geometric and mechanical qualities for automotive use.

The support must allow the passage of the exhaust gases without causing any prohibitive increase in the back-pressure at the exhaust, which would be detrimental to engine performance. It must also offer a satisfactorily developed surface with

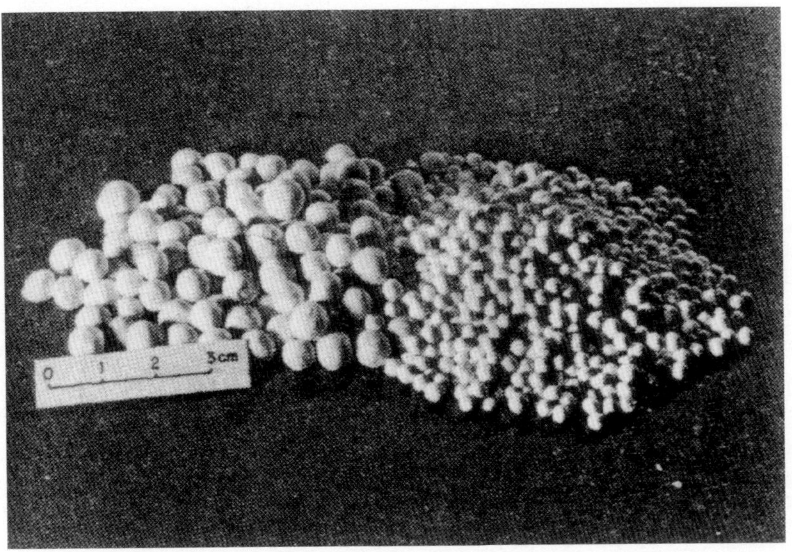


***a***: bowl-granulated alumina pellets

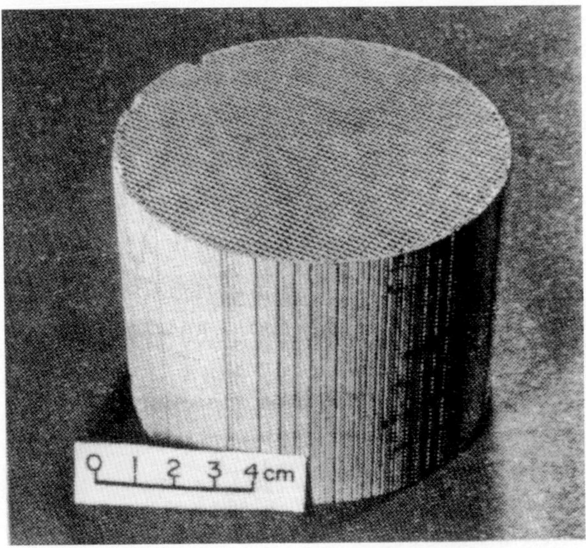


***b***: monolith support

**Fig 12.6** Catalyst supports. *IFP Photos*

pore characteristics that ensure proper dispersion[2] of the active phase, as well as sufficiently rapid mass transfer. An optimal pore distribution is a bimodal distribution of the pores that allows both proper diffusion of the gaseous reagents and adequate dispersion of the catalytic species (macroporous fraction with average diameter 1 to 2 μm and microporous fraction around 20 nm) [228].

The mechanical properties required are resistance to crushing and attrition (wear by friction) for bead catalysts. The support must also withstand the thermal shocks caused by sudden changes in engine operations. A low heat capacity also helps to respond rapidly to catalyst light-off during starting.

Catalysts used on automotive vehicles have particulate supports (pellets or extrudates) or are of the "monolith" type (Fig. 12.6). Since the catalytic reactions depend on the partial pressures of the reactants, the reaction rates decrease as the pollutants are depleted. Despite a high rate at the start, a sufficient length of reactor is necessary to obtain an overall conversion ratio of more than 90%. This is because, as opposed to a chemical reactor, it is not possible here to recycle the fractions that have not reacted.

### 12.5.2 Particulate supports

Particles of porous ceramic are made in the form of buttons, cylindrical extrudates, or pellets less than 5 mm in diameter. The usual form consists of small alumina pellets with a large surface area formed from the $\gamma$ transition phase, which can be doped by certain elements (BaO, $La_2O_3$, etc.) to improve its mechanical properties or its thermal stability. The beads, obtained by bowl granulation or oil drop coagulation, display the following properties [3]:

- mean diameter — 2.3 to 3.1 mm
- bulk density — 0.45 to 0.70 $g/cm^3$
- specific surface area (BET) — 80 to 150 $m^2/g$
- pore volume — 0.6 to 1.2 $cm^3/g$

Advances related to these supports concern the reduction of their density, the increase of their pore volume and their specific surface area, and a slight decrease in their grain size distribution [297]. Their high temperature stability has also been enhanced by various additives.

### 12.5.3 Monolith supports

These are one-piece supports made of ceramic or metal.

2. Fraction of the mass of active species accessible to the gas phase.

#### 12.5.3.1 Ceramic monoliths

In spite of tests on other materials (alumina, zirconia, mullite, aluminum titanate, silicon carbide) [146], the ceramic used is nearly always cordierite [158], $2MgO \cdot 2Al_2O_3 \cdot 5SiO_2$.

It consists of a phase of the triple magnesia/silica/alumina system mixed with traces of spinel and alumina [158]. These materials are cheap and readily available. The catalyst is fabricated from a mixture of clay (e.g. kaolinite), talc, silica, and alumina. The component materials are reduced to a powder (grain size $<50$ μm in diameter) and then incorporated with a bonding agent (e.g. methylcellulose or carboxy methylcellulose), a lubricant (e.g. ethylene glycol) that facilitates shaping before firing, and fluxing agents (alkaline and alkaline earth hydroxides) to favor sintering. The mass thus prepared is extruded into its final shape. Pre-sintering eliminates the volatile compounds such as the bonding agents and lubricants. The subsequent firing cycle at high temperature (between 800 and 1300 to 1450°C) produces a porous material capable of holding the catalyst mixture, but possessing a BET surface area that is too small to ensure its satisfactory dispersion. This ceramic offers the advantage of having a very low thermal expansion coefficient, which confers excellent thermal shock resistance. Its melting point of about 1450°C enables it to preserve sufficient elasticity up to around 1300°C to resist permanent deformation [110] in normal engine running conditions, although local melting may occur as a result of carburation or ignition incidents.

Another ceramic, a mixture of mullite, $\beta$-$Al_2O_3$, and aluminum titanate has a softening point 200°C higher than that of cordierite [198], where it decomposes into rutile and $\alpha$-$Al_2O_3$. Its higher density and specific heat may be a drawback to warming up when starting, and are not offset by its greater resistance to high-temperature excursions. This ceramic is virtually unused today.

The monoliths used are cylinders with circular, oval, or "racetrack" cross-sections. They contain several small parallel triangular- or square-section channels in a honeycomb arrangement. The "racetrack" shape is most widely used, with a cross-section of about 120 cm$^2$ (170×80 mm) for engines around 100 kW. For larger engines (3 and 3.5 liter cylinder displacement), two identical monoliths are placed in parallel [377]. The volume used varies between 0.02 and 0.03 dm$^3$ per kW of engine output. The diameter of the support is the most important factor in reducing the pressure drop at a given volume of catalytic converter (influences by a magnitude of about 4), in comparison with the length and number of channels per cm$^2$ [60].

The section formed from two combined triangles is used in a number of models [2] to match the shape of the transmission tunnel, while offering the largest possible passage cross-section [394]. If need be, two monoliths are placed in series in the envelope, separated by a spacer ring of aluminum titanate [149].

Advances in support fabrication have succeeded in reducing their pressure drops and increasing their mechanical strength [59]. A reduction of the intrinsic porosity of the material is favorable to its mechanical behavior [106]. Decreasing the wall thicknesses (down to 0.10 mm) tends to improve both the pressure drop and the speed of warmup by reducing the heat capacity of the support [390 and 391]. Cordierite supports also display better high-temperature behavior than certain metallic structures which undergo irreversible deformation above 1200°C [109].

The main characteristics of ceramic monoliths are listed below [109 and 297]:

| | |
|---|---|
| • number of cells per $cm^2$ | 46 or 62 |
| • wall thickness (mm) | 0.10, 0.15 or 0.30 |
| • porosity (%) | about 30 |
| • geometric surface area ($m^2$/liter) | 2.19 or 2.79 |
| • material density (g/$cm^3$) | 1.68 |
| • bulk density (g/$cm^3$) | 0.58 or 0.41 |
| • mass specific heat Cp (cal/g°C) | 0.20 |
| • volume specific heat (cal/$cm^3$°C) | 0.086 |
| • radial thermal conductivity (cal/cm · s°C) | 0.005 |
| • thermal expansion coefficient ($10^{-6}$/°C) | 0.7 |
| • maximum service temperature | about 1100°C |
| • size of macropores | 7000 to 10,000 Å |
| • size of micropores | 70 to 90 Å |
| • BET surface area ($m^2$/g) | $<1$ |

#### 12.5.3.2 Metallic monoliths

Following a number of unsuccessful attempts to make monoliths of monel alloy [258], metal monoliths are now fabricated from very thin (40 to 50 μm thick) stainless steel sheets (containing chromium and aluminum). This steel grade, with a ferritic structure [291] displays excellent resistance to corrosion by hot exhaust gases up to 1100°C [73]. Due to the aluminum content of at least 4%, the sheets are coated with a protective layer of alumina by oxidation at high temperature. The additional 0.2 to 0.3% zirconium also increases the resistance to oxidation at high temperature, and prevents grain enlargement [40]. The addition of calcium also enhances the adhesion of the oxide coat. A relatively high yttrium content (≈0.3%), (Fecralloy type) improves the durability of the material in contact with hot exhaust gases. Because of the cost of yttrium, this value is often limited to 0.05%, and is replaced by 0.02% by Mischmetall, a blend of cerium-rich rare earths that also prevents grain enlargement [40]. After annealing around 1200°C, the sheets are corrugated on a special rolling mill to yield a sinusoidal or trapezoidal structure. They are assembled by electron beam welding or more often by brazing [268] under vacuum at about 1200°C directly on the outer envelope, thus avoiding the installation of a pad to absorb expansion (Section 12.7 below) [258]. To avoid deformation over time due to thermal cycles, brazing is usually recommended [342]. A brazed assembly can be placed directly at the exit of the exhaust manifold, which is excellent for reducing light-off time (Section 12.9 below) [342]. At equivalent outer cross-sections, the opening offered to the gases is larger (after applying the catalyst wash-coat, this ranges from 57% for ceramic to 72% for metal) [257], which reduces the pressure drops at the exhaust [127] and makes it possible, for example, to gain 4 kW on a 160 kW engine [285]. The sheets are wound in the form of a spiral or S-shape, the latter displaying better mechanical endurance [285]. The use of split sheets (500,000 slits in a 2-liter matrix), by increasing turbulence, helps to increase the effectiveness of contact between the gas to be treated and the catalyst, thus reducing the volume and weight of the catalytic converter. This technique is unfeasible with the ceramic formed by extrusion [259 and 260].

The average characteristics of the metallic material are listed below [40, 109, 268, and 297]:

| | |
|---|---|
| • composition | 15 to 20% Cr, 4 to 5% Al, 0 to 2% Si, 0.1 to 0.3% Y, Fe q.s.p. 100% |
| • number of cells per $cm^2$ | 62 or 93 |
| • wall thickness (mm) | 0.05 |
| • geometric surface area ($m^2$/liter) | 3.2 |
| • material density (g/$cm^3$) | 7.2 |
| • bulk density (g/$cm^3$) | 1.25 |
| • mass specific heat Cp (cal/g°C) | 0.11 |
| • volume specific heat (cal/$cm^3$°C) | 0.05 to 0.08 |
| • radial thermal conductivity (cal/cm · s°C) | 0.03 |
| • thermal expansion coefficient ($10^{-6}$/°C) | 12 |
| • maximum service temperature | about 1100°C |

These supports are more expensive but have greater mechanical strength than ceramic monoliths. They allow greater flexibility in the choice and density of the channels [226]. In addition to the advantage of a smaller volume (by about 55%), which they offer over conventional ceramics (25% in comparison with the new ceramics) [268], they offer a reduction in pressure drop at the exhaust [357] of about 15 to 20% after deposition of the wash-coat [258]. Their better thermal conductivity reduces the risks of local overheating that is liable to cause melting, and their lower heat capacity reduces their light-off time in starting, the primary reason for their development. Their elevated temperature behavior appears to be inferior to that of cordierite [109, 112], and the risks of detachment of the wash-coat are estimated to be greater despite tests that tend to discount this risk [127]. A well, there are risks of oxidation and corrosion at high temperature, especially after contact with the halogenated acids that convey the precious metals at the time of impregnation [40].

These sheets, like the ceramics, are coated with a layer of $\gamma$ alumina before impregnation with precious metals [291]. The choice of refractory steels containing some aluminum allows the formation of a very adhesive alumina-rich oxide film on the surface, which favors the adhesion of the wash-coat [258]. Y and Ce type additives also enhance the epitaxic growth of crystals (whiskers), which serve as anchoring points [234 and 342].

Another technique is to wind flat sheets coated with the wash-coat and impregnated with the precious metals, which are thus distributed more uniformly. Corrugated and flat sheets are alternately wound to form a honeycomb structure. Since brazing and welding are impractical in these circumstances, the structure is assembled by pins or rivets, which are then welded to the outer envelope [227]. Brazing and the insertion of intermediate flat sheets can be avoided by stacking plates with dual perpendicular corrugations, arranged in opposing corrugations [358].

### 12.5.4 Active species

Despite several attempts to develop cheaper catalysts based on oxides of more commonly-used metals, only catalysts based on precious metals are used industrially today, because no other compound is appropriate for reliable three-way catalysis.

Compared with metallic oxides, precious metals have high intrinsic activity, display activity at relatively low temperatures, and preserve this activity at higher temperatures by resisting the sintering that tends to reduce their specific surface area. They also display better resistance to poisoning by the ever-present sulfur in the fuels.

Metallic oxides that have demonstrated the best activity in the laboratory belong to the group of transition metals. They include $Co_3O_4$, CuO, $Cr_2O_3$, ZnO, and $MnO_2$, which are used alone or combined with other oxides. Their minimum light-off temperatures are all about 100°C higher than those of corresponding precious metals. Their lower specific activity also means the use of quantities of active species that are two or three times larger for the same conversion rates. However, the prohibitive obstacle to the use of metallic oxides derives from their lack of stability at high temperature and their high sensitivity to sulfur. Advances achieved in this area by the use of more stable mixed oxides of the perovskite type are still inadequate for practical applications [297]. Attempts to replace platinum and rhodium by palladium and tungsten, or rhodium by a $Pt/MoO_3$ combination, in order to reduce the precious metal contents, have not yet succeeded [80].

Oxidation catalysts contain, as active elements, platinum and palladium, either alone or in combination. To oxidize CO, olefins or methane, the initial activity of palladium is higher than that of platinum. This activity is practically identical for oxidizing aromatics and platinum is better for oxidizing paraffins [143]. Since the catalytic reaction always begins with an adsorption stage, which demands prior dehydrogenation for saturated hydrocarbons, catalysts that are well known for the dehydrogenating activity, such as platinum, prove to be the most effective. Between 600 and 900°C, platinum undergoes rapid sintering in an oxidizing medium, but slower sintering in a reducing medium [340]. By contrast, palladium resists sintering better in an oxidizing medium and, combined with a suitable wash-coat, displays equivalent performance to the platinum/rhodium pair in terms of duration [338]. However, in the presence of poisons like lead and phosphorus, which irreversibly block the active sites of the catalyst, platinum is deactivated much more slowly than palladium [246, 338, and 340]. Palladium also has a lower conversion rate for $NO_x$ and CO on the rich side of stoichiometry [338]. The role of platinum in bimetallic catalysts is essentially to reduce activity losses by poisoning. However, despite these shortcomings, attempts are being made to develop palladium/rhodium catalysts to replace the platinum/rhodium combination with virtually identical performance and the benefits of lower cost of palladium [340].

In three-way catalysts, it is necessary to add rhodium to the platinum/palladium pair, which is normally sufficient for oxidation catalysts. This is because the activity of Pt and Pd is insufficient to reduce NO to $N_2$ due to the inhibiting action of CO on these catalysts. Rhodium has a greater storage capacity for oxygen and helps to widen the applicable fuel/air ratio window [262]. In addition, rhodium is immune to the inhibiting effect of CO and it also produces less $NH_3$ during excursions with 'rich' mixtures [49]. On the other hand, rhodium is sensitive to poisoning by lead and phosphorus. In an oxidizing medium, it is oxidized at high temperature to $Rh_2 0_3$, which may form solid solutions with the alumina of the support. This oxide can also deactivate the platinum crystallites by coating them [297].

Ruthenium appears to be the best catalyst for reducing NO to $N_2$ [146]. It is not used in practice because it presents the drawback of forming volatile oxides in an oxidizing medium [49], which have not yet been stabilized successfully in the form of mixed oxides with La, Ba, or Mg [323]

## 12.5.5 Catalyst additives

In addition to the alumina support and precious metals, automotive post-combustion catalysts may contain a wide variety of additives, such as Ni, Ce, La, Ba, Zr, Fe, and Si.

These elements play different roles:

- reinforcement of catalytic action
- stabilization of the support
- inhibition of the sintering of precious metals

Nickel in particular reinforces the activity of platinum and palladium for reducing NO [52]. It can also catalyse the water/shift reaction of CO in a reducing medium and also serve as a buffer to diminish the effect of fuel/air ratio fluctuations about stoichiometry, by oxidizing and by reducing. It is also proposed as a 'scavenger' (Section 12.11.3 below) to reduce $H_2S$ emissions, but it is little used in Europe due to its reputation as a harmful substance. Iron and cerium display similar behavior to nickel, with a lesser tendency to be deactivated by reaction with the alumina of the support [297]. Cerium oxide has several effects: it prevents sintering of the alumina of the wash-coat, it decreases the reactions between rhodium and alumina, and it catalyses the water/shift reaction, going easily from valency 4 to valency 3 [52]. Cerium oxide is nevertheless sensitive to sintering at temperatures lower than for alumina.

Lanthanum, added to palladium, helps to improve its performance in the reduction of NO in a reducing medium. It offers a higher conversion rate in the water/shift reaction and the steam reforming of hydrocarbons, and the hydrogen thus supplied can also reduce NO more easily [253].

Lanthanum, barium, zirconium, and silicon are primarily ionic stabilizers of the alumina phases. Silicon proves to be a better stabilizer against sintering of alumina and cerium oxide, while lanthanum prevents the enlargement of the platinum crystallites [124]. The prior incorporation of rhodium in a $ZrO_2$ support then installed in the $\gamma Al_2O_3$ matrix helps to prevent the diffusion of rhodium in the $\gamma Al_2O_3$. It thus increases the resistance of the catalyst to oxidation at high temperature, while preventing contact between the rhodium and the rare earth oxides present in the alumina, which would diminish the activity of the rhodium [369].

## 12.6 Preparation of supported catalysts

### 12.6.1 Application of the wash-coat

Since the developed surface of the supports, both ceramic and metallic, is much too small to guarantee proper dispersion of the precious metals ($\approx 0.2$ m$^2$/g) [228] it is necessary to apply a coating to the walls of the channels before impregnation. This coating is an alumina coat with a large surface area (100 to 200 m$^2$/g BET (Section 8.9.1)) that is evenly divided (wash-coat) and ranges from 20 to 50 $\mu$m in thickness, which increases the developed surface area of the support by a factor of about 100 [158]. This coat accounts for about 5 to 20% of the mass of the support. The property of adhesion of the wash-coat to the monolith channel walls is extremely important for the maintenance of catalyst effectiveness over time, due to the risks of cracking and detachment of the active layer, particularly if the thermal expansion coefficients of the support and the adhesion coat are very different [357]. A wash-coat formula with a low modulus of elasticity may be advantageous in this case to prevent the formation of microcracks [111].

The wash-coat is applied in three steps: the preparation of a liquid precursor for the coat, the immersion of the support in this preparation, followed by the drying and sintering of the combination on the monolith. The liquid precursors include solutions of aluminum hydrochloride, $Al_2(OH)_5Cl$, hydrosols of alumina or sometimes silica or zirconia, or aqueous suspensions of $\gamma$ alumina that are obtained by grinding alumina to a size close to that of the pores of the monolith (<5 μm) to facilitate adhesion. The adhesion of the suspensions is sometimes promoted by additives (sodium silicate, proteins, synthetic resins), added to the suspension or first deposited on the support before the application of the wash-coat. The addition to the suspension of aluminum nitrate, which decomposes when raised to about 500°C, improves the adhesion of the particles. In addition, small additions of $CeO_2$ (4.5% by weight of the wash-coat in the form of nitrate) [228] and of BaO (<1% by weight of the monolith) help to slow down the sintering of the alumina and to increase the dispersion of the precious metals. This technique thus helps to reduce the initial platinum contents by half [80] while maintaining overall high temperature stability [189]. According to Japanese authors, the effectiveness of cerium oxide as an oxygen storage buffer is improved if it is first deposited on the support in a layer separate from the wash-coat containing the catalyst at the rate of 20% by weight of the wash-coat [169]. A doubling of the specific quantity of wash-coat, despite the slight increase in the pressure drop, increases the conversion rate of CO and $NO_x$ and improves endurance behavior thanks to the additional $CeO_2$ that stores oxygen [108]. Some formulas thus incorporate up to 7% by weight of cerium and 7% by weight of lanthanum in the support [47].

The solutions generally demand several applications, whereas a single one suffices for suspensions and hydrosols. This deposition is carried out by dipping in the liquid precursor or by the injection of this suspension into the channels of the monolith. To clear the channels, the excess suspension is removed by blowing with compressed air or by using a centrifuge. The precursor is then dried at around 100 to 150°C with hot air blowing in the channels to prevent the migration of the wash-coat. With hydrosol precursors, the addition of hexamethylene tetramine helps to reduce the shrinking of the colloidal micelles on drying, which tends to decrease the BET surface area [357]. With thin-wall monoliths, whose water retention rate is insufficient for successful deposition of the same quantity of wash-coat by dipping, additional spraying of the suspension may be necessary after a first drying [166].

For metallic monoliths, the adhesion of the wash-coat is more delicate, because the metal surface is smoother. It is absolutely essential to eliminate any trace of grease and it is often advantageous to oxidize the metal surface.

### 12.6.2 Incorporation of catalysts

The content of active species (Pt, Pd, Rh) in automotive catalysts varies considerably. Catalysts deposited on pellets or extrudates may contain 0.07 to 0.22% by weight (10 to 30 $g/ft^3$) of platinum/palladium, with a Pt/Pd ratio ranging from 15/1 to 1/3 [201]. Suitable deposition techniques help to concentrate the active species on the surface of the pellets for maximum effectiveness.

After the application of the wash-coat, the monolith is impregnated by dipping or injection using a solution containing salts of precious metals (e.g. $H_2PtCl_6$, $PdCl_2$,

$Rh(NO_3)_3$, and $RhCl_3$ or acetone solutions containing $(n\text{-butyl}_4N)_2Rh_2(CO)_2Br_8$ or $H_2PtCl_6 \cdot 6H_2O$) [246]. During drying, to prevent the migration of the catalyst species to the ends of the channels (detrimental to the uniformity of distribution of the catalysts), it is often necessary to fix the active compounds before raising the temperature [357]. The acidity of the impregnation medium has a strong influence on the depth of penetration of the catalyst in the support [146]. This depth must remain small to guarantee good contact with the gaseous reactants, but nevertheless it must be sufficient to prevent entrainment by abrasion and contact with poisonous lead and phosphorus. The chloroplatinic acid would thus attack the alumina to form a compound, $PtCl_4$, that would remain on the surface. When the catalyst is first mounted on the vehicle, the precious metal chlorides are not always reduced and the initial activity is not optimal. The reduction of these salts by reducing agents in the exhaust causes the formation of chlorine, which is strongly adsorbed and decreases the initial CO conversion rate accordingly . Ceramic monoliths must be raised to 500 to 600°C to desorb this chlorine completely.

For platinum and palladium, prior reduction of the salts in the metallic state is achieved by passing a stream of $H_2/H_2O$ at 75°C through the channels. Another technique suggested is to pass through a stream of $H_2S$ to fix the precious metals on the surface in the form of a colloidal precipitate of sulfides, which are then thermally decomposed. This would help to prevent the enlargement of the precious metal crystallites [146]. Additives such as nickel are added in the form of nitrates in aqueous solution and this operation is followed by calcination [52] and reduction to the metal state.

Another technique is to deposit the wash-coat and the active species simultaneously, particularly if deposition is carried out from hydrosols mixed with the catalyst precursors. This technique could however present the drawback of yielding catalyst species that are partly covered by the wash-coat [357].

## 12.7 Installation of catalyst in the exhaust line

The support, impregnated with its catalyst, is incorporated in a metallic casing designed to keep it in place on the exhaust line and to prevent any damage. This casing, which is usually made of austenitic or ferritic nickel/chromium refractory stainless steel [175], is prepared from two stamped half-shells. It matches the shape of the corresponding support, with an inlet cone and an outlet cone, often with a 7 degree taper [285]. It replaces the muffler previously installed on the exhaust. The position of the catalytic muffler in the exhaust system represents a compromise. Catalyst light-off time, which must be as short as possible after a cold start, indicates that the muffler should be placed as near as possible to the engine while protection against the maximum permissible risk-free temperatures for the catalyst bed (800 to 900°C) [306] indicates a more remote location. Double-wall connecting tubes are sometimes used to accelerate this light-off [337]. The casing also has a double wall [337] with internal acoustic and thermal insulation. The thermal shield avoids an excessively high outside temperature caused by heat radiation at full load and improves catalyst light-off when the engine is started.

Metallic monoliths are directly brazed to the casing [258]. For ceramics, however, to keep the monolith in place, to prevent its damage by vibrations, and to preserve the tightness around the monolith by absorbing the differential expansions of the ceramic and the metal (which are more difficult to offset for the oval and 'racetrack' shapes than for the circular cross-section), a pad of soft material is inserted between the monolith and the casing (Fig. 12.7). This pad, which first consisted of a metal wire weave or knit, is now a heat-resistant cushion based on ceramic fibers of aluminum silicate bonded by an acrylonitrile bonding agent and containing 45 to 60% by weight of vermiculite particles (mica) [377]. This complex material has a high swelling coefficient and preserves its resiliency at high temperature [104]. It expands up to around 750°C and then shrinks [377]. The pad is reinforced on the edges by a fiberglass cord to prevent erosion by the gas stream [175]. In addition to its function of maintaining the monolith, the cushion guarantees the tightness around the ceramic and reinforces the thermal insulation of the support. To keep this cushion in place and to guarantee better rigidity, it may be necessary to provide the metal casing with ribs. If so, these should be oriented inward and should be as wide as possible [360].

Beaded catalysts are placed in the jacket between two perforated plates with the gases flowing down through the catalyst bed (Fig. 12.8).

The volume of beads is usually matched to the engine cylinder displacement.

For metallic monoliths, the casing is made of austenitic refractory steel that has an expansion coefficient higher than that of the ferritic monolith, which minimizes differences in expansion at high temperature between the inside and the outside of the muffler [257].

To obtain an optimal conversion ratio in the monolith and uniform aging of the catalyst system, it is essential to distribute the gas stream uniformly through the catalyst [377]. The 'racetrack' shape (advantageous for installation below the car body) with a single fluid inlet is unfavorable in this respect.

## 12.8 Catalyst poisoning

Catalysts tend to be deactivated by the action of the different elements present in the fuel (Pb, S, halogens) or the lubricant (P, Ca, Zn, B). The deactivation rate varies according to whether the poison acts by combination with the active phase of the catalyst or by mechanical action by blocking the pores of the catalyst and hindering the access of the gas to the active sites [297].

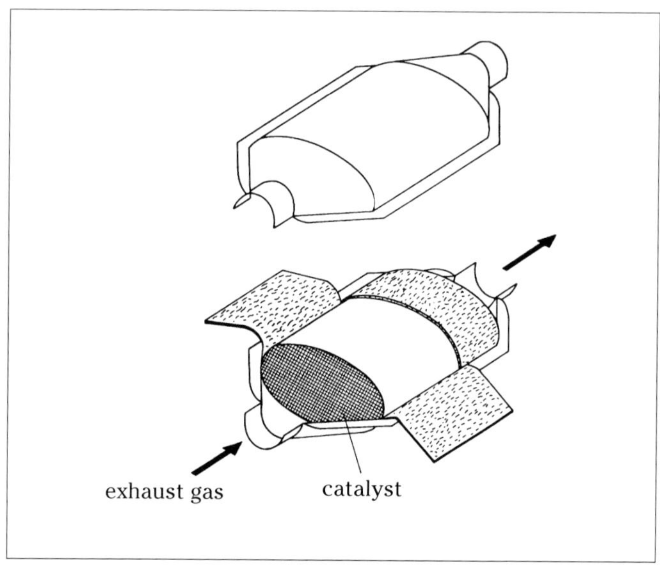


**Fig 12.7** Installation of the monolith in the casing [187]

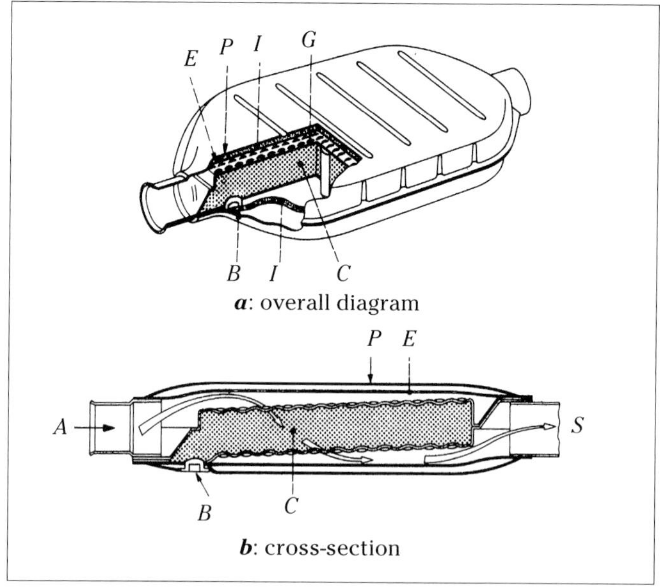


| | | | |
|---|---|---|---|
| *A* | gas inlet | *G* | metal grids |
| *B* | filling plug | *I* | insulation |
| *C* | catalyst | *P* | external protection |
| *E* | muffler casing | *S* | gas outlet |

**Fig 12.8** Catalytic muffler for beaded catalyst [297]

## 12.8.1 Lead poisoning

### 12.8.1.1 Lead compounds formed

Various lead compounds (oxides, halogenides, and sulfates) are responsible for lead poisoning. Lead-based anti-knock additives in fact contain halogenides (chlorides and bromides) enabling the lead to volatilize in the exhaust. After combustion of the gasoline, these compounds give rise to lead oxide (PbO) and to the acids HCl and HBr [295]. The combustion of the sulfur molecules of the fuel and of the phosphorus additives in the lubricant also generates $SO_2$ and phosphorus oxides. At the high temperatures of the combustion chamber, the possibilities of the species combining together are limited by the thermodynamics and the high-temperature stability of lead, lead oxide, and hydracids [294]. However, the cooling of the gas in the exhaust circuit tends to give rise to reactions such as:

$$PbO + 2HCl \Rightarrow PbCl_2 + H_2O \tag{12.23}$$

$$PbO + 2HBr \Rightarrow PbBr_2 + H_2O \tag{12.24}$$

The transfer of lead between the combustion chamber and the catalytic converter begins with PbO, which is initially in vapor form. These vapors condense rapidly and at around 850 to 900°C they generate fine particles that are entrained by the gas stream or deposited on the walls of the exhaust circuit [296]. The attack of these particles or deposits by HCl or HBr begins at about 700 to 750°C and the chlorides and bromides formed condense between 200 and 300°C (Fig. 12.9).

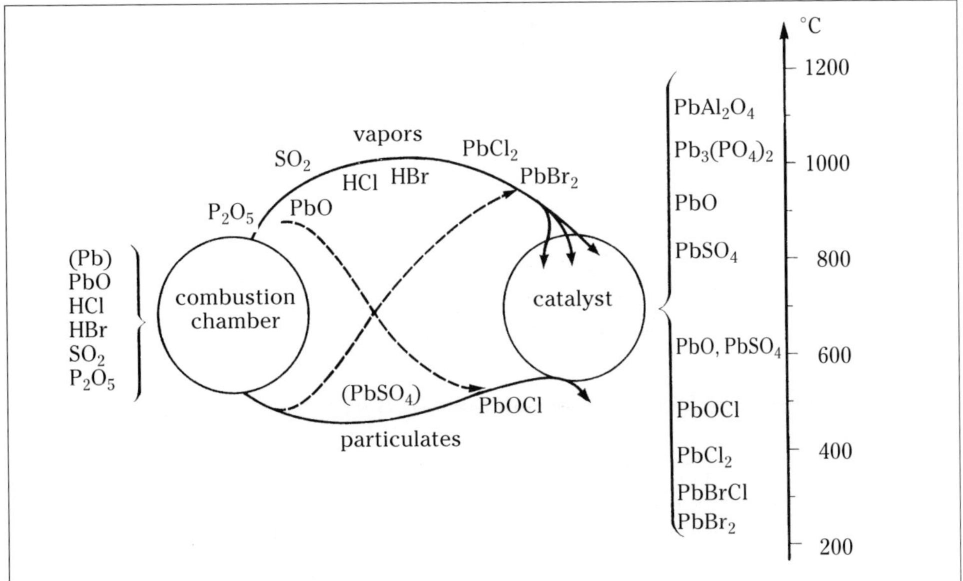


**Fig 12.9** Formation, transport and fixation of lead pollutants on automotive catalysts [296]

During the transfer, PbO in the particles or deposits can also react with the sulfur and phosphorus oxides. However, the formation of solid $PbSO_4$, which demands prior oxidation of $SO_2$ to $SO_3$ , remains very limited.

Depending on the temperature when it makes contact with the catalyst, lead is either in vapor form (PbO, $PbCl_2$, $PbBr_2$), or in the form of fine solid particles formed within the gas mass (PbO, $PbSO_4$, $Pb_3(PO_4)_2$), or even in the form of coarse particles detached from the walls of the exhaust manifolds.

The vapors penetrate deeply into the pores of the catalyst mass, while the particles remain on the surface of the support. When the exhaust gases containing the combustion products of the lead-based anti-knock mixture reach the catalyst, the following processes are liable to reduce catalytic activity [294]:

- the combining of lead with the active catalytic elements to form lead/precious metal alloys, accompanied by reduced catalytic activity corresponding the lead content
- inhibition of oxidation reactions by preferential adsorption of halogenated compounds
- chemical attack of precious metals by halogenated hydracids, causing a loss of active elements in the most sensitive zones
- acceleration of the sintering of precious metals (coalescence of microcrystallites of platinum or palladium on the surface of the alumina)
- mechanical effects resulting from the accumulation of lead deposits on the catalyst surface: pore clogging, embrittlement of the supports (melting of the monolith or attrition of the pellets)

Measurements on old catalysts have shown that most of the lead is deposited on the support, and that only a small amount of lead is deposited on the precious metal crystallites [41].

Among the reactions that contribute to the fixation of lead in the catalyst, the most important concern the formation of sulfates and oxysulfates according to reactions (12.25), (12.26), and (12.27):

$$PbCl_2 + SO_3 + H_2O \Rightarrow PbSO_4 + 2HCl \qquad (12.25)$$

$$PbO + SO_3 \Rightarrow PbSO_4 \qquad (12.26)$$

$$n PbO + PbSO_4 \Rightarrow n PbO, PbSO_4 \qquad (12.27)$$

These reactions are facilitated considerably by the presence of the catalyst which activates the reaction:

$$SO_2 + 1/2 O_2 \Rightarrow SO_3 \qquad (12.28)$$

The layer of lead sulfate that forms around 550°C may crack around 600°C, which makes it more permeable and partly restores the HC oxidation activity [117]. However, this cannot restore more than 80% of the initial activity and this non-uniform restoration occurs at the cost of methane and other alkanes.

Other reactions, such as addition, participate in lead fixation:

$$nPbO + PbCl_2 \Rightarrow nPbO,PbCl_2 \quad (12.29)$$

Lead oxide can also react with phosphorus oxides:

$$3PbO + P_2O_5 \Rightarrow Pb_3(PO_4)_2 \quad (12.30)$$

At very high temperature, some of these species formed at lower temperatures may decompose (for example, by reaction (12.26) in the reverse direction). The decomposition products are removed or absorbed by the support by reactions of the following type (12.31):

$$PbO + Al_2O_3 \Rightarrow PbAl_2O_4 \quad (12.31)$$

All the compounds mentioned above have been found by analysis in spent catalysts from engines running on leaded fuels [296]. The majority consists of oxysulfates, phosphates, and oxides. However, very little sulfate, $PbSO_4$, is found. The mass of lead retained in these different forms in the catalyst is greater if the catalyst has operated at higher temperature. The maintenance of lead in the vapor state (by means of 'scavengers') favors this fixation of lead [296]. The high temperatures and the presence of halogens facilitate the penetration of lead into the catalyst bed. Thermal desorption of the lead deposited on the catalyst takes place in two steps: around 400 to 500°C, most of the lead is eliminated, leaving a practically monomolecular layer on the surface [41 and 296]; this layer then disappears at about 1150°C. On platinum, the action of lead is therefore mainly harmful below 500°C [295].

#### 12.8.1.2 Mechanisms of deactivation by lead

The harmful effect of lead may be due to coating of the catalyst or to clogging of the pores of the support. In the oxidation of CO it has been pointed out that under a monomolecular layer ($\leqslant 1\%$ PbO) lead did not exert a harmful effect, but could on the contrary, lower the catalyst light-off temperature [295 and 296]. Beyond a single layer, the CO conversion reaction is inhibited. For high PbO concentrations (5% or more), pore clogging is responsible for lowering the conversion rate.

Catalysts poisoned by a chemical effect connected with the covering of the precious metal crystallites can be regenerated by heating to about 500°C in a lead-free atmosphere. To open the pores clogged by lead sulfate deposits, however, temperatures of at least 900°C must be reached.

The poisoning effect of lead is more pronounced on palladium than on platinum, especially at low temperature. Attempts were made to regenerate catalysts poisoned by lead by washing the catalyst with acetic acid. This achieved partial regeneration, but required the dismantling of the system [146]. In traffic conditions, a residual lead content of 3 mg/liter does not raise any problems, even with endurance, whereas 10 mg/liter causes deactivation of precious metal catalysts [386].

#### 12.8.1.3 Effect of 'scavenging' halogenides

Catalyst poisoning by lead is seriously aggravated by the presence of halogens. The initial activity is lower than in the presence of pure lead, due to the inhibition caused by the halogens, which are selectively adsorbed, whereas the lead tends to cover the catalyst uniformly [49]. This effect is more pronounced with palladium than with platinum [201, 295, and 296].

#### 12.8.1.4 Lead-resistant catalysts

Conventional three-way catalysts based on precious metals tend to resist the presence of lead in the fuel as long as the exhaust gases reach them at a temperature of about 500°C (hence in non-urban traffic) and if the leaded fuels were free of halogen 'scavengers' [295]. Fuel containing 0.15 g/liter of pure lead results in a 20% loss of CO activity after 40,000 km, which rises to a 40% loss under the same conditions in the presence of 'scavengers'. Engine tests at *IFP* have also demonstrated that the use of pure tetraethyl lead did not cause any deterioration to the engine [294]. By placing the catalytic converter very near the exhaust manifold, high temperatures are maintained allowing the elimination of lead. With richer mixtures, moreover, secondary air injection [184], which favors the combustion of unburnt HC, also helps to obtain the requisite temperature level [294]. Lead-resistant three-way catalysts based on $AB_2O_3$ type perovskites have also been patented [146]. The B sites consist of Co substituted by 1 to 20% Ru or Pt and the A sites are occupied by a mixture of rare earths. Development work on these catalysts has now been suspended, since the general use of unleaded gasoline makes them less attractive. Besides, their activity is low compared with that of precious metals and they exhibit poor elevated temperature behavior and a fairly high light-off temperature.

### 12.8.2 Phosphorus poisoning

Contamination by phosphorus stems both from impurities in the fuel and from additives (zinc dialkyldithiophosphates) in the lubricant. The phosphorus content of unleaded fuels is variable but low (≈0.02 mg/liter) compared with lubricants (≈1.2 g/liter). It can be estimated that in 80,000 km (50,000 miles), a three-way catalyst may be exposed to 13 g of P, of which 93% originates in the lubricant [344 and 388]. Phosphorus acts both on the accuracy of the oxygen probe and on the aging of the catalyst by reducing the CO conversion rate more than the NO conversion rate at stoichiometry. The chemical form in which the phosphorus is retained in the catalyst is still poorly known, although aluminum phosphate, zinc phosphate and alkaline earth phosphates have been identified [201]. By depositing on the surface of the wash-coat, the deposits progressively clog the pores of the catalyst [262 and 386] in the form of mixed calcium and zinc oxides or phosphates. In addition, a very close relationship exists between the drop in performance on CO, HC, and $NO_x$ and the phosphorus content of the lubricant [292]. Hence, the tendency is to reduce the phosphorus content in engine oils to the extent permitted by onset of wear.

### 12.8.3 Sulfur poisoning

Sulfur poisoning is mainly caused by transition metals, which easily form sulfates, rather than precious metals [146]. This formation of sulfates requires the oxidation of $SO_2$ to $SO_3$. The reaction is catalysed more easily by oxidation catalysts, but three-way catalysts exert less activity in this case due to the presence of rhodium [344]. However, $SO_2$ itself affects the activity of the three-way catalyst, by reducing the conversion rate of the three pollutants CO, HC and $NO_x$. Furthermore, in a rich mixture it blocks the water/shift reaction and steam reforming [344], and it tends to dissociate at the surface of the precious metals into oxygen and adsorbed sulfur, with the sulfur strongly bonded to the metal [33].

### 12.8.4 Silicon contamination

Silicon contamination is very rare and exceptional, because the contents are generally lower than 1 ppm. The accidental presence of silicon in a poorly identified soluble form in the fuels (up to 150 ppm of Si has been identified [89]) causes the formation of silica deposits on the alumina surface. With an Si content of 20 ppm, catalyst deactivation is already observed and if one-third of the alumina surface of a three-way catalyst is covered, virtually all activity is eliminated, although this can be regenerated by washing with hydrofluoric acid [89]. Silicon also causes damage to the oxygen probe by reducing the mass transfer rates.

## 12.9 Catalyst light-off

It was pointed out earlier (Section 10.14) that a large proportion of urban driving takes place without reaching the normal engine operating temperature. This is why most of the regulation tests of pollutant measurements (with or without catalyst) are performed from a cold start (Chapter 6).

At ambient temperature, a catalytic converter has no action on the pollutants emitted by the engine. The catalyst must reach a minimum temperature, between 200 and 300°C, to begin to act. Hence, the catalyst has a light-off period during which engine emissions are not treated, which is responsible for a large share of the emissions. Tests on different models show that, for the catalyst to reach 300°C, which approximately corresponds to conversion rates of 90%, it is necessary to drive 1 to 3 km in urban surroundings. This distance varies with the vehicle model and the outdoor temperature [45]. On the FTP cycle, the passage from the regulation temperature of 25°C to a temperature range between 13 and 17°C multiplies the HC emissions by a factor of 3 to 6 and the CO emissions by a factor of 4, while leaving $NO_x$ emissions unchanged [37].

This is why cold engine emissions after 40 s of idling in the ECE cycle (Chapter 6) are subject to regulation measurements at the exit of a catalytic converter [302]. By definition, the light-off temperature is the temperature at which a conversion rate of 50% is reached [267].

It has been observed that in the first 120 s of the ECE urban cycle (which lasts 13 min), about 50% of the CO, 75% of the HC, and 50% of the $NO_x$ are emitted (Fig. 12.10). This relative proportion of pollutants emitted during the first phases is still greater with oxygenated fuels [62], formaldehyde being the dominant compound with methanol fuel [140]. With M100 (Chapter 11), HCHO emissions are increased by a factor of 6 to 7 between FTP cold and warm cycles.

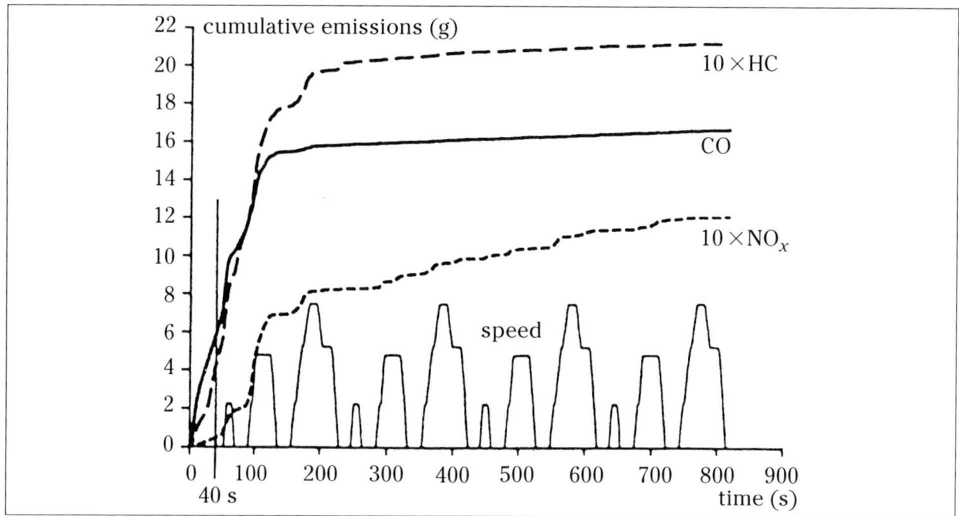


**Fig 12.10** Cumulative CO, HC and nitrogen oxide emissions as a function of time over the standard ECE cycle (vehicle with 2.2 liter engine, three-way catalytic muffler, emissions in the first 40 s not included) [302]

It is therefore vitally important to try to minimize the catalyst light-off period to meet the standards and also to reduce urban pollution.

The time required for a catalytic converter to become effective depends on the following:

- the inherent properties of the catalyst: its formula and its instantaneous state (state of oxidation, aging, compounds present on the surface)
- the exhaust gas composition
- the heat input by the exhaust gases: this depends on the engine settings (especially fuel/air ratio and spark timing), the heat transfer at the wall of the exhaust circuit, the distance between the exhaust manifold and the converter, and the characteristics of the converter itself (geometry, heat capacity, thermal insulation, thermal conductivity)

### 12.9.1 Influence of catalysts

In oxidation catalysis, palladium has a lower light-off temperature than platinum. In multi-metallic three-way systems, the Pt/Rh combination lights off at a lower temperature than Pt/Pd, Pd/Rh, and Pt/Pd/Rh systems [302]. The light-off temperature decreases with increasing dispersion of the platinum.

The increase in the precious metal concentration tends to lower the light-off temperature. On an aged catalyst, about 30°C can be gained by increasing the metal content from 0.53 to 2.12 g/liter.

To oxidize CO, the oxidation rate and the light-off temperature depend on the area exposed to CO and not on the size of the crystallites. An Arrhenius type relationship exists between this temperature and the dispersion of the platinum [302].

### 12.9.2 Action of support additives

Additives tend to inhibit the sintering of precious metals and slow their aging, and also tend to lower the light-off temperature. This temperature is thus lowered almost linearly as a function of the $CeO_2$ content [302], especially if the size of the cerium oxide particles is smaller. The other additives, which are added in particular to promote the oxygen storage capacity (e.g. $Fe_2O_3$) or to stabilize the precious metals (rare earth oxides), reduce the light-off temperature. In addition, we have already pointed out that a very low lead content can also lower it [295 and 296].

### 12.9.3 Effect of gas phase composition

When the engine is started, the initial gas phase flowing through the catalytic converter contains a variable amount of CO, $O_2$, NO, and unburnt HC depending on the extent of the initial enrichment (effect of the choke), which depends on the ambient temperature and pressure. A high oxygen content and a low CO content (as in the diesel engine) lower the light-off temperature of oxidation catalysts [395].

The composition of the unburnt hydrocarbons also varies with the composition of the fuel used. Other species, for example $SO_2$, may be present in variable amounts. It has been shown that a high olefins content reduces the light-off temperature, which is actually raised by a high aromatics content [303].

The reaction of the catalysts to these factors is obviously not systematic, but also depends on the formulas used and their state of aging at start up.

#### 12.9.3.1 Effect of fuel/air ratio

For a conventional Pt+Pd oxidation catalyst used without auxiliary air on a lean burn engine, the light-off temperature rises sharply with cold start enrichment [302]. This effect is less on a three-way catalyst containing rhodium, since Rh is less sensitive than Pt and Pd to the inhibiting effect of CO (Sections 12.3.1 and 12.5.4). Conversely, with a platinum oxidation catalyst, as the CO content rises from 0.5% to 7% the temperature to obtain 50% conversion rises from 160 to 300°C [302].

Besides CO, unburnt hydrocarbons may exert a variable inhibiting effect depending on their composition and concentration. Like CO, NO also delays light-off, whereas the oxygen content tends to have a favorable effect.

However, the sulfur content of the fuel apparently has no effect on light-off [302].

To control as rapidly as possible the fuel/air ratio of mixtures in looped control systems, which depends on the performance of the oxygen sensor, the $\gamma$ sensor can be heated electrically to reach its optimal temperature quickly [340].

#### 12.9.3.2 Role of the surface texture of the catalyst

A catalyst with a larger developed surface area tends to have a lower light-off temperature, but this quality is maintained for a shorter time [391]. In practice, a catalyst exhibits starting behavior that depends substantially on its previous history. The light-off temperature is higher if the catalyst has previously undergone thermal treatment in oxidizing conditions, but it is lowered if this treatment has taken place in reducing conditions [302].

Deposits of metals and metalloids (for example, Pb, P, S and Zn) have a more irreversible effect. In general, the cumulation of thermal effects (sintering) and fouling by deposits of impurities result in a progressive rise of the light-off temperature, which could increase under very severe running conditions from 330°C after 1000 km to 370°C after 20,000 km [302].

### 12.9.4 Influence of support type and position

To reach the catalyst light-off temperature as quickly as possible after cold starting, the catalytic unit should be located very close to the exhaust manifold, should have a low heat capacity [391], and sometimes a high heat transfer coefficient [312]. These conditions are often contradicted by the risks of overheating during driving at full load. However, provided a temperature of 950°C is never exceeded for Pt/Rh systems, the advantage offered by a closer arrangement of the catalytic converter prevails over the deterioration of performance over time due to operation at high temperature [50].

A compromise is to separate the catalytic converter into two components: a mini-converter with low heat capacity, which is placed as near as possible to the exhaust manifold where it heats up faster thus reducing the starting CO and HC, and, further downstream, the main converter [56] (Fig. 12.11). For metallic monoliths, the starting converter can be placed very close to the engine because of its greater resistance to any overheating at high charge [268]. Composite solutions place a metallic mini-monolith, possibly heated by electric resistance [395], directly on the manifold with a ceramic monolith placed further downstream [19 and 127].

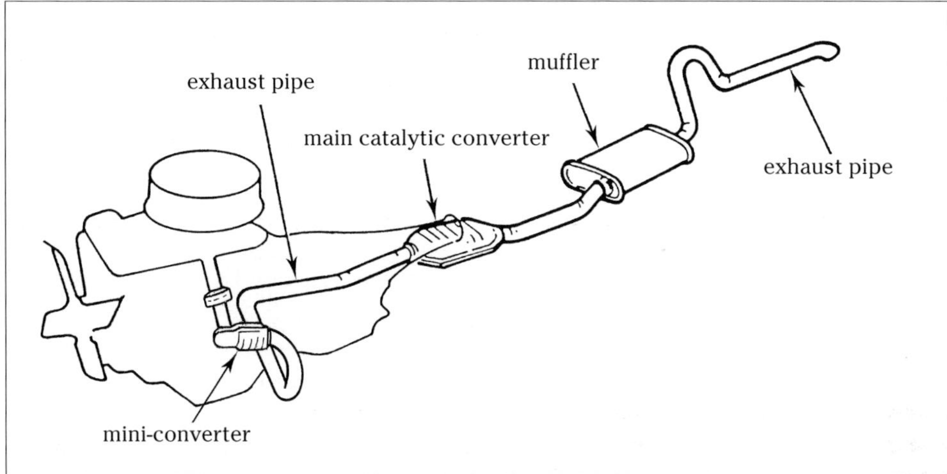


**Fig 12.11** Exhaust system with a mini-converter upstream from the main muffler [56] Reprinted with permission © 1983 *McGraw Hill Inc*

A method designed to bring the catalyst to its operating temperature before the engine is started is to use the energy from the battery to heat the overall catalytic system [132]. An electrically heated catalyst is now capable of reducing NMHC and CO emissions by 70% [396]: the catalyst is heated to 480°C in 42 s with a 4700 W electric heater. A wattage of about 5.5 kW applied for 15 s is generally adequate to raise the catalyst to about 300 to 350°C. The high power requirement raises serious questions about battery life [397]. To accelerate the warmup of the catalyst support, attempts have been made to make these supports of a conducting refractory material that displays sufficient electric resistivity to be heated by Joule effect under the same conditions. Thus porous catalyst elements based on silicon carbide have been made, which heat in less than 1 min with 1 kW of electric power [140].

For metallic monoliths, to reach the starting temperature more rapidly, the resistivity of aluminum-coated steel plates is exploited to heat the monolith by Joule effect [101]. With a power of about 3 kW, this system serves to raise the monolith to 350°C in 20 s [379]. However, the simple passage from ceramic to metal is insufficient to reduce cold emissions due to the enrichment of the mixture caused by the choke [206]. Consequently, to be able to cut CO and HC emissions by 50% after this 20 s time interval, it may sometimes be necessary to add air injection [395]. To do so, the metallic monolith is separated into two sections. The larger downstream section is not heated while the upstream section, which is about six times smaller, is heated [380]. An air flow of about 140 liters/min is injected between the two sections by a vane pump for 140 s for a two-liter engine [131]. This system also helps to reduce the initial cold start emissions of benzene and toluene by a factor of 3 and 5.

Power choppers help to supply the amperage necessary (700 to 800 A) [379]. Other configurations propose a metallic mini-monolith heated electrically upstream from the conventional ceramic monolith [164].

In the field of ceramic monoliths, attempts have been made to reduce the wall thicknesses (down to 0.10 mm) [390] to lower the heat capacity of the units. Furthermore, the development of metallic monoliths has been sparked by the advantage of lower heat capacity rather than higher mechanical strength. The thermal insulation of the casing accordingly reduces the light-off time and enhances the effectiveness of the catalyst [226].

To maintain the monoliths in the metal casings of the catalytic converter, the use of cushions of mineral fibers, rather than metal lattices (Section 12.7 above), provides greater thermal insulation and faster light-off of the monolith [234 and 304]. In some cases, it may be necessary to thermally insulate the connecting pipe between the exhaust manifold and the converter [234]. Double-thickness lightweight thin-walled connecting pipes in particular help to reduce both the thermal conductivity and the heat capacity of the system [261]. A better design of the gas streams also allows a gain in temperature [13]. The splitting of the catalytic converter into two successive components placed in series helps to improve the mixing of the gases in the catalytic space [13] and, above all, to favor the warmup of the upstream component, thus shortening the light-off time, as in the case of the mini-converter described above.

Another method to reduce the light-off time is to use a vane pump to send air downstream of the exhaust valves during the time the choke is on [394]. In this way, the combustion of the rich mixture in the exhaust manifold heats the catalyst more rapidly. The pump is driven by the engine using a transmission belt and an electromagnetic coupling, which is deactivated when the heating period is over. It has also been proposed to insert into the exhaust system, upstream from the catalyst, a small burner that is turned on 1 to 3 s before the engine starts. This burner, turned off after 20 s, needs 50 to 90 ml of gasoline and heats the catalyst up to 350°C.

Moreover, during cold starts, part of the unburnt HC in the exhaust, often consisting of unvaporized fuel droplets in these conditions, tends to condense on the intake manifolds. As the system heats up, this fuel is vaporized again and it strongly enriches the mixture fed to the engine resulting in increased unburnts in the exhaust during the period when the catalyst is not yet active. To overcome this drawback, one solution is to preheat partially (between 40 and 55°C) the intake manifold by a heating element consuming $\approx$20 A, which is disconnected when the coolant reaches between 60 and 65°C [165].

Another method to promote catalyst light-off is to misadjust the ignition point temporarily. An ignition delay causes delayed combustion with a temperature increase in the exhaust gases. Fresh air injection behind the exhaust valves favors the post-combustion of the unburnt HC and heats the catalyst faster. Heating time is accordingly shortened from 105 to 35 s [190] and HC emissions are cut to about 35% of the value obtained without the use of this arrangement, which is interrupted after 2 min. Combined with short-term enrichment of the mixture, this technique helps to raise the catalyst to 500°C in less than 90 s [12], which would otherwise require more than 3 min. This practice would help to avoid the use of the upstream mini-converter and the installation of the catalyst near the engine, thus avoiding any risk of overheating at full charge.

## 12.10 Catalyst wear

Besides the external causes of defective catalyst operation (disconnection of the oxygen probe, ignition failure, excessive oil consumption) [61 and 354], several mechanisms tend to deteriorate catalyst performance over time (Table 12.1) [47].

For correctly set engines with suitably mounted catalytic converters, the various types of pollution and mechanical deterioration are insignificant. Chemical and thermal factors are the main ones involved. However, despite the fears expressed on this subject, operation in conditions of full charge enrichment on expressways does not appear to jeopardize significantly the catalyst conversion rates [182].

**Table 12.1** Catalyst deactivation mechanisms

| | |
|---|---|
| **chemical mechanisms** | *poisoning:* adsorption or irreversible reaction on or with the surface<br>*inhibition:* competitive and reversible absorption of poison precursors<br>*restructuring* of catalyst surfaces caused by poisons<br>*physical or chemical clogging* of the porous structure of the support |
| **thermal mechanisms** | *sintering:* redispersions<br>*formation* of alloys<br>*modifications* of the support<br>interactions between base metals and precious metals<br>interactions between metals or oxides and support<br>oxidation (segregations of alloys)<br>surface orientation of noble metals<br>volatilization of metals |
| **pollution** | carbon deposits (coking) |
| **mechanical factors** | thermal shock<br>attrition<br>physical destruction |

Various forms of thermal deactivation may occur as the catalyst temperature rises (Table 12.2). Oxidation on the oxidizing side of the air/fuel ratio (with the formation of $Rh_2O_3$ on the surface with Pt/Rh systems, and of PdO with Pd/Rh systems) [252] appears to be the most important degradation factor, worse than the sintering and alloying of the precious metals or their interaction with cerium [47]. In particular, the rhodium oxide resulting from the oxidation of the metal is partly incorporated in the alumina crystal lattice [340] with a resulting increase in the Pt/Rh mass ratio, which could rise from 5.5 to 12 [334]. With monoliths, thermal deactivation is more concerned with the center of the support. On the other hand, poisoning mainly concerns the upstream part of the support with a uniform distribution of the various poisons [329].

**Table 12.2** Thermal deactivation processes [90]

| Temperature (°C) | Mechanism |
|---|---|
| 1300 | cordierite ⇒ mullite |
| 1200 | loss of wash-coat |
| 1100 | |
| | oxidation of Pt/Rh alloy |
| 1000 | |
| | $\gamma \Rightarrow \alpha$-$Al_2O_3$ |
| 900 | oxidation of Pt/Pd alloy |
| | sintering of $\gamma$-$Al_2O_3$ |
| 800 | |
| | reduction of Pt/Pd and Pt/Rh alloys |
| 700 | sintering of platinum |
| | $Rh/Al_2O_3$ reaction |
| 600 | $Ni/Al_2O_3$ reaction |

Another factor contributing to catalyst deactivation with time stems from their sintering, which causes a loss of active surface area. Reductions of the BET surface area from 22.3 to 14.6 $m^2/g$ have been observed after aging [334]. Usage of the catalyst at high temperature (900 to 1100°C) tends to accelerate sintering [118]. Aging of the catalyst system under severe operating conditions [228] (high temperature, ignition and fuel cutoffs, oil consumption) reveals rapid reductions of the developed specific surface area, accelerated sintering of the metals, the coalescence of the oxide and cerium particles, and alumina phase transformations (progressive passage from $\gamma$ and $\delta$ phases to $\theta$ phase). These developments cause an exponential increase in the light-off temperature and, after a short period of stability, the pollutant conversion rates are reduced. Driving conditions in cold countries, which require the prolonged use of the choke for short hops, accelerate deterioration of the catalysts, which can barely preserve their performance up to 80,000 km [207].

The highly reducing or oxidizing exhaust gases, which are at high temperature, cause the formation of alloys between active precious metals on the catalyst surface. To minimize these alloys, attempts have been made in the laboratory to deposit Pt (and especially Pd) and Rh on different supports [90], by first depositing Rh on $ZrO_2$, for example, before impregnating the $\gamma$ alumina [344]. One method to improve the time-related behavior of the catalysts is to increase (triple) the $CeO_2$ content of the wash-coat. The lower initial performance is compensated for by the maintenance of the dispersion of the metallic species that results from the stabilization by the cerium [267]. These improved catalysts help in particular to preserve high activity in the oxidation of CO and HC [328], even in acceleration at high speed. However, the wider dispersion of the platinum makes it much more sensitive to poisoning by residual lead [90].

Another mechanism involves the detachment of the wash-coat from the support. This can be caused by the transition between the $\gamma$-$Al_2O_3$ and the $\alpha$-$Al_2O_3$, which implies a transition from the cubic form to the octahedral form, accompanied by a volume reduction and a density increase that causes the bonding points to release from the support [90]. Cerium and the other lanthanides tend to inhibit this transition. These oxides, inserted between the planes of $\gamma$ alumina, tend to slow down the transition to the $\alpha$ form.

The amplitude and duration of excursions about stoichiometry in the rich and lean ranges is an important factor in performance loss. Consequently, the quality of the closed-loop fuel/air ratio control is crucial [130], especially with Pd/Rh systems [252]. In particular, a spent catalyst mounted on a vehicle that has good fuel/air ratio control yields better results than a newer catalyst coupled with poorer fuel/air ratio control [4].

The installation of two $\lambda$ probes, upstream and downstream of the catalytic converter respectively, combined with a suitable processing algorithm, should help to detect the operating quality of the catalyst, especially based on measurements during acceleration and at cruising speed [195].

Catalyst aging does not have a uniform effect on the different families of hydrocarbons. It is harmful for aromatics, with an increase that rises with the extent of alkylation. This effect on paraffins and olefins is more pronounced with higher molecular weight compounds [6].

## 12.11 Effect of catalysts on unregulate pollutants. Secondary pollutants out of catalytic converters

Although specially developed to act on the regulated pollutants, CO, HC and $NO_x$, catalytic purifiers also exert action on the other pollutants present at the engine exhaust. It is also important to determine whether the installation of catalytic converters does not risk emitting new pollutants, which are normally not emitted by unequipped vehicles.

It has also been found that, in the case of hydrocarbons, oxidation catalysts in particular do not demonstrate identical conversion rates for all the hydrocarbon classes [171]. Their reactivity is generally higher for unsaturated compounds. Vehicles equipped with catalysts emit far less reactive mixtures into the atmosphere and the real effectiveness of the catalytic converter is far superior to the value calculated from the mass conversion rate of total HC.

### 12.11.1 Oxygenated pollutants

These pollutants are primarily alcohols (methanol and ethanol) with engines supplied with a high proportion of these alcohols. The methanol conversion rates are higher than those of ethanol [229]. With platinum on alumina, 95% conversion is reached at 150°C for methanol and 240°C for ethanol [229].

The main pollutants concerned are aldehydes, for which 95% reduction rates have been observed on thermal reactors [61] and 50 to 80% rates on oxidation catalytic converters or oxidation plus reduction systems, with virtually total effectiveness on aromatic aldehydes [53]. For formaldehyde, a first step involves decomposition into CO and $H_2$, which are then oxidized on the platinum catalyst, the limiting step being the subsequent oxidation of CO [332]. It has also been demonstrated on an engine supplied with methanol [126] that aldehydes are partially eliminated in the exhaust and then completely destroyed by the catalyst [61]. On the FTP cycle, to improve the aldehyde conversion rate, it is necessary to place the catalyst as near as possible to the exhaust manifold [256]. After poisoning by lead, despite the reduction of the conversion rates, the catalyst preserves some effectiveness in eliminating aldehydes [255]. In the worst possible case, conversion to formaldehyde does not exceed 5% of the unburnt methanol [229]. On the other hand, design concepts for a lean burn engine, which are effective without a catalyst on the standard pollutants, proved to be harmful for aldehyde emissions due to their particular behavior as a function of fuel/air ratio [61]. This is why, with methanol fuel, the lean burn and oxidation catalyst system emits more aldehydes than the stoichiometric mixture and three-way catalyst system [240]. For this reason, with the three-way catalyst, it is preferable to have a fuel/air ratio setting that is slightly offset in the rich zone to minimize aldehyde emissions. Sufficient oxygen is required to complete oxidation without stopping at the aldehyde stage, but on the other hand, an excessively lean atmosphere must be avoided because the catalysts tend to lose their activity due to superficial oxidation [229].

With M85 fuel (Chapter 11), Pt and Pd based catalysts demonstrate the best activity in oxidizing methanol and minimizing the formation of formaldehyde [229]. This is in contrast to rhodium, which tends to oxidize more easily in a slightly lean mixture. However, with M100 fuels (Chapter 11) , precious metal catalysts containing rhodium prove to be even more effective, with conversion rates exceeding 90%, even with the Pd/Rh mixture at 9/1 with 0.35 g/liter on FTP cycle [288]. On the same cycle, a catalyst containing only 10 g/liter of silver displays an 88% conversion rate, with a 99% rate on HFET cycle (Section 6.2.1.3).

### 12.11.2 Oxidized sulfur pollutants

This class of pollutants refers to $SO_2$ and sulfates. Oxidation catalytic converters oxidize the sulfur compounds initially present in the fuel to the highest degree, producing $SO_2$, which normally accounts for 85% of the sulfur initially present in the fuel [311]. In conditions of excess air, this $SO_2$ is very easily converted to $SO_3$ and sulfates, especially if the catalyst contains platinum [63]. With the alumina and cerium in the wash-coat, $SO_3$ forms the corresponding sulfates, which are stored on the surface of the catalyst, or are again reduced to $SO_2$ in a subsequent passage with a richer mixture. The following occurs as a consequence:

- oxidation catalysts emit higher levels of sulfates than those found in the absence of a catalyst
- air pumps further increase the emission levels
- in contrast with three-way catalysts, sulfate emissions are unaffected by the presence or absence of a catalyst

The percentage of sulfur converted to the sulfate can rise from 0.4% of the sulfur present in the fuel for a vehicle not equipped with a catalyst to 9% for a vehicle equipped with an oxidation catalyst with additional air injection [61]. In the absence of air injection or with modulated air injection, this oxidation does not take place [61].

With diesel engines, to minimize the oxidation of sulfur to $SO_3$, it may be necessary to optimize the composition of the wash-coat by partly replacing the alumina by other inorganic oxides [394].

### 12.11.3 Reduced sulfur compounds

These compounds are hydrogen sulfide ($H_2S$) and carbonyl sulfide (COS), which can itself form $H_2S$ in contact with moist air. The corresponding emissions always occur in the presence of precious metals, usually with poorly-operating oxidation catalysts [86] and more easily with fresh catalysts than with spent catalysts [69].

On a platinum catalyst, $SO_3$ tends to be formed from $SO_2$ in the presence of oxygen stored on the catalyst under excess air conditions. However, when low-oxygen conditions are restored the $SO_2$ and $SO_3$ can be reduced to yield $H_2S$. This process appears to be promoted by a low gas flow rate (as in idling) [311] and by the presence of platinum [141]. Hydrogen sulfide emissions are ephemeral and extremely brief, with concentrations that are always far below the toxicity threshold. They sometimes occur in cold starting, but mostly in warm-engine idling at traffic lights after deceleration [349] or during parking, but very rarely in moving traffic [61]. The highest concentrations essentially appear when the mixture becomes rich after a long period of lean combustion [69]. These rich mixture conditions may occur when purging canisters limiting evaporative losses [99]. The total quantities of $H_2S$ emitted are very small and often difficult to measure. This is because the amount of sulfur retained during lean combustion is very small compared with the total amount of sulfur that has passed through the catalyst ($<2\%$) [86]. However, since these are emissions of odorous gusts of a product with a very low olfactory threshold (0.017 $\mu g/m^3$) [68], they are extremely unpleasant to the human nose. This is why catalyst formulas are designed to prevent these gusts of sulfur products under all circumstances.

Emissions of sulfur products result from the $SO_2$ stored on the catalyst during times when the fuel/air ratio is lean. During transitions to a rich mixture, the stored sulfur is reduced to $H_2S$ and COS [311], resulting in $H_2S$ emissions that may be three to ten times higher than the initial $SO_2$ concentration in the exhaust gas [349]. Lean burn is accompanied by the adsorption of $SO_2$ on the support surface [141], oxidation to $SO_3$ and storage in the form of cerium and aluminum sulfates, and cerium oxysulfate. In this respect, among the other rare earths, cerium displays high activity for promoting the storage and discharge of sulfur [33 and 86]. Rich mixtures are accompanied by reduction and the desorption of $H_2S$. Comparative tests show that, in a reducing atmosphere on pure $\gamma$ alumina, 34% of the sulfur leaves in the form of $SO_2$ and 40% in the form of $H_2S$. These figures are changed to 30 and 60% respectively on a mixed aluminium/cerium support [223]. Desorption is very rapid, but sufficient residence time is necessary in a rich mixture to desorb enough sulfur in reduced form to reach an odorous concentration in the exhaust due to the dilution at the exhaust exit [99]. For instance, hydrogen sulfide can be smelled during warm idling after high-speed driving, when dilution is low. Running on a low-sulfur fuel does not decrease the mass of sulfur adsorbed on the catalyst, but extends the time interval before saturation of the catalyst with sulfur.

Apart from the use of no-sulfur fuel, the measures taken to limit gusts of hydrogen sulfide include a restriction of rich mixture excursions by better closed-loop control of the fuel/air ratio, achieved by keeping the air/fuel ratio at $\lambda = 1 \pm 05$ [287]. Fuel feed cutoff in deceleration also helps to prevent the reduction of the sulfur compounds stored on the catalyst in these conditions [99]. Use is also made of catalyst formulas that limit the level of sulfur stored or contain a 'getter' or 'scavenger' like nickel [141], which forms a stable sulfide in a reducing mixture, but which oxidizes to $SO_2$ in a lean oxidizing mixture [349]. Furthermore, the formation of aluminum and cerium phosphates, especially when a catalyst is poisoned, reduces the possible mass of $SO_2$ stored and hence the $H_2S$ emissions during transition to a rich mixture [69]. In the course of catalyst attrition, to prevent any emissions of nickel [86] (considered harmful to health due to the possible formation of nickel carbonyl) [388], it is replaced by ferrites of divalent metals with the general formula $M_2^+Fe_2O_4$ [308]. Cobalt and copper ferrites, incorporated in the wash-coat, have been claimed to be as effective as nickel oxide. Copper, incorporated in the wash-coat in the form of nitrate, blocks $H_2S$ emissions, but unlike nickel, sharply reduces catalyst performance [123], except if added to the wash-coat in a different area from the one containing precious metals [67]. Among oxides, only germanium oxide, which, like nickel oxide, has a high melting point enabling it to resist aging, does not affect catalyst performance and demonstrates the same effectiveness for $H_2S$ [388]. By way of experiment, manganese was applied to a monolith coated on its upstream 5/6 with a wash-coat containing precious metals and on its final 1/6 with alumina containing 17% manganese oxide [67]. Attempts have also been made to develop formulas without a 'scavenger' for low $H_2S$ emissions. One technique consists in rapidly 'aging' the catalyst by favoring the enlargement of cerium oxide crystallites and thereby decreasing the surface area available for the adsorption of sulfur. By calcination up to around 870°C, the $H_2S$ emission peaks are reduced by 25% without perceptibly decreasing the effectiveness for CO, HC and $NO_x$ [86]. Formulas without cerium, which favor the water/gas shift reaction (Section 12.5.5 above) among other properties, have also been developed without diminishing the capacity to oxidize CO but also reducing the conversion of hydrocarbons, especially saturated HC [86]. The exchange of hydroxyl groups, which are located at the surface of the aluminum and cerium oxides and favor the adsorption of sulfur, also helps to reduce $H_2S$ emissions by decreasing the number and strength of the adsorption sites [223].

### 12.11.4 Nitrogen pollutants: cyanogen and hydrogen cyanide

The passage of a mixture of NO, CO, and $H_2$ on noble catalysts between 400 and 800°C can give rise to HCN [61]. In the laboratory, it was possible to obtain 700 ppm of HCN on oxidation catalysts at 700°C, but in actual conditions on a vehicle it has not been possible to exceed 1.5 ppm (3 mg/km), even in abnormally rich conditions. On a three-way catalyst, HCN is not found in a stoichiometric or very lean mixture, but it does appear in a rich mixture. Rhodium, added to favor the reduction of $NO_x$, can even promote the reduction to HCN, but only in conditions of exceptional maladjustment (disconnection of the oxygen probe simultaneous with excessive enrichment at idling). Despite all these factors, and even in the same maladjustment conditions, catalysts tend to reduce the emission levels found without catalyst [61 and 354].

### 12.11.5 Nitrogen pollutants: ammonia and amines

As for HCN, the formation of ammonia occurs by the reduction of the $NO_x$ at high fuel/air ratios. The main NO reduction reaction, favored by the presence of rhodium, involves hydrogen:

$$2NO + 5H_2 \Rightarrow 2NH_3 + 2H_2O \tag{12.32}$$

At a fuel/air ratio of 1, it is virtually non-existent because the $H_2$ concentration is practically nil, but mixture incursions into the rich zone can lead to the formation of ammonia [154]. The speed of response of mixture control systems, particularly in transient driving conditions, is therefore an essential factor for avoiding ammonia emissions. The maladjustment of control systems [61], the disconnection of the oxygen probe, and enrichment when idling all promote the formation of $NH_3$. On a catalyst containing rhodium, up to 300 mg/km has been observed under these conditions with undiluted gas contents liable to exceed the statutory environmental limits [61].

Amines are formed in circumstances identical to those that favor ammonia. However, very low concentrations of mono- and diethylamines have been detected in the range of 0.3 and 0.1 mg/mile on the FTP cycle [46]. These values are too low to be implicated in the formation of atmospheric nitrosamines [61].

### 12.11.6 Nitrogen pollutants: nitrous oxide

At the engine exit with a mixture burning at stoichiometry, $N_2O$ represents less than 1% of total NO and EGR also tends to reduce this concentration [300]. After passage on a three-way catalyst based on platinum/rhodium with light-off at around 360°C, the $N_2O$ content rises sharply and then drops below the initial value at about 460°C. On a vehicle equipped with closed-loop mixture control, the $N_2O$ contents tend to double or triple after a cold start. After a warm start, the increase in $N_2O$ is negligible. Consequently, most of the nitrous oxide emitted (less than 1% of NO) is discharged during the light-off period, for example on a vehicle driven slowly after a cold start [300].

### 12.11.7 Aromatic hydrocarbons

Special attention must be paid to benzene to make sure that, despite the great stability of the aromatic ring, it is totally oxidized in contact with the catalyst, like the other classes of hydrocarbons. Measurements have demonstrated that all the purifying systems designed tend to eliminate benzene in a higher proportion than that of the other aromatics and of hydrocarbons in general [61]. The conversion rates observed on injection engines equipped with three-way catalysts indicate that between 85 and 90% of the benzene is eliminated in comparison with unequipped vehicles [74], while the lean burn engine emits more benzene under these conditions than the conventional engine.

Another class of monitored aromatic hydrocarbons is represented by PAH. On thermal reactors [204] and on three-way catalysts, conversion rates of about 97 to 98% [61 and 74] have been observed for PAH, and the rates are always higher than 95% for most of the species and even higher than 90% for 1-nitropyrene [53].

It has also been demonstrated that the addition of three-way catalytic converters reduces the mutagenicity of exhaust gases by more than 90%, both in direct and indirect mutagenesis [74], virtually nullifying any mutagenicity at the catalyst outlet [53].

## 12.12 Oxidation catalysts

### 12.12.1 Spark ignition engines

The development of lean burn spark ignition engines has helped to meet the standards set by European Community legislation concerning nitrogen oxides. However, to eliminate the unburnt hydrocarbons generated in these conditions, it is necessary to add an oxidation catalyst. Requirements concerning this type of catalyst are less drastic than for three-way catalysis. Formulas without precious metals are not excluded here: at least the use of rhodium, which is the rarest (and the most expensive) of the three-way catalysts, is not indispensable [298 and 321]. However, the specified requirements for engine controls and the fact that lean burn engines responded only to the medium category defined by the legislation have made the oxidation catalyst unattractive for spark ignition engines in comparison with the three-way catalysts, which are already developed, because the small cost advantage does not appear to merit developing this alternative [130].

### 12.12.2 Catalysts for two-stroke engines

The composition of exhausts from two-stroke engines is significantly different from that of four-stroke engines (Section 10.8). They normally contain low $NO_x$ concentrations, so that an oxidation catalyst is adequate. However, they display an excess of unburnt hydrocarbons, which varies with time and in comparison with the oxygen present, and the additional pressure drop caused by the oxidation converter can increase internal recirculation and hence boost HC and CO emissions [250]. Except on special engines running mainly on a lean mixture (severe speed limit in Switzerland) [203], secondary air injection is therefore essential for effective catalytic combustion of these hydrocarbons [185]. Besides, the gases at the engine outlet are generally colder than on four-stroke engines, but once initiated, the combustion of the large quantity of hydrocarbons is liable to raise the catalyst temperature abnormally [352]. Secondary air injection facilitates temperature control. From the practical standpoint, one solution is to split the catalytic converter into two components: the first at the direct outlet of the exhaust manifold to facilitate the initiation of combustion, and the second further downstream after secondary air injection to complete the oxidation of the HC, with thermally-insulated connections. The catalytic element selected in this case is platinum, or even palladium, deposited on monoliths [352]. Palladium displays a fairly good capability for oxidizing HC, combined with a relatively low light-off temperature. In practice, it is possible to mount metallic catalytic converters on motor-cycles that are similar to the primary converters mounted on vehicles to accelerate light-off, by placing two in series if necessary. These converters have conversion rates of 88 to 99% for CO, and 88 to 96% for HC, with nitrogen oxides remaining unchanged [203].

### 12.12.3 Diesel exhaust oxidation

Diesel exhaust gases can also be treated by oxidation catalysts, particularly by catalytic monoliths similar to those used for spark ignition engines (flow through monoliths). These systems on regenerable filters (described below), which do not collect particulates, offer the advantage of not raising problems of regeneration and lower exhaust pressure drops. They were developed and used initially to limit the proportion of CO emitted by diesel engines operating in confined areas, such as mining machinery [162].

They essentially have the effect of oxidizing the extractable part (SOF) of the particulates without affecting elemental carbon. In fact, even by adding oxidation catalysts (incorporated in the fuel, for example), the carbon particles in the exhaust produce an aerosol that is too dilute to burn, without any need for accumulation on a filter [254]. But since SOF may represent the most harmful phase from the health standpoint, and also a very large fraction of the mass of particulates measured by regulation, these devices thus offer a positive way to satisfy the present legal limits [398]. Since the deterioration of particulate emissions has a stronger effect on SOF than on elemental carbon over time [95], the oxidation catalyst helps to guarantee good 'maintenance' of pollution control. SOF reductions of 40 to 90% have thus been measured [155]. It is also claimed that diesel catalytic oxidizers reduce exhaust odors.

Compared with the exhaust of spark ignition engines, diesel exhaust gases are characterized by a mixture containing a high proportion of residual oxygen, a lower content of CO and HC, and to a lesser degree, $NO_x$. They are also colder in urban driving (100 to 450°C) [24], reaching only 750°C on highways or expressways. This temperature level limits any possible oxidation to the adsorbed or gaseous organic substances and excludes elemental carbon. Besides, in comparison with gasoline engine exhaust, the diesel exhaust contains a higher sulfur content in the form of $SO_2$, of which the conversion to $SO_3$ must be minimized by the catalyst, because the sulfates and their associated water make a significant contribution to the mass of particulates collected by standard analytical methods (Chapter 11) [155 and 176].

Oxidizable organic species are present in the exhaust in three different forms:

- in the gas state, which can subsequently condense on the walls or on the carbon particles
- in the form of aerosol droplets in the exhaust
- already adsorbed on the particles

The relative proportions vary with temperature. The lower the temperature, the smaller the proportion of gas. Since oxidation reactions demand minimum residence time in contact with the catalysts, the species adsorbed on particles react more effectively, so that above 300°C, when the gas phase is larger, the performance of the converter declines despite the higher activity of the catalyst.

Besides, above 300°C the oxidation of $SO_2$ to $SO_3$ on precious metals becomes significant. Hence, an optimal temperature window exists for the oxidation catalyst. On the CFDS (Chapter 6) cycle it has accordingly been observed that an oxidation catalyst based on noble metals did not increase sulfate emissions, because on this cycle, the average temperature of the catalyst remains around 210°C [348]. The addition of rhodium to the platinum also slows down the oxidation of $SO_2$ [145]. However, on the 13-mode cycle [290] and on the MAN 'M' prechamber engine, catalytic converters equipped with precious metals all show an increase in the weight of particulates in all the modes generating a temperature above 350°C. The action is only positive in the other modes by the reduction of SOF, since the MAN engine emits a large amount of unburnt HC by virtue of its design [270].

As to mutagenicity, depending on the exhaust temperature, an increase in specific activity may be observed in certain operating modes. This factor becomes more important than the reduction of the mass of SOF emitted and the platinum catalyst favors the nitration and oxidation of the PAH. In other modes, the reduction of SOF prevails [163] and the PAH contents can be cut by half [145].

At low temperature (100 to 300°C), when idling for example, the HC and SOF appear to be reduced at the outlet of the oxidation catalyst. Although the light-off temperature is much lower thanks to a higher $O_2$ and lower CO partial pressure than in spark ignition engines [394], this reduction of HC and SOF more likely refers to an effect of adsorption of these pollutants [290]. During a sudden temperature rise to between about 450 and 500°C (acceleration and passage at high charge), an emission peak of HC and particulates is observed at the time of desorption. However, these transitory emissions, due to the time required to warm up the catalyst, remain low compared with those observed in the absence of catalyst [155], thus demonstrating the effectiveness of the catalyst. Also identified is an effect of adsorption of the oxidized sulfur species, either by adhesion of $H_2SO_4$ mist to the support at low temperature (<350°C), or by the formation at high temperature (>400°C) of aluminum sulfate by reaction with the wash-coat [156]. These sulfur species are salted out later at higher temperature once the support is saturated.

#### 12.12.3.1 Catalyst support

It is important to select a catalyst support that minimizes sulfate storage and salting out. During accelerations, $H_2SO_4$ mists can be emitted due to the thermal decomposition of aluminum sulfate formed at the surface of the wash-coat deposited on the support. Hence, wash-coats based on silica or titanium dioxide, which store fewer sulfates and $SO_2$, are preferable [24, 398, and 399].

Furthermore, if supports with a more sinuous geometry than once-through monoliths offer greater retention capacity for the species to be oxidized, the storage of carbon could cause the emission of gusts of black smoke by detachment during accelerations, or could even damage the support at high temperature by the accidental ignition of the deposited carbon [24]. This random salting out of soot on the catalyst supports can cause sudden variations in the measurements of the emitted particulates [22].

#### 12.12.3.2 Choice of catalytic species

The type of catalytic metal selected also affects the oxidation of $SO_2$ to sulfates. While at low temperature (200 to 300°C), platinum and palladium are minimally effective for this reaction, but at the temperatures above 400°C encountered in truck accelerations, platinum oxidizes $SO_2$ more strongly and palladium is preferable [24]. Palladium alone or the Pd/Rh combination are preferable to the Pt/Rh combination [22]. This is because, with a platinum catalyst on cordierite monolith and a fuel containing 0.25% by weight of sulfur, an increase in the mass of particulates collected is observed on most of the modes of the 13-mode cycle, essentially due to sulfate formation [162]. However, with the same type of catalyst and a fuel with an indeterminate sulfur content, a reduction in SOF of 70% is achieved between 170 and 250°C, which initially represented 34% of the particulates [7]. The effectiveness on particulates varies between 50% at high charge and 15 to 20% at low charge [8]. With a 0.03% sulfur fuel, the oxidation catalyst helps to drop from 0.32 to 0.24 g/kWh on the transient cycle [307]. The addition of a water scrubber (which is feasible and in use for stationary, rail, and mining machinery, and on fork-lift trucks) helps to boost the effectiveness on particulates from 70 [231] to about 95% [8]. The scrubbers also help to absorb the sulfuric acid droplets formed on the catalyst placed upstream [9].

On turbo-diesel passenger cars, diesel oxidation catalysts thus help to reduce emissions of CO by 30%, HC by 50%, and particulates and $NO_x$ by 10% [15 and 16]. The composition of the particulates is enriched with carbon at the expense of SOF, going from 72 to 85% carbon [222]. PAH are eliminated in a proportion ranging from 30 to 100% depending on the molecules. These catalysts, when installed on urban transit buses, help to reduce both particulates and PAH [17].

## 12.13 $NO_x$ treatment in diesel engines

The excess oxygen always present in the diesel exhaust has so far made it difficult to reduce $NO_x$ by the reducing components of the exhaust gas, as in the case of three-way catalysts. A number of rare tests claim to have achieved simultaneous conversion rates of 65% on NO and 85% on CO by means of a mixture of Cr, Cu, and Ag deposited on $\gamma$ alumina [200]. Other tests claim to use the particles that burn on filters undergoing regeneration to reduce $NO_x$ [391], but the regeneration times are short compared with engine operating times. Therefore, the reduction of nitrogen oxides by using additional chemical reducing agents is necessary wherever possible, for example in stationary or large diesel engines; this may offer an alternative to EGR without the drawback of increasing particulate emissions.

One technique proposed is the addition of ammonia, which passes together with the exhaust gases over catalysts such as transition metals or zeolites exchanged by metals [400], and displays a high ammonia absorption and hence storage capacity. To obtain nitrogen as the reaction product without excess ammonia consumption or the excessive formation of $N_2O$, it is necessary to comply with a narrow temperature range (200 to 300°C) and a narrow range of oxygen contents [66 and 191].

This helps to achieve conversion rates of 90 to 95% on a catalyst at 350°C [188] by controlling the ammonia flow rate to limit its residual content to 25 ppm [215]. Higher conversion rates are obtained at the cost of higher residual ammonia contents. Catalysts based on transition metals ($Fe_2O_3$, $Cr_2O_3$, $MnO_2$, $V_2O_5$, $Ag_2O$) have also been employed to activate the $NO/NH_3$ reaction. Special conditions of temperature and oxygen content are required to avoid producing high $N_2O$ concentrations [375]. This is because maximum effectiveness in the reduction of NO is always accompanied by the increased formation of $N_2O$ [66].

Another technique also uses catalysis by zeolites by causing NO to react with urea, which offers the advantage over ammonia of being neither toxic nor odorant. Urea can be dissolved in high concentrations in water and thus stored in a tank. The solution, when heated above 160°C, releases ammonia according to the reaction:

$$H_2N{-}CO{-}NH_2 + H_2O \Rightarrow CO_2 + 2NH_3 \qquad (12.33)$$

At very low spatial velocity, on a copper-exchanged zeolite [137], a conversion rate of 100% can be obtained, but the light-off temperatures are higher [137] and the yields decrease sharply at the spacial velocities routinely encountered in diesel exhausts [191].

Another absorbent investigated is cyanuric acid $(N-C-OH)_3$, a solid polymer which decomposes into isocyanic acid HNCO. The latter, by decomposing in turn around 320°C into ammonia and carbon dioxide, helps to reduce nitrogen oxides. Thus, NO is 95% converted in a reactor at 620°C, but this conversion rate decreases rapidly with temperature [48]. Consequently, apart from its high cost, this product demands temperature conditions that are incompatible with the operation of the automotive diesel engine [316].

## 12.14 Diesel trap oxidizers

Since the limits imposed on particulate emissions are becoming increasingly stringent, engine settings (Section 10.10) are no longer sufficient to reach the assigned levels, despite the contribution of electronics. This has led to the development of diesel engine outlet devices (especially traps) to collect these particulates and to prevent their release into the atmosphere.

Given the low overall density of the particulates emitted by diesel engines (0.075 g/cm$^3$), it is not possible to store the trapped soot on board, and to dump it (how?) from time to time at service stations, for example. Not only do the trapped particles cause back-pressures in the exhaust that are detrimental to engine operation, and that could boost the emissions of other pollutants, but the quantities collected build up at an alarming rate. On an automobile, this amounts to more than 13 liters after 5500 km[3]; and for a truck, the figure is in the neighborhood of 62 liters of soot after 1000 km[4]. Under these conditions, it is therefore essential to provide for regenerable trap systems, particularly by the continuous or periodic destruction of the soot collected.

Dust separation systems used in industry, such as cyclone separators, cannot be used on diesel engines due to the particle size distribution (70% $<$ 0.3 μm). Their average diameter of about 0.3 μm means that the diesel aerosol tends to behave like a gas. Cyclones are only feasible following a coagulation device placed between the engine and the trap. However, even if such systems operate adequately, the problem of eliminating the trapped soot would remain unsolved. Recycling of the soot to the intake is in fact impossible because the mineral ash could abrade the combustion chambers [217].

Despite these basic drawbacks, attempts have been made to develop no-regeneration systems. One example is a rotary monolithic filter, rotating slowly and permanently inside a casing, which filters the exhaust on one-third of its frontal surface. Compressed air is blown in countercurrent on the remaining two-thirds, and the soot detached is collected in a filter bag [216 and 217]. These attempts have not attracted significant development.

It is therefore essential to destroy the trapped soot, while avoiding an excessive accumulation in the trap. The best way to achieve this is to burn the soot using

3. Assuming that the automobile meets the previous regulations without filter of 0.37 g/km, and has to meet the new limit of 0.19 g/km, already after $\frac{1000}{0.37-0.19} \approx 5500 \text{ km}$, 1 kg of soot is recovered, occupying a volume of $\frac{1000}{0.075} \approx 13{,}300 \text{ cm}^3$.

4. A 40 t truck consuming an average of 2 liters/100 t × km [36] of 0.85 density diesel at about 35 MJ/liter [102], and considering an emission factor of 6 g/kg of diesel (Section 3.8.2) emits: $\frac{2 \times 40 \times 6}{0.85 \times 0.075} \approx 7.5$ liters of soot per 100 km. With an average engine efficiency of 25%, on the engine: $\frac{2 \times 40 \times 35 \times 0.25}{3.6} \approx 194$ kWh is recovered over 100 km.

If the exhaust regulation allows only 0.5g/kWh or $\frac{194 \times 0.5}{0.075 \times 1000} \approx 1.3$ liters of soot per 100 km, it is necessary to trap $7.5 - 1.3 = 6.2$ liters of soot per 100 km.

oxygen, which is always present in excess in the diesel exhaust. Even in the absence of a catalyst, diesel soot only starts to be oxidized around 380°C, and combustion only reaches an appreciable rate at about 550 to 600°C, becoming total around 700°C [97]. These temperature conditions are only exceptionally encountered in the exhaust of a diesel vehicle. Fig. 12.12 shows that, without a catalyst, the temperature required for combustion is only reached at maximum speed and full load.

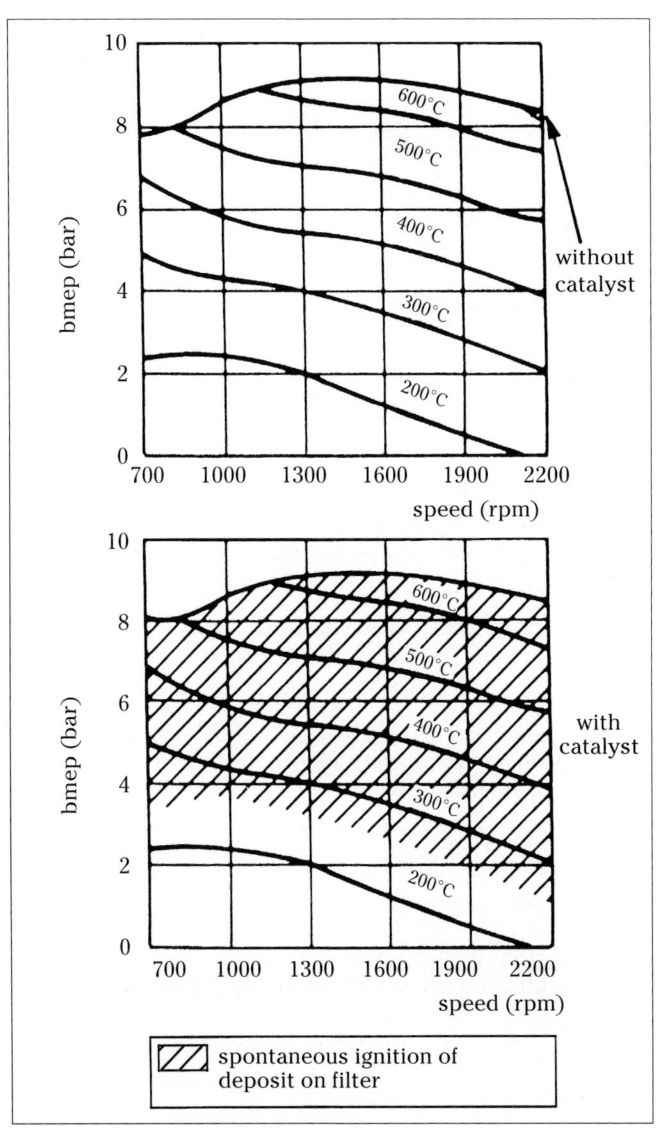


Combustion area cross-hatched

**Fig 12.12** Exhaust isotherms in a charge/speed diagram [97]

In the presence of a catalyst, the ignition temperature can be lowered to 170°C (incipient oxidation around 210 to 260°C), thus reaching an oxidation rate from 360°C that would otherwise only be obtained at 600°C without catalyst (Fig. 12.13).

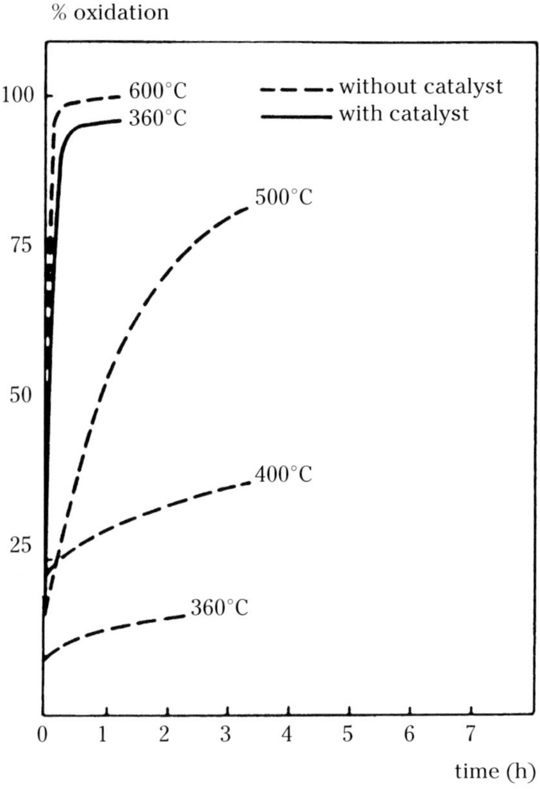


**Fig 12.13** Oxidation of diesel soot alone or mixed with an active phase (Pa-9), Thermogravimetry versus time [97] (*Procatalyse* Document)

## 12.14.1 Traps

The combustion of soot, even if facilitated by the addition of catalysts, remains a slow process, and its duration always exceeds the particulate residence time in the exhaust system. For kinetic reasons, it is therefore necessary to eliminate this soot in two steps: filtration and trapping of the particulates in the first phase, and then, once the critical mass sufficient to maintain combustion is reached, ignition and combustion in a second phase, making sure that the mass to be burned is not so large as to result in temperatures incompatible with the thermal resistance of the trap [98]. These traps must demonstrate high trapping efficiency combined with minimum pressure drops and good strength at elevated temperatures.

Non-woven felts must be discarded, because they collect the soot on the surface in the form of an impervious cake, rapidly causing prohibitive pressure drops [345]. Table 12.3 lists the characteristics of a number of available traps [370].

**Table 12.3** Diesel particulate traps [370]

| Type of trap | Efficiency (%) | Advantages | Drawbacks |
|---|---|---|---|
| ceramic monolith | 60 to 90 | • high efficiency<br>• moderate cost<br>• can be covered with catalyst | • moderate $\Delta P$<br>• high $\Delta P$ gradient<br>• subject to thermal shoc cracking |
| aluminated metallic sponge (precious metal catalyst) | 50 to 80 | • low $\Delta P$ gradient<br>• self-regenerable<br>• reduces HC, CO and odor | • moderate $\Delta P$<br>• low efficiency, especially at high speed<br>• produces sulfates |
| ceramic foam | 30 to 75 | • good thermal shock resistance<br>• can be covered with catalyst | • very high $\Delta P$<br>• regeneration difficult<br>• low efficiency |
| ceramic fiber sponge | >75 | • very high efficiency<br>• good thermal shock resistance | • fiber disintegration<br>• high $\Delta P$<br>• high $\Delta P$ gradient<br>• large volume and weight |
| woven silica fiber coil filter | >75 | • high efficiency<br>• low $\Delta P$<br>• good thermal shock resistance | • large volume demand |

#### 12.14.1.1 Trapping mechanisms

Three processes take place in any filter in the trapping of particulates belonging to an aerosol: diffusion, interception, and inertial impaction [27 and 360]. In Fig. 12.14, particle **1** has a low enough mass to follow a random route due to Brownian motion. This leads to its capture when in contact with the surface of a fiber or with a pore. Particle **2** is still small enough to have no inertia, but already too large to be sensitive to bombardment by the molecules of the gas (Brownian motion). It therefore follows the gas streams, and is captured if the gas stream falls into the diameter of a fiber or in the wall of a pore. Particle **3** is large, and has significant inertia, so that, when the stream to which it belongs approaches a wall or a fiber and is deflected, it leaves the stream to impact on the solid surface. The latter mechanism may trap the type **2** particles in the meanders of the pores.

These three trapping mechanisms are involved to a different extent according to the particle size, speed of the aerosol, and diameter of the fibers and pores. Diffusion predominates for small particles in a slow gas stream, with long residence time.

Interception is more effective when the ratio of particle size to pore or fiber size increases. Inertial impaction is predominant for high flow rates conveying larger or denser particles. As a rule, the particle deposition improves the trapping efficiency for particles that subsequently reach the trap [119]. However, excessive accumulation before regeneration can cause unforeseen detachment of the adsorbed particles (*blow off*) [20] with the consequence of the corresponding emissions [138].

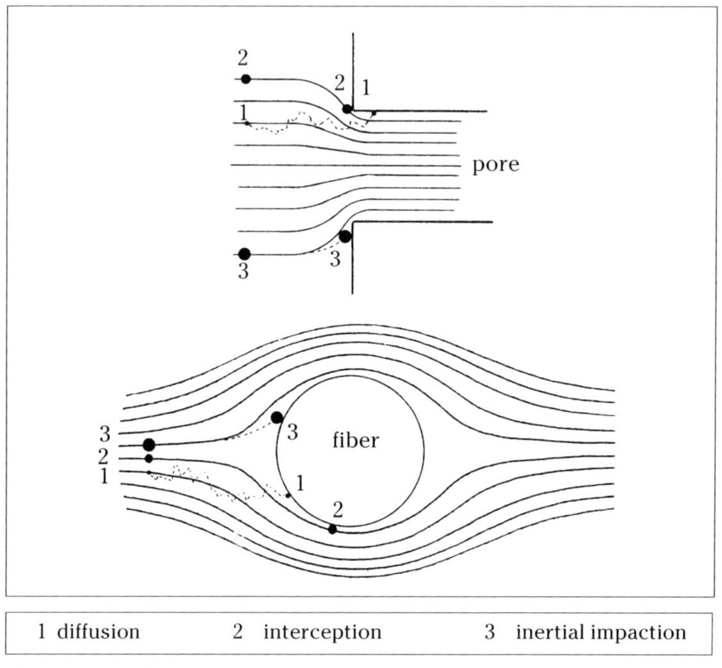


| 1 diffusion | 2 interception | 3 inertial impaction |
|---|---|---|

**Fig 12.14** Thermal reactor for oxidation of CO and HC [306]

It must also be pointed out that particulate traps can reduce unburnt HC emissions, especially if the trap is loaded with soot, but not immediately after a trap has just been regenerated [119]. Thus a 20% decrease in HC emissions has been detected before regeneration, and ≈12% of the PAH emitted by the engine could remain trapped on the soot [214].

The hydrocarbons thus adsorbed are first partly desorbed (20% of SOF at low charge and 7% at medium charge) when the trap temperature rises at the start of regeneration [212] and the rest (14% at low charge and 25% of SOF at medium charge) is then burned with the soot during the regeneration of the trap. However, this property depends strongly on the trap operating temperature. A transition from 145 to 230°C at the trap inlet reduces the trapping efficiency from 87 to 66% on volatiles, thus increasing by a factor of 2.5 the quantity of volatile material passing through the filter, with a possible tenfold increase in the volume of inhalable small particles (0.007 to 0.023 μm) in comparison with operation without a trap [319].

Among the PAH, it is mainly the heavy products ($>C_{20}$) that are retained on non-catalytic traps once their temperature exceeds 160°C. The trap has little effect at low charge, but a reduction of nearly 90% of PAH contents has been observed at medium charge [39 and 212]. Although, on the whole, the trap reduces total mutagenicity [220], which includes the majority of direct mutagenic products, the specific mutagenicity of the fraction of particulates not retained on the filter is higher [70 and 100]. This occurs because a large proportion of nitrogen and oxygen derivatives can be formed due to the longer residence time of the PAH hydrocarbons in the presence of nitrating and oxidizing agents contained in the exhaust [241]. On the other hand, the trap reduces the mutagenicity of the compounds remaining in the gas phase. A catalytic trap decreases the odor level [144]. At low charge, the adsorption of the hydrocarbons by the soot deposits in the trap helps to reduce the odor emitted (50% lower concentration at the olfactory thresholds) [289]. This effect disappears at medium and high charge. However, the subjective perception of the odor is different in the presence and in the absence of a trap [284].

Special traps, such as absorption on an oil surface, have been tested [224]. However, entrainment of the oil by the gas stream usually leads to an increase in the mass of particulates measured. Tests with plasma generation in an oil mist totally eliminate the soot in the oil, also reducing $NO_x$ and $SO_x$ at the rate of 70% [341]. The energy consumed is prohibitive and the problem of treating the residues collected has not yet been solved.

#### 12.14.1.2 Monolithic traps

This is the system currently most closely investigated and the most developed. These traps are derived from the supports used in three-way catalysts (*flow through monolith type*) by plugging one channel out of two, alternately at each end, in order to force the aerosol through the walls between the channels (*wall flow monolith*). Thus, cylindrical traps with total filtration have been obtained, which display excellent filtration efficiency (Fig. 12.15). Another rectangular type of filter monolith is made by the parallel assembly of cordierite plates with inlet holes for the gas to be filtered and outlet slits for purified gas [236 and 343].

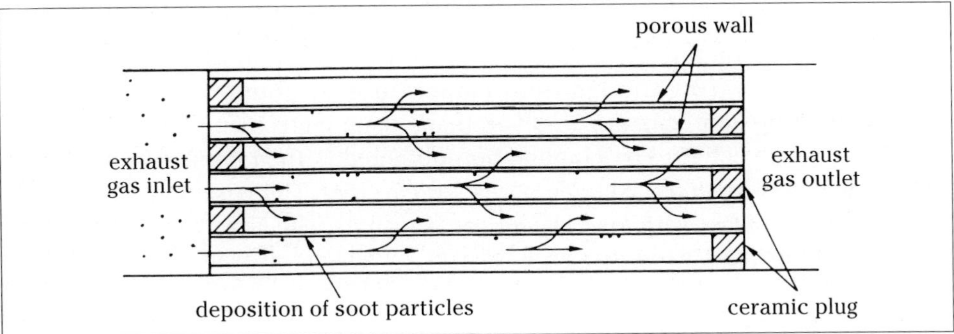


**Fig 12.15** Structure of monolith filters [98]

The porous walls obtained by extrusion have a smooth surface with a wide distribution of fine and irregular pores [27]. These pores, ranging in size from 10 to 35 μm on the average, are tortuous but do not all terminate on both sides of the wall. This type of filter is more suitable for low flow rates that are ideal for diffusion capture. Their good capture efficiency (over 60% and usually 80 to 90% retention rate) is obtained at the cost of fairly high pressure drops, increasing with the filter load. However, structures with low porosity (13 μm) and high filtration efficiency (90 to 95%) exhibit lower thermal shock resistance in endurance than more open structures (33 and 21 mm) that are less efficient (60 to 85%) [113]. The pressure drops can be minimized by the use of large trapping surfaces [324]. These large frontal areas, which are essential on trucks and buses, can be obtained by the combination of small monoliths cemented by a paste that is converted to cordierite when baked [107]. Despite the excellent trapping efficiency, very small particles (3.2 to 5.6 nm) may be found downstream of the filter; these particles have been reformed by nucleation from the volatile fraction [32 and 319].

The filter volume generally used is at least equal to the engine cylinder displacement [193], and for trucks, where size considerations are less critical, sometimes double the engine cylinder displacement to limit pressure drops to a reasonable level (about 10 kPa). The length and diameter of the filter are generally similar [320]. A large filter on an urban bus makes it possible to regenerate only once daily, upon returning to the garage [93].

#### 12.14.1.3 Ceramic foam traps

These traps consist of ceramic foams made from silicon carbide (SiC) [27] or cordierite [244 and 324]. They exhibit a fairly narrow distribution of wide and virtually circular pores, 250 to 500 μm in diameter, winding in depth, with few non-through channels. These filters appear to be more suitable for large flows. They offer low pressure drops and exploit the impaction trapping principle. Their retention rates are lower (60 to 70%) [20 and 351] than those of monoliths, but they are uncloggable. They can be installed in the form of filter cartridges. To reduce the pressure drops even further and improve the distribution of the mass of soot collected, non-through channels are provided in the cylindrical volume of ceramic foam [88]. This structure ensures more uniform propagation of the flame during regeneration, lowering the ignition temperature by about 50°C. The trap is manufactured by impregnating a polyurethane foam matrix with a ceramic paste (cordierite paste) [369]. The combination obtained is then calcined to obtain a cordierite foam with about 20 to 30 pores per $cm^2$ [85]. The retention rates of this type of trap are higher with lower linear gas velocities. The large volumes required make them more suitable for trucks and buses, on which the available space is less restricted [88].

Microporous foams have been made from cordierite matrices, which are then reinforced by mullite. These compositions are then equipped downstream with membranes, also of cordierite/mullite, designed to prevent the re-entrainment of the particles during excessive overloads of the filter before regeneration. They have an efficiency of 70 to 75% [138 and 139].

A similar technique uses steel wool pressed on a die [134]. The filtration properties depend here on the size of the steel wires and their pressing. Steel wool filters covered with alumina have also been prepared [333]. They are made from wires of Fecralloy or knit stainless steel, sometimes flattened and covered with wash-coat [76].

#### 12.14.1.4 Non-woven fiber traps

These traps consist of ceramic fibers wet calendered and bonded by a resin [27]. This structure has a very large number of fine pores (about 10 μm), distributed over a rather rough surface, with a very deep winding path. The filtration efficiency is higher with finer fibers, but at the cost of the strength of the filter in regeneration conditions [318]. Some models are prepared from paper of mullite fibers corrugated and wound on a die, yielding a structure with high porosity and high filtration efficiency [324]. However, the mechanical strength is much lower than that of extruded monoliths. Like the latter, they are more suitable for diffusion capture with low flow rates. The fibers are also used in the form of filter cartridges prepared by stacking several layers of non-woven ceramics 10 to 12 mm thick on a steel die drilled with holes [135]. This device displays better thermal shock resistance than monoliths. These thermal shocks can occur while idling after initiating regeneration when the filter, which is still not cooled, can reach prohibitive temperatures [120], or on the expressway when the accelerator pedal is released with the engine running at full speed, after a period of high acceleration to overtake [77]. The fibers selected are of silica or mixed aluminum and silicon oxides [120]. Before installation, they can be impregnated with refractory inorganic compounds. These dies lined with their fibers are assembled in a tube bundle placed in a casing that replaces the muffler, and are traversed by the exhaust gas from the outside to the inside [122]. The ceramic fibers undergo special treatment designed to make them bristle with a multitude of ultra-thin hairs to improve particle retention [194]. This type of trap has an average particulate retention rate of more than 80% on a transient cycle (Chapter 6).

Traps have also been made from steel sponges lined with $\gamma$ alumina [232]. The metal selected must resist oxidation in an oxidizing atmosphere at about 1000°C. The efficiency of this type of trap ranges between 68 and 80%.

#### 12.14.1.5 Electrostatic trapping

This technique is widely used in industrial dust separation. By capturing, coagulating, and re-entraining fine particles, the use of this technique results in a relatively high recovery efficiency in a cyclone located downstream. To avoid generating new pollutants by the action of an additional electric field (corona effect), which is applied upstream to charge the particles, it is necessary to use only the natural charge of the particles, which is mainly carried by carbon more than by SOF [179]. It has been demonstrated that more than 80% of the mass of particulates emitted is charged, each particle capable of carrying 1 to 5 elementary charges, either positive or negative [180]. For engines emitting mainly dry particulates, the process should eliminate 70 to 90% of the particulates. A voltage of 4000 V is applied to a stack of short tubes placed in parallel, which doubles the aeraulic diameter of the particles [346] and multiplies by 100 the average mass diameter of the particles re-entrained downstream of the agglomerator [180]. In addition to its low efficiency, this system raises practical problems due to the short-circuits caused by carbon deposits on the electrodes [224]. Electrostatic trapping also presents the drawback already mentioned of not dealing with the accumulated soot. The proposed solution of re-injecting the agglomerated particles into the engine air supply has not yet proved its feasibility [180]. In the automotive field, this trapping raises technical and safety problems due to the very high voltages required. These reasons have led to the virtually total abandonment of research in this area [64].

### 12.14.2 Trap regeneration

To remove the soot accumulated on the traps and especially to reduce the back-pressure generated by the deposits, it is necessary to burn the particles by using the excess oxygen present in the exhaust, either permanently or intermittently (depending on the back-pressure acceptable by the engine: 10 to 15 kPa). The combustion of the trapped soot must be conducted so as to be as fast and as complete as possible, but without incurring any risk of cracking the ceramic traps by excessive overheating. Accordingly, this demands a sound compromise between the light-off temperature, the oxygen concentration, the gas flow rate, and the mass of accumulated particulates. Regenerations carried out while idling (low flow rate) and at low soot loads are rapid and hence advantageous [314].

Two possibilities are available for this regeneration [283].

- The deposits can be heated to the ignition temperature of soot, between 550 and 600°C. The gases can be raised to this temperature by several means [125, 266 and 327]:
  - by running at full charge and high speed
  - by delaying injection
  - by pre-heating the intake air
  - by bypassing the turbo-charger and the downstream cooler [214]
  - by an electric resistance heater placed upstream of the trap
  - by a diesel or gas burner also placed upstream, fed by an air pump
  - by the same burners using excess oxygen present in the exhaust as comburent
  - by throttling the intake to increase the exhaust temperature

- by throttling the exhaust to increase the back-pressure and hence the exhaust temperature
- by a catalytic converter placed upstream of the trap, in which the exothermicity of the CO and HC oxidation reaction heats the effluent gases [186]: this heat input can be increased by altering the injection to increase the CO and unburnt HC content [371]
- by injection of combustible hydrocarbons upstream of the trap

- The soot ignition temperature can be lowered to about 250°C by means of catalysts:
  - placed on the trap
  - dissolved in the diesel
  - injected intermittently upstream of the trap

Intake throttling is one of the most effective means to raise the temperature of the trap [125], but many of the above methods can be combined in practice. The combustion of soot temporarily generates increased CO emissions (+70% for regeneration in the FTP cycle) [327], which generally remain lower than the regulation limits [121], and increased HC emissions due to the temporary evaporation of the adsorbed hydrocarbons that are released by the heating of the soot before combustion [121]. However, if two traps are used in parallel, these hydrocarbon emissions can be reburned in the combustion chamber by mixing the effluents from the regenerating trap with the exhaust recycled in the EGR circuit [310]. Yet the contribution of emissions due to regeneration does not significantly change the overall emissions [210]. Initiation by burner adds further pollutants. Progress has been achieved by reducing the dead volumes between the shutoff valve and the burner nozzle [361]. In this case, regeneration during an FTP cycle temporarily causes a 25 to 50% increase in CO and HC, but distributed over the entire period, this corresponds to about 8% of the limit values. Regeneration while idling does not alter the HC and $NO_x$ emissions normally obtained while idling, but temporarily increases the CO emissions tenfold [53].

Trap regeneration by these processes thus helps to obtain a service life on trucks and buses of up to 100,000 to 150,000 km [119]. After this period of time, however, the trap must be replaced because of the irreversible increase in the pressure drop due to plugging by incombustible materials (for example, mineral ash). This ash originates both in the metallic additives in the lubricant and the sulfur in the fuel. To ensure the required trap life, it is therefore necessary to use ash-free lubricants and low-sulfur fuels. In a 3000 h test, the trap accumulates 1.2 kg of incombustible product with a lubricant containing 1.6% ash and a fuel containing 0.21% sulfur. This mass drops to 65 g with an ash-free lubricant and a 0.03% sulfur fuel [30].

It also appears that it is not always advantageous to have a filter with a large particulate trapping capacity before an excessive pressure drop requires its regeneration. In this case, in fact, the size of the mass of soot to be burned risks demanding excessively long regeneration times [138], and generating excessive temperatures that are detrimental to the mechanical strength of the trap [120]. The large capacity of the filter is also accompanied by an excessively high inertia of the system, which is unfavorable to rapid initiation of combustion. Similarly, excessively thick connecting pipes between the engine and the trap are detrimental to the speed of ignition of the soot during regeneration [281]. Since the combustion rate drops progressively as the reaction advances, traps are not generally cleaned completely to their initial state to avoid excessively long regeneration [245].

On turbo-charged engines, to keep the filter at the highest possible temperature and to prevent cooling by expansion in the turbo-charger, the filter is generally placed between the engine and the turbine [1 and 282]. However, this raises the risk of breaking the turbine blades in the case of attrition of the monolith. This arrangement also raises difficulties in transient conditions, where the thermal inertia of the ceramic trap hampers the acceleration response of the turbo-charger. This can be overcome by dividing the mass of the particulate trap by four [172]. This is why some manufacturers place the trap at the exit of the turbo-charger [128], sometimes with a back-pressure valve at the turbo outlet before the trap to initiate its regeneration (see below) [336].

#### 12.14.2.1 Thermal regeneration

Compared with the other regeneration techniques, thermal regeneration raises problems of thermal stability. These problems are attenuated by using traps with low thermal expansion coefficients [103]. During successive combustions, these traps are subject to high-temperature fatigue combined with vibration fatigue [105]. The exhaust flow rate also influences the thermal level of the catalyst support. A high flow rate cools the support at the time of combustion, but could prevent combustion from initiating. Doubling the flow rate thus increases soot accumulation by 40% without any risk of thermal fracture [181]. Increasing the average pore size also increases the supportable peak temperature and the level of soot accumulation [181].

Thermal regeneration demands a sufficient temperature and oxygen content to burn the soot particles. A higher temperature is required with a lower $O_2$ content: 570°C for 6% $O_2$ and 750°C for 2% $O_2$ [271]. This minimum temperature of 570°C is due to the activation energy of the soot ignition reaction (Fig. 12.16).

With turbo-charged engines, the higher residual oxygen content in the exhaust causes lower ignition temperatures than in naturally aspirated engines [282]. During regeneration, the engine operating conditions should not be suddenly changed. For instance, sudden braking, sudden idling, or coast down could reduce the cooling by decreasing the gas flow. The increase in the oxygen content also favors combustion, and this can cause cracking of the trap [245]. Systems such as a trap bypass, which functions during excessive temperatures at the trap exit (also reached at full charge in uphill driving), must be provided in this case [277]. If need be, this system also makes it possible to restore the maximum torque, which is reduced by progressive

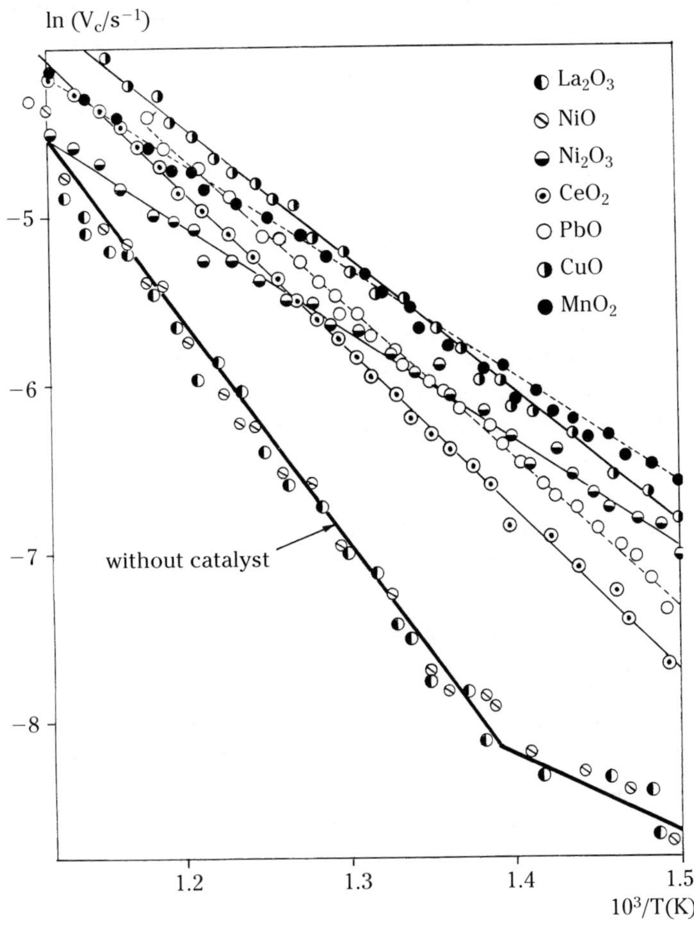


**Fig 12.16** Apparent combustion rates, Combustion in $O_2$ of soot from α-methylnaphthalene ($PO_2$ = 21 kPa) [65]

clogging of the trap [276]. Conversely, in deceleration, shutting off the fuel feed brings pure and cold air to the trap, which is suddenly cooled. To prevent this from happening, a bypass valve actuated by releasing the accelerator pedal helps to maintain the trap temperature [264] (this action is inhibited while idling).

Furthermore, difficulties in propagating combustion may occur with monoliths. Once the first soot has been burned in the front area of the trap, the superheated combustion gases tend to cross the walls that are thus liberated instead of licking and igniting the soot further downstream. These hot gases could melt the downstream part of the trap, which is still loaded with soot on the other side of the wall [128].

One method to overcome this drawback is to reverse the gas streams during regeneration (Fig. 12.17). In this case, the hot gases first cross the wall and are then heated by the combustion of the first soot, which are now located downstream of the trap when it is in filtration operation in a place where they are found in larger quantities than upstream [168]. They then lick the soot not yet burned that is located 'upstream'. This technique demands a slightly higher thermal energy for initiation, because the filter wall must first be raised to the ignition temperature. In the reverse system, for example, it takes 48 s instead of 27 s to reach 650°C [128]. This process helps to shorten the time required for regeneration and, by blowing the air necessary for combustion in countercurrent flow, it simultaneously eliminates any mineral ash that may have accumulated on the filter walls [168].

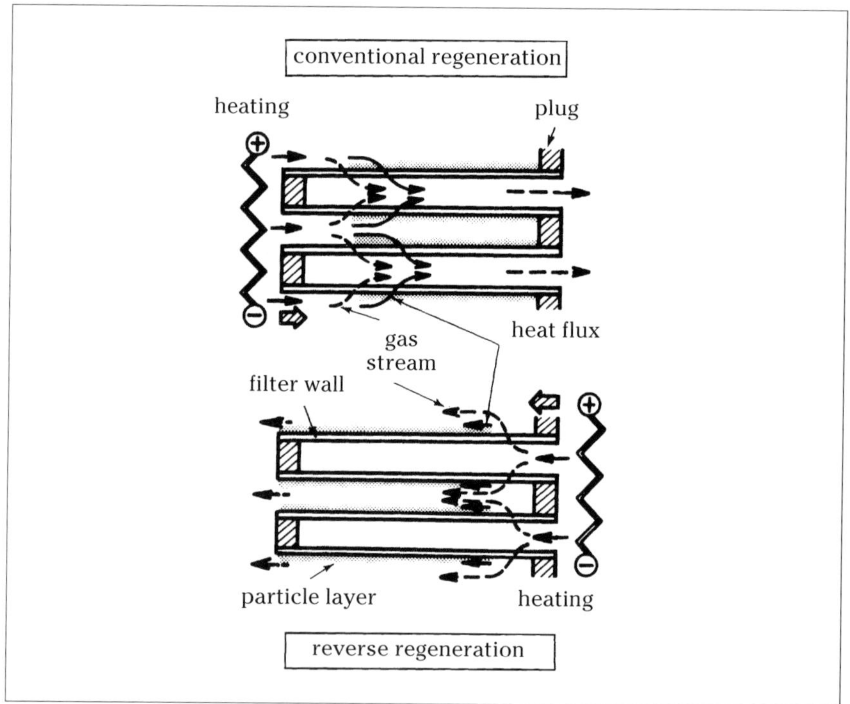


**Fig 12.17** Conventional and reverse regeneration [128]
Reprinted with permission © 1990 *Society of Automotive Engineers Inc*

*A. Initiation by burner*

Burners fed with propane and diesel have been developed and tested [327], with ignition by spark or by catalysis [232]. Burners installed on coaches for air-conditioning or heating of the coolant for cold-weather starting [96] have thus been used to trigger regeneration [114 and 353]. A heating capacity of about 15 kW appears to be sufficient for a 12 liter ceramic trap [239]. Several types of arrangements have been developed: trap bypass during regeneration [25]; two traps placed in parallel,

one in service and the second in regeneration [325]; and without bypass but with burner in series in front of the trap to be regenerated. The first two alternatives require corresponding valves [224]. The two traps in parallel can be operated simultaneously outside regeneration periods [114, 152 and 239] and the initiation of combustion can be further facilitated by using traps with a catalyst deposit and low sulfur diesel [96]. The burner placed in-line does not require a bypass, but its operation is complicated by the fact that it must operate in very different engine conditions causing consumption that is higher than with the burner with bypass (3.3% overconsumption instead of 1.8%) [305]. The in-line burner must raise the entire exhaust flow to the regeneration temperature of about 540°C. Consequently, it is more appropriate to the case of the urban bus which regenerates its trap on completion of its daily service [93]. With an in-line burner using excess oxygen in the exhaust, both as a comburent and to burn the soot, the burner can only be ignited with reduced torque output from the engine [199]. By contrast, the burner with bypass operates in conditions that are virtually independent of the engine operating conditions. It heats the air conveyed by a pump, which is used for the combustion of the soot, to the ignition temperature of the soot [55]. To avoid excessively high temperature peaks during soot combustion, the thermal power of the burner is reduced once the temperature of 750°C has been reached in the trap, while maintaining the comburent air flow rate [325]. With a truck, this solution enables it to return easily to its home base in case of damage to the trapping and regeneration system [320]. This device is also energy-saving: a 3 kW burner with an air pump delivering 7 $m^3/h$ suffices, whereas an in-line burner would demand 23 kW with a 20 $m^3/h$ pump [305]. Swirl chamber burners are generally selected for their compactness [205].

The system with a bypass naturally gives rise to unfiltered emissions during the regeneration period. For a vehicle emitting 0.3 g/km of particulates with regeneration every 150 km, the emissions according to the FTP cycle would be an average of 8% higher. During the regeneration period (estimated at 9 min), the instantaneous particulate emissions would rise by 26%, and CO emissions by 17% [305].

The propane burner includes the actual torch, a one-liter propane tank sufficient for 80,000 km, an air pump, and a buffer air tank [225]. The air pump can be discarded in some cases if the residual oxygen content in the exhaust is sufficient [360]. To facilitate the initiation of combustion, a rotary nozzle actuated by an electric motor enables the flame to sweep the whole frontal area of the trap to be regenerated and to raise it to between 900 and 1100°C in a few seconds. It is nevertheless necessary to keep the air supply to the burner on permanently to prevent the particles from fouling the spark plug and gas feed lines. Even if the burner uses the excess air in the exhaust, a small permanent air feed is necessary to keep the nozzle clean ($\approx$600 liters/h) [199]. The corresponding air pump may demand a power input from 0.7 to 3 kW [224]. The same sweep system is used for a diesel fuel burner, which also requires compressed air atomization of the fuel that is supplied by a low-pressure pump [320] and pre-heating of the comburent air to facilitate ignition. The nozzle is flushed by an air flow when not in operation to prevent possible clogging by particles [361]. The burner must also have adjustable power (by a ratio of 4) and, for an in-line system, it must remain unaffected by the pressure pulses generated by the engine [93].

The burner can be triggered when the back-pressure limit is reached [55], which is set according to the gas flow rate through the trap, as measured by a Venturi [239]. It can also be controlled by a timer, based on the loading time of the trap to be regenerated, if the running conditions are reproducible and perfectly known [114]. On urban buses, with engines idling a great deal of the time, once the back-pressure limit has been exceeded, measures have been taken to ensure that the burner is not ignited with the engine idling [135] or in deceleration. In this case, a glow plug is powered for 40 s to initiate regeneration. A safer system to guarantee ignition of the burner and thus to avoid additional pollution is to use a high-energy spark plug [361], fed with 14 kV for 10 $\mu$s with a 2 mm air gap. However, outside periods of actuation, this ignition plug must be protected by a mask to avoid deposits on the electrodes. If, during regeneration, the driver has to re-accelerate the vehicle, the burner is then switched off, and regeneration, which lasts about 8 to 10 min, resumes at the next idling [78].

Although complicated and expensive, the burner regeneration system is generally used on trucks because, in this case, regeneration can be achieved in all conditions. Above all, this is the system that least penalizes fuel consumption, a very important factor for long-distance transport [320].

### *B. Initiation by electric heating*

Several electric systems have been tested: cigarette lighter type spiral resistors, diesel glow plugs, and resistance wires applied to the trap to be regenerated [326]. The first were rapidly abandoned, and the plugs, even introduced in threes uniformly spaced in the monolith, often proved to be incapable of initiating combustion without the addition of a catalyst to the fuel. As in the case of the burner, the trap is bypassed during regeneration; the flow is cut off, the resistor first raises the trap to the desired temperature, and then, with the valve partly open, a portion of the exhaust gas is used to burn the soot [20]. At the beginning of the operation, to prevent exhaust leaks from cooling the trap while it is being heated, the tightness of the bypass valve is very important [21].

To save electric power taken from the battery, the necessary resistors are placed as near as possible (a few mm) upstream of the filter. They are more efficient if in direct contact with the filter, but are damaged faster by oxidation [167]. They can be subdivided into elements that are uniformly distributed and activated in succession [128 and 214]. Wires consuming about 400 W for a few seconds are, during operation, covered with soot that burns first and initiates combustion [383]. The maximum temperatures reached during combustion of the soot ($\approx$1000°C) can be lowered to around 650°C by using diesel with additives (80 mg/liter of Mn+20 mg/liter of Cu) [358].

To improve combustion efficiency, a flow distributor [20] of perforated plate is placed upstream of sheathed spiral resistors adjoining the front side of the trap [28]. In this case, it is necessary to input 5.5 W/cm$^2$ of frontal surface area for the monolith being regenerated, which may demand at least 3 kW for several minutes for a 30 cm diameter trap (about 130 A at 24 V). For a 127 mm diameter trap, six elements covering 60 cm$^2$ and consuming 60 W/cm$^2$ ensure initiation [128] in six times 30 s. Placed on a trap regenerated in a bypass, a 3 kW resistor with energy supplied by a 6 m$^3$/h air fan is sufficient to initiate regeneration [305]. Electrical initiation of regeneration proves to be advantageous for fork-lift trucks because it can be carried out with the engine idling at the end of daily service in a special regeneration room [231]. Plug-in filters are also available for rapid dismantling and regeneration in an auxiliary hot air furnace [39].

One technique available to lower the instantaneous electric power demand is sequential regeneration of the trap [289]. To initiate combustion, each channel of a monolith trap demands about 10 W on a resistor inserted into the channel. On a bus, for example, the trap is divided into six segments each alternately consuming about 1300 W for 40 s, a power level compatible with the capacity of the battery; combustion then continues for 120 s.

In another configuration associated with the rectangular monoliths mentioned earlier, and regenerated by blowing countercurrent air, the electrical initiation resistor (with Inconel shielding) is placed in a casing that is located at the base of the monolith and which collects the soot entrained by blowing. This technique helps to avoid the thermal shocks to which the monolith will be subjected during combustion and only requires a low-power resistor (200 W instead of 1 kW) [236 and 343].

Regeneration on a truck could thus mean an additional 1.8% of consumption at full charge, and on a bus, 5% on the ADB cycle (Chapter 6) with a 4 kW resistor [209]. The initiation of regeneration is then automatically actuated from a threshold value that depends on the pressure drop, the engine flow, and the trap temperature. An electric fan delivering 300 liters/min simultaneously conveys the combustion air [28].

A system for electric pre-heating of the intake air (24 kW at 24 V for 5 min) may suffice to raise the temperature of the gas reaching the trap to 520°C. However, it is only valid while idling, when the intake air rate is minimal [358].

### C. *Heating by dielectric losses*

Electric resistance heating (as with burner systems) has the drawback of uselessly heating the thermal mass of the monolith, whereas it is much more important to raise the soot itself to the ignition temperature. It was accordingly decided to try to exploit the properties of microwaves for selective heating of the soot, which absorbs the waves, with an energy efficiency of between 60 and 70% and at a frequency of about 2.45 GHz. This is achieved without heating the cordierite ceramic, which is practically transparent to microwaves [92] due to its low dielectric constant and its low dielectric loss factor [366]. In addition, the metal casing of the trap allows confinement of the microwaves, preventing their escape to the exterior and reflecting them on the trap. A magnetron is therefore placed upstream of the trap and connected to it by an axial waveguide. During regeneration, the exhaust flow is partly bypassed, the magnetron supplies a power of 1 kW for 400 to 600 s, to raise the soot to the requisite temperature, and the exhaust flow is then restored for combustion. To improve the uniformity of heating (carried out in a domestic oven by rotation of the target or of the emitter), attempts were made to place microwave receivers at regular intervals on the upstream side of the monolith. The choice was ferrites, which have good dielectric properties and high magnetic losses. Their magnetic susceptibility is also nullified by heating when they reach the Curie point, offering greater safety in the case of overheating. Thus the conventional ceramic plugs placed upstream of the monolith, obstructing one channel out of two (Fig. 12.12), are replaced by a cordierite-based ceramic composition blended with a ferrite [366]. These plugs allow the initiation of combustion of the soot deposited in each channel and power is thermostatically cut off when the Curie point is reached. This system is currently under investigation by automobile manufacturers [18].

*D. Electrostatic initiation*

An annular ceramic monolith open at both ends (of the three-way catalyst type), fitted at its center with an electrostatic charge electrode (Fig. 12.18), would allow continuous combustion of the soot produced by a diesel engine [51]. Efficiency of 90% would be possible without excessive pressure drop, because the ceramic is open at both ends. The voltage applied is about 20 to 25 kV (applied to the plugs) and the power required is about 2 W per engine kW, or 200 W for the average automobile. Even in the case of a retention defect and combustion during sudden accelerations, there would always be some agglomeration of the particles making their atmospheric dispersion more difficult. The mechanism involved is still not clearly understood and it appears that negatively-charged oxygen facilitates the oxidation of the soot at lower temperature.

*E. Intake throttling*

By throttling the engine intake, the fuel/air ratio is increased, making it possible to reach sufficient exhaust temperatures in a wider range of engine operating conditions than with operation at full charge. This is because throttling reduces the pressure in the intake manifold, thus introducing additional pumping work. To offset the loss of power, the tendency is to increase the quantity of fuel injected, thus increasing the exhaust temperature [224]. However, a sufficient oxygen content (2 to 5%) must be preserved in the exhaust to prevent the excessive formation of smoke and particulates [360]. The regeneration rate first increases with the temperature rise, but above a peak ($\approx$600), the combustion rate remains independent of temperature [245]. Once combustion has been initiated, the throttle valve is opened fully to obtain a sufficient air flow to maintain combustion.

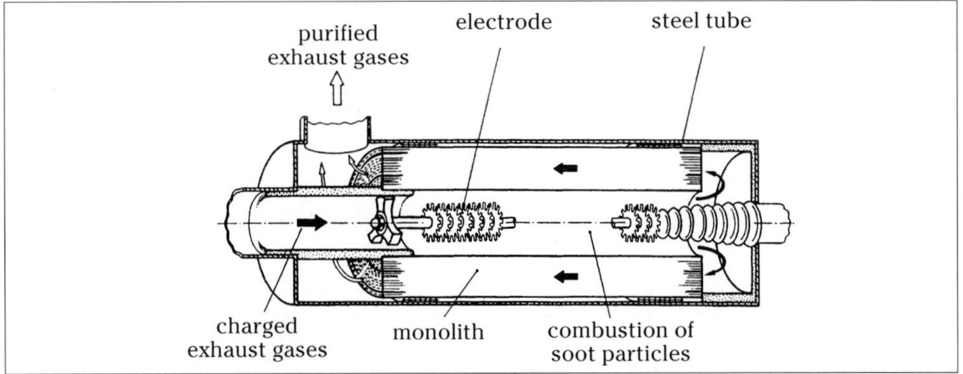


**Fig 12.18** Electrostatic initiation diesel trap [51]

*F. Exhaust throttling*

This process increases the amount of residual gases in the combustion chamber and generates higher temperatures in the chamber at the start of the compression phase, with a decrease in volumetric efficiency and of shaft horsepower, and an increase in pumping work in the cycle that is dissipated in the form of heat in the exhaust. This heat is added to that due to the loss of efficiency in these conditions [278]. This process occurs naturally due to progressive plugging of the pores of the trap, which both increases the back-pressure and decreases the gas flow cooling the trap [382]. A loaded trap decreases the power available due to the back-pressure, so that, to maintain speed, the engine is subject to a higher specific charge, giving rise to a higher exhaust temperature and increased consumption ($\approx$8%). A properly loaded trap can thus be regenerated at about 30 km/h [1]. Mounted on a truck, this system, combined with the bypass, can be actuated by an upper back-pressure limit that opens the bypass while awaiting a sufficient exhaust temperature (for example, high acceleration, uphill driving). The valve then closes and sends the hot exhaust to the trap to initiate combustion [346]. However, the back-pressure established cannot exceed a maximum, at the risk of decreasing the vehicle's driveability. As in the case of the burner, it may be necessary to eliminate the effect of the back-pressure valve in unfavorable conditions (prolonged idling in dense traffic), and electronic regulation is accordingly necessary to avoid jerky driving, due to the closure of the valve when the temperature required for regeneration is insufficient [336]. At the same time, it is necessary to adjust the EGR valve as the back-pressure increases [327], and to modify the air/fuel ratio to recover a sufficient oxygen concentration to burn the soot [278]. It is also important to avoid reaching the smoke limit, and thus overload the traps [273] which could crack when combustion begins [272]. The butterfly valve is preferably installed upstream of the trap to avoid whistling in the exhaust when turned on [272]. Throttling is preferably carried out at zero charge to avoid causing excessive thermal loads on the components of the combustion chamber [278].

To prevent exhaust overheating during regeneration, the size of the orifice restricting the flow must be modulated according to the engine speed by controlling the position of the flap to keep the exhaust pressure constant. Depending on this position, the quantities of fuel injected must also be adjusted to limit the fuel/air ratio and to avoid smoke emissions [273]. The trap inlet temperature must be limited at the start of regeneration to 650°C to avoid overheating, which could damage the trap during combustion that starts at about 550°C [272]. During the few minutes that regeneration lasts, consumption rises 30%, but this means an overall extra consumption of less than 1%. This throttling system presents the drawback of being limited to naturally aspirated engines [64].

## 12.14.3 Catalytic regeneration

The use of catalysts is designed to reduce the soot ignition temperature. As mentioned earlier (Sections 10.6.1 and 11.2.5.1), metallic additives already reduce particulate emissions in the absence of a trap. Yet this effect is insufficient to meet the standards. For example, it has been claimed that emissions can be reduced 20% by adding 0.08% manganese to the fuel [382].

### 12.14.3.1 Catalytic traps

These catalytic traps, made from compressed steel fibers, have a lower retention rate than monoliths, especially at high speed [370]. The fibers are covered with a wash-coat impregnated with precious metals and behave like platinum oxidation catalysts. They allow regeneration around 350°C for naturally aspirated engines, and around 400°C for turbo-charged engines [42]. From 350°C, a temperature easily reached in high acceleration or uphill driving [370], they form sulfates [20] that increase the mass of particulates measured [270]. Thus, downstream of the trap on a transient cycle, the particulate mass found may be greater than that obtained without a trap and consists of 60% sulfates [386]. A tripling of sulfate emissions can be observed with this type of trap [76]. On the other hand, they offer the advantage of easily oxidizing the SOF fraction of the particulates, including the PAH [212] with 50 to 80% efficiency, and, if the exhaust temperature is sufficient (>200°C [380], around 80 to 90 km/h), they are self-cleaning without increasing the pressure drop [77]. Monolith traps impregnated with catalysts based on the platinum/vanadium/silver mixture have only succeeded in lowering the ignition temperature to 400 to 450°C [327]. On these types of trap, coating by non-precious metals lowers the light-off temperature by 80°C. Followed by a deposit of precious metals, this temperature drops to 380°C, with the additional removal of CO and unburnt HC [79]. Monoliths impregnated with transition metals, pure or mixed with precious metals, cut particulate emissions by a factor of 30, and only convert to sulfuric acid between 2 and 10% of the initial sulfur. In these conditions, the transition metals lower the light-off temperature to about 420°C [57]. In these conditions, a soot oxidation intermediate would be the $NO_2$ formed on the precious catalyst (especially $Pt/Al_2O_3$).

However, it is impossible to find an active catalyst for this reaction which does not strongly oxidize $SO_2$ to $SO_3$ [54].

Ceramic foams impregnated with catalysts are regenerated on a vehicle around 360°C and on buses and trucks slightly below 500°C with approximately 50% efficiency [244]. These cordierite foams containing a titanium oxide support impregnated with $CuCl_2-KCl-NH_4VO_3$ or with $CuCl_2-KCl-(NH_4)_6Mo_7O_{24}$ allow operation with continuous regeneration for an exhaust gas temperature of 460°C [369]. Similarly, catalytic coatings based on $V_2O_5$ lower the ignition temperature by 100°C [133].

Metal sponges impregnated with precious metals help to reduce emissions of particulates, PAH and their nitrogen derivatives, and the corresponding mutagenicity [377].

A system combining ceramic traps impregnated with precious metals, low-sulfur diesel and temperature maintenance of the trap by bypass in deceleration was reported to be detrimental to driveability and demands excessively long regeneration times [264].

### 12.14.3.2 Catalytic additives

During the progressive loading of the catalyst-impregnated traps with soot, the catalyst is gradually covered with soot and only the first layer of soot deposited remains in contact with the catalyst [360]. The catalyst is thus masked and cannot ensure the contact between oxygen and soot at its surface to initiate combustion. One way to overcome this drawback is to provide the catalyst at the right time, by placing it in the fuel, so that it is deposited simultaneously with the soot to facilitate the latter's ignition. The regeneration rates observed in this case are higher than those corresponding to the deposited catalyst [20].

Catalytic additives can either be dissolved in the fuel or added immediately upstream of the trap to be regenerated. In the former case, it is important to ensure that the combustion in the chamber preserves the catalytic properties needed. Moreover, the additives used must not cause wear of the engine or the emission of harmful unregulated pollutants such as heavy metals and halogenated acids [121]. The retention of additives in the form of ash in the traps avoids the dispersion of harmful elements such as manganese into the atmosphere (limited in California to 1 $\mu g/m^3$), but causes progressive clogging of the pores [320]. Thus it is found that, with 80 g/liter of Mn (which lowers the ignition temperature to about 370°C), the exhaust only discharges 94 $\mu g/m^3$ of Mn, more than 95% of the metal being retained on the trap, and 2.4% in the lubricant [57]. A large proportion ($\approx$ 85%) of the additive remains trapped in the form of oxides, and in these conditions it is estimated that, by adding 0.08% Mn to the fuel, the exhaust would contain emissions of about 1 to 1.5 mg/mile of Mn [383]. Contrary to lead, which tends to form an impervious layer of $PbSO_4$ on the surface of the trap [361], the Mn/Cu mixture tends to produce flaky, non-adhering ash, which does not increase the pressure drop of the trap, and which is not dispersed into the atmosphere [249]. Other measurements on diesels with Pb, Mn, Fe, and Ce added show that over 90% of the metal added remains trapped on the filter [235] (over 95% for Ni and Ci) [305].

The compounds tested include oxides of transition metals like NiO, $Ni_2O_3$, PbO, CuO, $MnO_2$, $CeO_2$, and $La_2O_3$. Table 12.4 gives a list of compounds added to the soot with their capacity to reduce the soot ignition temperature. While some compounds reduce the light-off temperature, they do not necessarily accelerate the soot combustion reaction. Fig. 12.16 shows the soot oxidation rates catalysed by different metallic oxides. The activity of $La_2O_3$ and NiO is virtually nil, while that of $CeO_2$ is still weak compared with CuO and $MnO_2$ [65].

**Table 12.4** Relative activity of different inorganic compounds added to carbon [254 and 360]

| Additive | Lowering of ignition temperature (°C) | Relative oxidation rate (1) |
|---|---|---|
| Na | 92 | 230 |
| Ca | 124 | 4 |
| Zn | 130 | – |
| Mn | 130 | 86,000 |
| Fe | 131 | – |
| K | 137 | – |
| $NH_4$ | 137 | – |
| $Sn^{2+}$ | 153 | – |
| Ni | 162 | – |
| Pb | 180 | 470,000 |
| Cu | 284 | 500 |
| Ba | – | 100 |
| Au | – | 240 |
| V | – | 340 |
| Ag | – | 1340 |
| Cs | – | 64,000 |

(1) By comparison with pure graphite.

Oxidation tests, followed by thermogravimetry, on soot obtained from diesels to which Ca, Ba, Fe, and Ni salts have been added, show that the reaction occurs in two steps, a first fast step below 500°C, and a second slower one. The metals act on the two oxidation steps. They lower the activation energy of the first step, and without altering that of the second step, they increase the reaction rate. Barium proves to be the most effective, followed by calcium and iron, with nickel having the weakest effect [243]. Note that the ash of diesel soot often naturally contains a low calcium content (up to 0.18% by mass) that originates in the lubricant additives [269], and this could contribute to the initiation of combustion. At the rate of 40 mg/liter [72], manganese helps to lower the ignition temperature by 65 to 80°C, and copper and lead help to lower it by 150°C [224]. Diesel fuel containing 0.13 g/liter of lead and 0.07 g/liter of copper allows regeneration at 190°C, corresponding to a lowering of 236°C [361]. With 66 mg/liter of metal (Cu or Ni) in octoate form, this temperature is reduced from 510 to between 280 and 310°C [305].

Manganese can play a catalytic role in the nitration of PAH [72] and thus increase the specific mutagenicity of SOF, although by retention in the trap the total mutagenicity is reduced. With diesels to which $4.83 \cdot 10^{-4}$ mol/liter of metal has been added, ignition temperatures have been reduced by 100°C for Cu and Fe, and by 40 to 60°C for Pb and Mn [235], compared with temperatures of between 415 and 520°C without catalyst. The additives also cut regeneration time in half.

The permanent use of additives in the fuel is a simple solution, but presents the drawbacks of uselessly adding the product outside regeneration periods, a product whose consumption and corresponding emissions should be minimized. Although lead remains totally trapped in the filter and substantially lowers the ignition temperature (by 170°C for 0.25 g/liter of diesel in the form of lead tetraethyl) [360], experiments with lead were discontinued for psychological reasons, at the time that it was banned from automotive gasolines [326]. Additives based on copper naphthenate can cause the precipitation of sludge in the fuel tanks [327], especially if storage duration exceeds two months, unless the fuel contains additives that deactivate the copper (additive containing 3.4% by mass of Cu [218] for a Cu concentration of 100 ppm) [362]. Mixtures of cerium and manganese have also proved to be advantageous [326]. However, these products tend to generate metallic deposits on the injection nozzles and glow plugs [192]. A soluble additive based on copper and manganese (34.4 mg/ml of Mn and 9.3 mg/ml of Cu) added at the rate of 0.1% by volume to diesel fuel lowers the light-off temperature from 600 to 420°C, and reduces particulate emissions by 70% at the outlet of the ceramic monolith; 99.8% of the Mn remains in the trap in the form of $MnSO_4$ and 97.8% of the Cu is also retained [192]. A fuel containing 80/20 mg/liter of Mn/Cu lowers the ignition temperature from 500 to 350°C. On mine machines tested according to the MTU cycle (Chapter 6), it thus allows continuous regeneration by stabilizing the back-pressure in the exhaust and by minimizing the thermal stresses on the trap [208].

For questions of long-term stability, it may be necessary to inject the additive into the fuel just before it enters the engine. This is done by a pump fed by an auxiliary tank. It is important to prevent uninjected fuel from returning to the main tank, at the risk of a progressively increasing additive concentration [382]. An organic additive based on iron, probably ferrocene[5] [251] is thus added periodically at the fuel tank exit from a pressurized container and a valve controlled by microprocessor. The addition of iron may have two effects: it may favor the combustion of the particulates deposited on the trap, or it may form particulates of a different structure, easily burnable, inside the combustion chamber.

5. Iron dicyclopentadienyl.

With the fiber coil filters mentioned earlier, different additives injected upstream from the trap to be regenerated (injection actuated by a pressure drop exceeding a preset limit) help to initiate the combustion of the soot deposited on the ceramic fibers. Depending on the type of product, the ignition temperature obtained is different: 380°C for CuCl, 310°C for $CuCl+NH_4NO_3$, 230°C for $Cu(ClO_4)_2 \cdot 6H_2O$, and 150°C for the mixture of $Fe(NO_3)_3 \cdot 9H_2O$, $C_5H_8O_2$ (acetylacetone), $C_4H_8O_2$ (dioxanne) and water (iron acetylacetonate) [121]. Among these additives, the choice falls preferably on those that emit a minimum or no hydrochloric acid, such as acetylacetonates, with the knowledge that the nitrates will release some nitrogen oxides at the time of regeneration. To ensure uniform combustion of the soot, great care must be taken to ensure proper product atomization on the entire surface of the trap to be cleaned. This is because, since the relationship between the pressure drop and the trap load is hyperbolic, the lowering of this pressure drop after regeneration does not prove complete cleaning of the fouled filter [121]. This type of process has been progressively abandoned in favor of the prior deposition of a film of copper oxide on the ceramic fibers making up the trap, to lower the soot auto-ignition temperature. Before regeneration, this catalyst is activated by the injection of a small amount of acetylacetone into the trap casing from an auxiliary tank. This injection, actuated by the increase in the pressure drop in the exhaust, is delayed to the next engine idling period and until the trap temperature reaches 160°C. The volume of acetylacetone injected (≈10 ml) converts the CuO to acetylacetonate and water:

$$CuO + 2C_5H_8O_2 \Rightarrow Cu(C_5H_7O_2)_2 + H_2O \tag{12.34}$$

When the engine is again in service, the trap temperature reaches 250°C, soot combustion is initiated, as well as the combustion of the adsorbed hydrocarbons, and the copper acetylacetonate returns to the CuO state. To renew and clean the surface of the CuO, which may be fouled by deposits, 1% of copper oxalate ($CuC_2O_4$) and an emulsifier are added to the acetylacetone [122 and 325]. A tank containing 7 to 9 liters of mixture suffices for 60,000 km, or one year of service for a bus [194]. This type of catalysis causes emissions of copper into the atmosphere, but at the exhaust exit they remain less than 0.45% on the average, and the maximum (regeneration) is 2.1% of the maximum permissible concentration in a working atmosphere (MAC value).

Another system uses cerium naphthenate as the catalyst, injected permanently into the fuel at the rate of 25 to 150 ppm of $CeO_2$. The catalytic solution is then combined with the exhaust throttling described above [275]. In urban service, a bus accordingly runs 98% of the time in normal operation, about 1% of the time with throttling, and less than 1% with trap bypass [279]. A higher cerium concentration lowers the light-off temperature: 480°C for 150 ppm and 525°C for 50 ppm. In the same concentrations, cerium proves to be more effective than copper [282]. In the higher concentrations, however, the trap is progressively clogged due to the residues of stagnant cerium ash on the trap, which cause a progressive increase in pressure drop at the rate of 1 hPa every 100 km. This clogging does not appear at 50 ppm [279]. This also shows why there are few emissions of inorganic compounds, such as cerium, in the atmosphere.

### 12.14.4 Diesel traps: unsolved problems

While diesel traps are not a priority for passenger vehicles, they will certainly have to be mounted on trucks and urban buses. In this case, problems of longevity and reliability will predominate. A truck that drives 250,000 km without servicing can emit 2800 t of exhaust gases during this period, depositing 250 kg of soot in the trap and requiring 2000 regeneration cycles [392]. Simultaneously, apart from the metallic additives that may be added for regeneration (of which the ash must be kept onboard the vehicle for pollution considerations), other metallic ash—that originates in the lubricants, and to a lesser degree in the fuel, and from engine wear [313]—accumulates on the trap in combination with the sulfates generated by the diesel sulfur content. This combination of ash, the emissions of which have been estimated at 17 g/1000 km on trucks [313], can irreversibly cover the catalysts deposited on the catalytic traps [315], and multiply the pressure drop on a vehicle by a factor of 1.4 after 16,000 km. This problem can only be solved by developing low-ash or no-ash lubricants with organic additives [315] and by a systematic filter replacement at a predetermined frequency [370].

Added to these problems of progressive clogging are the problems of mechanical strength, connected with the many regeneration cycles, the rapid fluctuations in exhaust temperature (100 to 700°C), and with the vibrations to which the traps are subjected. To reduce these thermal shock risks, it has been suggested that traps be split into two upstream and downstream parts: the gas filtered by the upstream part creates a blanket of hot gases around the overall system, limiting the thermal stresses [392].

As to regeneration, electric initiation systems appear to be less complicated and hence more reliable, but their energy demand may be prohibitive. Burners employ a well-known technology and represent the most advanced systems, but they are complicated and expensive. They are also liable to fouling and demand periodic maintenance. Also necessary are valves, sensors, actuators, algorithms, and control arrangements that guarantee total safety and avoid sending fuel into the trap in the case of a burner ignition defect, which would run the risk of igniting the entire system [370].

Catalytic regeneration using diesel fuel with additives, apart from the problems already listed of trap clogging and fuel storage stability, is liable to cause emissions of heavy metals if the fuel is also supplied to vehicles not equipped with traps [370]. The injection of the additive onboard the vehicle also raises the problem of the handling of concentrated metallic solutions, which are generally toxic.

As to passenger vehicles, the complexity of the systems (for example, initiation of combustion and necessary regulation) and their cost have discouraged the use of diesel-powered passenger cars vehicles in the United States [327].

# REFERENCES

[1] J. Abthoff et al., (1985), "The regenerable trap oxidizer, an emission control technique for Diesel engines", *SAE Paper* No. 850015, 11 p.

[2] J. Abthoff et al., (1990), "New developments in catalytic converter technology as demonstrated by Mercedes-Benz 300 SL and 300 CE", *SAE Paper* No. 900267, 7 p.

[3] J.R. Adomaitis et al., (1980), "Improved pelleted catalyst substrates for automotive emission control", *SAE Paper* No. 800084, 12 p.

[4] J.R. Adomaitis and R.M. Heck, (1988), "Vehicle control strategies, effect on catalyst performance", *SAE Paper* No. 881597, 12 p.

[5] P. Advenier et al., (1990), "Le Diesel automobile face à la réduction des émissions, évolution des moteurs, influence des caractéristiques du gazole", *SIA Int. Conf.*, Lyon, 13/14 June, *Paper* No. 90064, pp. 43-53.

[6] S. Andersson et al., (1991), "The effect of catalyst ageing on the composition of gasoline engine hydrocarbon emissions", *SAE Paper* No. 910174 (SP-863), 39-45.

[7] G.E. Andrews et al., (1987), "Diesel particulate SOF emission reduction using an exhaust catalyst", *SAE Paper* No. 870251, 10 p.

[8] G.E. Andrews et al., (1988), "Diesel emission reduction using a catalyst and water scrubber for underground mine operations", *Proc. IMechE*, **202**, 233-242.

[9] Anon., (1977), *Epurateur/laveur de gaz Diesel, Percevault Anti-pollution SA.*

[10] Anon., (1989), "SWRi exhaust particulate filter", *J. APCA*, 39, 1234-1235.

[11] Anon., (1989), "Katalysatortechnik für V8 Ottomotoren im Bootbetrieb", *MTZ*, **50**, 205-206.

[12] Anon., (1991), "Mercedes-Benz stellt Katalysator-Systeme der Zukunft vor", *MTZ*, **52**, 267.

[13] Anon., (1989), *L'échappement et les calories, SIA Conf.*, February, pp. 72-80.

[14] Anon., (1990), "Les émissions de particules des moteurs Diesel", *Rev. Techn. Diesel*, (161), 16-23 and (162), 82-88.

[15] Anon., (1990), "Turbodieselmotor von BMW mit Katalysator", *ATZ*, **92,** 257.

[16] Anon., (1990), "BMW präsentiert Turbodiesel Modelle mit Katalysator", *MTZ*, **51,** 81.

[17] Anon., (1990), "MAN Dieselmotor mit Katalysator im Linienbus", *ATZ*, **92,** 753.

[18] Anon., (1991), "Les jaune et noir se mettent au vert", *J. de l'Automobile*, (294), 17-20.

[19] Anon., PSA, (1991), *Une stratégie pour l'environnement, Direction de la Communication PSA.*

[20] M. Arai et al., (1987), "Development and selection of Diesel particulate trap regeneration system", *SAE Paper* No. 870012 (SP-702), 27-36.

[21] M. Arai, (1990), "Particulate regeneration improvements on actual vehicle under various conditions", *SIA Int. Conf.*, Lyon, 13/14 June 1990, *Paper* No. 90093, pp. 221-226, and *SAE Paper* No. 900328 (SP-816), 141-150.

[22] M. Arai, (1991), "SOF reduction and sulfate formation characteristics by Diesel catalyst", *SAE Paper* No. 910328 (P-240), 135-143.

[23] G. Arendt and H.J. Decker, (1986), "Luftqualität in Fahrgasträumen", *Forschungsvereinigung Automobiltechnik e.V. (FAT) Schriftenreihe*, No. 59, 94 p.

[24] D.J. Ball and R.G. Stack, (1990), "Catalyst considerations for Diesel converters", *SAE Paper* No. 902110 (SP-839), 11 p.

[25] A. Balzotti et al., (1990), "Italian city buses with particulate traps", *SAE Paper* No. 900114 (SP-816), 79-86.

[26] E. Barbera and F. Cavallino, (1990), *Evolution of the spark ignition and Diesel engines in relation with the anti-pollution legislation, 10th AGELFI Symp.*, Ostende, 11/12 October, 106 p.

[27] M.A. Barris et al., (1987), "Material characterization of Diesel particulate trap alternatives", *SAE Paper* No. 872246, 12 p.

[28] M.A. Barris and G.J. Rocklitz, (1989), "Development of automatic trap oxidizer muffler systems", *SAE Paper* No. 890400, 69-86.

[29] M.A. Barris, (1900), "Durability studies of trap oxidizer systems", *SAE Paper* No. 900108 (SP-816), 7-20.

[30] M.A. Barris et al., (1991), "The influence of lubricating oil and Diesel fuel on ash accumulation in an exhaust particulate trap", *SAE Paper* No. 910131 (P-240), 19-28.

[31] C. Bassoli et al., (1979), "Exhaust emissions from a European light duty turbocharged engine", *SAE Paper* No. 790316 (SP-442), 19 p.

[32] K.J. Baumgard and D.B. Kittelson, (1985), "The influence of a ceramic particle trap on the size distribution of Diesel particles", *SAE Paper* No. 850009, 12 p.

[33] D.D. Beck et al., (1991), "The impact of sulfur on three-way catalysts, storage and removal", *SAE Paper* No. 910844, 14 p.

[34] C. Bertoli et al., (1989), *Performance evaluation of particulate traps for passenger car Diesel engines, 12th ASME Annual Energy Sources Technology Conf.*, Houston, Texas, 22/25 January, pp. 27-35.

[35] W.D. Bond, (1972), "Quick heat intake manifolds for reducing cold engine emissions", *SAE Paper* No. 720935, 19 p.

[36] Y. Bonnetain et al., (1980), "Le poids lourd, conception et fonctionnement", *IRT Information Report* No. 18, 176 p.

[37] J.N. Braddock, (1981), "Impact of low temperature on 3-way catalyst car emissions", *SAE Paper* No. 810280, 28 p.

[38] R.L. Bradow and F.D. Stump, (1977), "Unregulated emissions from three-way catalyst cars", *SAE Paper* No. 770369, 7 p.

[39] F. Brear, (1991), *An introduction to Diesel exhaust aftertreatment technology with special reference to the control of particulates, A short course on Diesel particulates*, University of Leeds, 8/12 April, 38 p.

[40] U. Brill et al., (1988), "Werkstoffe für Metallträger von Automobil Abgaskatalysatoren", *MTZ*, **49,** 365-368.

[41] J.P. Brunelle et al., (1980), "The desactivation of automotive postcombustion catalysts by lead from gasoline", in: *"Catalyst Desactivation",* B. Delmon, Elsevier Science Publications, Amsterdam, pp. 233-250.

[42] M.F. Buchmann and B.E. Enga, (1983), "Catalytic Diesel particulate control system design and operation", *SAE Paper* No. 830080 (SP-537), 23-36.

[43] M.F. Buchmann and B.E. Enga, (1984), "Regeneration behavior of light duty catalytic trap oxidizer systems", *SAE Paper* No. 840080 (P-140), 71-78.

[44] E.R. Budd and B.E. Enga, (1984), "Catalytic particulate control for off-highway Diesels", *SAE Paper* No. 840170, 79-87.

[45] D. Burch and P. Riedwyl, (1988), *Toute la vérité sur le catalyseur*, Touring Club Suisse, 88 p.

[46] S.H. Cadle and P.A. Malawa, (1980), "Low molecular weight aliphatic amines in exhaust from catalyst-equipped cars", *E.S.&T.*, **14,** 718-723.

[47] L.A. Carol et al., (1989), "High temperature desactivation of three-way catalysts", *SAE Paper* No. 892040, 14 p.

[48] J.A. Caton and D.L. Siebers, (1989), "Reduction of nitrogen oxides in engine exhaust gases by the addition of cyanuric acid", *J. Eng. Gas Turbine Power*, **111,** 387-393.

[49] M.L. Church et al., (1989), "Catalyst formulations 1960 to present", *SAE Paper* No. 890815, 7 p.

[50] M.L. Church et al., (1991), "Operating temperature effects on catalyst performance and durability", *SAE Paper* No. 910845, 9 p.

[51] M. Cikanek, (1990), "Kombifilter löst Ruß-Problem bei Diesel-Pkw", *VDI Nachrichten*, (33), 25.

[52] B.J. Cooper and L. Keck, (1980), "NiO incorporation in three-way catalyst systems", *SAE Paper* No. 800461, 10 p.

[53] B.J. Cooper and P.R. Shore, (1989), "Catalytic control of mutagenic exhaust emissions from gasoline passenger cars", *SAE Paper* No. 890494, 15 p.

[54] B.J. Cooper and J.E. Thoss, (1989), "Role of NO in Diesel particulate emission control", *SAE Paper* No. 890404, 12 p.

[55] G.M. Cornetti et al., (1989), "Development of a ceramic particulate trap for urban buses", *J. Eng. Gas Turbine Power*, **111,** 398-403.

[56] W.H. Crouse and D.N. Anglin, (1977), *Automotive Emission Control*, McGraw Hill, New York, 278 p.

[57] E.D. Dainty et al., (1987), "Diesel emissions reduction employing catalysts or a fuel additive", *SAE Paper* No. 870014 (SP-702), 57-65.

[58] A.M. Danis et al., (1985), "Effect oc eramic monolith particulate filters on Diesel exhaust odorant and irritant species", *SAE Paper* No. 850011, 13 p.

[59] J.P. Day, (1990), "The design of a new ceramic catalyst support", *SAE Paper* No. 902167 (SP-839), 7 p.

[60] J.P. Day and L.S. Socha, (1991), "The design of automotive catalyst supports for improved pressure drop and conversion efficiency", *SAE Paper* No. 910371, 10 p.

[61] P. Degobert, (1985), "Action des pots catalytiques sur les polluants non réglementés", *Revue Inst. Franç. du Pétrole*, **40,** 635-648.

[62] P. Degobert, (1987), "Comportement des pots catalytiques en présence de carburants oxygénés", *Revue Inst. Franç. du Pétrole*, **42,** 255-266.

[63] P. Degobert, (1987), "Pollution secondaire des pots catalytiques, action sur les polluants non réglementés", *Poll. Atmosph.*, Special Issue November, pp. 286-296.

[64] J. Delsey, (1990), (unpublished documents).

[65] G.G. de Soete, (1988), *Catalysis of soot combustion by metal oxides, Comb. Inst. Western States Sect. Meeting*, Salt Lake City, 21/22 March, 44 p.

[66] G.G. de Soete, (1990), "Nitrous oxide formation and destruction by industrial NO abatement techniques", *Revue Inst. Franç. du Pétrole*, **45,** 663-682.

[67] J.C. Dettling et al., (1990), "Control of $H_2S$ emissions from high-tech TWC converters", *SAE Paper* No. 900506, 9 p.

[68] M. Devos et al., (1990), *Standardized Human Olfactory Thresholds*, IRL Press, Oxford, 165 p.

[69] A.F. Diwell et al., (1987), "The impact of sulphur storage on emissions from three-way catalysts", *SAE Paper* No. 872163, 10 p.

[70] L.D. Dorie et al., (1987), "Collection and characterization of particulate and gaseous phase hydrocarbons in Diesel exhaust modified by ceramic particulate traps", *SAE Paper* No. 870254, 13 p.

[71] L.D. Dorie et al., (1987), "Characterization of mutagenic subfractions of Diesel exhaust modified by ceramic particulate traps", *E.S.&T.*, **21,** 757-765.

[72] W.M. Draper et al., (1987), "Impact of ceramic trap and manganese fuel additive on the biological activity and chemical composition of exhaust particles from Diesel engines used in underground mines", *SAE Paper* No. 871621, 18 p.

[73] C.A. Dulieu et al., (1977), "Metal supported catalysts for automotive applications", *SAE Paper* No. 770299, 8 p.

[74] K.E. Egebäck and B.M. Bertillson, (1983), *Chemical and biological characterization of exhaust emissions from vehicles fueled with gasoline, alcohol, LPG and Diesel*, Report snv pm 1635, National Swedish Environment Board.

[75] K.D. Emmenthal and I. Geiger, (1989), "Entwicklungsstand eines alternativen Magersmotors", *Automobil-Industrie*, (3), 279-287.

[76] B.E. Enga et al., (1982), "Catalytic control of Diesel particulate", *SAE Paper* No. 820184, 63 p.

[77] B.E. Enga and J.F. Platosh, (1985), "The development of a passive particulate control system for light-duty vehicles", *SAE Paper* No. 850018 (P-158), 153-160.

[78] B.E. Enga et al., (1990), "Development of a simplified Diesel particulate filter regeneration system for transit buses", *SAE Paper* No. 900326 (SP-815), 127-130.

[79] B. Engler et al., (1986), "Catalytically activated Diesel particulate traps, New development and applications", *SAE Paper* No. 860007, 9 p.

[80] B. Engler et al., (1987), "Three-way catalyst performance using minimized rhodium loadings", *SAE Paper* No. 872097, 7 p.

[81] B.H. Engler, (1988), *Katalysatoren zur Reduzierung von Schadstoffen in Autoabgasen*, Umwelt Special "Luftreinhaltung", June, pp. 22-28.

[82] B. Engler et al., (1988), *Aspects généraux des concepts catalytiques pour la diminution des constituants nocifs dans les gaz d'échappement des automobiles, Int. SIA Conf. "Le moteur à allumage commandé de la prochaine décennie"*, Strasbourg, 18/19 Mai 1988, Ing. Automobile, 311-317.

[83] B. Engler et al., (1988), *Optimisation des métaux nobles pour les catalyseurs trois voies, Int. SIA Conf., "Le moteur automobile de la prochaine décennie, quels matériaux?"*, Orléans, 8/9 November, pp. 123-128.

[84] B. Engler et al., (1989), *High-tech three-way catalysts and $H_2S$ suppression, 3rd Int. Symp.*, "Highway Pollution", München, 18/22 September, 2 p.

[85] E. Erben et al., (1988), "Untersuchung zur Verminderung der Dieselpartikelemission von Nutzfahrzeugen mittels Schaumkeramik", *MTZ*, **49,** 511-512.

[86] M.V. ERnest, (1989), "Development of beaded three-way catalysts with reduced $H_2S$ emissions", *SAE Paper* No. 892042, 13 p.

[87] W.D.J. Evans et al., *Catalytic exhaust emission control, progress in the application of catalysts in Europe, IMechE Conf. "Vehicle emissions and their impact on European Air Quality"*, London, 3/5 November 1987, Paper No. C337/87, pp. 281-293.

[88] J.P. Gabathuler et al., (1991), "New developments of ceramic foam as a Diesel particulate filter", *SAE Paper* No. 910325 (P-240), 99-108.

[89] H.S. Gandhi et al., (1986), "Silicon contamination of automotive catalysts", *SAE Paper* No. 860565, 10 p.

[90] H.S. Gandhi, (1987), "Technical considerations for catalysts for European market, *IMechE Conf. "Vehicle emissions and their impact on European Air Quality"*, London, 3/5 November, *Paper* No. C344/87, pp. 295-303.

[91] C.P. Garner and J.C. Dent, (1988), "A thermal regeneration model for monolithic and fibrous Diesel particulate traps", *SAE Paper* No. 880007, 61-76.

[92] C.P. Garner and J.C. Dent, (1989), "Microwave-assisted regeneration of Diesel particulate traps", *SAE Paper* No. 890174, 8 p.

[93] H. Garthe, (1989), "Rußfiltertechnik für Nutzfahrzeug Dieselmotoren", *Verkehr und Technik*, 7, 257-261.

[94] R.A. Gast, (1975), "Pulsair, A method for exhaust system induction of secondary air for emission control", *SAE Paper* No. 750172, 15 p.

[95] A.P. Gill, (1988), "Design choices for 1990's low emission Diesel engines", *SAE Paper* No. 880350, 20 p.

[96] L. Goldberger et al., (1990), "Field evaluation of a Diesel particulate trap system for a 6V 92TA transit bus engine", *SAE Paper* No. 900112 (SP-816), 47-66.

[97] E. Goldenberg et al., (1983), "Dépollution des gaz d'échappement des moteurs Diesel au moyen de pots catalytiques", *Revue Inst. Franç. du Pétrole*, **38,** 793-805.

[98] E. Goldenberg and P. Degobert, (1986), "Filtres à activité catalytique pour moteur Diesel", *Revue Inst. Franç. du Pétrole*, **41,** 797-807.

[99] I. Gottberg et al., (1989), "Sulphur storage and hydrogen sulphide release from a three-way catalyst equipped car", *SAE Paper* No. 890491, 7 p.

[100] L.D. Gratz et al., (1991), "The effect of a ceramic particulate trap on the particulate and vapor phase emissions of a heavy duty Diesel engine", *SAE Paper* No. 910609 (P-240), 251-272.

[101] B. Grosch, (1991), "Optimierte Katalysatortechnik", *ATZ*, 93, 329-330.

[102] J-C. Guibet and B. Martin, (1987), *Carburants et moteurs*, Editions Technip, Paris, 903 p.

[103] S.T. Gulati, (1983), "Thermal stresses in ceramic wall flow Diesel filters", *SAE Paper* No. 830079 (SP-537), 11-22.

[104] S.T. Gulati and R.P. Merry, (1984), "Design considerations for mounting wall flow Diesel filters", *SAE Paper* No. 840074, 10 p.

[105] S.T. Gulati and J.D. Helfinstine, (1985), "High-temperature fatigue in ceramic wall flow Diesel filters", *SAE Paper* No. 850010, 7 p.

[106] S.T. Gulati, (1985), "Long-term durability of ceramic honeycombs for automotive emissions control", *SAE Paper* No. 850130, 16 p.

[107] S.T. Gulati, (1986), "Strength and thermal shock resistance of segmented wall flow Diesel filters", *SAE Paper* No. 860008 (SP-172), 11-18.

[108] S.T. Gulati et al., (1989), "Improvements in converter durability and activity via catalyst formulation", *SAE Paper* No. 890796, 8 p.

[109] S.T. Gulati et al., (1990), "High-strength behavior of ceramic versus metal substrates", *SAE Paper* No. 902170 (SP-839), 10 p.

[110] S.T. Gulati and R.D. Sweet, (1990), "Strength and deformation behavior of cordierite substrates from 70 to 2550 °F", *SAE Paper* No. 900268, 6 p.

[111] S.T. Gulati et al., (1991), "Optimization of substrate/washcoat interaction for improved catalyst durability", *SAE Paper* No. 910372, 13 p.

[112] S.T. Gulati et al., (1991), "High-temperature creep behavior of ceramic and metal substrates", *SAE Paper* No. 910374, 14 p.

[113] S.T. Gulati and D.L. Sherwood, (1991), "Dynamic fatigue data for cordierite ceramic wall flow Diesel filters", *SAE Paper* No. 910135 (P-240), 49-62.

[114] K. Ha and A. Lawson, (1989), "Development of a Diesel particulate trap system for a 6V-92TA engine", *SAE Paper* No. 890402, 151-158.

[115] K. Ha et al., (1991), "Particulate trap technology demonstration at New York city transit authority", *SAE Paper* No. 910331 (P-241), 165-182.

[116] K. Ha et al., (1991), "Demonstration of durable retrofit Diesel particulate trap systems on an urban bus and class 8 truck", *SAE Paper* No. 910332 (P-240), 273-280.

[117] R.H. Hammerle and Y.B. Graves, (1983), "Lead accumulation on automotive catalysts", *SAE Paper* No. 830270, 10 p.

[118] R.H. Hammerle and C.H. Wu, (1984), "Effect of high temperatures on three-way catalysts", *SAE Paper* No. 840549, 6 p.

[119] H.O. Hardenberg et al., (1987), "Urban bus application of a ceramic fiber coil particulate trap", *SAE Paper* No. 870011 (SP-702), 17-25.

[120] H.O. Hardenberg et al., (1987), "Experiences in the development of ceramic fiber coil particulate traps", *SAE Papers* No. 870015 (SP-702), 67-78.

[121] H.O. Hardenberg et al., (1987), "Particulate trap regeneration induced by means of oxidizing agents injected into the exhaust gas", *SAE Paper* No. 870016, 11 p.

[122] H. Hardenberg, (1989), "Das keramische Wickelfilter mit katalytischer Regeneration für Mercedes-Benz Nutzfahrzeuge", *Verkehr und Technik*, 7, 213-218.

[123] M.A. Härkönen et al., (1990), "Prevention of hydrogen sulphide formation on three-way catalysts", *SAE Paper* No. 900498, 10 p.

[124] M.A. Härkönen et al., (1991), "Thermal behavior of metallic TWC, Evaluation of the structural and performance properties", *SAE Paper* No. 910846, 13 p.

[125] H. Harndorf and H. Daudel, (1988), *Möglichkeiten der thermischen Regeneration von Rußfiltern mit motorischen Maßnahmen, Tagung "Rußminderung bei Dieselfahrzeugen"*, Essen (Haus der Technik), 24/25 February, 16 p.

[126] M.S. Harrenstien et al., (1979), "Determination of individual aldehyde concentrations in the exhaust of a spark-ignited engine fueled by alcohol/gasoline blends", *SAE Paper* No. 790952, 10 p.

[127] P.N. Hawker et al., (1988), "Metal supported automotive catalysts for use in Europe", *SAE Paper* No. 880317, 18 p.

[128] K. Hayashi et al., (1990), "Regeneration capability of wall flow monolith Diesel particulate filter with electric heater", *SAE Paper* No. 900603 (SP-816), 203-210.

[129] E. Heck et al., (1989), "Motorkonzept mit Oxydationskatalysator", *MTZ*, **50,** 101-108.

[130] R.M. Heck et al., (1989), "Platinum versus palladium three-way catalysts, Effect of closed loop feedback parameters on catalyst efficiency", *SAE Paper* No. 892094, 19 p.

[131] M.J. Heimrich, (1990), "Air injection to an electrically-heated catalyst for reducing cold start benzene emissions from gasoline engines", *SAE Paper* No. 902115 (SP-839), 12 p.

[132] M.J. Heimrich et al., (1991), "Electrically-heated catalyst system, conversions on two current technology vehicles", *SAE Paper* No. 910612, 19 p.

[133] H. Hiereth and G. Withalm, (1988), "New results of passenger car Diesel engines pressure wave supercharged with and without a particulate trap", *SAE Paper* No. 880005, 25-30.

[134] W. Held, (1985), "Wege zur Minderung der Partikelemission beim Stadtlinienbus", "Emissionsminderung Automobilabgase, Dieselmotoren", *VDI Berichte* No. 559, 445-458.

[135] W. Held, (1988), *Partikelverminderung bei Nfz-Dieselmotoren durch Abgasnachbehandlung, Tagung "Rußminderung bei Dieselfahrzeugen"*, Essen (Haus der Technik), 24/25 February, 14 p.

[136] W. Held and A. König, (1989), "Laboruntersuchungen von Abgaskatalysatoren", *MTZ*, **50,** 111-113.

[137] W. Held et al., (1990), "Catalytic $NO_x$ reduction in net oxidizing exhaust gas", *SAE Paper* No. 900496, 7 p.

[138] R.L. Helferich et al., (1989), "Evaluation of a stacked element Diesel particulate trap using a newly developed membrane covered ceramic foam filtering media", *SAE Paper* No. 890787, 12 p.

[139] R.L. Helferich et al., (1991), "Regeneration performance of a catalysed versus a non-catalysed ceramic membrane Diesel particulate trap", *SAE Paper* No. 910327 (P-240), 121-134.

[140] K.H. Hellman et al., (1989), "Resistive materials applied to quick light-off catalysts", *SAE Paper* No. 890799, 10 p.

[141] M.G. Henk et al., (1987), "Sulfur storage and release from automotive catalysts", *SAE Paper* No. 872134, 8 p.

[142] D.M. Herod et al., (1973), "An engine dynamometer system for the measurement of converter performance", *SAE Paper* No. 730557, 8 p.

[143] J.B. Heywood, (1988), *Internal combustion engine fundamentals*, McGraw Hill, New York, 930 p.

[144] A.J. Hickman and C. Jaffray, (1986), Performance and durability of a catalyst trap oxidizer installed on a city bus for 65,000 miles of revenue service, *SAE Paper* No. 860138 (P 172), 133-141.

[145] O. Hiemesch et al., (1990), "Das BMW Abgasreinigungskonzept für Dieselmodelle", *MTZ*, **51,** 196-200.

[146] J.W. Hightower, (1976), "Catalysts for automobile emission control", in: *Preparation of Catalysts*, B. Delmon, Elsevier Science Publications, Amsterdam, pp. 617-636.

[147] N. Higuchi et al., (1983), "Optimized regeneration conditions of ceramic honeycomb Diesel particulate filters", *SAE Paper* No. 830078 (SP-537), 1-10.

[148] L.J. Hillenbrand and D.A. Trayser, (1982), "A concept for catalysed ignition of Diesel soot", *SAE Paper* No. 811236, 11 p.

[149] K.G.L. Hockel et al., (1990), "Das Katalysatorkonzept des neuen BMW 325i", *MTZ*, **51,** 528-534.

[150] E. Hoepke, (1989), "Partikelfilter für Omnibusse und Kommunalfahrzeuge", *ATZ*, **91,** 680-683.

[151] E. Hoepke, (1989), "Zweites Omnibus Forum des TÜV Baden", *Verkehr und Technik*, **7,** 294-297.

[152] E. Hoepke, (1989), "Dieselpartikelfilter für Nutzfahrzeuge", *Verkehr und Technik*, **7,** 333-334.

[153] E. Hoepke, (1990), "MAN Dieselmotor mit Katalysator im Linienbus", *ATZ*, **92,** 753.

[154] S. Hori et al., (1990), "Analysis of $NH_3$ emission characteristics from three-way catalyst cars", *Int. J. Vehicle Design*, **11,** 188-200.

[155] M. Horiuchi et al., (1990), "The effects of flow through type oxidation catalysts on the particulate reduction of 1990's Diesel engines", *SAE Paper* No. 900600 (SP-816), 183-193.

[156] M. Horiuchi et al., (1991), "Sulfur storage and discharge behavior on flow through type oxidation catalyst", *SAE Paper* No. 910605 (P-240), 215-222.

[157] R.W. Horrocks, (1987), "Particulate control systems for Diesel engines", *IMechE Conf. "Vehicle Emissions and Their Impact on European Air Quality"*, London, 3/5 November, *Paper* No. C349/87, pp. 319-334.

[158] J.S. Howitt, (1980), "Thin wall ceramics as monolithic catalyst supports", *SAE Paper* No. 800082, 9 p.

[159] J.S. Howitt and M.R. Montierth, (1981), "Cellular ceramic Diesel particulate filter", *SAE Paper* No. 810114, 9 p.

[160] J.S. Howitt et al., (1983), "Application of a ceramic wall flow filter to underground Diesel emissions reduction", *SAE Paper* No. 830181 (SP-537), 131-139.

[161] W. Hühn, (1988), *Aspekte zur Verminderung der Partikelemission von Dieselmotoren im Gabelstapler, Tagung "Rußminderung bei Dieselfahrzeugen"*, Essen (Haus der Technik), 24/25 February, 14 p.

[162] G. Hunter et al., (1981), "The effect of an oxidation catalyst on the physical, chemical and biological character of Diesel particulate emissions", *SAE Paper* No. 810263, 29 p.

[163] G. Hunter et al., (1981), "The effects of fuels on Diesel oxidation catalyst performance and the physical, chemical and biological character of Diesel particulate emissions", *SAE Paper* No. 811192, 15-36.

[164] R.G. Hurley et al., (1990), "Evaluation of metallic and electrically-heated metallic catalysts on a gasoline fueled vehicle", *SAE Paper* No. 900504, 8 p.

[165] D. Hütterbräucker and J. Henke, (1990), "Verringerung der Kaltstartemission durch partielle Saugrohrvorwärmung an der Mercedes-Benz Vierzylinder-Einspritzmotoren", *MTZ*, **51,** 316-317.

[166] M. Ichimura, (1991), "Coating experience on thin wall substrates", *SAE Paper* No. 910373, 4 p.

[167] T. Igarashi et al., (1990), "Current situation and problems of Diesel particulate trap", *JSAE Rev.*, **11,** 13-17.

[168] T. Igarashi et al., (1991), "Development of Diesel particulate trap systems for city buses", *SAE Paper* No. 910138 (P-240), 83-92.

[169] K. Ihara et al., (1990), "Improvement of three-way catalyst performance by optimizing ceria impregnation", *SAE Paper* No. 902168 (SP-839), 7 p.

[170] M.N. Ingalls and R.I. Bruetsch, (1980), "Evaluation of a low sulfate emission control system", *SAE Paper* No. 800821, 19 p.

[171] M.W. Jackson, (1978), "Effect of catalytic emission control on exhaust hydrocarbon composition and reactivity", *SAE Paper* No. 780624, 24 p.

[172] E. Jenny et al., (1989), "The transient behavior of supercharged passenger car Diesel engines fitted with particulate traps", *SAE Paper* No. 890171, 137-149.

[173] J.H. Johnson et al., (1981), "The engineering control of Diesel pollutants in underground mining", *SAE Paper* No. 810684, 46 p.

[173] F.W. Kaiser and S. Pelters, (1991), "Comparison of metal supported catalysts with different cell geometries", *SAE Paper* No. 910837 (SP-863), 179-193.

[174] D. Kattge, (1988), "Advanced canning systems for ceramic monoliths in catalytic converters", *SAE Paper* No. 880284, 9 p.

[175] D.A. Ketcher and R.W. Horrocks, (1990), *The effect of fuel sulphur on Diesel particulate emissions when using oxidation catalysts, IMechE Seminar, "Fuels for automotive and industrial Diesel engines"*, London, 19/29 November, pp. 1-7.

[177] J.B. King et al., (1970), "The 1970 General Motors emission control systems", *SAE Paper* No. 700149, 13 p.

[178] J. Kitagawa et al., (1991), "Electric heating regeneration of large wall flow type DPF", *SAE Paper* No. 910136 (P-240), 63-72.

[179] D.B. Kittelson et al., (1986), "Electrostatic collection of Diesel particles", *SAE Paper* No. 860009, 11 p.

[180] D.B. Kittelson et al., (1991), "Further studies on electrostatic collection and agglomeration of Diesel particles", *SAE Paper* No. 910329 (P-240), 145-163.

[181] J. Kitagawa et al., (1990), "Analyses of thermal shock failure on large volume DPF", *SAE Paper* No. 900113 (SP-816), 67-77.

[182] H. Klingenberg et al., (1988), "Einfluß verschiedener Katalysatorkonzepte auf die Abgasemissionen bei realen Straßenfahrten", *MTZ*, **49,** 69-70.

[183] H. Klingenberg, (1988), "ASU-Methode für Fahrzeuge mit Katalysator", *Automobil-Industrie*, (1), 29-36.

[184] E. Koberstein et al., (1980), "Catalytic purification of automotive exhaust gases under European conditions", *SAE Paper* No. 800394, 8 p.

[185] E. Koberstein and H.D. Pletka, (1982), "Exhaust purification with small 2-stroke engines, A challenge for catalytic systems", *SAE Paper* No. 820279, 11 p.

[186] E. Koberstein et al., (1983), "Catalytically activated Diesel exhaust filters, Engine test methods and results", *SAE Paper* No. 830081 (SP-537), 37-43.

[187] E. Koberstein, (1984), "Abgaskatalysatoren/Bauarten, Funktionen, Verfügbarkeiten, Emissionsminderung Automobilabgase, Ottomotoren", *VDI Berichte* No. 531, 385-401.

[188] E. Koberstein et al., (1985), "Einsatz von Abgasnachbehandlungseinrichtungen", "Emissionsminderung Automobilabgase, Dieselmotoren", *VDI Berichte* No. 559, 275-296.

[189] E. Koberstein and B. Engler, (1987), "The use of three-way catalysts under extreme operation conditions", *IMechE Conf. "Vehicle emissions and their impact on European Air Quality"*, London, 3/5 November, *Paper* No. C347/87, pp. 275-279.

[190] K. Kollmann, (1990), *Die Erfüllung verschärfter Anforderungen bei der Abgasreinigung mit Hilfe moderner Motortechnologien, 10th AGELFI Symp.*, Ostende, 11/12 October, pp. 13-31.

[191] A. König et al., (1988), "Katalytische Stickoxidverminderung bei Dieselmotoren", *VDI Berichte*, (714), 309-326.

[192] A.G. Konstandopoulos et al., (1988), "Ceramic particulate traps for Diesel emissions control, effect of a manganese copper fuel additive", *SAE Paper* No. 880009, 99-107.

[193] A.G. Konstandopoulos and J.H. Johnson, (1989), "Wall flow particulate filters, their pressure drop and collection efficiency", *SAE Paper* No. 890405, 99-121.

[194] W.D. Korner, (1990), "Les moteurs VI modernes sous l'aspect des émissions à l'échappement, problèmes et perspectives d'avenir", *SIA Int. Conf.*, Lyon, 13/14 June, *Paper* No. 90094, pp. 281-295.

[195] J.W. Koupal et al., (1991), "Detection of catalyst failure on vehicle using the dual oxygen sensor method", *SAE Paper* No. 910561 (SP-863), 135-146.

[196] O. Kruggel, (1985), "Untersuchungen zur Stickoxidminderung an Großdieselmotoren", "Emissionsminderung Automobilabgase, Dieselmotoren", *VDI Berichte* No. 559, 459-478.

[197] O. Kruggel, (1988), "Untersuchungen zur Stickoxidminderung an schnelllaufenden Großdieselmotoren", *MTZ*, **49,** 23-29.

[198] J.E. Kubsh and D.J. Weissert, (1987), "High-temperature substrates and washcoats for auto exhaust emission control", *SAE Paper* No. 872131, 11 p.

[199] P. Kugland et al., (1991), "Cleaner Diesels, full flow soot filter regeneration system", *SAE Paper* No. 910133 (P-240), 37-42.

[200] M. Kulazynski et al., (1988), "Auswahl eines Katalysators zur Beseitigung toxischer Bestandteile des Abgase von Diesel Motoren", *Chem. Ing. Techn.*, **60,** 644-645. (MS 1693/88, 23 pp.)

[201] J.T. Kummer, (1980), "Catalysts for automobile emission control", *Prog. Energy Comb. Sci.*, 6, 177-199.

[202] I. Kurki-Suonio et al., (1988), "Einfluß der Abgasrückführung und des katalytischen Nachbrenners auf die $NO_x$ und PAK Gehalte der Abgase eines Dieselmotors", *MTZ*, **49,** 31-35.

[203] F.J. Laimböck and C.J. Landerl, (1990), "50 cc two-stroke engines for mopeds, chainsaws and motorcycles with catalysts", *SAE Paper* No. 901598 (SP-835), 41-61.

[204] J.L. Laity et al., (1973), "Mechanisms of polynuclear aromatic hydrocarbon emissions from automotive engines", *SAE Paper* No. 730835, 10 p.

[205] H. Langen and P. Reiser, (1988), *Zur thermischen Regenerierung von Rußfiltern, Tagung "Rußminderung bei Dieselfahrzeugen"*, Essen (Haus der Technik), 24/25 February, 17 p.

[206] J. Laurikko, (1986), *The evaluation of two different automotive catalytic converters at low ambient temperature, Proc. ENCLAIR '86*, Taormina, Italy, 28/31 October, pp. 227-236.

[207] J.K. Laurikko, (1991), "On the road durability and performance of TWC exhaust emission control under real Nordic driving conditions", *SAE Paper* No. 910172 (SP-863), 13-21.

[208] A. Lawson et al., (1985), "Performance of a ceramic Diesel particulate trap over typical mining duty cycles using fuel additives", *SAE Paper* No. 850150 (P-158), 117-130.

[209] A. Lawson et al., (1990), "Demonstration of durable retrofit Diesel particulate trap systems on an urban bus and class 8 truck", *SAE Paper* No. 900110 (SP-816), 35-45.

[210] T.D. Laymac et al., (1991), "The measurement and sampling of controlled regeneration emissions from a Diesel wall flow particulate trap", *SAE Paper* No. 910606 (P-240), 223-236.

[211] J. Lemaire, (1989), *Purification of Diesel engine exhaust, contribution of cerium-based additives*, Japan Soc. Lubrication Eng., Tokyo, 18 October, 35 p.

[212] G. Lepperhoff and G. Kroon, (1985), "Impact of particulate traps on the hydrocarbon fraction of Diesel particles", *SAE Paper* No. 850013, 12 p.

[213] G. Lepperhoff, (1985), "Verminderung von Partikeln im Abgas", "Emissionsminderung Automobilabgase, Dieselmotoren", *VDI Berichte* No. 559, 99-115.

[214] G. Lepperhoff, (1988), *Möglichkeiten zur Verminderung der Partikelemission, Schmieröleinfluss und Partikelfilter mit selbsttragender Regeneration, Tagung "Rußminderung bei Dieselfahrzeugen"*, Essen (Haus der Technik), 24/25 February, 17 p.

[215] G. Lepperhoff and J. Schommers, (1988), "Verhalten von SCR-Katalysatoren im dieselmotorischen Abgas", *MTZ*, **49**, 17-21.

[216] Y.A. Levendis et al., (1990), "Development of a self-cleaning particle trap for Diesel engine particulate control", *SAE Paper* No. 900601 (SP-816), 195-201.

[217] Y.A. Levendis et al., (1991), "Evaluation of a self-cleaning particulate control system for Diesel engines", *SAE Paper* No. 910333 (P-240), 183-194.

[218] M.D. Levin et al., (1990), "Copper fuel additives as part of a particulate emission control strategy", *SAE Paper* No. 901619, 14 p.

[219] M.D. Levin and D.E. Koehler, (1990), "An experimental evaluation to determine the effect of an organometallic fuel additive on particulate trap regeneration", *SAE Paper* No. 900920, 6 p.

[220] I.E. Lichtenstein, (1981), Effect of catalyst on PAH content of automotive Diesel exhaust particulate, in: *"Polynuclear aromatic hydrocarbons, physical and biological chemistry"*, M. Cooke et al., *6th Int. Symp.*, Battelle, Columbus, 27/29 October, pp. 461-470.

[221] J.W.S. Longhurst, (1989), "Autocatalysts and motor vehicle emission control", *Clean Air*, **19,** 14-22.

[222] G. Lonkal and O. Hiemesch, (1990), "Le concept de dépollution BMW des véhicules automobiles diesel", *SIA Int. Conf.*, Lyon, 13/14 June, *Paper* No. 90058, pp. 209-215.

[223] E.S. Lox et al., (1989), "Development of scavenger-free three-way automotive emission control catalysts with reduced hydrogen sulfide formation", *SAE Paper* No. 890795, 12 p.

[224] O.A. Ludecke and D.L. Dimick, (1983), "Diesel exhaust particulate control system development", *SAE Paper* No. 830085, 21 p.

[225] O.A. Ludecke and D.L. Dimick, (1984), "Diesel exhaust particulate control by monolith trap and fuel additive regeneration", *SAE Paper* No. 840077, 9 p.

[226] R. Lylykangas and P. Lappi, (1991), "How to achieve optimum physical properties in the metal catalyst", *SAE Paper* No. 910614, 10 p.

[227] M. Määttänen and R. Lylykangas, (1990), "Mechanical strength of a metallic catalytic converter made of precoated foil", *SAE Paper* No. 900505, 9 p.

[228] G. Mabilon et al., (1989), "Ageing of an autocatalyst under simulated high-speed conditions", *3rd Int. Symp., "Highway Pollution"*, München, 18/22 September 1989, 8 p, *Sci. Tot. Environm.*, **93,** 223-230.

[229] R. W. McCabe et al., (1990), "Laboratory and vehicle studies of aldehyde emissions from alcohol fuels", *SAE Paper* No. 900708, 14 p.

[230] D.L. McKinnon et al., (1989), "Diesel particulate filter underground trial at Brunswick mining and smelting's No. 12 mine", *SAE Paper* No. 891846, 10 p.

[231] D.L. McKinnon et al., (1991), "A Diesel particulate filter system using assisted regeneration for mechanical handling equipment", *SAE Paper* No. 910134 (P-240), 49-62.

[232] M.A. McMahon et al., (1982), "Alumina-coated metal wool as a particulate filter for Diesel-powered vehicles", *SAE Paper* No. 820183 (P-107), 23-33.

[233] S.H. Mansouri et al., (1982), "Divided-chamber Diesel engine, (1) A cycle simulation which predicts performance and emissions", *SAE Paper* No. 820273, 30 p.

[234] D. Maret, (1988), *La ligne d'échappement du véhicule dépollué, matériaux, réalisation et endurance, SIA Int. Conf., "Le moteur automobile de la prochaine décennie, quels matériaux?"*, Orléans, 8/9 November, pp. 129-138.

[235] B. Martin and D. Herrier, (1990), *Efficiency of fuel additives on Diesel particulate trap regeneration, IMechE Seminar, "Fuels for automotive and industrial Diesel engines"*, London, 19/29 November, pp. 77-84.

[236] A. Matsunuma et al., (1991), "Status of particulate trap system for a heavy-duty Diesel truck", *SAE Paper* No. 910132 (P-240), 29-38.

[237] H. May, (1984), "Technische Möglichkeiten zur Reduzierung der Schadstoffen emissionen von Kraftfahrzeugen", *ATZ*, **86,** 5-10 and 75-78.

[238] A. Mayer and E. Pauli, (1988), "Emissions concept for vehicle Diesel engine supercharged with COMPREX", *SAE Paper* No. 880008, 77-89.

[239] S. Meinrad and C. Giorgio, (1989), "Laboratory results in particulate trap technology", *SAE Paper* No. 890170, 11-18.

[240] H. MENRAD et al., (1988), "Methanol vehicles of Volkswagen, A contribution to better air quality", *SAE Paper* No. 881196, 12 p.

[241] P.R. Miller et al., (1983), "The effects of a porous trap on the physical, chemical and biological character of Diesel particulate emissions", *SAE Paper* No. 830457, 29 p.

[242] N. Miyamoto et al., (1987), "Characteristics of Diesel soot suppression with soluble fuel additives", *SAE Paper* No. 871612, 7 p.

[243] N. Miyamoto et al., (1988), "Catalytic effects of metallic fuel additives on oxidation characteristics of trapped Diesel soot", *SAE Paper* No. 881224, 7 p.

[244] T. Mizrah et al., (1989), "Open-pore ceramic foam as Diesel particulate filter", *SAE Paper* No. 890172, 19-27.

[245] Z.N. Mogaka et al., (1982), "Performance and regeneration characteristics of a cellular ceramic Diesel particulate trap", *SAE Paper* No. 820272 (P-107), 65-87.

[246] D.R. Monroe and M.H. Krueger, (1987), "The effect of Pt and Rh loading on the performance of three-way automotive catalysts", *SAE Paper* No. 872130, 8 p.

[247] X. Montagne et al., (1990), *Caractéristiques des essences et composition des gaz d'échappement, 10th AGELFI Symp.*, Ostende, 11/12 October, pp. 205-218.

[248] R.M. Montano et al., (1989), "Simultaneous reduction of soot and $NO_x$ in Diesel engines by homogeneous catalysis of group platinum metals", *SAE Paper* No. 891634, 10 p.

[249] M.R. Montierth, (1984), "Fuel additive effect upon Diesel particulate filters", *SAE Paper* No. 840072 (P-140), 1-14.

[250] J.J. Mooney et al., (1975), "Catalytic control of two-stroke motorcycle exhaust emissions", *SAE Paper* No. 750910, 7 p.

[251] E. Müller et al., (1989), "Diesel-Partikelfiltersystem mit additivgestützter Regeneration", *ATZ*, **91,** 674-679.

[252] H. Muraki et al., (1990), "The effect of palladium on the performance of three-way catalyst", *SAE Paper* No. 900610, 7 p.

[253] H. Muraki, (1991), "Performance of palladium automotive catalysts", *SAE Paper* No. 910842, 10 p.

[254] M.J. Murphy et al., (1981), "Assessment of Diesel particulate control, direct and catalytic oxidation", *SAE Paper* No. 810112, 11 p.

[255] G.J. Nebel, (1981), "The effect of misfueling on aldehyde and other auto exhaust emissions", *J. APCA*, 31, 877-879.

[256] R.J. Nichols et al., (1988), "A view of flexible fuel vehicle aldehyde emissions", *SAE Paper* No. 881200, 8 p.

[257] K. Nishizawa et al., (1989), "Development of improved metal supported catalyst", *SAE Paper* No. 890188, 8 p.

[258] M. Nonnenmann, (1985), "Metal supports for exhaust gas catalysts", *SAE Paper* No. 850131, 8 p.

[259] M. Nonnenmann, (1989), "Neue Metallträger für Abgaskatalysatoren mit erhöter Aktivität und innerem Strömungsausgleich", *ATZ*, 91, 185-192.

[260] M. Nonnenmann, (1990), "New high-performance gas flow equalizing metal supports for automotive exhaust gas catalysts", *SAE Paper* No. 900270, 9 p.

[261] T. Nording, (1991), "Neuartiges Konzept für isolierte Abgaskrümmer, Vorrohre und Katalysatoren", *MTZ*, **52,** 206-210.

[262] K. Obländer et al., (1984), "Der Dreiwegkatalysator, Eine Abgasreinigungstechnologie für Kraftfahrzeuge mit Ottomotoren", "Emissionsminderung Automobilabgase, Ottomotoren", *VDI Berichte* No. 531, 69-96.

[263] S.H. Oh et al., (1981), "Mathematical modelling of fibrous filters for Diesel particulates, theory and experiment", *SAE Paper* No. 810113, 12 p.

[264] H. Oikawa et al., (1990), "Catalyst-assisted regeneration system for a Diesel particulate trap", *SAE Paper* No. 900324 (SP-816), 109-117.

[265] P. Öser, (1979), "Catalyst systems with an emphasis on three-way conversion and novel concepts", *SAE Paper* No. 790306, 14 p.

[266] P. Öser and U. Thoms, (1983), "Particulate control systems for Diesel engines using catalytically-coated and uncoated traps with consideration of regeneration techniques", *SAE Paper* No. 830087, 97-110.

[267] P. Öser and H. Völker, (1987), "Optimization of catalyst systems with emphasis on precious metal usage", *SAE Paper* No. 872096, 7 p.

[268] P. Öser, (1988), "Novel autocatalyst concepts and strategies for the future with emphasis on metal supports", *SAE Paper* No. 880319, 21 p.

[269] K. Otto et al., (1980), "The oxidation of soot deposits from Diesel engines", *SAE Paper* No. 800336 (P-86), 277-289.

[270] K.N. Pattas et al., (1984), "Comparative measurement of the efficiency of catalytic afterburning devices on a heavy-duty Diesel engine", *SAE Paper* No. 840171 (P-140), 89-96.

[271] K.N. Pattas et al., (1985), "A new approach to the oxidizing behavior of a porous ceramic Diesel particulate trap", *SAE Paper* No. 850012, 8 p.

[272] K.N. Pattas et al., (1986), "A trap oxidizer system for urban buses", *SAE Paper* No. 860136 (P-172), 127-132.

[273] K.N. Pattas et al., (1986), "Forced regeneration by exhaust gas throttling of the ceramic Diesel particulate trap", *SAE Paper* No. 860293 (P-172), 195-201.

[274] K.N. Pattas et al., (1987), "Operation characteristics of the ceramic Diesel particulate trap during forced regeneration", *SAE Paper* No. 870252 (SP-702), 113-122.

[275] K.N. Pattas et al., (1987), "Size determination of the ceramic Diesel particulate trap", *SAE Paper* No. 870253 (SP-702), 123-126.

[276] K.N. Pattas et al., (1988), "Ceramic trap regeneration rate control through bypass technique", *SAE Paper* No. 880004, 17-24.

[277] K.N. Pattas et al., (1989), "Computational simulation of the ceramic trap transient operation", *SAE Paper* No. 890403, 87-98.

[278] K.N. Pattas et al., (1989), "The effect of exhaust throttling on the Diesel engine operation characteristics and thermal loading", *SAE Paper* No. 890399, 59-68.

[279] K.N. Pattas et al., (1990), "On-road experience with trap oxidizer systems installed on urban buses", *SAE Paper* No. 900109 (SP-816), 21-33.

[280] K.N. Pattas et al., (1990), "Transient performance prediction of trap oxidizer systems", *SAE Paper* No. 900322 (SP-816), 87-98.

[281] K.N. Pattas et al., (1990), "Exhaust temperature response of trap oxidizer systems", *SAE Paper* No. 900323 (SP-816), 99-107.

[282] K.N. Pattas and A.M. Stamatelos, (1991), "A trap oxidizer system for the turbocharged Diesel engine", *SAE Paper* No. 910137 (P-240), 73-81.

[283] E. Pauli et al., (1984), "The calculation of regeneration limits of Diesel particulate traps for different regeneration methods", *SAE Paper* No. 840075 (P-140), 35-42.

[284] V. Pellegrin, (1986), "The retrofitting of a catalytic trap oxidizer to a metropolitan transit coach", *SAE Paper* No. 860135 (P-172), 117-125.

[285] S. Pelters et al., (1989), "The development and application of a metal-supported catalyst for Porsche's 911 Carrera 4", *SAE Paper* No. 890488, 15 p.

[286] R.C. Peterson, (1987), "The oxidation rate of Diesel particulate which contains lead", *SAE Paper* No. 870628, 20 p.

[287] R.S. Petrow et al., (1989), "Vehicle and engine dynamometer studies of $H_2S$ emissions using a semi-continuous analytical method", *SAE Paper* No. 890797, 10 p.

[288] G.K. Piotrowski and J.D. Murrell, (1987), "Catalysts for methanol vehicles", *SAE Paper* No. 872052, 18 p.

[289] F. Pischinger et al., (1990), "Modular trap and regeneration system for buses, trucks and other applications", *SAE Paper* No. 900325 (SP-816), 119-126.

[290] B.C. Porter et al., (1991), "Engine and catalyst strategies for 1994", *SAE Paper* No. 910604, 14 p.

[291] A.S. Pratt and J.A. Cairns, (1977), "Noble metal catalyst on metallic substrates", *Plat. Met. Rev.*, 21, 74-83.

[292] W.H. Preston et al., (1987), "An investigation into lubricant-related poisoning of automotive three-way catalysts", *IMechE Conf. "Vehicle Emissions and Their Impact on European Air Quality"*, London, 3/5 November, *Paper* No. C348/87, pp. 305-318.

[293] M. Prigent et al., (1977), "A three-wat catalytic muffler using progressive air injection for automotive exhaust gas purification", *SAE Paper* No. 770298, 8 p.

[294] M. Prigent, (1980), "Emploi des catalyseurs de post combustion automobile avec des carburants à basse teneur en plomb", *Poll. Atmosph.* (85), 122-127.

[295] M. Prigent, (1982), "Catalyseurs de post combustion utilisés avec des carburants à basse teneur en plomb", *La Revista dei Combustibili*, **36,** 381-388.

[296] M. Prigent et al., (1983), "Lead-tolerant catalysts for Europe, The behavior of precious metals on alumina pellets when used with 0.15 or 0.40 g/l lead in gasoline", *SAE Paper* No. 830269, 9 p.

[297] M. Prigent, Les catalyseurs de post combustion automobile, Cycle de perfectionnement, "Catalyseurs Industriels", ENSIC, Nancy, 39 p.
(1984/1985), "Aperçu sur les problèmes de catalyse dans les pots catalytiques d'automobiles", *Revue Inst. Franç. du Pétrole*, **40,** 393-409.

[298] M. Prigent, (1988), *Pots catalytiques, les alternatives au pot trois voies fonctionnant à richesse, 1,00 régulée, Conf. "Le moteur à allumage commandé de la prochaine décennie"*, Strasbourg, 18/19 May, Ing. Automobile, pp. 252-258.

[299] M. Prigent, 1988, *Le traitement catalytique des gaz d'échappement, TEC 88 Symp. "Matériaux"*, Grenoble, 13 October, 17 p.

[300] M. Prigent and G. de Soete, (1989), "Nitrous oxide $N_2O$ in engine exhaust gases, A first appraisal of catalyst impact", *SAE Paper* No. 890492, 11 p.

[301] M. Prigent, (1989), "La réduction des émissions des véhicules à essence", *Poll. Atmosph.* (121), 38-42.

[302] M. Prigent et al., (1990), "Principaux facteurs agissant sur la température de mise en action des catalyseurs d'échappement", *SIA Conf. "Equip Auto"*, Paris, 23/25 October 1989, *Paper* No. SIA 89077, pp. 277-282, and Ing. Automobile, January/February, pp. 65-70.

[303] M. Prigent et al., (1990), "Engine bench evaluation of gasoline composition effect on pollutant conversion rate by a three-way catalyst", *SAE Paper* No. 900153, 6 p.

[304] J. Quarg, (1987), "Zur Berechnung des Wärmeüberganges in Abgaskrümmmern", *LTZ*, **48,** 291-293.

[305] V.D. Rao et al., (1985), "Advanced techniques for thermal and catalytic Diesel particulate trap regeneration", *SAE Paper* No. 850014, 17 p.

[306] B. Raynal, (1982), "Moteurs thermiques et pollution atmosphérique, origine et réduction des polluants", *Techn. de l'Ing.*, Leaflet B 378,1, 26 p.

[307] R.R. Richards and J.E. Sibley, (1988), "Diesel engine emissions control for the 1990's", *SAE Paper* No. 880346, 16 p.

[308] J.S. Rieck et al., (1989), "Development of non-nickel additives for reducing hydrogen sulfide emissions from three-way catalysts", *SAE Paper* No. 892095, 6 p.

[309] R.C. Rijkeboer et al., (1986), "The catalytic trap oxidizer on a city bus, A Dutch demonstration programme", *SAE Paper* No. 860134, 10 p.

[310] J.J. Rim, (1991), "Reduction of Diesel particulates, unburned hydrocarbons and nitrogen oxides from Diesel exhaust gases", *SAE Paper* No. 910335 (P-240), 205-214.

[311] H. Rohlfing et al., (1989), "Nebenreaktionen am Abgaskatalysator", *MTZ*, 50, 269-272.

[312] M.J. Ryan et al., (1991), "Light-off performance of catalytic converters, the effect of heat/mass transfer characteristics", *SAE Paper* No. 910610, 12 p.

[313] R. Sachdev et al., (1983), "Effect of ash accumulation on the performance of exhaust particulate traps", *SAE Paper* No. 830182, 141-152.

[314] R. Sachdev et al., (1984), "Analysis of regeneration data for a cellular ceramic particulate trap", *SAE Paper* No. 840076 (P-140), 43-54.

[315] K. Saito et al., (1988), "Fuel and lubricant effect on durability of catalytic trap oxidizer (CTO) for heavy-duty Diesel engines", *SAE Paper* No. 880010, 109-114.

[316] H. Schindlbauer et al., (1988), "Verminderung der Stickoxidemissionen durch chemische Nachbehandlung der Abgase", *MTZ*, **49,** 161.

[317] H.D. Schuster, (1985), "Verminderung der Partikelemission am Pkw-Dieselmotor", "Emissionsminderung Automobilabgase, Dieselmotoren", *VDI Berichte* No. 559, 117-137.

[318] J. Scott McDonald, (1981), "Experimental evaluation of fibrous filters for trapping Diesel exhaust particulates", *SAE Paper* No. 810956, 37-49.

[319] J. Scott McDonald, (1983), "The effect of operating conditions on the effluent of a wall flow monolith particulate trap", *SAE Paper* No. 831711, 14 p.

[320] J. Scott McDonald, (1988), "Development of a particulate trap system for a heavy-duty Diesel engine", *SAE Paper* No. 880006, 31-59.

[321] R.A. Searles, (1988), "Car exhaust pollution control, lean burn engines and the continuous requirement for platinum-containing autocatalysts", *Plat. Met. Rev.*, **32,** 123-129.

[322] R.E. Seiter and R.J. Clark, (1978), "Ford three-way catalyst and feedback fuel control system", *SAE Paper* No. 780203, 15 p.

[323] M. Shelef and H.S. Ghandhi, (1974), "The reduction of nitric oxide in automobile emissions", *Plat. Met. Rev.*, **18,** 2-14.

[324] O. Shinozaki et al., (1990), "Trapping performance of Diesel particulate filters", *SAE Paper* No. 900107 (SP-816), 1-5.

[325] M. Signer, (1989), *Partikelfiltersysteme für Stadtbusse, Kommunalfahrzeuge und Verteilerfahrzeuge, Symp. "Dieselmotorentechnik" Ostfildern*, Stuttgart, 7/8 December, 19 p.

[326] G.M. Simon and T.L. Stark, (1985), "Diesel trap regeneration using ceramic wall flow traps, fuel additives and supplemental electrical igniters", *SAE Paper* No. 850016, 25 p.

[327] G.M. Simon and T.L. Stark, (1986), "Diesel exhaust particulate control techniques for light-duty trucks", *SAE Paper* No. 860137, 23 p.

[328] J.F. Skowron et al., (1989), "Effect of ageing and evaluation conditions on three-way catalyst performance", *SAE Paper* No. 892093, 12 p.

[329] G. Smedler et al., (1991), "Spatially-resolved effects of deactivation on field aged automotive catalysts", *SAE Paper* No. 910173 (SP-863), 23-37.

[330] L.R. Smith and F.M. Black, (1980), "Characterization of exhaust emissions from passenger cars equipped with three-way catalyst control systems", *SAE Paper* No. 800822, 21 p.

[331] L.R. Smith and P.M. Carey, (1982), "Characterization of exhaust emissions from high mileage catalyst-equipped automobiles", *SAE Paper* No. 820783, 19 p.

[332] D. Sodhi et al., (1990), "The kinetics of formaldehyde oxidation and emissions reduction in methanol fueled vehicles", *J. Air Waste Managem. Assoc.*, **40,** 352-356.

[333] K.J. Springer and R.C. Stahman, (1977), "Removal of exhaust particulate from a Mercedes 300D Diesel car", *SAE Paper* No. 770716, 24 p.

[334] G. Smedler et al., (1990), "Thermal desactivation of a three-way catalyst, changes of structural and performance properties", *SAE Paper* No. 900273, 11 p.

[335] A. Stawsky et al., (1984), "Evaluation of an emission control strategy for underground Diesel mining equipment", *SAE Paper* No. 840176 (P-140), 139-160.

[336] P. Stiglic et al., (1989), "Control considerations for an on-line, active regeneration system for Diesel particulate traps", *J. Eng. Gas Turbine Power*, **111,** 404-409.

[337] P.D. Stroom et al., (1990), "Systems approach to packaging design for automotive catalytic converters", *SAE Paper* No. 900500, 13 p.

[338] J.C. Summers et al., (1989), "Durability of palladium only three-way automotive emission control catalysts", *SAE Paper* No. 890794, 16 p.

[339] H. Suto et al., (1991), "Evaluation of Diesel particulate filter systems for city buses", *SAE Paper* No. 910334 (P-240), 195-205.

[340] J.C. Summers et al., (1990), "The role of durability and evaluation conditions on the performance of Pt/Rh and Pd/Rh automotive catalysts", *SAE Paper* No. 900495, 16 p.

[341] N. Suzuki et al., (1991), "Simultaneous removal of $NO_x$, $SO_x$ and soot in Diesel engine exhaust by plasma oil dynamics means", *SAE Paper* No. 910562 (SP-863), 147-152.

[342] T. Takada and T. Tanaka, (1991), "Development of a highly heat resistant metal-supported catalyst", *SAE Paper* No. 910615, 8 p.

[343] K. Takesa et al., (1991), "Development of particulate trap system with cross-flow ceramic filter and reverse cleaning regeneration", *SAE Paper* No. 910326 (P-240), 109-120.

[344] K.C. Taylor, (1984), *Automobile catalytic converters*, Springer Verlag, Berlin, 54 p.

[345] L.P. Tessier et al., (1980), "The development of a high efficiency Diesel exhaust particulate filter", *SAE Paper* No. 800338 (P-86), 7 p.

[346] D.P. Thimsen et al., (1990), "The performance of an electrostatic agglomerator as a Diesel soot emission control device", *SAE Paper* No. 900330 (SP-816), 173-182.

[347] W.B. Thompson, (1966), "The General Motors air injection reactor air pump", *SAE Paper* No. 660108, 10 p.

[348] T.J. Truex et al., (1980), "Sulfate in Diesel exhaust", *E.S.&T.*, **14,** 1118-1121.

[349] T.J. Truex et al., (1987), "The chemistry and control of $H_2S$ emissions in three-way catalysts", *SAE Paper* No. 872162, 10 p.

[350] Y. Tsukasaki et al., (1990), "Study of mileage-related formaldehyde emission from methanol-fueled vehicles", *SAE Paper* No. 900705, 6 p.

[351] J.J. Tutko et al., (1984), "Feasibility of ceramic foam as a Diesel particulate trap", *SAE Paper* No. 840073 (P-140), 15-24.

[352] H. Uchiyama et al., (1977), "Emission control of two-stroke automobile engine", *SAE Paper* No. 770766, 9 p.

[353] T.L. Ullman et al., (1984), "Preliminary particulate trap tests on a 2-stroke Diesel bus engine", *SAE Paper* No. 840079 (P-140), 55-69.

[354] C.M. Urban and R.J. Garbe, (1980), "Exhaust emissions from malfunctioning three-way catalyst-equipped automobiles", *SAE Paper* No. 800511, 11 p.

[355] C.M. Urban et al., (1983), "Diesel car particulate control methods", *SAE Paper* No. 830084, 87-96.

[356] C.M. Urban and R.D. Wagner, (1985), "Evaluation of heavy-duty engine exhaust particulate traps", *SAE Paper* No. 850147, 8 p.

[357] J.C.C. van den Donck, (1987), "L'application de catalyseurs sur les supports monolithiques", *Mémoire de chimie minérale*, 28 p.

[358] H.C. Vergeer et al., (1985), "Electrical regeneration of ceramic wall flow Diesel filters for underground mining applications", *SAE Paper* No. 850152 (P-158), 143-151.

[359] A. Verma, (1991), "Rib selection to ensure optimum monolith stresses in catalytic converters", *SAE Paper* No. 910376, 7 p.

[360] W.R. Wade et al., (1981), "Diesel particulate trap regeneration techniques", *SAE Paper* No. 810118, 22 p.

[361] W.R. Wade et al., (1983), "Thermal and catalytic regeneration of diesel particulate traps", *SAE Paper* No. 830083 (SP-137), 61-85.

[362] K. Walker, (1990), *Recent developments in fuel additives to assist particulate trap regeneration, 10th AGELFI Symp.*, Ostende, 11/12 October, pp. 303-310.

[363] M.P. Walsh, (1989), "Worldwide developments in motor vehicle Diesel particulate control", *SAE Paper* No. 890168, 9 p.

[364] M.P. Walsh, (1989), "Worldwide developments in motor vehicle Diesel particulate control", in: *Man and his ecosystem*, Vol. 4, Ed. L.J. Brasser, Elsevier Science Publications, Amsterdam, pp. 435-440.

[365] M.P. Walsh, (1991), "Diesel particulate control around the world", *SAE Paper* No. 910130 (P-240), 1-18.

[366] F.B. Walton et al., (1990), "Controlled energy deposition in Diesel particulate filters during regeneration by means of microwave irradiation", *SAE Paper* No. 900327 (SP-816), 131-140.

[367] F.B. Walton et al., (1991), "On-line measurement of Diesel particulate loading in ceramic filter", *SAE Paper* No. 910324 (P-240), 93-98.

[368] C.Z. Wan and J.C. Dettling, (1986), "Effective rhodium utilization in automotive exhaust catalysts", *SAE Paper* No. 860566, 7 p.

[369] Y. Watabe et al., (1983), "Trapless trap, A catalytic combustion system of Diesel particulates using ceramic foam", *SAE Paper* No. 830082 (SP-537), 45-59.

[370] C.S. Weaver, (1983), "Trap oxidizer technology for light-duty Diesel vehicles, status, prospects and current issues", *SAE Paper* No. 831713, 18 p.

[371] C.S. Weaver, (1984), "Particulate control technology and particulate standards for heavy-duty Diesel engines", *SAE Paper* No. 840174, 109-125.

[372] C.S. Weaver et al., (1986a), "Feasibility of retrofit technologies for Diesel emissions control", *SAE Paper* No. 860296 (P-172), 19 p.

[373] C.S. Weaver et al., (1986b), "Ways to control Diesel emissions", *Automotive Eng.*, **94,** 47-51.

[374] C.S. Weaver, (1989), "Feasibility of emissions control for off highway Diesel engines", *SAE Paper* No. 890169, 123-135.

[375] W. Weisweiler et al., (1988), "Selektive katalytische Reduktion von Stickoxiden", Staub, 48, 119-126.

[376] H. Weltens et al., (1988), "Design of exhaust gas catalyst systems for European applications", *SAE Paper* No. 880318, 11 p.

[377} R. Westerholm et al., (1986), "Chemical analysis and biological testing of emissions from a heavy-duty Diesel truck with and without two different particulate traps", *SAE Paper* No. 860014, 11 p.

[378] W.A. Whittenberger and J.E. Kubsh, (1990), "Recent developments in electrically-heated metal monoliths", *SAE Paper* No. 900503, 10 p.

[379] W.A. Whittenberger and J.E. Kubsh, (1991), "Electrically-heated metal substrate durability", *SAE Paper* No. 910613, 6 p.

[380] J. Widdershoven et al., (1986), "Possibilities of particle reduction for Diesel engines", *SAE Paper* No. 860013, 12 p.

[381] B. Wiedemann et al., (1983), "Regeneration of particulate filters at low temperatures", *SAE Paper* No. 830086, 20 p.

[382] B. Wiedemann et al., (1984), "Application of particulate traps and fuel additives for reduction of exhaust emissions", *SAE Paper* No. 840078, 17 p.

[383] B. Wiedemann and K.H. Neumann, (1985), "Vehicular experience with additives for regeneration of ceramic Diesel filters", *SAE Paper* No. 850017, 21 p.

[384] B. Wiedemann, (1985), "Rußfiltertechniken für Fahrzeug-Dieselmotoren", "Emissionsminderung Automobilabgase, Dieselmotoren", *VDI Berichte* No. 559, 139-156.

[385] A.J.J. Wilkins and N.A. Hannington, (1990), "The effect of fuel and oil additives on automobile catalyst performance", *Plat. Met. Rev.*, **34,** 16-24.

[386] V.W. Wong et al., (1984), "Effects of catalytic wire mesh traps on the level and measurement of heavy-duty Diesel particulate emissions", *SAE Paper* No. 840172 (P-140), 97-107.

[387] W.T. Wotring et al., (1978), "50 000 mile vehicle road test of three-way and $NO_x$ reduction catalyst systems", *SAE Paper* No. 780608, 21 p.

[388] T. Yamada et al., (1990), "Development of non-Ni low $H_2S$ Pt/Rh/$CeO_2$ TWC catalyst", *SAE Paper* No. 900611, 8 p.

[389] H. Yamamoto et al., (1990), "Reduction of wall thickness of ceramic substrates for automotive catalysts", *SAE Paper* No. 900614, 9 p.

[390] H. Yamamoto et al., (1991), "Warm-up characteristics of thin-wall honeycomb catalysts", *SAE Paper* No. 910611, 8 p.

[391] K. Yoshida et al., (1989), "Simultaneous reduction of $NO_x$ and particulate emissions from Diesel engine exhaust", *SAE Paper* No. 892046, 12 p.

[392] S.V. Yumlu, (1988), "Particulate traps, some progress, some problems", *SAE Paper* No. 880347, 8 p.

[393] W. Zahn et al., (1989), "Die Abgasreinigung der neuen Mercedes-Benz 300 SL-24 und 500 SL, Aufbau und Wirkungsweise", *MTZ*, **50,** 247-254.

[394] P. Zelenka et al., (1990), "Reduction of Diesel exhaust emissions by using oxidation catalysts", *SAE Paper* No. 902111, 11 p.

[395] P.A. Weber et al., (1992), "Fuel effects on emissions from an advanced technology vehicle", *SAE Paper* No. 922245 (SP.938), 23-31.

[396] K. Hamai et al., (1992), "Effects of clean fuels (reformulated gasolines, M85, and CNG) on automotive emissions", *SAE Paper* No. 922380, 14 p.

[397] W.A. Whittenberger et al., (1992), "Experiences with 20 user vehicles equipped with electrically-heated catalyst systems", *SAE Paper* No. 920722 (SP.910), 123-131.

[398] M.K. Khair et al., (1992), "Design and development of catalytic converters for Diesels", *SAE Paper* No. 921677 (SP.931), 199-209.

[399] R. Beckmann et al., (1992), "A new generation of Diesel oxidation catalysts", *SAE Paper* No. 922330 (SP.938), 101-117.

[400] J. Walker and B.K. Speronello, (1992), "Development of an ammonia/SCR $NO_x$ reduction system for a heavy-duty natural gas engine", *SAE Paper* No. 921673 (SP.931), 171-181.

# Economic challenges 13

## 13.1 Introduction

Compiling the overall economic cost of automotive air pollution, including calculating the benefits and extra costs incurred by engine fine-tuning, retrofit technologies, or pollution control systems, is not an easy task because of the inadequacy of short-term economic calculations.

An objective economic balance has to consider problems of universal importance such as the global warming of the atmosphere and its economic consequences, and acid rain and its effect on the forestry economy. In connection with health, the extra cost paid by drivers for pollution control must be offset against the burden of health care expenditures shouldered by social security institutions. Another important item is the cost of maintaining monuments and buildings that are degraded by air pollution of automotive origin.

This chapter provides further details about the estimated costs of the different solutions discussed in the previous chapters, but without claiming to draw overall financial conclusions due to the impossibility of objectively comparing the benefits anticipated with their corresponding costs.

## 13.2 Cost of improvements made to spark ignition engines

We showed earlier (Chapter 10) that modifications to the engine architecture and tuning arrangements help substantially to improve the level of pollutants emitted. While alterations to the engine architecture (to increase swirl, for example) represent initial manufacturing costs that ultimately have minimal repercussions on consumer cost, the improvement in the accuracy of tuning by using several electronically-controlled sensors and actuators could raise the cost to the level of systems that include three-way catalysts. For example, these measures include variations in the volumetric ratio, accurate control of the fuel/air ratio in the carburetted mixture, variation of the quantity of exhaust gas recirculation according to engine conditions, separate cooling circuits for the cylinder head and the engine bloc, individual control of the quantities of fuel injected into each cylinder to control idling, and so on [35].

### 13.2.1 Cost of injection systems

The replacement of inaccurate carburetors by injection systems is a prerequisite, not only for the installation of three-way catalysts, but also for more accurate mixture control in lean burn engines. On a car, the replacement of a carburetor by a single-point injection system usually means an additional tax-inclusive cost to the consumer of 2300 French francs (Table 13.7). This figure rises to 3000 French francs exclusive of tax for multi-point injection (Table 13.9).

## 13.3 Cost of improvements to diesel engines

As with spark ignition engines, changes to diesel engines and their tuning make considerable use of electronics with the corresponding sensors and actuators. These changes aim to achieve the following [11]:

- Vary the injection advance according to the driving conditions.
- Vary the air/fuel ratio according to the driving conditions by means of variable-geometry turbo-chargers.
- Improve the atomization of the diesel with very high-pressure injection pumps that closely control the injection timing characteristics. Electronic injection offers independent control of the flow rate, injection timing, and even the pressure level.
- Control the inlet temperature according to engine conditions: the cooling of warm intake air to reduce $NO_x$ and the heating of cold air to reduce HC.

All these complex technologies incur the additional costs listed in Table 13.1. The extra cost of electronic injection has also been estimated at 2000 French francs for light-duty vehicles, and 4000 French francs for trucks and buses [16].

**Table 13.1** Estimated costs of new diesel technologies [11]

| Equipment | Extra cost (%) | | (%) |
|---|---|---|---|
| | Equipment | Engine | Engine price |
| **injection:** | | | |
| • present pump | 0 | 0 | 12 |
| • high-pressure pump | 34 | 4 | 16 |
| • high-pressure pump with electronic advance variator | 260 | 12 | 27 |
| **turbo-charger:** | | | |
| • conventional turbo-charger | 0 | 0 | 2 |
| • variable geometry turbo-charger | 450 | 8 | 9 |
| **particulate trap** | – | 100 | 100 |

**Table 13.2** Figures for different purification alternatives [42]
(Prices in French francs, exclusive of tax)

| Technology | | Extra cost of vehicle |
|---|---|---|
| three-way converter: | • + single-point injection<br>• + multi-point injection | 4000 to 5500<br>5000 to 6500 |
| catalytic oxidizer + lean burn: | + carburettor + Pulsair + EGR<br>+ single-point injection + Pulsair + EGR<br>+ very lean + multi-point injection | 2600 to 3000<br>4250 to 4650<br>5400 to 5800 |
| open-loop three-way converter + carburettor | | 1950 to 2400 |

**Table 13.3** Comparison of the price of vehicles sold in Germany in 1988 with and without catalytic converters [41] (*Source AECC*)

| Model | Cylinder displacement | Extra cost catalytic converter (DM)(1) | (%)(2) |
|---|---|---|---|
| Ford Ghia | 1368 | 490 | 2.5 |
| VW Polo Fox | 1035 | 490 | 3.7 |
| VW Polo CL | 1035 | 490 | 3.5 |
| VW Polo Fox | 1263 | 720 | 5.2 |
| VW Polo CL | 1263 | 720 | 4.2 |
| Alfa Romeo 33 | 1474 | 950 | 4.9 |
| Alfa Romeo 33 | 1700 | 790 | 3.6 |
| Alfa Romeo 75 | 1767 | 1110 | 4.4 |
| Audi 80 | 1760 | 500 | 2.1 |
| Mercedes 190E | 1977 | 1049 | 3.0 |
| VW Golf CL | 1760 | 950 | 4.9 |
| VW Golf GTi | 1760 | 1850 | 7.7 |
| VW Passat | 1760 | 950 | 4.2 |
| Opel Ascona GLS | 1984 | 1800 | 7.1 |
| Alfa Romeo | 2464 | 1801 | 5.3 |
| BMW M 53li | 3406 | 950 | 1.7 |
| BMW 655 CSi | 3406 | 950 | 1.2 |
| Mercedes 190E | 2276 | 1049 | 2.8 |
| Mercedes 230E | 2276 | 1049 | 2.7 |
| Mercedes 300E | 2932 | 1049 | 2.0 |
| Porsche 924S | 2449 | 1365 | 2.8 |
| Opel Omega 3000 | 2935 | 0 | 0 |
| Opel Senator | 2935 | 0 | 0 |

(1) 1 DM ≈ 3.37 French francs.
(2) % increase over model without catalytic converter

## 13.4 Economic consequences of the introduction of catalysts

In terms of tonnage sold, the automotive catalyst market has long overtaken sales of catalysts to the chemical and petroleum industries. The catalytic oxidizers initially installed on US cars, which contained an average of 1.8 g of precious metal per vehicle, have already sparked a 20% increase in the world production of precious metals [25].

At 1986 prices, the cost of installing oxidation catalysts was estimated at £50 sterling. This figure rose to £475 sterling for the installation of three-way catalytic converters [33]. Depending on the severity of the prevailing standards, the extra costs applicable to vehicles range between 2000 and 6500 French francs (Table 13.2) [42]. The catalyst itself actually costs about 600 French francs (Table 13.10). Table 13.4 and 13.5 and Fig. 13.1 show the prices of the different components of the catalyst systems, with the support accounting for 15 to 20% of the cost, whereas precious metals represent between 40 and 70% of the total amount.

In Germany, the additional cost of clean cars was estimated in 1986 at an average of 1200 DM [44], a value equivalent to the French estimate of 4510 French francs exclusive of tax for a vehicle not originally equipped with an injection system (Table 13.7). The catalytic converter itself costs about 200 to 250 DM [44], or approximately 655 French francs (Table 13.7). German experience in fact reveals an average additional cost of about 3.5% for 1988 models [41], when both versions (with and without a catalytic converter) are offered on the market (Table 13.3).

On vehicles already well equipped, like BMWs, the catalytic converter represents a negligible extra cost. On French cars, on which the cost of injection is virtually equivalent to that of the catalytic converter (Table 13.9), the additional cost ranges between 5 and 10% of the vehicle price exclusive of tax (Table 13.5), depending on whether or not an injection unit is to be installed on the mass-produced vehicle. To the production cost of the systems supplied by equipment manufacturers must be added the installation and test costs borne by the automobile manufacturers, and this could practically double the cost of the catalytic converter exclusive of tax (Table 13.7) and explains the estimated additional cost to the consumer of about 6000 French francs per vehicle.

In addition, Table 13.6 gives the forecasted additional cost in dollars for the future solutions planned for California, including the various possible motor fuels. In 1985, the market for catalytic converters in France for 1995 was estimated at 910 million French francs exclusive of tax, assuming that all automobiles would be equipped with three-way catalysts [39]. In Europe, the installation of three-way catalysts on all vehicles produced will cost about 6.5 billion US dollars per year according to 1986 forecasts, to which an equivalent amount would have to be added for maintenance [38].

**Table 13.4** Cost breakdown of catalytic converter components [39] (Prices in 1985 French francs exclusive of tax)

| Converter component | Three-way catalytic oxidizer | Catalytic trap converter |
|---|---|---|
| support | 100 | 100 |
| impregnation costs | 275 | 185 |
| precious metals | 175 | 50 |
| casing | 200 | 200 |
| **total** | 655 | 535 |

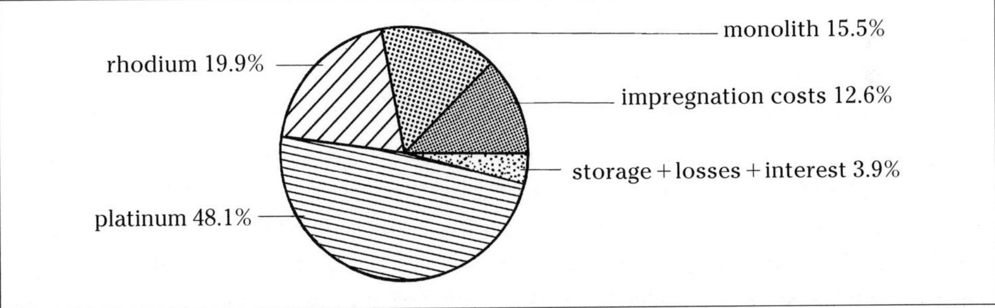


**Fig 13.1** Cost breakdown of a three-way catalyst [41]

**Table 13.5** Example of incidence on selling price, exclusive of tax, of costs of mounting catalytic trap oxidizer + EGR on different vehicles with or without factory injection [32]. (Assumed price of catalyst + EGR 2600 to 3000 French francs) (Vehicle price in 1985 French francs exclusive of VAT, 33.3%)

| | Engine displacement ($cm^3$) | Vehicle price | Percentage increase | |
|---|---|---|---|---|
| with factory injection | 1590 | 54,163 | 4.80-5.53 | |
| | 1590 | 58,214 | 4.46-5.15 | |
| without factory injection | | | with injection mounted | without injection mounted |
| | 1700 | 51,012 | 9.01-9.80 | 5.09-5.88 |
| | 1900 | 59,864 | 7.68-8.35 | 4.34-5.01 |
| | 1600 | 50,187 | 9.16-9.96 | 5.18-5.97 |

**Table 13.6** Additional costs in US dollars of low-emission vehicles [9] (CARB estimates , Value August 1990)

| Motor fuel | Category | | | |
|---|---|---|---|---|
| | TLEV | LEV | ULEV | ZEV |
| gasoline | 70 | 170 | 170 | – |
| methanol/ethanol | 200 | 270 | 370 | – |
| liquefied petroleum gas | 600 | 700 | 870 | – |
| compressed natural gas | 1000 | 1200 | 1200 | – |
| electricity | – | – | – | 1350 |

**Table 13.7** Breakdown of additional costs to the consumer [39] (Prices in 1985 French francs, with VAT at 33.3%)

**cars equipped with injection:**

- three-way catalyst (including λ sensor) .......... 2 500 F tax inclusive
- safety shields .......... 250 F tax inclusive
- installation and functional tests .......... 250 F tax inclusive

**total** .......... 3 000 F tax inclusive

**cars not equipped with injection (first breakdown):**

- three-way catalyst .......... 2 500 F tax inclusive
- addition of single-point injection compared with carburettor.......... 2 300 F tax inclusive
- EGR .......... 700 F tax inclusive
- safety shields .......... 250 F tax inclusive
- installation and functional tests .......... 250 F tax inclusive

**total** .......... 6 000 F tax inclusive

**cars not equipped with injection (second breakdown):**

- three-way catalytic converter.......... 655 F exclusive of tax
- addition for single-point injection compared with carburettor.......... 1 400 F exclusive of tax
- improved ignition .......... 50 F exclusive of tax
- safety shield + wiring .......... 150 F exclusive of tax

sub-total for supplies .......... 2 555 F exclusive of tax
manufacturer value added .......... 2 555 F exclusive of tax

total additional cost ex-manufacturer .......... 4 510 F exclusive of tax
VAT at 33.3% .......... 1 501 F

total additional cost to consumer .......... 6 011 F tax inclusive

**rounded off to .......... 6 000 F tax inclusive**

**Table 13.8** Distribution of noble metals in ores [25] (Weight percent)

| Noble metal | Origin | | |
|---|---|---|---|
| | Canada | Russia | South Africa |
| platinum | 43.4 | 30 | 64.05 |
| palladium | 42.9 | 60 | 25.61 |
| iridium | 2.2 | 2 | 0.64 |
| rhodium | 3.0 | 2 | 3.20 |
| ruthenium | 8.5 | 6 | 6.40 |
| osmium | – | – | 0.13 |

**Table 13.9** Comparative costs of installation components of a three-way catalytic converter [32]. (Selling price exclusive of tax in 1984 French francs)

| | |
|---|---|
| catalyst and support | 1500 to 2000 |
| casing | 200 |
| oxygen sensor | 200 |
| single-point injection | 2000 |
| or | |
| multi-point injection | 3000 |

**Table 13.10** Cost of the precious metals fraction of different catalysts [17] (Basis \$19/g (Pt), \$4.8/g (Pd) and \$42/g (Rh))

| Pt/Pd/Rh ratio | Content (g/l) | Cost (\$/l) |
|---|---|---|
| 5/0/1 | 1.4 | 32.5 |
| | 1.06 | 24.4 |
| | 0.70 | 16.3 |
| 10/0/1 | 1.4 | 30.1 |
| | 1.06 | 22.6 |
| | 0.70 | 15.1 |
| 14.4/0/1 | 1.4 | 29.3 |
| | 1.06 | 22.0 |
| | 0.70 | 14.7 |
| 0/5/3 | 1.4 | 24.4 |
| | 1.06 | 19.8 |
| | 0.70 | 13.2 |
| 0/5/1 | 1.4 | 15.5 |
| | 1.06 | 11.6 |
| 2.5/0/1 | 0.82 | 21.2 |
| | 0.62 | 15.9 |
| | 0.41 | 10.6 |
| 1/0/0 | 1.4 | 27.2 |
| | 1.06 | 20.4 |
| | 0.70 | 13.6 |
| 3/1/0 | 1.4 | 22.1 |
| | 1.06 | 16.6 |
| 2/1/0 | 1.4 | 20.4 |

Automobiles tuned at an fuel/air ratio of 1 and equipped with three-way catalysts consume a few per cent more fuel than leaner burning vehicles [33].

### 13.4.1 Availability of precious metals

Precious metals are usually found in ores in combination with other metals, such as nickel. In the Republic of South Africa, extraction is mainly carried out to recover the metals from the platinum mine (with the precious metal contents of ore at 8 to 10 g/t). The corresponding ore is found in a saucer-shaped deposit about 500 km in diameter [12]. A second more readily-accessible deposit is found under the first at a depth ranging between 1300 and 1750 m, with ambient temperatures of 55°C demanding cooled ventilation air [13].

In Russia (Urals) and Canada (Ontario, Manitoba), precious metals are recovered as by-products of copper and nickel ore extraction (sulfides), with an the precious metals content of the ore at about 6 g/t. In this case, production depends on the market for less noble metals such as nickel and copper.

The relative proportions of precious metals in the ores are often different from those required by three-way catalysts. Pt/Pd weight ratios of 2/1 are found in oxidation catalysts, and Pt/Rh ratios of 5/1, and Pt/Pd/Rh $\approx$10/4/1 (Section 12.6.2) in three-way catalysts. In fact, South African mines deliver a Pt/Pd/Rh blend in a ratio of 12.5/5/1, with the lower deposit being slightly richer in rhodium, which corresponds to a higher extraction price. Table 13.8 gives the metals distribution of three ores of different origin.

The consumption of rhodium is mainly due to automotive catalysts (Table 13.11), whereas platinum accounts for only about 40% of this consumption. However, according to the ratio present in the mine and the relatively low consumption of palladium in automotive catalysis, the surplus palladium justifies a lower market price. This is even more true of Russian ores, which contain 12 to 15 g/t of noble metals with a Pt/Pd ratio of 1.3 [13]. The higher demand for rhodium, causing a sharply higher market price, justifies the efforts made to minimize the rhodium content of catalysts [12]. However, the precious metal stockpiles appear to be adequate to guarantee decades of consumption in automotive catalysts [25].

#### 13.4.1.1 Platinum market

The supply of platinum to the Western world amounted to 130 t in 1991 and 118 t in 1992. The main producers are the Republic of South Africa for 75%, and Russia for 19%, with the rest of the world producing 6% (Canada, USA, Colombia, Zimbabwe, Australia).

Apart from automotive catalysts, which account for over 40% of demand (Table 13.11 and Fig. 13.2), platinum is also used in jewelry (jewels, watches) (37%), as a catalyst in the chemical industry (6%), the petroleum industry (3%), the electrical industry (6%), the glass industry (4%), and as investments (3%) [13].

Platinum demand for automotive catalysts is rising fast in Europe with the arrival of the new 1993 standards. In Germany and the Netherlands, and now in the whole of the EEC, 95% of new cars on the road are already equipped with catalysts. The figure is 100% in Switzerland, Austria, Sweden, and Norway. Thus platinum demand in western Europe for automotive purposes is expected to rise from 11 t in 1990 to 21 t in 1993.

Platinum demand in Japan for automotive catalysts was 12.3 t in 1990. In the United States and Canada, the production of cars is declining, even in transplanted Japanese firms, but manufacturers are inclined to increase their catalyst precious metals contents to meet increasingly strict longevity standards. Despite this, demand declined to 21 t in 1990, the level at which it is likely to remain for some time.

The advent of fuel cells would alter the physiognomy of the market. The electrodes from the first three plants producing phosphoric acid cells (one of 4.5 and two of 11 MW) demanded more than 300 kg of platinum. It is estimated that, around 1995, about one hundred fuel cell power plants are expected in Europe, Japan, the United States, and the Far East. If these projects materialize, the annual demand for platinum, which is about 50 t today, could grow tenfold in the next decade [13].

*Platinum price trends*

Starting at about $5 per gram in the early 1970s, the average price reached its highest level in 1986 (over $19/g or more than $600/oz), and then dropped from 1989 ($17/g) to 1992 ($11/g). Prices fluctuate widely according to the economic situation (fears of recession, etc.) and in line with international events (the Gulf War, developments in the political situation in South Africa, the disintegration of the USSR, etc.) as users often make precautionary purchases, which tends to push prices upward.

#### 13.4.1.2 Palladium market

The supply of palladium amounted to 115 t in 1991 and 121 t in 1992. The main supplier is Russia with 52% of the market, followed by South Africa with 35%, and by North America with 10%. Two-thirds of Russian palladium is exported to Japan, which is developing palladium/rhodium catalysts and uses a great deal of palladium in the manufacture of electronic components.

Automotive catalysts represent only a small share of the palladium market (less than 10%) (Table 13.11 and Fig. 13.3). Half of the palladium used goes to the electrical industry, much of it to Japan for the manufacture of electronic components. Palladium is also largely used, especially in Germany, to make dental alloys in combination with silver, gold, copper, and tin, since these alloys are less expensive than gold alloys.

*Palladium price trends*

The price of palladium, which was fixed at about \$1.3/g in the early 1970s, reached a peak in 1989 at \$5.5/g or \$170/oz. It then fell in 1990 to \$3.7/g and to \$2.85/g in 1992. Since 95% of the palladium supplied in 1990 is a by-product of nickel metallurgy, there is no risk of production drying up if the bottom falls out of the palladium market.

#### 13.4.1.3 Rhodium market

In 1992, 11.75 t of rhodium reached the market. The Republic of South Africa supplied 54%, Russia 41%, with the remainder was supplied by North America. Most of the rhodium (87%) (Table 13.11 and Fig. 13.4) is used in the composition of automotive catalysts, where rhodium has so far proved to be irreplaceable for reducing $NO_x$ in three-way catalysts. The other uses cover catalysts for the chemical industry and electronic components.

Faced with the strong market demand for automotive catalysts, precious metals mining companies are seriously tempted to boost their production of rhodium. Because of the price prevailing in 1990, the value of rhodium sales rose to 75% of the value of platinum sales at one-tenth of the volume. However, while they could pursue this further, the mining companies refuse to increase their platinum production merely to have more by-product rhodium, because this would cause platinum prices to collapse [13].

*Rhodium price trends*

Starting at a price of \$19/g in the early 1970s, the price of rhodium held at around \$38/g (\$1200/oz) from 1986 to 1989, and then suddenly climbed to a peak of \$160/g in mid-1990, subsequently falling to \$145/g and then to \$80/g in 1992. This sudden rise could be due to the strategic stockpiling of rhodium by the US Department of defense [13]. Efforts to reduce the specific quantity of rhodium in catalysts are also counteracted by the precautionary maintenance of the present contents to guarantee the catalyst's longevity as demanded by toughened standards.

#### 13.4.1.4 Recovery of platinum and precious metals

A growing share of platinum demand can be satisfied by recovery from spent catalytic converters (Table 13.11). However, since wrecks only reach the scrap market eight to ten years after their first registration, recovery now happens only in the United States and Japan, with installations being set up in Germany. In the USA, recovery prices range from \$10 to \$17 per converter depending on the rhodium content. It is estimated that the converter recovery value represents about half of the total wreck [13]. However, 10% of the wrecks still go to the scrap heap with their catalytic converters.

In 1990 (Table 13.11), a significant amount of palladium ($\approx$ 2.5 t) was recovered in the United States and Japan from catalytic converters from wrecks, which were initially equipped with palladium-based trap oxidizers.

**Table 13.11** World consumption of precious metals in catalytic converters [13] (in metric tons)

| Metal | Platinum | | | Palladium | | | Rhodium | | |
|---|---|---|---|---|---|---|---|---|---|
| Year | (1) | (2) | (3) | (1) | (2) | (3) | (1) | (2) | (3) |
| 1981 | **19.90** | 0.00 | 26 | – | – | – | – | – | – |
| 1982 | **20.30** | 0.31 | 28 | – | – | – | – | – | – |
| 1983 | **20.06** | 0.93 | 30 | – | – | – | – | – | – |
| 1984 | **26.10** | 1.40 | 32 | – | – | – | – | – | – |
| 1985 | **30.40** | 2.18 | 35 | – | – | – | **4.20** | 0 | 55 |
| 1986 | **35.61** | 2.95 | 40 | **8.24** | 1.24 | 9 | **5.85** | 0 | 70 |
| 1987 | **39.03** | 3.58 | 38 | **8.40** | 1.56 | 8 | **7.03** | 0.09 | 76 |
| 1988 | **40.90** | 4.98 | 36 | **8.09** | 2.02 | 8 | **7.22** | 0.22 | 76 |
| 1989 | **45.26** | 5.44 | 42 | **8.24** | 2.18 | 8 | **8.21** | 0.22 | 81 |
| 1990 | **47.28** | 6.53 | 42 | **9.64** | 2.49 | 9 | **10.26** | 0.34 | 85 |
| 1991 | **48.82** | 6.68 | 39 | **11.5** | 2.64 | 10 | **9.39** | 0.50 | 87 |
| 1992 | **51.47** | 7.62 | 43 | **15.39** | 2.95 | 19 | **9.42** | 0.62 | 87 |

(1) Consumption (2) Recovery (3) Percentage of consumption

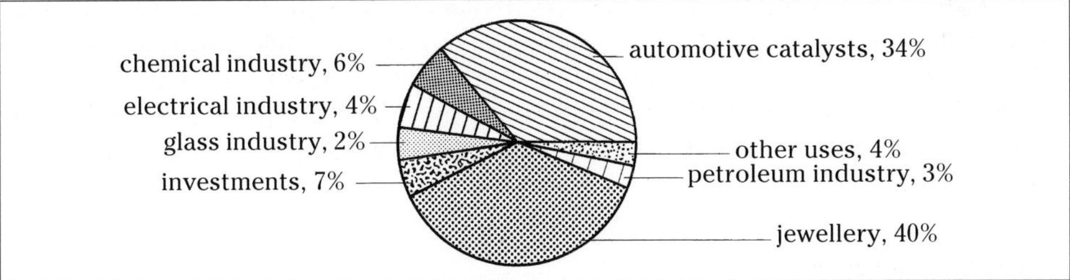


**Fig 13.2** Breakdown of platinum consumption in the Western world in 1992 [13]

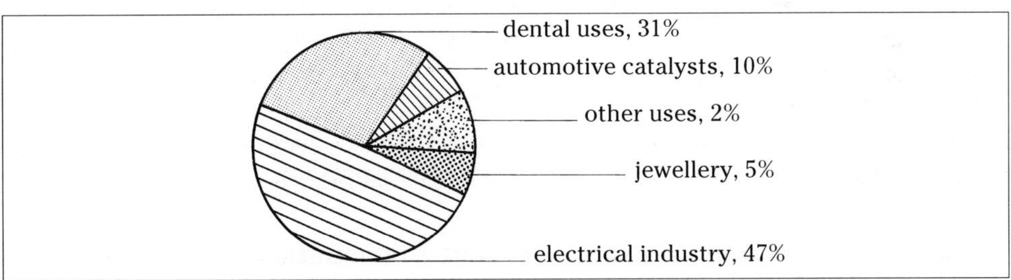


**Fig 13.3** Breakdown of palladium consumption in the Western world in 1992 [13]

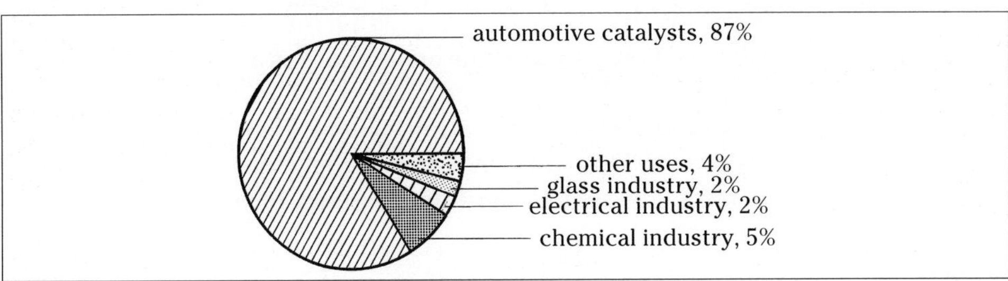


**Fig 13.4** Breakdown of rhodium consumption in the Western world in 1990 [13]

Given the prices reached by rhodium, its recovery from spent catalytic converters is a profitable business.

## 13.5 Additional costs incurred by diesel traps

The cost of a particulate trap system for buses, consisting of a dual trap with bypass regeneration burner, has been estimated at 25,000 DM (or about 80,000 French francs) [45]. For mass-produced diesel vehicles, the extra cost of the trap system with in-line burner is estimated at about 5% of the vehicle price [20].

Installation of a ceramic trap on a bus already in service has been estimated to cost US$1000 in terms of outlay, accompanied by an annual US$400 to cover depreciation and maintenance [55] (Table 13.12).

On diesel loaders used in Canadian nickel mines, equipped with monolith traps automatically regenerated due to the high exhaust temperature, the following annual costs (in Canadian dollars) were estimated for the equipment on a loader:

- annual amortization of trap purchase (four traps per year and per loader) 4000
- trap installation costs 180
- trap operating and maintenance costs 2080
- extra cost of fuel (to overcome trap pressure drop) 430

total extra cost (per loader per year) 6690

This total annual extra cost of about 35,000 French francs should be compared with the savings realized in the mine (amounting to Canadian $27,500 or 137,000 French francs per year per loader). In fact, the reduction of the diameter of the ventilation ducts and the reduction in size of the blowers mean savings in depreciation, power consumption, and maintenance, plus lower heating costs for a smaller ventilation air throughput [26].

A US assessment concerns all trucks and buses in circulation (250,000 registered per year driving an annual 50,000 miles): Each vehicle has a service life of six years, with an assumed trap price of US$3000, replaced once during the truck lifetime. By its regeneration and the pressure drop it causes, the filter implies extra fuel consumption of 5%. After the first six years, the additional extra cost paid by the US truck and bus industry would amount to about 2 billion dollars [56]. These figures should be compared with the French situation, where annual coach and bus registrations range between 3200 and 3600, truck registrations are at about 40,000 units of more than 5 t, and semi-trailer tractors about 15,000 [16].

The microwave system for trap regeneration is estimated to cost about US$200, or 1200 French francs, for the magnetron alone, with a replacement cost of US$60 [19].

**Table 13.12** Cost of particulate traps installed on buses [16 and 54]
(Prices in 1985 French francs exclusive of tax)

| Cost item | System selected | | | |
|---|---|---|---|---|
| | **Monolith + burner** | **Monolith + additive** | **Catalytic 'sponge'** | **DB 'fiber coil'** |
| **initial cost to manufacturer:** | | | | |
| • trap | 1200 | 1200 | 4000 | 1360 |
| • casing and tubes | 480 | 480 | 480 | 480 |
| • additive tank + pump | | 640 | | |
| • sensor and safety elements | | 240 | | |
| • regeneration and control systems | 1440 | | 560 | 1280 |
| • modifications to vehicle | 800 | 800 | 800 | 800 |
| COST TO MANUFACTURER | 3920 | 3360 | 5840 | 3920 |
| **labor for assembly (h):** | 4 | 2 | 4 | 4 |
| • cost at 100 F/h | 400 | 200 | 400 | 400 |
| • overheads (40%) | 160 | 80 | 160 | 160 |
| TOTAL COST TO MANUFACTURER | 4480 | 3640 | 6400 | 3920 |
| • manufacturer margin (20%) | 896 | 728 | 1280 | 896 |
| • tooling unit cost | 800 | 800 | 800 | 800 |
| • R&D unit cost | 2400 | 1600 | 800 | 2400 |
| COST TO DEALER | 8576 | 6768 | 9280 | 8576 |
| • dealer margin (20%) | 1715 | 1353 | 1 856 | 1715 |
| COST TO CONSUMER | 10 291 | 8121 | 11 136 | 10 291 |
| **operating costs:** | | | | |
| • vehicle lifetime (km) | 400,000 | 400,000 | 400,000 | 400,000 |
| • vehicle lifetime (years) | 10 | 10 | 10 | 10 |
| • maintenance cost per 100,000 km | 200 | 560 | 200 | 100 |
| • consumption: | | | | |
| • basic value (liters/100 km) | 40 | 40 | 40 | 40 |
| • extra consumption due to trap (%) | 3.9 | 2.5 | 2.5 | 1.25 |
| • diesel cost (F/liter inclusive of tax) | 3.5 | 3.5 | 3.5 | 3.5 |
| • trap replacement/cleaning: | | | | |
| • lifetime (km) | 270,000 | 160,000 | 250,000 | 160,000 |
| • number of replacements | 1 | 2 | 1 | 2 |
| • cost of replacement | 3800 | 3800 | 9500 | 4200 |
| • cost of cleaning | | 672 | | |
| **extra operating cost:** | | | | |
| • if cleaning | | 1691 | | |
| • if replacement | 2644 | 2384 | 2436 | 1580 |

## 13.6 Cost of periodic inspection of pollution control systems

The basic aim of pollution control systems is not to have them operate correctly when they leave the assembly line, but to help reduce the pollutants emitted by the vehicles on the roads. This is why the different countries concerned are trying to set up systems for the periodic inspection of the effectiveness of the retrofit and tuning technologies and the purifying systems. The exorbitant cost of the organizations needed for efficient inspection has so far delayed their implementation.

In the United States, the I/M inspection program is under the authority of the different states. The FTP procedure was considered too expensive. Early attempts were made to replace it by short idling early-warning tests, which are not very effective for distinguishing vehicles that do not meet FTP limits, especially if the vehicles tested are not correctly preconditioned [23]. The price of a short test is about US$10 and the average costs for reconditioning are about US$140. However, since this concerns a small number of vehicles, the impact on the reduction of total emissions is rather small and the total cost is more than US$8000/t of HC not sent into the atmosphere, based on the cost of inspection alone (US$10) [23]. Adding the reconditioning costs gives the figures in Table 13.13.

**Table 13.13** Cost of periodic inspections

| Cost of inspection (US$) | Cost of repair (US$) | Emission reduction on repaired vehicles (g/mile) | | Cost/benefit (US$/t) | |
|---|---|---|---|---|---|
| | | HC | CO | HC | CO |
| 10 | 136 | 0.048 | 1.10 | 12,753 | 561 |

A more recent survey in the State of Maryland estimates the inspection cost at US$20/year per vehicle. The total cost of the program, estimated at US$7500/t of HC not emitted, is considered much less profitable than the reduction of HC emissions from stationary sources [34].

With the advent of onboard computers, it is possible to install permanent monitoring of pollution control systems with onboard diagnosis. This system is two to three times more effective than idling tests [23].

After a transitory period up to 1996, the *EPA* has imposed the Onboard Diagnostic on models produced in 1994. The onboard systems will be checked as part of the inspection program [9].

In Germany, it was not possible to implement the following ASU[1] procedure recommended by the TÜV [24]: after conditioning the vehicle at 50 km/h on a chassis

1. Special exhaust gas inspection.

dynamometer, it is driven at 50 km/h while measuring CO, HC, and $NO_x$, followed by CO and HC measurements while idling for gasoline vehicles, and smoke measurement at full charge maximum speed for diesel vehicles. The cost of an installation to perform these tests (chassis dynamometer, analyzers) for a very large market is between 100,000 and 150,000 DM, not including structural work and civil engineering. Germany would need 34,000 installations of this type [7] with the necessary technical and administrative personnel. An annual tax of about one billion DM would be needed to finance this program, which was rejected by German manufacturers. Their counterproposal involves ten measurement points. It consists of a visual inspection of the good working order of the components, combined with measurements while idling and during free acceleration of CO, HC, and smoke, excluding $NO_x$ without the use of a chassis dynamometer. This should cost about 15,000 DM in investment outlay per installation and represent 30 DM per car and 100 DM per truck/bus, for 30 min of inspection. To this argument, the TÜV retort that on a chassis dynamometer with automated analyzers, inspection would only last 10 min and cost about 25 DM.

## 13.7 Costs incurred by improvements to motor fuels

### 13.7.1 Gasoline fuels

The advent of catalytic converters, especially three-way catalysts incorporating platinum, absolutely demands that the engine run on fuel containing no lead anti-knock additives. The lowering of the octane number, which results from the elimination of this additive, implies higher fuel consumption by the automobile. To recover the same anti-knock properties without these additives, so as to preserve the efficiency of the high compression ratio of today's engines, it is therefore essential to modify refining patterns. Yet the sophistication of refining methods for increasing the 'clear' octane number of the products means higher consumption of crude oil.

Given the price and the cost of these modifications in energy terms, it was necessary to find a compromise to reconcile the total cost of increasing the anti-knock qualities of fuels without additives with the cost of additional consumption by the vehicles resulting from the deterioration in fuel performance.

An car efficiency parameter (CEP) was accordingly defined as the variation in the mass consumption of gasoline per unit variation in RON octane number, a value assumed to be constant in the 90 to 100 RON interval [3]. This value of the CEP ranges between 0.4 and 1.6, with an average of 1.0.

The energy optimum, an index that minimizes the total consumption of crude oil so that an automobile with a CEP of 1 drives a given distance while burning 1000 t of gasoline, is 94.5 RON and 84.5 MON [29 and 39] (Fig. 13.5).

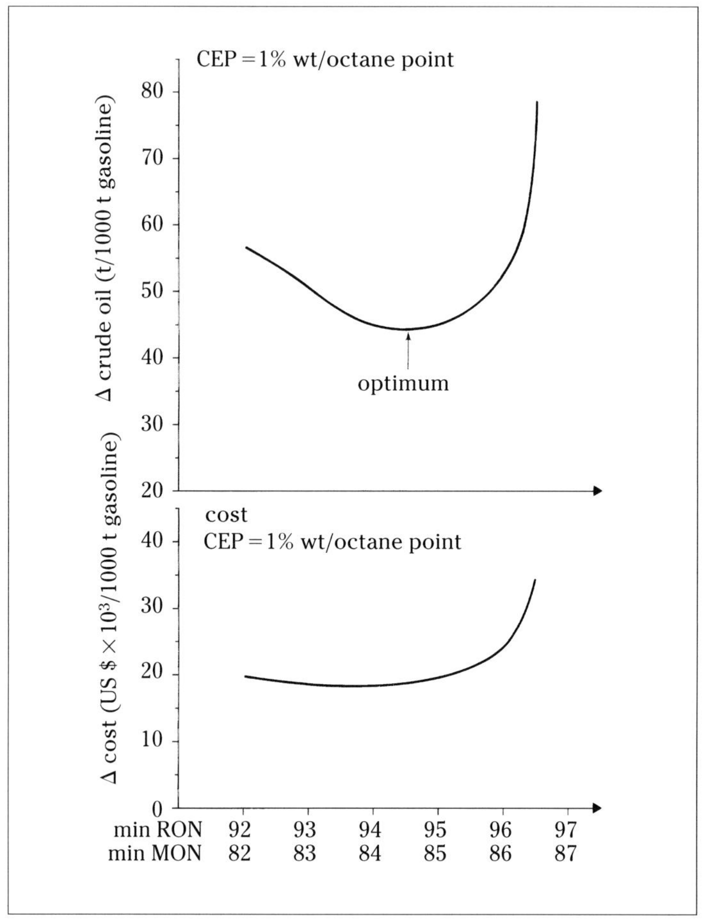


**Fig 13.5** Minimum consumption of crude oil and cost [29]. Unleaded gasoline

At this energy low, the increase in crude oil consumption over unleaded gasoline containing 0.4 g/liter of Pb amounts to 44 t of crude oil to manufacture 1000 t of gasoline. This extra consumption is reduced over the years due to economic advances in refining processes.

The economic optimum, an index that minimizes the total annual extra cost (extra refining cost, including capital amortization, operating costs, and the cost of crude oil + extra cost to consumer, including the increase in consumption) was calculated at 93.5 RON and 83.5 MON (Fig. 13.5). Under these conditions, for 1000 t of gasoline produced annually, the additional cost over leaded gasoline is about US$20,000, and the corresponding additional investments range between 26 and 46 million US dollars [29].

Negotiations between European refiners and automobile manufacturers have culminated in the definition of a euro-premium gasoline (Eurosuper) with octane numbers of 95 RON and 85 MON, a figure with a slight advantage in favor of reduced vehicle consumption.

To raise the clear octane number, which ranges around 91 RON ex-refinery, it is necessary to add oxygenated compounds (methanol, ethanol, tert butyl alcohol, MTBE, ETBE) which help to gain three octane points; the additional two points are gained by modifying the refining schemes incorporating aromatization, alkylation, and isomerization units.

To achieve this, isomerization and alkylation units are being built in the different French refineries (Lavéra, Gonfreville, La Mède, Grandpuits, Feyzin) to meet the demand for unleaded fuels, of which 6 Mt was produced in 1992 (in a total automotive gasoline market of ≈18 Mt), representing a 30% increase over 1991 [14].

This restructuring of refining capacities completes the transformations of the French refining industry, faced in the 1980s with a shrinking market for heavy products (heavy fuel oil and, to a lesser extent, home-heating oil) due to the transition to nuclear-generated electricity. This market structure also means increased imports of automotive fuels (≈3.5 Mt in 1990).

In early 1991, the share of unleaded gasoline represented about 20% of the gasoline market. It was then available in 46% of the sales points of the distribution network, with 98 RON unleaded premium accounting for 92% of sales as against 8% for 95 RON Eurosuper [14].

Eurosuper was introduced into France for use on relatively recent vehicles not yet equipped with catalysts. These vehicles, whose valve seats do not need lead as a fuel, and whose plastic feed circuits are resistant to oxygenated compounds, still have compression ratios demanding a high octane number.

In view of the price fluctuations generated by world market changes and external events (Gulf War for example), leaded premium gasoline was priced in 1993 (ex-refinery exclusive of tax) around 1.14 French francs/liter. In the same conditions, Eurosuper cost 0.12 French franc/liter more and 98 RON premium an average of 0.08 French franc/liter more than Eurosuper.

Added to these prices exclusive of tax are the miscellaneous taxes that more than triple the ex-refinery price of leaded premium (78% tax on the tax-inclusive consumer price). With unleaded fuels, to avoid the use of leaded gasoline in vehicles equipped with catalysts, the overall taxes were reduced to bring the consumer price to a lower level. This brings the multiplication factor of the Eurosuper ex-refinery price to less than 2.5 (71.1% tax on the tax-inclusive consumer price). In early 1991, the average tax-inclusive prices in French francs/liter were 5.27 for leaded premium, 5.09 for Eurosuper, and 5.20 for 98 RON unleaded gasoline.

#### 13.7.1.1 Reformulated gasoline

The future fuels of the coming decade will have to satisfy environmental requirements as well as the quality criteria hitherto prevailing. In particular, they will have to display lower aromatics[2] and olefins[3] and lower vapor pressures[4]. These changes will undeniably have an influence on refining schemes. The bulk of the aromatics is generated in catalytic reforming, where the severity will have to be reduced and which will have to be supplemented by alkylation reactions. The olefins are mainly present at the exit of fluid catalytic cracking, of which the production will have to be aimed more towards light products such as propylene and butylenes, which are raw materials for the production of the ethers MTBE and ETBE [15]. Isomerization and alkylation units will also have to be developed.

A US survey on this subject [37] shows that, added to the present production cost of gasoline at 0.16 French franc/liter[5] over the price of crude, is another 0.12 French franc/liter corresponding to investment increments and operating costs to obtain reformulated gasoline (Table 13.14). This would boost the pump price in the United States by 12.5 to 33%. Some estimates of the total cost to the US refining industry hint at 20 billion dollars [22].

**Table 13.14** Cost of motor fuels in the year 2000 in gasoline equivalent [9], CARB estimates, August 1990 value, US$1 = 6 French francs

| Fuel | Price | |
|---|---|---|
| | **US$/gallon** | **French francs/liter** |
| gasoline | 1.35 to 1.45 | 2.14 to 2.29 |
| methanol | 1.44 to 1.49 | 2.28 to 2.36 |
| ethanol | 2.33 | 3.69 |
| liquefied petroleum gas | 0.98 | 1.55 |
| compressed natural gas | 0.84 | 1.33 |
| electricity | 0.59 | 0.93 |

#### 13.7.1.2 Oxygenated fuels

Contrary to ethers (MTBE, ETBE, TAME), the alcohols methanol and ethanol, despite their high mixture octane number, are rarely used as replacement fuels due to their high volatility and their affinity for water. This volatility can sharply increase evaporative emissions, and the effect of reducing CO emissions by lean burn is only valid on older vehicles, which are tuned rich and not equipped with mixture control.

2. <20 to 25% instead of the current 35 to 50% and less than 1% benzene instead of the present 5%.
3. <5% instead of the present 8 to 10%.
4. Reid vapor pressure limited to 62 instead of 65 kPa today in summer in France.
5. Based on US$1 = 6 French francs.

Despite these imperfections, many attempts are being made in the United States, Brazil, and France to promote the use of alcohol as a motor fuel, based on the fact that fermentation ethanol is a renewable energy source (from corn in the United States, sugar cane in Brazil, beets or wheat in France). However, ethanol only starts becoming economically profitable with a crude oil price per barrel exceeding US$40 [10] because it costs between 3 and 3.5 French francs/liter [1], based on a guaranteed EEC wheat price of 1250 French francs/t [46]. This price would drop to 1.6 French francs/liter based on a world wheat price of 500 French francs/t for plants manufacturing 130,000 t/year. Hence, its use is subject to the extent of tax relief granted by governments.

Methanol itself has progressively been discarded in favor of ethers obtained particularly from methanol. The quantity introduced into European gasoline dropped from 750,000 t in 1987 to 200,000 t in 1988. Its price of about 9 French francs/liter makes it prohibitive for use as a fuel in pure form, unless the price per barrel of crude exceeds US$50 [5]. However, ethers like MTBE do not raise any problems of vapor pressure, have a favorable mixture octane number, and can be added to the fuel in a content of up to 15% by volume[6], corresponding to about 2.7% oxygen in the gasoline (the EPA demands at least 2% oxygen in reformulated gasoline). These ethers are produced by the addition of the alcohols methanol and ethanol to olefins from steam crackers and catalytic crackers or, for MTBE, from butanes and isobutene. The price ratio between MTBE and gasoline is higher than 1.4 [5].

Given the increasing price of methanol and the availability of large stocks of wine alcohol in the EEC (900,000 t, growing by 200,000 t/year), which are sold by auction, it is advantageous to convert MTBE production plants to make ETBE. If taxation on fuel alcohol, similar to that on diesel, is extended to ethanol used to manufacture ETBE, the latter would cost about 2000 French francs/t [18]. With a tax rebate of 1.5 French francs/liter of ethanol, ETBE would cost 2200 French francs/t from wheat and 1400 French francs/t from beets (to be compared with the 1991 cost of premium at 1200 French francs/t exclusive of tax).

#### 13.7.1.3 Incidence on distribution costs

Although the total amount of automotive fuels placed on the market varies only slightly, the availability to the consumer of a larger number of grades of automotive fuels, leaded regular gasoline, leaded premium, Eurosuper, and 98 RON unleaded premium, instead of the former two grades, means additional costs of storage in refineries, in tank farms, and in service stations, and a corresponding change in the configuration of these service stations.

This situation of co-existence of four grades of automotive fuels is obviously transitional, but this phase is liable to last at least ten years before all the vehicles on the road are equipped with catalytic converters.

---

6. 10% in the present EEC regulations.

The costs incurred include rinsing and cleaning of the installations that previously conveyed leaded fuels to allow the distribution of unleaded fuels meeting the specifications (Pb content, 0.013 g/liter).

Table 13.15 lists a number of costs of installing systems necessary for the distribution of unleaded fuels [30]. In France, the extra distribution costs were estimated in 1988 at 1 French franc/liter, a figure expected to decline with the increase in volumes distributed [4].

**Table 13.15** Unit investment costs for storage and distribution facilities [30], Prices in 1983 US$

| Equipment | Capacity | Cost |
|---|---|---|
| storage and blending tanks, including necessary piping | 5000 to 20,000 $m^3$ | 80 to 150 $/$m^3$ |
| tank truck | 35 $m^3$ | 50,000 to 100,000 |
| tanker loading system: ramp, piping, meters, loading arm | | 100,000 to 120,000 |
| service station tank with piping and gasoline pump meter | | 15,000 to 20,000 |
| refuelling nozzle | | 100 to 150 |

## 13.7.2 Diesel fuels

The average price of diesel ex-refinery in 1993 was 1.22 French francs/liter. After adding miscellaneous taxes, which multiplied the base price by a factor of 2.9 (<65% taxes on the tax-inclusive price), the average consumer price was around 3.5 French francs/liter in 1993.

The Domestic Tax on Petroleum Products (TIPP) applied to diesel was raised in February 1990 to bring it closer to European conditions.

The improvement in diesel properties to meet pollution regulations essentially concerns the reduction of sulfur contents, to allow the use of oxidation catalysts based on precious metals without forming sulfuric acid, and a reduction in aromatics contents to reduce particulate emissions. With the amendment of the *Clean Air Act*, the *EPA* intends to limit sulfur contents to 0.5% by weight and aromatics to 10 to 20% by volume [15]. These new limits will demand more hydrodesulfurization and hydrotreating with a more severe selection of cuts intended for road diesel, thereby narrowing the refiner's leeway.

In the United States, it was estimated that the transition from diesel containing 0.25% sulfur to a diesel containing 0.05% sulfur would cost US$700 to 2000 per ton of diesel. An additional cost of US$26,000 to 554,000/t would be added to this desulfurized diesel to reduce aromatics from 32, to 10% [27].

The forthcoming limits in Europe are slightly less severe, but they are set at 0.2% by weight. A European survey [47] shows that desulfurization to 0.05% sulfur for a capacity of 1 Mt/year would cost US$14.4/t of diesel. This figure rises to US$26.3 and to US$31.8 if the aromatics content is simultaneously reduced to 20 and 10% respectively. It is estimated in France that the total investment for a dozen units would be about 3 billion French francs, with a price increase of 0.10 French franc/liter of diesel for the consumer [6].

### 13.7.2.1 Oxygenated diesel fuels

Alcohols can be used as replacement fuels in diesel engines, but only after a thorough transformation of the engine, involving a lowering of the compression ratio and the addition of ignition by spark plug. Vegetable oils have been proposed, but their viscosity and low temperature behavior are unfavorable.

By contrast, the methyl esters of fatty acids, obtained by transesterification of rapeseed oil with to methanol in particular, are excellent diesel fuels. However, the synthesis process leaves glycerin as a co-product in a proportion of 10% of the ester produced, and the economics of the process depends on the utilization of this glycerin. Today, with a world rapeseed oil price of 2400 French francs/t, depending on whether the glycerin is sold at 9000 or 6000 French francs/t, the ester production cost oscillates between 1.7 and 1.9 French francs/liter[7], a value that is uncompetitive considering the diesel price of 1.3 French francs/liter. Only tax relief aligning the taxation on the ester to that on home-heating oil would serve to lower the cost to 1.21 French francs/liter.

## 13.8 Costs incurred by evaporation control systems

The cartridges needed to recover fuel vapors emitted and the necessary pipes and gaskets on the vehicle have been estimated to cost about US$20 [43] or 200 DM [28] per vehicle, and this cost could be partly offset during the ten years of the vehicle's lifetime by the amount of fuel recovered (US$19) [21] and [28]. The cost of the onboard system would amount to US$190/t of fuel recovered [43].

The equipment for the service stations installing the complete recovery system ('Stage II') (Section 10.12) would cost US$5700 to 14,800 per station, or US$1470 per ton of fuel recovered [8] and [43]. The twin-pipe refueling nozzle would cost US$125, or US$75 more than the conventional nozzle [8]. The oil companies believe that the investment required to cover all the service stations of Western Europe

7. Even 2.6 French francs/liter on a plant manufacturing 25,000 t/year.

(≈2.45 billion dollars) is prohibitive to deal merely with emissions of 1.7% of total hydrocarbon emissions [48]. On the contrary, they recommend the installation of larger-volume (≈5 liters) ( Section 10.12) activated carbon canisters on the vehicle, estimated to cost US$20 to 80 per vehicle. The total cost is accordingly estimated at US$335 to 1340 per ton of hydrocarbons recovered, compared with about US$5000 per ton to equip the service stations [2]. This opinion is not shared by the automobile manufacturers who estimate a US cost of US$35 per vehicle added to a capital cost of one billion dollars, increased by 250 million dollars or US$16.5 per vehicle for inspection [31]. Apart from the fact that the effects of the equipment at service stations will be felt sooner than the equipment on vehicles, they estimate the total cost for service stations at 0.4 billion dollars, whereas, for vehicles, this cost would be 3.34 billion dollars. In Germany, despite the contrary opinion of the oil industry (*MWV*), the cost of the service station alternative (1960 to 3100 DM) is also considered to be cheaper per ton of gasoline recovered than the cost of the vehicle alternative (2600 to 4550 DM) [49].

## 13.9 Conclusion

As pointed out at the beginning of this chapter, it is difficult to compile a completely balanced economic cost for pollution control systems. American mathematical models have estimated that the elimination of 1000 t of diesel particulates would avoid the death from cancer of 56 persons per year, indicating a 'saving' ranging from 4 to 17 million dollars per 1000 t of diesel particulates. The effect on the other causes of mortality (bronchitis, asthma) would add a saving of US M$794 for each $\mu g/m^3$ of particulates removed [50]. Besides these health benefits, it is essential to consider the soiling caused by diesel soot and the lessening of atmospheric visibility. Lowering the ambient particulate rate by 1 $\mu g/m^3$ saves between US M$37 and M$100 per year for cleaning and US$2000/t for the improvement in visibility [50]. These economies easily counterbalance the extra costs incurred by the installation of traps on urban buses [51]. Another factor in these savings is the ventilation of road tunnels due to reduced emissions in the tunnels. It is estimated that if particulate traps become mandatory from 1995 on, the fresh air requirements of tunnels could be cut by 30 to 45% [36].

On the other hand, this collective benefit offered to the social community is unfortunately not always favorably perceived by consumers and the authorities. The additional cost of the traps, when added to the higher price of the diesel engine in comparison with the gasoline engine, has already eradicated the production and sale of diesel-powered automobiles in the United States. This occurred in an economic context in which gasoline has again become relatively cheap. The factory price for mounting a diesel trap would have had to have stayed under US$150 to be accepted by consumers [53].

Yet the extra costs borne by consumers for catalytic converters or diesel traps must be seen in relative terms, by comparing them with the costs of the other prestige options offered in manufacturer's brochures: automatic transmission (≈7500 French francs), metallized paint (1600 to 4700 French francs), electric sun roof (4500 to 5500 French francs), seat heaters (2500 to 3800 French francs), tinted windows (1500 French francs), power steering (2500 French francs), electric window operators and rearview window defrosting (1600 to 5500 French francs), light alloy wheels (1700 to 6000 French francs), and headlight washers (1600 French francs). These options do not always enhance driving safety and environmental protection may well merit an equivalent financial sacrifice on the part of the consumer.

## REFERENCES

[1] Anon., (1986), "Quel avenir pour les carburants alcoolisés?", *Pet. Inf.*, November, pp. 29-36.

[2] Anon., (1987), "Volatile organic compound emissions in Western Europe, Control options and their cost-effectiveness for gasoline vehicles, distribution and refining", *CONCAWE Report* No. 6/87, 24 p.

[3] Anon., (1980), "The rational utilization of fuels in private transport (RUFIT), Extrapolation to unleaded gasoline case", *CONCAWE Report* No. 8/80, 21 p.

[4] Anon., (1988), "Les carburants, ça change!", *Pet. Inf.*, May, pp. 6-7.

[5] Anon., (1990), "Situation actuelle et perspectives des composés oxygénés dans les carburants", *Actualité Chim.*, July/September, pp. 174-190.

[6] Anon., (1991), "La réduction du soufre dans les carburants, quelles solutions et pour quels coûts?", *Pet. Inf.*, July/August, pp. 28-29.

[7] Anon., (1991), "Defekten Katalysatoren und rußenden Dieselmotoren auf der Spur", "Weiteerentwicklung der ASU II ist bereits geplant", Viel Schlupflöcher für Abgassünder, Leichte Prüfung für Leichtgewichte, *VDI Nachrichten*, 27 September, pp. 9-11.

[8] T.C. Austin and G.S. Rubinstein, (1985), "A comparison of refueling emissions control with onboard and stage II systems", *SAE Paper* No. 851204, 30 p.

[9] W. Berg, (1991), "Die neue 'Abgas-Gesetzgebung' der USA", *VDI Fortschritt-Berichte* (150), 154-239.

[10] W.E. Betts, (1991), "Automotive fuels for the future", *Pet. Rev.*, June, pp. 284-287.

[11] M. Bidault, (1990), "La réduction des émissions des moteurs de véhicules industriels", *SIA Int. Conf.*, Lyon, 13/14 June, *Paper* No. 90099, pp. 265-279.

[12] M.L. Church et al., (1989), "Catalyst formulations 1960 to present", *SAE Paper* No. 890815, 7 p.

[13] J.S. Coombes, (1991), *Platinum 1992*, Johnson Matthey, London, 56 p.

[14] Comité Professionnel du Pétrole, (1990), *Pétrole 1990*, Éléments statistiques, 275 p.

[15] E.A. Corbett, (1990), "Fuels for tomorrow, Oil Gas J.", *Special Issue*, 18 June, pp. 33-57.

[16] P. Degobert and J. Delsey, (1986), *Réduction des émissions Diesel*, Proc. ENCLAIR '86, Taormina, Italy, 28/31 October, pp. 217-226.

[17] B. Engler et al., (1987), "Three-way catalyst performance using minimized rhodium loadings", *SAE Paper* No. 872097, 7 p.

[18] A. Forestière et al., (1989), *L'ETBE, Un avenir pour l'éthanol, 5th European Conf.*, "Biomass for Energy and Industry", Lisboa, 9/13 October, 5 p.

[19] C.P. Garner and J.C. Dent, (1989), "Microwave assisted regeneration of Diesel particulate traps", *SAE Paper* No. 890174, 8 p.

[20] H. Garthe, (1989), "Rußfiltertechnik für Nutzfahrzeug Dieselmotoren", *Verkehr und Technik*, **7,** 257-261.

[21] J.A. Gunderson and D.K. Lawrence, (1975), "Control of refueling emissions with an activated carbon canister on the vehicle", *SAE Paper* No.750905, 22 p.

[22] J. Gurney, (1990), "The US clean air act, Mandate for reformulated gasoline", *Pet. Rev.*, December, pp. 606-608.

[23] H.M. Haskew et al., (1987), "I/M effectiveness with today's closed-loop systems", *SAE Paper* No. 871103, 25 p.

[24] D. Hasssel et al., (1986), *Cost-optimized periodical inspection, A necessary prerequisite for realization of the EC resolutions for motor vehicle exhaust gas legislation*, Proc. ENCLAIR '86, Taormina, Italy, 28/31 October, pp. 203-215.

[25] J.W. Hightower, (1976), "Catalysts for automobile emission control", in: *Preparation of Catalysts*, B. Delmon, Elsevier Science Publications, Amsterdam, pp. 617-636.

[26] J.S. Howitt et al., (1983), "Application of a ceramic wall flow filter to underground Diesel emissions reduction", *SAE Paper* No. 830181 (SP-537), 131-139.

[27] M.C. Ingham and R.B. Warden, (1987), "Cost-effectiveness of Diesel fuel modifications for particulate control", *SAE Paper* No. 870556, 11 p.

[28] G. Lach and J. Winckler, (1990), "Kraftstoffdampf-Emission von Personenwagen mit Ottomotoren", *ATZ*, **92,** 388-396.

[29] R. Kahnitz et al., (1983), "Assessment of the energy balances and economic consequences of the reduction and elimination of lead in gasoline", *CONCAWE Report* No. 11/83R, 47 p.

[30] R. Kahnitz et al., (1984), "Effect of the introduction of unleaded gasolines on the gasoline storage/distribution system", *CONCAWE Report* No. 2/84, 16 p.

[31] L.B. Lave et al., (1990), "Controlling emissions from motor vehicles", *E.S.&T.*, **24,** 1128-1135.

[32] G. Le Baill, (1985), *Rapport parlementaire sur les formes de pollution atmosphérique à longue distance dites "pluies acides"*, 310 p.

[33] J.W.S. Longhurst, (1989), "Autocatalysts and motor vehicle emission control", *Clean Air*, **19,** 14-22.

[34] V.D. McConnell, (1990), "Costs and benefits of vehicle inspection, A case study of the Maryland region", *J. Environm. Management*, **30,** 1-15.

[35] R.J. Menne, (1988), "Magerkonzepte, Eine Alternative zum Dreiwegkatalysator", *MTZ*, **49,** 421-427.

[36] W. Meyeroltmanns, (1991), "The influence of decreasing vehicle exhaust emissions on the standards for ventilation systems for urban road tunnels", *Tunnel Underground Space Technol.*, **6,** 97-102.

[37] K. Owens, (1990), "Will reformulated gasolines cross the Atlantic?", *Pet. Rev.*, September, pp. 451-453.

[38] F. Perrin-Pelletier, (1986), *Coût de réduction des émissions en provenance des voitures*, Proc. ENCLAIR '86, Taormina, Italy, 28/31 October, pp. 157.167.

[39] J.M. Poutrel, (1986), "Impacts économiques pour la filière automobile et le secteur du raffinage distribution de la réglementation anti-pollution", *BIPE Report*, 111 p.

[40] J.M. Poutrel, (1987), "Enjeu économique de la réduction des polluants", *Poll. Atmosph.*, Special Issue November, pp. 15-24.

[41] M. Prigent, (1988), *Le traitement catalytique des gaz d'échappement*, TEC 88 Symp. "Matériaux", Grenoble, 13 October, 17 p.

[42] M. Prigent, (1988), *Pots catalytiques, Les alternatives au pot trois voies fonctionnant à richesse 1.00 régulée, Conf. "Le Moteur à Allumage Commandé de la Prochaine Décennie"*, Strasbourg, 18/19 May, Ing. Automobile, pp. 252-258.

[43] C.H. Schleyer and W.J. Koehl, (1986), "A comparison of vehicle refueling and evaporative emission control, Methods for long-term hydrocarbon control progress", *SAE Paper* No. 861552, 14 p.

[44] R.A. Searles, (1986), *Application of exhaust catalysts for Europe, The effets on costs and performance*, Proc. ENCLAIR '86, Taormina, Italy, 28/31 October, pp. 169-178.

[45] M. Signer, (1989), *Partikelfiltersysteme für Stadtbusse, Kommunalfahrzeuge und Verteilerfahrzeuge, Symp. "Dieselmotorentechnik" Ostfildern*, Stuttgart, 7/8 December, 19 p.

[46] B. Torck and P. Renault, (1988), "Les biotechnologies, un avenir pour une nouvelle chimie et pour l'énergie", *Ann. Mines*, October/november, pp. 73-84.

[47] C.W.C. van Paassen et al., (1989), "Costs to reduce the sulphur content of Diesel fuel", *CONCAWE Report* No. 10/89, 38 p.

[48] E. van Veen, (1986), *VOC's emissions inventory and control of emissions from gasoline distribution systems*, Proc. ENCLAIR '86, Taormina, Italy, 28/31 October, pp. 271-280.

[49] H. Waldeyer et al., (1990), "Emissionsminderung beim Tanken, Vergleich tankstellen- und fahrzeugzeitiger Techniken", *Verlag TÜV Rheinland*, 148 p.

[50] M.P. Walsh, (1983), "The benefits and costs of light-duty Diesel particulate control", *SAE Paper* No. 830179 (SP-537), 19 p.

[51] M.P. Walsh, (1985), "The benefits and costs of Diesel particulate control, (3) The urban bus", *SAE Paper* No. 850148 (P-158), 8 p.

[52] C.S. Weaver, (1989), "Feasibility of emissions control for off highway Diesel engines", *SAE Paper* No. 890169, 123-135.

[53] C.S. Weaver, (1983), "Trap oxidizer technology for light-duty Diesel vehicles, Status, prospects, and current issues", *SAE Paper* No. 831713, 18 p.

[54] C.S. Weaver, (1984), "Particulate control technology and particulate standards for heavy-duty Diesel engines", *SAE Paper* No. 840174, 109-125.

[55] C.S. Weaver et al., (1986), "Feasibility of retrofit technologies for Diesel emissions control", *SAE Paper* No. 860296, 19 p.

[56] S.V. Yumlu, (1988), "Particulate traps, some progress, some problems", *SAE Paper* No. 880347, 8 p.

# 14 Summing up

Upon completion of this book, several questions remained unanswered:

- Will the legislation enacted in the various countries and the implementation of pollution control techniques contribute to a decrease in air pollution?
- Is the selected target (the automobile) the priority target?
- Are the pollutants initially selected (CO, HC, $NO_x$, particulates) the most harmful?
- Should carbon dioxide emissions and their consequences on the greenhouse effect be assigned priority?
- Is the effect of the unit decrease in vehicle emissions not liable to be submerged by the larger number of units in circulation?
- Is availability of precious metals sufficient for their general use in the pollution control systems of vehicles?
- Is the inspection of emissions on a sampling of new vehicles effective for reducing general pollution?
- Do diesel-powered automobiles have a future in light of the possible tightening of pollution standards?
- Will new fuels reduce the level of emissions?
- Will new modes of power (electric vehicles) have a positive impact on the environment?

*Impact of pollutant reductions*

From the outset of European Community legislation, the allowable limits for HC and $NO_x$ have been progressively reduced. To meet the standards, it is possible to intentionally reduce HC at the expense of the reduction of $NO_x$, progressively increasing the $NO_x$/HC ratio. HC in particular is implicated in the formation of ozone (Section 2.3.2) and in California considerable emphasis has been laid on reducing VOC to control photochemical smog. In some circumstances, increasing the $NO_x$ concentrations at constant HC concentration can help to reduce the ozone concentration; at constant $NO_x$ concentration, the reduction of HC may have no effect whatsoever [14]. In the cities, the results vary with the fluidity of the traffic and the HC/$NO_x$ ratio [24]. In slow dense traffic (HC/$NO_x$ ratio $\approx$10), a reduction of hydrocarbon and/or nitrogen oxides causes a decrease in atmospheric ozone. In fluid traffic (HC/$NO_x$ ratio $\approx$3), a 50% reduction in $NO_x$ can more than double the ozone concentration [23]. This occurs even with an oxygenated fuel like methanol [3].

Hence $NO_x$ control is much more effective than HC control. Consequently, the amalgam hitherto made between HC and $NO_x$ appears to be the wrong way to act on air pollution levels.

On the other hand, as already pointed out earlier with diesel engine exhausts, means similar to catalytic converters are not yet available to eliminate $NO_x$ emissions. If tuning and retrofit technologies prove to be inadequate to satisfy the standards, the maintenance of the diesel engine will ultimately only be justified by its smaller contribution to the greenhouse effect.

*The automobile and the greenhouse effect*

$CO_2$ emissions have not been considered in this work. Carbon dioxide, which is a normal product of the combustion of carbonaceous products, has not been considered as a pollutant. The CFC stored in the air-conditioners mounted on 90% of US vehicles makes a stronger contribution to the greenhouse effect over the lifetime of the automobile than all the $CO_2$ emitted in the exhausts [1]. Discounting CFC, European estimates indicate that automobile traffic is more or less responsible for 10% of the human contribution to the global greenhouse effect [16]. Carbon dioxide emissions are directly proportional to the fuel consumption of carbon-bearing fuels and to the mileage traveled by vehicles. The advancements made during the energy crises and the development of diesel technology for private automobiles represent favorable trends.

Gases other than $CO_2$ also contribute to the greenhouse effect. Although vehicles with three-way catalytic converters emit more $CO_2$ than unequipped vehicles (5 to 10% due to slightly higher consumption and conversion of the pollutants to $CO_2$), their overall contribution is smaller [13].

Although diesel combustion uses a fuel that emits more $CO_2$ than gasoline, expressed as g/kg burned [1], its higher energy efficiency may prove to be advantageous for the reduction of $CO_2$ emissions and thus offset its disadvantages in terms of particulates and $NO_x$. However, given the relatively high contribution of $NO_2$ to the greenhouse effect, the direct injection diesel engine could be less advantageous than the gasoline engine with three-way catalyst [13].

*Impact of fuel modifications*

Contrary to expectations and for reasons similar to those mentioned earlier ($HC/NO_x$ ratio in the atmosphere), substituting methanol for conventional hydrocarbon fuels in modern vehicles with catalytic converters may not have a beneficial effect on the ambient ozone concentrations [6]; this effect is partly due to the higher emissions of formaldehyde in the presence of methanol.

On the other hand, modifications to conventional motor fuels (lower aromatics and sulfur contents, lowering of gasoline vapor pressures) cannot have other than a beneficial effect.

*Overall impact of reducing individual emissions*

The efforts expended by manufacturers, who are under pressure from lawmakers, have reduced and continue to reduce the emissions per unit of distance traveled for each vehicle. This reduction is measured on new vehicles by standardized procedures and route cycles.

In Europe, however, given the rate of new vehicle registration, the general use of pollution control systems on vehicles is liable to take a decade or so.

Furthermore, the user does not always drive his vehicle in accordance with the test conditions, often far from it. Due to tuning and adjustments designed to meet the statutory standards, expressway driving at 100 miles per hour, which is unrelated to test cycles, generates mileage emissions that could be three times higher than the limit values [20]. In addition, the driver does not always keep his vehicle in good working order, that is to say correctly tuned. We have already discussed the difficulty of installing generalized inspection systems, chiefly due to their prohibitive cost. In fact, only these inspections could ensure the permanent effectiveness of the tuning adjustments and control systems.

The pollution control efforts concern primarily the reduction of individual emissions. In fact, the number of cars on the road is steadily increasing. This figure rose from 50 million vehicles in 1950 to 350 million in 1988, and is expected to reach 500 million units around the year 2000 [10]. Despite the larger number of vehicles in circulation, if an overall reduction of the various pollutants is imposed in the developed countries (in Germany for the year 2000, 82% reduction of CO, 78% of HC, 83% of $NO_x$, 63% of particulates, 90% of benzene, 73% of PAH, and even 15% of $CO_2$ [11 and 12]), this will not apply to the other countries currently enlarging their vehicle fleets. In the developing countries, essentially in gigantic megalopolises, the number of vehicles grew by 105% between 1970 and 1980, compared with 52% in Western Europe [7]. These vehicles are often badly maintained, overloaded, supplied with bad fuel (low RON leaded gasoline, high sulfur and low cetane diesel), and the renewal rate is half of that in the industrialized countries.

*The electric car alternative*

The electric car, which generates no pollutant emissions, is often suggested as the final solution to the question of air pollution by the automobile. In fact, it simultaneously solves the problem of exhaust emissions, and for gasoline-powered vehicles, the evaporative losses from the vehicle and from the transportation and distribution installations (tank farms and service stations). If this solution effectively reduces pollution locally, that is to say behind the vehicle, this cannot be extrapolated in general terms if one considers the air pollution caused by the production of the electrical energy on which the vehicle is designed to run.

Only the production of electrical energy by nuclear means, from hydropower plants such as in Norway, or from solar energy by charging conventional storage batteries, or after the conversion of water by electrolysis to hydrogen to feed fuel cells, will we be capable of meeting the 'zero pollution' objective. These solutions are faced on the one hand with a reluctance to expand the number of nuclear power plants, as well as the currently prohibitive cost of fuel cells, and also with the difficulties encountered by onboard hydrogen storage.

In the case of conventional electricity generation by thermal power plants, the corresponding pollution will depend on the type of generator (boiler, gas turbines), the fuel used (fuel oil, gas, coal), and the control systems installed in the power plants. In converting the emission factors of the power plants (in g/kWh) into the g/km traveled by the electric vehicle, it is necessary to account for the succession of energy efficiencies (energy transmission, battery charge/discharge, electric motors). The relatively low total efficiency of the electric vehicle supplied with thermally-generated electricity is also liable to be a handicap in comparison with the diesel vehicle, if greenhouse effect problems assume primary importance.

The modeling of California conditions (no diesel-powered engines) shows that the advent of the electric vehicle will sharply reduce CO and HC emissions. Depending on the pollution control equipment at the power plants, $NO_x$ emissions may rise or fall, and $SO_2$ and particulate emissions have significant chances of increasing [22].

Even if the electric vehicle retains its potential as a short-range urban vehicle, it cannot become a highway vehicle because of its present inability to compete with vehicles using internal combustion engines. The electric vehicle's motor, battery or fuel cell system, and limited fuel storage capacity cannot compete with the internal combustion engine in terms of volume and mass per unit of energy developed.

*Towards the regulation of automotive traffic?*

The increasing number of vehicles in circulation worldwide (50 million vehicles in 1950 and 567 million in 1991, and how many more around the year 2000?) goes hand in hand with the growth of the world population and its greater concentration in the cities. On the other hand, it has not been accompanied by a concomitant growth in roads (22 vehicles per km in the United States, over 40 in Europe, and 60 in Germany) [17].

Pollution problems are felt on a worldwide scale due to their repercussions on the Earth's climate. Automotive transportation is not the main culprit (how many diesel vehicles would be needed to match to pollutant emissions of the burning oil wells of Kuwait?). It is therefore essentially in cities subject to dense traffic that the highest levels of automotive pollutants are to be found.

The anarchical growth of the megalopolis is tending to aggravate this situation by increasing pollutant emissions, some of which (like CO) are higher while idling, but in any case, all are extremely high in relation to the mileage traveled. Added to these consequences of pollution are the economic disadvantages: enormous fuel consumption in liters/100 km, time wasted in traveling from place to place, and corresponding psychological stress, especially when trying to find some place to park the vehicle.

To dissuade and limit these short hops (half of the source-to-destination routes traveled do not exceed 5 km) [17], the cities have already taken measures of varying effectiveness: driving on alternate days (Athens, Singapore), entry tolls for the large built-up areas (Netherlands), surtax levied on the fuel above an annual mileage limit (Switzerland, 15,000 km/year).

In recent decades, despite the foreseeable clogging of urban roads, everything has been designed for the anarchical growth of the automobile in the urban sector to the detriment of collective transport. Priority has been given to the construction of urban expressways before the establishment of communal transport on proper tracks (Metros, trams, trains) that are more convenient and faster. Since they are more profitable due to their enormous turnover, supermarkets and shopping malls have been installed on the outskirts of the cities in places that are only accessible by automobile, while neighborhood stores are gradually disappearing.

Moreover, inter-city transport of goods is increasingly carried out by road, instead of rail or waterway, causing huge traffic jams on expressways in countries like Germany, which nevertheless has a well-developed expressway network. In addition, commercial and industrial firms tend to deal with their transport requirements with their own fleet of trucks. Thus, in Germany, 60% of industrial trucks and 40% of commercial trucks return empty to their home base.

Therefore, it is necessary to alter habits and to reverse the trends. Reserving the inner cities for communal transport, electric vehicles, pedestrians, and bicycles would not only reduce chemical pollution but also pollution from noise. Communal transport should serve the shopping centers on the outskirts and should be designed to accommodate the merchandise purchased by patrons (carts that can enter buses and Metros?) or offer electric mini-vehicles that can be borrowed by customers to take their shopping home.

However, this can only be a long-term affair. In Germany, the switching from road to rail of 10% of the road goods traffic would require a fivefold increase in the tonnage currently transported by the Bundesbahn. A better rationalization of the transportation system would therefore be advisable. This could be done by limiting the range of unrestricted competition, which is responsible for the current anarchy in the transport sector. The road freight exchanges that have been progressively abandoned should be re-activated. Production complexes, whose specialized units are dispersed over long distances for profitability considerations, should take into account the harmful effects generated by the resulting transportation and the cost of the necessary road infrastructures. Freight exchanges could thus help to limit the inevitable two-way goods traffic generated by orders from customers for products manufactured nearby but ordered from distant commercial centers.

## REFERENCES


[1] C.A. Amann, (1990), "The passenger car and the greenhouse effect", *SAE Paper* No. 902099, 20 p.

[2] C. Barrier-Lynn et al., (1990), "Les industries automobiles française et allemande face aux nouvelles normes anti pollution", *Poll. Atmosph.* (126), 193-205.

[3] T.Y. Chang et al., (1989), "Impact of methanol vehicles on ozone air quality", *Atmos. Environm.*, **23,** 1629-1644.

[4] C.I. Davidson et al., (1986), "Indoor and outdoor air pollution in the Himalayas", *E.S.&T.*, **20,** 561-567.

[5] P. Degobert, (1989), "Les polluants atmosphériques anthropogènes", *Journées CNRS/PIREN*, Réactions des êtres vivants aux changements de l'environnement, 30 November/1 December, pp. 51-61.

[6] A.M. Dunker, (1989), "The relative reactivity of emissions from methanol-fueled and gasoline-fueled vehicles in forming ozone", *GMR Report* No. 6604 ENV 270, 1989, p. 21, *E.S.&T.*, **24,** 853-862.

[7] R. Joumard, (1989), "Pollution de l'air due au trafic dans les pays en voie de développement", *Recherche Transports Sécurité*, (22), 29-34.

[8] H. Heitland et al., (1990), "Einfluß des zukünftigen Pkw Verkehrs auf die $CO_2$ Emission", *MTZ*, **51,** 66-72.

[9] J. Lambert et al., (1986), "Prévisions globales des émissions de polluants automobiles en France à l'horizon 2000", *INRETS Report* No. 2, 69 p.

[10] J.W.S. Longhurst, (1989), "Autocatalysts and motor vehicle emission control", *Clean Air*, **19,** 14-22.

[11] N. Metz, (1989), *Highway emissions of regulated and some unregulated exhaust components in West Germany from 1970 to 2010, 3rd Int. Symp.*, "Highway Pollution", München, 18/22 September, 10 p.

[12] N. Metz, (1990), "Entwicklung der Abgasemissionen des Personenwagen Verkehrs in der BRD von 1970 bis 2010", *ATZ*, **92,** 176-183.

[13] L. Michaelis, (1991), *Global warming impacts of transport, INRETS Conf. "Transports et Pollution de l'Air"*, Avignon, 10/13 September, 9 p.

[14] J.B. Milford et al., (1989), "A new approach to photochemical pollution control, Implications of spatial patterns in pollutant responses to reductions in nitrogen oxides and reactive organic gas emissions", *E.S.&T.*, **23,** 1290-1301.

[15] A. Milhau and O. Boulhol, (1990), "L'automobile, une source de pollution majeure", *Air Environnement*, (10), 4 p.

[16] A. Saje, (1991), *Vehicle emissions, the consumer and industry, finding the balance, INRETS Conf. "Transports et Pollution de l'Air"*, Avignon, 10/13 September, 5 p.

[17] H. Schneider, (1991), "Auto und Umwelt, Perspektiven für das Jahr 2000", *ATZ*, **93,** 354-362 and 448-455.

[18] L.M. Thomas, (1989), "A US perspective on hydrocarbon controls at service stations", *CONCAWE Report* No. 11/89, 13 p.

[19] H. Waldeyer et al., (1985), "Abgas-Emissionsszenario für den Pkw-Verkehr in der Bundesrepublik Deutschland unter Berücksichtigung der Beschlüsse der EG-Umweltministerkonferenz", *TÜV Rheinland Report*, October, 29 p.

[20] M.P. Walsh, (1989), *Vehicle pollution control in Europe, The local and global significance, 3rd Int. Symp., "Highway Pollution"*, München, 18/22 September, 10 p.

[21] M.P. Walsh, (1989), "Controlling motor vehicle emissions, an assessment of the implications for climate modification", *Plat. Met. Rev.*, **33,** 194-212.

[22] Q.Wang et al., (1990), "Emissions impacts of electric vehicles", *J. Air Waste Managem. Assoc.*, **40,** 1275-1284.

[23] F.J. Wiesmann et al., (1991), "Ozonbildung durch anthropogene Stickstoffoxid- und Kohlenwasserstoffemissionen", *Staub*, **51,** 35-41.

[24] N.E. Gallopoulos, (1992), "Bridging the present to the future in personal transportation, the role of internal combustion engines", *SAE Paper* No. 920721 (SP. 910), 195-206.

# Abbreviations, acronyms and symbols

| | |
|---|---|
| **2T** | two-stroke |
| **4T** | four-stroke |
| **ACEA** | Association des Constructeurs Européens d'Automobiles |
| **ACS** | American Chemical Society |
| **ADB** | advanced design BUS |
| **ADR** | Australian Design Rules |
| **AECC** | automobile emission control by catalysts |
| **AFNOR** | Association Française de Normalisation |
| **Ag** | silver |
| **AGELFI** | AGIP/Elf/Fina |
| **Al** | aluminum |
| **API** | American Petroleum Institute |
| **APPA** | Association pour la Prévention de la Pollution Atmosphérique |
| **As** | arsenic |
| **ASME** | American Society of Mechanical Engineers |
| **ASU** | Abgassonder Untersuchung |
| **ATZ** | Automobil Technische Zeitschrift |
| **Au** | gold |
| **AVL** | Anstalt für Verbrennungsmotoren List |
| **B** | boron |
| **Ba** | barium |
| **BaP** | benzo(a)pyrene |
| **BAPMON** | background air pollution monitoring network |
| **BeP** | benzo(e)pyrene |
| **BET** | Brunauer Emmet Taylor |
| **bhp h** | brake horse power hour |
| **BIPE** | Bureau d'Informations et de Prévisions Economiques |
| **bmep** | brake mean effective power |
| **BMFT** | Bundes Ministerium für Forschung und Technologie |
| **BMW** | Bayerische Motoren Werke |
| **Br** | bromine |
| **C** | carbon |
| **Ca** | calcium |
| **CAAFI** | compressed air assisted fuel injection |
| **CARB** | California Air Research Board |
| **CCMC** | Committee of Common Market Automobile Constructors |
| **Ce** | cerium |
| **CEA** | Commissariat à l'Energie Atomique |
| **CEP** | car efficiency parameter |
| **CERNE** | Centre d'Etude de Recherche des Nuisances et de l'Environnement |
| **CFC** | chlorofluorocarbons |
| **CFDS** | congested freeway driving schedule |
| **CFR** | cooperative fuel research |
| **CFV** | critical flow Venturi |
| $CH_3CHO$ | acetaldehyde |
| $CH_4$ | methane |
| **CITEPA** | Centre Interprofessionnel Technique d'Etudes de la Pollution Atmosphérique |
| $(CN)_2$ | cyanogen |
| **CNG** | compressed natural gas |
| **CO** | carbon monoxide |
| **Co** | cobalt |
| $CO_2$ | carbon dioxide |
| **COHb** | carboxyhaemoglobin |
| **CONCAWE** | Group for Conservation of Clean Air and Water in Europe |
| **COS** | carbon oxysulfide |
| **Cr** | chromium |
| **CRC** | Cooperative Research Committee |
| **Cs** | cesium |

| | |
|---|---|
| **$CS_2$** | carbon disulfide |
| **CSR** | Chambre Syndicale du Raffinage |
| **Cu** | copper |
| **CUE** | crowded urban expressway |
| **CVCC** | compound vortex controlled combustion |
| **CVS** | constant volume sampler |
| **d** | day |
| **DCM** | dichloromethane |
| **DDA** | Detroit Diesel Allison |
| **DDS** | durability driving schedule |
| **DEFORPA** | Dépérissement des Forêts Attribué à la Pollution Atmosphérique |
| **DGMK** | Deutsche Gesellschaft für Mineralöl und Kohlechemie |
| **DI** | direct injection |
| **DIS** | diffusional and inertial spectrometer |
| **DM** | Deutsche Mark |
| **DMSO** | dimethyl sulfoxide |
| **DNA** | deoxyribonucleic acid |
| **DNPH** | 2,4-dinitrophenyl hydrazine |
| **DNSH** | 1-dimethylamino naphthalene-5-sulfonyl hydrazine |
| **DOAS** | diesel odor analytical system |
| **DRG** | ex-Democratic Republic of Germany |
| **E.S.&T.** | Environmental Science and Technology |
| **E85** | 85% ethanol fuel |
| **EAA** | electric aerosol analyzer |
| **EACN** | European Air Chemistry Network |
| **EAEC** | |
| **ECC** | European Coordination Committee |
| **ECD** | electron capture detector |
| **ECE** | Economic Commission for Europe |
| **EEC** | European Economic Community |
| **EGR** | exhaust gas recirculation |
| **EMEP** | European Monitoring Environmental Programme |
| **ENCLAIR** | energy and cleaner air |
| **EOT** | exclusive of tax |
| **EPA** | Environmental Protection Agency |
| **ETBE** | ethyl tertbutyl ether |
| **EUDC** | extra urban driving cycle |
| **EUREV** | Enquête sur l'Usage Réel des Véhicules |
| **F** | French franc |
| **Fe** | iron |
| **FID** | flame ionization detector |
| **FISITA** | Fédération International des Sociétés d'Ingénieurs des Techniques de l'Automobile |
| **FNG** | fuel natural gas |
| **FPD** | flame photometer detector |
| **FRG** | ex-Federal Republic of Germany |
| **FTIR** | Fourier transform infrared |
| **FTP** | Federal Test Procedure |
| **GC** | gas chromatography |
| **GM** | General Motors |
| **GNC** | gaz natural carburant |
| **GREF** | Groupe de Recherche et d'Etude des Forêts |
| **GSM** | Groupement Scientifique Moteur |
| **Gt** | gigaton |
| **h** | hour |
| **$H_2$** | hydrogen |
| **$H_2O$** | water |
| **$H_2S$** | hydrogen sulfide |
| **$H_2SO_4$** | sulfuric acid |
| **HBr** | hydrobromic acid |
| **HC** | hydrocarbons (unburnt) |
| **HCHO** | formaldehyde |
| **HCl** | hydrochloric acid |
| **HCN** | hydrogen cyanide |
| **hp** | horse power |
| **HPLC** | high performance liquid chromatography |
| **HWFET** | highway federal economy test |
| **IAPAC** | injection assistée par air comprimé |
| **ICOMIA** | International Council of Marine Industry Association |

| | |
|---|---|
| **IDI** | indirect injection |
| **IFP** | Institut Français du Pétrole |
| **I/M** | inspection and maintenance |
| **IMechE** | Institution of Mechanical Engineers |
| **INCOLL** | inertia collection |
| **INRETS** | Institut National de Recherches et d'Etudes sur les Transports et leur Sécurité |
| **INRS** | Institut National de Recherche de Sécurité |
| **INSERM** | Institut National de la Santé et de la Recherche Médicale |
| **IPSN** | Institut de Protection et de Sûreté Nucléaire |
| **IR** | infrared |
| **Ir** | iridium |
| **IRT** | Institut de Recherche des Transports |
| **ISO** | International Organization for Standardization |
| **IUR** | International Union of Railways |
| **J. APCA** | Journal of the Air Pollution Control Association |
| **K** | potassium |
| **KfZ** | Kraftfahr Zeuge |
| **kWh** | kilowatt hour |
| **La** | lanthanum |
| **LCPP** | Laboratoire Central de la Préfecture de Police |
| **LEV** | low emission vehicle |
| **LHD** | load haul dump |
| **LHVP** | Laboratoire d'Hygiène de la Ville de Paris |
| **LKW** | Last Kraft Wagen |
| **LPG** | liquefied petroleum gas |
| **LSC** | low-speed cycle |
| **M100** | 100% methanol fuel |
| **M15** | 15% methanol fuel |
| **M85** | 85% methanol fuel |
| **MAN** | Maschinenfabrik Augsburg Nürnberg |
| **MBT** | maximum brake torque |
| **MBTH** | 3-methyl-2-benzothiazolone hydrazone |
| **Mg** | magnesium |
| **MMT** | methylcyclopentadienyl manganese tricarbonyl |
| **Mn** | manganese |
| **Mo** | molybdenum |
| **MON** | motor octane number |
| **MS** | mass spectrometry |
| **Mt** | megaton |
| **MTBE** | methyl tertbutyl ether |
| **MTU** | Michigan Technical University |
| **MTZ** | Motor Technische Zeitschrift |
| **MVEG** | motor vehicle emission group |
| **MWV** | Mineralöl Wirtschaft Verband |
| **N** | nitrogen |
| **$N_2O$** | nitrous oxide |
| **Na** | sodium |
| **NASA** | National Aeronautics and Space Administration |
| **NATO** | North Atlantic Treaty Organization |
| **NDIR** | non-dispersive infrared |
| **NDUV** | non-dispersive ultraviolet |
| **$NH_3$** | ammonia |
| **Ni** | nickel |
| **NIOSH** | National Institute for Occupational Safety and Health |
| **NM** | new model |
| **NMHC** | non-methanic hydrocarbons |
| **NMOG** | non-methanic organic gases |
| **NMR** | nuclear magnetic resonance |
| **NO** | nitric oxide |
| **$NO_2$** | nitrogen dioxide |
| **$NO_3H$** | nitrous acid |
| **NOAA** | National Oceanic and Atmospheric Administration |
| **$NO_x$** | nitrogen oxides |
| **NPD** | nitrogen phosphorus detector |
| **NTIS** | National Technical Information Service |
| **NV** | new vehicle |
| **NYCC** | New York city cycle |
| **$O_2$** | oxygen |
| **$O_3$** | ozone |
| **OECD** | Organization for Economic Cooperation and Development |
| **OEV** | ordonnance sur les échappements des véhicules |

| | |
|---|---|
| **P** | phosphorus |
| **Pa** | pascal |
| **PAH** | polynuclear aromatic hydrocarbons |
| **PAN** | peroxyacetyl nitrate |
| **Pb** | lead |
| **PCDD** | polychlorodibenzo dioxins |
| **PCDF** | polychlorodibenzo furans |
| **Pd** | palladium |
| **PDP** | positive displacement pump |
| **PHS** | Public Health Service |
| **PIXE** | particle-induced X-ray emission |
| **PKW** | Personen Kraft Wagen |
| **ppb** | parts per billion (10-9) |
| **ppm** | parts per million (10-6) |
| **ppmC** | ppm related to atoms of carbon |
| **ppmV** | ppm related to volume |
| **PROCO** | programmed combustion |
| **PSA** | Peugeot Société Anonyme |
| **Pt** | platinum |
| **PTFE** | polytetrafluoroethylene |
| **PVC** | polyvinyl chloride |
| **r** | richness: fuel/air ratio |
| **Rh** | rhodium |
| **RON** | research octane number |
| **Ru** | ruthenium |
| **RVP** | Reid vapor pressure |
| **RWTÜV** | Rheinland Westfalen TÜV |
| **S** | sulfur |
| **SAE** | Society of Automotive Engineers |
| **SET** | sulfate emission test |
| **SHED** | sealed housing for evaporative determination |
| **SI** | spark ignition |
| **Si** | silicon |
| **SIA** | Société des Ingénieurs de l'Automobile |
| **Sn** | tin |
| **$SO_2$** | sulfur dioxide |
| **$SO_3$** | sulfur trioxide |
| **SOF** | soluble organic fraction |
| **$SO_x$** | sulfur oxides |
| **SPIN** | Service de Protection des Installations Nucléaires |
| **StVZO** | Straßen Verkehrs- Zulassungs-Ordnung |
| **TAME** | tertioamylmethylether |
| **TCCS** | Texaco controlled combustion system |
| **TCDD** | 2,3,7,8-tetrachlorodibenzo-p-dioxin |
| **TCDF** | 2,3,7,8-tetrachlorodibenzo furan |
| **TDC** | top dead center |
| **TEA** | thermal energy analyzer |
| **TEOM** | tapered element oscillating microbalance |
| **TI** | tax inclusive |
| **Ti** | titanium |
| **TIPP** | taxe intérieure sur les produits pétroliers (domestic tax on petroleum products) |
| **TLEV** | transitory low-emission vehicle |
| **TNO** | Toegepasst Natuurwetenschaplijke Onderzoek |
| **TOE** | total organic extract |
| **TSP** | total suspended particulates |
| **TÜV** | Technische Überwachung Verein |
| **UBA** | Umwelt Bundes Amt |
| **UDDS** | urban dynamometer driving schedule |
| **UHC** | unburnt hydrocarbons |
| **UIC** | Union Internationale des Chemins de Fer |
| **UK** | United Kingdom |
| **ULEV** | ultra low emission vehicle |
| **US** | United States |
| **USPHS** | United States Public Health Service |
| **USSR** | Union of Soviet Socialist Republics |
| **UTAC** | Union Technique de l'Automobile et du Cycle |
| **UV** | ultraviolet |
| **V** | vanadium |
| **VAT** | value added tax |
| **VDI** | Verein Deutscher Ingenieure |
| **VHSV** | volumetric hourly space velocity |

**VN** véhicule neuf
**VOC** volatile organic compounds
**VROM** Ministerie van Volkhuising, Ruimtelijke Ordening en Milieubeheer
**VW** Volkswagen

**W** tungsten
**WHO** World Health Organization
**WSL** Warren Spring Laboratory

$\lambda$ air/fuel ratio

**Y** yttrium

**ZEV** zero emission vehicle
**Zn** zinc
**Zr** zirconium

$\Delta$**P** pressure difference (pressure drop)
$\mu$**m** micrometer

# Index

ACHEVÉ D'IMPRIMER
EN JUIN 1995
PAR L'IMPRIMERIE NOUVELLE
45800 SAINT-JEAN-DE-BRAYE
N° d'éditeur : 907
Dépôt légal 1995 : n° 27016
IMPRIMÉ EN FRANCE

Typesetting and diagram
MACH3, 60720 BURY